Bank Management and Financial Services

Clanrye International,
750 Third Avenue, 9th Floor,
New York, NY 10017, USA

ISBN: 978-1-63240-777-1

Cataloging-in-Publication Data

Bank management and financial services / edited by Perry Stinson.
p. cm.
Includes bibliographical references and index.
ISBN 978-1-63240-777-1
1. Bank management. 2. Finance. 3. Financial services industry. I. Stinson, Perry.
HG1615 .B36 2019
332.1--dc23

For information on all Clanrye International publications
visit our website at www.clanryeinternational.com

CLANRYE INTERNATIONAL

Printed in China.

Bank Management and Financial Services

Perry Stinson

CLANRYE
INTERNATIONAL
www.clanryeinternational.com

Contents

Preface

I am honored to present to you this unique book which encompasses the most up-to-date data in the field. I was extremely pleased to get this opportunity of editing the work of experts from across the globe. I have also written papers in this field and researched the various aspects revolving around the progress of the discipline. I have tried to unify my knowledge along with that of stalwarts from every corner of the world, to produce a text which not only benefits the readers but also facilitates the growth of the field.

Financial services refer to the economic services delivered by the finance industry across multiple businesses and organizations like banks, insurance companies, stock brokerages, etc. In banks, besides the primary functionalities of storing, lending and borrowing money, financial services also include making investments across many industries and companies, capital generation, insurance facilitation and fund transfer. This book presents the key concepts and theories essential to the field of bank management and financial services. Constant effort has been made to make the understanding of the difficult concepts as easy and informative as possible. Banking professionals, financial advisors, experts and students alike will be benefited by an in-depth study of this book.

Finally, I would like to thank all the contributing authors for their valuable time and contributions. This book would not have been possible without their efforts. I would also like to thank my friends and family for their constant support.

Editor

A Study of Factors Affecting Organizational Commitment among Bank Officers in Pakistan

Khaliq IH[1]*, Naeem B[2] and Khalid S[3]

[1]*Pacific Western University (USA), Warid Telecom, Pakistan*
[2]*Department of Management Sciences, COMSATS Institute of Information Technology, Lahore, Pakistan*
[3]*Department of Education, University of Sargodha, Sargodha, Pakistan*

Abstract

There has been lesser evidence regarding the factors driving the commitment from countries like Pakistan. The purpose of present research was to find out the factors affecting the organizational commitment of the officers in the banking industry of Pakistan. The hypothesized relationship between variables rests on the foundations of social exchange theory, the perceived organizational support theory, and the Gouldner's norm of reciprocity. The quantitative data was collected through self-administered closed ended questionnaire. The questionnaire was filled by 47 Grad II officers of different banks in the Metropolitan city of Lahore. The criteria for inclusion in sample were those having passed their probationary period. The data was analyzed using SPSS version 16.0. The correlations showed that the strength of relationship between factors affecting commitment and organizational commitment is higher. There are five factors which affect the organizational commitment of bank officers. These factors include organizational rewards both monetary and non-monetary, supervisor support, career development opportunities, work-family support, and favorable job conditions. The results of study may be beneficial for devising such policies as to reduce the employees' turnover which has been an area of major concern for the human resource professionals especially in the context of Pakistani banking sector.

Keywords: Organizational commitment; Banks officer; Pakistan

Introduction

The construct, "organizational commitment" has been a subject of interest for those studying the organizational psychology. Organizational commitment involves the loyalty of employees' to the organization, their readiness to put exertion on organization's behalf, the level of coincidence of personal goals with the organization, and an aspiration to continue employment with the organization. However, there is a disagreement on the definition and the way of measurement of the construct. Since commitment involves a psychological state, which is a main source of disagreement on the definition of commitment. Further differences stem from the antecedents causing the commitment and by the behaviors depicting the commitment [1-4]. Despite the differences in definitions of organizational commitment [5]; the one given Modway is considered to be most acceptable which defines organizational commitment as the might of an individual's identification with, and involvement with an organization.

Organizational commitment has three basic components; (a) identification, a strong faith and reception of goals as well as values of an organization (b) effort, an eagerness to put effort for the goals of organization (c) loyalty, an intention to remain part of the organization.

There are many factors which affect the organizational commitment of employees. These include the financial inducements [6]. Among other factors inducing organizational commitment are, good relations between supervisors and employees, good career opportunities [7], role in organizational goal setting, lesser ambiguity in role [8], and fairness in appraisal of performance [9].

Literature review and hypothesis development

It has been widely held in the literature that the organizational rewards indicate that the organization gives importance to the contribution of employees towards the organization [2]. The organizational rewards show that the organization investing in the employees. Further, rewards indicate that organization appreciates and recognizes its employees [10,11]. These kinds of rewards develop a perception of support from the employees of organization in the minds of worker, making them committed to the organization. Fasolo argues that organizational support must enhance employees' thinking that organization regards them as good performer and honors their achievements, helping employees to increase esteem [9]. The fairness in recognition and rewards signals out the care organization gives to the employees.

Landsman concluded that the belief of employees about the fairness in the distribution of rewards and punishments leads to higher commitment of employees with the organization [12]. The organizational commitment is enhanced in this manner by their mental satisfaction with the job. Therefore, following hypothesis is proposed:

H1: Higher the Organizational reward (monetary and non-monetary), higher the organizational commitment of employees.

Researcher indicates that supervisors are the agent of the organization. Higher level of support from supervisors shows support from the organization itself [2,13]. Landsman tested the relationship of supervisor support with organizational commitment [12]. It was found that better supervisor support develops a perception among employees that organization values them. Such a feeling hinders employees to leave the organization. Hence, supervisor support plays a major role in developing the organizational commitment among employees.

***Corresponding author:** Imran Hameed Khaliq, Pacific Western University (USA), Warid Telecom, Pakistan, E-mail: imranhameedkhaliq@gmail.com

Therefore, supervisor support is an important factor affecting organizational commitment. It is hypothesized that:

H2: Higher the support from supervisor, higher the organizational commitment.

Tansky and Cohen found that the provision of career development opportunities is important for enhancing commitment of employees to the organization [14]. They suggested that it is important for an organization to have a formal program aimed at the development of career of employees. Such a program may necessarily be developed and designed to aid the workers in their goals within and outside the organization. These kinds of activities on the part of organization retain employees for the longer period of time and help them attain future plans.

The training activities not only develop employees and refine their acumen but also improve their job satisfaction and organizational commitment [15-17].

Harel and Tzafrir held that the provision of career development plans results into the tightened psychological contract and makes employees committed to their organization [15]. A feeling among employees to grow with the organization, commits them to the organization [18]. It has further been argued that the activities aimed at the development of career of employees convey to the employees that they are valued. These efforts on the part of organization are thus reciprocated by the employees. Employee development opportunities are taken as positive actions on the part of organization towards employees. In the light of above discussion we hypothesize [19]:

H3: Higher the provision of career development opportunities, higher the organizational commitment.

Family is an important aspect of lives employees. Those highly contented and satisfied in their family life perform better in their workplace. If the employees get support for their family issues from their organization, they will reciprocate in the form of higher commitment to the organization. Work-life balance and benefits enhance organizational commitment [20]. It has been suggested theoretically that work-life benefits enhance the perceived organizational support which in turn is related to organizational commitment positively and negatively to the turnover intentions [21].

According to Grover and Crooker the provision of work-life benefits is related to higher level of commitment and lesser turn over intentions among employees. It was suggested by them that the work life benefits indicate that the organization cares about the employees' well-being and enhance attachment to the organization. In a further study, Allen concluded that those organizations which give more work life benefits to the organization are regarded as family supportive organizations [22]. Moreover, it was held that family leave, flexible timings and condensed schedules of work are positively related to higher organizational commitment and lesser intentions of turnover.

H4: Higher the work-family support, higher the organizational commitment.

Job conditions mean security, autonomy and empowerment that an employee assumes while performing job. Job conditions are favorable if it carries above mentioned elements. According to Rosseau, security of job means that the organization wishes to retain employee as organization's member even in distress conditions. The theory of social exchange comes into action here. The exchange occurs. The employees in exchange become loyal to the organization and do not think of turning over. Another important aspect of job conditions is the empowerment of employee. Empowerment means the power to take actions independently. The employees are delegated powers to make decisions independently. These kinds of actions on the part of organization communicate to the employees that they are being trusted by the organization, and hence become committed to the organization. Therefore, we hypothesize:

H5: Higher the favorable job conditions, higher the organizational commitment (Figure 1).

Methodology

The study aims to delineate the factors affecting organizational commitment among bank officers in Pakistan. Survey research was used so that data could be collected at a less cost within a short period of time. Moreover honest responses could be encouraged because of the anonymity of the respondents.

Population of the present study consists of all Grade–II officers inducted through management trainee officers. The sample was

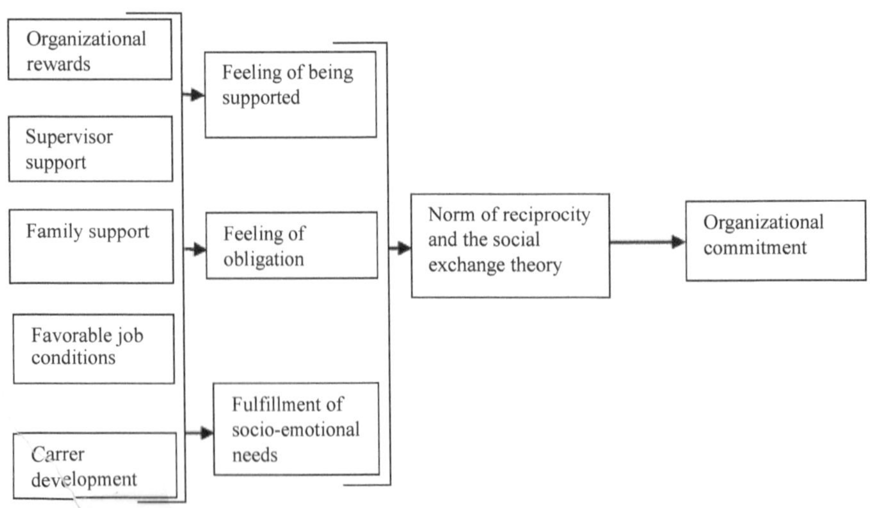

Figure 1: The following schematic model summarizes all the above discussion.

A Comparative Study of the Public and Private Sector Bank with Special Reference to Punjab National Bank and HDFC Bank

Agrawal P[1]*and Yadav AK[2]

[1]Research Scholar, Department of Business Administration, DDU Gorakhpur University, Gorakhpur

[2]Associate Professor, Department of Commerce, DDU Gorakhpur University, Gorakhpur

Abstract

After passing of nationalization the Indian banking system has considerably developed with a large network of branches and wide range of financial instruments. As banking industry is growing today with a rapid speed and competition it has more than 11,75,150 employee and has a 1,09,811 branches across India and 171 branches in abroad and have managed deposits of Rs. 67504.54 billion and bank credit of Rs. 52604.59 billion. The net profit of banks operating in India was Rs. 1027.51 billion against RS. 9148.60 billion turn over during 2012-13.

Banking sector has a very important place in our Indian economy. The amount of the profit indicates the efficiency of the organization the larger the profit higher the growth rate. The profitability depends on the effective utilization of funds to procure maximum profit for growth. . The present research paper is an effort to make a comparative study between the Growth rate in Punjab National Bank and HDFC Bank. As a study of Growth analysis of both the banks for a period of 10 years, i.e., from 2004 to 2014 is made. The main parameters of growth in banks are Net profit growth, Net assets growth, ROA (Return on Assets) and NPA.

Keywords: Growth; Net assets; Net profit; Future value; Present value; Compound annual growth rate (CAGR); Return on assets (ROA); Non performing assets (NPA)

Introduction

Banking is a single industry incorporating a dozen businesses, such as corporate banking, investment banking, small business banking, wealth management, capital markets and so on. Further one of these is retail banking, which is characterized by large numbers of customers, accounts and transactions, a variety of products and services, a high level of dependency on technology and terrific levels of cooperation between banks, retailers, businesses and consumers [1].

Banks have more capacity than they can use; consumers will need a bank account to receive government benefits; and banks continue consolidating into a small number of large banks. This consolidation may be a good thing, or it may be a bad thing. Certainly, smaller banks will have to develop successful strategies to compete with large banks, and such competition will benefit customers. One hope could be that even if we do end up with a handful of banks, they will at least compete with each other, and not enjoy comfortable, begin competition between themselves. But that might be a dream. We must have real competition.

After passing of nationalization the Indian banking system has considerably developed with a large network of branches and wide range of financial instruments. As banking industry is growing today with a rapid speed and competition it has more than 11,75,150 employee and has a 1,09,811 branches across India and 171 branches in abroad and have managed deposits of Rs. 67504.54 billion and bank credit of Rs. 52604.59 billion. The net profit of banks operating in India was Rs. 1027.51 billion against RS. 9148.60 billion turnover during 2012-13 [2]. Banking sector has a very important place in our Indian economy. The amount of the profit indicates the efficiency of the organization the larger the profit higher the growth rate. The profitability depends on the effective utilization of funds to procure maximum profit and growth.

As regards Punjab National Bank, it was established in 1895. Bank has strong capital base with capital adequacy ratio 12.89% as in March 2014. The bank has paid-up capital of 370.91 crore as on march 2014, with more than 120 years of purposeful existence, more than 8.9 crore customers through 6200 branches it has grown. As regards HDFC Bank, it was established by Reserve Bank of India in 1994 [3]. It was the first bank to get the approval by RBI to set up as Private Sector Bank. The paid up share capital as on march 2015 is Rs.501,2990,634, its capital adequacy ratio as on March 2014 is 16.1% and it has 3659 branches with 11766 ATMs [3,4].

This research paper is an effort to make a comparative study of the Growth rate in Punjab National Bank and HDFC Bank. As a study of Growth analysis of both the banks for a period of 10 years, i.e., from 2004 to 2014 is made [5,6]. The main parameters of growth in banks are Net profit growth, Net assets growth, ROA (Return on Assets) and NPA. The statistical analysis is made on the bases of annual compound growth rate and NPA on mean, standard deviation, coefficient of correlation.

Objectives of the Study

1. To review the growth rate of both the banks under study
2. To compare the growth between in private (HDFC Bank) and public sector (PNB) bank

Research Methodology

The present study is secondary data based collected from various

***Corresponding author:** Agrawal P, Research Scholar, Department of Business Administration, DDU Gorakhpur University, India
E-mail: registrarddugu@gmail.com

journals, reports of RBI and annual reports of banks, moneycontrol.com. The study period is limited, from 2004-05 to 2013-14.

Concept of Growth

Growth is the concept for banking sector to grow in a profitable manner, in assets, in number of branches and networks in number of ATMs, in capital adequacy ratio, but less in percentage of NPA.

Every year targets are fixed by the banks to achieve it, various types of scheme are launched, and interest on deposits and loans are adjusted. The increase in business per employee of the bank in comparison to the previous year is evaluated. Operating profits, net profits, earning per share, dividend per share, return on capital employed, return on equity, interest coverage ratios are the other yardsticks to measure the growth of a business entity over a period of time. Growth also means to compare the net profit of current year to the previous year's profit.

All of these mostly depend upon the factor which is very important in the recent scenario is the customer satisfaction and prompt services of banks. The technology factor also affects the growth very hardly. The bank which gives the prompt services to the customers they grow rapidly on every parameter of growth.

Net assets growth comparison

Net assets is the sum of asset side of the balance sheet excluding any provision for depreciation fund or the assets shown at book value less depreciation charges, or the market value of the asset to be disposed off less any expected loss or provision against that asset. This total of the asset side exclude the fictitious assets if there is any shown in the asset side of the balance sheet like preliminary expenses, discounts on issue of shares or debenture, interest paid out of capital etc. Net assets include both types of assets i.e., fixed asset, as well as, the current asset possessed by the business entity owned by the concerned. These assets provides the base for making the concern capable for carrying out its business activities for earning revenue and consolidate its position in the years to come. These assets are possessed by the business from various sources shown in the liability side of the concern i.e., owners funds and borrowed funds or the internal resources of the business created out of profits. As regarding Net Assets of Punjab National Bank & HDFC Bank Limited, it has been computed by deducting all liabilities from total assets and shown in Table 1 [5-7].

Table 1 reveals that Net Assets of Punjab National Bank indicated a Compound Annual Growth Rate (CAGR)of 15.5% whereas that of HDFC Bank indicated an annual compound growth rate of 25.4%. All this indicate that net assets of HDFC Bank Limited increased quicker than that of Punjab National Bank Limited. Growth rate of Net Assets of Punjab National Bank and HDFC Bank has been computed by way of annual compound growth rate with the help of the following formula:

$$CAGR = \left(\frac{Ending\ value}{Begining\ value}\right)^{\left(\frac{1}{\#of\ years}\right)} - 1$$

That is CAGR = $(FV/PV)^{1/n} - 1$

Where FV = Future Value

PV = Present Value

n = Number of Years

Using logarithms Growth rate is calculated as

Growth rate of Punjab National Bank = 15.50 (%)

Growth rate of HDFC Bank = 25.4%

As regarding Net Assets Growth of Punjab National Bank & HDFC Bank Limited, it has been computed with the help of geometric mean and has been shown in Figure 1.

Net profit/loss growth rate

Net income is what remains out of a company's revenue after subtracting all costs. It is also referred as net profit, earnings, or the bottom line. Net Income, that is not paid out in dividends is added to retained earnings.

Increasing (decreasing) net income is a good (bad) sign for a company's profitability [8]. Companies with consistent and increasing net income over time are looked at very favorably by stockholders.

Net profit is another base for comparing the performance of these two banks PNB and HDFC. Net profit growth in respect of Punjab National Bank and HDFC Bank has been calculated by taking Net Profit after Tax, so as to adjudge the absolute growth of net profit after tax [9,10].

As per Table 2, it can be observed that the net profit of PNB was 141012 lac in 2004-05 and it rose to 334258 lac in 2013-14 which is 1.37 times but the growth of HDFC is much higher than PNB as HDFC has a net profit of 66556 lac in 2004-05 and it rose to 847838 lac in 2013-14 which is 11.73 times. Net profit growth rate of PNB is 9.01% and the HDFC is 28.98%. This implies that the performance of HDFC is better times as PNB in the corresponding years. In 2012-13 and in 2013-14 PNB has shown a negative growth in the profit which is -2.7 and -29.5

Year	Punjab National Bank			HDFC Bank		
	Net Assets (in Lacs)	Total Assets (in Lacs)	% of Net Assets	Net Assets (in Lacs)	Total Assets (in Lacs)	% of Net Assets
2004-05	816130	12624128	6.46	452028	5142900	9.76
2005-06	937636	14526738	6.45	529960	7350639	9.53
2006-07	1043546	62422149	6.42	643315	9123561	7.05
2007-08	1231835	19902036	6.19	1149724	13317661	8.63
2008-09	1465363	24691862	5.93	1505273	18327077	8.21
2009-10	1772292	29663277	5.97	2152249	22245857	9.67
2010-11	2150856	37832526	5.68	25,37927	27735260	9.1
2011-12	27,81707	458,19401	6.06	29,92468	33790951	8.85
2012-13	31,24805	477,44819	6.54	36,21414	40033189	9.04
2013-14	34,48714	549,01174	6.28	4347863	49159950	8.84

Source: Annual Reports of Punjab National Bank and HDFC Bank - various issues.

Table 1: Net Assets.

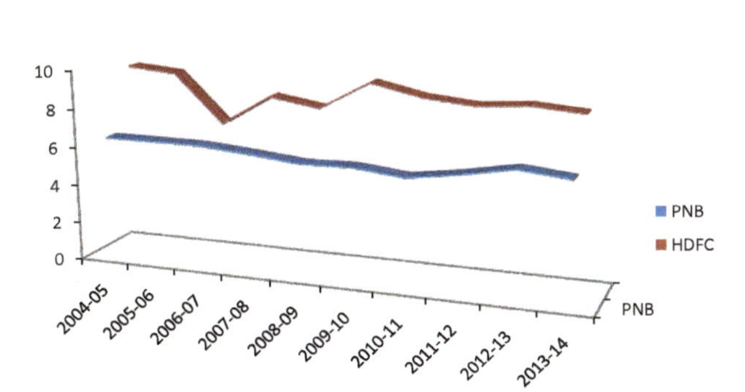

Note: Net assets % growth-year wise-has been shown in Figure 1.

Figure 1: Net Assets Growth of PNB and HDFC Bank.

Year	PNB		HDFC	
	Net Profits in lac	% Increase over Previous Years	Net Profits in lac	% Increase over Previous Years
2004-05	141012	------	66556	------
2005-06	143931	2.07	87078	30.83
2006-07	154008	7.00	114155	31.08
2007-08	204876	33.0	159018	39.31
2008-09	309088	50.86	224494	41.17
2009-10	390536	26.35	294870	31.34
2010-11	443350	13.52	392640	33.15
2011-12	488420	10.16	516709	31.59
2012-13	474767	-2.7	672628	30.17
2013-14	334258	-29.5	847838	26.04

Source: Annual Reports of Punjab National Bank and HDFC Bank - various issues.

Table 2: Net Profit Growth of PNB and HDFC Bank.

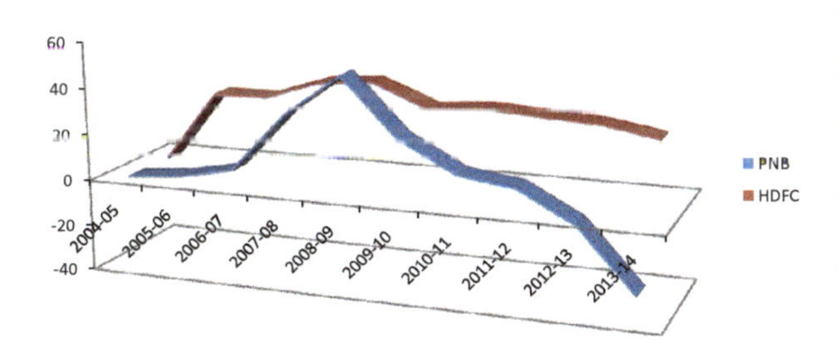

Note: Net Profit is shown in % form in Figure 2.

Figure 2: Net Profit of PNB and HDFC Bank.

respectively, as compared to HDFC it is very low. The growth rate of PNB is 15.5% and HDFC growth rate is 25.4%. The net profit of both the banks HDFC indicate annual compound growth rate of 28.98% where as PNB shows 9.01% (Figure 2).

Return on assets

Return on Assets (ROA) shows the rate of return (after tax) being earned on all of the firm's assets regardless of financing structure (debt vs. equity). It is a measure of how efficiently the company is using all stakeholders' assets to earn returns [11]. Because ROA can differ significantly across firms, ROA is often used to compare a company over time or against companies that have similar financing structures [12,13].

A bank's ROA is typically well under 2%. This ratio measures the return on assets employed or efficiency in utilization of the assets. It is arrived at by dividing net profit by total assets.

Return on Assets=Net Profit/Total Assets × 100

The figures in Table 3 show the fluctuations in ROA of both banks. Return on Assets of PNB is lower in comparison to HDFC. In 2009-10 the ROA of PNB is highest 1.31% and of HDFC's is 1.32%. In 2013-14 the ROA of HDFC is 1.72%, which is highest among above years; but PNB's ROA is 60%, which is lowest among above years. Therefore, in comparison to PNB, HDFC utilizes its assets more efficiently and gives better performance (Figure 3).

NPA (Non Performing Assets)

A debt obligation where the borrower has not paid any previously agreed upon interest and principal repayments to the designated lender for an extended period of time. The Non-Performing Asset is therefore not yielding any income to the lender in the form of principal and interest payments [14].

Types of NPA

Gross NPA: Gross NPAs are the sum total of all loan assets that are classified as NPAs as per RBI guidelines as on Balance Sheet date. Gross NPA reflects the quality of the loans made by banks. It consists of all the nonstandard assets like as sub-standard, doubtful, and loss assets. It can be calculated with the help of following ratio:

Gross NPAs Ratio = Gross NPAs/Gross Advances

Net NPA: Net NPAs are those type of NPAs, in which the bank has deducted the provision regarding NPAs. Net NPA shows the actual burden of banks. Since in India, bank balance sheets contain a huge amount of NPAs and the process of recovery and write off of loans is very time consuming [15]. The provisions the banks have to make

Year	PNB	HDFC
2004-05	1.11	1.29
2005-06	0.99	1.18
2006-07	0.21	1.25
2007-08	1.02	1.19
2008-09	1.25	1.22
2009-10	1.31	1.32
2010-11	1.17	1.41
2011-12	1.06	1.52
2012-13	0.99	1.68
2013-14	0.60	1.72

Source: Annual Reports of Punjab National Bank and HDFC Bank - various issues

Table 3: Return on Assets (%).

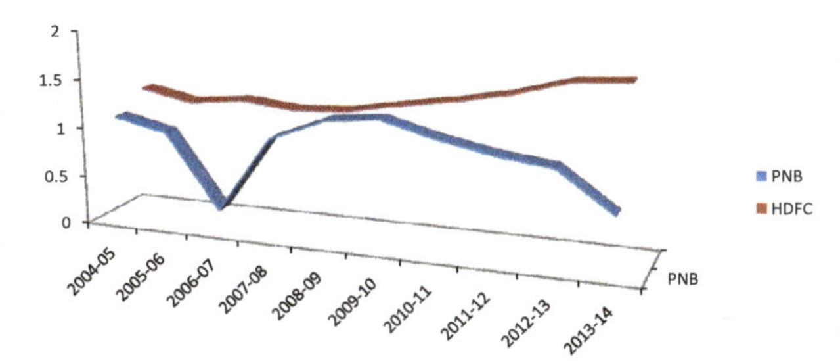

Note: Return on Assets has been shown in % form in Figure 3.

Figure 3: Return on Assets in PNB and HDFC Bank.

against the NPAs according to the central bank guidelines are quite significant. That is why the difference between gross and net NPA is quite high. It can be calculated as per following:

Net NPAs = Gross NPAs – Provisions/Gross Advances – Provisions (Table 4)

As shown in Table 5 bank wise mean standard deviation and coefficient of variation of Net NPA ratio of the selected banks. HDFC have the lowest mean value and standard deviation as for as 0.336 and 0.14998 respectively. Coefficient of variation of PNB is 0.9046 which is very high as compared to HDFC. This means that HDFC is managing its NPA in better manner. The net NPA ratio is shown in Figure 4 year wise.

Analysis and Findings

Net assets of HDFC show annual compound growth rate of 25.4% which is much higher than PNB that is 15.5%. While comparing the net profit of both the banks, HDFC indicate annual compound growth rate of 28.98% whereas PNB shows 9.01% so there is a huge difference between profits of these two banks, as the net profit of PNB in year 2013 and 2014 indicate negative growth rate from corresponding years.

Looking at the next basis which is Return on assets, HDFC grew from 1.29% to 1.72% but PNB went down stairs from 1.11% to 0.60%. So as in comparison to PNB, HDFC utilizes its assets more efficiently and giving better performance. Further the Net NPA ratio of both the banks indicate the true story of the banks that how much loans are bad and how much is recovered, who is managing its NPA more efficiently to lower it down to maximize the true profit shown in Tables 4 and 5. PNB has higher coefficient of variation in Net NPA ratio that is 0.90461 whereas HDFC has 0.46853 having large gap. So every basis of data establishes that HDFC as compared to PNB. Therefore, it can easily be concluded that growth in private sector (HDFC) banks is better than public sector (PNB) banks.

Banks	Mean	Standard Deviation	Coefficient of Variation
PNB	1.012	0.9266	0.90461
HDFC	0.336	0.14998	0.46853

Table 4: Analysis of NPA of PNB and HDFC Bank.

Banks	Mean	Standard Deviation	Coefficient of Variation
PNB	1.012	0.9266	0.90461
HDFC	0.336	0.14998	0.46853

Table 5: Analysis of NPA of PNB and HDFC Bank.

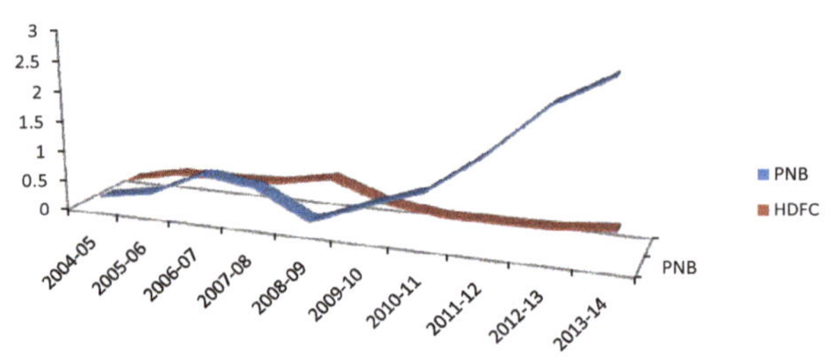

Note: Net NPA is shown in % form in Figure 5.

Figure 4: Net NPA of PNB and HDFC Bank.

References

1. Apropos (2004) The Soundness of Public Sector Banks. Finance India: 12.
2. Bhole LM (2000) Financial Institution and Markets. Tata McGraw Hill Publications Ltd, New Delhi.
3. Garima C (2014) Preformance Comparision of Private Banks with Public Sector Banks. International Journal of Emerging Research in Management and Technology.
4. Desai, Vasant (1997) Indian Financial System, Himalaya Publishing House, New Delhi.
5. Dutt, Ruddar, Sundaram KPM (2003) Indian Economy, S. Chand and Company Pvt. Ltd, New Delhi.
6. Gupta R, Sikarwar NS (2013) A Comparative Study of Growth Analysis of Punjab National Bank of India and HDFC Bank Limited. IJAIEM 2: 60-68.
7. Gupta SP (2000) Statistical Methods. S. Chand and Sons, New Delhi.
8. Gupta, Shashi K, Aggarwal, Nisha, Gupta, Neeti (2004) Financial Institutions and Markets. Kalyani Publishers, New Delhi.
9. Horne, Van JC (2000) Financial Management and Policy. Prentice Hall of India, New Delhi.
10. Jain TR, Khanna OP (2007) Indian Financial System, V. K. Publications, New Delhi.
11. Uma K (2009) Indian Economy, Performance and Policies. Academic Foundation (8th eds.), New Delhi.
12. Khan MY (1996) Indian Financial System. Tata McGraw-Hill Publishing Company Ltd, New Delhi.
13. Kothari CR (2006) Social Banking and Profitability. Arihant Publishers, Jaipur, Delhi.
14. Mangal SK, NP (1988) Reading in Financial Management. Printwell Publishers, Jaipur.
15. Vaish MC (2005) Money, Banking & Finance. Vikas Publishing House Pvt. Ltd, New Delhi.

Customers' Switching Intention in Oman's Banking Industry

Al Ghammari KA and Ahmed EM*

Binary University, Faculty of Business, Multimedia University, Malaysia

Abstract

Throughout early 2012, Oman allowed the Islamic banking for the first time as a response to a public demand during what was called "Arab spring". Consequently, this study presumed that, such new entry will create impact on the customers' switching intention as customers may intent to switch to the new Islamic banks. The main objective of this study is to identify the factors that influencing customers' intention to switch banks in general and the impact created by the need to Islamic banking in Oman in particular.

Nonetheless, the initial literature reviews has not cited the need for Islamic banking products among the common switching factors; however, face to face interviews with bank customers revealed that, the need for Islamic banking product was one of the influencing factors. Therefore, it has been added to this study as variable to test the expected influence and the impact on switching intention without going deeply into the concept of Islamic banking.

The method used is qualitative approach in the form of interview with focus groups, in this respect, face-to-face interviews of selected customers from 6 different banks in Oman were conducted to show the impact on customers' intention to switch conventional banks to Islamic banks. The interview outcome assisted to get a richness and depth of data and information on the impact created by the introduction of Islamic banking in Oman on customers' intention to switch conventional banks to Islamic banks. The interview outcomes suggest that more than half of respondents are inclined to transfer to Islamic banking despite the fact that 64% are satisfied with their current banks. Hence, it can be concluded that faith has an influence on customer decisions and that is considered to be the impact created by the Islamic banking on Oman's banking industry.

Keywords: Impact; Islamic banking; Customers' intention to switch banks; Oman's banking industry

Introduction

The behaviour of customers' switching is a prevailing global phenomenon spread among banking customers who tend to move from one bank to another in searching of more appealing and attractive services. Such behaviour is caused by dissatisfaction with their primary banks. During 2008, the rate of customers who had changed their banks was one out of ten constituting about 10%. However, this number increased to 18.3% during 2011.

According to the World Retail Banking report (2013) [1], nearly 10% of customers claim that they are likely to switch their banks in the near future. Besides, almost 41% are not sure if they want to continue dealing with their current bank. It should be noted that bank switching has a dangerous impact on the monetary state of the service providers including revenues, profit, and market share volume [2].

In this respect, the banking sector in Oman is relatively small, and the Omani people are highly interrelated. Consequently, the word of mouth and the social media are considerably powerful tools that shape the overall bank customer's perception of the service provider in the country. In addition, there is a belief in Oman that it is necessary to change a bank in order to find more attractive offers and consumer loans at competitive terms.

Moreover, Oman has recently allowed the Islamic Banks to operate in the country's banking sector. Hence, the first Islamic bank began to operate in the country in December 2012. During the time of "Arab Uprising," the Omani authorities acknowledged the social demand of the Omani citizens for Islamic banking as Oman is an Islamic country. It is believed that many bank customers will migrate to Islamic banks seeking to satisfy their religious beliefs. Finally, this study is desirable as there are no academic studies related to the research topic carried out in Oman to the best of knowledge so far.

For few decades, the rate of customers' retention has been one of the main concerns of all commercial banks around the globe due to the increased number of customers switching their banks on a regular basis because of various reasons. Needless to say, Sultanate of Oman, as a significant element of business community, is, of course, not necessarily immunized against such negative phenomena despite all the efforts that have been done to overcome this problem so far. Considering this aspect in broad terms, the objective of the presented study is to examine the major factors and reasons which instigate customers and motivate them to switch banks operating within the territory of Oman in general and the impact of the need to join the newly introduced Islamic banking of the Omani banking industry.

Islamic banking *vs.* conventional banking: cost of finance

As Islamic banking does not accept interest from money provided, or an item/possession(s) given as collateral, the cost of financing is differential in nature. This is majorly dependent on the social facet, where one draws his/her ideals and perspectives. From the viewpoint of the common customer or accountholder, Islamic banking provides an ideal avenue, through which loans can be procured at economically more reasonable terms and conditions as opposed to conventional banking. In the latter, an account holder has to deal with the fact that any loan or financing procured, necessitates the presence of either

***Corresponding author:** Elsadig Musa Ahmed, Binary University, Faculty of Business, Multimedia University, Malaysia
E-mail: elsadigmusa@yahoo.com

collateral or compounded interest rates. These rates are often higher than that acquired through account holding (savings), hence, the critic of not gaining much, but actually building the banking sector through increased profits from loans provided [3].

In Sudan, Pakistan and Iran, through full government intervention, Islamic banking has become the main model of banking within their territorial boundaries. The costs of financing would be in favour of the Islamic model of banking as opposed to conventional banking. The converse is true with reference to other parts of the global arena, where conventional banking is the dominant mode of banking and commercial interactions. In such a case scenario, the costs of financing would be greater on Islamic banking, whereas their source of funding would be limited. This is because existent conventional banking systems, basing their operation-ability on profit and interest making, essentially provide the lions-share of capital to existent banking and financial institutions. Consequently, Sharia-compliant banking institutions are not able to finance their operations with such monies, hence necessitating the raising of capital from other sources. Additionally, there is the fact that the lack of interests on ventures undertaken would further limit their sources of capital, compensation and asset basis, providing high rates and costs of financing [4].

Are Islamic windows as effective as full-fledged Islamic banks?

The three nation-entities (Sudan, Pakistan and Iran) are predominantly the only arenas, where full-fledged Islamic banking thrives, with the government implementing a greater compliance of Sharia Law with respect to their banking industries. Fully-fledged Islamic banks are, however, present in various other nation-entities, though not with the same impact as that experienced in the aforementioned two states. These banks are vital in enhancing the banking capacities of Muslim populations within various regions, providing requisite financing and account holding services and products. Islamic windows, even when enhanced to the best possible levels, are not as effective as fully-fledged Islamic banks. The former are unable to fully shield themselves from any transactions, deals, investments and ventures, which may inadvertently in one way or another entail that which is considered Haram, as adequately as the latter [5].

Can Islamic banking, as a system replace conventional banking in Muslim countries?

This is possible, in a localised or national point of view, and eventually regionally and globally. Muslim nations, apart from Sudan, Iran and Pakistan, are indeed faced with considerable challenges, with respect to their overall replacement of existing conventional banking systems with Islamic, Sharia-compliant banking systems. This is due to the nature of the foundation of their individual financial and banking sectors. As former colonies or trust lands, the majority of the existing Muslim nations were founded on conventional banking and finance systems, which are traceable to their colonising nations' financial organisations. These parent organisations, being styled along Western Capitalism were fundamentally influenced and, hence, rooted in the accumulation of wealth [6]. This necessitated the utility of interest-based loans, asset and venture financing, capital accumulations, as well as capital sourcing. These principles were ideally passed on to the resultant banks, which engaged in similar practices, the form of religious ideals held notwithstanding. Due to the lack of greater accessibility to adequately available optional banking systems, the young (recently independent) nation-states had to engage interactively with such entities in their processes of finance, banking, investment and even funding of governance.

In addition, with the increased utility of such conventional systems, they became entrenched and, difficult to do away with within a short time-frame, let alone based on religious principles and ideals. Their economies had to run, sustain and support the national growth; hence, this could not be risked at the expense of changing existing systems of banking. With a gradual shift of economic practices, Islamic banking may lay a strong foundation for itself, especially in nation-entities with strong economic muscle and flexibility [7].

Additionally, with a fundamental stake in global trade and commerce, such nations may withstand the pressure and competition from conventional banking. In conclusion, the less economically strong nation states, specifically those dependent on Western trade and aid in terms of funding and logistical support, may find it an uphill task to achieve, as their economic basis is controlled and, influenced by conventional banking systems rooted in Western Capitalism.

Meanwhile, Islamic banking incorporates various aspects of Islamic faith and religion into the trade and commercial aspects of banking. Oman, like many of her neighbours, is a Muslim nation, with the majority of nationals being Muslims [8,9]. This underscores the introduction of Islamic banking in the country. From the social perspective, Islamic banking not only brings on board religious values practiced by the larger sections of the population, it also serves as a bridge between religious teachings and believers' practices [9].

Based on the above perspective, it is obvious that in theory, researchers would contemplate a positive relationship between Islamic banking and the customers' intentions to switch accounts. However, this study paints a different image of the situation. Respondents appeared unconvinced that Islamic banks are actually cheaper than conventional banking, and that these unique institutions have a bright future in the banking world. Equally unimpressive among the features of Islamic banks are the ethical and transparency aspects. Based on the overall response of interviewees, Islamic banks are unlikely to fully replace other conventional banking institutions in the unlikely situation that the other banks were phased out.

An inverse linear relationship between Islamic banking (and its perspectives) and customers' intentions to switch accounts is indicative of low satisfaction levels with the unique features offered by the Islamic banks. In practice, this relationship would result in greater intention to switch accounts among Islamic bankers. For implementers of this banking system, it is apparent that there is need for review of the specific features that cause discontent, or better explain the various aspects of the business that are not easily understood by the customer base and certainly can be achieved through raising the level of customer awareness.

Qualitative Approach

This study applied the qualitative approach as the method of analysis in terms of interview to focus groups to measure the impact created by introducing the Islamic bank system on customers' switching intention on Omani banking industry. In this respect the use of the interviews can help to gather valid and reliable data that are relevant to the research questions and objectives [10]. In addition, these authors further stated that, the nature of any interview should be consistent with the research questions, objectives, purpose and strategy. Furthermore, the same writers categorized three types of interviews; structured interviews, semi-structured interviews and unstructured interviews.

In this regard, in an exploratory study, semi-structured interviews has been used in order to understand the relationships between variables such as those revealed from a descriptive study, therefore, and since this study is exploratory in nature and this study generated several themes, factors and questions from the literatures review, a semi-structured type has been adopted.

Interview process

Based on the themes, factors and questions generated from the literature reviewed a set of 15 semi-structured questions has been developed and e-mailed to 4 bank customers from the researcher e-mail address book as a pilot test. All the 4 customers' responses were received and based on their feedback, the interview questions were modified and two questions out of 15 questions were found repeated and accordingly dropped.

Thereafter, 14 bank customers were randomly selected from different banks in Oman and appointments for face-to-face interviews were arranged and agreed. Prior to the interview's date the set of the interview's questions was sent to them through an e-mails in order to ensure the preparedness of the interviewees.

Upon the completion of the 14 interviews, the respondents' feedback was recorded, coded and translated into transcripts.

Interviews' participants' selection and sampling

According to Creswell [11-13], selecting the appropriate candidates for interviews is very critical. The study therefore should use one of the various types of sampling strategies such as criterion based sampling or critical case sampling in order to get reasonable qualified candidates that will provide the most credible information to the study. Creswell also suggests the significance of getting participants who will be willing to openly and honestly share information and experience.

Moreover, there are different ways in which interview participants can be selected. However, selecting interview participants and contacting them depends on several factors including the researcher's skills, time, budget, study objectives, and which organisations and managers are willing to cooperate [14]. Moreover, the way of defining and choosing interview participants and the way of contacting them depends on which types of information are needed and how the data will be used [15].

In this study, conducting interviews with banks' customers was undertaken on a small scale with respect to the idea that the customers' switching phenomenon is investigated mainly from the customers' perspective and also taking a note of the relevant literatures from other banking industries.

Ethical considerations

According to Gregory [16], a set of ethical consideration plays a role in a qualitative research method. This study took into consideration the ethical principles in order to conduct the research in an ethical way and responsible way. The respondents were free to choose whether to participate in the study or even to terminate their participation. Informed consent was first obtained before any participant was involved in the study.

Meanwhile, all the participants were informed of the nature of this research study, but more importantly, they were informed about the expected outcome once the study is completed. The contact address of the study's researcher and the University accompanied the questionnaires. The researcher received a number of e-mails from the banks customers showing their interest to share more personal banking experience and also wanted to know the end results and findings of this study.

Further, the second principle considered in this study methodology is the principle of beneficence and justice. The duty of the researcher was to do well and practice equality in order to avoid bias. Effective confidentiality procedures were considered in the research. The responses were not linked to any name or financial institution thus the report maintained the anonymity. As it was in the qualitative approach, quantitative approach was as well guided by ethical principles.

Qualitative Analysis Results and Discussion

This section interprets the results generated through interview with focus groups concerned the study by using qualitative method in terms of interview.

Customers are becoming more aware of banking relationships and are taking greater control of them. They tend to switch banks, change their behaviour and demand improvements in order to get satisfaction and have their needs met. In response, banks have to re-evaluate their assumptions and make fundamental changes in the way they interact with customers. They need to provide the customers with greater flexibility, control and choice as well as reconfigure their business models around the needs and demands of the customers. Modern customers are becoming less loyal and the number of those who are switching their main bank is constantly growing.

In order to get data for analysis, this researcher conducted 14 face-to-face interviews of selected customers from 6 different banks in Oman. They helped to get a richness and depth of data [17]. In this respect, face-to-face interviews enable the interviewer to observe and listen at the same time, to establish rapport with the respondent and to ask complex questions. They also allow getting the formulation of scientific generalizations and are helpful at the exploratory stage of research [18].

It is believed that customer satisfaction is the main factor that influences customers' decision to switch the main bank. Effective satisfaction creates loyalty among customers. Hence, satisfaction is a critical scale of how well customers' demands and needs are met. At the same time, customer loyalty is considered to be a measure of how likely a customer is to repeat the use of services and products as well as engage in relationship activities [19].

Customers' switching experience/intention and factors

It should be mentioned that 36% of respondents claimed that they have switched a bank during the past 5 years; the same quantity remained loyal to their main bank. The interview results show that 5 participants are going to switch their main bank because of service issues, high loan interest rates, the need for Islamic banking, and the relationships with bank staff. Nine interviewees expressed no intention to change the bank. Participants' desire to change their main bank is shown in Table 1.

This finding is in line with the finding of past studies as shown in the literature analysis that the overall proportion of customers planning to change their main banks has increased since 2011. A total

Response	Number of interviewees	Participants %
Yes	5	36%
No	9	64%

Table 1: Interviews Result for Customers' Switching Intention.

of 50% of customers find that the need for Islamic banking charges and fees the leading drivers of attrition. More and more often, customers use the service of two, three, or even four banks [20]. Meanwhile, the predominant feedback of the interview participants showed that they maintain between 1 and 2 accounts, and the reasons are as follows: one source of income and loan commitments, one account participants, two and more account participants, segregation between salary and other incomes (Table 2).

In this regard, when respondents were asked about their opinion concerning the most important factors that may influence their intention to switch their main bank, they repeatedly commented that the customer service and transaction speed are the most important factors for the bank switch. However, there were some other factors mentioned, including: accuracy, easy access, loan interest rates, service, quality, the need for Islamic banking, problem solving, product/service varieties, facilities, speed, location/convenience, communication/open-door, attractive offers (competitions), innovative products, and respect (staff conduct/attitude).

It has been found that quality, trust, satisfaction and behavioural intentions are significant factors which affect switching barriers prediction. However, satisfaction appears to be the strongest factor [21]. The analysis of relevant literature has shown that a reduction in customer switching can be more profitable than reducing costs or gaining market. The participants frequently commented that the existing loan commitments and relationship with bank staff are the most important factors to stay with their main banks in spite of being not fully satisfied with overall bank services. However, they also mentioned other factors including switching costs, resistance to change/laziness, proximity (convenience), the need for existing products, new life insurance as well as lack of competitive offers. The process of switching from one bank to another is described as an easy one with little concern about the documentations. Only 2 participants (14%) followed the idea that this process it difficult as it takes time and effort. The interview results have shown that the barriers and costs associated with bank switch are clearance of existing loans, fees and interests, new life insurance costs and others (Table 3).

Moreover, Colgate and Lang [22] carried out the study that investigated the reasons why customers did not switch their main bank. They identified the two most important barriers of switching banks including apathy and negative reasons for customers staying with their current bank (e.g., switching costs such as money, time, and psychological costs). A relationship variable was also mentioned as one of the key factors. It was also stated that repeated purchase does not necessarily indicate loyalty. Service recovery efforts are believed to be related to organisations' desire to rectify, amend and restore one loss caused by a service failure.

Number of Participants	Number of banks	Reasons for maintaining bank account
6	1	Loan commitments Good service One source of income
5	2	For Salary Credit and Other Income Different Products More Access to ATMs
3	3	For Salary, Savings and Other Needs Relationship with other Banks Branch Managers

Table 2: Reasons for maintaining one or more bank accounts.

Switching's barriers	Participants %
Clearance of Existing Loans	42%
Time and Efforts (new approvals)	15%
Interests and Fees	15%
New life Insurance Cost	14%
No Barriers/No Idea	14%

Table 3: Barriers Associated with Bank Switch.

Customers' perception towards Islamic banking products

Participants often expressed serious concerns about the full compliance of Islamic banking with Shariah principles. Thus, 5 interviewees (36%) agreed that with the entry of Islamic Banking to Oman, the Islamic banking in general is fully complying with "Shariah" principles. This opinion was based on the country Mufti and Shariah Scholars. Three interviewees (21%) expressed disagreements due to loan renaming and bank circumvents. Doubts were shown by 6 interviewees (43%) as they believed that Islamic banking is trying to legitimize banking transactions. Participants showed a mix of views whether many customers will migrate to Islamic banking or not. Hence, 50% of participants suggested the idea that customers will migrate because of religious reasons, opportunities for businessmen, new employees, something new in the market, dissatisfaction with the conventional banks as well as high belief in the concept of "Halal" and "Haram". Four interviewees (30%) disagreed with customer migration to Islamic banking as they believed that they provide limited services and products and that banks are unable to provide financial solutions and credibility. It was also explained by the fact that many customers are unaware of Islamic banking, have misconceptions about Islamic bank functioning, or feel the need to clear the existing consumer loans commitments. 20% expressed doubts as they claimed that customers who feel a need in special products and services and have individual beliefs may migrate. However, they also agreed that religious orientation, financial solutions, Shariah compliance and credibility may influence customers' intention to switch.

Furthermore, it was revealed that the most important factors that motivate a conventional bank customer to migrate to an Islamic bank are religious reasons, low loan interest rates, and better customer service. However, better financing rates/terms, "Halal" banking services and awareness were also mentioned. In spite of having Islamic banks, many Muslim customers are still banking with conventional banks. Participants' opinion concerning this issue widely differs. The main reasons which influence customers' decision to deal with conventional banks are as follows: the need for easy cash (consumer loans), existing consumer liabilities, limited products, high administrative fees (cost of borrowing), quality service and relationship, awareness about Islamic banking, scepticism, the strength of promotional activities of conventional banks, customers will think on the benefits rather than anything else, and no difference between Islamic and conventional banking in the content (only name/form). Most participants (86%) claimed they would not migrate even in case the cost of borrowing is higher in Islamic bank.

The final question of the interview was concerning being a customer of a conventional bank with Islamic window and the desire to migrate to a full-fledged Islamic bank. 11 participants (79%) said that they would not migrate, explaining that the Islamic window meets their needs; they get the same benefits from both conventional and Islamic products/services and remain loyal to the main bank. Only 3 participants (21%) doubted and said that their decision would depend on incentives and offers.

In this respect, the data gathered from face-to-face interviews shows that 50% of all respondents state that they have switched a bank during the past 5 years. At the same time, the rest of respondents have confessed that they remained loyal to their conventional banks. Further interviews results have showed that 33% of the participants were about to switch their main bank. The reasons for such decisions are rather diverse and, among others, include the issues related to negative experience with service and technical support, and high rates of loan interest. Some of them mentioned that switching of banks is needed for further financial requirements especially the Islamic products and therefore they switched to Islamic banks. The rest of the respondents indicated that the relations with bank staff to have been the reason for leaving.

Moreover, the results showed positive customers' attitude towards Islamic banking in general as 56% of the respondents are interested in switching to Islamic Banks. It should be recalled that the main objective of this study is to identify the factors that influencing customers' intention to switch banks. However, during early 2012, Oman allowed the Islamic Banking for the first time as a response to a public demand during what was called "Arab spring". Therefore, this study presumed that, such new entry will have an impact on the customers switching intentions as customers may intent to switch to the new Islamic banks. Nonetheless, the initial literature reviews has not cited the need for Islamic banking products among the common switching factors; however, face to face interviews with bank customers revealed that, the need for Islamic banking product was one of the influencing factors. Therefore, it has been added to this study as variable to test the expected influence on switching intention without going deeply into the concept of Islamic banking.

Conclusion and Implications

This study concludes that customers tend to switch their main bank, and they usually have more than 1 account due to loan commitments, two and more account participants, segregation between salary and others. Meanwhile, trust, quality, the customer service, behavioural intentions and transaction speed have proven to be the key factors which influence customers' desire to switch. In this respect, the process of switching is considered to be an easy one. Moreover, it was discovered that customers express concerns about the full compliance of Islamic banking with Shariah principles. Finally, better customer service, low loan interest rates and religious beliefs motivate customers to migrate from a conventional bank to an Islamic one.

It should be recalled that to reflect the impact of Islamic banking entry in Oman on customers' intentions to switch banks. Literature analysis showed that customers' awareness of the prevalence of interest-based business contracts within traditional banking institutions forced a lot of Muslim customers to switch to Islamic banks (Omar 2008). However, the quality of services, costs, and benefits are equally important factors. One of the main reasons why the participants of focus groups wanted to change their main bank was the need for Islamic banking products (34%). This percentage sounds reasonable, especially taking into consideration the momentum of the new launch of Islamic banking in Oman and the tendency to try new products. The overall customers' perceptions towards the entry of Islamic Banking to Oman banking sector is positive.

Meanwhile, the findings indicated that 40.7% of interviewees expressed neutral attitude towards full compliance of Islamic banks with Shariah (Islamic) principles. The main reason is that Islamic banking is new for Oman market, and the awareness level needs more time to mature. 25% of respondents believed that Islamic banking is less costly and more ethical and transparent than conventional banking. However, only 26.3% of participants claimed that Islamic banking products and services are very different from those of conventional banking. At the same time, the literature review indicates on the contrary views.

Moreover, the study predicts great potential for Islamic banks as more than one third of respondents showed an intention to change their banks to Islamic banking in Oman, and only 13.2% spoke against this idea. Almost half of the respondents supported the idea of using services of Islamic banking, even if the service costs would be higher than those in traditional banks.

Even though the concept of Islamic banking is new to most Omani citizens, the customers' expectations are high as they believe that this type of banking will substantially reduce loan fees and suit their religious beliefs. Most Islamic banks in Oman are new and have a limited number of branches across the country, and it might be difficult for them to reach customers who live in distant areas. In this regard, the interview outcomes suggest that more than half of respondents are inclined to transfer to Islamic banking despite the fact that 64% are satisfied with their current banks. Hence, it can be concluded that faith has an influence on customer decisions.

Moreover, the customers' intention to switch their current bank is influenced by the perception of a number of factors, such as the need for Islamic banking products, fees, service quality, competition, convenience of services, barriers associated with bank switch, bank employee performance and relationships with customers, and transparency of terms and conditions. However, the need for Islamic banking products and services has been found to be the major factor that influences the customers' intention to switch their banks.

This is the main driving force for customers to develop the intention to change their banks in future as the majority of the respondents showed an interest in Islamic banking products. Therefore, it is essential for all banks to satisfy their customers' needs and consider their individual religious beliefs. Islamic banking is a new concept in Oman, which is only starting preparations for the future operations. Conventional banks need to be proactive in addressing the needs of Islamic banking products before those customers switch to Islamic Banks.

Based on the above perspective, it is obvious that theoretically the researchers in a Muslim country like Oman would contemplate positive relationship between the need for Islamic banking products and the customers' intentions to switch bank accounts. However, this study presents a different image of the situation. Participants often expressed serious concerns about the full compliance of Islamic banking with Shariah principles (43%) as they believed that Islamic banking is trying to legitimize the banking transactions. Most participants (86%) claimed they would not prefer Islamic bank if it has higher loan interest rates. Furthermore, the majority of participants (79%), perceived the Islamic 'window' as good as the full-fledged Islamic bank and appeared unconvinced that Islamic banks are actually cheaper than conventional ones. Therefore, they will not give preference to it.

The above-mentioned results allow concluding that, the Islamic banking in Oman is expected to face a plenty of challenges and customers' perception is one of the major concerns. Islamic banking in Oman needs to put a lot of efforts into educating the community and promoting the level of awareness about the faith and essence of Islamic banking.

References

1. World Retail Banking Report, 2013.

2. Zeithaml VA, Bitner MJ, Gremler DD (2009) Services marketing: integrating customer focus across the firm. McGraw-Hill Education, Singapore.
3. Rosly SA (2009) Critical issues on Islamic banking and financial markets: Islamic economics, banking and finance, investments, Takaful and financial planning. House Publishers, Bloomington.
4. Warde I (2009) Islamic finance in the global economy. Edinburgh University Press, Edinburgh.
5. Chapra MU, Khan S, Al Shaikh-Ali A (2008) The Islamic vision of development in the light of maqasid al-Shariah.
6. El-Gamal M (2010) Limits and dangers of Sharia Arbitrage. In: Ali N (ed.), Islamic finance: current legal and regulatory issues, Islamic Finance Project/ Islamic Legal Studies/Harvard Law School, Cambridge, pp: 117-131.
7. Jairus B (2007) Islam, the Mediterranean and the rise of capitalism. Historical Materialism 15: 47-74.
8. Sangeetha K, Pria S (2012) Resources Affecting Banks' CSR in Sultanate of Oman: A Stakeholders' Perspective. Electronic Journal of Business Ethics and Organization Studies 17: 31-40.
9. Khan S (2012) Factors responsible for making consumer attitude towards Islamic banking. Arabian Journal of Business and Management Review 2: 136-146.
10. Saunders M, Lewis P, Thornhill A (2000) Research methods for business students. (2nd edn.), Prentice Hall, Harlow.
11. Creswell JW (2007) Qualitative inquiry & research design: choosing among five approaches. (2ndedn), Sage, Thousand Oaks.
12. Bryman A (1988) Quantity and Quality in Social Research. London: Unwin Hyman.
13. Bryman A (2004) Social Research Methods. (2nd edn), Oxford: Oxford University.
14. Ferreira L, Merchant K (1992) Field research in management accounting and control: a review and evaluation. Accounting Auditing and Accountability Journal 5: 3-34.
15. Silverman D (2013) Doing qualitative research: A practical handbook. SAGE Publications Limited.
16. Gregory I (2003) Ethics in research. Bloomsbury Publishing, London, UK.
17. Newton N (2010) The use of semi-structured interviews in qualitative research: strengths and weaknesses.
18. Designing structured interviews for educational research (1997) Research & Evaluation.
19. Mohsan F, Nawa MM, Khan MS, Shaukat Z, Aslam N (2011) Impact of customer satisfaction on customer loyalty and intentions to switch: evidence from banking sector of Pakistan. International Journal of Business and Social Science 2: 263-270.
20. Global Consumer Banking Survey (2012) The customer takes control.
21. Kaur G, Sharma RD, Mahajan N (2012) Exploring customer switching intentions through relationship marketing paradigm. International Journal of Bank Marketing 30: 280-302.
22. Colgate MR, Lang B (2001) Switching barriers in consumer markets: an investigation of the financial services industry. Journal of Consumer Marketing 18: 332-347.

selected based on the willing of respondents to participate in the study. The criteria for the inclusion of respondents were that those having passed their probationary period. A total of 60 respondents filled the questionnaire selected from the metropolitan city of Lahore, from three different banks.

The questionnaire consisted of 47 closed ended questions on five point Likert scale. For the measurement of organizational commitment, 13 items were included in the questionnaire. The items for the measurement of organizational commitment were based on the Mowday's most widely use measure of organizational commitment [23]. A total number of 34 items were included for the measurement of factors affecting organizational commitment. The items measuring factors were based on the instrument developed by Eisenberger et al. [2]. Since both the questionnaires have been widely used in studies, therefore there was no problem of reliability and validity. The data were analyzed using SPSS version 16. The following section presents the analysis of discussion.

Data Analysis and Discussion

The following Table 1 shows the correlations among the factors affecting the organizational commitment. As cursory look at Table 1 shows that there are significant correlations among the factors affecting the organizational commitment and the construct of organizational commitment. The organizational rewards (both monetary and nonmonetary) have positive correlation strength of 0.383 at significance level of 0.05. The level of supervisor support is also positively correlated with organizational commitment having a value of 0.372 at $p \leq 0.05$. This is in line with the study of Landsman [12]. According to Landsman supervisor support is correlated to organizational commitment at a level of 0.26 [12]. The results on the third factor of work-family support also show that is positively and significantly correlated to organizational commitment having strength of 0.468 at $p \leq 0.01$. This result confirms the study of Dockel who that the support and organizational commitment have a correlation of 0.31. Further correlations are also in line with the other findings.

They found correlations of 0.26. According to another research study the results are confirming the theoretical background. The third factor affecting the organizational is career opportunities. Career opportunities are strongly correlated to the organizational commitment with value of 0.626 at $p \leq 0.01$. The fact that career opportunities are correlated with organizational commitment is also support by Dockel. However Dockel found the value of correlation to a lower level of 0.34. The results also confirm the argument of Opkara that the feeling among employees to grow with the organizational commits them to the organization [18]. The fifth and the last factor which is significantly and in fact highly correlated to organizational commitment are job conditions. The value of correlation between organizational commitment and job conditions is 0.637 at $p \leq 0.01$. This is in contrast to Dockel who found no significant correlation between job characteristics and organizational commitment. But at the same time results confirm that finding of Steers, concluding there is a significant relationship between job conditions and organizational commitment (Table 1).

Table 2 shows the regression results. The independent factors explain a variation of up to 38% in the dependent variable of organizational commitment. Having a look at the regression coefficients tells that the all the factors positively affect the dependent variable of organizational commitment. If the organizational rewards are increased by 1% the level commitment will be enhanced by 2%. We can therefore claim that higher the organizational reward, higher the organizational commitment thus supporting our first hypothesis. This result is consistent to our theoretical framework and confirms the previous studies of Landsman and Fasolo [9,12].

The second regression coefficient relates to supervisor support. It tells that while the level of supervisor support towards employees increases by 1%, the level of employee commitment increases by a considerable level of 16%. These results supplement the previous studies of Eisenberger et al. [2,13]. Hence we can conclude that higher supervisor support is regarded as support by the organization itself. Therefore, higher the supervisors' support, higher the organizational commitment.

	OC	OR	SS	WFS	CO	JC
OC	1	0.383*	e.372*	0.468**	0.626**	0.637**
OR	0.383*	1	0.402*	0.590**	0.540**	0.276
SS	0.372*	0.402*	1	0.341*	0.476**	0.478**
WFS	0.468**	0.590**	0.341*	1	0.460**	0.425**
CO	0.626**	0.540**	0.476**	0.460**	1	0.615**
JC	0.637**	0.276	0.478**	0.425**	0.615**	1

*Correlation is significant at the 0.05 level (1-tailed).

**Correlation is significant at the 0.01 level (1-tailed).

OC: Organizational Commitment; OR: Organizational Rewards; SS: Supervisor Support; WFS: Work-family support; CO: Career; Opportunities; JC: Job Conditions.

Table 1: Correlations

		Unstandardized Coefficients		Standardized Coefficients	
Model		B	Std. Error	Beta	T
1	Constant	10.964	8.977		1.221
	OR	0.022	0.337	0.013	0.066
	SS	0.166	0.333	0.087	0.499
	WFS	0.388	0.549	0.127	0.708
	CO	0.608	0.404	0.31	1.505
	JC	0.833	0.369	0.445	2.259

Dependent Variable: OC; F = 4.679; Adjusted R Square = 0.384; Significance =0.004.

OC: Organizational Commitment, OR: Organizational Reward, SS: Self Support, WFS: Work Family Support, CO: Career Opportunities, JC: Job Conditions

Table 2: Regression coefficients.

The third factor of work family support showed a beta coefficient of 0.388. Organizational commitment is positively affected by the support from organization in family issues. Our third hypothesis proposing higher the support in family matters, higher the organizational commitment also stands accepted confirming the previous researches [20,22].

The regression result show that our hypothesis stating that higher growth opportunities lead to higher organizational commitment of employees. An increase of 1% in the growth opportunities enhances the organizational commitment to 60%. The results thus validate the previous studies that there is positive relationship between organizational commitment and growth opportunities.

There is evidence that highly favorable job conditions lead to higher organizational commitment among the employees. The beta coefficient (Table 2) shows that our proposed hypothesis is supported. The results of regression analysis are in line with the previous studies. The interpretations of regression analysis hold true if for one factor affecting organizational commitment, the effect of other four factors is held constant (Table 2).

We analyzed the effect of factors effecting the organizational commitment of bank officers. The data analysis validates the conclusions of previous researches [24-26]. It has been found that there is direct positive effect of various factors on the commitment of banks officers. Another study was conducted on radiographers to find the effect of factors affecting the commitment of radiographers [26]. The findings of this study are also consistent with the said study. However, we did not find any previous study to have been conducted on bank officers.

The underlying theoretical framework to this study holds that through provision of various facilities to the employees, their level of organizational commitment enhances as a matter of phenomenon of norm of reciprocity. According to proposition of social exchange theory, individuals who receive good treatment from others are likely to repay. This exchange may be called as the phenomenon of reciprocity [3].

Such exchange occurs in organizations as well. In this exchange employees contribute to the achievement of organizational goals, put extra effort, and stick with the organization after having supported by the organization [2,24]. The results show that bank officers get more committed based on certain factors validating the exchange and reciprocity phenomenon.

Conclusion and Recommendations

We have investigated those factors which affect the organizational commitment of bank officers. This research happens to be unique in the context of Pakistan. The factors having positive impact on organizational were proposed on the basis of social exchange theory and the reciprocity norm. The results of our investigation show that the relevant factors must be promoted to enhance the commitment of officers. The employees in turn are likely to put more effort, and are likely to be attached with the organization for longer time.

The researchers recommend that in order to strengthen the commitment of employees with their organization, the factors responsible for enhancing the commitment must be strengthened. Lew found that committed employees are very beneficial for the organization [25]. In this research, we conclude that if the organization cares for officers, they will repay with stronger commitment to their bank. Thus phenomenon of reciprocity happens to be proved in true sense. The organizations should provide clear and easy career paths to the employees. Among the rewards may include both monetary and non-monetary benefits. Another are of support may be the extension of support beyond the work to the family.

References

1. Blau PM (1964) Exchange and power in social life. Wiley, New York.
2. Eisenberger R, Huntington R, Hutchison S, Sowa D (1986) Perceived Organizational support. Journal of Applied Psychology 71: 500-507.
3. Gouldner AW (1960) The norm of reciprocity: A preliminary statement. American Sociological review 25: 161-178.
4. Meyer JP, Allen NJ (1991) A three-component conceptualization of organizational commitment. Human Resource Management Review 1: 61-89.
5. Mathieu JE, Zajac D (1990) A review and meta-analysis of the antecedents, correlates, and consequences of organizational commitment. Psychological Bulletin 108: 171-194.
6. Guzzo RA, Noonan KA, Elron E (1994) Expatriate managers and the psychological contract. Journal of Applied Psychology 79: 617-626.
7. Wayne SJ, Shore LM, Liden RC (1997) Perceived organizational support and leader member exchange: A social exchange perspective. Academy of Management Journal 40: 82-111.
8. Jones B, Flynn DM, Kelloway EK (1995) Perception of support from the organization in relation to work stress, satisfaction and commitment. In: Sauter, Murphy (eds.) Organizational risk factors and job stress. pp: 41-52.
9. Fasolo P (1995) Procedural Justice & Perceived organizational support: Hypothesized effects on job performance. In: Cropanzano, Kacmar (eds.) Organizational politics, justice and support pp: 185-195.
10. Eisenberger R, Cummings J, Armeli S, Lynch P (1997) Perceived organizational support, discretionary treatment, and job satisfaction. Journal of Applied Psychology 82: 812-820.
11. Shore LM, Shore TH (1995) Perceived organizational support and organizational justice. In: Cropanzano, Kacmar (eds.) Organizational politics, justice, and support: Managing the social climate of the workplace pp: 149-164.
12. Landsman MJ (2008) Pathways to Organizational Commitment. Administration in Social Work 32: 105-132.
13. Levinson H (1965) Reciprocation: The relationship between man and organization. Administrative Science Quarterly 9: 370-390.
14. Tansky JW, Cohen DJ (2001) The Relationship Between Organizational Support, Employee Development, and Organizational Commitment: An Empirical Study. Human Resource Development Quarterly 12: 285-300.
15. Harel GH, Tzafrir SS (1999) The effect of human resource management practices on the perceptions of organizational and market performance of the firm. Human Resource Management 38: 185-199.
16. Kalleberg AL, Moody JW (1994) Human resource management and organizational performance. American Behavioral Scientist 37: 948-962.
17. McEvoy MG (1997) Organizational change and outdoor management education. Human Resource Management 36: 235-250.
18. Okpara JO (2004) Job Satisfaction and Organizational Commitment: Are there differences between American and Nigerian Managers Employed in the US MNCs in Nigeria? Academy of Business & Administrative Sciences, Briarcliffe College, Switzerland.
19. Nadler L, Nadler Z (1989) Developing human resources. (3rdedn) Jossey-Bass, San Francisco.
20. Casper WJ, Harris CM (2008) Work-life benefits and organizational attachment: Self-interest utility and signaling theory models. Journal of Vocational Behavior 72: 95-109.
21. Rhoades L, Eisenberg R (2002) Perceived Organizational Support: A Review of the Literature. Journal of Applied Psychology 87: 698-714.
22. Allen TD (2001) Family-supportive work environments: The role of organizational perceptions. Journal of Vocational Behavior 58: 414-435.
23. Mowday RT, Porter LW, Steers RM (1982) Employee-organizational Linkages:

The psychology of commitment, absenteeism, and turnover. San Diego, Academic Press, CA 88: 1315-1317.

24. Somech A, Bogler Ronit (2002) Antecedents and consequences of Teacher organizational and professional commitment. Educational Administration Quarterly 38: 555-577.

25. Lew TY (2009) The Relationships between Perceived Organizational Support, Felt Obligation, Affective Organizational Commitment and Turnover Intention of Academics working with Private Higher Educational Institutions in Malaysia. European Journal of Social Sciences 9: 72-87.

26. Makanjee CR, Hartzer YF, Uys IL (2006) The effect of perceived organizational support on organizational commitment of diagnostic imaging radiographers. Radiography pp: 118-206.

Bankers on Board, Banks as Shareholders and Firm's Performance: Case of the Tunisian Listed Companies

Affes H and Hakim NH*

Lecturer at the Faculty of Sciences, Faculty of Economics and Management of Sfax, University of Sfax, Tunisia

Abstract

Unlike the Anglo-Saxon countries, where business financing is made through the financial markets, Tunisian banks play a more important role than the financial markets in funding the firms. In addition to their function as lenders, they can participate in the capital of companies and/or serve on their boards. Our results on a sample of 14 listed companies on the Tunisian Stock Exchange (STE) during the 2003/2009 period show that banks play an important role in the governance of the Tunisian firms and affect their performance. Based on this sample, we performed regressions of these two governance variables (banking participation in the firms' equity and boards) on the firms' accounting and stock performance. The obtained results show that, firstly, the banking investment in the firms' share capital has a negative impact on the accounting performance measured by the ROA and the ROE and positively on the stock market performance (Tobin's Q and Marris) and, secondly, the banking presence in the board of directors has both a positive and negative impact on the accounting performance on the stock market performance.

Keywords: Bankers on board; Banks as shareholders; Firm's Performance; Anglo-Saxon

Introduction

Nowadays, the corporate finance researches attach great importance to the role of banks in the management of enterprises [1-3]. In fact, companies resort to banking indebtedness. The nature of the relationship between banks and enterprises depends on the country and the existing regulations. Unlike Germany and Japan, where financing takes place via banks, the Anglo-Saxon financial markets play an important role in the funding and control of companies. German companies maintain long term relationships with a Bank called "Hausbank". A fundamental characteristic of these banks is their participation in the companies' capital and funding them Moreover, the Japanese Keiretsu system enables banks to become shareholders and members in the Board of Directors. The bank ownership is a very widespread phenomenon in the Japanese banking systems and the continental Europe. The theory recognizes the ability of the bank holdings on the liabilities of big businesses to improve the control system of the leaders. Moreover, the presence of banks in the capital of companies improves the quality of information they have, which leads to a more efficient control of the investment activities. The banking participation in the companies' capital enables them to acquire data related to the internal functioning of the company, the sector and competition. This piece of information does not exist in the accounting and financial documents which are usually possessed by banks.

Unlike the studies dealing with the effect of composition of the Board of Directors and the structure of property on performance, the ones conducted about the effect of the presence of banks in both the Board of Directors and in the structure of property on performance are few. Indeed, the scarcity of studies has led to the present research.

The agency theory assumes that there are conflicts of interest between the shareholders and the creditors. The control exercised by the banks on companies helps reduce the agency costs [4]. Therefore, according to the assumption of control, the presence of the banks in the Board of Directors reduces the agency costs and improves the company's value. On the other hand, under the assumption of the agency costs of debt-equity, the banks' presence in the Board of Directors negatively impacts the company's value. On the other hand, according to the assumption of the agency costs of debt-equity, the banks' presence in the Board of Directors negatively effects on the company's value. Bubna and Radhakrishnan [5] showed that there are information asymmetries between the shareholders and the creditors. According to this hypothesis, the presence of banks in the board of directors reduces the information asymmetries between the firms and the creditors and consequently improves the companies' value.

The existence of conflicts of interest between the shareholders and the creditors is reduced by a set of internal and external mechanisms. The board of directors and ownership structure are two alternative mechanisms of governance and control. Besides these two internal governance mechanisms, the presence of banks in the board of directors and ownership structure are also two governance mechanisms since this presence is associated with a reduction of the agency costs due to the conflicts of interest between the shareholders and the creditors.

The practice of the banks' participation in the firms' capital depends on the country considered. Actually, in France, for example, banks are under no obligation to participate in the firms' capital. However, the American legislation and more particularly the Glass-Steagall Act (1933) prevents banks from participating in the firms' capital. Recently, the American legislation, through the Gramm-Leach- Bliley Act, has given commercial banks the opportunities to participate in the capital of firms. Besides, Germany, which encourages the banks' participation in the companies' capital, introduced some restrictions which were discussed in the Bundestag (1977). A very recent study has revealed that the Monopoly Commission limited the banks' participation to the amount of 5% of the companies' capital. The banking regulations in

***Corresponding author:** Hakim NH, PhD, Faculty of Economics and Management of Sfax, Lecturer at the Faculty of Sciences, University of Sfax, Tunisia
E-mail: nourchenehamza@gmail.com

Tunisia, and more specifically article 21 of Act No. 2001-65 of 10 July 2001 about the credit institutions, stipulate that a credit institution may hold directly or indirectly more than 30% of the capital of the same company.

Literature Review

Banks' participation in the firms' capital in the different theories

Jiang et al. state that the presence of the banks as creditors and shareholders is explained by both the agency and the information asymmetry theories [3]. The banking representation in the companies' capital is beneficial insofar as it helps reduce the conflicts of interest and the information asymmetries between the shareholders and the creditors.

In the agency theory: Being at the same time lenders and shareholders, banks face an apparent conflict of interest and may therefore give their own interests at the expense of the interests of the ordinary shareholders. This apparent conflict between banks and shareholders generates agency costs. However, Petersen and Rajan stipulates that the banks' participation in the capital helps reduce the agency costs when banks act in the interests of the shareholders [6]. Furthermore, he asserts that their presence in the capital improves the flow of information between companies and banks, which therefore reduces the conflicts of interest between the shareholders and the creditors.

Apart from the benefits of the agency cost reduction of the bank shareholding, banks buy the companies' shares when they have the private information that makes them believe that these companies' shares are undervalued. In fact, when banks possess such inside information, they will have the opportunities and incentives to acquire the undervalued shares of these firms to generate capital gains.

Most of the studies point out that the reduction of the agency problems between banks and firms explain the positive relationship between the bank shareholding and the companies' performance. In accordance with this hypothesis, Flath [7] states that the largest creditors in the keiretsu member companies, highly indebted and with strong growth prospects have majority stakes.

Gonzalez states that a bank's decision to raise or reduce the banking debt about the acquisition of capital is operated by the market to know which of the two potential motivations explains the banks' participation in the companies' capital [8]. The author shows that the market explains the banks' participation in the capital together with the reductions of the banking debts by the rise of the agency costs. However, both the banks' stake and the rising banking debt are considered by the market as elements indicating that the bank possesses positive information about the company's prospects. According to this explanation, the companies' abnormal stock returns regarding the announcement of the banks' participation in the capital differ depending on the decision about the banking debt.

The acquisition of the shares by the banks is a mechanism to reduce agency costs. In other words, this acquisition of shares of firms by banks or the participation of the banks in the capital of companies is the result of increases in the costs of Agency Gonzalez [8]. According to this principle, a fall of profitability or a rise of the risk raises the agency costs between the bank and the firms and justifies the involvement of the banks in the capital [7].

Gonzalez states that it is impossible to predict the reaction of the share price when banks participate in the companies' capital when the prospects are unfavorable (lower profitability and/or higher risk under the assumption of the agency costs) or better (higher profitability and/or lower risk under the assumption of the information asymmetry) [8].

Jiang W, Li K, Shao P stipulate that if the origin of the banks' participation in the capital is a rise of the agency costs, then banks may reduce their debt to firms because of these costs [3]. Actually, high agency costs that emerge when companies announce they are insolvent cause an increase of the capital share held by banks and reduce their debt in companies [9-11].

Gonzalez F expects some financial exchange making it possible to reduce the agency costs between the shareholders and the creditors. Moreover, he found that, in countries where banks' participation in the capital is permitted, banks buy the companies' shares and reduce debts in the defaulting firms if they expect a decline of profitability and/or a rise of the company's risk [8].

The agency theory stipulates that the companies' returns on the shares decline following the announcement of the banking participation in the capital preceded by reductions in banking indebtedness. In fact, Gonzalez F showed that the banks' participation in the capital followed by a decline of the banking debts gives negative information to the market about the companies' profitability and risk [8].

Jiang et al. Suggest that the presence of the creditors in the ownership structure enables them to control the leaders and prevents the leaders and/or the large shareholders from taking action which expropriate the creditors [3]. Kalyani examined the effect of the strong relationship between banks and enterprises on the funding constraints. The conflicts of interest between the shareholders and the creditors are a funding constraint. The author also found that the banking participation in the companies' capital helps eliminate the conflicts of interest between the shareholders and the creditors and consequently reduces the resulting agency costs.

In the information asymmetry theory: Gonzalez stipulates that banks may acquire the shares of undervalued companies where they are better informed about the firms' quality (information asymmetry hypothesis) [8]. Under this assumption, the rise of the expected profitability and/or the reduction of the company's risk explain the banks' participation in the capital of firms, while providing capital gains for banks [12]. In other words, the under-valuation of the companies' shares induces banks to participate in their capital. In fact, any participation in the capital is based on the fact that the bank has positive internal information about the company's future. This assumption therefore expects that the decision by the Bank to acquire shares is linked to the expectations of a greater profitability and/or a lower company's risk [8]. Jiang et al. showed that keeping shares and debts given to creditors provides the shareholders with an informational advantage which helps them to choose the borrowers with a lower default risk [3]. From the capital point of view, the institutions participating in the companies' capital will be more informed than the other shareholders due to their effort and their better access to the leaders.

Taking into account the debt, it appears that the syndicated loans are private mechanisms through which confidential information about the company is revealed to the lenders. The creditors' dual position enables them to acquire more information and look for companies having better credit quality, which will consequently reduce the debt cost. Furthermore, by holding a fraction of the capital in the companies, a bank gets new information about the firms' quality, which will help the companies raise their debt with banks [6,13]. On the basis of this theory

Gonzalez [8] states that the bank which possesses private information about the firm's prospects should participate in the companies' capital so as to get capital gain.

The presence of banks in the board of directors as seen by the various theories

In the agency theory: The agency theory assumes that there are conflicts of interests between the shareholders and the creditors that can be solved through a set of internal or even external mechanisms among which we can cite the presence of banks in the Board of Directors. Actually, this presence is beneficial since, according to the agency theory, it minimizes the potential conflicts between the shareholders and the creditors. The presence of banks in the Board ensures a better control. The benefits related to the control exercised by the banks on business help reduce the agency costs [4].

Randall and Strahan [4] argue that American banks are board members because they are concerned only by their function as lenders. On the other hand, this study reveals that one third of the American companies have a Board of Directors dominated by a bank suggesting that the benefits associated with the control by banks help reduce or even eliminate the costs generated by the conflicts of interests. Contrary to what exists in Germany and the Japan, this low percentage is due to the protection of the creditors' rights.

Furthermore, Randall and Strahan found a negative relationship between the presence of banks in the companies' boards of Directors and the conflicts of interests between the creditors, among other things, banks and shareholders [4]. Actually, banks are present in the companies' Boards of Directors if the conflicts of interests between the shareholders and the banks are not very important. In fact, to better defend and act in the shareholders' interests, banks expressed interests have interest in joining the Board of Directors. Randall and Strahan argue that the banks must join the Board of Directors to avoid the conflicts of interests that arise between the banks and company's shareholders [4]. However, Byrd and Mizruchi state that the appointment of banks in the Board of Directors goes against the shareholders' interests [14].

The control hypothesis underlines the role the banks' representatives on the Board of Directors in controlling the leaders. According to this control hypothesis, banks generally that lie ahead for the companies' Board of Directors with lots of agency problems. Moreover, on the basis of the control hypothesis, the banks' membership in the Board of Directors reduces the agency costs and improves the company's value.

The hypothesis of the agency costs, debt, and equity underlines the agency problems between the lenders and the shareholders, and the role of the representatives of the banks in the worsening of these problems. The lenders and shareholders have conflicts because of their different choices of risk which are caused by their different payment structures. In fact, while the lenders prefer a lower risk, the shareholders prefer a higher risk. According to this hypothesis, the fact the banks become members of the Board of Directors negatively affects the market value of equity capital and shows a low market capitalization.

In the theory of the information asymmetry: The hypothesis of the information asymmetry focuses on the role of the banks' representatives to collect information on the company and transmit it to the lender who, in turn, reduces the extent of the information asymmetry between the lender and the company and facilitates external financing. This is beneficial for companies which a greater information asymmetry and financial difficulties [5]. In this scenario, firms with large information problems are more likely to have bank representatives on their boards of directors. Moreover, this information asymmetry hypothesis also provides that companies with a bank representative on their boards have fewer financial constraints and a higher value [5].

Banking participation in equity and performance

Meckling argues that the agency relationship between the shareholders and managers, on the one hand, and between the shareholders and creditors, on the other hand, generates conflicts of interest which involve the agency costs [15]. First, the conflicts between the shareholders and the managers can be reduced by a set of internal and external mechanisms. Then, some researchers state that the conflicts of interest between the shareholders and the creditors are eliminated if banks occupy a dual position as shareholders and creditors [16,17]. As a consequence, the presence of banks in the companies' ownership structure is a way to reduce the conflicts of interest between the shareholders and the creditors.

The banking control of the managers is very common within the Japanese companies. Moreover, the important disciplinary role exerted by banks is put forward as one of the determining factors of the Japanese firms' efficiency. The Japanese companies, which belong to a "keiretsu", are controlled by the main banks which are at the same time shareholders and creditors Kang, Shivdasani, Kaplan, Minton, Morck, Nakamura showed that the major Japanese banks play a crucial role in corporate governance [18-20].

A great deal of research underlines the relationship between the banks' participation in the capital and the firms' performance. However, the obtained results are contradictory, as some have found a linear relationship while others have demonstrated a nonlinear relationship. Banks play a dual role as they are considered at the same time shareholders and creditors. In fact, this dual role affects their motivation to defend the shareholders' interests and, therefore, the company's value [20]. In Japan, Morck, Nakamura, Shivdasani showed that there is a convex relationship between the banks' participation in the companies' capital and their value [1]. This relationship is negative in the case of low levels of equity participation.

Cable showed the existence of a significant positive relationship between the banks' participation in the capital and the profitability of large industrial companies [21]. Gorton, Schmid, Nibler, Perlitz, Seger found a positive relationship between the control by a bank and performance [22-25]. In fact, they found that banks' participation in the companies' capital improves performance when measured with the ROE. Zoido studied the role of the shareholder banks in the industrial companies and showed that the banks exercise their right of control over the decisions taken by companies [26]. Their control is reflected in the low cost of project funding and in the way in which companies solve their financial problems. Pushner found a positive relationship between banks' equity participation and the efficiency of the Japanese companies [27].

On the other hand, Weinstein and Yafeh studied the effect of stable relationships between banks and companies and found that companies which maintain stable relationships do not get higher profits than those that do not have stable relationships but have the same growth rate [28]. Gorton and Schmid found a positive relationship between the banks' participation in the companies' equity and their performance [29]. Lehmann and Weigand reached the same conclusions as those of Gorton and Schmid except that the first used the ROA as an alternative measure of performance [30].

In contrast, in Germany, Weinstein, Chirinko, Kang found a negative relationship between the capital share held by the bank and performance [28,31,32]. Moreover, Emmons, Schmid found a roof-shaped relationship (U-shaped) between performance and the percentage of capital held by the bank, which confirms the managerial hypothesis [33].

Using a sample of 142 companies during the period 1999-2002, Palenzuela, Iturriaga, Tejerina found that banks play a crucial role in corporate governance in Spain [34]. In fact, banks not only act as creditors but can grab a share of the capital as they can serve on the Board of Directors. The authors also claim that control through banks has an impact on the companies' performance. Palenzuela, Iturriaga, Tejerina conducted a comparative study on the bank shareholding between companies in which control comes from banks and those in which control is not confined to banks and found that for the first category of companies, the bank shareholding reduces the performance, however, for the second category of companies, the bank shareholding positively affects performance [34].

On a sample of 94 German companies during the 1992/1996 period, Chirinko and Elston found that the relationship between the Bank shareholding and performance is nonlinear [31]. The sample of Gorton and Schmid consists of two sub samples [22]. The first consists of 88 companies and analysis refers to the year 1974. The second sample consists of 66 companies and relates to the year 1985. They use the capital share held by the Bank as a variable representing the ownership structure and the ROA and ROE as alternative measures of accounting performance.

Gorton and Schmid showed that the relationship between the bank shareholding and performance is based on three hypotheses; the alignment of interests, the opposite or the divergent interests and the managerial hypothesis [22]. Each hypothesis can be associated with an infinite number of explanations. The alignment of interest hypothesis assumes that the capital share held by the bank will be positively related to performance. The argument that corresponds to it is that of aligning the shareholders and creditors' interests. The divergence of interest hypothesis predicts that an increase of the share capital held by the bank is associated with a decrease of performance. The divergence of interests between banks and other shareholders explains this inverse relationship. The third assumption is that the relationship between the capital share held by the bank and performance is nonlinear. In fact, performance decreases and then rises again. This assumption is similar to the managerial one supported by Morck and Nakamura or to the one that tested the effect of the managers' capital participation on performance [20].

Jiang et al. [3] Showed that the relationship between the capital shares held by the bank and the ROE is not linear, in other words, it rises then falls. On the other hand, in a study conducted during the 1965/1990 period, Chirinko and Elston [31] found no relationship between the capital share held by a bank and the performance measured by the ROA.

On a sample of Japanese companies, Wenlian studied the impact of bank's main shareholding on the performance during the 1977/1987 period [35]. In this regard, he conducted a comparative study between affiliated and independent firms and found that the former have a lower performance compared to the latter. By examining a sample of Japanese firms over the 1971/1981 period, Nakatani [36] stated that firms which have relationships with banks have a lower profit and growth rate and a lower performance than independent firms.

In affiliated companies or companies belonging to a group, such as Keiretsu, banks act primarily to save the companies in difficult situations [37]. However, in independent companies, the banking role is rather to defend the creditors' interests and not the shareholders'. Gonzalez [8] analyzed the impact of bank's participation in the capital on a sample of companies in Spain over 1992/1998 period and found that firms in which banks participate in the capital show high levels of profitability and low risk levels.

All these empirical studies show that the affiliated companies reported low cash flow and do not guarantee better performance than the independent ones due to the expropriation of the main bank. Indeed, Morck et al. [1] showed that the major banks maximize their interests through their presence as shareholders and a creditor in companies.

Nachane et al. [38] found a nonlinear relationship between the participation of the major banks and the firm's performance measured by Tobin's Q. Indeed, at low levels of participation of banks in the capital, an increase of this share lowered performance as measured by Tobin's et al. [39] examined a sample of German companies and found that most of the banking ownership in the capital of companies has a positive effect on the equity value measured by the Market to book ratio. They distinguished between majority-shareholder banks and other banks and found that they both have a positive impact on the performance of large listed companies.

The studies focused on the performance difference between the affiliated and independent firms [28,36,40]. Moreover, Gorton et al. [22] state that the relationship between the banks' participation and firm's performance is based on three assumptions. The first assumption is that of the alignment of the banks' interests with the shareholders'. According to this hypothesis, the relationship between the banking participation in the capital and the firm's performance is positive. The higher this share held by banks is, the more the latter ones use their power and information they have to control the managers and the higher the firms' performance will be:

Hypothesis 1: The relationship between the banking stake in the capital and the firms' performance is on the rise (interest convergence hypothesis or the interest alignment).

The second hypothesis is of the different or opposing interests. In fact, banks' interests do not coincide with the shareholders'. The presence of banks as creditors and shareholders and in front of a non-competitive capital market, banks act like monopolists which use their power to extract firms' annuity at the expense of the shareholders, which negatively affects the performance.

Hypothesis 2: The relationship between the banking participation in the capital and the firm's performance is falling (hypothesis of conflicting interests)

Hypothesis 3: The relationship between the banking participation in the capital and the firm's performance falls and then rises again (managerial hypothesis)

The banking presence in the board of directors and performance

A great deal of research has shown a relationship between the presence of the bank in the board of directors and the firms' performance. The results were contradictory. Some found a linear relationship while others found the opposite.

Rosenstein and Wyatt [41] indicated that the proportion of outside directors is positively related to profitability. This positive relationship has an impact on the appointment of a new financial director. The authors add that these outside directors are elected for their expertise. Financial outside directors provide financial security for the business [42-45].

On a sample of 55 Japanese companies, Naohito et al. [46] showed that the presence of banks in the companies' boards of directors helps them better control the leaders. On the other hand, Nachane et al. [38] showed that the presence of banks on the companies' boards of directors has a positive impact on the company's performance due to their expertise.

In the United States, banks do not have the right to participate in the capital of non-financial companies but are often members of the Board of Directors. According to Santos and Rumble [47], the 100 largest US banks control 10% of the voting rights of the 500 non-financial companies of the Standard and Poor's index. They also found that, for some companies of S&P 500, banks hold more than 20% of the voting rights.

Randall and Strahan [4] examined the impact of banks as directors and found that US banks are more likely to sit on the boards of stable large-sized firms which have high proportions of tangible assets and use less short-term funding. On a sample of Japanese firms over the period 1981-1987, Morck and Nakamura [20] examined the impact of the presence of banks in the companies' boards of directors on the firm's value and found that their appointment does not maximize the value.

On a sample of German companies, Dittmann et al. [2,48] found a negative relationship between the banking presence in the firms' board of directors and the performance measured by Tobin's Q. This may be due to the fact that banks, as directors, serve their interests rather than the shareholders'. Actually, banks do not act in the shareholders' interests. Similarly, Güner et al. [49], using a sample of US companies, found that the presence of commercial banks in the boards of directors has a negative impact on the market performance (Tobin's Q). Moreover, Mitchell and Walker (2008) on a sample of 2746 Compustat companies during 2002, found that the presence of banks in the boards of directors has a negative impact on the market performance (Tobin's Q). However, Loderer and Peyer [50] found no significant relationship between the banking presence in the board and Tobin's Q.

On the other hand, Lehmann and Weigand [30] showed that there is a positive relationship between the banking presence in the board and performance. Moreover, [19], on a sample of Japanese companies, stated that appointing banks in the boards of directors improves following a low market performance. In addition, the authors found that the firm's performance improves after banks are appointed in the companies' boards of directors. On the other hand, Byrd and Mizruchi [14], by examining a sample of US companies, found that there is a negative relationship between the banking presence in the board of directors and the firms' performance.

Hypothesis 4: The banking presence on the board has a negative impact on the companies' performance (Table 1).

Methodology

Sample presentation

The aim of our research is to analyze the impact of the banking presence in the capital and in the firms' boards of directors on their accounting and market performance. For this reason, a sample of 14 listed companies on the Tunis Stock Exchange (TSE) is used. As the sample characteristic, the study examined 14 TSE listed firms on the over a 7-year period from 2003 to 2009, which amounts to 98 observations. In this research, two types of data are taken into account: financial data and data related to the composition of the board and ownership structure. Financial data are collected from companies' financial statements published by the CMF. As for the composition of the board and ownership structure, all the necessary data were collected from the value sheets available within the Tunis stock exchange (TSE). By performing Fisher's test (F-test), it is assumed that our model is either a fixed or random individual effect model. The specification of these effects according to Hausman's test (1968) tells indicates that the models that fit the sample data structure are fixed effect models.

Model, variables and measures: $PERF_{it} = \alpha_0 + \alpha_1$ Percent bankers $+ \alpha_2$ Bankshr $+ \alpha_3$ TCA $+ \alpha_4$ LNTA $+ \alpha_5$ (VentesN-VentesN-1/Ventes N-1) $+ \mu_t$

In order to test the hypotheses related to the impact of the banking presence in the firms' boards of directors and in the ownership structure on performance, econometric estimation techniques on panel data were chosen. Our model is a fixed effect panel data model with $PERF_{it}$ the performance measured through the ROE, ROA, Tobin Q and arris $\alpha_{0..........}$ $\alpha_{5:}$ The estimation techniques $\mu_{t:}$ The regression residue.

Variables: The variables used in this study are connected with the board of directors, namely the banks' presence as administrators and the ownership structure, such as the banking participation in the companies' capital. Besides, two other control variables have been included in models, namely the sales growth rate, the company's and the Board's size.

Performance measures

A/Accounting performance: The ratio of the overall asset returns or the "returns on assets" (ROA)

This ratio is measured by the ratio of the net income to the total assets. It is the return on assets, which generally shows accounting profitability.

-The ratio of net income or "return on equity" (ROE)

This ratio, which is measured by the ratio of net income to equity, expresses financial profitability. The problem with this ratio is that it can give a distorted picture of profitability since a high ratio may be the result of a low level of funds.

Hypotheses	Expected signs
H1: The relationship between the banking participation in the capital and the firms' performance is pointing upwards (interest convergence hypothesis or interest alignment)	+
H2: The relationship between the banking participation in the capital and the firms' performance is pointing downwards (conflicting interest hypothesis)	-
H3: The relationship between the bank participation in the capital and the firms' performance falls then rises (managerial hypothesis)	-/+
H4: The relationship between the banking presence in the companies' boards of directors and performance is negative	-

Table 1: The banking presence on the board has a negative impact on the companies' performance.

B/The stock market performance: - The Tobin's Q

We think it is more appropriate to use, besides the accounting measures, a performance measure, such as Tobin's Q, which reflects the future. The Tobin's Q reflects the financial market forecasts of future growth and potential profitability of a firm. This ratio is measured by the ratio between the sum of the market values of securities held by financial investors and the amount of capital these investors invested.

The value of the invested capital is measured by the replacement cost of the financial assets. The asset market value is obtained by reducing the book value of the market capitalization debt. In practice, such a measure is difficult to use because of the data unavailability. Therefore, we use a proxy, such as the ratio (market value of equity debt book value) divided by the book value of the total assets.

-The Marris ratio

The Marris ratio, which is the ratio of the bank market capitalization to equity at the book value, is itself an indicator that reflects the opportunities for growth. When this ratio is greater than 1, the bank creates value; otherwise, it would destroy it (Table 2).

Results and Interpretations

Descriptive statistics

The descriptive statistics supplied in this table show that the average performance measured by the ROA is 2.88%, -4.95% for the ROE, 30.62% for the Tobin Q and 2.2729 for Marris ratio. Since the Marris ratio is above 0.1, therefore, the company creates value. According to the descriptive statistics, it can be deduced that the banking presence in the capital and in the Board of Directors of the Tunisian companies improves their stock market performance (Tobin Q and MARRI) and decreases their accounting performance measured with the ROA and ROE. The average growth rate of these companies is about 5.67% and the average company's size measured by the natural logarithm is equal to 11.44, (that is 92985.607D. This proves that the Tunisian companies in our sample are larger compared to the companies in the study by Byrd DT, Mizruchi [14] of which the natural logarithm of the total assets is of the order of $4.381 79.9179 (Table 3).

Regarding the Board of Directors' characteristics, its average size, which is equal to 9.651, has between 5 and 12 members. Therefore, the Tunisian companies apply the standards for the size of their Boards of Directors. This table shows that banks' shareholding (bankshr) is on average 28.09% whereas their presence in the companies' Board of Directors (percent bankers) is 23.61%. As a consequence, the Tunisian companies apply the standards regarding the participation of the banks in their capital (the Act of July 10, 2001 states that a credit institution may hold more than 30% in a company).

Correlation matrix

Impact of the accounting performance: The regression results show that the presence of banks as shareholders has a negative and significant effect on performance, as measured by the ROA, and negative and significant, as measured by the ROE. On the other hand, their presence, as administrators, has a positive and significant effect on these two accounting performance measures. The negative relationship between the banking participation in the Tunisian companies' capital and performance is consistent with the study of [28,31]. This waning relationship is explained by the hypothesis of conflicting interests. Actually, the banking interests do not coincide with the other shareholders' interests. The positive relationship between the banking presence in the Boards of Directors of the Tunisian companies and their performance is explained by the hypothesis of reducing information asymmetries and the agency costs between the shareholders and the creditors. On the other hand, there is a positive relationship between the control variables and the accounting performance measured with

Variables	Significance	Measure
Dependent variables		
ROA	Return on Assets	Net profit/Total Assets
ROE	Return on Equity	Net profit/shareholders' equity
Qt	Tobin Q	Log ((market capitalization + total assets-equity Total Assets
m	Marris Ratio	Equity market value/equity accounting value
Independent variables		
Pb	Banks in the board of directors	The number of banks in the BOD/Size of the Board of Directors
Bs	The banking participation in the capital	Capital share held by banks
Control variables		
Tc	Sales growth rate	Sales(N) - Sales (N-1)/Sales (N-1)
LNTA	Company's size	Natural logarithm/total Assets
TCA	Board of directors' size	Overall number of directors

Table 2: Variables and measures.

Variable	Obs	Mean	Std. Dev.	Min	Max
ROA	112	0.0288339	0.0865126	-0.2160268	0.2408826
ROE	112	-0.0495427	1.243811	-12.38258	1.69165
qt	112	0.3062448	0.4328689	-1.166932	1.539912
m	112	2.272955	2.211723	-2.207259	14.76769
Tc	112	0.0567431	0.3087398	-0.976528	1.72802
Pb	112	0.236104	0.1316899	0.0833333	0.6666667
LNTA	112	11.4402	0.9501768	9.507106	13.41303
bs	112	0.2809241	0.1592075	0.0189	0.622
TCA	112	9.651786	2.082574	5	12

Table 3: Descriptive statistics.

	ROA	ROE	qt	m	tc	pb	LNTA	bs	TCA
ROA	1.0000								
ROE	0.4376	1.0000							
qt	0.5881	0.1378	1.0000						
m	0.4029	-0.1536	0.6833	1.0000					
tc	0.0827	0.1277	0.0074	0.0004	1.0000				
pb	-0.4987	-0.1865	-0.1448	-0.1172	0.2188	1.0000			
LNTA	-0.1288	0.0008	-0.1241	0.0561	-0.1288	-0.0111	1.0000		
bs	-0.3785	-0.1761	-0.2429	-0.0708	0.1862	0.5194	0.0407	1.0000	
TCA	0.0289	-0.0312	0.0364	0.0455	-0.2538	-0.3115	0.2674	-0.1440	1.0000

Table 4: Correlation matrix.

	Accounting measures		Stock market measures	
	ROA (Fixe)	ROE (Fixe)	Q de Tobin (Fixe)	Marris (Fixe)
Constant	-0.573043*** (-2.63)	-2.836517 (-0.41)	-2.675348* (-1.74)	-44.17712*** (-5.20)
Tc	0.0254476* (1.98)	0.4819129 (1.19)	0.0121155 (0.13)	0.1290398 (0.26)
Pb	0.1751591* (1.93)	7.080454** (2.47)	-0.4462486 (-0.69)	-7.207806** (-2.03)
LNTA	0.0474531*** (2.65)	0.1881522 (0.33)	0.2997068** (2.37)	4.144513*** (5.94)
Bs	-0.1346005 (-1.59)	-4.841608* (-1.81)	0.3478799 (0.58)	8.233562** (2.49)
TCA	0.055512 (0.71)	0.303707 (0.12)	-0.4523465 (-0.82)	-1.626315 (-0.53)
***Significant at 1%; **Significant at 5%, *Significant at 10%				

Table 5: Regressions results of the governance variables by banks (Bank participation in the capital and in the Board of Directors of firms) and the control variables on the performance measures.

the ROA and ROE. This applies particularly to the company's size, that of the Board of Directors and the sales growth rate (Table 4).

Impact on the market performance: The regression results show that the presence of banks, as shareholders, has a positive but insignificant effect on the stock market performance as measured by Tobin's Q and a positive and significant impact measured with the Marris ratio. On the other hand, their presence, as administrators, has a negative and insignificant effect on Tobin Q and negative and significant impact on the Marris ratio. The positive relationship between the banking participation in the companies' capital and performance is explained by the hypothesis of conflicting or aligned interests. The negative relationship between the banking presence in the firms' boards of directors and their performance is explained by the worsening of agency problems or interest conflicts between the shareholders and the lenders. In fact, the sources of conflict between the lenders and the shareholders are mainly due to the different choices of risk: if the lenders prefer a lower risk, shareholders prefer a higher one. On the other hand, there is a positive relationship between the sales growth rate, the firm's size and the stock market performance. However, the Board of Directors' size has a negative and significant effect on the performance measured by Tobin Q and the Marris ratio (Table 5).

Conclusion

In this study, we investigated the impact of the banking participation in the capital and in the Board of Directors on the performance of the Tunisian companies. The results show that the Tunisian companies, which apply the standards related to the capital share held by banks (that is 28.09% against 30% of the share capital of a company), are characterized by a low presence of banks in their boards of Directors (that is 23.61%). Moreover, the results show that the boards of directors of these companies are characterized by a fairly high size.

The Tunisian companies have a poor accounting and stock market performance. The results showed that the effect of the banking presence in their boards of directors is positive and significant for the accounting performance (ROA and ROE), and negative and insignificant for Tobin Q and negative and significant for the Marris ratio.

References

1. Morck R, Nakamura M, Shivdasani A (2000) Banks, ownership structure, and firm value in Japan. Journal of business 73: 539-567.
2. Dittmann I, Maug E, Schneider C (2006) Bankers on the boards of German firms: Causes and consequences.
3. Jiang W, Li K, Shao P (2010) When shareholders are creditors: Effects of the simultaneous holding of equity and debt by non-commercial banking institutions. Review of Financial Studies 23: 3595-3637.
4. Randall KS, Strahan PE (1999) Bankers on Boards: Monitoring, Conflicts of Interest, and Lender Liability. Journal of Financial Economics 62: 415-452.
5. Bubna A, Radhakrishnan G (2012) Bank involvement in firm Management, Panacea or a Pain? India Finance Conference, IIM Calcutta.
6. Petersen MA, Rajan RG (1994) The benefit of firm-creditor relationships: evidence from small business data. Journal of Finance 49: 3-37.
7. Flath D (1993) Shareholding in the keiretsu, Japan's financial groups. The Review of Economics and Statistics 249-257.
8. Gonzalez F (2006) Banks equity investments: Reducing agency costs or buying undervalued firms? The information effects. Journal of Business Finance and Accounting 33: 284-304.
9. Franks JR, Nyborg KG (1996) Control rights, debt structure, and the loss of private benefits: the case of the U.K. insolvency cod. Review of Financial Studies 9: 1165-1210.
10. Gilson SC, John KL, Larry LHP (1990) Troubled debt restructurings: An empirical study of private reorganization of firms in default. Journal of Financial Economics 27: 315-353.
11. James C (1995) When Do Banks Take Equity in Debt Restructurings? The Review of Financial Studies 8: 1209-1234.
12. Iqbal Z, Shetty S (2002) An investigation of causality between insider transactions and stock returns. Quarterly Review of Economics and Finance 42: 41-57.
13. Berger AN, Udell GF (1995) Relationship lending and lines of credit in small firm finance. Journal of Business 68: 351-382.
14. Byrd DT, Mizruchi MS (2005) Bankers on the board and the debt ratio of firms. Journal of Corporate Finance 11: 129-173.

15. Meckling J (1976) Theory of the firm: Managerial behavior, agency costs and ownership structure. Journal of financial economics 3: 305-360.

16. Dewatripont M, Tirole J (1994) The Prudential Regulation of Bank. Cambridge, MA: MIT Press.

17. Rajan RG (1992) Insiders and outsiders: The choice between informed and arm's length debt. Journal of finance 47: 1367-1400.

18. Kang JK, Shivdasani A (1995) Firm Performance, Corporate Governance, and Top Executive Turnover in Japan. Journal of Financial Economics 38: 29-58.

19. Kaplan SN, Minton AB (1994) Appointments of outsiders to Japanese boards-determinants and implications for managers. Journal of Financial Economics 36: 225-258.

20. Morck R, Nakamura M (1999) Banks and Corporate Control in Japan. Journal of Finance 54: 319-339.

21. Cable J (1985) Capital market information and industrial performance: The role of West German banks. Economic Journal 95: 118-132.

22. Gorton G, Schmid FA (1996) Universal banks and the performance of German firms. Journal of Financial Economics 58: 29-80.

23. Nibler M (1995) Bank Control and Corporate Performance in Germany: The Evidence. University of Cambridge.

24. Perlitz M, Seger F (1994) The Role of Universal Banks in German Corporate Governance. Business and The Contemporary World 6: 49-67.

25. Seger F (1997) Banken, Erfolg und Finanzierung, Deutscher Universitäts Verlag, Wies-baden.

26. Zoido ME (1998) Un estudio de las participaciones accionariales de los bancos en las empresas españolas. Investigaciones económicas 22: 427-467.

27. Pushner GM (1995) Equity ownership structure, leverage, and productivity: Empirical evidence from Japan. Pacific-Basin Finance Journal 3: 241-255.

28. Weinstein D, Yafeh Y (1998) On the costs of a bank-centered financial system: Evidence from the changing main bank relationships in Japan. Journal of finance 53: 635-672.

29. Gorton G, Schmid F (2000) Universal banking and the performance of German firms. Journal of financial economics 58: 29-80.

30. Lehmann EE, Weigand J (2000) Does the governed corporations perform better? Governance structures and corporate performance in Germany. European Finance Review 4: 157-195.

31. Chirinko SR, Elston JA (2006) Finance, control and profitability: The influence of German banks. Journal of Economic Behavior and organisation 59: 69-88.

32. Kang J, Stulz R (2000) Do banking shocks affect borrowing firm performance? An analysis of the Japanese Experience. Journal of Business 73: 1-23.

33. Emmons WR, Schmid FA (1998) Universal banking, control rights, and corporate finance in Germany. Federal Reserve Bank of St. Louis Review 80: 19-42.

34. Palenzuela AV, Iturriaga LFJ, Tejerina FG (2008) Banks as shareholders: The Spanish model of corporate governance. Nova Science Publishers pp: 55- 82.

35. Wenlian G (2008) Banks as lenders and shareholders: Evidence from Japan. Pacific-Basin Finance Journal 16: 389-410.

36. Nakatani I (1984) The economic role of financial corporate grouping. In Aoki M (Ed), The economic analysis of the Japanese firm, North-Holland: Amsterdam pp: 227-258.

37. Troege M (2000) Should banks be allowed to own equity in non-financial firms? Mimeo Northwestern University.

38. Nachane DM, Ghosh S, Ray P (2005) Bank nominee directors and corporate performance: Micro-evidence for India. Economic and Political Weekly 40: 1216-1223.

39. Edwards J, Nibler M (2000) Corporate Governance in Germany: The Role of Banks and Ownership Concentration. Economic Policy 15: 237-267.

40. Prowse SD (1992) The structure of corporate ownership in Japan. Journal of Finance 47: 1121-40.

41. Rosenstein S, Wyatt JG (1990) Outside directors, board independence, and shareholders wealth. Journal of financial economics 26: 175-191.

42. Mace MLG (1971) Directors: myth and reality. Division of research graduate school of business administration, Havard University, United States.

43. Pfeffer J (1972) Size and composition of corporate boards of directors: The organization and its environment. Administrative Science Quarterly 17: 218-228.

44. Baysinger BD, Butler HN (1985) Corporate governance and the board of directors: Performance effects of changes in board composition. Journal of Law, Economics and Organizations 1: 101-124.

45. Kesner IF (1988) Directors' characteristics and committee membership; An investigation of type, occupation, tenure and gender. Academy of Management Journal 31: 66-84.

46. Naohito A, Noel G, Kastsuyuki K (2005) Executive pay in Japan: the role of bank-appointed monitors and the Main Bank relationship. Japan and the World Economy 17: 371-394.

47. Santos JAC, Rumble AS (2004) The American Keiretsu And Universal Banks: Investing ,Voting And Sitting On Non Financials' Corporate Boards. Journal Of Financial Economics 80: 419-454.

48. Dittmann I, Maug E, Schneider C (2005) Bankers and the performance of German firms. Working paper.

49. Guner AB, Malmendier U, Tate G (2005) The impact of boards with financial expertise on corporate policies. NBER Working Paper No. 11914.

50. Loderer CF, Peyer U (2001) Board overlap, seat accumulation and share prices. European Financial Management 8: 165-192.

Consumers' Perceptual Biasness in Debit Cards of Indian Banks

Prasad S*

Associate Professor in Marketing, Regional College of Management, Bhubaneswar, India

Abstract

Debit cards are highly attractive to convenience driven consumer markets. As banks explore potential debit based loyalty system therefore convenience and control seeking consumers found debit cards as more attractive option. This card business depends on very reliable and secure technology and requires a very strong connectivity backbone. The topic taken for the research is a recent issue related to the debit card and the preference of customers towards different types of debit cards of different banks. Primary data has been collected through questionnaire of sample taken from the market which is a replica of the universe (Population of India). By the primary data the profile of customer being selected which are highly affected by the utility of the debit card. Hence the research justifies that the factors responsible for selecting a debit card are favourability, situational, recognize and bias. MDS (Multi-dimensional scaling) technique has been taken to study the perception of the customer for different brands of debit cards especially the public sector and private sector banks. The study has given an idea about the high inclination of customers towards private sectors debit cards than public sectors one.

Keywords: Consumer; Perceptual biasness; Debit cards; Multi-dimensional scaling; Indian banks

Introduction

Indian financial institutions like banking is the lifeline of the nation has helped in developing the major sectors of the economy and usher in a new dawn of progress on the Indian economy. The sector has created the hopes and aspirations of millions of people into reality in the world. But it has control the miles of difficult terrain and suffers under the foreign rules and the pangs of partition. Recently Indian banks have adopted the modern technology and can strongly compete with modern banks of the world [1]. The economic reforms of have presented a challenge before Indian banking sector to make continuous innovation with the pace of new technological change. The technological advancement and adoption is purely based on the consumers' acceptance and positive response. Traditionally, banks were only concerned with the stereotyped activities like acceptance of deposits and lending surplus money to the customer at some rate of interest and the common products being availed by banks were savings account, current account, term deposit account and lending products like cash credit and term loans. It becomes very much necessary for the today's banks to offer the services by taking into account the customer's needs, preferences, perceptions and convenience [2]. Customer is now enjoying the facilities of banks like anywhere, anytime banking. Internet banking has changed the bank market dramatically. Innovative banking services like plastic cards introduced in the market which has changed the customer lifestyle by making them more dynamic. Today's customer mostly made the transactions through plastic cards and most preferably the highly acceptable debit cards. Consumers are trying to code, categorize and evaluate economic outcomes and frame the transaction which determines the benefits and the level of satisfaction they expect to receive [3]. The process of payment mode serves to influence outcome perceptions of the customers.

Electronic banking has a wider scope which has adopted by the banking sector now days. Banks have developed various sophisticated products to meet the basic requirements of their customers. Indian banking sector has faced a dramatic change with the advent of tech savvy private sector banks and foreign banks. Public sector banks have created a large network of traditional branches to approach their customers from urban to rural as compared to the private and foreign players. Information technology has made a revolutionary to deliver the banking products and services efficiently and effectively. The new private and foreign bankers on the basis of adoption of new technological services like plastic cards, personal computer banking, electronic funds transfer, internet banking can able to connect maximum number of customers in spite of having less physical presence. Now public sector banks are equally trying to move towards electronic banking, which leads to the remarkable development with respect to its operational efficiency, customer services, employee productivity and banking profitability. Now banks are bringing flexibility in their distribution channel by reengineering their services.

There is a rising acceptance of debit cards in retail locations which has increased the debit cards transactions. Highest number of consumers and merchants acceptance of plastic cards has changed the way to move beyond the traditionally geographic located merchant base to modern arena of transactions. The demand for debit cards has grown rapidly among consumers as these are more convenient than other payment options and cost effective for merchants. Consumers with the limited access to existing payment methods find a debit card is the most suitable instrument for the latest transactions. Debit cards' superiority over credit cards as the most acceptable form of electronic payment at the point of sale and it becomes a primary consumer choice which requires relatively little scrutiny for acceptance. Debit card users who have the knowledge of hidden cost associated with the credit cards are rationally choose to use debit card to minimize the transaction costs. The drawbacks like binding limit in credit cards are converting customers to rely more on debit cards.

Objectives

Debit card plays a vital role in plastic cards which has changed the

***Corresponding author:** Saraju Prasad, Associate Professor in Marketing, Regional College of Management, Bhubaneswar, Odisha-751023, India
E-mail: saraju_prasad@rediffmail.com

future of banking sector and positioned as a multiple service provider instruments for the consumer. It can able to change the perception of both customers and merchant by reducing the complexities in the financial transactions and became a strong instrument in banking operations. Keeping in view of the above discussion the present study has made an attempt to study the profile of customers using debit cards different banks. Also the study gives idea about the factors creates biasness to select the debit cards of any banks and the customers' perception about the different brands of debit cards.

Methodology

The research design is mostly based on the consumers' decision on different debit cards on the basis of banks like public and private sectors. For literature review articles are mostly taken from published journal of e-journal sites. Sampling methods used for this research is stratified sampling one (respondents mostly in the twin city Bhubaneswar and Cuttack of Odisha i,e. an state in Eastern India). Questionnaire method was used to collect the data from the market from 400 respondents during the period of January to February 2016. Pilot survey has been conducted to know the acceptance of debit cards of different banks and their relative importance for the customers. Considering the feedback of the respondents questionnaires are being designed to apply different statistical tools for inference. Statistical tools like factor analysis and multi-dimensional scaling techniques are used to interpret the data by data analysis through the statistical software SPSS.

Literature Review

Customer perceives that private sector banks provide better services in terms of facilities than the public sector banks. Although public sector banks have a strong presence in terms of branches in the market, but now days they are facing stiff competition from private sector banks in terms of quality of services they offered [4]. High level of customers' adoption of online banking systems because of perceived usefulness, ease of use, awareness of technology and less perceives risks on customer to accept online banking system [5]. Extending technology driven products for farmers will enhance the brand image of commercial banks and helps to enlarge the base of operation to attract more farmers to commercial banks [6]. Adoption of new technological in banks are always assets to a bank which will reduces the cost in long runs like years of operation of the technology, urban location, deposits ratio and expenses ratio [7]. Internet banking has become an important medium to sell the products and services of banks to stay profitable and successful [8]. Domestic and foreign banks are providing five basic services associated with internet banking like to view account balances and transaction histories, paying bills, transferring funds within accounts, requesting for credit card advances and ordering checks quickly [9]. Now days customers' can able to do anytime and anywhere banking through internet banking services provided by the banks through their websites [10]. With the advent of new technologies in banking sectors consumers' can able to do e-banking through the internet services and applications in mobile phones. The main motivation factors for the consumers to use internet banking are the speed, the convenience of remote access, seven days and twenty four hours availability of services and the price incentives [11]. The easier accessibilities of the banking products and services facilitates the adoption of internet banking by consumers [12]. The services offered by the banks like internet banking, automated tailor machine (ATM) and phone banking are substitute to each other [13]. Consumer will prefer highly to a particular types of internet banking services where the consumer familiarity is highest [14]. Clients' usage rate of banking products and services through internet banking depends upon the attitude customers' towards it [15].

Consumers' influenced towards internet banking through document accessibility of internet, awareness of e-banking and resistance to change. Sellers' support plays a vital role on clients' usage of internet banking [16]. All the financial institutions has accepted that smart card technology as a viable retail point of sale transactional alternative and a right replacements for cash in everyday exchange situations around the world [17].

Credit card is right kind of plastic card for those customers who use it to increase their purchasing power [18]. Plastic cards of different banks provide new packages to attract the customers like tele-ticketing, offers, insurance coverage and reward points etc. Debit cards penetrate very rapidly in the consumers' market while Rysman clarified through his research that demographic variables have high impact on consumer choice for any brand of credit cards [19,20]. Hayashi, Sullivan and Weiner (2003) examined that consumers have given equal importance on adoption of debit cards as well as direct deposit and electronic bill payment [21]. Credit card holders are influenced more by the informal sources than the mass media and are using credit cards because of ease of payment and risk of carrying cash [22]. Older adults use credit cards with similar frequency to younger adults when circumstances and opportunities for consumption in both the groups are similar [23]. Lots of factors are responsible for the growing demand of plastic cards like rapid expansion, increasing acquisitive middle class, growing demand of expenses towards travel and entertainment, sophisticated merchant establishment and more transparency in financial system [24]. There is an increase usage of credit cards in developing countries because of increased level of socio-economic and technological development [25].

In twenty first century plastic cards as an efficient electronic payment system changed the market into a cashless society by reducing the transactions through coins and notes [26]. The changing utility of the smart card can be able to deal with the transaction of non financial data which has changed the purchase system through collection and exchange [27]. This change affected the retailers through their store and office upgradation, replacement of point of sales terminals and giving training to the cashiers which has indirectly created a substantial cost to accept the smart cards. The latest features of plastic card like pay later, pay now and pay before has created future prospects by the development of the cashless society [28]. The authorization system quality can be measured through two major considerations like the enhancement of customer's quality service by reducing the waiting time at the point of sale and by reducing the risk of bad credit transactions [29]. Any banks credit and money supply can be controlled through the amount of credit have given to individuals as well as households [30]. There is a negative relationship exist between the usage of consumer's bankcard and store cards during transaction as store cards plays a substitute of bank cards [31]. The evidence of credit cards explosive growth in numbers and amount of transactions indicates the benefits derived by the customers and merchants [32]. Consumers considers few factors like income level, fees for service network, add on card facility availability, revolving credit facility, insurance facilities, cash withdrawal charges, lost card liabilities for selecting the best credit card provider [33]. Consumer perceived now days that credit card is the convenient substitute for carrying cash and a right kind of credit facilities for a short period [34].

The advent of innovations in information and communication technology has changed the usage of credit card which indirectly encourages the customer for compulsive buying [35]. These cards have changed the horizon with various features like identity proof, storage for bank data, e-purse, finger print, health record, blood group and license details of each individual [36]. Worthington et al. Customers feel comfortable to hold and use of the credit cards for spending on travel and entertainment purpose [37]. The multiple cardholders are always feeling comfortable to spend more through a specific credit card called main card which indirectly gives benefit to the card issuer [38]. Customers are willing to use the mobile phone credit card which can able to carry highest amount of information related to transactions [39]. The variations in number of credit card holders depends upon the number of times customers using the cards for the services like number of time missing payments, frequency of use, entertainment expenditures, and petrol purchase [40].

VISA and Master Card both the organizations are responsible for any kind of international payment system and both of them act as franchisers, lending their names to credit and debit cards of respective member banks and act as a guarantor of payment to merchants which will receive the cards [41]. Both VISA and Master card are not credit or debit card companies but functioning for bankers to provide a global network to give authorization, clearing and settlement of card transactions for both credit and debit cards. Less educated, lower income groups, middle-aged and owner of fewer credit cards are mostly using the cash transactions [19]. In other way debit and credit card users are mostly younger, highly educated and holds more numbers of credit or debit cards. The rising interest of customers towards debit cards is because of combination of factors like ease of availability of cards, profile of customer inclined towards debit averse and zero interest rates on cards [42]. Todays' competitive market customers are financially so much sophisticated and eager to use the latest technology plastic card like debit cards to avoid interest due to credit cards which shows that the amount of spending is more on credit cards but the number of transactions is more on debit cards [43]. The emerging trend in India shows a greater importance of debit card in daily lives which capture the market in places like supermarkets, petrol stations, convenience stores where most transactions are done by cashes or cheques in earlier days [44]. The high acceptability of debit cards with comparison to credit cards is because of few factors like assurance of payments to retailers, use interest free period to avoid high interest cost, reduce annual charges, easy electronic fund transfer, point of services offer a huge acceptance of debit cards, cutting down the cost associated with the paper based clearing and payment services [45]. Information and technology has given a great change on Indian banking sector for their survival and growth in the advancements of plastic cards which has the bright future prospects of e-payments market in India [46]. Manivannan In the entry level debit cards are used only by higher income groups residing in urban areas or cities but now it has widely accepted to fixed income groups or salaried classes and also the customers staying in rural areas [47].

Particular	Category	Frequency	Percentage
Annual Income in Rs.			
	Less than 5 Lac	16	4
	5Lac to 8 Lac	26	6.5
	8Lac to 10Lac	122	30.5
	10Lac above	236	59
Age			
	20-25	15	3.75
	25-30	77	19.25
	30-35	104	26
	35-40	204	51
Occupation			
	Student	11	2.75
	Salaried Employee	124	31
	Businessman	145	36.25
	Professional	120	30
Family size(2+)			
	Bachelor	15	3.75
	Married with no kid	72	18
	Married with one kid	168	42
	Married with two kids	145	36.25

Table 1: Demographic profile of respondents.

Results and Analysis

Demographic profile

The respondents selected for the debit card holders are mostly income level above Rs.10 Lacs (59%) followed by Rs.8 to 10 Lacs (30%). 77% of the total respondents are in the age group of 30 to 40 year. There is almost equi-proportionate of salaried employees, professionals and businessman and around 78% of them are married and having one or two kids (Table 1).

Different brands of debit cards

Out of 400 respondents, 39.5% and 13.5% of respondents are using debit cards exclusively and 46.5% are both from private and public sector banks. 36.25% of respondents are using the Industrial Credit and Investment Corporation of India (ICICI) a private sector bank followed by 26% by Housing Development Financial Corporation (HDFC) a private sector bank shown in Table 2.

Factor analysis

This research focused mostly to the customer perception towards selecting a debit card. Several statements are generated from the variables to measure attitude of the respondents on a 5-point Likert scale. These scores are measured though the factor analysis to know the utility of each factors.

Table 3 depicts the variables under each of the four desired factors. The first factor 'favorability' identified with acceptance, high level of discounts in brand of debit card, transaction in ATM (Automated Tailored Machine), discounts on the basis of point system and international transaction. The second factor 'situational' explains the selection of a brand of debit card depends upon number of ATMs and distance of ATM from residence. The third factor 'recognize' explains the cash back reward system and unlimited transactions. The fourth factor 'bias' explains the debit card is selected because of influence of family and most popular bank.

Ranking has made on the basis of highest factor loadings generated by the different factors. In the Table 4 customers have given highest factor loading score to the factor like 'favorability' followed by 'situational', 'recognize' and 'bias' respectively.

Banks	Frequency	Percentage
Private Sector	158	39.5
Public Sector	55	13.75
Both	187	46.75
Debit Cards of different banks		
ICICI(Private Sector)	145	36.25
HDFC(Private Sector)	96	24
SBI(Public Sector)	89	22.25
PNB(Public Sector)	35	8.75
Others(both Public and Private)	35	8.75

Table 2: Profile of respondents using different brands of debit cards.

Favorability F1	Most of the transaction this brand of debit card is highly acceptable (S3)
	High level of discounts can be available in this brand of debit card (S4)
	Transaction in ATM (Automated Tailored Machine) is quite safety (S5)
	Discount can be available on the basis of point system available in the debit card. (S6)
	Any international transaction can be possible through this debit card (S7)
Situational F2	Selection of a brand of debit card depends upon the number of ATM branches (S1)
	Selection of a brand of debit card depends on the distance of ATM from
	Residence (S2)
Recognize F3	Cash back reward system available with this debit card (S10)
	Unlimited transaction can be possible through other banks ATMs (S11)
Bias F4	You select the debit card because of the influence of family or relatives (S8)
	You select the debit card because of most popular bank (S9)

Table 3: Factors generated through the variables of debit card.

Factors	Factor loadings of each factor	Ranking on basis of score
F1(Favorability)	3.351	1
F2(Situational)	1.759	2
F3(Recognize)	1.622	3
F4(Bias)	1.426	4

Table 4: Ranking of factors on high factor loads.

Multi-dimensional scaling (MDS)

The result of the multidimensional scaling in terms of stress value is 0.15 which is acceptable and the R^2 value is 0.92 or 92% which is also accepted. The perceptual image about the different brand of debit cards is represented in two-dimensional space. Multi-dimensional scaling technique can able to generate the different coordinates created on the basis of the responses. The coordinates created are represented in Figure 1 i.e. X co-ordinates and Y co-ordinates for SBI is (-0.19, -1.42), for HDFC is (1.42, -0.11), for ICICI is (0.16, 1.36) and for PNB is (-1.39, 0.17).

The Figure 1 shows the perceptual image which gives the pictorial representation of the different brands of debit cards. The above image shows that customers prefer primarily ICICI followed by HDFC, PNB and finally SBI debit card respectively.

Concluding Observation

It was observed through the factor analysis the importance of each variable for the decision of consumers to select any brands of debit cards. The relative importance of the variables can able to generate the factors. The first factor 'favorability' identified with acceptance, high level of discounts in brand of debit card, transaction in ATM, discounts on the basis of point system and international transaction. The second factor 'situation' explains the selection of a brand of debit card depends upon number of ATMs and distance of ATM from residence. The third factor 'recognition' explains the cash back reward system and unlimited transactions. The fourth factor 'biasness' explains the debit card is selected because of influence of family and most popular bank. The perceptual map created through the multi-dimensional scaling technique showed that customers are more inclined towards private sector banks rather than the public sector one. It gives the idea that people prefer the private banks especially ICICI the most. In the meanwhile other banks like HDFC, PNB and SBI should give better facilities in order to capture attention of the customers. Hence the research concludes that customer look after the 'favorability' in terms of benefits and 'situation' in terms of facilities factor while selecting any particular brand of debit card.

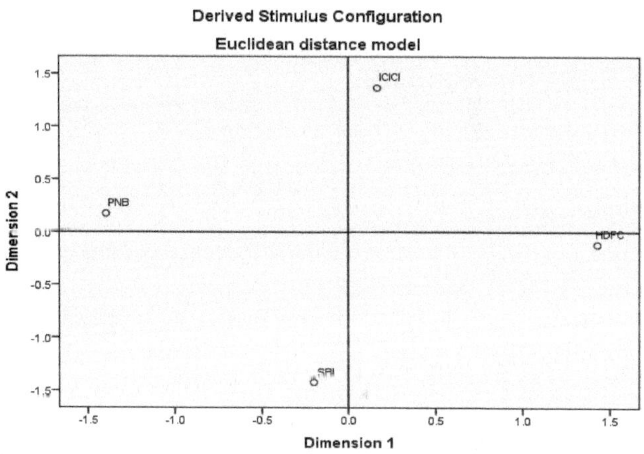

Figure 1: Pictorial representation of the different brands of debit cards.

Limitations and Directions for Future Research

As the research conducted in two cities of eastern part of India greater number of customers and more brand of debit cards can be considered for the further research. Here mostly young generation and mostly middle class respondents considered for the research work. Various categories of customers with upper class segment can be considered for the further research.

References

1. Caskey JP, Sellon Jr GH (1994) Is the Debit Card Revolution Finally Here? Economic Review - Federal Reserve Bank of Kansas City pp: 79-95.
2. Zinman J (2004) Why use debit instead of credit? Consumer choice in a trillion-dollar market. Federal Reserve Bank of New York Staff Reports No.191.
3. Thaler RH (1999) Mental accounting matters. Journal of Behavioral Decision Making 12: 183-206.
4. Simon LM (2012) A Study on Customer Perception Towards Services Provided By Public Sector Bank and Private Sector Bank. Paripex - Indian Journal Of Research 1: 113-115.
5. Safeena R, Date H, Kammani A (2011) Internet Banking Adoption in an Emerging Economy: Indian Consumer's Perspective. International Arab Journal of e-Technology 2: 56-61.
6. Rama PP (2004) Product Innovation–A Suggestion from a Reader: KCC vs. ATM. Bank Quest April 75: 29-31.
7. Habib S (2012) Internet Banking in India Consumer Concerns and Bank Marketing Strategies. Research Journal of Management Sciences 1: 20-24.
8. Christopher G, Mike C, Visit L, Amy W (2006) A Logit Analysis of Electronic Banking in New Zealand. Int. J. Bank Market 24: 360-383.

9. Chou DC, Chou AY (2000) A Guide to the Internet Revolution in Banking. Information Systems Management 17: 47-53.

10. Grabner-Krauter S, Faullant R (2008) Consumer acceptance of internet banking: the influence of internet trust. International Journal of bank marketing 26: 483-504.

11. Centeno C (2004) Adoption of Internet services in the Acceding and Candidate Countries, lessons from the Internet banking case. Telematics and Informatics 21: 293-315.

12. Durkin M, Jennings D, Mulholland G, Worthington S (2008) Key influencers and inhibitors on adoption of the Internet for banking. Journal of Retailing and Consumer Services15: 348-357.

13. Calisir F, Gumussoy CA (2008) Internet banking versus other banking channels: Young consumers' view. International Journal of Information Management 28: 215-221.

14. Maenpa K, Kale SH, Kuusela H, Mesiranta N (2008) Consumer perceptions of Internet banking in Finland: The moderating role of familiarity. Journal of Retailing and Consumer Services 15: 266-276.

15. Sohail, SM, Shanmugham B (2003) E-banking and customer preferences in Malaysia: An empirical investigation. Information Sciences 150: 207-217.

16. Nilsson D (2007) Internet Banking and the Impact of Seller Support and Third Party. Journal of Internet Banking and Commerce 12: 1-9.

17. Plouffee CR, Yandenbosch M, Hulland J (2000) Why Smart cards have failed: looking to consumer and merchant reactions to a new payment technology. International Journal of Bank Marketing 18: 112-123.

18. Vora S and Gidwani R (1993) Plastic at a premium. Business India pp: 95.

19. Carow Kenneth A, Staten AS (1999) Debit, credit, or cash: survey evidence on Gasoline Purchases. Journal of Economics and Business 51: 409-421.

20. Rysman M (2004) Competition between Networks: A Study of the Market for Yellow Pages. Review of Economic Studies 71: 483-512.

21. Hayashi F, Sullivan R, Weiner S (2003) A guide to the ATM and Debit Card Industry. Economic Review. Federal Reserve Bank of Kansas City pp: 1-44.

22. Barker T, Sekerkaya A (1992) Globalization of credit card usage: The case of a Developing Economy. International Journal of Bank Marketing 10: 27-31.

23. Mathur A, George P Moschis (1994) Use of Credit cards by older Americans. Journal of Services Marketing 8: 27-36.

24. Almeida M (1995) The Future's in Cards. Business India pp: 113-116.

25. Kaynak E (1995) Correlates of credit card acceptance and usage in an advanced developing Middle Eastern country. Journal of Services Marketing 9: 52-63.

26. Worthington S (1995) The Cashless Society. Internal Journal of Retail and Distribution Management 23: 31-40.

27. Worthington S (1996) Smart cards and retailers who stands to benefit? International Journal of Retail and Distribution Management 24: 27-34.

28. Gambhir AC (1989) Credit cards in India, Punjab National Bank Monthly Review 11: 413-420.

29. Leung WK, Lai KK (2001) Improving the quality of the credit authorization process. International Journal of Service Industry Management 12: 328-341.

30. Azhagaiah (2002) Credit creations through plastic money. Yojana 46: 33-34.

31. Lee J, Kwon Kyoung-Nan (2002) Consumers' use of credit cards: store credit card usage an alternative payment and financing medium. Journal Consumer Affairs Winter 36: 239-262.

32. Chakravarti S (2003) Theory of Credit Card Network: A Survey of The Literature. Review of Network Economics 2: 50-68.

33. Saha TR (2003) The Booming Credit Cards business of Indian Banking. The Management Accountant 38: 371-374

34. Easwar SA, Rawani NK (2004) Credit Card on a growth trajectory. Chartered Financial Analyst pp: 50-53.

35. Park HJ, Burns LD (2005) Fashion orientation credit card use, and compulsive buying. Journal of Consumer Marketing 22: 135-141.

36. Al-Alawi AI, Al Amer AM (2006) Young generation attitudes and awareness towards the implementation of smart card in Bahrain: An Exploratory study. Journal of computer science 2: 441-446.

37. Worthington S, Stewart D, Lu X (2007) The adoption and usage of credit cards by urban affluent consumers in china. International Journal of Bank Marketing 25: 238-252.

38. Devlin FJ, Worthington S, Gerrand P (2007) An Analysis of main and subsidiary credit card holding and spending. Journal of Bank Marketing 25: 89-101.

39. Amin H, Pagar SJ (2008) Factors affecting the intentions of customers in Malaysia to use mobile phone credit card. Management Research News 31: 493-503.

40. Gan LL, Maysami R, Koh CH (2008) Singapore Credit cardholders: ownership, usage patterns, and perceptions. Journal of Services Marketing 22: 267-279.

41. George P (1995) The Card Major Lead the Way. Business World p: 116.

42. Bhargava S (2004) Debit cards: A rule generation plastic money. Chartered Financial Analyst pp: 47-50.

43. Joshi G (1996) Variants in Plastic. Dalal Street Investment Journal 10: 50-51.

44. Maganty KK (1996) Changing dimension. Analyst pp: 95-96.

45. Radhakrishan R (1996) Debit Cards. PNB Monthly Review pp: 309-317.

46. Kaur M, Kaur K (2008) Development of plastic Cards Market: Past, future scenario in Indian Banks. Asia-Pacific Business Review 4: 62-74.

47. Manivannan P (2013) Plastic Money a way for cash Less Payment System. Global Research Analysis 2: 10-12.

An Analytical Study on Trends and Progress of Indian banking Industry

Malyadri P[1]* and Sirisha S[2]

[1]*Principal, Government Degree College, Osmania University, Hyderabad, India*
[2]*Assistant Professor, ITM-Business School, Warangal, India*

Abstract

Financial sector plays a pivotal role in the economic development. It is generally agreed that a strong and healthy banking system is a prerequisite for sustainable economic growth. Banks in India have been undergoing major challenges in the dynamic environment over the past few years as it is evident from several parameters, including No. of offices, No. of employees, Business per employee, Profit per employee, Net Worth, Deposits, Investments, Advances, Interest income, Other income, Interest expended, Operating expenses, Cost of Funds (CoF), Return on advances adjusted to CoF, Wages as % to total expenses, Return on Assets, CRAR and Net NPA ratio In order to resist negative shocks and maintain financial stability, it is important to identify theprofile of the banks. The current study is mainly concerned with the analysis of comparative profiles of Public Banks, Private Banks and Foreign Banks in India during the period of 2006-13 that reflects the impact of new competitive environment on the bank's performance in terms of various selected parameters. The Data was collected through secondary sources from Trend and Progress Report of RBI and the tool used for data analysis of the profile of bank group wise is Compound Annual Growth Rate (CAGR) which is expressed in percentages. The results have found strong evidence that the Private Sector Banks surpasses the other bank groups and topped the position in all the parameters, while Public Sector Banks and Foreign Banks are just competing for the 2nd and the 3rd position.

Keywords: Commercial banks; Public sector banks; Private sector banks and foreign banks; NPA

Introduction

It has been around one and half decade since financial sector reforms were initiated in India. As banks are the major segment of the financial sector in India, reform measures are primarily aimed at improving the performance of the banking sector. An efficient banking system has significant positive externalities, which increases the efficiency of economic transaction in general. The first deals with the history part since the dawn of banking system in India. Government took major step in the 1969 to put the banking sector into systems and it nationalized 14 private banks in the mentioned year. This has been elaborated in Nationalization Banks in India. The last but not the least explains about the scheduled and unscheduled banks in India. Section 42 (6) (a) of RBI Act 1934 lays down the condition of scheduled commercial banks

It is believed that private ownership helps to improve efficiency and performance of bank and accordingly, the Indian government started diluting its equity in PSBs from early 1990s in a phased manner. The privatization of Indian banks really helped to improve their efficiency and performance. Liberalization and Globalization ushered in by the government in the early 90s have thrown open many challenges to the Indian financial sector. Banks, amongst other things, were set on a path to align their accounting standards with the International standards and by global players. They had to have a fresh look into their balance sheet and analyze them critically. In this background, this article is designed to give an outline of profile of ban group wise in Indian banking industry. Banks that employ IT solutions are perceived to be 'futuristic' and proactive players capable of meeting the multifarious requirements of the large customer's base. Private Banks have been fast on the uptake and are reorienting their strategies using the internet as a medium The Indian banking has finally worked up to the competitive dynamics of the 'new' Indian market and is addressing the relevant issues to take on the multifarious challenges of globalization.

Need for the Study

Banking business has done wonders for the world economy. The intensifying competitive environment in the banking sector forcing the banks to focus in their operations. The profile of the banks plays an important role in the performance of the banks and measuring the relative profile of bank group wise has gained academic attentions over the years. Various parameters have been used to determine the profile of the banks. Evaluating the profile of the commercial banks is important to depositors, owners, potential investors, managers and of course, regulators.

Objective

1. To explore the concentration of profile of Public sector banks, private sector banks; and Foreign banks
2. To analyse the comparison of performance of Nationalized Banks, State Bank Group, old Private sector Banks, New Private Sector Banks and Foreign Banks.

Review of Literature

Over the past decade, there has been a considerable growth in studies addressing the profile of the banks. Various studies conducted and numerous suggestions were sought to bring effectiveness in the working and operations of banks. Some of the studies are as follows:

***Corresponding author:** Malyadri P, Principal, Government Degree College, Osmania University, Patancheru, Hyderabad, India
E-mail: drpm16@gmail.com

Dipasha Sharma, Anil K Sharma, Mukesh K Barua in their study discussed that both the frontier approaches, parametric and non-parametric, are gaining an edge over the traditional financial performance measures. In the non-parametric approach, data envelopment analysis (DEA) is widely applied to measure a bank's efficiency and productivity [1].

Siraj and Sudarsanan Pillai, in their paper determined that asset quality and efficiency of bank is highly correlated. Against this backdrop, this paper investigates the growth of selected NPA variables and compares it with banking performance indicators [2]. Variables that impact NPA of banks is assessed and based on its growth rate, inference is generated. The analysis focused on identifying relative efficiency of different bank groups in managing their NPA.

Singh analysed the profitability management of banks under the deregulated environment with some financial parameters of the major four bank groups i.e. public sector banks, old private sector banks, new private sector banks and foreign banks, He emphasized to make the banking sector competitive in deregulated environment and prefer non-interest income sources [3].

Souza, in his study evaluated the performance of public sector banks, private sector banks and foreign banks during the period 1990-1991 to 1999-2000. The efficiency of the banking system was measured in terms of spread/working fund ratio and turnover/employees ratio [4].

Kannan and Aditya Narain made an attempt to identify the factors influencing spreads of scheduled commercial banks in India and concluded that nonperforming asset effect bank spread.

Centric to the ratio analysis, these studies have customized and blended financial ratios in a model form to examine and predict the financial health. Similarly, comparative performance, recovery performance, cost reduction, productivity and efficiency are vital areas which have been considered by various analysts. With inquisitiveness the present study has been undertaken with specific objectives as envisaged in the objectives of the study [5].

Research Methodology

Data collection and sources of data

The study is based on secondary data collected from the select bank records and other secondary sources like research papers, review papers, published papers of related Banks,. Banks' websites, periodicals, Bank's publications, newspapers etc. A list of the related articles from various journals is also used to develop the basic idea about the particular topic. This paper uses the Compound Annual Growth Rate (CAGR) Method and Ranking method to analyse the profile of banks. The study covers for the period of 8 years data from 2005-06 to 2012-13.

Data analysis and interpretation

Customer deposit is a major part of total liabilities of any bank and it is a major source of fund for banks. Since deposit is the main concern for any bank therefore it becomes important to examine the deposit of each bank groups in India. Customer deposits provide funds for investment and financing. Growth in customer deposits is a positive indicator of banking growth. Bank group-wise, public sector banks accounted for the largest CAGR (56.19 per cent) in total deposits followed by private sector banks (54.57 per cent). Foreign banks showed the lowest CAGR (49.77 Percent). High levels of public deposit ensured that most of the banks had a comfortable liquidity profile.

It is observed from the Table 1 that the scheduled commercial bank offices in the country showed CAGR of 6.12%, over a period of eight years and for this growth the major contribution is observed from the growth in the new private sector banks. It is also observed from the Table 2 that there is a continuous increase in number of offices in scheduled commercial banks and this is as a result of continuous increase in number of offices of all bank group wise that is in case of public sector banks, private sector banks and foreign banks.

Capital adequacy ratio is a measure of a bank's financial health and it measures the performance of a bank's capital. It reflects the soundness of a financial institution. It is expressed as a percentage of a bank's risk weighted credit exposures. This ratio is used to protect depositors and promote the stability and efficiency of financial systems around the world. A Bank shall maintain a minimum ratio between its total regulatory capital (the numerator) and the aggregate of its risk weighted on balance sheet assets and risk weighted off-balance sheet assets less approved deduction. The Ratio is provided by equity plus reserves over total assets. It is shown in the Table 3 that the CAGR of foreign banks is 4.04% as compared to public sector banks and private sector banks where it is 0.21 and 3.88 respectively. The Capital to Risk weighted Assets Ratio (CRAR) profile of SCBs remains comfortable and much above the minimum regulatory requirements of 9%. The decline in the capitalization level of the nationalized banks, is attributable largely to strong credit growth.

Total operating expenses includes staff costs, general and administrative Expenses. A lower Operating Expense (OE) shows better control and highlights higher earnings. Operating Expense (OE) differentiates between low efficiency and high efficiency bank. Table 4 shows, Bank Group wise operating expenses. In case of private sectors banks the operating expenses increased significantly over the period of eight years i.e. from 2006-2013 and overall there was an increase by 50.29%.

It is observed from Table 5 that the rate of distribution of employees in new private sector banks is high as compared to any other bank group. The trend of number of employees during the study period is highly volatile. In case of Nationalized banks it is observed that there was a

Bank Group Wise	2005-06	2006-07	2007-08	2007-09	2009-10	2010-11	2011-12	2012-13	CAGR (%)
Nationalised Banks	1080072	1360724	1679993	21057056	25839338	31265862	35969893	41272523	57.68
SBI and Associates	542409	633476	773875	10070415	11080856	12458624	14050241	16184449	52.88
Public Sector Banks	1622481	1994200	2453868	31127471	36920194	43724487	50020134	57456972	**56.19**
Old Private Sector Banks	130456	138249	165589	1992735	2298969	2641571	3158914	3738964	52.11
New Private Sector Banks	298000	413738	509444	5371041	5929038	7386018	8586960	10219391	55.56
Private Sector Banks	428456	551987	675033	7363776	8228007	10027588	11745874	13958355	**54.57**
Foreign banks	113745	150750	191161	2140764	2320995	2406668	2769477	2879997	**49.77**
Scheduled Commercial Banks	2164682	2696937	3320062	40632011	47469196	56158743	64535485	74295324	**55.58**

Table 1: Trends in Deposits Relating to Bank Group Wise During 2006 to 2013.

Bank Group Wise	2005-06	2006-07	2007-08	2007-09	2009-10	2010-11	2011-12	2012-13	CAGR (%)
Nationalised Banks	35858	37431	39234	41041	43690	46462	50713	54478	5.37
SBI and Associates	14130	14673	15846	16938	18390	19338	20256	21301	5.26
Public Sector Banks	50168	52104	55080	57979	62080	65800	70969	75779	**5.29**
Old Private Sector Banks	4819	4826	4690	4952	5273	5090	5673	6283	3.37
New Private Sector Banks	2016	2598	3632	4336	5243	7007	8297	9718	21.73
Private Sector Banks	6835	7424	8322	9288	10516	12097	13970	16001	**11.22**
Foreign banks	259	272	279	295	310	318	323	334	**3.23**
Scheduled Commercial Banks	57262	59800	63681	67562	72906	78215	85262	92114	**6.12**

Table 2: Trends in Bank Group Wise Number of Offices During 2006 to 2013.

Bank Group Wise	2005-06	2006-07	2007-08	2007-09	2009-10	2010-11	2011-12	2012-13	CAGR (%)
Nationalised Banks	12.27	12.37	12.13	13.24	13.18	13.47	13.03	12.26	-0.01
SBI and Associates	11.95	12.30	13.21	13.96	13.46	12.25	13.70	12.67	0.73
Public Sector Banks	12.17	12.36	12.51	13.49	13.27	13.08	13.23	12.38	**0.21**
Old Private Sector Banks	11.69	12.08	14.08	14.74	14.85	14.55	14.12	13.73	2.03
New Private Sector Banks	12.60	11.99	14.39	15.33	18.03	16.87	16.66	17.52	4.21
Private Sector Banks	12.42	12.10	14.34	15.23	17.43	16.46	16.21	16.84	**3.88**
Foreign banks	13.02	12.39	13.08	14.19	17.26	16.97	16.75	17.88	**4.04**
Scheduled Commercial Banks	12.32	12.28	13.01	13.97	14.54	14.19	14.24	13.88	**1.50**

Table 3: Trends in Bank Group Wise CRAR During 2006 to 2013.

Bank Group Wise	2005-06	2006-07	2007-08	2007-09	2009-10	2010-11	2011-12	2012-13	CAGR (%)
Nationalised Banks	25548	27268	29670	354160	407922	538193	574753	647182	49.78
SBI and Associates	15760	15987	16993	200877	252828	291459	327299	370940	48.41
Public Sector Banks	41308	43255	40003	555037	660749	820652	002052	1018122	**49.27**
Old Private Sector Banks	3089	2967	3235	39392	47153	56000	65404	77459	49.59
New Private Sector Banks	8949	12353	17032	178401	181357	220064	274898	327392	56.82
Private Sector Banks	12038	15320	20267	217794	228510	276064	340301	404851	**55.18**
Foreign banks	5854	7745	10353	122984	111019	125686	133367	142882	**49.09**
Scheduled Commercial Banks	59201	66319	77283	895814	1000279	1231403	1375720	1565855	**50.59**

Table 4: Trends In Bank Group Wise Operating Expenses During 2006 to 2013.

Bank Group Wise	2005-06	2006-07	2007-08	2007-09	2009-10	2010-11	2011-12	2012-13	CAGR (%)
Nationalised Banks	473725	473179	466400	462926	473041	471727	494520	507694	0.87
SBI and Associates	270608	255699	242029	268598	266605	283375	279809	293965	1.04
Public Sector Banks	744333	728878	708429	731524	739646	755102	774329	801659	**0.93**
Old Private Sector Banks	51138	48667	48700	51341	55052	55380	62589	66208	3.28
New Private Sector Banks	59367	88617	110123	142237	133280	162573	185695	203733	16.66
Private Sector Banks	110505	137284	158823	193578	188332	217953	248284	269941	**11.81**
Foreign banks	22117	28426	33969	29582	28012	28041	25907	25384	**1.74**
Scheduled Commercial Banks	876955	894588	901221	954684	955990	1001096	1048520	1096984	**2.84**

Table 5: Trends in Bank Group Wise Number of Employees 2006 to 2013.

decrease in number of employees in the year 2007 when it is compared to 2006 then again there was increase in number of employees in 2008 as compared to 2007 then again there was a slight decrease in 2009 as compare to 2008. From the year 2010 to 2013 there was continuous increasing trend. In case of SBI and Associates there was a continuous decrease in the year 2007 and 2008 as compared to the base year then there was a marginal increase in the year 2009 but again in 2010 it decreased. In the year 2011 the number of employees increased but again in the year 2012 the analysis showed a decreasing trend and it again picked up in the year 2013. Public sector banks also showed the same trend as SBI and Associates till 2009. In case of old private sector banks only in the initial year of the study that is from 2006 to 2007 the number of employees decreased otherwise till 2012 it showed increasing trend then later on in the year 2013 there was a decrease in number of employees. In case of New Private Sector banks there was a drastic increasing trend and as result the private sector banks CAGR was at 11.81. In case of Foreign Banks from the year 2006 to 2008 there was increase in the number of employees but it has decreased in 2009 and 2010, later on 2011 to 2013 it was continuously increasing, and the scheduled commercial banks continuously increased during the study period.

Table 6 Reflects that the new private sectors are maintaining high net worth CAGR as compared to other banks which has been followed by the Foreign banks CAGR. The public sector banks showed the lowest CAGR i.e. 56.24. The analyses shows that during the period of eight years study the bank group wise has resulted in a continuous increase in net worth.

Bank Group Wise	2005-06	2006-07	2007-08	2007-09	2009-10	2010-11	2011-12	2012-13	CAGR (%)
Nationalised Banks	77384	92689	113079	1359202	1572758	2059079	2483255	2832832	56.84
SBI and Associates	37660	42941	61706	724216	837256	843942	1072494	1253189	54.98
Public Sector Banks	115044	135630	174785	2083419	2410014	2903020	3555749	4086022	**56.24**
Old Private Sector Banks	9684	10736	15315	174765	201706	237982	278963	330127	55.45
New Private Sector Banks	34140	39736	76056	996686	1199839	1385664	1592952	1929461	65.59
Private Sector Banks	43823	50473	91371	996686	1199839	1385664	1592952	1929461	**60.5**
Foreign banks	24314	33075	49332	599368	691760	810507	936917	1073817	**60.56**
Scheduled Commercial Banks	183181	219179	315488	3679473	4301613	5099192	6085618	7089300	**57.93**

Table 6: Trends in Bank Group Wise Net worth During 2006 to 2013.

Bank Group Wise	2005-06	2006-07	2007-08	2007-09	2009-10	2010-11	2011-12	2012-13	CAGR (%)
Nationalised Banks	0.89	0.94	1.01	1.03	1.00	1.03	0.88	0.74	-2.28
SBI and Associates	0.87	0.86	0.97	1.02	0.91	0.79	0.89	0.88	0.14
Public Sector Banks	0.88	0.92	1.00	1.03	0.97	0.96	0.88	0.78	**-1.50**
Old Private Sector Banks	0.64	0.78	1.14	1.15	0.95	1.12	1.20	1.26	8.84
New Private Sector Banks	1.22	1.09	1.13	1.12	1.38	1.51	1.63	1.74	4.54
Private Sector Banks	1.07	1.02	1.13	1.13	1.28	1.43	1.53	1.63	**5.40**
Foreign banks	2.08	2.28	2.09	1.99	1.26	1.75	1.76	1.94	**-0.87**
Scheduled Commercial Banks	1.01	1.05	1.12	1.13	1.05	1.10	1.08	1.03	**0.25**

Table 7: Trends in Bank Group Wise Return on Asset (ROA) During 2006 to 2013.

Bank Group Wise	2005-06	2006-07	2007-08	2007-09	2009-10	2010-11	2011-12	2012-13	CAGR (%)
Nationalised Banks	408796	452981	536018	6550419	8281248	9503797	10899479	12861079	53.89
SBI and Associates	224761	211875	263823	3576239	3874734	3856967	4173221	4729979	46.35
Public Sector Banks	633557	664856	799841	10126658	12155981	13360764	15072700	17591058	**51.51**
Old Private Sector Banks	45254	43647	54080	723926	834993	926545	1093333	1344993	52.80
New Private Sector Banks	135314	171008	224498	2341385	2706176	3294031	4166489	4916070	56.69
Private Sector Banks	180568	214655	278578	3065312	3541169	4220576	5259822	6261063	**55.78**
Foreign banks	52384	71471	98910	1303537	1592909	1654993	2006511	2280631	**60.27**
Scheduled Commercial Banks	866508	950982	1177330	14495506	17290059	19236333	22339033	26132752	**53.08**

Table 8: Trends in Bank Group Wise Investments During 2006 to 2013.

Bank Group Wise	2005-06	2006-07	2007-08	2007-09	2009-10	2010-11	2011-12	2012-13	CAGR (%)
Nationalised Banks	734608	957877	1203678	15197619	18430819	23102793	27253162	30935500	59.61
SBI and Associates	371679	482270	593722	7394499	8579368	9941536	11519913	13792240	57.10
Public Sector Banks	1106288	1440146	1797401	22592117	27010187	33044329	38773075	44727740	**58.80**
Old Private Sector Banks	82957	92887	111670	1285039	1540853	1846473	2300795	2699373	54.54
New Private Sector Banks	230005	321865	406733	4468237	4783556	6128967	7363235	8733113	57.55
Private Sector Banks	312962	414751	518402	5753276	6324409	7975440	9664030	11432486	**56.79**
Foreign banks	97562	126339	161133	1653846	1632604	1955106	2298488	2636799	**51.00**
Scheduled Commercial Banks	1516811	1981236	2476936	29999239	34967200	42974875	50735592	58797025	**57.96**

Table 9: Trends in Bank Group Wise Advances During 2006 to 2013.

Table 7 is displaying the data related to return on assets (ROA) of public, private, and foreign banks during the period of 2006-2013. The ROA is a functional indicator of bank's profitability. ROA reflects bank's management ability to utilize the bank's financial and real investment resources to generate profits. This ratio is used to know the earning capacity of profit of a bank by using its assets and can be calculated as the after tax net profit percentage to total assets. Here, private banks have high ROA than public and foreign banks, which means they are using their assets efficiently. It refits the efficiency with which banks deploy their assets.

Table 8 is showing the data related to investment of Scheduled Commercial banks during the period of 2006-2013. This is one of the important segments of total assets which are used for different areas. Here, foreign banks have the high investment than private banks and public banks which mean foreign banks make more investment than private banks and public banks from their assets in other areas.

Table 9 is depicting the data regarding advances of bank group wise during the period of 2006-2013. Here, Nationalised banks have high Advances which mean that Nationalised banks grant more advances than private and foreign banks. The above analysis reveals that all most all the bank group wise increased their advances every year from 2006 to 2013 except the foreign bank has decreased its advances in the year 2010 as compared to 2009.

Comparison of bank group wise performance in terms of NPA reflects the profitability of loan portfolios of banks since less NPA contributes to higher interest income. Table 10 is demonstrating the data related to NPA to advances during the period of 2006-2013. This

Bank Group Wise	2005-06	2006-07	2007-08	2007-09	2009-10	2010-11	2011-12	2012-13	CAGR (%)
Nationalised Banks	1.16	0.94	0.77	0.68	0.91	0.92	1.44	2.00	7.05
SBI and Associates	1.63	1.32	1.43	1.47	1.50	1.49	1.76	2.04	2.84
Public Sector Banks	1.32	1.06	0.99	0.94	1.10	1.09	1.53	2.02	**5.46**
Old Private Sector Banks	1.66	0.96	0.66	0.90	0.82	0.53	0.58	0.77	-9.16
New Private Sector Banks	0.78	0.97	1.21	1.40	1.09	0.56	0.42	0.45	-6.64
Private Sector Banks	1.01	0.97	1.09	1.29	1.04	0.56	0.46	0.52	**-7.96**
Foreign banks	0.83	0.73	0.77	1.81	1.82	0.67	0.61	1.01	**2.48**
Scheduled Commercial Banks	1.22	1.02	1.00	1.05	1.12	0.97	1.28	1.68	**4.08**

Table 10: Trends in Bank Group Wise Non Performing Assets (NPA) During 2006 to 2013.

Bank Group Wise	2005-06	2006-07	2007-08	2007-09	2009-10	2010-11	2011-12	2012-13	CAGR (%)
Nationalised Banks	88574	110720	142647	1838924	2080289	2563064	3411767	3911088	60.56
SBI and Associates	49301	53465	70428	891958	979537	1098281	1435552	1637677	54.94
Public Sector Banks	137874	164185	213075	2730882	3059826	3661345	4847318	5548765	**58.7**
Old Private Sector Banks	10372	11474	14614	187898	204975	232989	325802	399275	57.83
New Private Sector Banks	24851	38092	56377	662816	623090	734142	1019752	1265589	63.44
Private Sector Banks	35223	49567	70991	850714	828064	967131	1345555	1664864	**61.93**
Foreign banks	12291	17924	24417	303220	263897	284931	359966	422486	**55.61**
Scheduled Commercial Banks	185388	231675	308482	3884816	4151786	4913407	6552839	7636115	**59.17**

Table 11: Trends in Bank Group Wise Interest Income During 2006 to 2013.

Bank Group Wise	2005-06	2006-07	2007-08	2007-09	2009-10	2010-11	2011-12	2012-13	CAGR (%)
Nationalised Banks	12379	14264	20979	263936	304996	287249	325766	370370	52.93
SBI and Associates	9526	9420	11818	160727	183937	192400	178231	197442	46.07
Public Sector Banks	21905	23684	32797	424662	488932	479649	503997	507812	**50.21**
Old Private Sector Banks	1221	1568	2184	27821	31518	30286	33948	41452	55.37
New Private Sector Banks	6870	10745	14822	150781	172713	178447	216532	256475	57.22
Private Sector Banks	8091	12313	17006	178602	204231	208734	250480	297927	**56.95**
Foreign banks	5371	7044	10588	148940	99513	110118	108950	112127	**46.2**
Scheduled Commercial Banks	35368	43041	60391	752204	792676	798501	863437	977866	**51.433**

Table 12: Trends in Bank Group Wise Other Income During 2006 to 2013.

Bank Group Wise	2005-06	2006-07	2007-08	2007-09	2009-10	2010-11	2011-12	2012-13	CAGR (%)
Nationalised Banks	52464	69353	101093	1316762	1457115	1641351	2397280	2813956	64.51
SBI and Associates	28040	32607	47809	617704	662285	670179	888609	1065334	57.57
Public Sector Banks	80504	101960	148902	1934467	2119401	2311530	3285889	3879290	**62.32**
Old Private Sector Banks	6247	7055	9960	128340	140760	147681	225057	278598	60.75
New Private Sector Banks	15261	25802	38535	441234	371296	423810	642787	792733	63.85
Private Sector Banks	21507	32856	48495	569574	512056	571491	867843	1071332	**62.99**
Foreign banks	5149	7603	10604	128191	89379	106227	149824	187406	**56.72**
Scheduled Commercial Banks	107161	142420	208001	2632232	2720836	2989248	4303557	5138027	**62.22**

Table 13: Trends in Bank Group Wise Interest Expended During 2006 to 2013.

ratio is used to know the asset quality, which is based on loan portfolio. Here, public sector banks have high ratio than other banks which means the asset quality of public banks is poor among other scheduled commercial banks. The nationalized banks are more exposed to high potential losses in case of defaults.

The above given Table 11 shows the new private sector banks CAGR is high as compared to other bank group. In the above analysis it is noticed in all bank group wise the interest income during the period of study is gradually increasing, except in the year 2010 the private sector a foreign banks has shown a declining figure. In case of private sector banks the declining figure is due to decrease in case of new private sector.

Table 12 Shows that in case of other income earned by the banks the new private sector bank has the highest CAGR during the period of study. If we observe, the nationalised banks during the period of study increased continuously except in the year 2011, in case of SBI & Associates there was decrease in the other income in the year 2007 and 2012. In case of old private sector banks there was continuous increase during the study period, except in the year 2011. In case of foreign banks the decreasing trend was in the year 2010 and 2012.

The above given Table 13 reflects that the interest expended in nationalized banks has more CAGR as compared to other bank group wise. From the above analysis it is clear that in all bank group wise during the period of study the interest expenditure has increased, except in the year 2010, where the foreign banks interest expenditure has declined as compared to 2009 and the same in case of private sector banks.

Bank Group Wise	2005-06	2006-07	2007-08	2007-09	2009-10	2010-11	2011-12	2012-13	CAGR (%)
Nationalised Banks	21.42	17.94	14.05	13.31	13.65	16.41	12.20	11.81	-7.17
SBI and Associates	24.35	21.55	15.89	15.06	17.10	19.97	17.42	16.20	-4.97
Public Sector Banks	22.48	19.15	14.66	13.88	14.79	17.50	13.72	13.09	**-6.54**
Old Private Sector Banks	18.93	16.89	13.67	13.26	14.57	16.75	13.00	12.28	-5.27
New Private Sector Banks	9.54	9.36	9.56	10.17	12.10	13.83	11.97	11.40	2.25
Private Sector Banks	12.15	10.93	10.35	10.83	12.73	14.53	12.22	11.61	**-0.57**
Foreign banks	18.22	20.08	19.95	19.44	23.48	23.30	20.35	18.22	**0**
Scheduled Commercial Banks	20.11	17.32	14.01	13.60	14.85	17.22	13.73	13.02	**-5.29**

Table 14: Trends in Bank Group Wise Wages as % of total expenses During 2006 to 2013.

Bank Group Wise	2005-06	2006-07	2007-08	2007-09	2009-10	2010-11	2011-12	2012-13	CAGR (%)
Nationalised Banks	4.27	4.80	5.82	6.09	5.37	4.93	6.22	6.39	5.17
SBI and Associates	4.84	4.75	5.90	6.00	5.32	4.85	5.66	5.96	2.64
Public Sector Banks	4.46	4.79	5.85	6.06	5.35	4.91	6.06	6.27	**4.35**
Old Private Sector Banks	4.77	4.98	6.20	6.67	6.13	5.66	7.10	7.27	5.41
New Private Sector Banks	4.14	5.24	6.11	6.15	4.42	4.27	5.45	5.77	4.24
Private Sector Banks	4.35	5.18	6.13	6.27	4.83	4.60	5.84	6.12	**4.36**
Foreign banks	3.63	4.03	4.33	4.46	2.83	3.11	3.88	4.05	**1.38**
Scheduled Commercial Banks	4.39	4.82	5.80	5.99	5.10	4.75	5.90	6.12	**4.24**

Table 15: Trends in Bank Group Wise cost of funds During 2006 to 2013.

Bank Group Wise	2005-06	2006-07	2007-08	2007-09	2009-10	2010-11	2011-12	2012-13
Nationalised Banks	383.07	490.01	618.28	783.16	935.86	1152.54	1278.50	1422.3
SBI and Associates	337.79	436.35	565.06	650.22	737.43	790.48	913.80	1019.7
Public Sector Banks	366.61	471.18	600.10	734.35	864.34	1016.67	1146.80	1274.7
Old Private Sector Banks	417.33	474.93	569.32	638.43	697.49	810.41	872.30	972.4
New Private Sector Banks	889.39	830.09	831.96	691.80	803.80	831.30	858.90	930.3
Private Sector Banks	670.94	704.19	751.42	677.60	772.70	826.00	862.30	940.6
Foreign banks	955.41	974.77	1037.10	1282.74	1411.39	1555.50	1956.20	2173.3
Scheduled Commercial Banks	419.80	522.94	643.24	739.80	862.30	990.30	1099.50	1213.3

Table 16: Trends in Bank Group Wise Business per employees During 2006 to 2013.

It has been observed from the above Table 14 that almost all the banks had shown a declining trend in case of wages as percentage to total expenses, except the New Private Sector banks. There are many fluctuations in the above trend, in case of Nationalised banks, SBI and Associate and old private sector banks there was a continuous declining trend from the year 2007 to 2009 then in the year 2010 and 2011 there was an increasing trend, but again in the year 2012 and 2013 there was a decreasing trend. If we look at new private sector banks the scenario is different, there is a continuous increase from the year 2006 to 2011, except in the year 2007 later on in the year 2012 and 2013 there was a fall in the trend. In case of Foreign banks, the wages as percentage to total expenses has increased in the year 2007 when it compared to 2006 but in the year 2008 an 2009 it has decreased, and again in the year 2010 it has increased but in the year 2011 it has reduced and again there was a raise in the year 2012 and fall in the year 2013.

The above Table 15 gives the details of cost of funds for a period of eight years i.e. from 2005-06 to 2013-14 where, the foreign banks are showing the low cost of funds with a CAGR of 1.38% . There are many ups and downs in the trends of cost of funds during the study period. In case of Nationalised banks and old private sector banks there was a continuous increase in the cost of funds from 2006 to 2009 later on in the year 2010 and 2011 there was a fall in the cost of funds again increased in the year 2012 and 2013. In case of SBI and Associates the cost of funds reduced in the year 2007 as compared to 2006 and increased in the year 2008 and 2009 as compared to 2007 and again reduced in the year 2010 and 2011 and there on increased in the year 2012 and in the year 2013. In case of new private sector banks the cost of funds increased from 2006 to 2009 and in the year 2010 and 2011 it has been decreased and again increased in the year 2012 and 2013. In case of foreign banks there was a continuous increase in the cost of funds from 2006 to 2009, in the year 2010 it reduced as compared to previous years but again from the year 2011 to 2013 there was a continuous increase in the cost of funds.

If we look at 8 years historical performance of different types of players in the banking industry, foreign banks has grown its business per employee by the highest rate CAGR i.e. 10.82%. There was a continuous increase in the trend of business per employee during the period of study in case of public sector banks and Foreign banks, but when it comes to private sector banks there was a fall in the year 2009 and this is as a result of fall in new private sector bank (Table 16).

It is revealed from the above facts that the foreign banks are at number position in case of profit per employee as compared to other two players in the banking industry i.e. public and private sector banks. The profit per employee is not in a similar trend in case of all bank group wise during the study period, in case of Nationalised banks there was a continuous increase in the profit per employee from the year 2006 to 2011, but in the year 2012 and 2013 it has been reduced. In case of SBI and Associates there was a continuous increasing trend in profit per employee till the year 2010, in the year 2011 it has been reduced but again in the year 2012 and 2013 it has shown an increasing trend.

Old private sector banks showed increasing trend till the year 2009 and in the year 2010 it has decreased but again from the year 2011 to 2013 it resulted in increasing trend. In case of New private sector banks the profit per employee decreased in the year 2007 as compared to 2006 and increased in the year 2008 and again decreased in the year 2009, from the year 2010 to 2013 there was a continuous increasing trend. In case of foreign banks there was a continuous increase, except in the year 2010.

It has been observed and derived from the analysis over sample period, that the Changes over the past eight years i.e., from 2005-2006 to 2013-2014 in the banking system have been drastic. The above ranking is done based on the CAGR of each parameter. The results show that public, private and foreign banks has different rankings based on different parameters such as No. of offices, No. of employees, Business per employee, Profit per employee, Net Worth, Deposits, Investments, Advances, Interest income, Other income, Interest expended, Operating expenses, Cost of Funds (CoF),Wages as % to total expenses, Return on Assets, CRAR and NPA ratio. Private sector banks are at first on the base of return on total assets (ROA), Number of offices, Number of Employees, Non Performing Assets (NPA), Interest Income and other income. Based on CRAR, cost of funds, operating expenses, Investments, Net worth, Interest expended, Business per employee, profit per employee and Wages as % of total expenses, Business per employee Foreign Banks are at the first as compared to public bank and private banks Findings.

On the basis of results and analysis, the following are the findings

1. It has been found that the new private sector banks have shown the highest annual expansion in terms of number of branches vis-à-vis old private sector banks.
2. The capitalization profile of private banks continues to be better than that of Public Sector Banks, with the private banks CRAR at around 3.88% and that of PSBs at around 0.21%. However, continuous government support (via capital infusion) to enable PSBs maintain a minimum Tier I capital of 7% is likely to result in these banks being able to maintain a comfortable capitalization profile over short to medium term.
3. Bank group-wise, public sector banks accounted for the largest CAGR (56.19 per cent) in total deposits followed by private sector banks (54.57per cent). Foreign banks showed the lowest CAGR (49.77 Percent)
4. Private sector banks have very good Return on Assets (ROA) as compared to other bank group during the study period of eight years i.e. from 2005- 06 to 2013-14.
5. As far as interest income is concerned, private banks are ahead in the race by reporting 61.93% growth, followed by pubic banks (58.7%) and then by foreign banks (55.61%).
6. Foreign banks have the highest business per employee as well as profit per employee.
7. The NPA of public sector bank was also significantly higher than that of private and foreign banks, which indicates the asset quality of public banks is comparatively poor.

Recommendations

Based on the findings of study the following are few suggestions to the Indian banking Industry, which helps them to improve their performance and efficiency and make them fit to compete in this competitive global scenario.

1. As the ROA i.e. Return on assets is the parameter that indicates the efficiency of banks management in utilization of its assets, it is advised that the public sector banks should take care regarding this parameter in general, and in particular it is in the case of nationalized banks where there is a need for improvement.
2. In case of cost of funds there is a need for both public sector banks and private sector banks to work upon this parameter because it shows on the higher side when it is compared to the foreign banks.
3. Having high ratio 11th of Non Performing Asset i.e., NPA is a sign of poor asset quality and in this study it is noticed that there is a high NPA in public sector banks as compared to private sector banks and foreign banks, and this high NPA's in public sector banks is due to high NPAs in nationalized bank, so there is a need for nationalized banks to focus on this parameter in particular and public sector banks in general, as the simple reason is that the asset quality effects the performance of the banks
4. In case of business per employee the private sector banks are at the back end when it is compared with the other bank groups in the study, this point out that there is a need for private sector banks to look into this matter.
5. When we take profit per employee into consideration, the foreign banks are at front position so it is an indication to both the bank groups i.e. public sector and private sector to try to with stand with the foreign banks in the global scenario.

References

1. Sharma D, Sharma AK, Barua MK (2013). "Efficiency and productivity of banking sector. A critical analysis of literature and design of conceptual model", Qualitative Research in Financial Markets 5: 195-224.
2. Siraj KK, Pilla PS (2013) "Efficiency of NPA Management in Indian SCBs –A Bank-Group Wise Exploratory Study", Journal of Applied Finance & Banking 3: 1792-6580.
3. Ranbir S (2003) 'Profitability Management in Banks under Deregulated Environment', IBA Bulletin 115: 19-2
4. Souza D' (2002) "How well have public sector banks done? A Note", Economic and Political Weekly 23: 245-256.
5. Kannan R, Narain A (2001) "Determinants of net interest margin under regulatory requirements, an economic study', Economic and Political Weekly 4: 337-344.

Evaluating Performance of Commercial Banks in Pakistan: "An Application of Camel Model"

Ishaq AB, Karim A, Ahmed S and Zaheer A*

Department of Finance, Army Public College of Management and Sciences (APCOMS), University of engineering and technology, Taxila, Pakistan

Abstract

Banking sector plays a vital role in the economic growth. In this paper, an effort has been made to assess the financial execution of the ten commercial banks working in Pakistan and the data has been taken for seven years i.e., 2007-2013. Moreover, data were also assembled from articles, papers, the World Wide Web (Internet), Specialized International Journals, and relevant previous studies. In the present study an endeavor was made to evaluate the execution and financial accuracy of commercial banks using CAMEL approach. CAMEL is the supervisory and administrative framework implemented by State Bank of Pakistan. It consists of five critical indicators to assess the soundness and execution of the bank. These segments are Capital adequacy, Asset quality, Management, Earning and Liquidity. The Capital adequacy, Asset quality, Management efficiency, Earning and Liquidity are taken as independent variables (financial measures) with a view to study their impact on the firm's performance. Earnings per share (EPS) is used as a dependent variable. Measurable apparatuses like descriptive statistics, Correlation and regression analysis were used to gauge the execution of the banks. The results show that total deposit to equity, non-performing loans to gross advances, non-performing loans to equity, Admin Exp to Interest Income Ratio, Gross Advances to Total Deposits Ratio were significantly but negative correlated with a bank's performance. The Return on Assets and Return on Equity were significantly and positively correlated with a bank's performance. The interest income to total assets ratio is statistically insignificant with bank's performance, whereas the regression result show that INT is statistically significant with bank's performance. The cash ratio is also showing insignificant correlated bank's performance, whereas the regression result shows that the cash ratio is statistically significant with a bank's performance.

Keywords: Capital Adequacy; Asset Quality; Management Efficiency; Earnings and Profitability; Liquidity; Bank's Performance (earning per share)

Introduction

Financial Sector is important for the economic development and prosperity of the country. Financial sector works as the backbone of the economy that controls the money supply. The Banks accept funding from surplus monetary units as deposits and give it to Business and Industries as advances. Banking is a very important sector because the development of the finance, and particularly the banking system, promote economic growth. Banks are important for the economy and organizations in particular at the time of declines and money related crisis. Industrial, agricultural and commercial development of a country is not imaginable without an efficient banking system. Sometimes bank truly don't respond to the crisis, comparing the later past financial crisis 2007-09, it makes the condition more terrible for economic improvement. Therefore, it is significant to observe the performance of the banks with the administrative prerequisites [1].

The financial resources of the country can be properly utilized through banks because they serve as a backbone of the financial sector. The banking sector has attracted a huge amount of investments and expanded to a great extent. Nowadays banks are not only restricted to financial intermediary services, but also involved in providing specialized services to their customers in order to meet ever changing customer needs as the banking industry is innovating rapidly [2].

A bank is an institution which receives deposits from customers and gives loan to the institutions [3]. The word bank implies an association where individuals and business can contribute or borrow money; transform it to foreign cash and so forth. As indicated by the Halsbury's Law of England "A Banker is an individual, partnership or corporation, whose sole or predominating business is banking, that is, the receipt of money on current or deposit account and the payment of cheques drawn by and the collection of cheques paid in by a customer".

Hilton Banking Commission defines Bank or Banker in the following words "Every person, firm or company using in the description or its title, Bank or Banker or Banking and accepting deposits of money subject to withdrawal by cheque, draft or order".

In the viewpoint of the above mentioned definitions, a straightforward and short definition is that the Bank is an establishment which deals in cash and credit. Furthermore a bank accepts deposits in reserve funds and current records at a lower rate of interest or benefit and gives advances to those who need it, and representatives at a higher proportion of interest or benefit. Likewise, it exchanges money for the customers across different cities and countries furthermore, it performs different other agency services for income purpose.

According to the Banking Ordinance 1962 (Pakistan) defines banking as "Accepting for the purpose of lending or investment of deposits of money from public, repayable on demand or otherwise and withdrawal by cheque, draft, order or otherwise". The significance of the financial sector in the monetary advancement can't be denied. The

***Corresponding author:** Adnan Zaheer, Department of Finance, Army Public College of Management and Sciences (APCOMS), University of Engineering and Technology, Khadim Hussain Road, Rawalpindi, Taxila, Punjab, Pakistan
E-mail: adnan_zaheer2009@hotmail.com

banking segment in its ability of intermediation between the borrower and the loan specialists facilitates the monetary exercises as a piece of the banking sector [4].

Financial segment in broad and banking segment in particular is one of the energetic elements for the economic development of the country. So it is important to control and regulate bank processes by an apex Bank to make sure customer's safety, strengthen and promote soundness, stability and efficiency of the banking system. This helps to decrease the hazards of banks becoming bankrupt [5]. Banks are well-known as financial intermediaries their role is to sell its own obligations and to buy from others. All over the world the banking segment is known for the appropriation of multidimensional techniques occasionally with fluctuating degrees of achievement. Banks are vital for the efficient functioning of budgetary markets as they serve as stores of fundamental monetary data and can conceivably alleviate the issues made by data asymmetries. Central bank needs such great disclosures for early identification of issues confronted by banks in the business and decreases the seriousness of business sector disturbances.

As per the report issued by Pakistan and Gulf economist on FEB 21st, 2015, the banking industry of Pakistan consists of 55 banks that include 5 public sector banks, 5 Islamic banks, 17 private banks, 6 foreign banks, 8 development financial institutions, 4 specialized banks and 10 micro finance banks.

Above mentioned banks provide a diverse type of products and services to their customers in order to attain long term growth. If the financial segments do not perform well and maintain the liquidity for unseen events than they can take cash from the central bank as per rules and procedure. It is the obligation of the state bank to take quick, appropriate action to avoid the bank managers and proprietors from assuming excessive risks.

The State Bank of Pakistan has increased and strengthened its capacity by acquiring new skills, improve the quality of the existing human resource base, implementing technology and re-engineering business processes. The financial soundness indicators show a healthy and sound banking system with a high degree of financial stability. Pakistan's Banking sector adopted some changes which were presented in the early 1990s and transformed into a decently sorted out, sound and strong accounting framework. The most recent extensive evaluation done mutually by the World Bank and IMF in 2004 reached at the following conclusion "For arriving at changes have brought about a more viable and focused money related framework specifics. The essential government managing an accounting framework has been changed into one that is overwhelmed under the control of the private division The lawmaking system and the State Bank of Pakistan's directing limit have been enhanced essentially. Because of this, the money related division is sounder and shows an expanded strength to stuns."

Formally banking begins in Pakistan during the time of British pioneers in the South Asia. After autonomy from the British Raj in 1947, and the origin of Pakistan as a country in the globe, the extent of banking segment in Pakistan has been expanding and stretching continuously. Pakistan's most seasoned bank is the State Bank of Pakistan, which is also the central bank of the country. Before freedom on August 14, 1947, the Reserve Bank of India was the national bank of what is presently Pakistan. After freedom, Muhammad Ali Jinnah took activities to secure a national bank in Pakistan, which brought about the new establishing of the State bank of Pakistan, with its home office to be situated in Karachi. Just 7% of the population utilizes the banks, has enormous potential yet this needs to be pushed somewhat further. Thus, the efficient performance of the banking sector is imperative for the smooth functioning of the Pakistan economy.

The research describes the financial performance of the banking segment by utilizing CAMEL model including Capital adequacy, Asset quality, Management efficiency, Earnings & Profitability and Liquidity to assess the financial performance. The significance of this study is valuable for helping business financiers to know the qualities and shortcomings for defining methodologies and polices that will push a successful and sound money framework. Regulators have enlarged bank supervision by utilizing CAMEL model to evaluate and assess the performance and financial soundness of the bank's activities [6].

The CAMEL Model was developed in 1979. This model is recommended by the US Federal Reserve and the Uniform Financial Institutions Rating System (UFIRS). This model was employed in the US financial institutions and then all around the world. This model consists of five indicators that are Capital adequacy, Asset quality, Management efficiency, Earnings & Profitability and Liquidity. The CAMEL framework emphasizes on the five parameters of the banking system by looking at its profit and loss statement to assess financial performance and balance sheet to assess the financial position of the banks [7]. CAMEL model is basically a methodology commonly used to measure the performance of banking segment in and outside India [8]. The different researchers have analyzed the overall financial performance of major private sector banks in India through the application of CAMEL Model [9].

Aspal and Dhawan analyzed the performance of banks in India, Reserve Bank of India has prescribed two supervisory models (Capital Adequacy, Asset Quality, Management, Earning, Liquidity, Systems and Controls) and CACS (Capital Adequacy, Assets Quality, Compliance, Systems and Controls) [10]. The study focused on the CAMEL model to assess the performance of Old Private Sector Banks in India. The CAMEL model is very famous among controllers because of its effectiveness. This model is very good for the evaluation of the performance of the banks. CAMEL model was implemented by North America Bank regulators to judge the financial and administrative reliability of commercial loaning organizations. This model assesses the general condition of the bank, its qualities and shortcomings [11].

Numerous researchers have conducted research to assess the performance of commercial banks by adopting the CAMEL model. Bodla and Verma, Gupta and Kaur, Dash and Das, Kaur have investigated the performance of Indian public sector banks, private sector banks and foreign banks by using the different ratios in CAMEL model [9,12,13]. The time period of their studies was different, however the findings reached by them was more or less similar. Sushendra and Kumar used CAMEL framework and they have broken down the performance of the State bank of India group. They utilized different ratios to gauge the State bank group's performance under each of the CAMEL parameters and presumed that a State bank of Travancore secured first position in all classifications. The real disadvantage of the study was that it was restricted to the state bank group.

CAMEL is a systematic methodology recommended by Moody's to evaluate a bank's general security, solidness and soundness. Banks are performing essential and a significant part in economic and capital development because of the inborn nature, in this way banks ought to be given more consideration than whatever other kind of the monetary unit in an economy. Assessment of financial performance of the banking sector is a powerful measure and pointer to check the soundness of economic activities of an economy. The five parameters of the CAMEL model used to evaluate the operating soundness, financial performance, financial condition and regulatory compliance of the banking organization [14].

CAMEL model is essentially a proportion based model utilized for assessing the performance of banks and is utilized for ranking or rating of the banks. CAMEL model is the instrument which is utilized in the critical investigation of the statement of financial position of banks and the presentation of such examination to provide the evaluation of the strength of the banks. In the present examination work, CAMEL model has been utilized as a measuring rod to gauge the Capital adequacy, Asset quality, Management efficiency, Earnings and Liquidity of five nationalized banks [15]. The performance of the banking segment under CAMELS model, which includes analysis and assessment of the five fundamental dimensions of banking operations. Thus the CAMEL model includes set of performance measures that provide a comprehensive view of the banks [16].

According to the Lakhtaria Ratio examination is the best tool for investigating the performance and productivity of the banking sector [17]. The CAMEL indicators include Capital adequacy, Asset Quality, Management efficiency, Earnings and Liquidity. According to the previous studies, it is clear that there are many studies carried out on banks in different countries. However, a detailed study has not yet been carried out in Pakistan to assess the performance of the banks. The purpose of this research is to analyze the Financial Performance of the 10 Commercial Banks working in Pakistan by adopting the CAMEL Model. It is an appropriate and simple model to evaluate the financial and managerial assessment of institutions based on Capital adequacy, Asset quality, Management efficiency, Earnings and Liquidity [18].

Controllers have enlarged bank supervision by utilizing CAMEL (Capital adequacy, Asset quality, Management competency, Earnings and Liquidity) model to evaluate and assess the performance and monetary soundness of the exercises of the bank. CAMEL is an acronym for a rating model through which banks are evaluated and given a rating focuses on the premise of different parameters [1].

Gap analysis

Banking sector acts as a backbone of the economy. The Financial resources of the country are allocated through banks. Moreover, banking sector acts as a heart through which money is injected into the economy. Therefore, it needs continuous performance evaluation. CAMEL model is a useful tool for performance evaluation and examining the soundness of banks. After 1980s noticeable loan losses occurred and banks collapsed, therefore, need of banking supervision has increased [2]. This model is used worldwide. In developed countries a lot of research has been carried out on the application and usefulness of camel model. In Pakistan there is no significant research carried out by utilizing Camel Model. Scholars in Pakistan used camel Model as ratio analysis by comparing one bank to another bank or one sector to another sector to find out the performance of the banks. They didn't find out the impact of the CAMEL model on bank performance. Alam, Raza and Akram, made comparison of public vs private commercial banks [19]. Usman and Khan evaluated the performance of Islamic and conventional banks [5]. Shar, Shah and Jamali, evaluated bank performance pre and post nationalization of the banking sector in Pakistan by adopting the CAMEL model [20]. Kouser, Aamir, Mehvish and Azeem adopt the CAMEL analysis of Islamic and Conventional Banks in Pakistan [21]. In existing literature other researchers used one component of CAMEL model to measure the bank performance. Bokhari, Ali and Sultan, used one component of CAMEL model, i.e. Capital adequacy to find out the impact on bank performance [22]. The focus of this research is to analyze the impact of different components of the CAMEL Model on the performance of 10 commercial banks operating in Pakistan and data is taken from 2007 to 2013.

Problem statement

What are the key factors that affect bank's performance? In previous studies key factors that affect bank's performance have not been identified. In this research key factors effecting bank's performance will be analyzed.

Research question

In recent years, the financial system, especially the banks has undergone numerous changes in the form of reforms, regulations & norms. CAMEL's framework for the performance evaluation of banks is an addition to this. From the above problem statement, following are the questions of this research are as follow:

a) What is the impact of Capital Adequacy on the financial performance of Banks?

b) How does Asset Quality impact on the financial performance of Banks?

c) Does Managerial Efficiency influence on the financial performance of Banks?

d) How Earnings & Profitability affects the financial performance of Banks?

e) Whether or not Liquidity affects the financial performance of Banks?

Scope of research

The scope of the research is restricted to the ten commercial banks operating in Pakistan due to the unavailability of data and time constraints. This study aims to evaluate financial performance by focusing on all five parameters of Camel Model i.e. Capital adequacy, Asset quality, Management Efficiency, Earnings & Profitability and Liquidity. However there are different ratios that can be used to analyze these parameters.

Research objectives

This study is aimed to analyze the Camel model in banking sector of Pakistan during the period 2007-2013. Specifically, the following objectives of the study are:

a) To investigate the capital adequacy of selected Commercial banks.

b) To consider Asset Quality of selected Commercial banks.

c) To analyze the Management Efficiency of selected Commercial banks.

d) To explore the Earning and profitability of selected Commercial banks.

e) To study the Liquidity of selected Commercial banks.

Significance of study

Evaluation of the organization's overall performance and observing the financial condition is essential to owners, potential investors, depositors, managers and, of course, the regulators [23]. The study is conducted to analyze the performance of banks with respect to a Camel model. This research is focused on CAMEL Model as it emphasizes on different indicators that are specifically important for safety and soundness of the banking industry.

This research will provide insight to shareholders and investors about the key factors that affect the bank performance. It will enhance their knowledge beyond the typical information like financial statement and disclosure which are made by banks in their annual statements. On the basis of information investors will take a more valuable decision to invest in a certain Bank.

The findings of this research will contribute to the existing literature on bank performance as well as bridge the knowledge gap currently exists related to bank performance measures available.

It will help the regulators in making appropriate rules and regulations, mitigate the potential risk of failures and take corrective actions. It will also helpful to formulate appropriate policies on how these can be improved upon.

Moreover, it will be beneficial for management to formulate a proactive strategy for survival and long term growth of the organization. It will also helpful for the reader to know the specific details of the model which in turn lead to identifying the strengths and weaknesses of the banks, it will give a better understanding and knowledge about the performance of the banking industry particularly in Pakistan. Further the study outcomes may be used as a basis for future research.

Delimitation of the study

a. The focus of study is a commercial bank's performance operating in Pakistan only.

b. Time and resources constraints.

c. The system under examination relates just to banks, however, it can be utilized for performance assessment of other money related organizations.

d. The study is totally done on the premise of ratios ascertained from the financial records.

e. It is impractical to get an individual meeting with the top administration representatives of all banks under study.

Review of the Literature

General

This chapter comprises of previous studies and their findings related to the independent variables that are used in this study with respect to their relationship with the dependent variable to measure the bank's performance. The theoretical framework and hypothesis that have been drawn on the basis of the results of the past studies have also been included.

Azizi and Sarkani research is carried out to assess the performance of Mellat Bank by adopting the CAMEL model [24]. Statistical tools were applied to analyze the data. The outcomes show that there is a significant and positive association between the indicators of liquidity, management efficiency and earnings quality with financial execution. According to the Chen the research is carried out to examine the relationship between CAMEL parameters and bank execution to advice supervisors to give careful consideration to the CAMEL model to improve competitiveness of banks [25].

Said and Saucier applied the CAMEL model to assess the execution of Japanese Commercial banks in terms of Capital adequacy, Asset quality, Management efficiency, Earnings ability and Liquidity position. Prasuna evaluates the performance of 65 Indian banks using the CAMEL model and conclude that innovative products, better service quality, and better bargains were beneficial because of the prevailing tough competition.

Sarker analyzed Bangali Islamic banks with the help of the CAMEL model which help the regulators to set Shariah benchmark to supervise and inspect Islamic banks and financial institutions from an Islamic perspective [26]. Nurazi and Evans find that capital adequacy ratio, asset quality, administration, earnings, liquidity and bank size are statistically significant in explaining bank failure [27].

Gupta evaluates the performance of 30 Indian commercial banks adopting CAMEL model data is taken for 2003-2007 and give rating to top five and bottom five banks [9]. According to the Goyal, the CAMEL model is a tool to measure the performance of the banks in terms of Capital adequacy, Asset quality, management efficiency, Earnings quality and Liquidity [28]. San and Phing found that the application of CAMEL framework is useful for banks in analyzing financial health, diagnoses which help in taking preventive measures, after testing the impacts of CAMEL norms on the performance of SBI Groups [29]. Reddy and Prasad applied CAMEL model for analyzing performance of rural Indian banks [30].

Olweny and Shipo took into account factors that result into bank collapse [31]. They came to the conclusion that Asset Quality and Liquidity are responsible for Kenyan bank failures. Bhayani carried out research to analyze the execution of new private sector banks by adopting the CAMEL model [32]. Four prominent private segment banks are Unit Trust of India, Industrial Development Bank of India, Housing Development Finance Establishment, and Industrial Credit & an Investment Corporation of India had been taken as a sample.

Biswas analyzes the execution of two public sector banks. The researcher compares the performance of Andhra Bank and Bank of Maharashtra by utilizing the CAMEL model [33]. The research is carried out for the period of 2011-2013 and the data were taken from the annual reports of the banks. Kabir and Dey carried out research to measure the execution of Private, Commercial banks of Bangladesh by adopting the CAMEL Model [34]. The outcomes show that the national banks of all around the globe have enhanced their supervision quality and methods.

Keovongvichith analyzed the performance of the Laotian Banking Sector during 2005-2010 by adopting the CAMEL model [35]. Altan, Yusufazari and Beduk, carried out research to investigate the execution and financial soundness of state owned and private owned banks operating in Turkish for the period 2005-2012 by applying the CAMEL model [36]. Camel model includes five important parameters that are Capital adequacy, Asset quality, Management efficiency, Earnings quality and Liquidity. According to the Mohiuddin study is carried out to assess the financial execution of the two major banks NCB and PCB operating in Bangladesh [37]. In this research CAMEL model is utilized, the latest model of financial analysis. The outcome shows that the position of the banks is comprehensive and satisfactory in terms of their Capital, Asset quality, Management efficiency, Earnings quality and Liquidity.

Muhmad and Hashim this research is carried out to analyze the performance of domestic and foreign bank operating in Malaysia by utilizing a CAMEL framework. The data is taken from 2008 to 2012 and regression analysis was used. The outcome shows that capital, asset quality and liquidity have a significant effect on the execution of Malaysian banks [38].

Ebrahimi, Nasab and Javaheri analyze the effect of Privatization of Banks on CAMEL Model. The data is taken from 2004 to 2014 and T-test is used to examine the data [39]. The result demonstrates that privatization has significant effect on ratio of return on equity and asset quality and other indicators CAMEL are not changed. Gebba and Ahmed analyze the execution of privatized financial institutions operating in Egypt by utilizing the CAMEL model [40]. The outcome reveals that there is a significant difference between the performance of the banks before and after privatization. Mishra analyzed the performance of different Indian public and private sector banks over the decade 2000-2011 using CAMEL approach and found that private sector banks are at the top of the list, with their performances in terms of soundness being the best.

EPS

Earnings per share show the return earned per share. This proportion measures the market worth of the shares of the organization (Banks). Higher earnings per share show better future prospects of the Banks. EPS shows whether the acquiring force of the bank has expanded or not [41].

This proportion shows the productivity of the firm on per Equity Share basis. This proportion measures the income available to an equity shareholder on a per share basis [42]. Furthermore, earnings per share (EPS) show how much income has been produced per share of stock amid the reported period. As an organizations income increase, earnings per share looks better and the firm issue more shares, increases the quantity of shares outstanding [43]. Earnings per share can be calculated as net income divided by the aggregate number of shares outstanding.

Earnings per share or (EPS) show a part of any company's total earnings, its net taxes, dividends on preferred stock, that are allocated to each share of common stock. EPS can be calculated by dividing net income earned by the company in a specific reporting period. (Normally it is quarterly or annually) by the total number of shares outstanding during the same reporting period. For the reason number of outstanding shares may be fluctuate. So a weighted average is generally used. E.g., a company ABC reported its net income of $6 Million and its number of shares outstanding during that time was 15 Million, after calculation it shows an EPS of $0.40 of the company for that period.

EPS = 6,000,000/15,000,000 shares = **$0.40**

According to past studies on EPS, it shows that EPS as a forecaster of share price has produced mixed results. EPS can be considered as a significant predictor when the firm increases its EPS repeatedly over a longer period of time. So many news releases have reported that so many firms did not see any increase in the share price even though their quarterly EPS increased. So it indicates that EPS might not be a good quality forecaster for share prices for a shorter period of time [44].

Earnings per share is an important factor which analyzing the impact of financial leverage on a firm [45].

Earnings per share is the measure of income every outstanding share of an organization's stock [46]. The equity stockholders are the sole claimants of the net incomes of the company after giving outflows of dividend to the preference stockholder. The importance of this proportion is that higher the earnings per share, the more is the possibility for a greater rate of dividend and also of retained earnings, to build up the internal strength of the corporation, consequently greater EPS would increase the market price and the other way around [47].

An earnings per share is a ratio which the stockbrokers and financiers will watch sensibly and deliberate it while determining the market worth of the equity share. Earnings per share is calculated as net income minus dividends on preferred stocks and then divided by average outstanding shares. The income received by a corporation after meeting cost of manufacture, then interest, devaluation and tax goes to the equity shareholders. These earnings are referred to as earnings per share [48]. EPS is a sequence proportion of income after tax divided by issued common stocks. EPS shows the amount that is going to be distributed among shareholders. EPS reflects future income or capital gain or loss [49].

Capital adequacy

The capital adequacy proportion is a complete index to mirror the danger of banks, additionally the bank's resource-obligation administration some of the benchmark targets. In handy utilize, the banks are not just utilizing the capital adequacy degree to gauge their own danger, additionally through this objective correlation of the pointers with industry, so that the capital adequacy proportion has a general importance [50]. Capital adequacy refers to the measure of value capital and different securities which a bank holds as stores against hazardous resources as a support against the probabilities of bank disaster [51]. The "Basle Committee" (focused on the Bank for International Settlements), which was initially settled in 1974, is a panel that speaks to national banks and financial supervisory powers of the major industrialized countries (the G10 nations). The board of trustees frets about guaranteeing the power supervision of banks on a worldwide premise by setting and advancing universal norms. Its central hobby has been in the territory of capital adequacy proportions.

In 1988, the board issued an announcement of standards, managing capital adequacy degrees. This announcement is known as the "Basle Capital Accord". It contains a prescribed methodology for computing capital adequacy proportions and suggested the least capital adequacy degree for universal banks. The Accord was produced so as to enhance capital adequacy degrees (which were thought to be too low in a few banks) and to help institutionalize the universal administrative practice. It has been embraced by the OECD nations and numerous creating nations. The Reserve Bank applies the standards of the Basle Capital Accord in New Zealand. Post the money related emergency, there has been a rise in regulation and diverse steps taken to save the breakdown of banks and make the country's economy robust to endure slowdowns. The Capital structure is likewise a vital variable in deciding imports and trades. Rating models in view of a framework called CAMEL (Capital adequacy, Asset quality, Administration, Profit, Liquidity) was actualized to help the RBI recognize the banks that required help. It is paramount, that here, Capital Adequacy was thought to be a top component. It is the extent of Entire Capital (worth) to the danger weighted assets [52]. Various examination studies have highlighted the essentials of the CAR (Capital Adequacy Ratio) in keeping money area.

The financial structure of the money related establishments is not the same as the capital structure of the non-monetary organizations because of the administrative effect on the money related foundations; most likely because of the certainties that are installed in light of the fact that structure, capacities and targets of banks are truly unique in relation to non-budgetary organizations. In this way literature recognizes the three classes through which CAR (Capital Adequacy ratio) and its determinants can distinguish these are; inner bank strategies and considerations, market forces, and the administrative prerequisites [53].

In recent years, financial emergencies have become to be progressively regular and progressively extravagant to manage. Prudential regulation of banks is supposed to avoid and reduce the occurrence of such emergencies. The group of concerns that vanishes under the heading of bank capital adequacy has gotten a lot of consideration from regulators, bankers and scholastics in recent years and is likely to proceed as a subject for civil argument for a long time to come [54]. Administrative prerequisite is vital part which majorly contributes the Capital Adequacy Ratio (CAR) in the banking segment. Administrative power set the CAR which gets to be committed to the banks to conform to that base degree.

In CAR determination administrative pressure is essentially variable, however, State bank of Pakistan decides the capital adequacy degree, yet in the couple of countries capital adequacy proportion is situated out by the agencies and supervisory advisory groups for bank to bank [22]. The Basle Capital Accord is a worldwide standard for the figuring of capital adequacy degrees. Accord prescribes least capital adequacy proportions that banks ought to meet. The Reserve Bank applies the basic norms indicated in the Accord to banks enlisted in New Zealand. This serves to advance strength and productivity in the money related framework, and guarantees that banks conform to by and large acknowledged universal benchmarks. In the banking sector, capital is usually controlled by a State Bank of the country in order to mitigate bank solvency problems.

It is the ratio which safeguards the banks against excess leverage, bankruptcy and keeps them out of trouble. This is the index administrative establishments utilization to focus the ideal measure of cash (i.e. Equity, retained earnings, and other reserves) that a bank must have the capacity to take certain levels of danger imperiling deposit funds, or its presence [55]. Capital adequacy ratio (CAR) is one of the measures which guarantee the monetary soundness of banks in retaining a sensible measure of misfortune [56]. It is defined as the ratio of bank's capital in relation to its current liabilities and risk weighted assets. Risk weighted assets are a measure of amount of bank assets, adjusted for risks. Capital adequacy of a commercial bank can be measured by computing a number of ratios, such as, capital adequacy ratio, return on equity, leverage ratio and net worth protection [34].

An appropriate level of capital adequacy ensures that the bank has sufficient capital to expand its business, while at the same time its net worth is enough to absorb any financial downturns without becoming bankrupt. It is the ratio which defines the bank's capability to meet the time liabilities and other risks such as credit risk, market risk, and operational risk [57]. According to the State Bank of Pakistan all banks must have a minimum capital adequacy ratio of 10% so those banks whose CAR is at present less than 10% are advised to meet the shortfall so they can easily operate their functions effectively and efficiently. The Capital base of money related foundations encourage contributors in shaping their danger observation about the establishments. Additionally, it is the key parameter for financial managers to keep up sufficient levels of capitalization.

Additionally, other than engrossing unanticipated stuns, it flags that the foundation will keep on honoring its commitments. Capitalism is the foundation of bank's quality, and it gives a method for reacting to opportunity and much of the time, goes about as a cushion against instability, unanticipated misfortunes, and in the occasion of distinctive zones to keep working whist issues are being determined. Capital has been utilized as the best parameter for measuring banks' execution and the measure of capital a bank has on its balance sheet decides the soundness and strength of the bank and its capacity to shield its moneylenders from the vulnerabilities of the economy [58]. A popular indicator of capital adequacy is Total Deposit to Total Equity ratio.

Total deposit to total equity ratio: The part of the deposit in the budgetary structure is essential [59]. Funds placed into an account at a financial institution to raise the credit balance of the account. Down payment installment gave ahead of time to back the plan to finish a commercial transaction. A bank deposit means the placement of funds in an account with a bank or other budgetary establishment. Bank Deposits are the primary way of funding and this is considered as the cheaper cost of funds. The more deposits will be changed into advances, the higher the interest margin and benefit. In this manner deposits have positive impact on productivity of the banks [60].

The basic purpose of bank deposit is to create a maturity mismatch between its resources and obligations by obtaining funds from the general public having excess funds and allocating these funds in the form of loans to the side in deficit. In the event that it is expected that banks have the capacity to contribute their money at the market interest rate, they make benefits from both deposits and credits by paying rates beneath the market rate to investors and charging rates over the market rate from the borrowers [61]. The underdeveloped countries are facing a lot of challenges and poverty. In Nigeria the financial system and specifically the bank deposits have been identified as a key component in the growth process and poverty mitigation. Bank deposits in emerging countries play a vital role and assist in economic expansion [62].

Bank deposits have a significant relationship with market share. Banks having a higher market share are in a better position to attract more deposits. Due to increased market share they are safer and mitigate the element of risk in deposit growth [63].

Deposits are usually known as an inexpensive source of funds instead of borrowings and other similar financial instruments. In order to avoid bank failures, it is important for banks to maintain a significant level of capital adequacy. When deposits expand, banks ought to be more managed and controlled to ensure the depositors rights, and to shield a bank from bankruptcy [54].

According to Soyemi, Akinpelu and Ogunleye banks perform as a financial mediator, play a vital role in converting deposits into financial resources, they obtain funds from individuals with excess liquidity and lend to those with insufficient liquidity thereby facilitating capital formation and trade [64]. Biswas and Koufopoulos, demonstrate that better observing incentives (due to higher capital) fascinates more deposits and hence surplus extraction [65].

Total deposit consists of foreign exchange deposit, time deposit and Demand deposit [66]. Demand deposits are the placement of funds into a record that permits the investor to withdraw his or her finances from the record without notice or with under seven day's notification. Checking accounts are demand deposits. They allow depositors to withdraw funds whenever, and there is no restriction on the quantity of transactions an investor can have on these accounts [61].

Fundamentally the time deposit is an enthusiasm-bearing

investment account kept up by a bank or fiscal foundation for a fixed term whereby the depositor can withdraw the deposits when giving a notification. Time deposits by and large allude to investment accounts and banks and cash related establishments as a general rule oblige 30 days warning for withdrawal of these deposits. Individuals and associations consistently consider time deposits as "cash" or speedily open funds in spite of the way that they really are not payable on demand. The warning essential furthermore suggests that banks may study a discipline for withdrawing before a predefined date. Time deposits may pay high intrigue rates than interest deposits.

The study with respect to Gulf Corporation Council (GCC) banks by Alkassim finds that the higher capital proportion supports the productivity of Islamic banks. For conventional banks, deposits have direct connection; however, deposits of the Islamic banks have a negative effect on the profitability of banks [67]. Anyhow, the advances have a positive impact on the profitability of both Islamic and conventional banks.

Hunjra and Bashir carried out research to assess the financial performance of Islamic and conventional banks operating in Pakistan [68]. They used ratio analysis technique, nineteen ratios were used to measure the bank's performance and the data was taken from 2008-2012. The results of the capital ratios examination show that mean values of Total Deposits/Total Equity ratio and CCTE is higher in conventional banks than in Islamic banks. The p value shows that there is a significant difference between TDTER and CCTE of both Conventional and Islamic banks.

The division of the entire resource portfolio risk between depositors and shareholders is influenced by the total deposit/total equity ratio, representing the extent of gearing of the bank. The lower this ratio, the more likely is that the promised return to depositors can be met from the uncertain worth of the resource portfolio [69].

A number of researchers have examined the impact of Capital Adequacy on the profitability in commercial banks in different countries. The results varied from one research to another as follows.

Capital proportion has long been a significant apparatus for surveying capital adequacy and ought to catch the general well-being and soundness of banks. It is by and large accepted that very much promoted banks face lower expected expenses of monetary trouble and such margin will then be interpreted into high gains. In his investigation of the determinants of banks' execution in twelve countries chosen from Europe, Australia and North America, Bourke found a significant positive connection between capital adequacy and benefit. He demonstrates that the higher the capital proportion is the more productive a bank will be [70].

Capital Adequacy Ratio (CAR) is utilized as independent variable. The discoveries exposed that capital adequacy proportion has a significant effect on the benefit of commercial banks in Nigeria [71].

The outcomes revealed that there is a positive relationship between capital structure and monetary execution. Furthermore, the capital structure altogether effect on money related execution of the firm demonstrated that obligation resource proportion, obligation value proportion and long term obligation corresponded with gross benefit margin (GPM), net benefit margin (NPM), Return on Capital Employed (ROCE), Return on Asset (ROA) & Return on Equity (ROE) at significant level of 00.05 and 0.1 [72].

The data investigation demonstrated a positive and significant relationship between capital adequacy and the benefit of the bank. This infers that for deposit taking banks in Nigeria, capital adequacy assumes a key part in the determination of gains. It was found that financial and productivity is the marker of bank risk administration effectiveness and mitigate against misfortunes, not secured by current income [73].

Contrary to the above researchers, the outcomes portray a negative relationship between capital structure and bank execution as they show negative coefficients. The estimation of R square and balanced R square was low, and the study prescribes to be reached out to more variables as it can help to enhance the wellness of the model [74].

Capital adequacy measured by EA has a significant negative effect on bank execution measured by return on equity (ROE). The outcomes are consistent with Sehrish et al, and Hoffmann who discovered a significant negative relationship in the middle of capital and bank productivity. This implies that domestic business banks are functioning over-cautiously by neglecting possible profitable endeavor. It shows that, setting up the high capital, administrative necessity has a negative effect on bank's execution, if not balanced by expanding investments [75].

The regression analysis demonstrates a negative relationship between Capital Adequacy (Equity/Total Asset) and return on Asset (ROA) furthermore; this independent variable is statistically significant. This investigation recommends that when the Capital Adequacy expands, productivity will diminish. In other words, when the banks build the utilization of Equity, they will enroll more misfortunes. The clarification of this sensation can be firstly the sum they are paying to their shareholders as a dividend is greater than what they are creating from it as a benefit. Besides, the facts could confirm that they are utilizing retain earnings without putting it in a new arrangement that will give more benefit to the organization [76].

The general capital adequacy proportions of the study demonstrate that Shareholders Fund/Total Assets (SHF/TA) which measures the capital adequacy of banks (danger of default) have significant negative effects on ROA [77].

From the outcomes, the study demonstrated a negative, but significant association between the capital adequacy proportion (CAR) and execution (Return on Equity). The negative relationship suggests that, as more capital is set aside as a cradle for banks wellbeing; it influences the execution of Ghanaian banks. The results of the study, lies in the way that the negative relationship between capital adequacy and execution highlights the way that different endeavors by the controllers to audit regularly the capital base of the keeping money division is not borne out of the plan to enhance the gains of the banks. Rather to maintain stability, security against contributors and trust in the keeping money industry [78].

Asset quality

In the banking sector, asset quality refers to a review or an evaluation, which assesses the credit risk associated with any particular assets. Such type of assets normally requires payments of interest like a loans and investment portfolios. Asset quality connotes the level of money related quality of and dangers in a bank's resources, principally advances and investments. The support of asset quality is an essential feature of bank [79]. Asset quality of the bank is one of the main issues whenever research on banks is conducted [42]. How effective management is in controlling and monitoring credit risk can also have an effect on the what kind of credit rating is given. Asset quality is a facet of bank management entails the evaluation of assets of a firm to help the measurement of the level and size of credit risk associated with its operation [80]. The Asset quality highlights the amount of existing and potential credit risk related to the advancement and portfolios of investment, other property owned, and various assets, as well as some off-balance sheet transactions. An inspector's valuation of asset quality should consider the sufficiency of the loan and lease losses and measure the presentation to the counterparty, or debt or failure to pay under actual or implied contractual understandings. Every other risk that may influence the worth or attractiveness of the assets of an organization, which may include, however, not forced to, market, operating, strategic, reputation, or compliance risks must also be considered. One of the pointers for asset quality is the proportion of non-performing advances to aggregate credits (GNPA). The gross non-performing credits to gross advances proportion is more demonstrative of the nature of credit choices made by investors. Higher GNPA is demonstrative of poor credit choice making [81].

Numerous examines like; Kunt and Barr and Siems have recognized that asset quality is a statistically important predictor of bankruptcy for the reason of bank disasters and the failing banking establishments always have high levels of non-performing advances prior to failure [63,82].

Asset quality refers to the overall risk attached to the different assets held by an individual or an organization. This term is most usually used by banks to decide what numbers of their assets are at financial risk and how much allowance for potential losses they must have to make. The most common assets which require a strict determination of asset quality are loans, which may be non-performing assets if borrowers default on repayment commitments. Risk Managers frequently survey the quality of assets by assigning a numerical positioning to every asset depending upon the amount of risk is involved. The term asset quality and its administration decide, all things considered, the development and productivity of a firm. This is on the grounds that, the deteriorating estimation of resources specifically likewise influences different zones on the grounds that the credit misfortunes are for the most part discounted against capital [83].

Saksonova and Solovjova sees combining as an amalgamation or a combination in which all the joining organizations are legitimately broken down and another organization is shaped with the targets of upgrading execution through stable asset quality as one of the yardsticks [84].

The asset quality position measures the monetary proficiency of the business banks while the capital adequacy position measures the going concern of the business banks. However the capital adequacy position relies on upon asset quality because of incredible dangers confronting business banks, decrease in asset quality does build the capital adequacy position with a specific end goal to offer the banking protection against danger [85].

Asset quality is a standout amongst the most basic areas in deciding the overall condition of a bank. The primary element that influences the overall asset quality is the quality of the loan portfolio and the credit organization program. Advances normally consist of a major part of a bank's assets and carry the biggest amount of risk to their capital. Securities may also contain a huge segment of the assets furthermore contain huge amount of risks. Different things which can affect asset's quality are other land, different assets, Off-balance sheet items and, to a lesser degree, money and due from accounts, and fixed assets and properties.

It helps us to determine the strength of financial institutions against loss of value in the assets. Decline in the value of assets, being the main reason of banking problems, straightforwardly spread in other different areas, as losses are later on written–off against capital, which as a result threatens the earning capacity of an organization. With this background, the asset quality is gauged in connection to the level and seriousness of non-performing assets, sufficiency of provisions for bad advances, recoveries of credits, asset distribution. Despite the fact that the banking system is infected with a huge volume of Non-Performing Loans (NPLs), the seriousness of this issue has balanced out to some certain extent.

The level of non-performing credits in bank's advance portfolio depicts the quality of bank advances which gives an evidence of the profitability, bank lending activities; it obliges the provision for write-offs are either portions or the majority of the credits. The write-offs are losses that the banks ingest with its equity capital, thus the banks hesitant to go for new risks and new advances which are depicted as the credit crunch [86]. This is not to say that the issue of NPLs has taken an optional position. Sadly, it still remains the most dominant factor which affects the earning capability of banks. Popular indicators include non-performing loans to advance, advance default to total advances, and recoveries to credit default ratios.

Asset quality shows the level of financial strength and risk associated with the bank`s loan assets. It is one of the measurement tools which are normally used to find out the level of a bank's credit risk. Many researchers define the term asset quality helps to discover and evaluate the condition of bank's loan assets and how much weaker the assets are to risk exposure.

Maintaining sound asset quality includes cautious loan granting that must be performed and that which can increase the level of the bank's income base. On the other hand, unpredictable loan granting, takes the bank to poor asset quality which will reduce the income and profit, reserves and deposit dissipation, zero profit payout, disintegration of the capital base and negative shareholders' funds.

Managing non performing credits leads to high provisioning which influences profitability causing liquidity, impairment of shareholders' funds, weakening of capital and thus poor asset quality coming about into misery [87].

Supporting non Asset quality in this connection relates to the quality of the assets (advances) on a financial organization's balance sheet, taking into consideration the probability that a given credit will repay essential and interest on time. Reduced asset quality indicates that the institution must make provisions for consequent losses [88].

Bank asset quality not just influences the financial and operating performance of the bank itself, additionally further imagines on the soundness of the national financial framework [89]. Yin alluded that the weakening of asset quality from the ignorance of advance quality by banks is one of the primary reasons behind the Asian Financial Crisis.

Non-performing loans to gross advances: It is considered as the rate of nonperforming loans to gross advances. It shows the quality of portfolio credit of a bank. It assesses the asset quality which is fortified on the loan portfolio. It is very much useful for banks (Bank particular and macroeconomic reasons which influence the productivity of banks [90].

Non-performing assets by and large refers to those assets which stop to give any return to the bank. At the present time, NPAs is a major issue for the banks as it has ever been a main worry for the bank promoters and the government. However, capable banks have no reason to panic from the NPAs on the grounds that they can locate some different means of income to match these NPAs in the time of LPG [91].

A total of obtaining cash upon which the indebted person has not made his or her planned installments for almost 90 days. A nonperforming advance/Loan is either in default or near to being in default. When a credit is nonperforming, the chances that it will be reimbursed in full are thought to be significantly lower. In case the debt holder begins making installments again on a nonperforming advance, it is converted into a re-performing credit, regardless of the fact that the indebted person has not got up to speed with all the missed installments.

Credit business is the principle business for all commercial banks. Since banks utilize a major segment of their funds for giving credit to firms and people, so they confront the possibility that organizations or people might sometimes indicate unwillingness to repay such borrowed funds instantly. This behavior often exposes banks to losses from giving credit business [92].

The asset quality of the banking system has enhanced very much in recent few years. The percentage of Gross NPL to Gross advances for the commercial banks has decreased from 25 percent to fewer than 10 percent, while the provisions held by the banks against these NPLs covering around 70 percent of gross NPLs. Hence, the net NPL to the net advances proportion has demonstrated a remarkable decrease to 3 percent while is equivalent to international standards. The stream of NPLs has dropped to under 5 percent that implies that 95 percent of the credits in banks' portfolios are being completely serviced on time [93].

Bank nonperforming credits to aggregate gross advances are the benefit of nonperforming advances divided by the aggregate estimation of the credit portfolio (counting nonperforming credits before the finding of particular advance misfortune gaining). The advance sum recorded as nonperforming ought to be the gross estimation of the credit as recorded on the monetary record, not simply the sum that is still unpaid.

The provisions against non performing advances to gross advances proportion is a measure of the asset quality. Provision against non performing credits to gross advances has a strongly negative impact on return over assets for commercial banks in the Pakistan and, thus, the asset quality matters a lot for the sound financial performance [94].

To assess the asset quality, NPL/GA is favored over advance loss reserve to gross advances since the credit loss reserve is specifically reliant on a bank's profitability and banks with higher pre-provision income could make higher provisions and the other way around [95].

Yet another internal determinant of income of banks is the quality of current assets (NPA) which is characterized as the proportion of net non-performing assets to net advances. Other things being equal, a bank which keeps an eye on an aggressive approach towards lending is expected to have a more elevated amount of NPA moreover. This is because of the weakening in due diligence that is resorted to by banks for inviting more clients. Hence, NPA is taken as another descriptive variable.

Alhassan, Coleman and Andoh investigated for the factors that deteriote asset quality. They took into account, 25 banks in Ghana during financial crisis, data from 2005 to 2010 [96]. They came to conclusion that non-performing loans are a crucial determinant that deteriorates asset quality.

NPL to shareholders equity

Analysis of the nonperforming loans in the albanian banking system: The Albanian banking system continues to face serious difficulties in loan repayment. In fact it is evidence that the major part of problematic loans belongs to the corporate sector showing the real difficulties of the Albanian businesses in loans repayment. According to the national authorities the loans are classified in five categories in the Albanian banking system as shown below:

1. Standard loans, regular loans that do not present any difficulty in maturity and outstanding capital;
2. Follow up loans, these loans present the first signs of delays in repayment and are under supervision of banks, but still are not classified as problematic loans;
3. Substandard loans, are not classified as standard loans because of delays in repayment and are classified as problematic loans;
4. Doubtful loans are loans presenting significant delays in repayment, but the bank still hopes to collect them and are classified as problematic loans;
5. Lost loans are loans which cannot be collected from the banks and are classified as problematic loans [97].

A number of researchers have examined the impact of Asset quality on the profitability in commercial banks in different countries. The results varied from one research to another as follows.

According to the Nisar, Susheng, Ahmed, Ke this research investigated how bank-specific, industry-specific and macroeconomic factors have affected the profitability of the banking sector of Pakistan [98]. The empirical results obtained by applying Pooled Ordinary Least Squares (POLS) technique on panel data of all Pakistani scheduled banks over the period 2006 to 2013, show that profitability of Pakistani banking sector is negatively affected by Funding Cost (FC), Liquidity (LIQ), Non-performing Loans (NPL) and Administrative Expensive (ADETA), and Positively affected by Non-fund based services (NII), Capital Adequacy (CA) Banking Sector Development (LOAGDP) and Economic Growth (GDP).

This study embraced an explanatory approach by utilizing panel information investigation outline to satisfy the targets. Yearly financial statements of 38 Kenyan business banks from 2002 to 2008 were gotten from the CBK and Banking Survey 2009. A Multiple linear regression model is used to analyze the data. The examination demonstrated that all the bank particular components (Asset quality) had a statistically significant effect on performance [31].

The study established a descriptive design in its practice and the researcher decided to study business banks because of the accessibility of required information and easily accessible. All the 43 business banks in Kenya were focused on this study. Secondary information was taken from Central bank of Kenya Banks supervision reports. SPSS variant 200.0 was utilized for information examination. The t-test with a 5% level of significance was utilized as a part of the study and the connection coefficient (r), coefficient of determination and analysis of difference (ANOVA) was ascertained. The examination demonstrated that asset quality has a statistically significant effect on monetary execution [99].

This study will explore and analysis the effect of total credit to aggregate resources and aggregate investment to aggregate resources as an intermediary for resources quality (autonomous variables) on the bank`s performance measured by EPS, ROA, ROE and Book value per share (Dependent variable). Applying multi and simple linear regression investigation, the most significant result was that bank`s asset quality indicators by and large have a positive effect on the performance *[100]*.

The study embraced the utilization of ratios as a measure of bank execution and asset quality since it is an evident means for evaluating the organizations' level of exercises while the information were analyzed utilizing the Pearson correlation and regression tool of the SPSS 170.0. The discoveries revealed that asset quality had a statistical relationship and impact on bank execution [80].

The commercial bank's profitability is measured as return on equity (ROE) and net-interest margin (NIM). Result specifies that the asset quality, measured by the loan loss provisions has positive affects the execution of the banks [101].

Contrary to above researchers, the outcomes demonstrate that the effect of advances/resources proportion (LA) and credits under follow-up /advances proportion (LFA) as indicators of asset quality have a negative effect on benefit and significant at the 5% level of significance on organization profitability [60]. Furthermore, the aim of this study is to investigate the impact of internal and external causes which affect the profitability. Internal causes include Size (LNTA), Capital (CAP), Liquidity (LQD), debt to equity ratio (DE), Non-performing loans to Gross advances (NPL), portfolio composition (PC), Loans to Total Assets (LA) whereas external causes include Gross Domestic Product (GDP), Inflation (INF), and Unemployment (UNMP). Return on Assets and Return on Equity are used as a measure of profitability. Data is collected for twelve (12) variables of twenty one (21) banks, including four (4) public and seventeen (17) private banks, for the year of 2006-2011, from the annual reports of banks, index Mundi and financial statement analysis of the State Bank of Pakistan (SBP). Nonperforming loan and portfolio composition has negative significant relationship with the profitability [90].

Management efficiency

Efficient management is another most important factor behind the Performance of all banks. Management efficiency of the bank includes its administrative ability to react in diverse circumstances. The term management efficiency involves the capability of management in generating business and maximizing profits. A focal term 'administrative proficiency', which essentially indicates the capacity of a bank to increase benefits or minimize costs under given situations [102]. With increased competition in the Pakistani banking sector, the efficiency and effectiveness become the rule as banks constantly strive to improve the productivity of their employees. Presently the banks have extended their working hours. By the use of latest technology banks have improved their operating system. Management efficiency is a useful for the bank performance. Above all it is a qualitative factor which is applicable to institutions individually or can jointly use as an indicator of management efficiency. Expense ratio, earnings per employee, loan size and cost of unit per lent money is used as an alternate of the management efficiency. By the use of technology they are able to provide quick service in a short time, so now they are attracting customers and compete with each other on the basis of quickly and comfortably [103].

In the CAMEL model this parameter has an important position. It shows the management efficiency of the banks for better financial performance. The ratios which are used in this part are involved subject analysis to measure the efficiency and effectiveness of bank management. Bank management takes difficult decision depending on its risk perfection [30]. Administration's effectiveness is calculated as Assets turnover. The higher the proportion the higher administration efficiency is. As administrators make progress toward more profit, it is likely that they would expand the expense of intimidation, which would upgrade profits [104].

The two main questions are "what drives performance", and "what contribute to performance" are headed in the minds of managers. Finding or highlighting the source of better performance and adoption of right management strategies is very important to the managers. The performance of the management based upon the availability of useful information for decision making, measuring the performance will give the idea that what is their current performance level and what can be done to enhance their performance. By using this information to check what the current performance is thus can focus on those areas in which they are weak or the resources should be allocated. The focus has shifted to analyze the management performance over the last decade. While the management analyzes that how well the boards of directors are functioning, the diversity of its technical knowledge and its ability for making flexible and effective decisions.

Effective management is a required for the success of financial organization. It is difficult to make any comment related to the management efficiency on the basis of quantitative data because generally it is qualitative in nature [26]. The management efficiency is most important for the ensuring the bank stability and strength. Past studies are devoted to the evaluation of the performance of banks, due to the qualitative parameter it is not used to measure. More indicators should be used to evaluate the efficiency of management like operating expenses as percentage of assets, personal expense to average assets, and cost to income ratio [105].

Managing asset efficiency is very important because of its impact of the debt service ability of an organization. Better deployment of commercial resources can generate more profits. However the methods of administration proficiency are not same in past studies. There is a good spread among techniques which are used by different researchers in management efficiency. It is exciting to see that either the researchers have assumed or ignored the independence or interrelations while evaluating the execution of banks. Dave and Bhatt highlight the importance of the complex interrelation among the components, there was no good attempt was made to measure these types of interrelations. Monetary segment performance is reliant on management proficiency [106].

Olweny and Shipho suggest that the perceived notion that higher expenditure results with lower profits may not be straightforward as it seems, because higher amounts of expenses may be associated with higher volume of banking activities and therefore higher revenues [31]. The Management has been empirically evaluated by non-interest expense to the sum of net interest income and non-interest income, personal expenses to average assets and cost to income ratio [107].

Admin expenses to interest income ratio: The expenses that an organization incurs not directly tied to a specific function such as manufacturing/production or sales. These expenses are related to the organization as a whole as opposed to an individual department; also referred to as "administrative cost."(Investopedia)

"Overhead expenses also include selling & administrative expenses are those expenses that are incurred whether the firm produces any revenues or not". The common concept is that a high Cost Income Ratio is equal to low productivity and low efficiency [108]. Karim states that larger banks tend to be more cost efficient [109].

Administrative expenses as percentage of total assets have a negative impact on bank performance. The negative sign shows that the lack of ability in expense management in banks. If administrative costs are managed properly, if expenses, increase it will increase the interest margin of the banks and raise income. The coefficient sign which is negative shows that banks are incapable to pass its expenses to customers because of the competition [110].

Related to the cost to operate a business and are not directly attributable to the production of goods or services. The Administrative expenses are linked to the business as a whole. It is not assigned to the individual section as a complete. These expenditures are essential costs which are associated with the administrative, clerical, and over-all functions of the corporate. Rent of the building, utilities or salaries of the employees are the type of administrative expenses and these are not involved in production of goods. These expenses incurred in controlling and directing as a business, but cannot be easily identified with the financing, marketing or production operations. The salaries of top level management (executive cost of services) an example of managerial expenditure. Admin overheads usually include the costs, which offer a wide benefit to the business. Cost of utilities is the most common example of administrative expenses.

Gross advances to total deposit ratio: Gross advance amount means the sum payable to the payee or for the payee's account as consideration for a transfer of structured settlement payment rights before any reductions for transfer expenses or other deductions to be made from such consideration. The aggregate estimation of private home loan credits progressed by social orders in the period, including advances for house buyers, further advances, remortgages and so on.

A commonly used statistic for assessing a bank's liquidity by dividing the banks total loans by its total deposits. This number, also known as the LTD ratio, is expressed as a percentage. If the ratio is too high, it means that banks might not have enough liquidity to cover any un-foreseen fund requirements; if the ratio is too low, banks may not be earning as much as they could be (Investopedia).

Operation ineffectiveness is also positive and significantly related to loan-to-deposit spreads banks with higher costs apparently tend to operate with higher margins [111].

The coefficient to the loan-to-deposit ratio (L/D) carries a positive sign and is statistically significant in all of the specific expense items equations and it is significant at the one percent level in the overall expense equation [112].

Find an inverse relationship between productivity growth and growth of loan to deposit ratio. This could be due to the fact that banks with rapid expansion in loan activities follow less stringent lending criteria and thus are exposed to higher credit risk resulting in higher loan losses [113].

Burki and Niazi analyzed the impact of financial reforms on the efficiency of state, private and foreign banks of Pakistan by using data of 40 banks for the period 1991-2000 [114]. They found a positive impact on bank size, interest income to earning assets and loans to deposit ratio on estimated efficiency scores.

A number of researchers have examined the impact of Management Efficiency on the profitability in commercial banks in different countries. The results varied from one research to another as follows.

Evaluation of management efficiency is important for banks, because it has a direct impact on the overall performance of an institution. On the basis of past performance directors evaluate management and also with the deliberated direction which is provided by the management. The check that is the incentive of management is according to the objective of institution safety and reliability. The arguments go to measure the management's quality requires the deep evaluation of the management system. To measure the management performance on single quantitative technique is not sufficient. Effective administration is one of the utmost significant factors which define the profitability of banks and looks one of the difficult issues to find with the financial ratios

The research is carried out in Kenya the results found that Management efficiency has a significant impact on the performance of commercial banks [115]. During the period of 2005 to 2009 the researchers evaluated the performance of Islamic and Conventional banks by applying the CAMEL model. They found that Islamic banks performed better and as they have high liquidity as compared to the conventional banks. After the study it is realized that conventional banks are pioneer in management and have a good earning ability [116]. There is a very strong relationship between bank performance and the management efficiency through the expenses of management [117]. Management efficiency has a positive influence on the bank profitability; however the impact of only management efficiency is statically significant [118].

The study utilized correlation and linear regression analysis. Return on Assets (ROA) and Earnings Yield (EY) are utilized as intermediaries of inward and outer profitability respectively. The outcomes of the regression investigation recommend that bank size, liquidity and administration effectiveness have a statistically significant effect on bank performance as Return on Assets [119].

Earnings and profitability

Earning Quality demonstrates the capability of a bank to earn regularly. It also defines the sustainability and progress in earnings in the future [15]. The quality of earnings is a very significant factor which shows the aptitude of a bank to earn consistently. It fundamentally defines the profitability of the banks [42].

The most generally acknowledged measure of the execution of commercial banks is current productivity (Earnings). There are different indicators and measures of profitability. The most important indicators are Return on Assets (ROA) and Return on Equity (ROE). Essentially, the ROA measures net income divided by aggregate resources. The ROE is the proportion of aggregate net income to the banks' value capital [120]. Benefits add to while misfortunes bring about the disintegration of the capital base of a banking organization. Earnings and profitability are normally measured as far as returns received on resources or capital employed [121].

The amount of profit produced by the company during a specific period of time, usually presented on a quarterly or, annual base. Profit ordinarily indicates to after-tax income. Eventually, business income is the primary determinant of its share price, on the grounds that profit and the circumstances, identifying them can demonstrate whether the business will be productive and effective over the long haul. Solid profit and benefit profile of banks reflects the capacity to help present and future operations. All the more particularly, this decides the ability to absorb misfortunes, finance its extension, pay profits in the form of dividends to its shareholders, and develop a sufficient level of capital. Administration's Efficiency is ascertained as the proportion of Interest Income over Interest Cost, this degree will indicate how well a money related organization has the capacity to utilize its assets and liabilities internally. Also, as the objective is to earn more from the investment that have been made, the higher this degree for an organization the more effective it is in creating more benefit over its operating expenses [76].

The organizations are required to increase high earnings and profitability in order to avoid capital base losses. Although diverse indicators are utilized to fill the need, the best and most generally utilize indicator is a Return on Assets (ROA). Profitability is a quantitative measure of the administration's capacity to use stakes effectively to make esteem for shareholders and keep up and enhance capital soundness. In the same setting, in the investigation of profitability, it will be critical to focus the degree of enhancement (sorts and sources) of earnings streams. It is reasoned that productive banks have a tendency to acquire high bank appraisals, and bankrupt banks appear to have issues creating satisfactory benefits [122].

Financial performance will look at the statement of an accounting summary that specifies a business organization's revenues, expenses and net income. Profitability is the most important for stockholders of a bank because it reflects what the bank is earning on their investments [123]. Earnings and profitability ratios are used to measure the ability of the bank to earn a profit compared to their expenses. It shows the bank's overall efficiency and performance as it examines the bank's investment decisions as compared to their debt situations [124].

Profitability is the profit earning capacity, which is a crucial element contributing to the survival of the organizations. The perpetual existence of the organizations relies on upon the profit earning capacity of the firm, which is likewise thought to be the primary figure affecting the reputation of the firm. The borrowing limit of the firm is likewise measured by Profit. Subsequently, it is considered as the principle, consider deciding the capital structure of the firm. Profit comprises of two words, the profit and ability. Along these lines, it is important to separate in the middle of profit and profitability at this crossroads. Profit, from the bookkeeping perspective, is arrived at by deducting from the aggregate income of an undertaking all sums consumed in procuring that wage, though productivity can be measured as far as profit demonstrated as a percentage of sales known as profit margin. Profitability pretty much relies on the good use of assets and human resource. It is beneficial to build creation limit and utilization propelled innovation to chop down the expense of generating and compensation cost with a specific end goal to expand profitability against the venture, as well as for investor's return perspective [125].

The profitability and earnings are measured on the basis of most common ratios such as Return on Assets (ROA), Return on Equity (ROE) and Interest Income to Total Assets Ratio.

Return on equity: This proportion shows the management productivity in utilizing the bank funds in attaining a profit [126]. A definitive reason for any benefit looking for the association is to make riches for its proprietors. It is the objective of a street vendor, and in addition to a vast listed organization. The main contrast is that the street vendor works for the advantage of one individual, though a listed organization works for the advantage of an extensive number of shareholders. Shareholder value is made when the equity returns of an organization surpass the expense of that value. It can likewise be depicted as the present estimation of all future money streams, less the expense of obligation [127].

Performance measurement systems were produced as a method for observing and maintaining organizational control, which is the methodology of guaranteeing that an association goes for systems that prompt the accomplishment of its general objectives and destinations. It is further clarified by Ongore and Kusa that ROE is the proportion of Net Income after Taxes divided by Total Equity Capital. It shows the rate of profit earned for the invested put resources in the bank by its stockholders. Performance measures, the key tools for performance measurement systems, assume a crucial part in every association as they are frequently seen as forward looking pointers that aid administration to foresee an organization's financial execution and commonly uncover the requirement for conceivable changes in operations [128].

However, the decision of performance measures is a standout amongst the most critical challenges facing organizations. Ineffectively picked performance measures routinely make the wrong flags for administrators, prompting poor choices and undesirable results. There are tremendous hidden expenses in using the wrong performance measures. Shareholders pay the charge every day as over investment and acquisitions that don't pay off and so forth. It is not that the administration is poor. Just, it is the wrongly picked execution measures, which thus push the administration to take improper choices Performance measures may be described as financial and non-financial. ROE ratio is the most usually used to evaluate the execution of banks and this proportion is critical in financial specialist's perspective [129].

ROE tells what rate of profit the organization makes for each financial unit of equity put resources into the organization. ROE doesn't indicate the amount of money will be coming back to the shareholders, since that relies on upon the organization's choice about dividend payments and on how much the stock cost increases in value. Nonetheless, it's a decent evidence of whether the organization is even capable of generating a return that is worth regardless of whatever danger the investment may involve. ROE is generally computed by dividing net profit by average shareholders' equity [130]. This ratio usually indicates the investor rate of return on their investment in the corporation

Interest income to total assets ratio: Interest Earning is a simple way of income for banks. Interest Income comprises of Interest on Deposits with RBI, Interest on Advances, Income from Investments, Discount on Bills and Other Inter-Bank Funds [42]. According to the Farooq in Islamic bank's income included in the markup income is considered as return on investment and invests in diverse modes of financing [131]. On the other hand, conventional banks usually earn income from the interest.

The term that organizations use on their income statement for reporting the interest earned on cash for the moment held in savings accounts or other investments. Since the interest wasn't a part of the original investment, they record it independently, as interest income. The amount of every gross investment, cash and equivalents, receivables, and different resources as they are exhibited in the accounting report.

In money related bookkeeping, asset is an economic asset. Anything tangible or intangible that is equipped for being possessed or controlled to deliver quality and that is held to have positive monetary worth is viewed as an asset. Just expressed, the resource's state value of possession that can be changed over into money (in spite of the fact that money itself is likewise viewed as an asset).

The statements of financial position of a firm record the monetary value of the assets which are held by the firm. It is cash and different resources having a place with an individual or business. Two noteworthy resource classes are tangible assets and intangible assets. Tangible resources contain different subclasses, including current resources and fixed resources. Current resources include cash, short-term investments, cash equivalents, stock inventory, accounts receivable. Fixed resources include such things as structures and equipment.

Return on assets: This ratio measures the ability of the company that how well management utilizes the organization's assets and also measure the effectiveness of the establishment in generating profits [132]. A financial proportion, the part of Return on Asset (ROA) is to show the rate of benefit which any organization/ association picks up against its whole capital investment. It is fairly known as net income (or pretax profit)/ total resources. ROA is a Profitability Ratio. ROA signifies bank's administration proficiency to produce revenue through utilizing the bank resource base and this is a key measure commonly used in the literature for assessing bank execution [133]. ROA is utilized by organizations and banks to outfit them with an important instrument for assessing their progress, including utilization of assets and financial quality [134]. Return on Assets (ROA) measures how profitable an organization is with respect to its aggregate assets. Thus, it measures how effectively an organization uses its assets. Return on assets (ROA) is an extensive measure of overall bank execution from an accounting viewpoint [135].

The assets of the organization consist of both obligation and equity. Both of these sorts of financing are utilized to run the operations of the organization. The ROA figure gives investors that how adequately the organization is changing over the cash it needs to put into net income. The higher the ROA ratio depicts that the organization is acquiring more cash for less investment and utilizing their assets productively. If one organization has a net income of $1 million and aggregate possessions of $5 million, its ROA is 20%; nonetheless, if an alternate organization procures the same sum, however has downright stakes of $10 million, it has an ROA of 10%. Taking into account this sample, the first organization is better at changing over its investment into a benefit. If this example truly considers it, administration's most paramount occupation is to settle on insightful decisions in apportioning its assets. Review that the return On Assets (ROA) is a sign of the operational productivity of the bank [136].

Anyone can make a benefit by throwing huge amounts of cash at an issue; however, not very many managers exceed expectations by making vast benefits with little investment. In banking perspective, this ratio indicates management ability to attract deposits at a reasonable cost and their investment to earn more profits. This ratio defines that how well the bank's assets are managed in order to maximize returns [137]. Financial measures of the bank performance are an important part of running a growing business, especially in the current economic environment. ROA is the indicator of measuring managerial efficiency. In ROA, the bank will know the efficiency and capability to convert its assets into net income. ROA is the ratio of net income to average total assets [138].

A number of researchers have examined the impact of on the Earnings & profitability in commercial banks in different countries. The results varied from one research to another as follows.

The reason for this study is to clarify the components which may have effects on the intellectual capital execution in UAE Banks over the period 2006-2009. The Multiple regression examination is utilized to test the relationship between intellectual capital execution as a dependent variable and certain independent variables. The outcomes demonstrate that earnings quality has a significant effect on intellectual capital execution in banks [139]. The outcomes demonstrate that productivity proportion (ROE), Market proportion (PBV), income from operations, and leverage proportion (DER) has a significant effect on earnings per share [140].

According to the Heikal, Khaddafi and Ummah research is carried out to find the impact of independents variable on a dependent variable. Return on Assets and Return on Equity are used as independent variables and income growth is taken as the dependent variable on automotive companies that were listed on Indonesia stock exchange [141]. The results show that Return on Assets and Return on Equity have a statistically significant impact on an income growth. Furthermore the study carried out by Olweny and Shipho, the outcome shows that there is a negative, but significant association between operational cost effectiveness and firm performance [31].

Liquidity ratios

Liquidity ratios are used to assess the overall administration of banks [142]. Liquidity is a measure of the capacity and straightforwardness with which resources can be changed over to money. Fluid resources are those that can be changed over to money rapidly if necessary to meet budgetary commitments [143]. Liquidity ratios measure a company's ability to pay off its short-term obligations. Liquidity ratios are a result of dividing cash and other liquid assets to the short term borrowings and current liabilities. The most common examples of liquidity ratios include the current ratio, quick ratio and working capital ratio.

Current ratio: Current ratio is a measure of company liquidity. Current ratio shows a company's ability to meet short-term debt obligations. The current ratio measures that a firm has enough assets to pay its liabilities for a year.

Quick ratio: Quick ratio is a measure of a company's ability to meet its short-term obligations. Quick assets include those current assets that can be easily converted to cash without significant decrease in their book value. Quick ratio is considered as a measure of a company's financial strength or weakness.

Working capital Working capital is the amount of current assets that are in excess of current liabilities. Working capital is often used to measure a firm's ability to meet current obligations. It measures how much liquid assets a company possesses to expand its business.

As it is clear at this point, liquidity is a standout amongst the most vital objectives of working capital administration and focal assignment of cash administration. Many authors have communicated their meaning of liquidity as a whole "a firm is fluid when it can pay bills on time without excessive expense" [144]. Liquidity can likewise mean the degree to how rapidly resources can be changed over into cash [145]. Solvency and liquidity are two ideas that are nearly related and reflect upon the activities of organization's working capital arrangement. As Maness and Zietlow have characterized; "a firm is viewed as solvent when its benefits surpass its liabilities" [144].

The term Liquidity demonstrates the capacity of a bank to meet its monetary obligations. Keeping up the right level of liquidity is vital for guaranteed development and profit. Banks should be more careful in investments in order to generate more profit on investment as well as to provide liquidity to the depositors. The High Liquidity proportion demonstrates the bank's proficiency [15].

A high level of liquidity must be maintained by any financial institution or bank in order to overcome the difficulties it may face in short term business activities, to minimize the chances of financial distress and exploit investment opportunities cash supply lines must be open. Ability to pay the day to day expenses indicates bank's liquidity position and also gratifies depositors demand for with drawls. To attain liquidity, the financial institution must focus on these three components: the highly liquid assets that can be easily converted into cash, access to the inter-bank market, their anticipated future cash inflow and outflow. Current status of liquidity is taken into account in relation to the liabilities of evaluating banks of liquidity. It also considers the ability of the bank to deal with the chances of unpredicted changes in its financial resources and the liquidation of its assets that will be affected by prevailing market conditions and minimum possible decrease in its earnings [1].

According to the Tesfaye, the conventional bank resources which are fluid incorporate money, reserves expressive an additional of stores required by law (i.e., trusts held in the record at the state bank), securities (e.g., regime obligation, commercial paper), what's more, interbank credits for a short period of time (one to three days) [146]. Moussa clarified that the practicality of business banks relies on upon the liquidity position of the bank [147]. As indicated by Kurawa and Abubakar liquidity essentially implies the capacity to change over an asset for cash with the least delay and least misfortune/cost [148]. Banks to a great extent work with the funds obtained from investors in the manifestation of demand and time deposit; thusly liquidity resources assume an essential part. These liquidity resources are the key balance sheet things which have the ability to keep up the confidence of investors which is the most significant intangible resource of the commercial banking business

Liquidity administration is an idea that is accepting genuine consideration everywhere throughout the world, particularly with the current money related circumstances and the condition of the world economy. A percentage of the striking corporate objectives incorporate the need to boost benefit, keep a high level of liquidity so as to ensure wellbeing, accomplish the largest amount of proprietor's net worth coupled with the fulfillment of other corporate targets. The significance of the liquidity administrator as it influences corporate benefit in today's business can't be over emphasized. The crucial part in overseeing working capital is obliged maintenance of its liquidity in regular operation to guarantee its smooth running and meets its commitment [149]. Liquidity assumes a critical part in the effective working of a business firm. The organization should guarantee that it does not suffer from lack-of or additional liquidity to fulfill its short-term obligations. A research of liquidity is important significance to both the inward and the outside examiners due to its nearby association with normal operations of a business. Dilemma in liquidity administration is to attain to required trade-off in the middle of liquidity and productivity.

The liquidity administration is an essential consider business operations. For the extreme survival of business, the firm ought to have an imperative level of liquidity. It ought to be neither extreme nor insufficient. Excessive liquidity implies an aggregation of perfect funds. Which may prompt lower productivity; expand speculation, and unjustified growth. While deficient liquidity brings about disturbances of business operations. A legitimate harmony between these two amazing circumstances accordingly ought to be kept up for effective operation of the business through aptitude full liquidity administration [126]. Disappointment of the bank to meet its commitment because of lacking liquidity will prompt poor credit value, defeat of investor's confidence or, on occasion lawful fall flat bringing about the conclusion of the bank. On the other hand, a high rate of liquidity is inappropriate, since inefficient resources produce nothing. The main part of the bank capital would be unnecessary tied up in current resources. It is consequently essential to come to convert stability between absence of liquidity and high liquidity [150].

Liquidity administration is one of the vital elements of bank's administration. It is important to avoid the liquidity shortfall, which can prompt the bankruptcy issue. Fluid resources, which can be easily changed over to money, are frequently connected to the lower rate of return. Henceforth, high liquidity would influence profitability adversely [151].

Cash ratio

The Liquidity of the organization can be tested through different ratios that include current ratio, quick ratio, working capital ratio and cash ratio as discussed earlier. well known indicator of liquidity is Cash ratio, it is defined as the ratio of cash and cash equivalents to net assets [152]. Moreover, cash ratio can be defined as, cash and marketable securities divided by the mean value of opening and closing total assets [153]. Furthermore, Chiang and Wang defined cash ratio as cash divided by assets [154]. The Cash proportion decides the extent to which an organization can quickly change their liquid resources into cash to meet the short term liabilities [150].

According to the Amuzu cash ratio is the most important indicator of liquidity used to measure for the amount of money available to adjust the current obligation (money/Total Current Liabilities) [155]. Cash ratio refers to the proportion of an organization's aggregate money and money equivalents to pay off its current liabilities. The money proportion is most regularly utilized as a measure of organization's liquidity. It can thusly figure out whether, and how rapidly, the organization can return its short term obligation. A solid money proportion is helpful to banks when choosing the amount of obligation, if any; they would be ready to reach out to the asking party. It is the most well-known ratio used to measure the liquidity position of any business [132].

Cash proportion is the ratio of an organization's money and money equivalent resources for its aggregate liabilities. Money proportion is a refinement of quick proportion and demonstrates the degree to which promptly accessible funds can pay off current liabilities. Money proportion is the most stringent and progressive of the three liquidity proportions (current, quick and money proportion). It just takes a look at the organization's most fluid short-lived resources – money and money reciprocals – which can be most effectively used to pay off current commitments [156].

A number of researchers have examined the impact of liquidity on the profitability in commercial banks in different countries. The results varied from one research to another as follows.

According to Anoh there is positive relationship between liquidity administration and the performance of banks [157]. Agbada and Osuji while leading a study on the efficacy of liquidity administration and banking execution, which is clear about the way that, there is a significant relationship between productive liquidity administration and banking execution and that effective liquidity improve the soundness of banks [158]. Akanbi and Ajagbe investigated the relationship between cash ratio and profitability of banks [159]. They used financial data of three Nigerian commercial banks from 1992 to 1999 and applied regression model. Researchers found that cash ratio and profitability are positively associated. Lartey, Antwi and Boadi tried to figure out the relationship between the liquidity and the profitability of banks verified on the Ghana Stock Exchange [160]. It was observed that for the period 2005-2010, both the liquidity and the gains of the listed banks were declining. Once more, it was additionally discovered that there was a very weak positive relationship between the liquidity and the gains of the listed banks in Ghana.

These discoveries support Bourke who discovered some proof of a positive relationship between fluid resources and bank benefit for

90 banks in Europe, Australia North America and from 1972 to 1981 [70]. In the perspective of the way that liquidity has some measure of direction on the productivity of a bank, it is imperative that banks deal with their liquidity exceptionally well. At the point when banks hold satisfactory fluid resources, their benefit would progress. Satisfactory liquidity helps the bank minimize liquidity danger and budgetary emergencies. The bank can assimilate any conceivable unforeseen stun brought on by the surprising requirement for a reduction in liabilities or the increment in resources side of the Statement of Financial Position. Then again, if fluid resources are held unreasonably, productivity could reduce. Fluid resources for the most part have no or minimal enthusiasm producing limit. The opportunity expense of holding low-return resources would in the long run exceed the advantage of any increment of the bank's liquidity flexibility as seen in financing market.

Olagunju, David and Samuel analyzed liquidity administration and business banks' profitability in Nigeria [161]. Discoveries of this study show that there is a significant relationship in the middle of liquidity and benefit. That implies benefit of business banks is fundamentally affected by liquidity and the other way around.

The relationship between liquidity and the benefit of oil and gas organizations recorded at Karachi Stock Exchange (KSE) Pakistan is presented by Saleem and Rehman general population for 26 oil and gas organizations traded every year were considered in the study [162]. Linear regression through SPSS was conducted. Report investigation was the principle research technique used to gather secondary information for the study. The money related reports of the 26 oil and gas organizations were considered and important liquidity and productivity proportions were computed. It was discovered that for the time of 2004 - 2009, there was a significant impact of liquidity ratio on the profitability of the organization. Zygmunt perceives the liquidity effect on productivity utilizing populace study, including all shine listed organizations for 9 years (2003 - 2011) utilizing Pearson's relationship coefficient and OLS regression model [163]. They find that, the empirical research over the liquidity effect on productivity, demonstrate the presence of statistically significant relationship in the middle of liquidity and benefit. The study inferred that the observational studies give the basis to finish up about the presence of liquidity effect on profitability.

Major Conclusions

The literature review on the determinants of the CAMEL model to assess the performance of banks has shown mixed results with respect to the significance and direction of their association. Some of the studies have shown significant and positive results of these variables with the firm's performance, whereas significant and negative results have also been found. The studies in the literature review showed that all components of CAMEL model have a significant effect on the bank's performance. In case of capital adequacy, asset quality and earnings & profitability, most of the studies showed these variables were positive and negative, but significantly related to the bank's performance, whereas studies on management efficiency and liquidity showed a positive and significant relationship with the bank's performance.

Theoretical Framework

The Theoretical framework is a diagram that indicates the variables and theoretical constructs of interest (Figure 1). The diagram is read from left to one side. The dependent variables are located on the right side and the independent variables are located on the left side. The arrow shows the relationship between independent and dependent variables. The arrow starts from the independent variable and finishes at the dependent variables. It demonstrates that the variance in the dependent variable is sequels to the changes in the independent variable. In the above given model, Capital Adequacy, Asset Quality, Management efficiency, Earnings & profitability and Liquidity are independent variables while, the Earnings per share as firm performance is a dependent variable. The model demonstrates

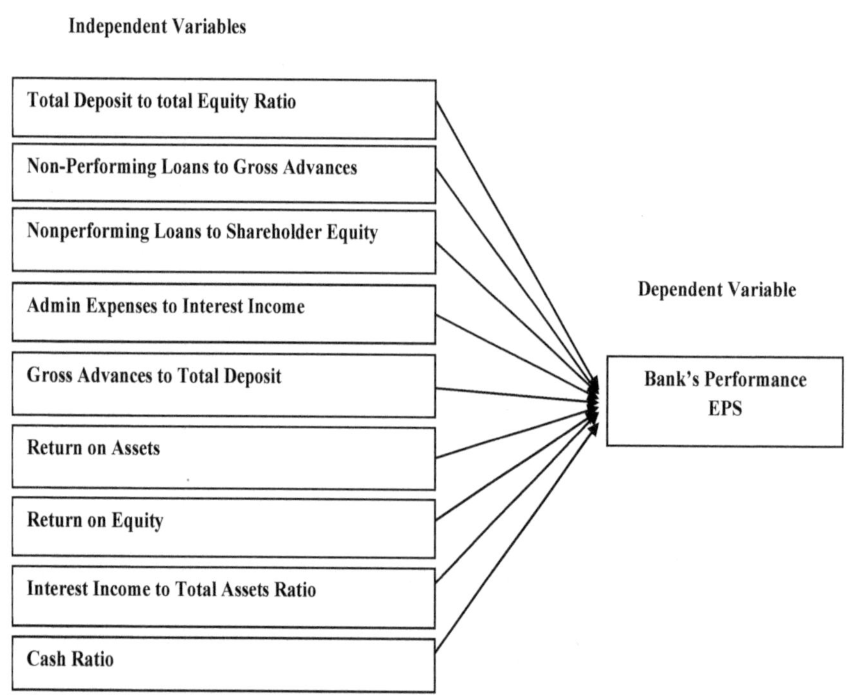

Figure 1: The variables and theoretical constructs of interest.

the effect of five independent variables on one dependent variable. The research model has been derived from the following studies: Momeni and HakimehGharibi, Kouser and Saba, Reddy, Ifeacho and Ngalawa, Jha and Hui, Thirunavukkarasu and Parthiban, Matthew and Esther, and Nagamani and Williams [18, 135,164-169].

Hypotheses

On the basis of the above literature review, the study has following hypotheses:

H1: There is a significant negative impact of Total Deposit to Total Equity ratio on the Bank's performance.

H1o: There is a significant positive impact of Total Deposit to Total Equity ratio on the Bank's performance.

H2: There is a significant negative impact of Non-performing Loans to Gross Advances ratio on the Bank's performance.

H2o: There is a significant positive impact of Non-performing Loans to Gross Advances ratio on the Bank's performance.

H3: There is a significant negative impact of Non-performing Loans to Shareholder Equity ratio on the Bank's performance.

H3o: There is a significant positive impact of Non-performing Loans to shareholder Equity ratio on the Bank's performance.

H4: There is a significant negative impact of Admin expense to interest income ratio on the Bank's performance.

H4o: There is a significant positive impact of Admin expense to interest income ratio on the Bank's performance.

H5: There is a significant negative impact of Gross advances to total deposits ratio on the Bank's performance.

H5o: There is a significant positive impact of Gross advances to total deposits ratio on the Bank's performance.

H6: There is a significant positive impact of Return on Assets on the Bank's performance.

H6o: There is a significant negative impact of Return on Assets on the Bank's performance.

H7: There is a significant positive impact of Return on Equity on the Bank's performance.

H7o: There is a significant negative impact of Return on Equity on the Bank's performance.

H8: There is a significant negative impact of Interest Income to Total Assets Ratio on the Bank's performance.

H8o: There is a significant positive impact of Interest Income to Total Assets Ratio on the Bank's performance.

H9: There is a significant positive impact of Cash Ratio on the Bank's performance.

H9o: There is a significant negative impact of Cash Ratio on the Bank's performance.

Research Methodology

This section gives the information about the methodology that is used to carry out the research: The main discussion is on the population, sample frame and size, sampling method, research design, research instruments and on the use of techniques that will be used to measure and interpret the variables of the study in the subsequent chapter of the research.

Sampling method

In this research non-probability sampling method is used.

Population: Banking sector of Pakistan is taken as population for this research; including listed and unlisted Banks that constitute the whole Banking industry of Pakistan.

Sample size: The sample frame consisted of the Commercial banks in Pakistan. The sample size of the research is ten commercial banks operating in Pakistan (Table 1).

Sampling technique: The main aim of sampling is to select a representative group of element that truly reflects the characteristics of the population. In this research convenient sampling technique was used, due to the reason that the research focuses on secondary data. The necessary data is available from the official website of the ten commercial banks, which meet the requirement of the study.

Data collection method

The proposed topic relates to Banking Sector of Pakistan. For this purpose, secondary data were used to assess the performance of the banks. The vital information is gathered from the financial statements of ten Pakistani banks over the period of 2007-2013. This data is used to calculate the key financial ratios of the selected Pakistani banks for the above mentioned period, as well as to assess the execution of these banks. Moreover, data were also assembled from articles, papers, the World Wide Web (Internet), Specialized International Journals, and relevant previous studies.

Research instruments: For this research secondary data is used for data collection of selected Commercial Banks in Pakistan. This research focuses ten commercial banks of Pakistan with respect to application of Camel Model. CAMEL model include Capital adequacy, Asset quality, Management efficiency, Earnings and Liquidity.

The variables

Referring to the prior studies, this thesis will employ two categories of variables in order to examine the profitability of the selected commercial banks. These categories are classified as dependent variables and independent variables. In the case of this study, ten (10) variables have been chosen: one dependent and nine independent (Table 2).

Capital adequacy: It is vital for a bank to maintain investors' confidence and preventing the bank from bankrupt. It shows the overall financial condition of banks and also the ability of administration to

No	Name of Banks	Remarks
1	Allied Bank Limited	
4	Askari Bank Limited	
3	Bank Al-Falah	
2	Bank Al-Habib	
5	Faysal Bank Limited	
6	Habib bank Limited	
7	KASAB Bank Limited	
8	Muslim Commercial Bank Limited	
9	National Investment Bank Limited	
10	United Bank Limited	

Table 1: Selected commercial banks.

overcome the need of additional capital [170]. Capital adequacy is measured by the degree of money to hazard weighted holdings. A solid capital adequacy proportion reinforces the confidence of investors in the bank. It is a measure of a bank's ability to meet its obligations relative to its exposure to risk. The capital adequacy proportion exists to guarantee that a bank has the capacity handle misfortunes and satisfy its commitments to account holders without stopping operations. Capital adequacy is a critical parameter for judging the quality and soundness of keeping money framework banks with a sensible Capital adequacy ratio can absorb the sudden misfortunes easily and their expense of funding is additionally lessened which at least enhance the benefit of banks [56].

The capital base of the banking sector facilitates depositors in forming their risk perception of the firm. Also, it is the responsibility of financial managers to retain adequate levels of capitalization. Moreover, if the banks absorbing unanticipated shocks, it indicates that the institution will continue to honor its obligations. The capital adequacy ratio is most widely used to assess the performance of the banks. According to the state bank of Pakistan, a minimum 10 percent CAR is required. Capital Adequacy can be the percentage ratio of a monetary organization's primary capital to its resources (advances and investments), utilized as a measure of its monetary strength and stability [171].

Capital adequacy finally determines that how well financial institutions can fight with shocks to their balance sheets. Thus, it is beneficial to track capital-adequacy ratios that take into account the most important financial risks that are interest rate risks, credit, and foreign exchange by allocating risk weightings to the organization's assets. Capital requirement is also known as capital adequacy. It is the amount of capital that a bank and other financial institutions have to hold as compulsory by the state bank of Pakistan. This is ordinarily communicated a capital adequacy degree that must be held at a rate of danger weighted resources. These prerequisites are instituted to guarantee that these establishments don't tackle overabundance influence and get to be insolvent. This ratio is mostly used to protect investors, promote the stability and efficiency of financial systems round the world [172].

Asset quality: Resources quality investigation serves to see how asset quality could affect a banks future profitability and capital adequacy. Hence, the asset quality examination is viewed as an integral part of a bank quantitative execution evaluation [173]. It considers the rate of bank credits which are an NPA (non-performing assets), high NPA suggests that advances given banks are of lower quality and in this manner not a decent thing for the bank. The Gross NPAs is measured as a percentage of net advances. The lower the ratio, the better the quality of advances [103].

The asset quality is an important indicator to measure the strength of a bank. The reason behind computing the asset quality is to determine the factor of non-performing assets (NPA) as a percentage of the bank total assets [174]. Asset quality determines the robustness of financial institutions against loss of value in the assets. The declining in value of assets, being a major source of banking complications, directly

Bank-Specific	Variables	Measures	Notation
Dependent Variable	Performance	Earnings per share $= \frac{\text{Net Income}}{\text{outstanding Shares}}$	EPS
Independent Variables	Capital Adequacy Ratio	$Total\ Deposit\ to\ Equity\ Ratio = \frac{Total\ Deposits}{Total\ Equity}$	CAR
	Asset Quality	Non-Performing Loans to Gross Advances $= \frac{\text{NPL}}{\text{Advacnes}}$ $Non\text{-}performing\ Loans\ to\ share\ holder\ equity = \frac{\text{NPL}}{\text{Equity}}$	AQ
	Management Efficiency	Admin expense to interest income $= \frac{\text{Admin expense}}{\text{Interest income}}$ Gross advances to total deposits $= \frac{Gross\ Advances}{\text{Total desposits}}$	ME
	Earnings Quality	Return on Assets $= \frac{\text{Net Income}}{\text{Total Assets}}$ Return on equity $= \frac{\text{Net Income}}{\text{Total Equity}}$ Interest Income to Total Assets Ratio $= \frac{\text{Interest Income}}{Total\ Assets}$	EQ
	Liquidity	Cash Ratio $= \frac{\text{Cash and Cash equivalents}}{\text{Current liabilities}}$	LQ

Table 2: The variables measures and their notation.

transfer into other areas, as losses are ultimately written-off against capital, which finally reduces the earning capacity of the institution. With this the asset quality is determined in relation to the level and severity of distribution of assets, recoveries, adequacy of provisions, non-performing assets, etc. Popular indicators of asset quality are loan default to total advances, recoveries to loan default ratios and non-performing loans to advance. Other indicators of asset quality are the ratio of non-performing loans to total loans (GNPA) and gross non-performing loans to gross advances ratio. NPLGA is more indicative of the quality of credit decisions made by bankers. Higher GNPA indicates the poor credit decision-making. According to the Aspal and Dhawan credit risk in the form of NPAs is one of the critical factors that have an effect on the financial well-being of a bank [10]. The extent of the credit risk depends on the quality of resources possessed by a bank.

Management efficiency: Management effectiveness is another significant component of the CAMEL Model. The proportion in this section includes subjective analysis to measure the productivity and effectiveness of administration [170]. It refers to the proportion of non- premium users like are done by bank higher rate of such use suggests that bank administration is bad at controlling the unnecessary costs. Management of financial institution is usually evaluated in terms of, asset quality, earnings and profitability, liquidity, capital adequacy. In addition, performance evaluation consists of the ability to plan and react to changing circumstances, technical competence, leadership, compliance with set norms and administrative ability. Basically, administration rating is simply a blend of execution in the aforementioned areas. Management efficiency is used to assess administration's quality; it involves analysis of efficiency of management in generating business (top-line) and in maximizing profits (bottom-line) [165].

Effective management is a standout amongst the most imperative components behind the financial institution's performance. Indicators of quality of administration, notwithstanding, are basically appropriate for individual organizations, and can't be effectively accumulated over the part. Moreover, given the subjective way of administration, it is hard to judge its soundness, just by taking a look at books of accounts of the banks. However, total expenditure to total income and operating expense to total expense helps in evaluating the administrative quality of the banking establishments. Efficient Administration is the most vital ingredient that ensures the smooth functioning of banks [103]. Numerous indicators, however, Admin Expense to Interest Income Ratio, Gross Advances to Total Deposits Ratio and Assets Turnover Ratio are measuring performance and soundness of the management. The bank management efficiency guarantees the growth and survival of a bank [175]. The management capability includes a variety of expenditures, such as salaries, employees compensation and training investment, reflects the administration policy stance. Aspal and Dhawan observed that the management efficiency is often expressed qualitatively through subjective evaluation of organizational discipline, management systems, quality of staff, control systems and others [10].

Earnings & profitability: The earnings quality is a very important measure that defines the capability of a bank to earn reliably. It determines the profitability of banks and explains its sustainability and progress in earnings in the future [170]. It refers to the net benefit that is made by a bank in the wake of taking into all components. Higher acquiring suggests the bank is doing great yet one ought to look whether this procuring is by virtue of center managing an account that is premium wage or different earnings. The earning quality is significant measure which shows the quality of income in terms of income generated from advancing operation by a bank. Aspal and Dhawan defined high earnings quality should reflect the firm's current operating performance and a good indicator of future operating performance [10]. Earnings and profitability are the single most considered figure in a company's financial accounts because they show a bank's profitability. Business quarterly and yearly incomes are normally contrasted with investigator appraisals and direction gave the business itself. Much of the time, when income doesn't meet both of those evaluations, a business' stock cost will have a tendency to drop. Then again, when real income beat gauges by a noteworthy sum, the offer cost will probably surge.

Earnings and profitability are the main source of the increase in capital base, is inspected with respects to interest rate policies and the adequacy of provisioning. Likewise, it additionally serves to help present and future operations of the Institutions. Indicators of earnings and profitability are ROA, ROE and Interest Income to Total Assets Ratio. The single best indicator used to measure earning is the Return on Assets (ROA), which is net income after taxes to total asset ratio. According to the Reddy High returns on asset means greater returns earned on assets deployed by the bank [165]. According to the Dang a consistent profit not only constructs the public confidence in the bank, but absorbs loan losses and provides sufficient provisions [2]. Profitability proportions measure the capacity of a company to produce profits from revenue and resources.

Solid earnings and profitability profile of banks mirror the capacity to help present and future operations. All the more particularly, this decides the ability to absorb misfortunes, fund its extension, pay profits to its shareholders, and develop an adequate level of capital. Being front line of defense against the destruction of a capital base from misfortunes, the requirement for high profit and earnings can scarcely be overemphasized. Although diversifying pointers are utilized to fill the need, the best and most broadly utilize indicator is a Return on Assets (ROA). ROA is employed by establishments and banks to outfit them with an important instrument for evaluating their progress, including utilization of assets and financial quality [134]. Then again, for inside and out examination, an alternate pointer Net Interest Margins (NIM) is likewise utilized. Chronically unfruitful money related establishment's hazard bankruptcy. Contrasted and most different pointers, inclines in gains can be hard to decipher for cars, abnormally high benefit can reflect excessive danger taking. To measure the profitability, Return on assets is characterized as the net benefits of the banks divided by the average aggregate resources. This ratio summarizes the capacity of the administration to create net income from the resources of the banks [176].

Liquidity: A firm ought to guarantee that it doesn't experience the shortage or an abundance of liquidity to meet its short-term obligations. An investigation of liquidity is of real significance to both the inward and the outside analysts due to its close association with day-to-day operations of an organization. Liquidity plays an important role in the effective running of a business firm [177]. Liquidity means the presence of the cash or near cash form. This ratio shows the capacity of the bank to pay off the liabilities when they mature. In other words, the liquidity means the capability of the bank to transform non-cash items into cash as they needed. It indicates the cash position of the bank. In other words, the capability of the bank meets its customers day to day cash needs [103]. Liquidity is the capacity of a financial establishment to respect all money installment duties as they fall due. These responsibilities can be met either by drawing from a stock of cash holdings, by utilizing current money inflows, by getting money or by changing over liquid resources into money.

Liquidity is an indispensable circumstance for any business. The inability to meet installment commitments on time can trigger liquidation and gives lenders the privilege to take ownership of the association's resources. Liquidity ratios are used to measure the position of the bank. The fluid resource contains a balance with institutions and money at call, cash in hand and short notice. The total resources contain the revaluation of all the resources [170]. Liquidity is considerably more essential for monetary establishments in light of the fact that they are especially powerless against sudden and prompt installment requests. This is the way of the loan making and deposit taking business. A bank can't stand to send away a client who needs to withdraw money from his record with a "possibly tomorrow". To stay in business, the bank must have the capacity to pay out legitimate withdrawals and credit asks for immediate.

In addition, in most of the everyday exchanges, the bank does not follow up for its own sake, e.g. Paying rent for bank workplaces or purchasing photocopy paper, yet rather works as a monetary mediator in the middle of savers and borrowers or as a payment agent for exchanges between organizations or people. Consequently, the disappointment of a huge money related organization can have expansive financial impacts on the whole national monetary framework. Indeed the disappointment of a little town bank will influence the dominant part of people in that town straightforwardly or in a roundabout way. Liquidity management has an important task to manage the appropriate liquidity in the banks due to competitive stress. The appropriate liquidity administration can be used to hedge Threat of liquidity and ensuring superior percentage of return on invested funds [174].

Data analysis tools

For the purpose of this analysis, financial ratios and statistical tools were applied to examine and compare the impact of independent variables on the dependent variables. Regression analysis is used in testing the hypotheses. The Pearson correlation coefficient is also used to examine the correlation between the study variables at the 5 % level of confidence according to the SPSS software package.

Descriptive statistics: Descriptive Statistics contain certain measures, such as measures of dispersion or variability (standard deviation, minimum variable, maximum variable, range) and central tendency (mean) that are used to describe a data set. According to the Trochim Descriptive measures summarize a particular data set that can either represent a sample or population used for the research [178].

The measure of central tendency defined as the sum of all values in a data set divided by the total number of values in that data set. Standard Deviation is the measure of dispersion of data from its mean. It is calculated by taking the square root of the whole equation in which the sum of squared deviations from the mean of data is divided by the total number of values in a data set minus one. A higher standard deviation shows a higher dispersion of data from its mean and vice versa. Range is the difference between the maximum value and the minimum value in a data set. It shows the gap between highest and lowest dispersion from the mean in the data set. Maximum Variable is the highest value in the data set. Minimum Variable is the lowest value in the data set.

Correlation analysis: Correlation Analysis is a statistical tool which is used to measure the strength of the relationship between two variables. It is used to accept or reject the hypothesis. In this study, the Pearson Correlation Method has been used, which is the most common technique to measure the linear relationship between the independent and dependent variables. The correlation coefficient is indicated by r. The correlation coefficient values are always between -1 to 1, i.e. $-1 < r > +1$.

A Pearson correlation matrix shows the strength, significance and the direction of the relationships among all the variables. The correlation is derived by measuring the variation in one variable along with the variation in another variable. A correlation coefficient may be positive, negative or zero. If a correlation value is positive, then it indicates that the direction of variation of both variables is the same. If a correlation value is negative, then it indicates that the direction of variation of both variables is opposite to each other. Zero value indicates no correlation between the two variables and this denotes that both moves randomly. One important thing to be kept in mind is the significance of the correlation, which reveals the probability of occurrence of correlation between the two variables. If the value of "r" is equal to 0.05 or less, then it means that 95% chance exists that the correlation is significantly or true and there are 5% chances that the correlation is insignificant. If the value of "r" is equal to 0.01 or less, then it means that 99% chance exists that the correlation is significantly or true and 1% chance that the correlation is insignificant. A significance value beyond 0.05 is not accepted in research studies and indicates that there is an insignificant relationship between two variables.

If the correlation coefficient value "r" is equal to 0, then no relationship exists between the two variables. If the value of "r" is in between 0.01 to 0.09, then a negligible positive relationship exists between the two variables. If the value of "r" is in between -0.01 to -0.09, then a negligible negative relationship exists between the two variables. If the value of "r" is in between 0.10 to 0.29, then a low positive relationship exists between the two variables. If the value of "r" is in between -0.10 to -0.29, then a low negative relationship exists between the two variables. If the value of "r" is in between 0.30 to 0.49, then a moderate positive relationship exists between the two variables. If the value of "r" is in between -0.30 to -0.49, then a moderate negative relationship exists between the two variables. If the value of "r" is in between 0.50 to 0.69, then a substantial positive relationship exists between the two variables. If the value of "r" is in between -0.50 to -0.69, then a substantial negative relationship exists between the two variables. If the value of "r" is in between 0.70 to 0.89, then a strong positive relationship exists between the two variables. If the value of "r" is in between -0.70 to -0.89, then a strong negative relationship exists between the two variables. If the value of "r" is in between 0.90 to 10.0, then a very strong positive relationship exists between the two variables. If the value of "r" is in between -0.90 to -10.0, then a very strong negative relationship exists between the two variables [179].

Regression analysis: It is a statistical tool that measures the dependency between the dependent variable and a series of independent variables. In this study, the linear regression analysis is used. In regression analysis, the regression coefficient R shows the overall strength of the association between the dependent variable and the independent variables. The R square is the coefficient of determination, which demonstrations the degree to which the regression equation can explain the difference in the dependent variable caused by the independent variables. The value of R square is in between 0 and 1. A model and its predictive ability are considered relatively better if the value of R square is closer to one.

Adjusted R square value indicates the resultant predictive ability of the model due to the addition or subtraction of independent variables into the model. Its value will decrease if the model's predictive ability is decreased, due to the addition of an independent variable into the model. The standard error of estimate is also known as the standard error of regression, shows the level of accuracy of the predictions stated by the model. It shows that at an average, how far are the values of the independent variables dispersed away from the regression line. A model having a relatively small value of the standard error of estimate is considered as a better model Table 3.

The Analysis of Variance (ANOVA) consists of the values of Sum of Squares, Mean Squares, F-Test, and p value. The value of Sum of Square indicates the amount of variation that exists between the values used in the model. The total sum of square value indicates the variation that exists within the observed data. A residual measure of the square indicates the variation that exists in the modeling errors. The sum of square value is compared with the total sum of square value and the residual sum of square value.

The degree of freedom refers to the number of observations among the sample that can be freely chosen from the total number of observations. The means of squares is the ratio of the sum of squares to the degree of freedom. The fitness of the whole regression model is specified by the F-test value. If the F-test value is significantly higher, then it shows that the dependent variable (Y) has a linear relationship with the independent variables of the model. It is not compulsory that a high F-test value means that all the independent variables have a linear relationship with the dependent variable. A high significant F-test may also show that only one independent variable has a linear relationship with the dependent variable.

The p value demonstrates that whether the overall regression model is statistically significant or not. If the p value is less than 0.05, then it indicates that the model is significant. The regression coefficient (Table 3) indicates that how each independent variable affects the value of the dependent variable. In the coefficient (Table 3), the values of unstandardized Coefficients, Standard error, t-value and significance are given. The unstandardized coefficient value indicates the strength of the relationship that exists between the dependent and the independent variable. The sign of the unstandardized coefficient shows the direction of the relationship. The standard error shows the precision of the strength of the relationship between the dependent and the independent variable. In other words, it shows the deviation from the parameters of its corresponding population.

The lower value of the standard error is better. The standardized coefficient beta value is useful because it allows comparison of those variables that are measured on a different scale. The standardized coefficient beta value indicates the change in the dependent variable due to the change in the standard deviations of the independent variables. The value of t statistics is important, as it decides whether a hypothesis will be accepted or rejected. If the t-value is above +2 or if it is below -2 then a null hypothesis is rejected, otherwise it cannot be rejected. The p value in the regression coefficient (Table 3) shows the statistical significance of the relationship between the dependent and the independent variable. The constant gives a prediction of the value of the dependent variable, when the value of all the independent variable's value is zero. If the significance value (p value) for any variable is above 0.05, then the relationship of that variable with the dependent variable is considered as statistically insignificant. If the significance value of any variable is below 0.05 then such a relationship is considered as statistically significant.

Variables	Mean	Std. Deviation
TDE	11.6264	5.0723
NPLG	0.1164	0.09412
NPLE	0.8129	0.83824
AEII	2.0767	0.65779
GATD	0.6866	0.1597
ROA	0.0063	0.01987
ROE	0.0641	0.30352
INT	0.0131	0.00603
CR	0.0953	0.034
EPS	7.1431	8.01579

Table 3: Descriptive statistics.

Results

Introduction

The reason for this portion meant to meet the general objective of assessing the execution of Pakistani commercial banks and secondly meeting the particular goal which was to create the impacts of CAMEL structure variables on bank execution. In this section objective is to examine the outcome and understanding whether there is a relationship between independent and dependent variable, whether the independent variables impacting on a dependent variable or not. To measure the relationship, Correlation and Regression investigation were utilized.

Descriptive statistics

The results in Table 3 shows the descriptive statistics applied to the data of the banking industry of Pakistan for the period 2007 to 2013. A total of 70 observations have been gathered from 10 commercial banks for the data analysis. The total deposit to equity ratio of the banking sector of Pakistan in seven years had a maximum value of 240.07 and the minimum value of 1.43. Average total deposits to equity ratio were 11.62. The standard deviation of total deposits to equity ratio was found to be 50.07.

The non-performing loans to gross advances had a maximum value of 0.40 and the minimum value of 0.62. Average non-performing loans to gross advances ratio was 0.11. The standard deviation was found to be 0.09. The non-performing loans to equity had a maximum value of 4.96 and a minimum value of 0.00. The Average value of nonperforming loans to equity was found to be 0.8129. The standard deviation was 0.83.

The administrative expenses had a maximum value of 3.65 and the minimum value of 0.62. The Average administrative expense ratio was 20.07. The standard deviation was found to be 0.65. The return on assets had a maximum value of 0.04 and the minimum value of 0.07. Average return on assets ratio was 0.006. The standard deviation was found to be 0.19. The return on equity had a maximum value of 0.28 and minimum value of 1.41. Average return on equity ratio was 0.06. The standard deviation was found to be 0.30.

The interest income to total assets had a maximum value of 00.04 and the minimum value of 0.00. The Average ratio was 0.01. The standard deviation was found to be 0.006. The cash ratio had a maximum value of 0.22 and minimum value of 0.03. The Average cash ratio was 0.09. The standard deviation was found to be 0.03. The earnings per share had maximum value of 24.47 and a minimum value of 4.54. Average earnings per share were found to be 7.14. The standard deviation was 80.01.

Inferential statistics

The Pearson's coefficient as shown in the Table 4 is used to verify the existence or non-existence of linear correlation between and among the quantitative variables indicated above of the 10 commercial banks for the period 2007 to 2013.

The correlation coefficient of total deposit to total equity with EPS is -0.337, which indicates that there is a moderate negative relationship exists between the two variables. The p value is 0.004 which is less the 0.01, indicating that the correlation value is significant at 99% confidence level. The direction of the correlation is negative, which shows that if one variable changes, the other variable changes in the opposite direction.

The correlation coefficient of Non-Performing Loans to Gross Advances with EPS is -0.458, which indicates that there is a moderate negative relationship exists between the two variables. The p value is 0.000 which is less the 0.01, indicating that the correlation value is significant at 99% confidence level. The direction of the correlation is negative, which shows that if one variable changes, the other variable changes in the opposite direction.

The correlation coefficient of Non-Performing Loans to shareholders equity with EPS is -0.472, which indicates that there is a moderate negative relationship exists between the two variables. The p value is 0.000 which is less the 0.01, indicating that the correlation value is significant at 99% confidence level. The direction of the correlation is negative, which shows that if one variable changes, the other variable changes in the opposite direction.

The correlation coefficient of Admin expenses to interest income ratio with EPS is -0.518, which indicates that there is a substantial negative relationship exists between the two variables. The p value is 0.000 which is less than 0.01, indicating that the correlation value is significant at 99% confidence level. The direction of the correlation is negative, which shows that if one variable changes, the other variable changes in the opposite direction.

The correlation coefficient of Gross Advances to total deposits ratio with EPS is -0.368, which indicates that there is a moderate negative relationship exists between the two variables. The p value is 0.002 which is less than 0.01, indicating that the correlation value is significant at 99% confidence level. The direction of the correlation is negative, which shows that if one variable changes, the other variable changes in the opposite direction.

The correlation coefficient of ROA with EPS is 0.743, which indicates that there is a strong positive relationship exists between the two variables. The p value is 0.000 which is less than 0.01, indicating that the correlation value is significant at 99% confidence level. The direction of the correlation is positive, which shows that if one variable changes, the other variable changes in the same direction.

The correlation coefficient of ROE with EPS is 0.441, which indicates that there is a moderate positive relationship exists between the two variables. The p value is 0.000 which is less than 0.01, indicating that the correlation value is significant at 99% confidence level. The direction of the correlation is positive, which shows that if one variable changes, the other variable changes in the same direction.

The correlation coefficient of interest income to total assets ratio with EPS is -0.092, which indicates that there is a negligible negative relationship exists between the two variables. The p value is 0.447 which is greater than 0.05, indicating that the correlation value is insignificant.

The correlation coefficient of cash ratio with EPS is 0.166, which indicates that there is a low positive relationship exists between the two variables. The p value is 0.169 which is greater than 0.05, indicating that the correlation value is insignificant.

Regression analysis

The model summary in the Table 5 provides the measures that show the extent to which the independent variables (predictors) can predict the dependent variable (outcome) and also how well the overall model used in our study fits (from the variable aspect). The value of R in the first column indicates the strength of the relationship between the dependent variable: banks performance measured through EPS and the independent variables included in the model: Capital Adequacy, Asset Quality, Management Efficiency, Earnings and Profitability and Liquidity. The proxies used to measure the independent variables have been mentioned in chapter 2. In addition, the Table 5 shows that the value of R is 0.944, which indicates that there is a strong relationship between the dependent variable and the independent variables. The value ofR^2 (R square) is 0.891, which indicates that 89.10% of the variance in the dependent variable is caused by the independent variables. The Table 5 shows that the F value is 54.664, which is a high value, having a significant value 0.0000, which is less than 0.05. This indicates that the overall model is significant at 95 % confidence level.

The Table 5 shows the regression coefficient of the model. It can be seen that the unstandardized coefficient value of Total Deposit to total Equity is -1.226. It indicates that a 1 unit increase in TDE will decrease the bank performance by 1.226 units. This result is statistically significant because the t-value is -9.418, which is beyond the range of -2 to +2. On this basis, the H1 cannot be rejected. The *p* value of TDE is 0.000. Thus, the regression result of TDE as a determinant of a bank's performance was statistically significant.

The unstandardized coefficient value of Non-Performing Loan to Gross Advances is -48.481. It indicates that a 1 unit increase in Non-Performing Loan to Gross Advances will decrease the value of a bank's

Variable	TDE	NPLG	NPLE	AEII	GATD	ROA	ROE	INT	CR	EPS
TDE	1									
NPLG	-0.342**	1								
NPLE	0.322**	0.586**	1							
AEII	0.204	0.438**	0.447**	1						
GATD	-0.391**	0.355**	0.212	0.013	1					
ROA	-0.148	-0.614**	-0.696**	-0.594**	-0.329**	1				
ROE	-0.104	-0.571**	-0.809**	-0.434**	-0.335**	0.823**	1			
INT	-0.019	-0.016	0.094	-0.550**	0.195	-0.034	-0.082	1		
CR	0.264*	-0.197	-0.145	-0.108	-0.360**	0.163	0.165	-0.096	1	
EPS	-0.337**	-0.458**	-0.472**	-0.518**	-0.368**	0.743**	0.441**	-0.092	0.166	1

**Correlation is significant at the 0.01 level (2-tailed).

Table 4: Correlation analysis.

Predictors	Outcomes		
	Beta	t	p
TDE	-1.226	-9.418	0.000
NPLG	-48.481	-6.444	0.000
NPLE	4.382	4.342	0.000
AEII	-2.186	-2.193	0.032
GATD	-20.412	-7.460	0.000
ROA	253.424	6.317	0.000
ROE	-9.403	-3.488	0.001
INT	-235.431	-2.802	0.007
CR	23.269	2.038	0.046

N = 70, F = 54.654, R Square = 0.891, Dependent variable EPS

Table 5: Coefficients.

performance by 48.481 units. This result is statistically significant because the t-value is -9.418, which is beyond the range of -2 to +2. On this basis, the H2 cannot be rejected. The *p* value of Non-Performing Loan to Gross Advances is 0.000, which is less than 0.05. Thus, the regression results of Non-Performing Loan to Gross Advances as a determinant of a bank's performance were statistically significant.

The unstandardized coefficient value of Non-performing Loan to Shareholder's Equity is 4.382. It indicates that 1 unit decrease in Non-performing Loan to Shareholder's Equity result in an increase in the value of a bank's performance 4.382. This result is statistically significant because the t value is 4.342, which is beyond the range of -2 and +2. On this basis, the H3 cannot be rejected. The *p* value of NPLE is 0.000, which is less than 0.05. Thus, the regression results of Nonperforming Loan to Shareholder's Equity as a determinant of a bank's performance were statistically significant.

The unstandardized coefficient value of Admin Expenses to Interest Income is -2.186. It indicates that a 1 unit increase in Admin Expenses to Interest Income will decrease the value of bank performance by 2.186 units. This result is statistically significant because the t-value is -2.193, which is beyond range of -2 to +2. On this basis, the H4 cannot be rejected. The *p* value of Admin Expenses to Interest Income is 0.032, which is less than 0.05. Thus the regression results of Admin Expenses to Interest Income as a determinant of a bank's performance were statistically significant.

The unstandardized coefficient value of Gross Advances to Total Deposits is -20.412. It indicates that a 1 unit increase in Gross Advances to Total Deposits will decrease in the value of a bank's performance by 20.412 units. This result is statistically significant because t-value is -7.460, which is beyond the range of -2 to +2. On this basis, the H5 cannot be rejected. The *p* value of Gross Advances to Total Deposits is 0.000, which is less than 0.05. Thus the regression results of Gross Advances to Total Deposits as a determinant of a bank's performance were statistically significant.

The unstandardized coefficient value of Return on Assets is 253.424. It indicates that a 1 unit increase in Return on Assets will increase in the value of a bank's performance by 253.424 units. This result is statistically significant because t-value is 6.317, which is beyond the range of -2 to +2. On this basis, the H6 cannot be rejected. The *p* value of Return on Assets is 0.000, which is less than 0.05. Thus the regression results of Return on Assets as a determinant of a bank's performance were statistically significant.

The unstandardized coefficient value of Return on Equity is -9.403. It indicates that a 1 unit increase in Return on Equity will decrease in the value of a bank's performance by 9.403 units. This result is statistically significant because t-value is -3.488, which is beyond the range of -2 to +2. On this basis, the H7 cannot be rejected. The *p* value of Return on Assets is 0.001, which is less than 0.05. Thus the regression results of Return on Equity as a determinant of a bank's performance were statistically significant.

The unstandardized coefficient value of Interest Income to Total Assets Ratio is -235.431. It indicates that a 1 unit increase in Interest Income to Total Assets Ratio will decrease in the value of a bank's performance by 235.431 units. This result is statistically significant because t-value is -2.802, which is beyond the range of -2 to +2. On this basis, the H8 cannot be rejected. The *p* value of Interest Income to Total Assets Ratio is 0.007, which is less than 0.05. Thus the regression results of Interest Income to Total Assets Ratio as a determinant of a bank's performance were statistically significant.

The unstandardized coefficient value of Cash Ratio is 23.269. It indicates that a 1 unit increase in Cash Ratio will increase in the value of a bank's performance by 23.269 units. This result is statistically significant because t-value is 20.038, which is beyond the range of -2 to +2. On this basis, the H9 cannot be rejected. The *p* value of Cash Ratio is 0.046, which is less than 0.05. Thus the regression results of Cash Ratio as a determinant of a bank's performance were statistically significant.

Clearly the outcomes demonstrated that all the CAMEL variables had a significant effect on the execution of banks amid the period under study at any rate, at 5% test level. This implies that CAMEL parameters influence the execution of commercial banks significantly.

Discussion

This section contains discussion on the basis of the findings of the study, which will lead to acceptance or rejection of the hypothesis. While drawing conclusions from the research, some important recommendations are formulated for future references / guidance.

H1: There is a significant negative impact of Total Deposit to Total Equity ratio on the Bank's performance.

H1o: There is a significant positive impact of Total Deposit to Total Equity ratio on the Bank's performance.

He first hypothesis of the study at hand states that the total Deposit to total Equity ratio has a significant impact on Bank's performance. As mentioned earlier in the Chapter 2, total Deposit to total Equity ratio has been used as a measure of Capital adequacy. For the purpose of testing the hypothesis, a regression model is used with intent to study the impact of Capital adequacy on Bank's performance. In the regression model, earning per share is used as a measure of the Bank's performance to test the significance of Capital adequacy with it. It is observed that Capital adequacy had a t-value -9.418 and its p value is 0.000. The t-value is beyond the range of -2 and +2, whereas the p value is below the significance level of 0.05. It is concluded that the null hypothesis can be rejected and at the same time the alternative hypothesis can be accepted. The results reflect a significant relationship between the dependent variable Bank's performance and the independent variable Capital adequacy. In other words, Capital adequacy has a significant impact on the bank's performance. Our Results are consistent with the studies of Pastory et al., Frederick, Guisse, Ikpefan, Barnor and Odonkor [74-78]. The Coefficient correlation value shows a negative relationship between Total Deposit to Total Equity ratio and the Bank's performance. It means that one variable is increasing and the other variable is decreasing. This implies that domestic banks are functioning over-cautiously by neglecting possible profitable endeavor. It shows that, setting up the high capital, administrative necessity has a negative effect on bank's execution, if not balanced by expanding investments. Moreover, when the Capital Adequacy expands, productivity will diminish. In other words, when the banks build the utilization of Equity, they will enroll more misfortunes. The clarification of this sensation can be firstly the sum they are paying to their shareholders as a dividend is greater than what they are creating from it as a benefit. Besides, the facts could confirm that they are utilizing retain earnings without putting it in a new arrangement that will give more benefit to the organization. Furthermore, the negative relationship suggests that, as more capital is set aside as a cradle for banks wellbeing; it influences the execution of banks. The results of the study, lies in the way that the negative relationship between capital adequacy and execution highlights the way that different endeavors by the controllers to audit regularly the capital base of the keeping money division is not borne out of the plan to enhance the gains of the banks. Rather to maintain stability, security against contributors and trust in the keeping money industry.

H2: There is a significant negative impact of Non-performing Loans to Gross Advances ratio on the Bank's performance.

H2o: There is a significant positive impact of Non-performing Loans to Gross Advances ratio on the Bank's performance.

The second hypothesis of the study at hand states that the NPL to Gross Advances ratio has a significant impact on Bank's performance. As mentioned earlier in the Chapter 2, NPL to gross advances ratio has been used as a measure of Asset quality. For the purpose of testing the hypothesis, a regression model is used with intent to study the impact of Asset quality on Bank's performance. In the regression model, earning per share is used as a measure of the Bank's performance to test the significance with it. It is observed that Asset quality had a t-value -6.444 and its p value is 0.000. The t-value is beyond the range of -2 and +2, whereas the p value is below the significance level of 0.05. It is concluded that the null hypothesis can be rejected and at the same time the alternative hypothesis can be accepted. The results reflect a significant relationship between the dependent variable Bank's performance and the independent variable Asset quality. In other words, Asset quality has a significant impact on the bank's performance. Despite the fact that our findings are consistent with the past studies [31,80,99,100] we have succeeded to find theoretical support for our results. The literature review on asset quality as a determinant of a bank`s performance indicates that it has a significant impact on the bank`s performance. Our correlation coefficient shows negative significance which means that when one variable moves in a direction the other variable moves in completely opposite directions. This is because when banks give loans to the individuals or to the firms and they cannot pay it back to the bank as per their understanding; it affects the bank's profitability and its earnings, the cost increases for the banks which ultimately decreases its earning capacity.

H3: There is a significant negative impact of Non-performing Loans to Shareholder Equity ratio on the Bank's performance.

H3o: There is a significant positive impact of Non-performing Loans to shareholder equity ratio on the Bank's performance.

The third hypothesis of the study at hand states that the NPL to shareholder's equity ratio has a significant impact on Bank's performance. As mentioned earlier in the Chapter 2, NPL to shareholders equity ratio has been used as a measure of Asset quality. For the purpose of testing the hypothesis, a regression model is used with intent to study the impact of Asset quality on Bank's performance. In the regression model, earning per share is used as a measure of the Bank's performance to test the significance with it. It is observed that Asset quality had a t-value 4.342 and its p value is 0.000. The t-value is beyond the range of -2 and +2, whereas the p value is below the significance level of 0.05. It is concluded that the null hypothesis can be rejected and at the same time the alternative hypothesis can be accepted. The results reflect a significant relationship between the dependent variable Bank's performance and the independent variable Asset quality. In other words, Asset quality has a significant negative impact on the bank's performance. The negative correlation between non-performing loans to shareholders equity and earnings per share shows that whenever non-performing loans increases earnings decreases because interest charged on loans is main source of income for banks. Whenever non-performing loans increases investor's confidence decreases and therefore they feel hesitate to invest in such circumstances. As investment decreases profitability also decreases and ultimately performance decreases.

H4: There is a significant negative impact of Admin expense to interest income ratio on the Bank's performance.

H4o: There is a significant positive impact of Admin expense to interest income ratio on the Bank's performance.

The fourth hypothesis of this study is Admin Expenses to Interest Income ratio, which has a significant negative association with the Bank's performance. As mentioned earlier Chapter 2, Admin Expenses to Interest Income has been used as a measure of the Bank's performance. For the purpose of testing the hypothesis, a regression model was used with the purpose to study the impact of Admin Expenses to Interest Income Ratio on Bank's performance. In the regression model, Admin Expenses to Interest Income was used as a measure of the Bank's performance to test the significance of the Bank's performance with it. It was observed that Admin Expenses to Interest Income had a t-value -2.193 and its *p* value was 0.032. The t-value is beyond the range of -2 and +2, whereas the p value was within the significance level of 0.05. It is concluded that the alternative hypothesis cannot be rejected and the same time the null hypothesis cannot be accepted as well, since the results reflects the significant relationship between the dependent variable Bank's performance and the independent variable Admin Expenses to Interest Income. In other words, there is a significant association between Admin Expenses to Interest Income with Bank's performance. The correlation results indicate that a significant negative and a substantial negative association exist between Admin Expenses to Interest Income and Bank's performance.

The correlation is negative because when the Admin Expenses to Interest Income increase the cost of the bank's increase which decreases the performance of Banks. Our findings (regression results for Admin Expenses to Interest Income and Bank's performance association) are consistent with the studies of Davydenko, Ongore, Sufian and Chong, and Aftab, Samad and Husain [110,115,117,118].

H5: There is a significant negative impact of Gross advances to total deposits ratio on the Bank's performance.

H5o: There is a significant positive impact of Gross advances to total deposits ratio on the Bank's performance.

The fifth hypothesis of this study is Gross Advances to Total Deposits Ratio which has a significant negative association with the bank's performance. As mentioned earlier Chapter 2, Gross Advances to Total Deposits Ratio has been used as a measure of the Bank's performance. For the purpose of testing the hypothesis, a regression model was used with the purpose to study the impact of Gross Advances to Total Deposits Ratio on Bank's performance. In the regression model, Gross Advances to Total Deposits Ratio was used as a measure of the Bank's performance to test the significance of the Bank's performance with it. It was observed that Gross Advances to Total Deposits Ratio had a t-value -7.460 and its p value was 0.000. The t-value is beyond the range of -2 and +2, whereas the p value was within the significance level of 0.05. It is concluded that the alternative hypothesis cannot be rejected and the same time the null hypothesis cannot be accepted as well, since the results reflects the significant relationship between the dependent variable Bank's performance and the independent variable Gross Advances to Total Deposits Ratio. In other words, there is a significant association between Gross Advances to Total Deposits Ratio with Bank's performance. The correlation results indicate that a significant negative and a moderate association exist between Gross Advances to Total Deposits Ratio and Bank's performance. The correlation is negative, which shows that one variable increase opposite variable decrease. The reason is that when deposit increase in banks and they are not properly utilized, than have to pay the interest on that deposit. When the banks pay interest with the utilization of deposit than cost increase, which decrease the earnings and finally it decrease the Bank's performance.

H6: There is a significant positive impact of Return on Assets on the Bank's performance.

H6o: There is a significant negative impact of Return on Assets on the Bank's performance.

The sixth hypothesis of the study at hand states that Return on Assets has a significant impact on Bank's performance. As mentioned earlier in the Chapter 2, Return on Assets has been used as a measure of Earnings & Profitability. For the purpose of testing the hypothesis, a regression model is used with the intent to study the impact of Earnings & Profitability on the bank's performance. In the regression model, earnings per share are used as a measure of the Bank's performance to test the significance of Earnings & Profitability with it. It was observed that Return on Assets had a t-value 6.317 and its p value is 0.000. The t-value is beyond the range of -2 and +2, whereas the p value is below the significance level of 0.05. It is concluded that the null hypothesis can be rejected and at the same time the alternative hypothesis can be accepted. The results reflect a significant relationship between the dependent variable Bank's performance and the independent variable Earnings & Profitability. In other words, Earnings & Profitability have a significant impact on the bank's performance. Our Results are consistent with the study of El-Bannany, Heikal et al. and Azizi and Sarkani [24,139,144]. The Coefficient correlation value shows a positive relationship between Return on Assets and the Bank's performance. It means that one variable is increasing and the other variable is also increasing in the same direction. It means that the management of the banks utilizes their assets efficiently and effectively.

H7: There is a significant positive impact of Return on Equity on the Bank's performance.

H7o: There is a significant negative impact of Return on Equity on the Bank's performance.

The seventh hypothesis of the study at hand states that Return on Equity has a significant impact on Bank's performance. As mentioned earlier in the Chapter 2, Return on Equity has been used as a measure of Earnings & Profitability. For the purpose of testing the hypothesis, a regression model is used with the intent to study the impact of Earnings & Profitability on the Bank's performance. In the regression model, earnings per share were used as a measure of the Bank's performance to test the significance of Earnings & Profitability with it. It was observed that Return on Equity had a t-value -3.488 and its p value is 0.001. The t-value is beyond the range of -2 and +2, whereas the p value is below the significance level of 0.05. It is concluded that the null hypothesis can be rejected and at the same time the alternative hypothesis can be accepted. The results reflect a significant relationship between the dependent variable Bank's performance and the independent variable Earnings & Profitability. In other words, Earnings & Profitability have a significant impact on the bank's performance. Our Results are consistent with the study of Taani and Banykhaled, Heikal et al. and Azizi and Sarkani [24,140,141]. The Coefficient correlation value shows a positive relationship between Return on equity and the Bank's performance. It means that one variable is increasing and the other variable is also increasing in the same direction.

H8: There is a significant negative impact of Interest Income to Total Assets Ratio on the Bank's performance.

H8o: There is a significant positive impact of Interest Income to Total Assets Ratio on the Bank's performance.

The eighth hypothesis of the study at hand states that the interest income to total assets ratio has a significant negative impact on Bank's performance. As mentioned earlier in the Chapter 2, interest income to total assets ratio has been used as a measure of a bank's performance. For the purpose of testing the hypothesis, a regression model is used with intent to study the impact of Earnings and Profitability on Bank's performance. In the regression model, earning per share is used as a measure of the Bank's performance to test the significance of earnings and profitability with it. It is observed that earnings and profitability had a t-value -2.802 and its p value is 0.007. The t-value is beyond the range of -2 and +2, whereas the p value is below the significance level of 0.05. It is concluded that the null hypothesis can be rejected and at the same time the alternative hypothesis can be accepted. The results reflect a significant relationship between the dependent variable Bank's performance and the independent variable earnings and profitability. In other words, earning and profitability have a significant impact on the bank's performance. The above mentioned results are consistent with the research carried out by Olweny and Shipho, the outcome shows that there is a negative, but significant association between operational cost effectiveness and firm performance as interest income is the main source of income for banks [31]. Interest income increases consequently profitability increases.

H9: There is a significant positive impact of Cash Ratio on the Bank's performance.

H9o: There is a significant negative impact of Cash Ratio on the Bank's performance.

The ninth hypothesis of the study at hand states that the cash ratio has a significant impact on Bank's performance. As mentioned earlier in the Chapter 2, cash ratio has been used as a measure of a bank's performance. For the purpose of testing the hypothesis, a regression model is used with intent to study the impact of cash ratio on Bank's performance. In the regression model, Earning per Share is used as a measure of the Bank's performance to test the significance of cash ratio with it. It is observed that cash ratio had a t-value 20.038 and its p value is 0.046. The t-value is beyond the range of -2 and +2, whereas the p value is below the significance level of 0.05. It is concluded that the null hypothesis can be rejected and at the same time the alternative hypothesis can be accepted. The results reflect a significant relationship between the dependent variable Bank's performance and the independent variable cash ratio. In other words, Liquidity has a significant impact on the bank's performance. Results are in accordance with previous studies carried out by Anoh, Agbada and Osuji, Akanbi and Ajagbe, Lartey et al., Olagunju et al. and Azizi and Sarkani [24,157-161]. These discoveries support Bourke who discovered some proof of a positive relationship between fluid resources and bank benefit for 90 banks in Europe, Australia North America and from 1972 to 1981 [70]. In the perspective of the way that liquidity has some measure of direction on the productivity of a bank, it is imperative that banks deal with their liquidity exceptionally well. At the point when banks hold satisfactory fluid resources, their benefit would progress. Satisfactory liquidity helps the bank minimize liquidity danger and budgetary emergencies. The bank can assimilate any conceivable unforeseen stun brought on by the surprising requirement for a reduction in liabilities or the increment in resources side of the Statement of Financial Position. Then again, if fluid resources are held unreasonably, productivity could reduce. Fluid resources for the most part have no or minimal enthusiasm producing limit. The opportunity expense of holding low-return resources would in the long run exceed the advantage of any increment of the bank's liquidity flexibility as seen in financing market.

Summary of discussion

To sum up, the correlation analysis and regression results have indicated that Bank's performance is significantly affected by Capital adequacy, Asset Quality, Management Efficiency, Earnings & Profitability and Liquidity. Although our correlation results have shown that interest income to total assets and cash ratio have a positive but statistically insignificant correlation with Bank‘s performance, However the regression results have shown that these two independent variables are statistically significant with a Bank‘s performance. On the basis of our findings, the hypothesis 1, 2, 3, 4, 5, 6, 7, 8, 9 have been accepted and confirmed to be true. It means that null hypothesis can be rejected and alternative hypothesis can be accepted because all hypotheses have statistical significance with Bank's performance (Table 6).

Conclusion

In this research, the impact of CAMEL model parameters on Bank performance has been analyzed. CAMEL model parameters, for example, Capital Adequacy, Asset quality, Management efficiency Earnings & Profitability and Liquidity are considered as independent variable while an earnings per share as a measure of bank performance is considered as the dependent variable. The sample size of this research is the 10 commercial banks operating in Pakistan. The financial data of 7 years (from 2007 to 2013) were collected from the official website of the banks, annual reports and from other related websites. The study utilized numerous statistical tools like regression analysis, descriptive analysis, and correlation analysis to analyze the data and interpret the findings. The results showed that total deposit to equity, non-performing loans to gross advances, non-performing loans to equity, Admin Expenses to Interest Income Ratio, Gross Advances to Total Deposits Ratio were significantly but negative correlated with a bank's performance. The Return on Assets and Return on Equity were significantly and positively correlated with a bank's performance. The interest income to total assets ratio is statistically insignificant with bank's performance, whereas the regression result show that INT is statistically significant with bank's performance. The cash ratio is also showing insignificant correlated bank's performance, whereas the regression result shows that the cash ratio is statistically significant with a bank's performance. The finding of this study was consistent with the finding of previous studies and sported the theories. It means that null hypothesis can be rejected and alternative hypothesis can be accepted because all hypotheses have statistical significance with the Bank's performance. It is concluded that at this point of time CAMEL model has a significant impact on Bank's performance. The findings of this research will be very helpful for the management of the banks in the banking industry of Pakistan, who can without any doubt focus on these key determinants of the CAMEL model to measure the performance and take appropriate decisions. The investors and shareholders can also assess the Bank's performance in order to make right and timely investment decisions.

Recommendations

On the basis of the findings of the study, it recommends that:

i) The banks should improve their capital base and maintain adequate capital adequacy ratio, lower the ratio more the performance of the banks.

ii) The bank should decrease their nonperforming loan in order to improve their asset quality and limiting the loan outstanding.

iii) The administration of the bank should manage the cost of the bank, and the cost to income ratio should be in a reasonable range. The administration of the bank should pay more consideration of its cost, and make sure the costs of the bank are utilized in the sensible way.

iv) The bank should increase their net profit and improve their net interest margin, and maximize the income of loan product.

v) The bank should try to get more deposits and keep the right

Hypothesis	Statement	Result
H1	There is a significant negative association between Total Deposit to Total Equity ratio and the Bank's performance.	Accepted
H2	There is a significant negative association between Non-performing Loans to Gross Advances ratio and the Bank's performance.	Accepted
H3	There is a significant negative association between Non-performing Loans to Shareholder Equity ratio and the Bank's performance.	Accepted
H4	There is a significant negative association between Admin expense to interest income ratio and the Bank's performance.	Accepted
H5	There is a significant negative association between Gross advances to total deposits ratio and the Bank's performance.	Accepted
H6	There is a significant positive association between Return on Assets and the Bank's performance.	Accepted
H7	There is a significant positive association between Return on Equity and the Bank's performance.	Accepted
H8	There is a significant negative association between Interest Income to Total Assets Ratio and the Bank's performance.	Accepted
H9	There is a significant positive association between Cash Ratio and the Bank's performance.	Accepted

Total number of Hypotheses: 9
Accepted: 9
Rejected: 0

Table 6: Summary of accepted/rejected hypothesis.

amount of liquid assets to increase its liquidity.

For asset quality banks need to enhance their procedures for screening, credit clients and observing of credit danger. This is a critical indicator on the grounds that the banks have confronted difficult issues with non-performing credits in the past which prompted the breakdown of numerous banks. Then again banks ought to concentrate on enhancing their capital levels so as to enhance their financial execution. This will empower the banks to be cushioned against outside stuns, as well as to exploit business open incredibly and expand their budgetary execution in the process. Income diversification can be accomplished by expanding interest income, charges and commissions and foreign exchange activities.

Recommendation for future studies

Further studies could use different ratios to represent each factor of CAMEL, for example, the shareholder's equity to assets ratio could represent the capital adequacy instead of the risk-weighted capital adequacy ratio. Also, more ratios could be included to represent each factor of CAMEL. Further studies also could extend the period of data observed and also change the frequency of data used and this might offer a different result. The restriction of the present study is that it is limited to the investigation of private sector banks working in Pakistan. The CAMEL model can be applied to the investigation of the financial execution of public sector banks and additionally non-banking financial organizations for further analysis. Accordingly, in the further research one may need to consider this examination as a source of perspective to extend the scope and enhance the consequences of the exploration (Appendix 1).

References

1. Babar HZ, Zeb G (2011) Does CAMELS system provide similar ratings as PACRA system in assessing the performance of banks in Pakistan? Umea journal of Business.
2. Dang U (2011) The CAMEL rating system in banking supervision: A case study. Arcada University of Applied Sciences, International Business.
3. Ally Z (2013) Comparative Analysis of Financial Performance of Commercial Banks in Tanzania. Research Journal of Finance and Accounting 4: 133-143.
4. Nazir MS, Alam A (2010) The Impact of Financial Restructuring on the Performance of Pakistani Banks: A DEA Approach. The IUP Journal of Applied Finance 16: 71-86.
5. Usman A, Khan MK (2012) Evaluating the financial performance of Islamic and conventional banks of Pakistan: A comparative analysis. International Journal of Business and Social Science 3: 253-257.
6. Misra SK, Aspal PK (2013) A CAMEL Model Analysis of State Bank Group. World Journal of Social Sciences 3: 36-35.
7. Tom KA (2012) Effects of camel variables on bank efficiency: a panel analysis of Kenyan Commercial Banks (Doctoral dissertation, University Of Nairobi) pp: 1-54.
8. Trivedi KRA (2011) Camel Model Analysis of Scheduled Urban Co-operative Bank in Surat City-A case study of Surat People's Co-operative bank. IOSR Journal of Business and Management pp: 48-54.
9. Gupta S, Verma R (2008) Comparative Analysis of Financial Performance of Private Sector Banks in India: Application of CAMEL Model. Journal of Global Economy 4.
10. Aspal PK, Sanjeev D (2014) Financial performance assessment of banking sector in India: A case study of old private sector banks. The Business and Management Review 5: 1-196.
11. Gaytan A, Johnson CA (2002) A review of the literature on early warning systems for banking crises. Central Bank of Chile.
12. Bodla BS, Verma R (2006) Evaluating Performance of Banks through CAMEL model: A case study of SBI and ICICI. The IUP Journal of Bank Management 3: 49-63.
13. Dash M, Das A (2009) A CAMELS analysis of the Indian banking industry. Social Science Research Network.
14. Gupta RC (2014) An analysis of Indian public sector banks using CAMEL approach. IOSR Journal of Business and Management 16: 94-102.
15. Nag AK, Khatik SK (2014) Analyzing soundness of nationalized Banks in India: A camel Approach. Applied Studies in Agribusiness and Commerce 8: 73-78.
16. Nimalathasan B (2008) A Comparative Study of Financial Performance of Banking Sector in Bangladesh-An Application of CAMELS Rating System. Annals of University of Bucharest, Economic and Administrative Series 2: 141-152.
17. Lakhtaria NJ (2013) A Comparative Study of the Selected Public Sector Banks through CAMEL Model. Paripex Indian Journal of Research 2.
18. Kouser R, Saba I (2012) Gauging the Financial Performance of Banking Sector using the CAMEL Model: Comparison of Conventional, Mixed and Pure Islamic Banks in Pakistan. International Research Journal of Finance and Economics 1: 67-68.
19. Alam HM, Raza A, Akram M (2011) A financial performance comparison of public vs private banks: The case of commercial banking sector of Pakistan. International Journal of Business and Social Science 2: 56-64.
20. Shar AH, Shah MA, Jamali H (2011) Performance evaluation of pre-and post-nationalization of the banking sector in Pakistan: An application of CAMEL model. African Journal of Business Management 5: 747-761.
21. Kouser R, Aamir M, Mehvish H, Azeem M (2011) CAMEL analysis for Islamic and conventional banks: Comparative study from Pakistan. Economics and Finance Review 1: 55-64.
22. Bokhari IH, Ali, SM, Sultan K (2012) Determinants of Capital Adequacy Ratio in Banking Sector: An Empirical Analysis from Pakistan. Academy of Contemporary Research Journal 2: 5-16.
23. Tamimi HA (2006) The determinants of the UAE commercial banks' performance: a comparison of the national and foreign banks. Journal of Transnational Management 10: 35-47.
24. Azizi M, Sarkani DYA (2014) Review Financial Performance of Mellat Bank According To Camel Model. A Journal of Multidisciplinary Research 3.
25. Chen FC (2014) The relationship between camel and Taiwanese banks performance: SBM network DEA approach. Actual Problems of Economics 154: 534-543.
26. Sarker AA (2006) CAMELS rating system in the context of Islamic banking: A proposed 'S' for Shariah framework. Journal of Islamic Economics, Banking and Finance 2: 1-26.
27. Nurazi R, Evans M (2005) An Indonesian study of the use of CAMEL (S) ratios as predictors of bank failure. Journal of Economic and Social Policy 10: 1-23.
28. Goyal S (2011) CAMEL model: A Tool to Measure Performance of Banks.
29. San OT, Phing NP (2013) Capital Structure Before and After Merger and Acquisition: Banking Industry in Malaysia. International Journal of Management Sciences and Business Research 2: 1-22.
30. Reddy DM, Prasad KVN (2011) Evaluating performance of Regional Rural banks: an application of CAMEL Model. Journal of Arts, Science & Commerce 2: 61-67.
31. Olweny T, Shipho TM (2011) Effects of banking sectoral factors on the profitability of commercial banks in Kenya. Economics and Finance Review 1: 1-30.
32. Bhayani SJ (2006) Performance of the New Indian Private Banks: A Comparative Study. Banking Review pp: 55-59.
33. Biswas M (2014) Performance Evaluation of Andhra Bank and Bank of Maharashtra with Camel Model. International Journal of Business and Administration Research Review 1: 220-226.
34. Kabir MA, Dey S (2012) Performance Analysis through CAMEL Rating: A Comparative Study of Selected Private Commercial Banks in Bangladesh. Journal of Politics & Governance 1: 16-25.
35. Keovongvichith P (2012) An analysis of the recent financial performance of the

Laotian banking sector during 2005-2010. International Journal of Economics and Finance 4: 148-162.

36. Altan M, Yusufazari H, Bedük A (2014) Performance Analysis of Banks in Turkey Using CAMEL Approach. In Proceedings of International Academic Conferences. International Institute of Social and Economic Sciences 2: 21-32.

37. Mohiuddin G (2014) Use of CAMEL Model: A Study on Financial Performance of Selected Commercial Banks in Bangladesh. Universal Journal of Accounting and Finance 2: 151-160.

38. Muhmad SN, Hashim HAB (2014) CAMEL Framework and Bank Performance: Evidence in Malaysia.

39. Ebrahimi SK, Nasab AB, Javaheri M (2015) The Impact of Privatization of Banks on CAMEL Indicators. Gmp Review 16: 201-209.

40. Gebba TR, Ahmed IE (2013) The Performance of Privatized Financial Institutions in Egypt: The Case of Alexandria Bank. Journal of Applied Finance & Banking 3: 245-269.

41. Tripathi D, Meghani K, Mahajan S (2014) Financial Performance of Axis Bank and Kotak Mahindra Bank In The Post Reform Era: Analysis On CAMEL Model. Economics and Applied Management Research 1: 1-34.

42. Chisti KA (2012) The impact of Asset Quality on Profitability of Private Banks in India. Journal of African Macroeconomic Review 2: 126-146.

43. Gyimah SF, Oscar AJ (2011) Effects of Share Pricing on Firms' Performance in Ghana. Journal of Economics and Sustainable Development 2: 140-153.

44. Irungu P (2013) Effect of Financial Performance Indicators on Market Price of Shares in Commercial Banks of Kenya. International Journal of Management and Business Studies 3: 72-77.

45. Thaddeus EO, Chigbu EE (2012) Analysis of Effect of Financing Leverage on Bank Performance: Evidence from Nigeria. Journal of Public Administration and Governance 2: 178-187.

46. Al Masum A (2014) Dividend Policy and Its Impact on Stock Price - A Study on Commercial Banks Listed in Dhaka Stock Exchange. Global Disclosure of Economics and Business 3: 9-17.

47. Srinivasan P (2012) Determinants of Equity Share Prices in India: A Panel Data Approach. The Romanian Economic Journal 46: 205-228.

48. Bhatt P, Sumangala JK (2012) Impact of Earnings per share on Market Value of an equity share: An Empirical study in Indian Capital Market. Journal of Finance, Accounting and Management 3: 1-14.

49. Silviana, Rocky (2013) Analysis of return on assets and earnings per share on the stock market in the banking companies in bursa efek Indonesia (Indonesia securities exchange). Journal of Global Business and Economics 7.

50. Yuanjuan L, Shishun X (2012) Effectiveness of China's Commercial Banks' Capital Adequacy Ratio Regulation: A Case Study of The Listed Banks. Interdisciplinary Journal of Contemporary Research in Business 4: 58-68.

51. Ezike JE, MO O (2013) Capital Adequacy Standards, Basle Accord and Bank Performance: The Nigerian Experience (A Case Study of Selected Banks in Nigeria). Asian Economic and Financial Review 3: 146-159.

52. Narasimhan VK, Goel M (2013) Capital Adequacy and its Relevance to the Indian Banking Sector: A Study of Four Indian Banks. International Research Journal of Social Sciences 2: 1-5.

53. Cecchetti SG, Li L (2005) Do capital adequacy requirements matter for monetary policy? National Bureau of Economic Research 46: 643-659.

54. Buyuksalvarci A, Abdioglu H (2011) Determinants of capital adequacy ratio in Turkish Banks: A panel data analysis. African Journal of Business Management 5: 11199-11209.

55. Charles O, Kenneth UO (2013) Impact of Credit Risk Management and Capital Adequacy on the Financial Performance of Commercial Banks in Nigeria. Journal of Emerging Issues in Economics, Finance and Banking 2.

56. Fatima N (2014) Capital Adequacy: A Financial Soundness Indicator for Banks. Global Journal of Finance and Management 6: 771-776.

57. Sangmi M, Nazir T (2010) Analyzing Financial Performance of Commercial Banks in India: Application of CAMEL Model. Pakistan Journal of Commerce & Social Sciences 4: 40-55.

58. Mathuva DM (2009) Capital adequacy, Cost Income ratio and the performance of commercial banks: The Kenyan scenario. The International journal of applied economics and Finance 3: 35-47.

59. Moussu C, Petit-Romec A (2014) Roe in banks: myth and reality. Social Science Research Network.

60. Alper D, Anbar A (2011) Bank Specific and Macroeconomic Determinants of Commercial Bank Profitability: Empirical Evidence from Turkey. Business and Economics Research Journal 2: 139-152.

61. Tynys L (2012) Estimating the value and interest rate risk of demand deposits in concentrated markets pp: 1-79.

62. Ogege S, Shiro AA (2013) Does depositing money in bank impact economic growth? Evidence from Nigeria. African Journal of Business Management 7: 196-205.

63. Kunt AD, Huizinga H, Bertay AC (2012) Do we need big banks? Evidence on performance, strategy and market discipline. Journal of Financial Intermediation 22: 532-558.

64. Soyemi KA, Akinpelu L, Ogunleye JO (2013) The Determinants of Profitability among Deposit Money Banks (DMBS) in Nigeria Post Consolidation. Global Advanced Research Journal of Economics, Accounting and Finance 2: 93-103.

65. Biswas S, Koufopoulos K (2013) Bank Capital Structure Relevance: is Bank Equity more Expensive than Deposits? pp: 1-28.

66. Chen YC, Chiu YH, Huang CW (2010) Measuring super-efficiency of financial and nonfinancial holding companies in Taiwan: An application of DEA models. African Journal of Business Management 4: 3122-3133.

67. Alkassim FA (2005) The profitability of Islamic and conventional banking in the GCC countries: A comparative study. Journal of Review of Islamic Economics 13: 5-30.

68. Hunjra AI, Bashir A Comparative Financial Performance Analysis of Conventional and Islamic Banks in Pakistan. Bulletin of Business and Economics 3: 196-206.

69. Lewis M, Davis KT (1987) Domestic and international banking. MIT Press, Business and Economics.

70. Bourke P (1989) Concentration and other determinants of bank profitability in Europe, North America and Australia. Journal of Banking & Finance 13: 65-79.

71. Abiola I, Olausi AS (2014) The Impact of Credit Risk Management on the Commercial Banks Performance in Nigeria. International Journal of Management and Sustainability 3: 295-306.

72. Nirajini A, Priya KB (2013) Impact of Capital Structure on Financial Performance of the Listed Trading Companies in Sri Lanka. International Journal of Scientific and Research Publications 3: 1-9.

73. Olalekan A, Adeyinka S (2013) Capital adequacy and banks' profitability: An empirical evidence from Nigeria. American International Journal of Contemporary Research 3: 87-93.

74. Pastory D, Marobhe M, Kaaya I (2013) The Relationship between Capital Structure and Commercial Bank Performance: A Panel Data Analysis. International Journal of Financial Economics 1: 33-41.

75. Frederick NK (2015) Factors Affecting Performance of Commercial Banks in Uganda: A Case for Domestic Commercial Banks. International Review of Business Research conferences, Mbarara, Uganda.

76. Guisse ML (2012) Financial Performance of the Malaysian Banking Industry: Domestic vs Foreign Banks. Doctoral dissertation, Eastern Mediterranean University, Sakarya, Gazimagusa.

77. Ikpefan OA (2013) Capital adequacy, management and performance in the Nigerian commercial bank (1986-2006). African Journal of Business Management 7: 2938-2950.

78. Barnor C, Odonkor TA (2013) Capital Adequacy and the Performance of Ghanaian Banks. Journal of Business Research 6: 105-117.

79. Gulia Y (2014) Financial Performance of Private Banks In India. Global Journal for Research Analysis 3: 1-14.

80. Abata MA (2014) Asset Quality and Bank Performance: A Study of Commercial Banks in Nigeria. Research Journal of Finance and Accounting 5: 39-44.

81. Manoj PK (2010) Financial soundness of old private sector banks (OPBs) in India and benchmarking the Kerala based OPBs: a 'CAMEL' approach. American Journal of Scientific Research 11: 132-149.

82. Swamy V (2012) Determinants of Bank Asset Quality and Profitability-An Empirical Assessment.

83. Baral KJ (2005) Health check-up of commercial banks in the framework of CAMEL: A case study of joint venture banks in Nepal. Journal of Nepalese Business Studies 2: 41-55.

84. Saksonova S, Solovjova I (2011) Analysis Of The Quality And Profitability Of Assets In The Banking System And The Impact Of Macroeconomic Factors On Its Stability-Case Of Latvia. In International Conference on Applied Economics pp: 537-548.

85. Pastory D, Mutaju M (2013) The Influence of Capital Adequacy on Asset Quality Position of Banks in Tanzania. International Journal of Economics and Finance 5: 179-180.

86. Alhassan AL, Brobbey FO, Asamoah ME (2013) Does Asset Quality Persist on Bank Lending Behavior? Empirical Evidence from Ghana. Global Journal of Management and Business Research Finance 13: 1-8.

87. Bebeji A (2013) Consolidation and Asset Quality Of Banks In Nigeria. International Journal of Business and Management Invention 2: 12-20.

88. Morgan JP (2010) All Eyes on Microfinance Asset Quality. Microfinance Global Valuation Survey.

89. Chaudhary S, Singh S (2012) Impact of Reforms on the Asset Quality in Indian Banking. International Journal of Multidisciplinary Research 2: 13-31.

90. Malik R (2013) Bank Peculiar and Macroeconomic Causes Which Affect the Profitability of Banks: Evidence from Banking Sector of Pakistan.

91. Uppal RK (2009) Priority sector advances: Trends, issues and strategies. Journal of Accounting and Taxation 1: 79-89.

92. Akpan ES, Riman HB (2012) Does Corporate Governance affect Bank Profitability? Evidence from Nigeria. American International Journal of Contemporary Research 2: 135-145.

93. Husain I (2005) Sustainable growth in the financial sector of Pakistan.

94. Nazir MS, Safdar R, Akram M I (2012) Impact of Global Financial Crisis on Banks' Financial Performance in Pakistan. American Journal of Scientific Research pp: 101-110.

95. Mirza N, Alexandre H (2009) Size, value and asset quality premium in European banking stocks.

96. Alhassan AL, Kyereboah-Coleman A, Andoh C (2014) Asset quality in a crisis period: An empirical examination of Ghanaian banks. Review of Development Finance 4: 50-62.

97. Shingjergji A (2013) The Impact of Bank Specific Variables on the Non Performing Loans Ratio in the Albanian Banking System. Research Journal of Finance and Accounting 4: 148-152.

98. Nisar S, Susheng W, Ahmed J, Ke P (2015) Determinants Of Bank's Profitability In Pakistan: A Latest Panel Data Evidence. International Journal of Economics, Commerce and Management 3: 1-16.

99. Kaddumi AD (2014) Effects of Asset and Liability Management On The Financial Performance Of Commercial Banks In Kenya.

100. Kaddumi TA (2015) Impact of Assets quality management on profitability and shareholders' Value-The case of Jordanian Listed Commercial Banks (2001-2012). American Academic & Scholarly Research Journal 7.

101. Tariq W, Usman M, Mir HZ, Aman I, Ali I (2014) Determinants of Commercial Banks Profitability: Empirical Evidence from Pakistan. International Journal of Accounting and Financial Reporting.

102. Kauko K (2007) Managers and Efficiency in Banking. Bank of Finland Research Discussion Paper 11: 1-33.

103. Vijayakumar A (2012) Evaluating performance of banks through camel model: a case study of State Bank of India and its associates. Online International Interdisciplinary Research Journal 2: 104-124.

104. Naceur SB, Kandil M (2006) The Impact of Capital Requirements on Banks' Performance: The Case of Egypt.

105. Avkiran NK, CAI LC (2012) Predicting bank financial distress prior to crises. In New Zealand Finance Colloquium.

106. Dave SR, Bhatt R (2008) Incorporating Intangible Aspects in Performance Evaluation of Indian Banks.

107. Poghosyan T, Cihak M (2011) Determinants of bank distress in Europe: Evidence from a new data set. Journal of Financial Services Research 40: 163-184.

108. Burger A, Moormann J (2008) Productivity in banks: myths & truths of the cost income ratio. Banks and bank systems 3: 85-94.

109. Karim MZA (2001) Comparative bank efficiency across select ASEAN countries. Asian Economic Bulletin 18: 289-304.

110. Davydenko A (2010) Determinants of bank profitability in Ukraine. Undergraduate Economic Review 7: 1-30.

111. Altunbas Y, Gardener EP, Molyneux P, Moore B (2001) Efficiency in European banking. European Economic Review 45: 1931-1955.

112. Rhoades SA (1980) Monopoly and expense preference behavior: An empirical investigation of a behavioralist hypothesis. Southern Economic Journal 47: 419-432.

113. Kumbhakar SC, Vivas AL, Lovell CK, Hasan I (2001) The effects of deregulation on the performance of financial institutions: the case of Spanish savings banks. Journal of Money, Credit and Banking pp: 101-120.

114. Burki AA, Niazi GSK (2006) Impact of financial reforms on efficiency of state-owned, private and foreign banks in Pakistan.

115. Ongore VO, Kusa GB (2013) Determinants of financial performance of commercial banks in Kenya. International Journal of Economics and Financial Issues 3: 237-252.

116. Jaffar M, Manarvi I (2011) Performance comparison of Islamic and Conventional banks in Pakistan. Global journal of management and business research 11: 60-66.

117. Sufian F, Chong RR (2008) Determinants of Bank profitability in a developing economy: Empirical evidence from the Philippines. Asian Academy of Management Journal of Accounting and Finance 4: 91-112.

118. Aftab N, Samad N, Husain T (2015) Historical Analysis of Bank Profitability Using CAMEL Parameters: Role of Ownership and Political Regimes in Pakistan. International Journal of Economics and Finance 7: 144.

119. Lipunga AM (2014) Determinants of Profitability of Listed Commercial Banks in Developing Countries: Evidence from Malawi. Research Journal of Finance and Accounting 5: 41-49.

120. Afolabi B, Adawale AA (2013) Measuring Bank Performance using the C.A.M.E.L. Analytical Technique in a Liberalized Economy: A Case Study of the Nigerian Economy (1971-2005).

121. Khalid U (2006) The effect of privatization and liberalization on banking sector performance in Pakistan. SBP Research Bulletin 2: 403-425.

122. Abdallah W (2013) The impact of financial and non-financial measures on banks' financial strength ratings: The case of the Middle East. University of Salford, Lancashire, United Kingdom.

123. Obamuyi TM (2013) Determinants of Banks Profitability in a Developing Economy: Evidence from Nigeria. Organizations and Markets in Emerging Economies 4: 97-111.

124. Nazir T (2010) Analyzing Financial Performance of Commercial Banks in India: Application of CAMEL Model. Pakistan Journal of Commerce & Social Sciences 4: 40-45.

125. Venkatesan T, Nagarajan SK (2012) An Empirical Study Of Profitability Analysis Of Selected Steel Companies In India. International Journal of Marketing, Financial Services & Management Research 1: 84-100.

126. Alshatti AS (2014) The Effect of the Liquidity Management on Profitability in the Jordanian Commercial Banks. International Journal of Business and Management 10: 62-72.

127. Wet DJ, Toit ED (2006) Return on equity: A popular, but flawed measure of corporate financial performance. South African Journal of Business Management 38: 59-69.

128. Maditinos D, Sevic Z, Theriou N (2006) A Review of the Empirical Literature on Earnings and Economic Value Added (EVA®) in Explaining Stock Market Returns. Which Performance Measure is More Value Relevant in the Athens Stock Exchange (ASE)? 5th Annual Conference of the Hellenic Finance and Accounting Association Thessaloniki, University of Macedonia, Greece.

129. Teker S, Teker D, Kent O (2011) Measuring Commercial Banks' Performances in Turkey: A Proposed Model. Journal of Applied Finance & Banking 1: 97-112.

130. Berzkalne I, Zelgalve E (2014) Return on Equity And Company Characteristics: An Empirical Study of Industries in Latvia. The 8th International Days of Statistics and Economics, Prague, Czech Republic.

131. Farooq M (2007) Forecasts of Future Profitability based on Disaggregated Earnings: A Comparative Analysis of Islamic and Conventional Banks. Journal of Managerial Sciences 7: 255.

132. Hossan F, Habib A (2010) Performance evaluation and ratio analysis of Pharmaceutical Company in Bangladesh. Department of Economic and Informatics, University West, Sweden.

133. Elsiefy E (2013) Determinants of profitability of commercial banks in Qatar: Comparative overview between domestic conventional and Islamic banks during the period 2006-2011. International Journal of Economics and Management Sciences 2: 108-142.

134. Haque A (2014) Comparison of Financial Performance of Commercial Banks: A Case Study in the Context of India (2009-2013). Journal of Finance and Bank Management 2: 01-14.

135. Jha S, Hui X (2012) A comparison of financial performance of commercial banks: A case study of Nepal. African Journal of Business Management 6: 7601-7611.

136. Petersen MA, Schoeman I (2008) Modeling of banking profit via return-on-assets and return-on-equity. In Proceedings of the World Congress on Engineering 2: 1-6.

137. Ahmeti S, Hoti A, Bekteshi SA (2014) Analysis of Financial Performance in the Banking System in Kosovo-the Period 2006-2012. Journal of Knowledge Management, Economics and Information Technology 4.

138. Socol A, Danuletiu AE (2013) Analysis of the Romanian Banks 'Performance through Roa, Roe and Non-Performing Loans Models. Annals Universities Apulensis Series Oeconomica 2.

139. El-Bannany M (2011) Earnings Quality and Other Factors Affecting Intellectual Capital Performance in Banks: The UAE Case. In Proceedings of the European Conference on Intellectual Capital p: 136.

140. Taani K, Banykhaled MHH (2011) The effect of financial ratios, firm size and cash flows from operating activities on earnings per share: (an applied study: on Jordanian industrial sector). International Journal of Social Sciences and Humanity Studies 3: 197-205.

141. Heikal M, Khaddafi M, Ummah A (2014) Influence Analysis of Return on Assets (ROA), Return on Equity (ROE), Net Profit Margin (NPM), Debt To Equity Ratio (DER), and current ratio (CR), Against Corporate Profit Growth In Automotive In Indonesia Stock Exchange. International Journal of Academic Research in Business and Social Sciences 4: 101-114.

142. Han Y, Kim MH, Kim WJ (2012) Determinants of profit efficiency: evidence from Korean savings banks. Applied Financial Economics 22: 1003-1016.

143. Farooq U, Maqbool MQ, Humanyun AA, Nawaz MS, Abbas M (2015) An Empirical Study on Impact Liquidity Risk Management on Firm Performance in the Conventional Banking of Pakistan. IOSR Journal of Business and Management (IOSR-JBM) 17: 110-118.

144. Maness TS, Zietlow JT (2004) Short Term Financial Management. South-Western Educational Publishing. Better world Books.

145. Howells PGA, Bain K (2005) The Economics of Money, Banking and Finance: A European Text. Pearson Education.

146. Tesfaye T (2012) Determinants of Banks Liquidity and their Impact on Financial Performance: empirical study on commercial banks in Ethiopia.

147. Moussa MAB (2015) The Determinants of Bank Liquidity: Case of Tunisia. International Journal of Economics and Financial Issues 5: 249-259.

148. Kurawa JM, Abubakar A (2014) An Evaluation of The Impact of Liquidity on The Profitability of Nigerian Banks. Journal of Management 2: 1-10.

149. Eljelly AM (2004) Liquidity-profitability tradeoff: an empirical investigation in an emerging market. International Journal of Commerce and Management 14: 48-61.

150. Donkor J, Kodua KT (2013) Profitability, Liquidity and Efficiency of Rural Banks: Evidence from Ghana. British Journal of Economics, Finance and Management Sciences 8: 1-11.

151. Al-Smadi MO, Al-Wabel SA (2011) The impact of e-banking on the performance of Jordanian banks. Journal of internet banking and commerce 16: 1-10.

152. Bokpin GA (2013) Corporate disclosure, transparency and firms' cash holdings: Evidence from the Emerging capital market of Ghana. Journal of Economics and International Finance 5: 106-113.

153. Yu Y, Jiang SJ (2010) Corporate life cycle and share repurchases: Evidence from the Taiwan Stock Market. African Journal of Business Management 4: 3139-3148.

154. Chiang YC, Wang CD (2011) Corporate international activities and cash holdings. African Journal of Business Management 5: 2992-3000.

155. Amuzu MS (2010) Cash flow ratio as a measure of performance of listed companies in emerging economies: The Ghana example.

156. Al Masum A, Johora FT (2015) Performance Evaluation of Selected Ceramic Companies of Bangladesh. Asian Business Review 1: 37-48.

157. Anoh A (2012) The impact of liquidity on the performance of commercial bank in Nigeria PLC: A case study of first bank of Nigeria PLC.

158. Agbada AO, Osuji CC (2013) The efficacy of liquidity management and banking performance in Nigeria. International Review of Management and Business Research 2: 223-233.

159. TA A, Ajagbe FA (2012) Analysis of monetary policy on commercial banks in Nigeria. African Journal of Business Management 6: 12038-12042.

160. Lartey VC, Antwi, S, Boadi EK (2013) The relationship between liquidity and profitability of listed banks in Ghana. International Journal of Business and Social Sciences 4: 48-56.

161. Olagunju A, David AO, Samuel OO (2012) Liquidity Management and Commercial Banks' Profitability in Nigeria. Research Journal of Finance and Accounting 2: 24-38.

162. Saleem Q, Rehman RU (2011) Impacts of liquidity ratios on profitability. Interdisciplinary Journal of Research in Business 1: 95-98.

163. Zygmunt J (2013) Does liquidity impact on profitability? 2nd International conference, Conference of Informatics and Management Sciences, ICTIC, Slovakia.

164. Momeni AR, HakimehGharibi GRJ (2014) Comparing The Performance Evaluation Of Tejarat And Mellat Bank Bay Camel Model. Indian Journal of Fundamental and Applied Life Sciences 4: 1071-1082.

165. Reddy SK (2012) Relative performance of commercial banks in India using CAMEL approach. Research Journal of Economics and Business Studies 2: 38-58.

166. Ifeacho C, Ngalawa H (2014) Performance of the South African Banking Sector Since 1994. Journal of Applied Business Research (JABR) 30: 1183-1196.

167. Thirunavukkarasu T, Parthiban E (2015) A Camel Model Analysis of Selected Public and Private Sector Banks. International Journal of Management and Social Sciences (IJMSS) 3: 422-437.

168. Matthew NG, Esther LA (2012) Financial Performance Comparison of Foreign VS Local Banks in Ghana. International Journal of Business and Social Science 3: 82-87.

169. Nagamani M, Williams M (2015) Comparison of the earnings of select commercial banks. International Journal of Research in Economics and Social Sciences 5: 14-18.

170. Prasad KVN, Ravinder G (2012) A camel model analysis of nationalized banks in India. International Journal of Trade and Commerce 1: 23-33.

171. Ogege S, Williams HT, Emerah A (2012) An empirical analysis of capital adequacy in the banking sub-sector of the Nigeria economy. International Journal of Economics and Finance 4: 208.

172. Aspal PK, Nazneen A (2014) An Empirical Analysis of Capital Adequacy in the Indian Private Sector Banks. American Journal of Research Communication 2: 28-42.

173. Elsiefy E (2013) Comparative Analysis of Qatari Islamic Banks Performance versus Conventional Banks Before, During and After the Financial Crisis. International Journal of Business & Commerce 3: 11-41.

174. Kumar S, Sharma R (2014) Performance analysis of top Indian Banks through camel approach. International Journal of Advanced Research in Management and Social Sciences 3: 81-92.

175. Karri HK, Meghani K, Mishra BM (2015) A Comparative Study on Financial Performance of Public Sector Banks in India: An Analysis on Camel Model.

176. De B (2012) Ownership effects on bank performance: A panel study of Indian banks. Indira Gandhi Institute of Development Research, Mumbai, India.

177. Ibe SO (2013) The Impact of Liquidity Management on the Profitability of Banks in Nigeria. Journal of Finance and Bank Management 1: 37-48.

178. Trochim W (2006) Descriptive Statistics. In Research Methods Knowledge Base.

179. Davis JA (1971) Elementary survey analysis. Englewood Cliffs, NJ: Prentice Hall.

Banking Liquidity and Stock Market Prices in ASEAN-3 Economies

Chung TF[1*] and Ariff M[2]

[1]Taylor's University, 47500 Subang Jaya, Selangor, Malaysia
[2]University Putra Malaysia, 43400, Serdang, Selangor, Malaysia

Abstract

The Global Financial Crisis has its origins in the surge in banking liquidity, which contributes to the volatility and instability of financial markets by affecting prices of financial instruments. This paper investigates the impact of banking liquidity, money supply and stock prices in ASEAN-3 economies. Although banking liquidity is widely attributed as one of the causes of financial instability, it is not fully verified or investigated despite earlier research attempts. The transmission channel of banking liquidity to banking credit is through net present value projects of firms. With higher net present value, this will support earnings and consequently share prices of firms will respond positively. This is the thesis statement of our paper and according to a major study, 52% of share returns emanate from macro-economic variables. To control for cross-section dependence and heterogeneity, this study use a panel data of 3 similar countries with 3 equations to study the relationship between money supply, liquidity and share prices over the period 2001:4 to 2012:2. Our findings show that banking liquidity is positively related to money supply with a positive impact on share prices.

Keywords: ASEAN-3; Liquidity; Bubble; Share prices; Dynamic OLS; Structural break; Bootstrapping

Introduction

This paper confirms findings on Friedman's proposal that liquidity is positively impacted by money supply, in discussing the money to liquidity nexus. Whenever the Federal Reserve raises the fund rate, this will cause price turbulence in the US financial markets [1]. Fair identified that monetary announcements by the Fed cause 30 per cent changes to stock prices [2]. In an earlier study, King suggests up to 52 per cent of share prices are from market-wide common factors while a later study by Bernanke and Kuttner says a one percent stock price increase is caused by a 25-basis point cut in the federal funds target rates [3,4]. It is for these reasons that monetary policy announcements are well scrutinized and intensely watched by media and market players. Our research objective is to look into how share prices react to monetary news on interest rates, liquidity and money supply. The third proposition of a money-liquidity nexus has not been verified by empirical studies. Money supply impact share prices through its impact on firms cost of capital and firms' capacity to raise new capital and invest, which in turn will affect consumption and economic growth through the wealth effect. When share prices fluctuate, this will impact on firms cost of capital and therefore money supply will have an impact on share price, the thesis statement of this paper.

Given the importance of the impact of money supply on share prices, policy makers are keen to know about the impact of monetary policy on share prices. Studies have shown that the size of the impact of monetary policy on share prices is significant and their effect is not symmetrical. During recession and amidst tight liquidity conditions, the impact of monetary policy on share prices doubles that of normal economic environment. The earlier finance literature, have linked share prices to market-wide macro factors as in the arbitrage pricing theory [5,6]. In macro-economics, the standard IS-LM model used Aggregate demand and Aggregate Supply (AD/AS) to identify the role of equity market in aggregate demand. In later models with better measurement techniques, these are further broken down into long-term and short-term dynamics.

In this paper, the monetary transmission mechanism to the share market is via bank credits to firms' earnings. This paper links the macro-economic aggregates of money supply to banking liquidity on to share prices in these three ASEAN countries (Malaysia, Singapore and Thailand). Finance theory has identified firm specific factors in share pricing equations, which are short-term in nature. In the longer-term, macro-economic factors will dominate share pricing. For successful investors, Musílek advise them to pay attention to price-shaping macro-economic factors [7]. Similar conclusions were also expressed by Flannery and Protopapadakis [8]. A breakdown of the determinants of share price movements attributed that 52 per cent are contributed by macro-economic factors, 10 per cent by industry factor and 38 per cent by firm specific factors.

GDP, money supply, liquidity, inflation and interest rates are the main macro-economic factors shaping share prices. Among the macro-economic factors, the money to liquidity nexus has yet to be fully verified in Friedman, while his proposition of a *negative* money supply effect on interest rate has been verified in a number of studies.

The main objective of this paper is to report evidence in support of money-to-banking-liquidity to stock price effect in each of three ASEAN countries chosen. These three countries are more homogenous in terms of open capital markets and have implemented large-scale financial liberalization since 1997. We apply recent econometric techniques using dynamic heterogeneous panel unit root estimations and cointegration tests to examine the dynamic relationship among stock price, liquidity and money supply in this paper.

Our paper is organized as below: A very brief discussion of the literature on money supply, liquidity and share prices is provided in Section 2. To prepare the data used in the test models, we transform the data as shown in Section 3. Section 4 contains a discussion of the findings and in Section 5 we conclude on our major findings.

***Corresponding author:** Tin-fah Chung, senior lecturer, Taylor's University, 47500 Subang Jaya, Selangor, Malaysia, E-mail: tinfah@yahoo.com

Literature Review on Money Supply, Liquidity, Share Price and Monetary Regime Changes

In this section, a brief literature review on money supply, liquidity, share price and monetary regime is carried out. The discussion on liquidity effect precedes our discussion on the link between banking liquidity and share prices in the context of monetary transmission mechanism in the latter part of the section.

Money supply effect in the transmission mechanism

A widely established representation in standard macroeconomics textbook, to show the effect on interest rates of a change in monetary policy (Friedman's interest effect) use:

$$M_t^d = a_1 + a_2 r_t + \varepsilon_t^d \quad (1.1)$$

$$M_t^s = b_1 + b_2 r_t + \varepsilon_t^s \quad (1.2)$$

$$\therefore M_t^d = M_t^s \quad (1.3)$$

where M^d indicates demand, M^s supply, M_t is the log of nominal money, r_t, is the nominal interest rate, while ε_t^d and ε_t^s are mutually correlated demand and supply shocks. r_t responds to shifts in money supply engineered by varying β_1 and the relation $dr_t/db_1=(a_2-b_2)^{-1}$means that the interest rate decreases when money supply increases, provided that $a_2<0$ and $b_2 <- a_2$. The liquidity effect is the negative reaction of changes to interest rate when there is a rise in money supply.

With a decline in interest rates and a corresponding reduction in discount rate (cost of equity) in future cash flow calculation, share prices are expected to rise. Sprinkel explicitly tested a model incorporating Simple Quantity Theory (SQT) as an asset pricing model [9]. With an increase in money supply, the portfolio will be thrown out of balance because the desired holding compared to actual cash holding is in disequilibrium. Since the stock of money must be held by some agents, the prices of other assets as well as goods and services for consumption are bid up to a new equilibrium level. Through this adjustment mechanism on stocks, money supply and stock prices is positively related. The above mechanism illustrates a combination of SQT and portfolio theory.

Liquidity serves as the missing link between money and aggregate demand. During boom conditions, increases in liquidity bolster investment and financial activities, when money supply is eased (Quantitative easing by the Fed in 2012). After the credit splurge of 1994-2004, which causes the asset price bubbles before the Global Financial Crisis [10], liquidity resurfaces as the focus of research and policy making. The interaction between liquidity and money supply is also the focus of post-Keynesian studies on the endogeneity of money.

Liquidity effect

The negative link between money supply and interest rates, as shown above, has been widely acknowledged by macroeconomists and policy makers. However, the positive liquidity effect link to income and inflation is not well established. Changes in the supply of money are, therefore, a proxy for likely changes in return on money holdings, which is the basis of why central bank uses statutory reserve requirements to control liquidity and money supply.

All market participants, such as institutions, dealers and wealthy individuals respond to money balance changes. Changes in stock prices and returns will result from this liquidity effect with an negative coefficient through this channel. Despite numerous attempts to measure to this liquidity effect, there has been little success, as the use of low frequency data will mix the effects of policy on economic variables with the effects of economic variables on policy. To overcome this, Hamilton tried to estimate the daily liquidity effect by estimating the response of federal funds rate to exogenous reserve supply shocks using daily data [11].

Share prices

Share prices are affected by a host of factors - macroeconomic, microeconomic, psychological and subjective factors. Both macroeconomic and microeconomic factors affect the direction and volatility of where stock markets are heading, notwithstanding the role given to psychological and subjective factors in the behavioural finance literature. The dominant role of macroeconomic factors on share prices is exemplified in the theory of Arbitrage Pricing Theory and tested in Chen et al. [6].

Among other studies that link share prices to macro factors are the following for:

Developed markets such as USA, Japan and Europe - Clare and Thomas and Flannery and Protopapadakis [8,12].

Developing markets in East Asia - Bailey and Chung, Mookerjee and Yu, Kwon and Shin, Ibrahim and Aziz (2003) [13-15].

Comparative markets - Cheung and Ng, Bilson, Wongbangpo and Sharma [16-18].

The theoretical underpinning of most of these studies that link macro factors to share prices can perhaps be seen in the portfolio model of Cooper [19]. In the model he assumes that individuals could hold wealth in two forms, money and common stock. A portfolio is said to be balanced when the marginal returns to holding these two assets are equal.

$$MNPS_t^M - \bar{P} = MNPS_t^r + \bar{r}_t^s \quad (2)$$

where, using the term of the author, the left side is the return to money asset and the right side is the return to stock asset;

$\bar{P}_t$ is anticipated percentage change in general price level;

$\bar{r}_t^*$ is the anticipated real pecuniary return of stocks (dividend plus change in stock prices);

$MNPS_t^s$ is marginal pecuniary return to the j-th asset (the risk of j-th assets is incorporated into its pecuniary returns.

$MNPS_t^M$ is implicitly a function of demand for money except for returns on alternative assets. In equilibrium, an underlying assumption is that the positive income effect on $MNPS_t^{M,S}$ cancel each other.

By re-arranging this equation, it could be shown that the stock return is:

$$\bar{r}_t^s = (MNPS_t^M - \bar{P}) - MNPS_t^s \quad (3)$$

Thus, Cooper's model is equivalent to the asset pricing model in finance, which provides the theoretical framework for this study. It would be interesting to examine the link between the liquidity effects from money supply affecting the stock prices, as proposed in this study [47].

The model of equity pricing used in finance with this kind of effect is:

$$P_0 = \sum_t^N = 1\frac{D_0(1+gt)^t}{(1+i_t+r_t)^t} \quad (4)$$

where P_0 is the current price of a share; D_0 is the dividend at time 0;

g is the constant growth rate of dividends; i_t is the risk-free rate at time t; and r_t is the equity risk premium at time t. By substituting EPS (payout ratio), the numerator may be replaced as (POR) . Thus, a proxy to represent EPS could be used to test if PO is significantly affected by earnings proxy using the IPI.

The equation "D=EPS (payout)", shows that stock prices are correlated with EPS. In this paper we used Industrial output (IPI as a proxy to represent corporate earnings, as payout ratios are unlikely to change in most economies. A lesson from the recent Global Financial Crisis (GFC) was that share prices lead earnings. The aftermath of the crisis has attracted a lot of rethinking on the impact of liquidity on money supply and share prices.

The Cooper model attempts to capture the relationship between money supply and stock prices as started by Sprinkel [9]. The imbalance in the financial sector and real sector resulting in liquidity surges that led to the GFC has revived interest in this relationship [10].

The ASEAN-3 (Malaysia, Singapore and Thailand) Economies

In 1967, the Association of Southeast Asian Nations (ASEAN) was inaugurated with four countries. Over time, this group has since expanded to include 10 countries. The aim of ASEAN is to create an integrated economic bloc and promote modernization so that political conflict will be minimized. Broadly, ASEAN can be divided into the more developed four core group which accounts for four per cent of world trade. These four countries have achieved a greater degree of economic and financial integration among themselves and with the developed countries. The remaining six rank lower in terms of development and modernization are at the peripheral.

The ASEAN countries can be divided into two major categories. The inner core group of four countries, accounts for four per cent of world trade, having achieved a greater degree of economic and financial integration among themselves and with the developed countries. However, the remaining peripheral six lag behind in development and modernization. The inner group is generally richer in income and more developed than those at the periphery. As the four core group adopt similar economic and financial regulations with the industrial countries, their financial integration is also higher. On the whole, the ASEAN group exports more merchandise goods over imports, while they are importers of commercial services.

From the mid-1980s, the inner four core group has embarked on capital market reforms to spearhead the development of the financial sector to the same level as those in developed countries. The banking sector has been the focus of these reforms as they bore the brunt of the financial crisis. The reforms have help to reduce the country's reliance on bank borrowings as a source of funding to equity and fixed-income markets to diversify the risks and tap on long-term funds for funding the infrastructure projects. Last year in 2015, the ASEAN group signed an agreement to form the ASEAN Economic Community. This will provide broad strategic measures from 2016-2025 to realize the following objectives: i) highly integrated and cohesive economy; (ii) competitive, innovative, and dynamic ASEAN; (iii) enhanced connectivity and sectoral cooperation; (iv) resilient, inclusive, people-oriented, and people-centered ASEAN; and (v) global ASEAN. This study using a panel of data from three inner core ASEAN countries (Malaysia, Singapore and Thailand) to investigate whether there is a significant relationship between stock prices and banking liquidity arising from their money supply in these core economies.

Methodology

Using cointegration analysis to test for a long-term relationship between share prices and underlying macroeconomic variables, we first conduct VECM test. In this test, Johansen cointegrating technique requires the variables in the model should be integrated of first order to pass a test of stationarity. A further vector autoregressive VAR-like model is applied [20,21].

In panel modeling, the estimator bias problem emerges for both static and dynamic models when we introduce heterogeneity in order to obtain different slope coefficient for the different cross section units [22].

Pool mean group (PMG) and mean group (MG)

To account for the different slopes in dynamic panels, two estimators were proposed by Pesaran [23]: the mean group (MG) estimator and the pooled mean group (PMG) estimator. The long-run parameters for the panel are estimated using an average of their long-run parameters from a regression using ARDL models of individual countries. Separate equations are estimated for each country and the distributions of their coefficients are examined across groups. It is one extreme of estimation because it just makes use of averaging in its estimation procedure. It does not consider any possibility of same parameters across groups.

In samples where there are a large number of observations and large number of groups, Pesaran added the PMGE estimator [23,24]. Both PMG and MG estimators are intermediate estimators because both used averaging and pooling in its estimation procedure. To account for variation in the intercepts, short-run dynamics and error variances across groups, Peseran proposed the PMGE estimator. It avoids the inconsistency problem from heterogeneous short-run dynamics in pooling the long-run parameters.

However, those with long-run dynamics are not allowed to differ across groups. Plus, the PMG relaxes the restriction on the common coefficient of short run while maintaining the assumption on the homogeneity of long run slope. The estimation of the PMG requires re-parameterization.

Estimator to account for dynamic fixed effects (DFEE)

To overcome the problems of the PMGE and MGE estimators, dynamic fixed effects estimator (DFEE) is also used to cross-checked the co-integrating vector. DFEE specifications control the country specific effects and rely on a pooling of cross-sections. To resolve the problem, the DFEE estimator also restricts the coefficient of co-integrating vector to be equal across all panels like the PMGE. In the PMGE model of Pesaran et al [23,24], an adjustment coefficient PMGE or error correction term, φ_i is computed. This φ_i indicates the amount of adjustment for each period.

The Hausman test is used to evaluate which estimator, MPG or PMGE is more appropriate. The Null hypothesis test for PMGE is that it is efficient and consistent against the alternative hypothesis: MGE is consistent. It allows for a choice between MGE and DFEE. To decide among the three different estimators, MGE, DFEE and PMGE, the Hausman test is used. As demonstrated by the Granger representation theorem [25], if these results show that the error correction term is significant, we can conclude there is cointegration.

The long run model in (5.1)

$$SP_{it} = \mu_{it} + \beta_{1t} LQ_{it} + \beta_{2t} MS_{it} + \beta_{3t} IPI_{it} + \varepsilon_{it} \quad (5.1)$$

will be transformed into the auto-regressive distributed lags ARDL (1,1,1) dynamic panel specification as follows:

$$SP_{it} = \mu_{it} + \lambda SP_{i,t-1} + \beta_{1t}LQ_{it-1} + \beta_{2t}MS_{it-1} + \beta_{3t}IPI_{it-1} + \varepsilon_{it} \quad (5.2)$$

By putting changing sign to the SPit, the model in (5.2) becomes

$$\Delta SP_{it} = \mu_{it} + (\lambda - 1)SP_{i,t-1} + \beta_{1t}LQ_{it-1} + \beta_{2t}MS_{it-1} + \beta_{3t}IPI_{it-1} + \varepsilon_{it} \quad (5.3)$$

From (5.2), by normalizing each coefficient of the right hand side variables by the coefficient of the SP_{t-1}, i.e (λ_i-1) or $-(1-\lambda_i)$ since $\lambda_i<1$,

Let $\phi_i = -(1-\lambda_i)$

$$\theta_{0i} = \frac{\mu_i}{1-\lambda_i} \quad \theta_{1i} = \frac{\beta_{10i}+\beta_{11i}}{1-\lambda_i} \quad \theta_{2i} = \frac{\beta_{20i}+\beta_{21i}}{1-\lambda_i} \quad \theta_{3i} = \frac{\beta_{30i}+\beta_{31i}}{1-\lambda_i}$$

By considering the normalized long run coefficient of (5.2), the error correction re-parameterization of (5.2) will be:

$$\Delta SP_{it} = \mu_{it} + \phi_i\left(SP_{i,t-1} - \theta_{0i} - \theta_{1i}LQ_{it} - \theta_{1i}MS_{it} - \theta_{1i}IPI_{it}\right) + \beta_{1t}\Delta LQ_{it} + \beta_{2t}\Delta MS_{it} + \beta_{3t}\Delta IPI_{it} + \varepsilon_{it} \quad (5.4)$$

←Long run relations→ ←Short run dynamics→

The MG estimator can easily be computed from the long run coefficient of parameters from the average of the parameter value for individual groups. For instance, the dynamic specification as follows:

$$SP_{it} = \mu_{it} + \lambda SP_{i,t-1} + \beta_{1t}LQ_{it-1} + \beta_{2t}MS_{it-1} + \beta_{3t}IPI_{it-1} + \varepsilon_{it} \quad (5.5)$$

The long-run parameter coefficient for equation above will be: $\theta_{0i} = \frac{\beta_{1i}}{1-\lambda_i}$

So, the whole long-run parameter will be represented as the average of long-run parameter across a group as follows: $\bar{\theta} = \frac{1}{N}\sum_{i=1}^{N}\theta_i \quad \bar{\mu} = \frac{1}{N}\sum_{i=1}^{N}\mu_i$

When the number of groups and cross sections is considerably large, the estimator for MG will be efficient even when the series is I(1). But the estimator tends to be biased when the number of time series observations is small.

The estimation of PMG and MG will be based on the error correction model in (5.4). The focus is on the long run coefficient (i.e θ_{1i}, θ_{2i}, θ_{3i} and θ_{4i}), which indicates the elasticity of LQ, MS and IPI factors towards the SP across different country stock markets. Due to the uniqueness of the operation for each country, the coefficient for each factor might vary across the panels. As the coefficient estimates are for long term equilibrium, it contains the theoretical information which is very important for each country's policy making. The error correction speed adjustment, ϕ_i also provides significant information to the investors: ϕ_i in equation (5.4) provides information on how long it is needed for the short run dynamics to return to long run equilibrium.

Normally, the short run coefficient usually will differ from the long run equilibrium affected by events like seasonality effect (noise), economic boom or recession. But, this temporaneous effects due to the short run dynamic result will eventually return to the long run equilibrium. The positive sign of the ϕ_i implies return to the long run relationships from points above the regression line [26]. The negative sign also shows the return to long run equilibrium but in opposite direction (from below). The ϕ_i is expected to be statistically significant as the insignificant coefficient of ϕ_i (i.e ϕ_i=0) implies the absence of long run equilibrium. In the absence of long run equilibrium, the results will be inconclusive theoretically.

Panel unit root tests

The existence of unit roots cannot be ruled based on a sufficient long panel dataset of 10 years. The panel unit root test is carried out using Maddala and Wu and Choi where the p-values of the test statistics for a unit root in each cross-sectional unit (the ADF-test or the PP-test) are shown [27,28].

The null hypothesis for both Fisher (P_λ) Chi-square panel unit root test are shown below:

- H_0: panel data has unit root (assumes individual unit root process)
- H_1: panel data has no unit root

We use the two different tests to confirm our results. The selection of the appropriate lag length was made using the Schwarz Bayesian Information Criterion.

Hypotheses

It is an empirical question [29-31], whether share returns are affected by economic indicators such as industrial production, inflation, interest rates, Treasury bill rate, liquidity, and money supply. King [3], and Thorbecke and Coppock have shown that share prices are affected by macroeconomic factors up to 50% and 32% respectively [32]. The use of cointegration will show whether these economic variables are cointegrated with into share prices. A system of equations comprising stock returns (P) and liquidity (LQ), is developed to be solved endogenously as follows [64]:

$$SP_{it} = f\left[LQ_{it}^{-}, MS_{it}^{+}, IPI_{it}^{+}\right] \quad (6.1)$$

$$LQ_{it} = f\left[MS_{it}^{+}, Y_{it}^{+}, LR_{it}^{-}\right] \quad (6.2)$$

$$MS_{it} = f\left[LQ_{it}^{+}, Y_{it}^{+}, TBR_{it}^{-}, SP_{it}^{+}, CPI_{it}^{+}, CPI(1)_{it}^{+}\right] \quad (6.3)$$

where SP_{it} is aggregate share price index, LQ_{it} is liquidity as proxied by reserve money, MS_{it} is money supply, IPI is industrial production index, Y is real GDP, LR is lending rate, TRB is Treasury bill rate and CPI is inflation. All variables are difference in log.

The operational model is parameterized as:

$$\ln SP_{it} = a_0 + a_1 \ln LQ_{it} + a_2 \ln MS_{it} + a_3 \ln IPI_{it} + e_{it} \quad (7.1)$$

$$\ln LQ_{it} = b_0 + b_1 \ln MS_{it} + b_2 \ln Y_{it} + b_3 LR_{it} + z_{it} \quad (7.2)$$

$$\ln MS_{it} = c_0 + c_1 \ln Y_{it} + c_2 \ln LQ_{it} + c_3 \ln SP_{it} + c_4 TBR_{it} + c_5 \ln CPI_{it} + v_{it} \quad (7.3)$$

This is used to test two separate set of hypotheses tests:

H_1: MS causes Liquidity

H_2: Liquidity causes Share Prices.

Data and variables

The data series from 2001:4- 2012:2 are sourced from Datastream and cross-checked against the dataset of International Monetary Fund (IMF) for external validity. Quarterly data are used for all three countries. As a proxy for earnings, we use the Industrial Production Index (IPI) which is highly correlated with national income, which in turn is known to determine the earnings of firms in a modern economy [47]. Hence, we use the log change of IPI as a proxy for earnings in the equation for asset pricing: if IPI goes up, the earnings of the firms go up.

Another variable liquidity is difficult to specify. In the literature, there are three alternative proxies: bid-ask spread used in market studies [33]; volume of transactions [34,35]; reserve money [36]. In this paper, we use reserve money as a proxy for banking liquidity, as the amount of liquidity in the banking system depends on how much reserves it has kept with the central bank [37-40]. In this sense, liquidity has an inverse relationship to reserves. All variables are seasonally adjusted where available and transformed to logarithmic form, with the exception of interest rates, which are the local 3-month Treasury bill rate, TBR and Lending Rate, LR [41,42].

Our literature review in section 2 show the relationship between share prices and corporate dividend. The relationship of the two depend in the long run on earnings of the corporations, which directly depends on IPI. There is a need to control for the effect of earnings on share prices and liquidity in the system of equations [43-46]. IPI is chosen as a proxy for earnings, after we confirm the cointegration tests between nominal GDP and IPI [47]. Finally, monetary regime changes and crises are controlled using dummies.

Descriptive statistics

Since the JB statistic for most variables are >5.9, they are not normally distributed, as the variables are skewed (>0, for normality should be close to 0). For the period 2001:4- 2012:2, the average Treasury bill and lending rate are 2.14 per cent and 6.04 per cent respectively. Inflation which is measured as mean difference in log CPI, averaged at 4.66 per cent during the period. DLSPRICE which measure share price returns, show a return of 2 per cent pa during the period, achieving a high of 27% during the boom conditions of 2003 and a low of 42% in the aftermath of 2008 share price correction (Table 1) [48-52].

Panel unit root tests using phillips-perron fisher tests

The tests on panel unit root tests are carried using Maddala and Wu and Choi [27,28].

Fisher tests as shown in Table 2.

We tested the following hypotheses:

H_0: the data series in the panel contains a unit root, against

H_1: at least one of the individual series in the panel is stationary

The decision criteria at the 10 per cent level is: accept null of non-stationary if: p-value >10 per cent and to reject null if: p-value <10 per cent, implying the data is stationary [53-55].

Other than LRGDP and LRLQ, the results in Table 2 show that all the variables contain a unit root at the one per cent and ten cent level of significance [56-58]. For money supply (LRM2), the Fisher chi-square statistic and Choi Z-statistic were 2.263 and 0.941 respectively, with p-values of 0.89 and 0.83, above the 10 percent level of significance. When the variables are first-differenced for testing, the alternative hypothesis of stationary is accepted, which leads us conclude that all variables are integrated of order one or I(1) (Table 2).

After testing for unit root and concluding that these variables are I(1), we carried out the Pedronic panel cointegration test.

Pedroni panel cointegration tests for money supply, liquidity and share price

The use of panel cointegration is to enable researchers to selectively pool information for common long-run relationships from across the panel, allowing for the associated short-run dynamics and fixed effects to be heterogeneous across different members of the panel [61].

This is implemented as a residual-based test of the null hypothesis:

Null: H_0: γ_i for all *i*.

Alternative: H_A: $\gamma_i=\gamma<1$ for all *i*.

The result of panel cointegration test for share price, liquidity and money supply based on Pedroni panel (v, rho, pp and adf) and group (v, rho, pp and adf) statistics shown in Table 3.

Lsprice: The *p*-value for Panel PP-statistics and ADF-statistics was <1% for within dimension and between dimension respectively. Thus we can reject the Null hypothesis of no cointegration. We can safely say that the common and individual auto regression coefficients are cointegrated. Similarly for Lrlq: *p*-values for group-pp for between dimension was less <1% and for lrm2, *p*-values for panel v-statistic was less <5%. Thus we can reject the Null hypothesis of no cointegration. We can safely say that the common and individual auto regression coefficients are cointegrated for share price, liquidity and money supply [27,28].

Results of Regression

The regression estimates are discussed in this section. The cointegrating equations using PMG, MG and DFE on panel data of 3 countries are presented next.

Cointegrating equations using PMG, MG and DFE on panel data - a comparison

The results from the long-run relationship of share price, liquidity and money supply are presented in Table 4a, and indicate that all

	LCPI	LR	LRGDP	LRIPI	LRLQ	LRM2	LSPRICE	DLSPRICE	TBR
Mean	4.66	6.04	6.73	0	4.64	7.03	5.39	0.02	2.14
Median	4.66	6	4.79	-0.01	5.55	7.93	4.85	0.03	2.28
Maximum	4.83	7.5	11.07	0.33	6.74	9.29	7.38	0.27	4.91
Minimum	4.51	5.3	4.36	-0.29	1.76	4.26	3.93	-0.42	0.21
Std. Dev.	0.08	0.67	2.92	0.14	1.86	1.9	1.14	0.1	1.15
Skewness	0.09	0.46	0.7	0.11	-0.61	-0.54	0.61	-1.04	-0.01
Kurtosis	1.84	1.91	1.51	2.4	1.52	1.52	1.69	6.64	2.23
Jarque-Bera	7.19	10.73	22.07	2.13	19.43	17.53	16.93	92.41	3.1
Probability	0.03	0	0	0.34	0	0	0	0	0.21
Sum	587.24	760.83	848	0.12	585.14	886.28	679.73	2.91	269.34
Sum Sq. Dev.	0.87	56.76	1063.96	2.37	430.78	450.85	163.68	1.36	165.6
Observations	126	126	126	126	126	126	126	126	126

Table 1: Descriptive statistics of the panel variables. Note: All variables are restated in logs except for TBR and LR. DLSPRICE is the difference in share prices measure the return in share prices The variables LSPRICE, LRM2, LRIPI, LRGDP, LCPI, TBR, LR and LRLQ represent Share price index, Money supply, Industrial production index, Income, Inflation, Treasury bill rate, Lending rate and Reserve money respectively.

Variables	Fisher chi-square statistic		Choi Z-statistic	
	Level	Difference	Level	Difference
LSPRICE	5.65265	30.1579***	-0.33782	-4.25075***
	-0.4632	0	-0.3677	0
LRM2	2.26398	48.5210***	0.94176	-5.72605***
	-0.8939	0	-0.8268	0
LRLQ	16.4100*	157.704***	-1.8	-10.6652***
	-0.0117	0	-0.0359	0
LRIPI	8.54115	136.321***	-1.00672	-10.3019***
	-0.2011	0	-0.157	0
TBR	2.59157	33.7573***	0.78759	-4.50771***
	-0.8581	0	-0.7845	0
LCPI	5.10797	57.1310***	0.18243	-6.21384***
	-0.53	0	-0.5724	0
LRGDP	17.4731***	180.647***	-2.60151***	-12.1164***
	-0.008	0	-0.0046	0
LR	3.2433	33.4376***	0.3815	-4.49963***
	-0.7777	0	-0.6486	0

Table 2: Panel Unit root tests – Fisher Phillips-Perron tests. Note: Numbers in parentheses are p-values. ***, ** denote significance at the 1 and 5 percent levels respectively. Δ denotes first difference. Both variables are taken in natural logarithms.

Alternative hypothesis: common AR coefs. (within-dimension)						
	LSPRICE		LRLQ		LRM2	
	Statistic	**Prob.**	**Statistic**	**Prob.**	**Statistic**	**Prob.**
Panel v-Statistic	0.60132	0.2738	-0.4235	0.6641	1.83068	0.0336*
Panel rho-Statistic	-0.8081	0.2095	0.45856	0.6767	1.62933	0.9484
Panel PP-Statistic	-2.1612	0.0153*	0.09237	0.6368	0.92784	0.8233
Panel ADF-Statistic	-3.0326	0.0012*	0.52307	0.6995	1.14167	0.8732
Alternative hypothesis: individual AR coefs. (between-dimension)						
	Statistic	Prob.	Statistic	Prob.	Statistic	Prob.
Group rho-Statistic	-0.0431	0.4828	-0.828	0.2038	1.9884	0.9766
Group PP-Statistic	-1.7587	0.0303*	-2.9274	0.0017*	1.01873	0.8458
Group ADF-Statistic	-3.0095	0.0013*	0.0376	0.1742	1.44894	0.9263

* denote significance of coefficients.

Table 3: Pedroni residual cointegration test values for the panel.

Variables	**MG**		**DFE**		**PMG**	
	Long Run Parameters					
	Coefficient	**p-value**	**Coefficient**	**p-value**	**Coefficient p-value**	**p-value**
LRLQ	-0.79	0.51	-0.63	0.37	-2.61	0.00
LRM2	1.59	0.01	1.14	0.00	2.61	0.00
LRIPI	0.84	0.00	1.17	0.00	1.07	0.00
	Average Convergence		**Parameters**			
φi	-0.44	0.00	-0.29	0.00	-0.30	0.15
	Short Run Parameters					
ΔLRLQ	0.38	0.03	0.15	0.09	0.42	0.00
ΔLRM2	-0.58	0.31	-0.63	0.39	-0.41	0.58
ΔLRIPI	0.47	0.12	0.37	0.01	0.46	0.17
Constant	-0.44	0.36	0.09	0.85	-0.34	0.27

* denote significance of coefficients.

Table 4a: 1st Equation – Share Price (LSPRICE).

variables have the correct hypothesized sign. In Table 4a, the long-run coefficients of LRM2, LRLQ and LRIPI seem to be consistent across the three estimators for LSPRICE. There is a negative relationship with liquidity (LRLQ) and positive relationship with money supply (LRM2) and industrial production index (LIPI). The symbol (φ_i) which measure the error correction term is negative and less than 1 in absolute sense. At the 1% level, φ_i is statistically significant for MG and DFE, but not for PMG (*p-value of* 15%) (Table 4a).

However, in the short run (SR), we can see the elasticity of LSPRICE as against LRLQ, LRM2 and LRIPI. The p value for ECT is 3%, 31% and 12%. The null hypothesis of cointegration is accepted for LRLQ (*p*<5%) and no correlation (*p*>10%*)* for money supply and industrial production index [62,63]. We conclude that in the short run (short term), ECT for LRM2 and LRIPI are not significantly affecting LSRICE. We can safely say that LSPRICE depends on the long run equilibrium of the combination between these variables (LRLQ, LRM2 and LRIPI).

The ECT coefficient of 0.44 reflects the period in which LSPRIC will return to equilibrium. Here, in the long run, it will take roughly

Variables	MG		DFE		PMG	
	Long Run Parameters					
	Coefficient	p-value	Coefficient	p-value	Coefficient p-value	p-value
LRM2	-0.29	0.64	0.93	0.21	0.44	0.08
LRGDP	2.13	0.10	0.54	0.24	0.53	0.10
LR	1.21	0.22	0.12	0.63	0.87	0.02
	Average Convergence		Parameters			
φi	-0.36	0.06	-0.08	0.12	-0.11	0.11
	Short Run Parameters					
ΔLRM2	0.69	0.01	0.70	0.00	0.83	0.00
ΔLRGDP	0.56	0.16	0.65	0.05	0.73	0.11
ΔLR	-0.46	0.33	-0.03	0.03	-0.30	0.30
Constant	-3.29	0.00	-0.50	0.00	-0.68	0.05

* denote significance of coefficients.

Table 4b: 2nd Equation – Liquidity (LRLQ).

Variables	MG		DFE		PMG	
	Long Run		Parameters			
	Coefficient	p-value	Coefficient	p-value	Coefficient p-value	p-value
LRLQ	0.98	0	0.14	0.43	1.01	0
LSPRICE	-0.26	0.38	0.11	0.27	0.13	0.02
LRGDP	2.52	0.38	1.5	0	-1.25	0
TBR	-0.12	0.35	0.02	0.68	0	0.76
LCPI	-3.65	0.28	-0.38	0.38	1.21	0
	Average Convergence		Parameters			
φi	-0.26	0.02	-0.08	0	-0.14	0.32
		Short Run	Parameters			
ΔLRLQ	-0.07	0.72	0.15	0.01	0.03	0.92
ΔLSPRIC	0.03	0.38	0.02	0.65	0.03	0.46
ΔLRGDP	-0.1	0.78	-0.15	0.02	0.01	0.96
ΔTBR	-0.02	0.02	0	0.93	-0.02	0
ΔLCPI	-1.03	0.22	-1.39	0.01	-1.42	0.04
Constant	0.39	0.72	-0.19	0.07	0.35	0.17

Table 4c: 3rd Equation – Money Supply (LRM2).

MG and DFE	MG and PMG
Ho: DFE estimator is efficient and consistent but MG is not efficieint.	**Ho**: PMG estimator is efficient and consistent but MG is not efficieint.
Eq1 : p-value=no values	Eq1: p-value=no values
Eq2: p-value=no values	Eq2 : p-value=no values
Eq 3: p-value=1.0 >0	Eq 3 : p-value=0.88 >0
For EQ1 and 2, no coefficients in common.and no tests conducted. For Eq3 - Since Ho is not rejected, DFE estimator is efficient and consistent than MG estimator	For EQ1 and 2, no coefficients in common and no tests conducted. For Eq3 : Since Ho is not rejected, PMG estimator is efficient and consistent than MG estimator
Overall Decision: Both DFE and PMG estimators are found to be more eficient and consistent than MG estimator in both Hausman tests, respectively. While PMG estimator dominates the DFE estimator because it permits heterogeneity in shor run coefficients. Hence PMG estimates should be relied upon, among the three estimators.	

Table 4d: Hausman test for selection between.

2.3 periods, or 2 quarters (referring to our data time scale in quarter) for LSPRICE to return to equilibrium if it deviates from regression line (taken as 1 / 0.44).

In Table 4b, the long-run coefficients of LRM2, LRGDP and LR seem to be consistent across the three estimators for LRLQ. There is a negative relationship with money supply (LRM2) and positive relationship with gdp (LRGDP) and lending rate (LR). The symbol (φ_i), the error correction term is negative and less than 1 in absolute sense. The ECT coefficient, φ_i are statistically significant for MG at 0.06 while for DFE and PMG are not significant since the p-values are 0.12 and 0.11 respectively (Table 4b).

In Table 4c, the long-run coefficients of LRLQ, LSPRICE, LRGDP, TBR and LCPI seem to be consistent across the three estimators for LRM2. There is a negative relationship with share price (LSPRICE), treasury bill rate (tbr) and inflation (LCPI) and positive relationship with liquidity (LRLQ) and gdp (LRGDP). The error correction term (φi) is negative and less than 1 in absolute sense. φi is statistically significant for MG and DFE at 2% and 8% respectively, while for PMG not significant at 32% (Tables 4c, 4d and 5).

In Table 5 statistics refer to final PMG regression of individual countries. We notice that in the long run, ECT for all countries are the same, while in the short run it differs. As each country is unique and heterogeneous, the short run is different. For LSPRICE, all countries (except Thailand) have p value of < than 1%. We conclude that, except for Thailand we do not accept the null hypothesis of no correlation for the ASEAN-3 countries. For LRLQ, (except Thailand), all countries have p-value of < than 1%. This means that, for all countries, we do not accept the null hypothesis of no correlation. For LRM2, all countries

LSPRICE												
Country	ECT	p-val	LRLQ	p-val	LRM2	p-val	LRIPI	p-val				
Malaysia	-0.10	0.01	0.20	0.26	0.93	0.09	1.01	0.03				
Singapore	-0.71	0.00	0.64	0.35	-0.52	0.56	-0.15	0.49				
Thailand	-0.07	0.31	0.42	0.22	-1.63	0.02	0.53	0.08				
LRLQ												
Country	ECT	p-val	LRM2	p-val	LRGDP	p-val	LR	p-val				
Malaysia	-0.09	0.04	1.05	0.00	1.44	0.01	0.02	0.01				
Singapore	-0.24	0.00	0.66	0.00	-0.11	0.39	0.88	0.06				
Thailand	0.00	0.84	0.77	0.00	0.84	0.00	-0.03	0.20				
LRM2												
Country	ECT	p-val	LRLQ	p-val	LSPRICE	p-val	LRGDP	p-val	tbr	p-val	LCPI	p-val
Malaysia	-0.02	0.10	0.11	0.08	0.09	0.02	-0.53	0.02	-0.03	0.15	-0.28	0.39
Singapore	0.02	0.42	0.42	0.00	0.03	0.34	0.04	0.75	-0.02	0.07	-1.34	0.02
Thailand	-0.42	0.00	-0.46	0.01	-0.04	0.32	0.54	0.00	-0.02	0.10	-2.65	0.00

Table 5: PMG Final Estimation of ECT and SR (individual countries).

(except Thailand) have p-value of >than 1%, which led us to accept the null hypothesis of no correlation [64].

However, the D1lrlq, D1lrm2, D1lripi denotes some very diverse patterns as can be seen in Table 5 above due to a heterogeneous panel of countries. For the dependent variable LSPRICE, LRLQ has no correlation because p-value is >10%, (accept Null hypothesis of no correlation) while the variables LRM2 and LRIPI are correlated with LSPRICE (reject Null hypothesis of no correlation because p-value is <10%) except for Singapore.

For the dependent variable LRLQ, LRM2 is correlated with LRLQ because p-value is <10%, (reject Null hypothesis of no correlation) while the variables LRGDP and LR are correlated with LRLQ (reject Null hypothesis of no correlation because p value is <10%) except for Singapore for LRGDP and Thailand for LR. In the case of the dependent variable LRM2, we conclude that:

- LRLQ is correlated with LRM2 (all countries, because p-value is <0.10)
- LSPRICE is correlated with LRM2 (except for Singapore) [64],
- LRGDP is correlated with LRM2 (except for Singapore),
- tbr is correlated with LRM2 (except for Malaysia and Thailand)
- LCPI is correlated with LRM2 (except for Malaysia)

Conclusion

This paper's findings are that money supply affects i) interest rates and ii) liquidity, while liquidity affect iii) share price, using estimators PMG, MG and DFE on a panel of three ASEAN countries. Although the money supply has been extensively covered in the literature and by policy maker, propositions (ii) and (iii) have not been verified. Therefore our findings on this are new in the literature and useful for policy makers.

Our findings confirm the existence of a long run cointegration relationship between share price and liquidity, money supply and industrial production index (IPI) and these are statistically significant. From the literature, empirical evidence has indicated that the Pool Mean Group (PMG) handles homogeneity/heterogeneity across panel data well, and our findings in the second equation confirm our research question that money supply causes liquidity in the short run. Liquidity causes money supply in the long run and is statistically significant. Following this, our second research question that liquidity causes share prices is also shown by the results from the first equation. In addition, while there exists a strong link between stock price and liquidity. Money supply and industrial production (proxy for earnings of firms) is significantly related in the long run, not in the short run, the latter being due to the money supply effect needing more time to convert credits to investments and then profits in the production process.

Acknowledgements

We are grateful for several critical comments of discussants and participants at two conferences (Global Finance and MFA) and staff seminars on three different versions of this paper. We take full responsibility for errors.

References

1. Fleming MJ, Remolona EM (1997) What moves the bond market? Federal Reserve Bank of New York Economic Policy Review, Newyork.
2. Fair RC (2002) Events that shook the market. Journal of Business 75: 713-731.
3. King BF (1966) Market and Industry Factors in Stock Price Behaviour. Journal of Business 39: 139-190.
4. Bernanke BS, Kuttner KN (2005) What Explains the Stock Market's Reaction to Federal Reserve Policy? Journal of Finance 60: 1221-1257.
5. Ross SA (1976) The Arbitrage Theory of Capital Asset Pricing. Journal of Economic Theory 13: 341-360.
6. Chen NF, Roll R, Ross SA (1986) Economic Forces and the Stock Market. Journal of Business 59: 383-403.
7. Musílek P (1997) Změny makroekonomických veličin a akciové kurzy. Finance a úvěr 47: 150-162.
8. Flannery MJ, Protopapadakis A (2002) Macroeconomic Factors do Influence Aggregate Stock Returns. Review of Financial Studies 15: 751-782.
9. Sprinkel BW (1964) Money and Stock Prices. Richard D. Irwin, Homewood III, New York.
10. Ariff M, Farrar J, Khalid AM (2012) Regulatory Failure and Global Financial Crisis. Edward Elgar Ltd UK and USA.
11. Hamilton J (1997) Measuring the Liquidity Effect. American Economic Review 87: 80-97.
12. Clare AD, Stephen HT (1994) Macroeconomic Factors, the APT and the UK Stock Market. Journal of Business Finance and Accounting 21: 309-330.
13. Bailey W, Chung YP (1996) Risk and Return in the Philippine Equity Market: A Multifactor Exploration. Pacific Basin Finance Journal 4: 197-218.
14. Kwon CS, Shin TS (1999) Cointegration and Causality between Macroeconomic Variables and Stock Market Returns. Global Finance Journal 10: 71-81.
15. Ibrahim MH, Aziz H (2003) Macroeconomic Variables and the Malaysian Equity Market A View Trough Rolling Subsamples. Journal of Economic Studies 30: 6-27.

16. Cheung YW, Ng LK (1998) International Evidence on the Stock Market and Aggregate Economic Activity. Journal of Empirical Finance 5: 281-296.
17. Bilson CM, Brailsford TJ, Hooper VJ (2001) Selecting Macroeconomic Variables as Explanatory Factors of Emerging Stock Market Returns. Pacific-Basin Finance Journal 9: 401-426.
18. Wongbangpo P, Sharma SC (2002) Stock Market and Macroeconomic Fundamental Dynamic Interactions: ASEAN-5 Countries. Journal of Asian Economics 13: 27-51.
19. Cooper RVL (1974) Efficient Capital Markets and the Quantity Theory of Money. Journal of Finance 29: 887-908.
20. Johansen S (1991) Estimation and hypothesis testing of cointegration vectors in Gaussian vector autoregressive models. Econometrica 59: 1551-1580.
21. Johansen S (1995) Likelihood-Based Inference in Cointegrated Vector Autoregressive Models. Oxford University Press, Oxford.
22. Pesaran MH, Smith RP (1995) Estimating long-run relationships from dynamic heterogeneous panels. Journal of Econometrics 68: 79-113.
23. Pesaran MH, Shin Y, Smith RP (1999) Pooled Mean Group Estimation of Dynamic Heterogeneous Panels. Journal of the American Statistical Association 94: 621-634.
24. Pesaran MH, Shin Y, Smith RP (1997) Pooled estimation of long-run relationships in dynamic heterogeneous panels. University of Cambridge, USA.
25. Engle RF, Granger CWJ (1987) Cointegration and Error Correction:Representation, Estimation and Testing. Econometrica 55: 251-276.
26. Blackburne EF, Frank MW (2007) Estimation of Nonstationary Heterogeneous Panels. The Stata Journal 7: 197-208.
27. Maddala GS, Wu S (1999) A Comparative Study of Unit Root Tests with Panel Data and a New Simple Test. Oxford Bulletin of Economics and Statistics 61: 631-652.
28. Choi I (2001) Unit Root Tests for Panel Data. Journal of International Money and Finance 20: 249-272.
29. Hardouvelis GA (1987) Macroeconomic Information and Stock Prices. Journal of Economics and Business 39: 131-140.
30. Keim DB (1985) Dividend Yields and Stock Returns: Implications of Abnormal January Returns. Journal of Financial Economics 14: 473-489.
31. Litzenberger RH, Ramaswamy K (1982) The Effects of Dividends on Common Stock Prices: Tax Effects or Information Effects? Journal of Finance 37: 429-443.
32. Thorbecke W, Coppock L (1996) Monetary Policy, Stock Returns, and the Role of Credit in the Transmission of Monetary Policy. Southern Economic Journal 62: 989-1001.
33. Amihud Y, Mendelson H (1986) Asset Pricing and the Bid-Ask Spread. Journal of Financial Economics 17: 223-249.
34. Amihud Y (2002) Illiquidity and Stock Returns: Cross-Section and Time Series Effects. Journal of Financial Markets 5: 31-56.
35. Chordia T, Subrahmanyam A, Anshuman VR (2001) Trading Activity & Expected Stock Returns. Journal of Financial Economics 59: 3-32.
36. Gordon DB, Leeper EM (2002) The Price Level, the Quantity Theory of Money, and the Fiscal Theory of the Price Level. NBER Working Paper 9084, National Bureau of Economic Research, Inc.
37. Anderson TW, Hsiao C (1982) Formulation and Estimation of Dynamic Models Using Panel Data. Journal of Econometrics 18: 47-82.
38. Effa B et al., (2011) Endogeneous Money Supply and Bank Stock Returns: Empirical evidence Using Panel Data. Applied Financial Economics 25: 345-356.
39. Badarudin E, Ariff M, Khalid A (2013) Post Keynesian money endogeneity evidence in G-7 economies. Journal of International Money & Finance 33: 146-162.
40. Brennan MJ, Chordia T, Subrahmanyam A (1998) Alternative Factor Specifications, Security Characteristics and the Cross-section of Expected Stock returns. Journal of Financial Economics 49: 345-373.
41. Bryant RC, Holtham G, Hooper P (1988) Consensus and Diversity in the Model Simulations. In Bryant RC, Henderson DW, Holtham G, Hooper P, Symansky SA (eds) Empirical Macroeconomics for Interdepent Economies. The Brookings Institution, Washington, D.C p: 27-62.
42. Cagan P, Gandolfi A (1969) The Lag in Monetary Policy as Implied by the Time Pattern of Monetary Effects on Interest Rates. American Economic Review 59: 277-284.
43. Carpenter S, Demiralp S (2006) The Liquidity Effect in the Federal Funds Market: Evidence from Daily Open Market Operations. Journal of Money, Credit, and Banking 38: 901-920.
44. Christiano LJ, Eichenbaum M, Evans CL (1996a) The Effects of Monetary Policy Shocks: Evidence from the Flow of Funds. Review of Economics & Statistics 78: 16-34.
45. Christiano LJ, Martin E (1992a) Liquidity Effects & the Monetary Transmission Mechanism. The American Economic Review 82: 346-353.
46. Christiano LJ, Martin E (1992b) Liquidity Effects, Monetary Policy and the Business Cycle. National Bureau of Economic Research Working Paper No. 4129 27: 1113-1136.
47. Chung TF (2013) A Test of their Linkage between Money Supply, Liquidity and Share Prices: An unpublished PhD thesis. The University Putra Malaysia, Serdang, Selangor, Malaysia.
48. Dhakal D, Kandil M, Sharma SC (1993) Causality between the Money Supply and Share Prices: a VAR Investigation. Quarterly Journal of Business and Economics 32: 52-74.
49. Fama EF (1990) Stock Returns, Expected Returns, and Real Activity. Journal of Finance 45: 1089-1108.
50. Geske R, Roll R (1983) The Fiscal and Monetary Linkage between Stock returns and Inflation. Journal of Finance 38: 1-33.
51. Gibson WE (1970b) Interest Rates and Monetary Policy. Journal of Political Economy 78: 431-55.
52. Kaldor N (1982) The Scourge of Monetarism. Oxford University Press, Oxford, New York.
53. Kraft J, Kraft A (1977) Determinants of Common Stock Prices in Time Series Analysis. Journal of Finance 32: 417-425.
54. Mehra YP (1993) The Stability of the M2 Demand Function: Evidence from an Error-Correction Model. Journal of Money, Credit and Banking 25: 455-460.
55. Mishkin FS (1998) The economics of money, banking, and financial markets. Columbia University: Addison Wesley Longman, USA.
56. Pedroni P (2004) Panel Cointegration: Asymptotic and Finite Sample Properties of Pooled Time Series Tests with an Application to the PPP Hypothesis. Economic Theory 20: 597-625.
57. Pesando JE (1974) The Supply of Money and Common stock Prices Further Observations on the Econometric Evidence. Journal of Finance 29: 909-921.
58. Rochon LP (2006) Endogenous Money, Central Banks and the Banking System: Basil Moore and the Supply of Credit. In Setterfield M, ed Complexity, Endogenous Money and Macroeconomic Theory (Edward Elgar, Cheltenham,UK).
59. Rozeff MS (1974) Money Stock Prices: Market Efficiency and the Lag in Effect of Monetary Policy. Unpublished doctoral dissertation, Graduate School of Management, University of Rochester.
60. Stock J, Watson M (1989) New Indices of Coincident and Leading Indicators. In Blanchard O & Fischer S (eds) NBER Macroeconomics Annual, Cambridge: MIT Press, USA.
61. Tainer EM (1993) Using Economic Indicators to Improve Investment Analysis. John Wiley & Sons, Inc, New York, USA.
62. Thornton DL (2007) Open Market Operations and the Federal Funds Rate. In Open Market Operations and the Financial Markets, the Bank of Finland, reprinted in the Federal Reserve Bank of St. Louis Review 89: 549-72.
63. Thornton DL (2001) The Federal Reserve's Operating Procedure, Nonborrowed Reserves, Borrowed Reserves and the Liquidity Effect. Journal of Banking and Finance 32: 155-167.
64. Effa ZB, Ariff M, Khalid AM (2011) Money Supply Endogeneity and Bank Stock Returns. Applied Financial Economics 21: 156-173.

Financial Ratios (Accounting Ratios) and Survival of Microfinance Institutions in Ghana

Sarkodie EE[1]*, Addai I[1] and Asiedu DK[2]

[1]*Department of Accounting Studies Education, College of Technology Education, Kumasi, Ghana*

[2]*University of Education, Winneba, College of Technology Education, Kumasi, Ghana*

Abstract

Accounting Ratio is a way of expressing the relationship between one accounting result and another, which is intended to provide a useful comparison. Accounting ratios assist in measuring the efficiency and profitability of a company based on its financial reports. Accounting ratios are important for financial decision making irrespective of the size of the institution. The Bank of Ghana has the constitutional mandate to oversee the activities of all financial institutions in Ghana including the Microfinance institutions. This core mandate of Bank of Ghana is basically guided by the use of accounting ratios. The ratios per their style have the power to determine the risk exposure of financial institutions. Over the past five years the Ghanaian economy has witnessed the collapse of certain microfinance institutions that the public assumed to be highly visible in the financial market. The study therefore provided a logistic regression model with 117 observations to determine whether accounting ratios have the power to predict the fortunes of microfinance institutions in Ghana. An increase in the current ratio reduces the log-odds of a firm's survival by -1.461987. An increase in the acid test ratio improves the log-odds of survival by 6.847345. An increase in the debt equity ratio increases the chances of survival of a firm by 1.055941. Current ratio and acid test ratio were statistically significant at 10 percent whilst debt equity ratio was statistically significant at 5 percent. The study implies that microfinance institutions should be mindful of the current ratio, acid test ratio and the debt to equity ratio.

Keywords: Financial ratios; Stock; Business; Microfinance; Enterprise

Introduction

A financial ratio or accounting ratio is a relative magnitude of two selected numerical values taken from an enterprise's financial statements (wiki). Accounting Ratio is a way of expressing the relationship between one accounting result and another, which is intended to provide a useful comparison. Accounting ratios assist in measuring the efficiency and profitability of a company based on its financial reports. Accounting ratios form the basis of fundamental analysis. An accounting ratio compares two aspects of a financial statement, such as the relationship (or ratio) of current assets to current liabilities. The ratios can be used to evaluate the financial condition of a company, including the company's strengths and weaknesses (Investopedia) [1].

Financial ratios quantify many aspects of a business and are an integral part of the financial statement analysis. Financial ratios are categorized according to the financial aspect of the business which the ratio measures. Liquidity ratios measure the availability of cash to pay debt. Activity ratios measure how quickly a firm converts non-cash assets to cash assets. Debt ratios measure the firm's ability to repay long-term debt. Profitability ratios measure the firm's use of its assets and control of its expenses to generate an acceptable rate of return. Market ratios measure investor response to owning a company's stock and also the cost of issuing stock. These are concerned with the return on investment for shareholders, and with the relationship between return and the value of an investment in company's shares. Financial ratios allow for comparisons;

1. Between companies
2. Between industries
3. Between different time periods for one company
4. Between a single company and its industry average

Ratios generally are not useful unless they are benchmarked against something else, like past performance or another company. Thus, the ratios of firms in different industries, which face different risks, capital requirements, and competition, are usually hard to compare.

The objective of this study was to find out whether accounting ratios have the capacity to tell the fortunes of microfinance institutions. The research questions that were asked included:

1. Does Current Ratio predict survival?
2. Does Quick Ratio predict survival?
3. Does Debt to Equity Ratio predict survival?

This study will contribute to microfinance management and policy making in the financial market at large.

Literature Review

Naser [1] conducted a study to find out if Financial Ratios Reliably Measure the Performance of Banks in Bahrain. The study covered the calculation of important financial ratios of major financial institutions in Bahrain as well as comparing their performance in the context of the global financial crisis. It also compared ratios of conventional banks with Islamic financial institutions in Bahrain. These ratios defined profitability, financial performance, size and type of banks. The result of the analysis of ratios for measuring financial performance showed

***Corresponding author:** Sarkodie EE, University of Education, Winneba, College of Technology Education, Department of Accounting Studies Education, Kumasi, Ghana, E-mail: effahsarkodie@yahoo.com

that there is corporate excellence in asset management and value equity shares. The study also recommended that the analysis could be used as a basis for preventative actions for future bankruptcy and market risk.

Lenders often rely on ratio analysis because it allows them to see how one's business is doing and how compare it compares to other businesses which they have loaned money to. The potential loan creditor also requires information about security that the Ratio Analysis can be provided [2].

Ratio analysis is a useful tool for business owners as well. It measures the health of the business whether it is a bank or a multinational corporation. It helps to measure the performance of the business, to diagnose potential problems and to see how well it is doing over time.

Finch [3] stated that financial ratios are one of the most common tools of managerial decision making. A ratio is to compare one number to another-mathematically, a simple division problem. Financial ratios involve the comparison of various figures from the financial statements in order to gain information about a company's performance. It is the interpretation, rather than the calculation, that makes financial ratios a useful tool for business managers. The future decisions can be evaluated in terms of measuring the behavior of the firm value, given a decision to be analyzed. However, examining historical financial statements analysis has the limitations in reaching the optimal financial decisions. Ratios may serve as indicators, clues, or red flags regarding not worthy relationships between variables used to measure the firm's performance in terms of profitability, asset utilization, liquidity, leverage, or market valuation [4].

Singh [5] in his study identified commonly used ratios in the lodging industry and discovered their importance for lodging financial executives. In his point of view, financial ratios have always been a valuable tool for lodging industry managers. Ratios allow the user to summarize and analyze related data to provide meaningful information for making decisions [6,7].

Problem Statement

Accounting ratios are important for financial decision making irrespective of the size of the institution. The Bank of Ghana has the constitutional mandate to oversee the activities of all financial institutions in Ghana including the Microfinance institutions. This core mandate of Bank of Ghana is basically guided by the use of accounting ratios. The ratios per their style have the power to determine the risk exposure of financial institutions [1]. Bank of Ghana is indeed noted for strict adherence to these accounting ratios. However, over the past five years the Ghanaian economy has witnessed the collapse of many microfinance institutions that the public assumed to be highly visible in the financial market. Some of these collapsed institutions include Noble Dream Microfinance, Above All Financial Services and KAD Microfinance. This study therefore tried to calculate some of these accounting ratios of microfinance institutions in Ghana including those that have collapsed and those that are still in operation. The study thereafter provided a logistic regression model to determine whether accounting ratios have the power to predict the fortunes of microfinance institutions in Ghana.

Methodology

Model specification

This study adopted Logistic regression modeling technique. The choice of this methodology is based on the fact that the regress and of the model is binary. The logistic regression is specified as

$$\ln[P_i/(1-P_i)] = \lambda_0 + \lambda_1 cr + \lambda_2 atr + \lambda_3 der + +\mu$$

Where: cr= Current ratio , atr= Acid Test Ratio, der=Debt Equity Ratio, μ= Error term, $\lambda_0..\lambda_3$ = The parameters to be estimated. $[P_i/(1-P_i)]$ = The Odds of survival of Microfinance institutions.

Definition of variables

Current Ratio is a relationship of current assets to current liabilities. Current Assets are the assets that are either in the firm of cash or cash equivalents or can be converted into cash or cash equivalents in a short time (say, within a year's time) and Current Liabilities are repayable in a short time. It is calculated as follows:

$$\text{Current Ratio} = \frac{\textit{current assets}}{\textit{current liabilities}}$$

The objective of calculating Current Ratio is to assess the ability of the enterprise to meet its short-term liabilities promptly. It shows the number of times the current assets can be converted into cash to meet current liabilities. As a normal rule current assets should be twice the current liabilities. Low ratio indicates inadequacy of the enterprise to meet its current liabilities and inadequate working Capital. High Ratio is an indication of inefficient utilization of funds. An enterprise should have a reasonable current ratio. Although there is no hard and fast rule yet a current ratio of 2:1 is preferable.

Acid Test Ratio: is a relationship of liquid assets with current liabilities and is computed to assess the short- term liquidity of the enterprise in its correct form.

This is calculated as follows:

$$\text{Acid Test Ratio} = \frac{\textit{current assets}}{\textit{current liabilities}}$$

Quick assets= Current assets – (stock + Prepaid Expenses) Liquid assets are the assets, which are either in the form of cash or cash equivalent or can be converted into cash within a very short period. Liquid assets include cash, bills receivable, marketable securities and debtors (excluding bad and Doubtful debts), etc. Stock is excluded from liquid assets as it may take some time before it is converted into cash. Similarly prepaid expenses do not provide cash at all and are thus excluded from liquid assets. A quick ratio of 1:1 is usually considered favorable, since for every rupee of current liabilities, there is a rupee of current assets. A high Acid Test ratio compared to current ratio may indicate under stocking while a low liquidity ratio while a low Acid Test ratio indicated overstocking.

Debt-Equity Ratio- It is computed to ascertain the soundness of the long-term financial position of the firm. This ratio expresses the relationship between debt (external equities) and the equity (internal equities) Debt means long term loans, i.e., debentures, long-term loans from financial institution. Equity means shareholders' funds, i.e., preference share capital, equity share capital, reserves less losses and fictitious assets like preliminary expenses. The ratio is ascertained as follows:

$$\text{Debt} - \text{equity Ratio} = \frac{\text{Debt}\left(\text{long} - \text{term loans}\right)}{\text{Equity}\left(\text{shareholders' Funds}\right)}$$

Higher Ratio indicates risky financial position while lower ratio indicates safe financial position. Acceptable Debt-Equity Ratio is 2:1 which means debt can be twice the equity. This ratio is significant to

Survive	Coef.	Std. Err.	z	P>|z|	[95% Conf. Interval]	
cr	-1.461987*	.7994525	-1.83	0.067	-3.028885	.1049107
acr	6.847345*	3.87012	1.77	0.077	-.7379499	14.43264
der	1.055941**	.3075388	3.43	0.001	.4531757	1.658706
_cons	-.9088469	.6503588	-1.40	0.162	-2.183527	.365833

*Significant at 10 percent, ** significant at 5 percent.

Number of observation = 117, Log likelihood chi square=35.18 Prob > chi^2 = 0.0000

cr= current ratio, atr= acid test ratio, der= debt-equity ratio, _cons=constant term

Table 1: Logistic Regression Results.

access the soundness of long –term financial position. It also indicates the extent to which firm depends upon outsiders for its existence. It portrays the proportion of total funds acquired by a firm by way of loans.

Data, population and sample

The study relied purely on cross sectional and secondary data collected from one hundred and seventeen microfinance institutions (117) in Ghana. The secondary source is from the annual audited accounts of these microfinance institutions. The population in this study includes all microfinance institutions in Ghana.

Results and Discussion

The table below is a logistic regression results which indicates that one hundred and seventeen microfinance institutions were used and there was no missing value. The log likelihood ratio of 35.18 with a chi square of 0.0000 is an indication that the model as whole fits better than a model with no predictors.

Number of observation = 117, Log likelihood chi square=35.18 Prob > chi^2 = 0.0000

cr= current ratio, atr= acid test ratio, der= debt-equity ratio, _cons=constant term

An increase in the current ratio reduces the log-odds of a firm's survival by -1.461987. That is as the firms' current assets increases too much relative to their current liabilities they stand the risk of collapsing. In other words, microfinance institutions may not be able to meet their liabilities if they create huge loans, which are usually a greater percentage of their current assets. Besides the current ratio proved statistically significant at 10 percent error level. This indeed, emphasizes that the variable is scientifically a true determinant of the log-odds of survival.

An increase in the acid test ratio improves the log-odds of survival by 6.847345. That is if microfinance institutions put much of their resources into very liquid assets then there is a higher possibility of its survival. This stems from the fact that microfinance institutions can easily lay hands on these liquid assets to settle their current liabilities. Therefore, to avoid risk of collapsing microfinance institutions must put resources into liquid assets. It is moreover, observed that, the acid test ratio is statistically significant at 10 percent error level.

An increase in the debt-equity ratio also enhances the log-odds of a firm's survival. From the Table 1 an increase in the debt equity ratio increases the chances of survival of a firm by 1.055941. This means that if the microfinance institution is able to access long term loans from other financial institutions, then it will enhance the firms chances of survival. Moreover, the debt-equity ratio is statistically significant at 5 percent error level.

Implications of the Study

The study implies that microfinance institutions should be mindful of the current ratio, acid test ratio and the debt to equity ratio.

Summary and Recommendations

Microfinance institutions may have at the heart to make profit by way of giving out several loans. However, increasing loans does not necessarily increase profit since the business can collapse through the loans giving. It is advised per the findings of this study that short term loans to customers would be of great advantage to the microfinance institutions. Also, microfinance institutions ability to invite long term loans from other financial institutions could be of great help to the microfinance institutions. This is because increasing long term loan accessibility can improve their chances of survival. In this regard an alliance of microfinance institutions would help form syndicate which can aid the assessment of long term loans from banks. Frequent monitoring of the microfinance institutions ratios would help to prevent collapsing.

References

1. Najjar NJ (2013) Can Financial Ratios Reliably Measure the Performance of Banks in Bahrain? Int J Eco Financ 5: 3.
2. Lambert RA, Larcker DF (1987) An analysis of the use of accounting and market measures of performance in executive compensation contracts, J Accont Res 2: 85-125.
3. Finch H (2005) Financial Ratios. Reference for business.
4. Murthy SRY (2004) Financial Ratios of Major Commercial Banks.
5. Ward S (2003) Is Your Business Sick? Give Your Business a Health Checkup with These Three Ratios.
6. Lang M, Maffett M, Owens E (2010) Earnings comovement and accounting comparability: The effects of mandatory IFRS adoption', Working paper, UNC-Chapel Hill.
7. Lynch RM, Willamson RW (1983) Accounting for Management. New York: McGraw-Hill.

A Study of use and Impact of Market Segmentation Practices on Bank Performance: With Special Reference to Commercial Banks in Colombia

Asiedu E*

Servicio Nacional De Aprendizaje (SENA) Neiva, Huila, Colombia

Abstract

The Banking and Financial Environment in Colombia has witnessed so many regulatory changes and competitive dynamics. This has made segmentation practices an imperative determinant in their service offering and development to its complex customers.

Approach: This study assessed the use and impact of market segmentation patterns and practices on the performance of selected banks in Colombia, post consolidation period of 2012 to date. The methods applied were both primary and secondary while the design was mainly exploratory, relating basic market segmentation variables like market share, geographical location and pricing to bank performance. Statistical test using Herfindal Hirchman Index (HHI) was designed to test for market concentration against bank's performance.

Objective: The idea behind this research was to assist managers, business students, and banking workers to understand the concept and impacts of marketing segmentation patterns and practices on banks performance.

Results: Findings from the study indicate that, segmentation practices have immensely impacted on the performance of the selected banks in Colombia. The study exposed that the banks have used segmentation practices to lower their overall operation unit cost, expand their market shares, retain their customers, better their communications, increase profitability and focus on their company. They are well positioned in capital strength and they are the best capitalized banks in Colombia, thanks to their segmentation strategy called data-informed strategy.

Conclusion: The study however concluded that there is a threshold point (37.2%) in which any further commitment of funds into market segmentation practice can lead to negative result.

Recommendation: It was recommended that less dominated banks can adopt acceptable corporate image, simple and flexible account opening formalities, just-in-time service delivery, employee-customer management, and effective and efficient use of referrals to win customer loyalty which tend to retain old customers and win new customers as well.

Keywords: Tier-1 capital ratio; Market segmentation; Commercial banks; Bank performance; Customer retention ability; Colombia

Introduction

Colombian banking industry and segmentation history

Developments in the financial and banking sector such as implementation of new technologies, constantly changing of customer needs, increase in the number of products offered and deregulation process have made segmentation practices very important in that sector. Banking and Financial sector in Colombia, South America, since the beginning of the 1990's has been characterised by its size, its oligopolistic and segmented structure, and has a history of segmenting market to meet their customer's satisfaction. Colombia, which is in the north-western corner of South America, is the 3rd most populous country after Mexico and Brazil in Latin America. It ranks as the 28th largest economy in the world according to 2015 Index of Economic Freedom with an overall percentage of 71.7 (+1.0) (The Heritage Foundation, 2015). The banking sector is the widest financial intermediary in Colombia's capital market. It is dominated by complicated financial conglomerates with different kinds of intermediaries.

The banking sector in Colombia like any other bank, have a history of segmenting their market on the basis of their service-offering such as saving patterns, level of income, demographic characteristics, professional calling, or risk preferences [1,2]. Banks whose market segmentation cut across all boundaries benefit from market share increment. In Colombia, banks such as Bancolombia have a wide market segmentation that cut across commercial banking, retail banking, construction banking, small business banking, treasury, off-shore commercial banking, government and institution banking, brokerage, credit card, manufacturing, investment banking, and leasing among others [3]. The purpose is to reduce expenses and achieve the objective of rendering services to a 'niche' or a given market.

Segmentation practices and patterns began in Colombia in as early as 1931 when Caja Agraria was established as an entity with public capital to serve the agricultural industry in the country. Bartel supported that the early history of the marketing discipline was focused on the sales of agricultural products. This bank at that time was tasked to refinance the debts of the coffee growers in the country. Banco Central Hipotecario (BCH) was also created in 1932 to purchase bad loans from commercial banks and mortgage. In 1951, Banco Popular was founded to grant credits to commerce and small urban businesses. 1953 saw Banco Cafetero created with the aim of financing the coffee

***Corresponding author:** Elvis Asiedu, B.Ed, MSc, and CMI Level 7, Management Studies, Servicio Nacional De Aprendizaje (SENA) Neiva, Huila, Colombia
E-mail: akwasiasiedu63@yahoo.com

growers in the country. Banco Ganadero in 1955-56 was established as a state-own institution targeting commercial cattle raisers in the country [4].

In the mid of 1980's, the financial system in Colombia were boosting of ninety-one (91) banks with an average of 46% GDP as assets equivalent. Out of the 91 banks, public-owned banks held 48% of the sector's assets with 20% GDP. Foreign Banks had 3% with 1% GDP; Domestic Private Banks had 20% with 9% GDP; Savings and Loans Corporations had 15% with an average GDP of 7% and others were 20% (9% GDP). The number of the bank institutions considerably grew up in the 1990's to 145 banks with total assets equivalent to 68% GDP [4-6]. However, the public-owned banks assets drastically fell to 13% as of 1995 due to the participation of other non-banking institutions whose assets rapidly grew from 20% between the 1986 to 1989 to 37% in 1990 [4]. This made the commercial banks to intensify their segmentation strategy to improve their performance. Asiedu supported that "segmentation strategy allows firms to understand customer value and identify the most profitable opportunities" [7].

In Colombia, banks such as BanColombia, S.A, Banco de Bogotá, S.A. and Davivienda, S.A. have adopted a segmentation strategy called data-informed strategy to develop their customer retention skills [4]. This data-informed strategy is used to reward and raise the moral of profitable customers who are loyal to the company. The data-informed segmentation allows firms to analyse how their customers think and make decisions about their products and services. This helps to customize products to suit the exact needs of consumers. Shaw et al. opined that commercial banks' capacity in terms of smooth payment system and resource allocation is important in every economy [2,8-10]. It is therefore necessary to adopt marketing segmentation practices as the main basis for allocating resources for marketing, service and delivery programs as well as product development [7]. This has brought the need for government in every country to draw regulatory models (frameworks) to control and guide their activities. The commercial banks domestic assets in Colombia as of 1999, was 50%. However, the bank's non-performing loans in Colombia as of 2014 were as low as 2.9% (The World Bank Groups, 2015).

Although the deregulation of Colombian financial industry since 1990 (Leg 45/1990) sought to reduce market segmentation, the new system continues to induce market segmentation with the aim of preventing competition [4]. Colombian banking and financial industry is known for their large volume of liquidity and bank deposit in the past due to their inappropriate market drives and design. The industry has witnessed so many regulatory changes and competitive dynamics making segmentation practices an imperative determinant in their service offerings and development to its complex customers. However, inn 2012, The Banker, Global Financial Intelligence in London reported that Bancolombia, Banco de Bogotá, Banco Davivienda, BBVA and Banco Occidente are the top most five banks within the Colombian banking sector. This has raised a concern to find out the market segmentation practices adopted by typical Colombian Commercial Banks, the benefits derived from market segmentation practices and the influences market segmentation practices have on customer loyalty through banks product and service offerings in Colombia.

Purpose of Study

The purpose of this study is to examine;

- ✓ The uses and impacts of market segmentation practices on bank performance with special reference to selected commercial banks in Colombia.
- ✓ To find out the market segmentation practices adopted by typical Colombian Commercial Banks.

Research objectives

The idea behind this research was to assist managers, business students, and banking workers to understand the concept and impacts of marketing segmentation patterns and practices on banks performance.

Research questions

- ✓ What market segmentation practices adopted by a typical Colombian commercial banks? Is there any relationship between segmentation practices and bank service offerings?
- ✓ Is there a positive relationship between market segmentation practices and bank performance?
- ✓ What benefits do the selected commercial banks in Colombia derive from market segmentation practices?

Significant of the Study

The paper will assist managers, business students, banking workers and general public in Colombia as well as other institutions interested in understand the concept of marketing segmentation, or segmentation practices and bank service offerings or its impacts on banks performance. Since the study seeks to address the benefits organisations derive from market segmentation, it wouldn't be surprised to see experienced and new researchers in the field of management making reference to it [11]. The study will also help students in their academic writings. Management and marketers in various financial institutions can adopt it as a yardstick to develop marketing strategies to achieve customer satisfaction to influence customer retention, loyalty and profitability.

The concept of market segmentation

The concept of Market Segmentation was first introduced into marketing terminology in 1956 by an American Marketing Professor, Wendell, Smith and was proposed as an alternative technique for market development where there are few competitors with identical products. Smith tried to define market segmentation as a condition of growth when core markets are developed on a generalised basis to the point where additional promotional expenditures are yielding diminishing returns [12]. This means that effective matching of firm's resources to target market segments can deliver the greatest return on marketing investment (ROMI). Day [2] perceived that market segmentation is a part of the bigger marketing plan adopted by companies to divide their markets into distinct groups on the basis of wants, needs, taste or behaviour for their different products and services.

The concept has common variables for consumer markets and it works for every company. It involves with the division of a broad target market into smaller segments to make marketing simpler and easier to undertake. According to Asiedu "segmentation is a management tool that enables firms to subdivide their market based on the same behaviour of consumers into discrete consumer groups [7]. He continued the tool can help firms to identify the unmet customer and employee needs and attend to the". This really shows that market segmentation form an important foundation for successful activities and strategies of every organisation.

Figure 1 demonstrates the common variables of market segmentation for consumer market.

The purpose of segmentation patterns in every aspect of business is to leverage limited (scarce) resources to focus on prospects customers who are likely to patronage its product offerings. This practice has enabled many organisations including financial institutions, to understand the elements of the marketing mix, distribution, price, promotion and products. It has helped many companies to design their products and services to suit the whims and caprices of different customers in the consumer market. Adewoye and Salami argued that effective and efficient segmentation practices enable financial institutions to maximise return for a given marketing expenditure [13]. The financial service requirements and its characteristics for consumers vary with age and that these differences could be used when developing marketing segmentation for such service [14].

Since financial institutions and many other companies have finite resources, it is however impossible to produce all possible products and services for everyone, all of the time. Therefore, the best thing to do most of the time is to provide selected offerings for selected groups of people. That's why different banks offer different products and services based on their geographical location, demography, and psychographic. This process enables firms to focus on the specific needs of customers in the most effective and efficient manner.

Onaolapo et al. advocated that the needs for segmentation practices by many firms are often influenced by the needs to satisfy customer's requirements [15]. Some customers require their companies to improve their cash flows, service delivery, and product quality. Bean and Ennis eloquently responded that a firm with limited resources needs to pick the best opportunities to pursue [16]. The tool allows banks to achieve their goals and objectives in terms of efficiency, sustainability and growth. Through segmentation, banks can carefully listen to their customers and respond to their wants and needs. Asiedu argued that the overall outcome is that the tool allows firms to provide great customer experience by satisfying the needs of customers with the idea that results are not important, rather the natural outcome of a job well done [7].

Asiedu encapsulated this in his work entitled **"Developing Market as a Source of Competitive Advantage: The Role of Management Tools"** by arguing that the concept of market segmentation is normally related to product differentiation since a firm needs to adopt different variations in its offerings to satisfy those segments [7]. He argued that if a firm adopt different versions of its product offerings, it allows the company to appeal to different market segments. Contrary to that, Cardozo perceived that if a firm start by adopting new products variations, it simply means that, such firm is using a product differentiation [17]. But if that same firm begin with the customers' needs, then that firm is using market segmentation approach. No matter the reasons for market partitioning, segmentation practices can only be feasible if the targeted market is accessible, identifiable and respond to the various marketing mix differently as offered in that particular sector. Agbo et al. among others indicated some causality between customer brand loyalty and profitability of the business [17,18]. This paper therefore seeks to explore how the banking sector in Colombia uses this tool (market segmentation) to administer its product offerings in a dynamic or different service market.

The process of market segmentation

The complexities involved in market segmentation process have made it an exacting activity. According to Griffith and Pol, the process involves greater customer variability, problems linked with the identification of the key differences between group of customers and multiple product applications [19]. Several academic pundits and market researchers have proposed myriad criteria that need to be met during segmentation process. Alfansi and Sergeant [20], in their studies came up with 6 criteria that must be met after they reviewed the works of scholars such as Frank et al. [20-24]. Alfansi and Sergeat criteria were based on accessibility, actionability, stability, responsiveness, sustainability and identifiability [20].

Wedel and Kamakura provided the most pertinent segmentation approach for financial and banking service sector. According to them, marketing segmentation bases can be classified based on "general" (that's independent of product/services) or "product-specific" and to the extent of each been observable (Figure 2) [25].

Scholars such as Dickens and Chappel et al. argued that the observable variables such as position in the family, life cycle, culture, gender, geographical location and income are potential criteria for marketing segmentation [26-31]. However, in the context of financial and banking sector, a number of research studies had revealed that there are differences in terms of purchasing and demographics. Though many scholars view demographic variables as too small, Alfansi and Sergeant maintained that demographic variable is very important and popular in marketing segmentation due to the following reasons; (i) easy and possible to conjunct demographic variables with other variables (ii) can easily be obtained (Figure 3) [20,32].

In the banking sector, segmentation is mostly limited to categories of commercial (corporate), and retail consumers. Commercial (corporate) customers are normally distinguished based on the sector they are affected and involved or based on their geographical range of activities. Meidan and Harrison argued on their part that demographic criteria such as income, age, profession, or wealth are very important for personal retail banking and credit card segment [33,34]. To talk about product-specific criteria under observable classification, Khermouch et al. detected that user-variables such as user status, user rate, loyalty, and stage of adoption are crucial factors for marketing segmentation [35-38].

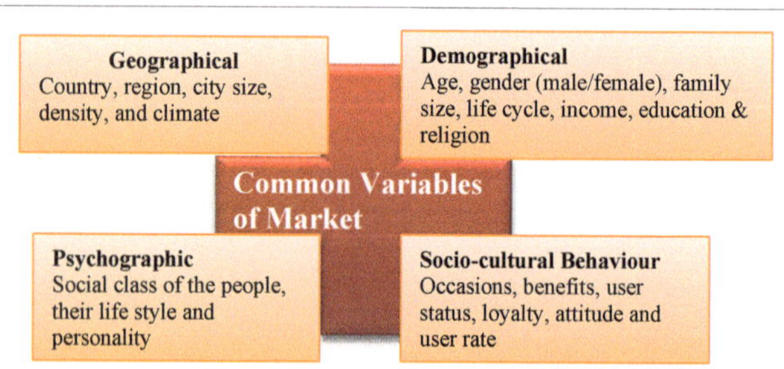

Figure 1: Common variables of market segmentation for consumer market.

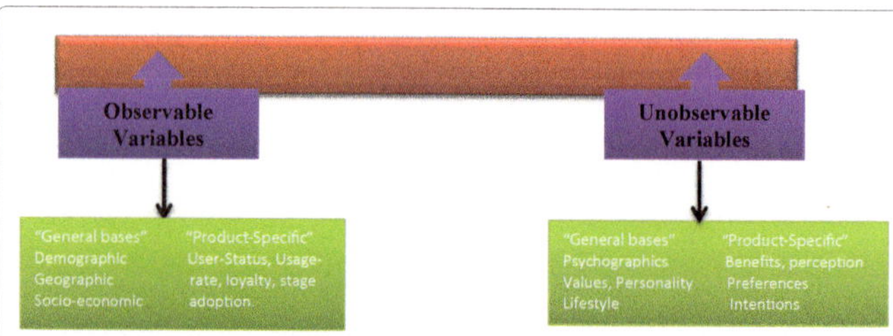

Source: Adapted from Wedel and Kamakura

Figure 2: Classification of segmentation variables.

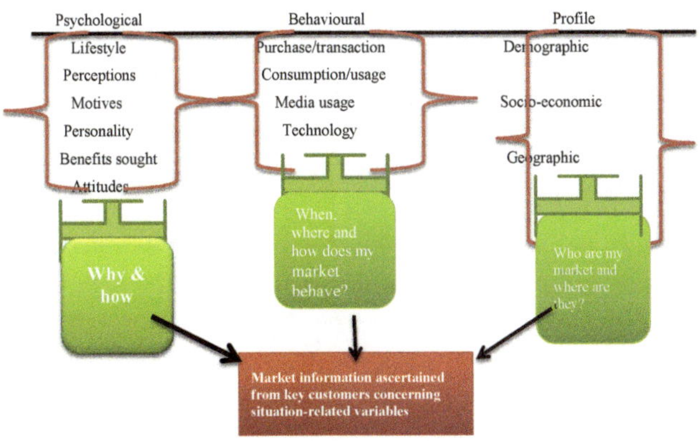

Figure 3: Shows the differing classification of consumer segmentation-bases.

Contrary to the above assessments, Evans et al. developed that unobservable classification must be taken into consideration during segmentation process for banking and financial service sector [39-42]. These scholars argued that general variables under unobservable segmentation classification such as personal values, personality, lifestyle or psychographic bases should be considered when segmenting market for banking companies. Harrison presented psychographic segmentation variables by using individual's perceived confidence and ability in dealing with financial issues, individual's own perceived knowledge and understanding of financial services as well as the expressed level of involvement and interest in financial service [34]. Harrison concluded his study with areas of four (4) segments and they are; (i) capital accumulators, (ii) financially confused, (iii) cautious investors and (iv) apathetic minimalists. Segmentation practices have benefited and proved its usefulness to many sectors and organisations. In Colombia, it has allowed banks such as Bancolombia, Banco de Bogotá, Banco Occidente, BBVA and Banco de D avivienda to increase their tier-1 capital and market share (The Banker Database, 2012).

To segment financial service markets, a firm must use market information ascertained from key customers concerning situation-related variables (criteria) and product. These are grouped as segmentation bases, and they include; **psychological criteria** (such as why does my market behaves the way it behaves?), **behavioural** (when, where and how does my market behave), **profile** (who are my market and where are they?). Kotler argued that a market segment consist of group of customers with similar features that are important in explaining their response to suppliers" market stimuli [43]. This really shows that important considerations should be made when choosing the differing bases for market segmentation.

Doyle observed the differing classification of segmentation bases and argued that market segmentation deals with a homogenous group of customers who react differently to distributional communication, promotion, pricing and other marketing mixes variables. When these variables (criteria) are applied, the impact is that it affords the marketers at the bank to dichotomies portions of the market from one customer needs to another to achieve corporate profit target [44].

To sum up everything in this section, there are two main basic approaches to segmenting a firm's market. They are break-down method and built-up method. Freytag and Clarke argued that the breakdown method is more recognised when segmenting consumer markets while built-up method is more recognised when giving general analysis based on identification of similarities. The built-up type is customer oriented as it seeks to put more emphasis on customer needs. According to Wind, the goal of market segmentation practices is to solve the conflict between the intentions of banks or any other organisation to satisfy their customers need; been it individual or group [17]. He further argued that it can also be sued to allocate marketing resources economically in time of limited resources (Table 1).

Market segmentation practices and bank service offerings

For successful bank service offerings, a segmentation practices plays a major role. It is a part of the bigger marketing plan that allows marketing managers to separate, identify and evaluate the layers of a market to design a marketing mix. Market Segmentation plan helps companies to focus on all the needs and wants of their customers. According to Asiedu, segmentation is seen as the bedrock of a firm's success in developing market [11]. However, it varies depending on the type of business and the objectives in which it focuses. Segmentation of banking products and services in Colombia has followed the trend of consumer banking segment, commercial banking segment and credit card segment with emphasis on psychographic, geographic, socio-cultural behaviour and demographic. Abel argued that the technique of partitioning a market discloses strategic and profit opportunities for new competitors to challenge market leaders in the system.

Before designing the segmentation plan, the marketing manager needs to accumulate enough information about the product-users variables; considering the geographical location of the business, its demography, and psychographic so that they can target the right market segment with appropriate strategy. Through market segmentation, financial institutions like the banks can be able to know the purchasing habits, needs, lifestyle, age and interests of their consumers and take them into consideration when designing products and services. The practices enable the industry to increase transparency through regulating the disclosure of information; albeit at the lower level. The essence of this is to retain customers, promote customer loyalty and satisfaction. Market segmentation practices allow banks to concentrate on serving the many needs of a specific customer group. The diagram summarises the benefits banks derive from practising market segmentation (Figure 4).

Bank Service Offerings can be defined as the services rendered to customers to satisfy their needs. Some of these services could be products or services related to banking such as leasing, cash management, investment banking, brokerage, factoring, portfolio, risk management, and trust services. However, bank service offerings differ from one geographical location to the other. That is why market segmentation is considered as the most sensitive part of marketing strategy since the practice is useful to describe and locate target segments and influence a firm's strategy. Banks' ability to know and understand their customer's level of needs and interest is important and beneficial in changing, and shaping the firm's product (service) portfolio. Bancolombia for example offers a large range of services and products to customers across all segments through 952 branches with 3,333 ATM's, mobile attention centres (718 Mobile Bank Units) and 1193 banking correspondents in Colombia. Bancolombia is the only commercial bank in Colombia with 65% geographical coverage in the whole country [3]. No wonder it is the largest banking company with widest market share in Colombia.

Also, knowledge about market segmentation can be helpful in terms of getting customers to support the firm's product and service offerings such as lending operations and deposit to help increase the bank's tier-1 capital. Tier-1Capital Ratio is designed to measure the financial strength (financial performance) of banks. Market segmentation practices do not only help banks to reposition their brand or develop new products but also ensure better communication between the two parties, thus, the bank and its customers. Asiedu argued in his conceptual framework called "**The Six Management Tools for Market Development**" that segmentation practices allows firms to develop pricing strategies and marketing campaigns to extract value from both low and high-profit income [7]. Bain and Company argued that making loyalty pay to its full potential require banks to master the five elements of reinforcing their brand, segmenting and targeting customers, transforming customer experience, enhancing product proposition, and improving scale capabilities. These five elements can effectively be done when there is proper marketing segmentation (Figure 5).

Hofstede et al. argued that many relate market segmentation practices to bank-service offerings on the basis of variables such as risk preferences, saving patterns, demographic features and level of income [1]. In the financial and banking industry, incidences of rising overheads expenditure are seen to be linked or related with segmentation practices. Segmentation practices under the banking sector can only be successful when marketers are able to identify individual similarities and differences within segments that have important effect on buying patterns. In this case, marketers need to segment the business environment by identifying group of customers with common interest in terms of gender (male or female), age, status, business, and aged.

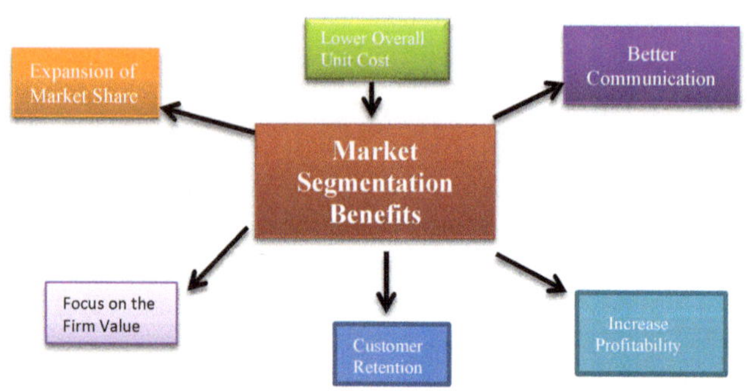

Figure 4: Benefits provided by market segmentation to banks.

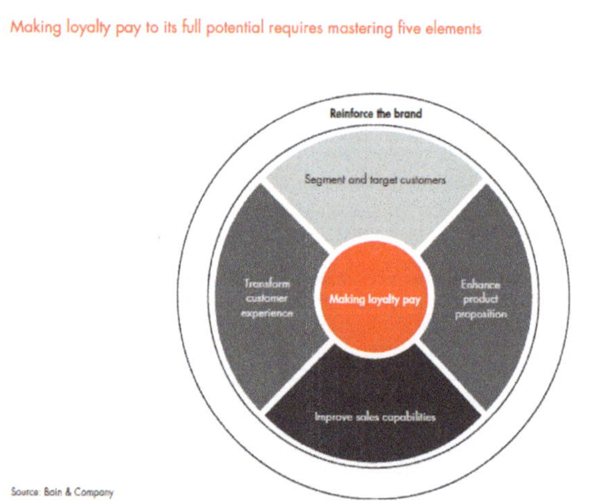

Figure 5: Making loyalty pay to its full potential requires mastering five elements.

After that, they will be able to know and understand their target market by identifying which group of customers their company aim for (that's; is it males or females, students or businessmen, and what target age group) . This will give the firm the chance to position their products or brand by creating concept to appeal to their target market. There are many theoretical models abound for the design of a successful segmentation plan in bank product and service offering. Scholars such as Cardozo and Wind identified a three-stage deign and Hofstede and Steenkamp as well as Petit and Brassington also designed a two-stage process based on the above characteristics [1,17,45]. Colombian banks mostly embark on segmentation with the aim of increasing market share, maximising profit, positioning products and finally enhancing turnover.

Petit and Brassington advocated that ideal market segmentation must go through at least two stages; namely; micro and macro segments stages. According them, while the micro-segments have substantial influence on the decision-making features, macro-segments have influence on buying situations [45]. From the print view of Ferrel and Pride market segmentation can be classified into consumer and industrial (Commercial) segments [46]. Though these theorists differ on certain points, there are basic tenets common to all and that is, to achieve the same objective based on location, size and usage rate adopted by Cardozo and Wind [17].

Most of the focuses of these theorists are meant to distinguish between specific individual customer needs, and the requirement for target market. Ovia and Cooper supported that organisational performance; customer retention and mass customization are likely to be improved whenever bank products and services are designed to satisfy customers' expectation within a market segment [47,48]. This implies that every market segment has its own features and strengths. It is therefore important for various bank marketers to study each segment carefully to know if the type and quality of products and services being rendered are in line with customers' expectation.

Bank performance and customer retention causality

Bank performance based on Key Performance Indicators (KPI) is influenced by the profitability of the company, its percentage of the market share, return on investment (ROM), return on assets (ROA), and return on equity (ROE) as well as its customer retention ability. In the words of Salami and Adeoti [49], the quantity and quality indicators of a bank performance are regulated by the profitability of the business and the risk which gives alternatives for assessing and evaluating the achievement of objectives through maximization of owners' wealth. After 2008-2009 global economic downturns, Colombia banks have shown a strong increase since 2011 by increasing their bank total asset (20.4%), loans (22.8%) in the same year [5,50]. The financial industry has grown in all segments with mortgage lending and consumer banking overtaking commercial lending. Banks have really benefited from effective market segmentation to increase their return on investment, tier-1 capital, return on assets and banking total asset.

Customer retention ability is defined as the ability of a bank to retain its customers based on the assessment of product or service quality. That's bank performance determines how loyal its customers are and it is normally measured in percentage of long term customers. This is very important because satisfied retained customers tend to lower cost (cost less), make valuable reference to new potential customers to increase banks market share, and spend more. However, banks can only perform well and satisfy their customers when there is proper market segmentation. Banks' ability to retain its customer's shows how satisfied their customers and brand loyalties are. Market segmentation can help banks to efficiently match their limited resources to target the market requirements and resource to reduce cost. It paves way to embrace consumer requirement that tends to increase customer satisfaction and retention. Banks can improve their customer retention through segmentation practices. Sylvia and Peter perceived that the ability of a bank to meet the needs of its customers (such as depositors and borrowers), stakeholders, shareholders, and employees show the performance level of the company [51]. In Colombia, the financial sector is quite profitable and credit quality is very strong due to the sound and healthy balance sheet from customers [5].

Colombian banking sector since the beginning of the 1990's have shown great consciousness towards the link between consumer retention and performance [4]. Banks such as Bancolombia, Banco de Bogotá, and BBVA among others have involved in cross selling, product bundling, and integrated computer system and loyalty programmes to attract more customers. Adewuyi propounded that customer loyalty to a bank service and product offering can be developed through employee and customer relation, quick delivery services, closeness to customer business outfits, corporate image built overtime, accessibility and referral, as well as relaxed account opening formalities [52].

Some scholars also link customer retention and bank performance to the company's value maximization in the stock market [7,15,48]. The approach is based on the interrelationship that exist between operational efficiencies changes, the prices of the company's stock in the market, exchange or change rate and the general economic situation. In Colombia, banks such as Bancolombia, Banco de Bogotá, Davivienda, BBVA and Banco de Occidente are more valuable in the stock market.

Although market behaviour towards stock price in theory, shows the performance level and how valuable the company is at the stock market, salient criteria needed for the calculation for banks in Colombia might not be available. And it is based on this assumption that made the researcher to use Profitability Ratio and Tier-1 Capital Ratio as alternative indicators for market value and financial performance. According to Onaolapo et al. [15], a sound financial (banking) system is built upon adequate and profitable capitalized banks. They continued that the use of ratios on performance evaluation covers the size of turnover, dividend or earnings per share, and return on capital profit margin. This signifies that the profit after tax, net interest margin and interest on income in the banking sector determines return on capital employed.

In an attempt to find out the impact of market segmentation patterns on banks successes in Colombia, key profitability ratios such as Tier-1 Capital ratio, Return on Equity (ROE), Net Interest margin and Net Operating Margin were applied. These were used as parameters to find out the impact of market segmentation patterns on the operational performance of the selected banks in Colombia.

Research Methodology and Design

Asiedu opined that "research aims decides what needs to be accomplished with the conduct of study" and Bhattacharya continued that keeping in mind the aims to be achieved [11,53]. The researcher explores which approach suits best the attainment of purpose. In an attempt to find out the impact of market segmentation patterns on banks performance in Colombia, key profitability ratios such as Tier-1 Capital, Return on Equity (ROE), Return on Assets (ROA), Net Interest margin and Net Operating Margin were applied. These were used as parameters to showcase the impact of market segmentation patterns on the operational and financial performance of the selected banks in Colombia. The variables for bank performance and segmentation targets like market share, profit and turnover, operating expenses, return on capital were all sourced from the 2014 annual reports of the five selected banks in Colombia. However, Tier-1 Capital Ratio was sourced from 2012 Bankers database. The study also linked basic criteria of market partitioning patterns with selected commercial banks' performance on customer loyalty, retention and profitability indices.

Out of the 21 commercial banks explored in Colombia, five (5) of them constituting 23.8% were selected for the study. The criteria for the selection of those five (5) banks were based on 2012 Tier 1 Capital Ratio and 2014 market share. Tier-1 Capital Ratio is used to measure the financial strengths or financial performance of banks based on regulator's view point. It is one of the most crucial indicators of financial performance in banking. Tier 1 Capital Ratio is a bank's core equity. The information regarding bank financial performance and segmentation targets such as Tier 1 Capital ($m), Assets ($m), Pre-Tax Profits ($m), Return on Capital (%), and Return on Assets (%), were taken from the 12/2012 Bankers database (Source: thebankersdatabase.com) of the selected commercial banks.

To test, analyse and measure the impacts of market segmentation practices on the selected banks performance in Colombia, Herfindahl Hirschman Index was adopted to calculate market concentration of the banking sector through the use of deposit size of the various selected banks from their 2014 Annual Report. The calculated figures were correlated with performance criteria through the use of spearman's rho test. Spearman's Correlation is non-parametric coefficient which is used to measure the strength of matched (association) of two variables. This test was done to draw the correlation between segmentation adoption and banks performance in Colombia. The analysis explains the strength of co occurrence (linkage) between bivariate in a form of -1 or +1. In this study, a positive correlation coefficient shows a positive relationship between market segmentation and bank performance.

However, a negative coefficient indicates a negative relationship between market segmentation and bank performance. For example if X_1 represent business development (or market share) as calculated using HHI and Y_1 represent the profitability rate among the selected commercial banks: with 'Z' representing a bivariate random sampled size. Therefore; $z(X_1, Y_1) \to (X_z, Y_z), \ldots\ldots(X_2, Y_2)$ can be determined. According to Hofstede et al. and Onaolapo et al. the calculation through this token hence ranks Herfindahl Hirschman Index (HHI) for →t=1, 2, 3, 4………. and period with Net Operating Margin (NOM), Return on Equity (RoE), and Net Interest Margin (NIM) for the various operational duration (period) of the selected commercial banks.

This can demonstrated mathematically as

$$p=\sum_{t=1}^{n}\left(\frac{[R(Y_1)-\frac{z+1}{2}]-\frac{z-1}{2}[R(X_1)\frac{z-1}{2}]}{z(z^2-1)12}\right) \tag{1}$$

Where;

P stands for = Spearman's correlation co-efficient

R (Y_1) = Rank of variable Y_1

R (X_1) = Rank of variable X_1 and

Z = Sample size.

Therefore, the equation was given as shown here below;

$$p=1-\sum\left(\left(\frac{R(Y_1)-R(X_1))^2}{z(z^2-1)}\right)\text{in a computed form...}\quad (2)$$

To make sure the information provided was reliable, valid and authentic, primary sources which focus on survey research strategy was conducted [7]. The customers of the selected banks constituted the target population for the study. The questionnaires were designed to solicit for customers opinions on the effects of segmentation practices on the selected banks' customer retention strategy. The data from the respondents were used to evaluate the successes of the selected banks. The criteria were used to surrogate customer defection ratio by management and bank consumer retention ability. The researcher used these questions to find out how this practice influences customer loyalty and retention in the banking and financial industry. The questions were both closed and opened ended and were designed to elicit customers views on branch loyalty, targeting and organisational product.

Findings and Discussion

This part of the study contains the findings obtained through analysis from Tier-1 Capital Ratio as of December, 2012 and Herfindal Hirschman Index as well as response rate from customers based on questionnaires to test customer retention and loyalty. It presents a detailed discussion from the results obtained while making reference back to the literature review earlier in this article.

Table 2 shows the results obtained using Tier-1 Capital Ratio and it indicates the top five banks performance in the financial industry as of 2012 in Colombia. The tier-1 capital ratio deals with tier-1 capital ($m), Assets ($m), pre-tax profits, return on capital (%), and return on assets (%). This ratio was used to find out if their business segment such as credit card banking, consumer banking, and commercial banking are accepted and supported by customers. No bank can increase its tier-1 capital without first getting customers to support and patronise its products and winning of customer loyalty rely on proper segmentation practices. The idea is to investigate on how marketing segmentation practices influence the financial performance of banks. This is because effective marketing segmentation allows banks to tailor their products and services such as lending operations and deposit to meet customer needs. Looking at the Table 2 on tier-1 capital ratio, thanks to Bankers Database, 2012, it could be seen that the return on capital on all the five (5) banks in Colombia were more than the minimum requirement of 6% as stated by Basel III (Table 2).

The stats according to tier-1 capital show that the largest bank in Colombia as of 2012 was Bancolombia. The second largest bank according to tier 1 capital is Banco de Bogotá, follow by Banco Davivienda, BBVA and Banco de Occidente. These banks are the best capitalized banks in Colombia as per their return on capital. They have higher capital than any other bank in Colombia. This results shows that these banks have advantage because it has a lower regulatory capital requirement due to their business segment. This reveals that these banks have been strong in their consumer banking segment, credit card segment and commercial banking segment. These banks based on their tier-1 capital have advanced on the five elements of winning customer loyalty and have begun to translate such loyalty to better their teir-1 capital and economic.

Also the researcher used Herfindal Hirschman Index to calculate the market share of these banks in 2014. The idea was to find out if these banks have greatly benefited from the use of market segmentation practices in terms of market share. It could be seen from the table that all the five (5) banks scored an index greater than half of the market share in Colombia. This simply shows that these five (5) commercial banks have total dominance in the banking and financial sector in Colombia, thanks to their effective and efficient segmentation patterns. The index

Base-type	Segmentation Criteria	Explanation
Psychological	Psychographic (lifestyle)	Banks can analyse consumers' interest, opinion and activities to understand their pattern of behaviour and lifestyle which affects their decision making processes and purchasing behaviour.
	Benefit Sought	Been able to understand customers purchasing motivation, it can be easy to have insight into the benefits they want from their used products.
Behavioural	Transaction/purchase	Information about customers' transactions and purchases provides very rich data for identifying profitable customer segment. This data can provide scope of analysis on who buys what, when and how (how much they spend and, how often), and what transaction channel did they use to purchase?
	Media usage	Information on what media channels are utilized, when, where, by whom and for how long. This provides useful data to find out the potentials of certain market segments.
	Product usage	Usually segments are obtained from analysing markets using their usage of product offering, product category and brand. This may be in the form of time of usage, frequency of usage, and situation of usage.
Profile	Lifestyle	Analysis on lifestyle is based on the principle that, customers need different products and services at different stages of their lives. For example; young couples, workers, retired.
	Demographic	The key criteria in this area are sex, age, profession (occupation), and religion, level of education, social class and income features. Many of these influences buyers ability to buy a certain product or service.
	Geodemographic	In the banking service context, this approach is very important. This is because it is presumed that there is a relationship between location and the type of house that people live in, and their buying behaviour.
	Geographic	The banking service during segmentation should also know and understand that the needs of potential customers in one geographical area are always different from those in another area. This stems from their custom, tradition and climate difference.

Table 1: Segmenting variables for consumer markets.

Rank	Bank	Tier-1 Capital $M	Assets $M	Pre-tax Profits	Return on Capital (%)	Return on Assets (%)
1	BanColombia	5120	55,272	1224.43	23.91	2.22
2	Banco de Bogotá	4657	45,444	1507.68	32.37	3.32
3	Banco Davivienda	2453	26,599	512.89	20.9	1.93
4	BBVA Colombia	1124	17,240	345.78	30.76	2.01
5	Banco de Occidente	1088	13,327	200.18	18.39	1.50

Source: thebankerdatabase.com Note: all data as of 12/12

Table 2: Top five banks in Colombia in 2012 based on tier-1 capital ratio.

score state that when a score is less than 100%, it means there is weak position. However, if the indexes are more than 100%, it shows strong result in the segmentation patterns and practices adopted by the banks or the monopoly of the market. When we also look market shares in total deposit as of 2014, it could be seen that five (5) banks in Colombia have excellent results in their segmentation patterns and practices. The results show that the marketplace of the banking and financial sector in Colombia is highly concentrated and the banks are characterised by its size, its oligopolistic and segmented structures (Table 3).

More so, in an attempt to test the relationship between bank performance and segmentation adoptions, Spearman's correlation coefficient was used. The result from the test showed a significant relationship that exists between the market share of the selected banks and their total (overall) expenses. The relationship according to the test was 0.581 which implies that banks with large market shares tend to lower their overall operation unit cost and increase profitability. This finding was done based on each bank's market position within the sampled banks. It consisted of both less-dominant and dominant companies in the sector.

The functional models such as quadratic, exponential equations and linear logarithm also proved that there is high contribution of 30.85% in the market share variation and this shows that the total (net) market expenses grow through different marketing segmentation practices among commercial banks in Colombia. It was reported that the five selected banks can still increase their market share until they get to their peak of 37.2%. However, any further increases above this point of 37.2% net (overall) expenses shows diminishing effect which in return diminishes the market share. The findings resulted that when market segmentation expenses is as high as 37.2% of total operating expenses, then benefits derivable can reach its extreme point where additional commitment of fund will reach a direction which can lead to negative result.

S/No.	Participants (Banks)	Deposit in 2014 (Annual Report)	Market Shares (In Total Deposit-A1%)	Square of Market Share ($A1^2$%)
1.	BanColombia, S.A	56231	30.05	903
2.	Banco de Bogotá, S.A	41512	22.18	491.95
3.	Banco de Davivienda, S.A	33773	18.05	325.80
4.	BBVA, S.A	32303	17.26	297.91
5.	Banco de Occidente, S.A	23323	12.46	155.25
	TOTAL	187142	100	HHI=2173.91

Source: Banks 2014 annual reports

Table 3: Total unconsolidated deposit and market share among sampled banks in Colombia.

Banks	Customer's with Active Accounts (Beginning of Period)	Sampled Customer with Active Accounts of Period	Degree of Customer Retention and Loyalty (%)
BanColombia, S.A	50	47	94%
Banco de Bogotá, S.A	50	40	80%
Banco de Davivienda, S.A	50	37	74%
BBVA, S.A	50	35	70%
Banco de Occidente, S.A	50	25	50%

Source: Response rate based on questionnaires to test customer retention and loyalty to bank branch/service 2015.

Table 4: Customer retention and loyalty ability based on selected banks.

To determine the impacts of market segmentation patterns and practices on customer retention and loyalty strategy on banks, the researcher employed a quantitative analysis by investigating the research question through questionnaires to test the five banks customer retention strategy. The table below shows the opinion of the respondents, and degree of customer retention ability for the sampled banks in Colombia.

From Table 4, it could be seen that, out of the 50 customers with active account as of the beginning of the period, 47 of them representing 94% have remained loyal to BanColombia. This shows that Bancolombia's business segment such as credit card, consumer banking and commercial banking segment have helped them to build an interactive relationship based on humanistic experience and trust. This shows that Market segmentation practices do not only help banks to reposition their brand or develop new products but also ensure better communication between the two parties, thus, the bank and its customers. Thus, segmentation allows banks to carefully listen to their customers and respond to their wants and needs. BanColombia's degree of customer retention and loyalty shows their ability to provide great customer experience by satisfying the needs of their customers. 40 (80%) for Banco de Bogotá, 37 (74%) for Banco de Davivienda, 35 (70%) for BBVA and 25 (50%) for Banco de Occidente show a massive impact of market segmentation patterns and practices among the banking and financial industry in Colombia.

To amass everything, the findings indicate that market segmentation practices have benefited these five banks, more than any other bank in Colombia in terms of financial performance and market share. Segmentation practices have led these banks to a more precise definition of the financial market in Colombia in terms of customer needs. The tool has improved the understanding of the management towards their customers. These five banks have used market segmentation practices to exploit and identity a niche market which most of the banks have ignored as not being large enough for them to make profit. This has helped the banks to acquire large market share in the financial and banking industry in Colombia. What the study figured out was that these five banks with large market tend to lower their overall operation cost and increase profitability. Market segmentation has benefited these banks to demonstrate high level of customer retention and loyalty.

Conclusion

This article has assessed the use and impacts of marketing segmentation practices on bank performance in Colombia. The study researched into the type of market segmentation practices adopted by typical Colombian banks, the impacts of market segmentation practices on bank performance on the selected banks in Colombia and the extent to which segmentation practices have influenced customer loyalty through banks product and service offerings.

The study revealed that market segmentation has benefited some section of the banking and financial industry in Colombia than others. That is, it has enabled the selected banks to dominate the market share and customer patronage. It was discovered that Segmentation of banking products and services in Colombia has followed the normal trend of business segment such as credit card segment, consumer banking segment and commercial banking segment with emphasis on psychographic, geographic, socio-cultural behaviour and demographic. Segmentation has allowed the banks to build an interactive relationship based on humanistic experience and trust.

Findings disclosed that the selected banks such as Bancolombia, Banco de Bogotá, Banco de Davivienda, BBVA, and Banco Occidente are well positioned in capital strength and they are the best capitalized banks in Colombia due to their business segments in terms of credit card, consumer banking segment and commercial banking segment. The study exposed that the banks have used segmentation practices to lower their overall operation unit cost, expand their market shares, retain their customers, better their communications, increase profitability and focus on their company. It was however revealed that Bancolombia is the largest bank with tier-1 capital of $5120 Million in Colombia.

Recommendations

Based on the above findings, it is recommended that carefully analysis of the operating environment should be made to ensure effective and efficient segmenting of bank's customer pool to help design its service and product offering. Dominated and less dominated banks can adopt acceptable corporate image, just-in-time service delivery, employee-customer relation, effective and efficient use of referrals and simple account opening formalities to win customer loyalty and satisfaction, which in return, helps to retain old customers and win customers as well.

References

1. Hofstede T, Steetkamp R, Gordon P (2002) International Market Segmentation-Issue & Perspectives. International Journal of Market Research 19: 185-213.
2. Day G (1990) Creating a Distribution Advantage. Channel Wave Software Inc.
3. Fitch Ratings Report (2012) Bancolombia.
4. Uribe JD (2000) The banking industry in Colombia: Competition, Consolidation and Systemic Stability.
5. (2013) IMF Country Report No. 13/50 Colombia: Financial System Stability Assessment. International Monetary Fund Publication Services, Washington D.C.
6. Claessons S (2009) Competition in the Financial Sector. Overview of the Competition Policy. IMF Working Paper WP/09/45, International Monetary Fund Publication Services, Washington D.C.
7. Asiedu E (2015) Supportive Organisational Culture & Employee Job Satisfaction: A Critical Source of Competitive Advantage. A Case Study in a Selected Banking Company in Oxford City-UK. International Journal of Economics & Management Science 2: 290-300.
8. Shaw ES (1973) Financial Deepening in Economic Development. Oxford University Press, New York, USA.
9. Soyibo A (2002) Importance of Financial Institutions in Strategic Management. A paper Presented at the Workshop on Strategic Management (Feb & Consult). Ijebu-Ode.
10. McKinnon RI (1973) Money and Capital in Economic Development. The Brooking Institutions, Washington D.C, NY.
11. Asiedu E (2015) Developing Market as a Source of Competitive Advantage: The Role of Management Tools. Elixir International Journal of Management Arts 88: 36319-36320.
12. Smith WR (1956) Product Differentiation and Market Segmentation as Alternative Marketing Strategies. Journal of Bank Marketing 21: 3-8.
13. Adewoye JO, Salami AO (2006) The Efficacy of Market Segmentation strategy in Nigerian Manufacturing Industries. A Case Study of Nigerian Bottling Company. International Journal of Environmental and Policy Issues.
14. Clarkson AH (1990) Competitive Strategies in Banking Services-Implications of Segmentation Analysis of Consumers by Age Groups. International Journal of Service Industry Management 1: 67-77.
15. Onaolapo AA, Salami AO, Oyedokun AJ (2011) Marketing Segmentation Practices & Performance of Nigerian Commercial Banks. European Journal of Economics. European Journal of Economics 29: 33-40.
16. Bean TP, Ennis DM (1987) Marketing Segmentation: A Review. European Journal of Marketing 21: 20-42.
17. Wind TY, Cardozo JS (1974) Threats to New Product Manufacturability and the Effect of Development Team Integration Process. Journal of Operation Management 17: 691-709.
18. Agbo JA, Onu E (2000) A Tactical Approach to Segmenting the Nigeria Market. Buisness & Management Journal 3: 25-28.
19. Griffith RL, Pol LG (1994) Segmenting Industrial Market. Industrial Marketing Management 23: 39-46.
20. Alfansi L, Sergeant A (2000) Marketing Segmentation in the Indonesian Banking Sector: The Relationship between Demographics and Desired Customer Benefits. International Journal of Bank Marketing 18: 64-74.
21. Baker MJ (1988) Marketing Strategy & Management. Macmillan Education. New York, USA.
22. Frank RE (1972) Market Segmentation. Prentice-Hall, Eaglewood, Cliffs, NJ.
23. Kotler P (1989) Marketing Management. Prentice-Hall, Englewood Cliffs, NJ.
24. Hiam A, Schewe CD (1993) Market Segmentation: Can It Work for Your Company? Incentive 167: 65-66.
25. Wedel M, Kamakura WA (1988) Marketing Segmentation: Conceptual and Methodology Foundations. Kluwer Academic Publishers, Boston, MA.
26. Dickens J, Chappel B (1977) Food for Freud? A Study of the Sexual Polarisation of Food and Food Products. Journal of the Market Research Society 19: 76-92.
27. Frank RE (1989) Market Segmentation Research. Findings & Implications, in Bass F.M. Applications of Science in Marketing Management. John Wiley & Sons, NY.
28. Lansing JB, Kish L (1957) Family Lifestyle as an Independent Variable. American Sociological Review 22: 512-519.
29. Lum T (1978) Segmenting and Constructing Markets. In Worcester: Downham RMJ (eds.), Consumer Market Research Handbook (2nd edn), Van Nostrand Reinhold Co (UK) Ltd, London.
30. Reading B (1988) Why it's time for Us to Save. The Sunday Times.
31. Monk D (1970) Social Grading on the National Readership Survey. Research Service Ltd, London.
32. McCam JM (1974) Marketing Segment Response to the Marketing Decision Variables. Journal of Marketing Research 11: 399-412.
33. Meidan A, Moutinho L (1988) Bank Customers Perception and Loyalty: An Attitudinal Research. European Marketing Academy Proceedings.
34. Harrison TS (1994) Mapping Customer Segments for Personal Financial Services. International Journal of Bank Marketing 12: 17-25.
35. Khermouch G (1960) The Marketers Take Over. Brand-Week 34: 28-35.
36. Twedt DW (1964) How Important is Marketing Strategy to the Heavy User? Journal of Marketing 28: 71-72.
37. Tucker WT (1964) The Development of Brand Loyalty. Journal of Marketing Research 1: 32-35.
38. Cunningham RM (1956) Brand Loyalty-What, Where, How, Much? Harvard Business Review 34: 116-128.
39. Evans FB (1959) Psychology and Objective Factors in Prediction of Brand Choice. The Journal of Business 32: 340-369
40. Pizam A (1972) Psychological Characteristics in Innovators. European Journal of Marketing 6: 203-210.
41. Ziff R (1971) Psychology for Market Segmentation. Journal of Advertising Research 2: 3-9.
42. Mitchell A (1983) The Nine American Lifestyles. Warner, New York.
43. Kotler P (2002) Marketing Management Analysis, Planning, Implementation and Control. Prentice Hill Inc, New Jersey, USA.
44. Doyle P (2004) Don't France m in Fragmented Market for Technology & Patent Acquisition Strategic Firms.
45. Brassington J, Pettit E (2006) Principles of Marketing Financial Times Management (4th edn.). Prentice Hall Inc, New Jersey, USA.
46. Ovia J (2004) IT Deployment as a Corporate Strategic in Repositioning Banks. Zenith Economic Quarterly 1.

47. Pride K, Ferrell N (1985) Marketing, Basic Concept & Decisions. Houghton Mifflin Company, Boston.

48. Cooper C (1993) Portfolio Management for New Products. Reading Ltd. Addition-Wesley.

49. Salami AO, Adeoti JA (2007) A Portfolio Management in Nigerian Banking Industry. A Case Study of Guarantee Trust Bank Plc. Bobcasts Journal of Management & Science 5.

50. Hamann F, Hernandez R, Silva L, Fernando TG (2013) Credit Pro-Cyclicality and Bank Balance Sheet in Colombia. Borradores de economia.

51. Sylvia CH, Peter SR (2013) Bank Management and Financial Service (7th edn). McGraw-Hill, International Edition, Texas, USA.

52. Adewuyi ID (2008) Marketing of Financial Services. Aseda Publishing. Mapo Ibadan-Nigeria.

53. Bhattacharya DK (2006) Research Methodology (2nd edn.). Excel Books, New Delhi, India.

11

How did the French and Belgian Equity Markets React to their Domestic Terrorist Attacks?

Veron JF, Wang I, Duong H, Dang VNT, Pham HNA, Wallace D and Ramiah V*

UniSA Business School, University of South Australia, Australia

Abstract

This paper investigates the effects of domestic terrorist attacks on the stocks listed on French and Belgian stock exchanges. We use two asset pricing models (CAPM and Fama-French Five-Factor Model) to assess how abnormal returns have changed following the attacks. We also estimate short-term and long-term changes in systematic risk around the attacks. Our findings show that the French sectors experienced mixed reactions following the Charlie Hebdo attack and were moderately affected by other terrorist attacks (Paris and Nice). Furthermore, the results indicate that Belgian sectors were sensitive to Brussels terrorist attack in terms of both risk and return.

Keywords: Terrorist attack; Abnormal return; Systematic risk; Equity market

Introduction

Terrorism has, more recently, become a global issue with an alarming escalation in the frequency of terrorist attacks. This has led to an increase in academics investigating the financial implications of terrorist attacks on stock market returns. For instance, using event study methodology, Ramiah and Graham [1], find that domestic terrorism in Indonesia can have a large impact on the risk and returns of the equity market. This impact is found to be greater than international terrorist events such as September 11 in the United States. We adopt a similar approach to separately examine the impacts of the Charlie Hebdo (occurred on 7 January 2015), Paris (13 November 2015) and Nice (15 July 2016) attacks in France in addition to the Brussels attack (22 March 2016) in Belgium on their respective equity markets. Our research provides empirical evidence of terrorist attacks on French and Belgian stock market returns and documents a guide for making investment decisions in the event of another terrorist attack.

Literature Review

The literature suggests that equity holders do not always react negatively to international terrorist activities and may become insensitive to them. Ramiah et al. [2], for instance, find that the Australian stock market was strongly affected by the September 11 attacks in the US, but was not significantly affected by subsequent attacks on Madrid, London and Bali. Graham and Ramiah [3] explain that this is due to investors having already incorporated geopolitical terrorist risk in their expectations. Later studies find similar effects in other markets such as Japan [3], Malaysia [4], Indonesia [1] and Singapore [5]. In the European context, one strand of literature supports the negative effect of terrorist events on stock markets [6] while another strand shows evidence of the positive impact of terrorist events on the stock market [7]. Chen and Siems [8] and Richman et al. [9] document the short term effect of September 11 on the global equity markets whilst other studies show that terrorist attacks tend to have sector-by-sector differences. For instance, Cam [10] shows that food, tobacco and real estate industries were affected by the September 11 attacks.

These studies show that equity markets can react differently to terrorist activities depending on where the attacks occur and the variability in risk and return can differ significantly across the sectors. The current literature indicates a lack of empirical evidence on the effects of terrorist attacks on the French and Belgian markets, hence our paper attempts to fill this gap.

Data and Methodology

We use the French and Belgian daily stock return indexes, the CAC40 and BEL20, respectively, as market proxies and three-month treasury bills as risk-free rates. The data, obtained from Datastream, are from January 2013 to July 2016 and consists 1201 French stocks and 159 Belgian stocks. These stocks are categorised into 40 sectors for France and 33 sectors for Belgium using GICS.

We follow the event study methodology of Brown and Warner [11] by calculating logarithmic daily returns for each stock, then adjust for the daily returns using two asset pricing models to obtain ex–post abnormal returns (AR). If the terrorist attack occurs during normal market trading hours, AR is calculated for the same trading date. Otherwise, AR is calculated from the next available trading day from the event date.

We start by calculating AR using the CAPM,

$$AR = R_{it} - \left(\beta_{it}^{0} + \beta_{it}^{1}\left(R_{mt} - R_{ft}\right)\right)$$

Where R_{it} is the stock return, R_{mt} is the market return, R_{ft} is the risk-free rate and β_{it}^{0} and β_{it}^{1} are the estimated parameters from a rolling CAPM over a period of previous 260 trading days.

The second model is the Fama-French Five-Factor Model (FF5FM) where the AR is estimated as follows:

$$AR = R_{it} - \left(\beta_{it1}^{0} + \beta_{it1}^{1}(R_{mt} - R_{ft}) + \beta_{it1}^{2}(SMB_t) + \beta_{it1}^{3}(HML_t) + \beta_{it1}^{4}(RMW) + \beta_{it1}^{5}(CMA_t)\right)$$

Where SMB_t is the size factor, HML_t is the book-to-market factor, RMW_t is the profitability factor, CMA_t is the investment factor, β_{it1}^{0} is

***Corresponding author:** Vikas Ramiah, Associate Professor, UniSA Business School, 37-43 North Terrace, City West Adelaide, South Australia 5000, Australia
E-mail: vikash.ramiah@unisa.edu.au

the sum of risk-free rate and the intercept α and $\beta_{it1}^{1}, \beta_{it1}^{2}, \beta_{it1}^{3}, \beta_{it1}^{4}$ and β_{it1}^{5} are the coefficients of R_{mt} - R_{ft}, SMB_t, HML_t, RMW_t and CMA_t respectively.

As there may be delayed responses when traders overreact or underreact to news of a terrorist event, we estimate the cumulative abnormal return (CAR) over five (CAR5), ten (CAR10) and fifteen (CAR15) days. To control for firm-specific news, we exclude companies that issue firm-specific information 15 days on either side of the terrorist event dates from the sectors. Firm-specific information is defined as any company press releases on the Euronext exchange.

To determine whether systematic risk of the French and Belgian sectors change, we follow the approach of Ramiah et al. [2] by fitting a multiplicative dummy variable into the CAPM to capture the change in risk following a terrorist attack. The dummy variable takes a value of one on the first trading day after the event and zero otherwise. We also calculate the long-term effects of these terrorist attacks on systematic risk using a multiplicative structural dummy variable, which takes a value of zero prior to each terrorist attack and one after the event.

Empirical Results

In general, our results show that French stock market reacts negatively on the first trading day following the French attacks while no statistically significant AR is observed on the Belgian stock market after the Brussel attacks (Table 1). We also observe that the French stock market tend not to experience any delayed reactions while Belgian stock market exhibits positive CAR5 and CAR10 from the event dates.

France

Table 2 displays statistically significant reactions (in %) from the French stock market following the attacks. Following the Paris attack, the results indicate that only the fixed line telecommunications industry experienced a statistically significant negative abnormal return of -2.95% (CAPM) and -4.04% (FF5FM) on the next trading day following the event with a negligible difference between the two models. This result is mainly driven by firm-specific news as the effects dissipates after controlling for firm-specific information.

When assessing delayed reactions, we find the mining industry exhibits a negative CAR5 of -10.58% (CAPM) and -8.85% (FF5FM) and CAR10 of -14.12% (CAPM) and -9.59% (FF5FM) from the event date. These results remain statistically significant even after controlling for firm-specific information (Table 3).

We find most French sectors to be sensitive to the Paris attack and relatively less so to the Charlie Hebdo and Nice terrorist events. Following the efficient market hypothesis (EMH), it is reasonable to hypothesise that returns will fall as a result of an increase in systematic risk following a terrorist attack. Following the Paris attack, we document an increase in short-term systematic risk in 28 sectors with the mining and fixed line telecommunications sectors experiencing the highest increase of 37.22 and 56.04 respectively (Figure 1). Based on Figure 1, indicating the change in long-term systematic risk, we conclude that the Paris terrorist attack did not influence the long-term risk structure.

Belgium

Statistically significant sectoral reactions (in %) following the

		CAPM				FF5FM			
Country	Date/Event	AR	CAR5	CAR10	CAR15	AR	CAR5	CAR10	CAR15
France	Charlie Hebdo	-0.01	0.11	0.69	-0.93	0.34	2.2	2.59	3.39
		(-0.08)	-0.27	(-1.07)	(-1.20)	-2.41	-5.53	-5.87	-4.33
	Paris	-0.44	-0.37	-0.49	-0.11	-0.4	0.54	0.64	-0.11
		(-3.76)	(-1.05)	(-1.00)	(-0.27)	(-3.66)	-1.59	-1.55	(-0.27)
	Nice	0.17	0.71	N/A	N/A	N/A	N/A	N/A	N/A
		-0.99	-2.1	N/A	N/A	N/A	N/A	N/A	N/A
Belgium	22-03-2016	-0.21	0.73	2	6.21	-0.07	0.34	1.51	3.78
		(-1.66)	-2.18	-3.12	-1.57	(-0.42)	-0.46	-1.17	-1.08

Table 1: Market Reaction following the Terrorist Attacks (t-stat in parenthesis).

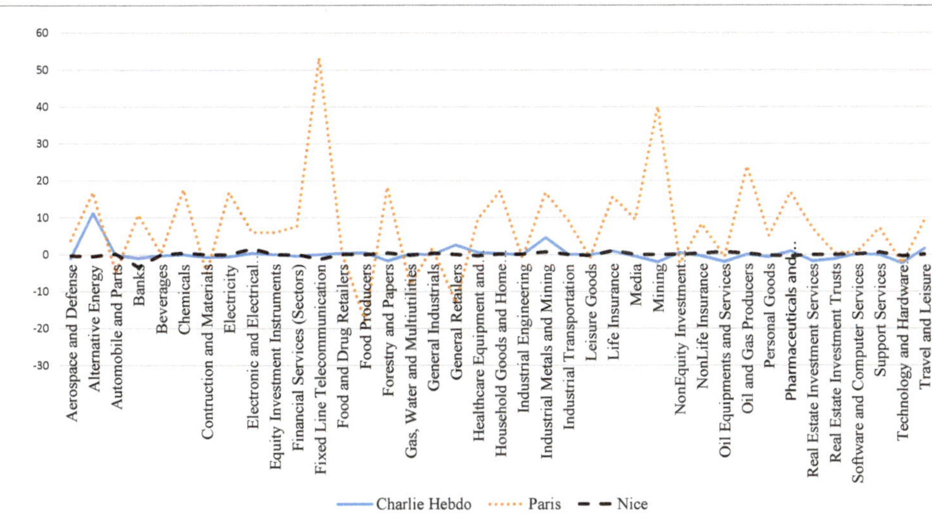

Figure 1: Changes in Systematic Risk following the Terrorist Attacks in France.

	CAPM				FF5FM	
Sector	AR	CAR5	CAR10	CAR15	CAR10	CAR15
France – Charlie Hebdo						
Alternative Energy	0.38	-1.27	-1.7	-22.2	2.05	-19.5
	-0.23	(-0.35)	(-0.36)	(-4.08)	-0.42	(-3.46)
Automobiles and Parts	-0.39	0.93	0.3	2.53	7.14	12.07
	(-0.36)	-0.4	-0.1	-0.7	-1.66	-2.46
Beverages	-0.02	0.01	0.65	1.4	3.06	4.51
	(-0.03)	-0.01	-0.38	-0.71	-1.62	-2.2
Financial Services	-0.26	-1.09	-3.79	-3.31	-1.43	0.23
	(-0.45)	(-0.92)	(-2.46)	(-1.75)	(-0.88)	-0.12
Gas, Water and Multi-utilities	0.03	1.07	-0.47	3.95	2.71	8.26
	-0.03	-0.52	(-0.17)	-1.13	-0.92	-2.36
General Retailers	1.85	0.17	-1.18	-2.17	0	-0.67
	-2.12	-0.09	(-0.47)	(-0.77)	0	(-0.20)
Industrial Metals and Mining	3.14	11.33	7.21	1.89	9.77	4.84
	-1.77	-2.98	-1.36	-0.31	-1.63	-0.68
Life Insurance	0.56	-0.12	0.02	0.15	7.05	10.02
	-0.64	(-0.08)	-0.01	-0.06	-1.85	-2.36
Media	-0.11	1.13	1.8	2.67	3.62	5.01
	(-0.19)	-0.9	-1.11	-1.45	-1.88	-2.2
Non-equity Investment Instruments	0.41	0.19	-0.27	0.2	3.6	5.42
	-1.98	-0.45	(-0.50)	-0.3	-2.16	-2.89
Personal Goods	-0.37	-4.17	-7.12	-8.47	-1.66	-2.39
	(-0.45)	(-2.47)	(-3.08)	(-3.05)	(-0.68)	(-0.87)
Real Estate Investment and Services	-1.26	0.53	0.42	5.75	3.3	10.06
	(-1.53)	-0.33	-0.19	-2.04	-1.32	-3.17
Real Estate Investment Trusts	-0.89	1.03	1.72	2.85	3.37	4.86
	(-1.43)	-0.81	-0.93	-1.26	-1.74	-2.07
France – Paris						
Fixed Line Telecommunications	-2.95	-2.52	-6.5	-4.4	-5.88	-4.86
	(-2.17)	(-0.95)	(-1.69)	(-0.98)	(-1.46)	(-1.02)
Mining	-2.52	-10.58	-14.12	-7.13	-9.59	-3.16
	(-1.66)	(-3.07)	(-2.75)	(-1.16)	(-1.96)	(-0.55)
Non-equity Investment Instruments	0.13	1.34	0.96	0.94	1.3	-0.79
	-0.44	-2.09	-1.17	-0.9	-0.64	(-0.38)
France - Nice						
Financial Services	4.36	2.32	N/A	N/A	N/A	N/A
	-5.62	-1.35	N/A	N/A	N/A	N/A
Fixed Line Telecommunications	2.4	5.72	N/A	N/A	N/A	N/A
	-1.59	-1.99	N/A	N/A	N/A	N/A
Software and Computer Services	0.25	2.87	N/A	N/A	N/A	N/A
	-0.46	-2.37	N/A	N/A	N/A	N/A

Table 2: Significant Sectoral Reactions following the Terrorist Attacks (t-stat in parenthesis).

	CAPM				FF5FM	
Sector	AR	CAR5	CAR10	CAR15	CAR10	CAR15
France – Charlie Hebdo						
Alternative Energy	1.16	4.43	5.53	-0.24	6.74	1.41
	-0.72	-1.48	-1.27	(-0.05)	-1.62	-0.29
Automobiles and Parts	-0.54	0.36	-0.74	0.16	6.81	10.61
	(-0.55)	-0.15	(-0.23)	-0.04	-1.43	-1.87
Beverages	-0.01	-0.17	0.3	1.22	2.58	4.16
	(-0.02)	(-0.11)	-0.14	-0.47	-1.17	-1.66
Financial Services	-0.26	0.07	-4.38	-4.53	-2.36	-1.4
	(-0.33)	-0.04	(-2.02)	(-1.70)	(-1.00)	(-0.49)
Gas, Water and Multiutilities	0	0.71	-0.94	6.1	-0.09	7.16
	0	-0.24	(-0.25)	-1.31	(-0.02)	-1.67
General Retailers	3.81	-0.14	-0.3	-2.38	-1.14	-4.03
	-2.34	(-0.04)	(-0.07)	(-0.50)	(-0.24)	(-0.76)
Industrial Metals and Mining	-0.99	24.16	18.17	14.39	22.62	18.69
	(-0.28)	-3.24	-1.86	-1.29	-2.12	-1.5
Life Insurance	N/A	N/A	N/A	N/A	N/A	N/A
	N/A	N/A	N/A	N/A	N/A	N/A
Media	-0.01	1.7	1.96	2.62	2.12	2.59
	(-0.01)	-1.06	-1.01	-1.28	-0.9	-0.95
Non-equity Investment Instruments	0.41	0.19	-0.27	0.2	3.6	5.42
	-1.98	-0.45	(-0.50)	-0.3	-2.16	-2.89
Personal Goods	-0.36	-6.41	-12.25	-13.65	-6.1	-7.28
	(-0.28)	(-2.40)	(-3.46)	(-3.30)	(-1.58)	(-1.71)
Real Estate Investment and Services	-1.88	2.16	2.09	9.59	4.79	13.31
	(-1.53)	-0.94	-0.64	-2.28	-1.43	-3.04
Real Estate Investment Trusts	-0.14	2.11	4.72	6.36	5.23	6.53
	(-0.06)	-0.44	-0.73	-0.87	-0.77	-0.84
France - Paris						
Fixed Line Telecommunications	N/A	N/A	N/A	N/A	N/A	N/A
	N/A	N/A	N/A	N/A	N/A	N/A
Mining	-4.08	-16.08	-21.87	-11.86	-16.95	-3.39
	(-1.68)	(-2.84)	(-2.60)	(-1.17)	(-1.91)	(-0.34)
Non-equity Investment Instruments	0.13	1.34	0.96	0.94	1.3	-0.79
	-0.44	-2.09	-1.17	-0.9	-0.64	(-0.38)
France - Nice						
Financial Services	7.24	4.21	N/A	N/A	N/A	N/A
	-5.94	-1.54	N/A	N/A	N/A	N/A
Fixed Line Telecommunications	3.82	8.57	N/A	N/A	N/A	N/A
	-1.6	-1.92	N/A	N/A	N/A	N/A
Software and Computer Services	0.13	2.97	N/A	N/A	N/A	N/A
	-0.15	(-1.57)	N/A	N/A	N/A	N/A
Belgium - 22 March 2016						
Aerospace and Defense	N/A	N/A	N/A	N/A	N/A	N/A
	N/A	N/A	N/A	N/A	N/A	N/A
Beverages	-0.31	-1.13	15.14	22.54	15.78	19.26
	(-0.17)	(-0.29)	-2.8	-3.55	-3.05	-3.36
Electricity	0.71	4.72	8.63	189.45	40.11	153.47
	-0.05	-0.14	-0.18	-3.24	-0.96	-3.11
Real Estate Investment and Services	N/A	N/A	N/A	N/A	N/A	N/A
	N/A	N/A	N/A	N/A	N/A	N/A

Table 3: Significant Sectoral Reactions Excluding Firm-Specific Information (t-stat in parenthesis).

terrorist attack in Belgium are shown in Table 2. Surprisingly, we find no statistically significant reactions on the first trading day following the attack. A plausible explanation is that the market had already anticipated the possibility of a terrorist attack due to the imposition of a security lock down on Brussels by the Belgian government. This lockdown was imposed founded on information received indicating that the city was a staging area for the terrorists responsible for the Paris attacks on 21 November 2015 with the Belgian government warning of a "serious and imminent" possibility of a Paris-style attack in Belgium.

However, we find evidence of a delayed response to the attack in the aerospace and defence, beverages, electricity and real estate investment

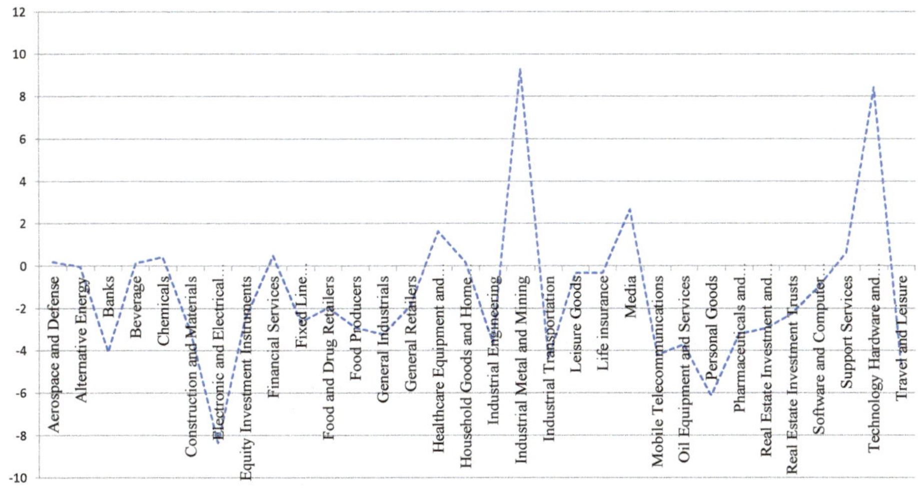

Figure 2: Changes in Systematic Risks following the Terrorist Attack in Belgium.

and services sectors. The electricity sector shows an exceptionally high positive CAR15 of 126.86% (CAPM) and 103.50% (FF5FM). The highly unusual CAR15 is caused by a company, 4Energy, in this sector which experiences a surge of 2300% in stock price rather than being affected by the terrorist attack.

The beverage sector also exhibits statistically significant positive CAR10 of 6.83% (CAPM) and 6.88% (FF5FM) and CAR15 of 8.14% (CAPM) and 7.22% (FF5FM) following the terrorist event. We propose that the positive results are due to an increase in demand for basic needs following extreme events such as this terrorist attack. Furthermore, we document the difference in CAR10 between the two models is insignificant.

Figure 2 displays the changes in systematic risks of the sectors following the terrorist attacks in Belgium. We exclude the electricity sector from our analysis because of the issue with 4Energy (as mentioned above). Surprisingly, ten sectors exhibit an increase in short-term systematic risk whereas 22 sectors experience a decrease in short-term systematic risk. In addition, we find 23 out of 33 sectors experience a decrease in long-term systematic risk. A plausible explanation is that investors have taken the terrorist risk into account in their investment portfolios appraisal.

Conclusion

Overall, our findings suggest that (1) the French terrorist attacks affect the French equity market immediately while the Brussels terrorist attack produced delayed reactions in securities listed on the Belgian stock exchange, (2) Belgian market sectors were relatively less sensitive to their domestic terrorist attack and (3) terrorist attacks do not always lead to an increase in both short-term and long-term systematic risk.

References

1. Ramiah V, Graham M (2013) The impact of domestic and international terrorism on equity markets: Evidence from Indonesia. International Journal of Accounting & Information Management 21: 91-107.
2. Ramiah V, Cam M, Calabro M, Maher D, Ghafouri S (2010) Changes in Equity Returns and Volatility across Different Australian Industries Following the Recent Terrorist Attacks. Pacific-Basin Finance Journal 18: 64-76.
3. Graham M, Ramiah V (2012) Global Terrorism and Adaptive Expectations in Financial Markets: Evidence from Japanese Equity Market. Research in International Business and Finance 26: 97-119.
4. Ramiah V (2012) The Impact of International Terrorist Attacks on the Risk and Return of Malaysian Equity Portfolios. Review of Pacific Basin Financial Markets and Policies 15: 145-171.
5. Ramiah V, Hui CWC (2015) Industry Effects of Recent Terrorist Attacks: Evidence from Singapore. Terrorism and the economy: Impacts on the capital market and the global tourism industry. Eleven International Publishing, Hague, Netherlands, pp: 41-76.
6. Barros CP, Gil-Alana LA (2009) Stock Market Returns and Terrorist Violence: Evidence from the Basque Country. Applied Economics Letters 16: 1575-1579.
7. Apergis E, Apergis N (2016) The impact of 11/13 Paris terrorist attacks on stock prices: Evidence from the international defence industry. Applied Economics Letters pp: 45-48.
8. Chen AH, Siems TF (2004) The effects of terrorism on global capital markets. European Journal of Political Economy 20: 349-366.
9. Richman V, Santos MR, Barkoulas JT (2005) Short- and Long-Term effects of the 9/11 Event: The International Evidence. International Journal of Theoretical and Applied Finance 8: 947-958.
10. Cam M (2008) The Impact of Terrorism on United States Industries. Economic Papers 27: 115-135.
11. Brown SJ, Warner JB (1985) Using daily stock returns: the case of event studies. Journal of Financial Economics 14: 3-31.

Audit Tenure, Rotation and Accounting Conservatism: Empirical Evidences from Nigeria

Babatolu Ayorinde[1] and Oyewo Babajide[2]*

[1]*Department of Accounting, Federal University of Agriculture, Abeokuta, Ogun State, Nigeria*

[2]*Department of Accounting, University of Lagos, Nigeria*

Abstract

Accounting regulators have, for many years, had concerns about the possible lack of Independence between auditors and their clients, which arises from a long-standing professional relationship between the two parties. The reservation stems from a widely-held belief that the risk of audit failure increases when an auditor and a client remain together for a long period of time. The possibility exists that auditors might get too familiar with their clients and in consequence loses professional scepticism and objectivity when the relationship goes on for too long. Stakeholders are therefore interested in if long-term relationship between companies and their auditors gives rise to closeness that impairs auditors' independence and reduces quality of audit work. With these in view, an attempt was made by the research to examine the link between audit tenure, rotation, and accounting conservatism using empirical data from Nigeria. Secondary data were randomly gathered by drawing 100 observations from the published financial statements of sample companies operating in the financial and non-financial sectors. Quantitative methods such as descriptive statistics, correlation, and multiple- regression analysis were used for data analyses. Findings were that; the tenure of auditor has a significant positive influence on firms accounting conservatism; the rotation of audit firms also significantly influences accounting conservatism. The study recommends the mandatory rotation of audit firms' lead engagement partner and the review partner on an engagement for publicly listed companies, and the strict prohibition of providing non-audit services by auditors to their clients to enhance auditors' independence and the quality of audit services.

Keywords: Audit failure; Audit tenure; Auditor rotation; Conservatism; Nigeria

Introduction

History is replete with recurring instances of prominent corporate failures and collapses that have ensued in recent times, raising serious concern about the authenticity and reliability of companies' financial statements. While the preparation of an accurate financial statement is a statutory duty vested on the company directors by S.334 (1) of the companies and allied matters Act [1], questions are further been put forward in respect of the quality and independence of external auditors who render assurance services. Accounting regulators have, for many years, had reservations about the independence gap that exist between auditors and their clients; this arises from a long-standing professional relationship between the two parties. Auditors working with clients for a long time would likely have increased specific knowledge about the activities of their clients, thereby increasing conservatism and result in a positive association between auditor tenure and accounting conservatism [2].

Attempts have been made by regulators to boost audit quality through formulation of rules impacting on auditors' independence. Concerns about auditors' independence were accountable in part for the development and passage of the Sarbanes Oxley Act of 2002 and the formation of the Public Company Accounting Oversight Board (PCAOB). The concern stems from a widely publicized belief that when an auditor gets too familiar with his client for a long period of time, it increases the risk of audit failure. There is every possibility that once auditors get too acquainted with their clients, they can lose professional scepticism and objectivity when such a relationship goes on for too long. It is of great interest to relevant stakeholders whether long-term relationships that exist between auditors and their client can bring about some level of closeness which can impair auditors' independence and reduces audit quality. To check this tendency, mandatory audit firm rotation has been suggested as a possible way out of it. The concept of mandatory auditors' rotation was introduced as a result of widely publicized corporate collapses that led to litigation. The topical issue of mandatory rotation of external auditor was perceived to be a way out of threat posed to the independence of an auditor as a result of the long relationship that may exist between the client and the auditor [3-5].

To ensure audit quality and investor confidence in the financial statements, a case could be made for mandatory rotation as an avenue to foster a more independent auditor-client relationship. In the mist of the scandals rocking Enron, the Comptroller General was directed by the Sarbanes-Oxley Act to study the merit and demerit of mandatory rotation. On the other hand, short term auditor-client relationships may also be associated with a high risk of audit failure due to an auditor's lack of familiarity with a client and its operations. The AICPA is of the view that new auditor-client relationships has more inherent risk, with reference to a study carried out by the SEC Practice Section, which came up with the findings that audit failures are three times more likely to occur in the case where the auditor is new to the client. Nonetheless, the Sarbanes Oxley Act requires audit partner rotation the question remains: what is the relation between audit firm tenure and audit quality?

There are two views on the issue of mandatory rotation of external auditors: one derives from the audit profession which is of the view

***Corresponding author:** Oyewo Babajide, Department of Accounting, University of Lagos, Nigeria, E-mail: meetjidemichael@ymail.com

that rotation is unnecessary because it would be costly to client and may reduce the quality of audits. The second perspective is from the regulators, which is in support of the rotation of the external auditors requiring audit firm to periodically let go of their client because of the notion that it could solve the problem of independence. It is against this background that the research attempts to empirically examine audit tenure, rotation and accounting conservatism using empirical data from Nigeria.

Review of Related Literatures

Conservatism has been seen as an integral part of accounting practice, which is usually expressed as the anticipation of losses and the non-recognition of profit [6]. Anticipating profits could be seen as recording profits before there is legal claim to their associated future cash flows and before the revenues are verifiable [7]. Financial Accounting Standards Boards (FASB) Statement of Concepts No. 2 justifies this behaviour by defining conservatism as "a prudent reaction to uncertainty to try to ensure that uncertainties and risks inherent in business situations are satisfactorily considered" [8]. Many construe this as traditional guidance for choosing between various methods of accounting for similar transactions. Conservatism suggests that when accountants are to make professional judgements and there is insufficient evidence as to information taking a position, the position to be taken should be the one which will less likely lead to overstatement of assets and income. Basu [9] viewed conservatism as representing the accountant's predisposition to involve a high sense of authentication to see good news as gains than to see bad news as losses. In other words, conservatism can be defined as accountants' asymmetric acknowledgment of unrealized gains and losses in reported earnings. Building on this interpretation, Basu [9] posits that accountants spot bad news in earnings more promptly than good news. Thus, if we are of the opinion that current equity returns efficiently put together good and bad news regarding firms' expected future cash flows, we expect that the slope coefficient and $R2$ in a regression of earnings on unexpected returns should be higher for firms with negative unexpected returns (proxy for "bad news") and lower for those with positive unexpected returns (proxy for "good news"). The empirical results from Basu [9] are consistent with this prediction. Basu's measures have been used in so many studies to assess the degree of accounting conservatism [10-14].

The importance of accounting conservatism principle in accounting practice cannot be over emphasized, as it is essential to understand the variance, and the inherent link between the traditional concept of accounting conservatism and the unevenness of recognition presented by Basu [9]. Going by how recent the literature is, the concept of conservatism was inconsistent across studies. The traditional conservatism is called ex ante conservatism [15-17], news independent conservatism [18] or unconditional conservatism [19-21]. Basu's concept of conservatism was referred to as ex-post conservatism, news-dependent conservatism [18], or conditional conservatism [17-19]. For the purpose of discussion, we will use the concept of unconditional and conditional conservatism throughout this study. Unconditional conservatism arose from policies that reduce earnings free of current economic news or from the application of generally accepted accounting principles (GAAP), denoting that aspects of the accounting process determined at the time of acquisition of assets and liabilities yield expected undervalued assets. Prompt expensing of the costs of most internally developed intangibles, accelerated depreciation of property, plant, and equipment, and historical cost accounting for positive net present value projects are examples of unconditional conservatism. As noted in Basu [9], since unconditional conservatism is independent of current-period news, it will lower the intercept in a regression of earnings on returns but will not affect the slope coefficient. That is, the implementation of unconditional conservatism will not have an impact on the relation between earnings and returns in the current period.

On the other hand, conditional conservatism implies that bad news is recognised asymmetrically compared to good news: which means that, book values are written down under unfavourable circumstances but not written up under favourable circumstances. Examples of conditional conservatism include, the market accounting rule for inventory, impairment accounting for long-lived tangible and intangible assets, and the asymmetric recognition of contingent losses and contingent gains. Thus, in an efficient market situation if good news and bad news are arrested promptly and totally in equity prices, the use of conditional conservatism will snowball to the slope coefficient in the regression of earnings on current returns being higher for firms with negative unexpected returns (proxy for bad news) than for those with positive unexpected returns (proxy for good news).

Only recently have researchers begun to study the interaction between the two types of conservatism. For example, Basu [22] notes that less conservative news-unrelated accounting allocation methods are more likely to result in asset write downs, and hence, greater asymmetric news-driven conservatism. DeAngelo [23] argued that audit firm size could be a surrogate of audit quality. Thus, big audit firms are expected to provide high quality earnings in financial statements. Consistent with this argument, Basu [22] demonstrated that the earnings reported by big auditees are more conservative than the earnings of non-big auditees. Earnings conservatism can be used by audit firms as a risk management strategy. Audit firms can maintain higher reported audit quality by demanding more conservative earnings for their clients even under the 'threat' of auditor independence.

To critically examine the relationship between audit firm tenure, audit firm rotation and conservatism as an intrinsic attribute of earnings quality, an in-depth understanding of earnings quality is essential. Most of the studies opined that, the quality of financial reporting depends on the company's management and the audit firm since financial statements are perceived as a joint product of the duo [24,25]. Supposing that auditor independence has a directly effect on the quality of an audit, this will imply that any such change in auditor independence will translate to a change in the quality of the financial statements, hence affects the quality of reported earnings. Proponents of auditor rotation are of this argument that auditors would provide more support for aggressive accounting by the client's management when their independence is compromised, which in due course result in failures to spot material errors [4]. Further, when the auditor-client relationship lengthens, management is likely to gain more reporting flexibility which could result in earnings management quality [26,27] opined that utmost criticism with respect to reduced auditor independence and its effect on earnings quality "seems to be premised on instances of overly aggressive reporting, whereby the underlying deterioration in the profitability of collapsing firms has been concealed". Aggressive reporting has been defined as using reporting methods that portray "the client's financial situation favourably when that method is not clearly indicated by the facts and relevant professional literature". The methods in totality are likely to result in an increase of earnings and/or liquidity in the sense that managers have incentives to partially estimate the future values in favour of current earnings [9].

The relationship between a long audit-client relationship and audit quality is not farfetched because economic, financial and social factors could drive the final result. Most empirical studies define audit quality relative to risk which is the risk that an auditor will fail to modify the opinion on audited financial statement that are materially misstated. If auditors are more independent, there is the likelihood that they will not compromise their integrity by attempting to manipulate earnings management, which would be shown in more income decreasing items being recorded [28]. Given that audit firm rotation impacts the independence of the auditor and also impact aggressive reporting, a variation in earnings depicting losses on a timely basis than gains would exist after audit firm rotation. Francis et al. [14] argued that conservative accounting results in higher accounting quality. This research takes the position that the level of earnings conservatism in reported earnings can be used to identify changes in the quality of those earnings after audit firm rotation.

Research Method

Population and sample of study

The population of the study consists of all quoted firms in Nigerian Stock Exchange. Samples were drawn from these sectors using the NSE classification of publicly quoted companies: Agriculture, Automobile and Tyre, Breweries, Building Materials, Chemical and Paints, Conglomerates companies, Food/Beverages and Tobacco, Construction, Healthcare, Industrial/Domestic Products, Packaging, Printing and Publishing, Textiles, Petroleum marketing companies, Banking, Insurance and others. 30 companies covering these sectors were randomly selected using the published financial statements for two years - 2009 and 2010. On the whole, 100 observations comprising of 50 from the financial sector and 50 from the non-financial sector were used.

Research hypotheses and model specification

The purpose of the present study was to investigate association between accounting conservatism (financial report quality) and audit tenure and rotation in Nigeria.

The following hypotheses have been formulated and expressed in the alternative form for the study:

H_1^1: The tenure of auditor exerts a positive influence on the firm's accounting conservatism.

H_1^2: The rotation of a firm's auditor exerts positive influence on its accounting conservatism.

H_1^3: Firm's accounting conservatism is positively associated with the rotation of audit partner.

The model adopted for the study started with a focus on measuring accounting conservatism (financial report quality) using total accruals, which were then partitioned into discretionary and non-discretionary accruals. Chen et al. [28] opined that the absolute discretionary accruals (ADA) which is a more popular and widely use indicator for measuring mangers accounting estimates and accounting choices. Thus, discretionary accrual was used to proxy accounting conservatism. In establishing discretionary accruals, we used the modified Jones model. Beaver and Ryan [20] identified the Jones model as a strong tool for measuring accounting conservatism (discretionary accruals). Dabor and Adeyemi [29] identified that the model uses components of annual financial statements such as turnover (Sales revenue), account receivables, profit and assets to establish discretionary accruals. Added to the above, the model establishes total accruals by subtracting cash flow from operations from net income before extraordinary items. Thus,

$$\text{TACC} = \text{EBEI- CFO} \tag{1}$$

Where TACC represents total accruals, EBEI is the net income before extraordinary items, and CFO is cash flow from operations. Total accruals are then partitioned into two components i.e non-discretionary accruals, which relate to normal activities of the company and discretionary accruals, which are determined according to the subjective reasoning of management. That is, discretionary accrual is a function of accounting conservatism (management choice of accounting policies) [30-32].

$$\text{TACC} = \alpha_0 + \alpha_1 (\Delta\text{REV-}\Delta\text{REC}) + \alpha_2\text{PPE} + \alpha_3\text{ROA}_{t-1} + e \tag{2}$$

Where ΔREV is change in revenue; ΔREC is change in accounts receivable; PPE means plants, property and equipment (Fixed Assets) and ROA is return on assets managed in the previous accounting period. All the variables that enter the equation are scaled by total assets (TA) of the previous year- $TA_{t-1.}$

The non-discretionary accruals portion (NDA) is also modelled as a function of the change in revenue, change in accounts receivable, plants, property and equipment and return on assets in the previous accounting period as follows;

$$\text{NDA} = \alpha_0 + \alpha_1 (\Delta\text{REV-}\Delta\text{REC}) + \alpha_2\text{PPE} + \alpha_3\text{ROA}_{t-1} \tag{3}$$

The difference between (2) and (3) above is the residual e, and this is the discretionary accruals (DA). Thus,

$$\text{DA} = \text{TACC} - [\alpha_0 + \alpha_1 (\Delta\text{REV-}\Delta\text{REC}) + \alpha_2\text{PPE} + \alpha_3\text{ROA}_{(t-1)}] \tag{4}$$

All the variables, except $ROA_{t-1,}$ are scaled by total assets in previous year.

In the light of the above and the research hypotheses we specified a multiple regression econometric model (4). By definition, multiple regression econometric models is one that seeks to explain change or variation in the values of one variable called the dependent variable(accounting conservatism) on the basis of changes in other variables known as the independent or explanatory variables (audit firm rotation and audit partner rotation). The assumption is that the dependent variable is a linear function of the independent variables. The function form of the model is express as follows;

$$\text{ACC} = f(\text{AUTEN,AUDROT, AUDPAT}) \tag{5}$$

The multiple regression with an error term (ε_t) is express in equation (6)

$$\text{ACC} = \alpha_0 + \beta_1\text{AUTEN} + \beta_2\text{AUDROT} + \beta_3\text{AUDPAT} + \varepsilon_t \tag{6}$$

Table 1 provides a summary of variable definitions and expected signs for relations.

The study used Descriptive Statistics, Correlation Analysis, and multiple Ordinary Least Square (OLS) Regression Analysis. The model was estimated using the ordinary least square (OLS) estimation technique with the aid of computer software (Eviews 7). The hypotheses stated was tested using the t-ratios obtained from the regression result. To ensure that our model is statistical and econometrically valid we conducted diagnostic test such as goodness fit and heteroscedaticity test.

Variables	Apriori Sign	Explanation
ACC		Accounting conservatism is measured as discretionary accruals(DA); $DA = TACC – [\alpha_0 + \alpha_1 (\Delta REV-\Delta REC) + \alpha_2 PPE+ \alpha_3 ROA_{t-1)}$
AUTEN	+/-	Auditor Tenure (number of years the current auditor has been firms). The following code was used to measure firms auditor tenure; we assign the values of "1" for Less than one year, "2" for more than one years but less than 3yeras and "3" for more three years.
AUDROT		Firms Auditor rotation. We use three dummy to proxy firms type of auditor rotation. These three dummy are express as follows; (i) AUDROTD1 = is assign the value of "1" when there is a change of auditor from non-big 4 to Big 4 (CROSS UP) otherwise "0" (ii) AUDROTD2 = is assign the value of "1" when there is a change of auditor from big 4 to non-Big 4 (CROSS DOWN) otherwise "0" (iii) AUDROTD3 = is assign the value of "1" when there is a change of auditor from big 4 to another Big 4 (LATERAL) otherwise "0"
AUDPAT		Firms Auditor partner rotation. The value of "1" is assign when there is a change of firms auditor partner, otherwise "0"

Table 1: Definition of Variables and Expected Signs.

	TENURE	AUDROTD1	AUDROTD2	AUDROTD3	ACC
Mean	4.5	0.02	0.02	0.55	97381941
Median	5	0	0	1	3925558
Maximum	5	1	1	1	3.36E+09
Minimum	1	0	0	0	-9072908
Std. Dev.	1.267304	0.140705	0.140705	0.5	4.04E+08
Skewness	-2.319302	6.857143	6.857143	-0.201008	6.737039
Kurtosis	6.57114	48.02041	48.02041	1.040404	50.39974
Jarque-Bera	142.7904	9228.828	9228.828	16.67347	10117.86
Probability	0	0	0	0.00024	0
Observations	100	100	100	100	100

Table 2: Descriptive statistics of study variables.

	TENURE	AUDROTD1	AUDROTD2	AUDROTD3	ACC
TENURE	1	-0.056647	-0.113293	-0.231144	0.051144
AUDROTD1	-0.05665	1	0.489796	-0.014358	-0.345209
AUDROTD2	-0.11329	0.489796	1	-0.014358	-0.345009
AUDROTD3	-0.23114	-0.014358	-0.014358	1	-0.043303
ACC	0.051144	-0.345209	-0.345009	-0.043303	1

Table 3: Correlation analysis between Audit Tenure, Rotation, and Accounting conservatism.

Data Presentation and Analysis

Descriptive statistical analysis

The descriptive statistical analysis result of variables is captured in Table 2. Result shows that the minimum audit tenure of firms quoted on the Stock Exchange is about a year while the maximum audit tenure is about 5 years. On average the audit tenure is about 4.5 years. 63 firms have had the same auditor from 2006 to 2010 which indicates No audit rotation. Hence majority of firms quoted on the Stock exchange do not rotate their auditors.

The minimum auditor rotation from non-big4 to big4 (AUDROTD1) is 0 while the maximum auditor rotation from non-big4 to big4 (AUDROTD1). It was observed that only one firm had changed from non-big4 to big4 audit firm. The minimum auditor rotation from big4 to non-big4 (AUDROTD2) is 0 while the maximum auditor rotation from big4 to non-big4 (AUDROTD2). It was observed that only three firms had changed from big4 to non-big4 audit firm. The minimum auditor rotation from big4 to big4 (AUDROTD3) is 0 while the maximum auditor rotation from big4 to big4 (AUDROTD3). It was observed that only six firms had changed from big4 to non-big4 audit firm. The jarque-Bera statistics revealed that all the variables are normally distributed.

Variable	Coefficient	Std. Error	t-Statistic	Prob.
C	-1.20E+08	1.59E+08	-0.755601	0.4518
TENURE	-34855898	30746418	-2.133657	0.0348
AUDROTD1	-6.67E+08	3.07E+08	-2.175414	0.0321
AUDROTD2	-7.01E+08	3.08E+08	-2.273202	0.0253
AUDROTD3	60897974	77439048	0.786399	0.4336
R-squared	0.373564	Mean dependent var		97381941
Adjusted R-squared	0.338767	S.D. dependent var		4.04E+08
S.E. of regression	3.74E+08	Akaike info criterion		42.36866
Sum squared resid	1.33E+19	Schwarz criterion		42.49892
Log likelihood	-2113.433	F-statistic		4.987863
Durbin-Watson stat	1.995234	Prob(F-statistic)		0.001080

Table 4: Ordinary Least Square regression result for 2009.

Inferential statistical analysis

Correlation analysis: In exploring the relationship between accounting conservatism and the variables used in the study, we carried out correlation analysis using Pearson product moment correlation method. The results are presented in the Table 3. There is a weak positive relationship of about 5% between accounting conservatism and audit tenure. An increase in audit tenure would lead to an increase in accounting conservatism. There is fairly weak negative relationship between accounting conservatism and auditor rotation from non-big4 to big4 (AUDROTD1) with correlation co-efficient of -0.35). With a correlation co-efficient of -0.35, the relationship between accounting conservatism and auditor rotation from big4 to non-big4 (AUDROTD2) is fairly weak and negative. There exists a weak negative relationship between accounting conservatism and auditor rotation from big4 to big4 (AUDROTD3) with a correlation value of 0.04.

An increase in auditor rotation from non-big4 to big4 audit firm, rotation from big4 to non-big4, or rotation from big4 to big4 should lead to a decrease in accounting conservatism.

Regression analysis: Regression Analysis for 2009- The result from the ordinary least square regression result is presented in Table 4. The coefficient of determination (R-Square) with a value of 0.37 means that about 37% of the total systematic variations in accounting conservatism(ACC), have been explained by the explanatory variables taken together. The Adjusted R-square shows that even after adjusting for the degree of freedom the model could still explain only about 33% of the total systematic variations in accounting conservatism (ACC) while about 67% of the systematic variation in accounting conservatism (ACC) was left unaccounted for by the model which has been captured by the stochastic disturbance term in the model. This implies that other factors apart from audit tenure and audit rotation affect accounting conservatism in Nigeria.

It was observed that the overall model was statistically significant since the calculated F- value of 4.92 was greater than the critical F-value at 5% level of significance. On the basis of the individual statistical significance, as shown by the t-ratios in the table above, it was observed that TENURE, AUDROTD1, and AUDROTD2 was statistically significant since their calculated t-values of 2.13, 2.17 and 2.27 respectively was greater than the critical t-value of 2.0 at 5% level of significance under the two tailed test. This means that TENURE, AUDROTD1, and AUDROTD2 had a significant impact on accounting conservatism while AUDROTD3 was not statistically significant since the calculated t-value of 0.78 was less than the critical t-value of 2.0 at 5% level of significance under the two tailed test (Table 5). The Durbin Watson statistics of 1.99 indicates the absence of first order autocorrelation of the stochastic variables inside the error term in the model.

Regression Analysis for 2010-The coefficient of determination (R-Square) with a value of 0.24 means that about 24% of the total systematic variations in accounting conservatism(ACC), have been explained by the explanatory variables taken together. The Adjusted R-square shows that even after adjusting for the degree of freedom the model could still explain only about 20% of the total systematic variations in accounting conservatism (ACC) while about 80% of the systematic variation in accounting conservatism (ACC) was left unaccounted for by the model. Overall, the model was statistically significant since the calculated F-value of 6.03 was greater than the critical F-value at 5% level of significance.

On the basis of the individual statistical significance, as shown by the t-ratios in the table above, it was observed that TENURE, AUDROTD1, and AUDROTD2 was statistically significant since their calculated t-values of 3.2, 1.85 and 2.02 respectively was greater than the critical t-value at 5% and 10% level of significance under the two tailed test. This means that TENURE, AUDROTD1, and AUDROTD2 had a significant impact on accounting conservatism while AUDROTD3 was not statistically significant since the calculated t-value of 0.97 was less than the critical t-value at 5% and 10% level of significance under the two tailed test. Thus, audit rotation from big4 to big4 audit firm has no significant impact on accounting conservatism. Furthermore, it was observed that TENURE, AUDROTD1, and AUDROTD2 had a negative relationship with accounting conservatism while AUDROTD1 had a positive relationship with accounting conservatism. The Durbin Watson statistics of 2.16 indicates the absence of first order autocorrelation of the stochastic variables inside the error term in the model.

Variable	Coefficient	Std. Error	t-Statistic	Prob.
C	1.90E+08	95851995	1.984407	0.0487
TENURE	-33668373	19164255	-1.756832	0.0806
AUDROTD1	-3.17E+08	98391253	-3.224391	0.0015
AUDROTD2	-55068027	83607088	-2.658653	0.0309
AUDROTD3	-22252045	62997046	-0.353224	0.7243
AR(1)	0.062273	0.073264	0.849981	0.3964
R-squared	0.119767	Mean dependent var		35373807
Adjusted R-squared	0.096105	S.D. dependent var		1.80E+08
S.E. of regression	1.71E+08	Akaike info criterion		40.78292
Sum squared resid	5.44E+18	Schwarz criterion		40.88471
Log likelihood	-3909.160	F-statistic		5.061543
Durbin-Watson stat	2.037436	Prob(F-statistic)		0.000225

Table 5: Pooled Ordinary Least Square regression result.

Pooled regression analysis: The coefficient of determination (R-Square) with a value of 0.119 means that about 12% of the total systematic variations in accounting conservatism(ACC), have been explained by the explanatory variables taken together. The Adjusted R-square shows that even after adjusting for the degree of freedom the model could still explain only about 10% of the total systematic variations in accounting conservatism (ACC) while about 90% of the systematic variation in accounting conservatism (ACC) was left unaccounted for by the model which has been captured by the stochastic disturbance term in the model. This implies that other factors apart from audit tenure and audit rotation affect accounting conservatism in Nigeria.

The F-statistics shows that the overall model was statistically significant since the calculated F- value of 5.06 was greater than the critical F-value at 5% level of significance. it was observed that TENURE, AUDROTD1, and AUDROTD2 was statistically significant since their calculated t-values of 1.75, 3.22 and 2.65 respectively was greater than the critical t-value at 5% and 10% level of significance under the two tailed test. Thus, audit rotation from big4 to big4 audit firm has no significant impact on accounting conservatism. Furthermore, it was observed that TENURE, AUDROTD1, AUDROTD2 and AUDROTD1 had a negative relationship with accounting conservatism. Durbin Watson statistics of 2.0 indicates the absence of first order autocorrelation of the stochastic variables inside the error term in the model.

Hypotheses testing

Hypothesis 1

H_1^1: The tenure of auditor exerts a positive influence on the firm's accounting conservatism.

The empirical result reveals that TENURE with a calculated t-value of 1.75 is greater than the critical t-values of 1.64 at 10% level of significance under the two-tailed test. Hence, we reject the null hypothesis and accept the alternative hypothesis that the tenure of auditor exerts a significant influence on firms accounting conservatism.

Hypothesis 2

H_1^2: The rotation of a firm's auditor exerts positive influence on its accounting conservatism.

The empirical result reveals that AUDROTD1 with a calculated t-value of 3.22 is greater than the critical t-values 1.64 at 10% level of significance under the two-tailed test. Hence, we reject the null hypothesis and accept the alternative hypothesis that the rotation of audit firms from Big 4 to Non-Big4 audit firms exerts a significant influence on firms accounting conservatism.

Hypothesis 3

H_1^3: Firm's accounting conservatism is positively associated with the rotation of audit partner.

The empirical result reveals that AUDROTD2 with a calculated t-value of 2.65 is greater than the critical t-values of 1.64 at 10% level of significance under the two-tailed test. Hence, we reject the null hypothesis and accept the alternative hypothesis that the rotation of audit firms from Non-Big 4 to Big4 audit firms exerts a significant influence on firms accounting conservatism.

Discussion of Findings

The study revealed that the tenure of auditor has a significant positive influence on firms accounting conservatism; conservatism increases as auditor tenure lengthens. This is consistent with the findings of Jenkins and Velur that conservatism increases as auditor tenure lengthens. The study also showed that the rotation of audit firms from Non-Big 4 to Big4 audit firms and from Big 4 to Non- Big4 audit firms has a significant influence on accounting conservatism which is in tandem with the findings of Sinnett that mandatory auditor rotation will adversely affect not only the auditors' accumulation of specific knowledge about their clients, but also auditors' independence because it undermines the incentives to build up a reputation for auditors' honesty, especially in the last period before rotation. Meanwhile, a newly appointed auditor might fail because of lack of a thorough understanding of the client. Incumbent auditors can profit from their learning curve effect in the detection of material errors or breach.

The study establishes the necessity to have properly defined maximum legal audit tenure, in order to minimize audit tenure elongation in Nigeria. There has been recent expression of concern by the Institute of Chartered Accountants of Nigeria, ICAN, that a long involvement of an individual or audit team with a client could lead to circumstances that could threaten objectivity and independence. It therefore suggested an orderly rotation of senior personnel serving on an audit engagement (section 4:76 of Rules of Professional Conduct for Members).

The study found out that long audit tenure impacts negatively on the quality of the auditor's report when the audit tenure is prolonged. This indicates that the longer the audit tenure, the lower the quality of audit. This disagrees with the findings of Ghosh and Moon, Carcello and Nagy [31] that prolongation of audit tenure increases audit quality because an auditor is able to gain firm-specific expertise and a better understanding of the client's business as the auditor's tenure. The study revealed that audit rotation can minimize the negative impact of long tenure, but the audit firms rather than audit partners should be rotated.

Conclusion and Recommendations

The study has attempted to empirically examine audit tenure, rotation and accounting conservatism in Nigeria. We therefore conclude that: the tenure of auditor has a significant influence on firms accounting conservatism; the rotation of audit firms from non-big4 to big4, rotation from big4 to non-big4, or rotation from big4 to big4 has a significant influence on accounting conservatism. In Nigeria, there exists a negative relationship between audit tenure and audit quality. This indicates that the longer the audit tenure, it may create familiarity threat by virtue of a close relationship with the client, its directors, officers or employees. The audit opinion of the auditor will favour the client, thus, impairing the independence of the auditor. Low-quality audits can mislead investors and result in misallocated resources. To ensure quality of audit and enhance auditor's independence, a period of five years has been suggested and adopted in some countries as the maximum audit tenure in an audite company for a principal partner of a firm.

The research contributes to knowledge in that it scientifically examines the connection between audit tenure, rotation and accounting conservatism. It also empirically established that the tenure.

The study recommends the mandatory rotation of audit firm lead engagement partner and the review partner on an engagement for publicly listed companies. A partner rotated after a pre-defined period should not resume the lead engagement role until a further period of time, say minimum of two years. The tenure of the Appointed Auditor should be one year in the first instance, renewable annually subject to satisfactory performance for 3 years and on no account should annual renewal extend the total tenure of the appointed firm or firms beyond 5 years. This is to ensure that the independence of the auditor is not placed in jeopardy. Professional bodies such as the Institute of Chartered Accountants of Nigeria (ICAN) should strictly ensure that their members who audit for their clients do not audit for more than three years at a stretch to preserve the independence of the auditor and his objectivity. There should be strict prohibition as to the provision of non-audit services by auditors to their audit clients. This could impair an auditor's independence. The auditor would lack independence if he represents an audit client before a law court on matters outside their main audit job such as maintaining or preparing the audit client's accounting records, preparing financial statements and originating source data underlying the audit client's financial statements.

References

1. (2004) Companies and Allied Matters Act (CAMA).
2. Jenkins D, Velury U (2008) Does auditor tenure influence the reporting of conservative earnings? Journal of Accounting and Public Policy 27: 115-132.
3. Jackson AB, Moldrich M, Roebuck P (2008) Mandatory audit firm rotation and audit quality, Managerial Auditing Journal 23: 420-437.
4. Myers J, Myers L, Omer T (2003) Exploring the term of the auditor-client relationship and the quality of earnings: A case for mandatory auditor rotation? The Accounting Review 78: 779-799.
5. Coopers P (2002) Mandatory rotation of audit firms: will it improve audit quality? New York.
6. Bliss J (1924) Management through accounts. New York: Ronald Press.
7. Watts R (2003) Conservatism in accounting Part1: Explanations and implications, Accounting Horizons 17: 207-221.
8. FASB (1980) Statement of Concepts No 2: Qualitative characteristics of accounting information, Financial Accounting Standard Board, Norwalk.
9. Basu S (1997) The conservatism principle and the asymmetric timeliness of earnings. J Account Eco 24: 3-37.
10. Givoly D, Hayn C (2000) The changing time series properties of earnings, cash flows and accruals: has financial reporting become more conservative?, J Account Eco 29: 287-320.
11. Ball R, Kothari S, Robin A (2000) The Effect of International Institutional Factors on Properties of Accounting Earnings. J Account Res 29: 1-51.
12. Chaney P, Philipich K (2003) The price-earnings relation in troubled times: the case of Arthur Andersen. Working paper, Vanderbilt University and The Ohio State University.
13. Krishnan G (2003) Audit quality and the pricing of discretionary accruals, Auditing: A Journal of Practice and Theory 22: 109-126.
14. Francis J, Olsson R, Schipper K (2004) Costs of capital and earnings attributes. The Accounting Review 79: 967-1010.
15. Giner B, Rees W (2001) On the asymmetric recognition of good and bad news in France, Germany and the United Kingdom, J Bus Financ Account 28: 1333-1349.
16. Pope P, Walker M (2002) Ex-ante and ex-post accounting conservatism, asset recognition, and asymmetric earnings timelines. Working Paper, Lancaster University.
17. Richardson G, Tinaikar S (2004) Accounting based valuation models: what have we learned? Accounting and Finance 44: 223-255.
18. Chandra U, Wasley C, Waymire G (2004) Income conservatism in the U.S. technology sector. Working paper, University of Rochester.
19. Ball R, Shivakumar L (2006) The Role of Accruals in Asymmetrically Timely Gain and Loss Recognition, J Account Res 44: 207-242.

20. Beaver W, Ryan S (2005) Conditional and unconditional conservatism: concepts and modelling, Review of Accounting Studies 10: 269-309.

21. Ryan S, Zarowin P (2003) Why has the contemporaneous linear returns earnings relation declined? The Accounting Review 78: 523-553.

22. Basu S (2001) Discussion of 'on the asymmetric recognition of good and bad news in France, Germany and the United Kingdom. J Bus Financ Account 28: 1333-1349.

23. DeAngelo L (1981) Auditor size and audit quality. J Account Eco 3: 113-127.

24. Antle R, Nalebuff B (1991) Conservatism and auditor-client negotiations. J Account Res 29: 31-54.

25. Hamilton J, Ruddock C, Stokes D, Taylor S (2005) Audit partner rotation, earnings quality and earnings conservatism, Working paper, and University of New South Wales, Sydney.

26. Davis LR, Soo B, Trompeter G (2000) Auditor tenure, auditor independence and earnings management. Working paper, Michigan Tech University and Boston College.

27. Kaplan S, Mauldin E (2008) Auditor rotation and the appearance of independence: Evidence from non-professional investors, J Account Public Policy 27: 177-192.

28. Chen K, Elder R, Hsieh Y (2007) Corporate Governance and Earnings management: The Implication of Corporate Governance Best Practice Principles for Taiwanese listed companies. J Contemp Acc Eco 3: 73-105.

29. Dabor E, Adeyemi S (2009) Corporate Governance and the Credibility of Financial Statements in Nigeria, J Bus Sys Governance and Ethics 4.

30. Ghosh A, Moon D (2005) Does auditor tenure impair audit quality? The Accounting Review 80: 585-612.

31. Carcello J, Nagy A (2004) Audit firm tenure and fraudulent financial reporting Auditing: A Journal of Practice and Theory 23: 55-69.

An Empirical Analysis of Liquidity, Profitability and Solvency of Bangladeshi Banks

Abdullah M*

Assistant Professor, Independent University, Dhaka, Bangladesh

Abstract

The financial sector of Bangladesh is small and underdevelopment and this sector resides of banking and an emerging capital market. The banking sector in the country comparatively more developed than the equity market, even though both are developing in international benchmark. In light of recent events that have taken place in the Bangladesh, the importance of knowing the financial position of banks is imperative for investors. Most investor use balance sheet, income statement, change in equity and statement of cash flow to calculate different ratios for technical analysis. Investor uses this ratio and trend analysis to invest in capital market. In this research I take 29 banks as sample size and calculate their different ratios. For examining the applicability of Altman's Z-Score model to forecasting banking failures. The emphasis of this research is to endorse the cogency of Altman's Z-Score model as a predictor of Bangladeshi bank failures. I after analyzing the all sample banks Z-Score I found that 7 banks are in healthy financial position and 22 banks are in insolvent during the time period of FY 2009-2014. Islamic or Sariah follower banks are doing better than conventional banks. Sate owned banks are doing better than before. This research indorses that those banks are in insolvent zone for their published financial review or trend statement. This supplementary material is probable to intensification stockholder assurance by their ability to make more conversant decisions.

Keywords: Financial performance; Liquidity; Bankruptcy; Bangladesh; Bank; Credit risk; Z-score; Bank profitability

Introduction

For bankruptcy companies in general and public shareholding will suffer financial distress. Not only owners are affected, but also other financial statements users, such as investors, creditors, and the economy in general will also be affected. Consequently, an early warning of bankruptcy could be taken as a precaution to be established to lower the risk and danger levels of company bankruptcy or distress. The motivation for this study arises from the arguments made by several authors who identified financial ratios and financial indicators that are used as a yardstick for bankruptcy prediction. It is based on where he compared a number of financial ratios of group of companies for the five years prior to bankruptcy period with another group of companies that are not bankrupt [1]. Then Altman [2,3], developed a model (Altmanz-score) which was the most renowned model in predicting company bankruptcy using financial ratios. Mr. Mahtab [4] has done another study and that was focused on Bangladeshi two groups of Banks, Conventional and Islamic Banks. So I focused my study on the performance evaluation of Bangladeshi Banks. I discuss about many ratios and performance indicator and compare their efficiency and effectiveness of operations of Banks in term of their return on investment, return on asset, return on equity and other company performance indicator. The research was based on secondary data and they are collected from five banks published annual reports. These data were analysed to test the financial performance of the banks by using ratio analysis which were selected by Altman Z score model. Those ratios are liquidity, profitability, efficiency and financial leverage. Working capital shows the position of a company's liquidity, efficiency, and overall health and it includes cash, inventory, accounts receivable, accounts payable and the portion of debt due within one year. Positive working capital generally indicates that a company is able to pay off its short-term liabilities almost immediately. Negative working capital generally indicates a company is unable to do so. The retained earnings of a company are the percentage of net income this is not paid out as dividends to its shareholders and it is retained to reinvest or to pay down debt that is accumulated over the year. The lower the outcome of ratio, the more a company is funding assets by borrowing or through retained earnings which again increases the risk of bankruptcy if the firm cannot meet its debt obligations. Companies with low profit margins tend to have high asset turnover, while those with high profit margins have low asset turnover. Companies in the retail industry tend to have a very high turnover ratio due mainly to cutthroat and competitive pricing. The measure of a company's financial leverage Debt-equity ratio relates the amount of a firms' debt financing with the amount of equity financing. CI Staff [5], indicator such as Earnings before Interest & Taxes to Total Assets is a variation on return on assets, and that show the efficiency of a company. This ratio assesses a firm's ability to generate profits from its assets before deducting interest and taxes. It Measures operating efficiency apart from tax and leveraging factors. It recognizes operating earnings as being important to long-term viability of banks and indicates a percentage of customer deposits; customer deposits as a percentage of total liabilities, and total equity as a percentage of total assets were computed to compare banks financial performance.

Problem Statement

The focus of my study is to apply an evolved model of Altman's Z score namely the 'Z" Score model [6] to failed banks. This model overcomes the manufacturing limitation of Altman's pioneering model and can be used on financial institutions. The main objective is to verify if the Z" Score is a true indicator of financial failure for a financial institution. The recent global crisis has demonstrated the importance

***Corresponding author:** Abdullah M, Assistant Professor, Independent University, Dhaka, Bangladesh, E-mail: htasfiq@gmail.com

of banks both at national and international levels. Business failures are a natural phenomenon in Bangladeshi economic system with firms entering and exiting as a function of overall business activity and expectations [7].

Corporate failure is the sequential conclusion due to systematic and non-systematic factors. Financial and accounting literature has over and over again renewed the confidence in ratio analysis as a proficient predictor of corporate failure. Nevertheless, more attention should be focused on the prediction of banking failures [8].

Financial performance is a subjective measure of how well a firm can use assets from its primary mode of business and generate revenues. The financial performance is also used as a general measure of overall financial health performance over the period. There are many different ways to measure financial performance. As far as ratios are concerned, there are numbers of ratios existing to evaluate the financial performance of a firm. These ratios can be classified into several categories such as liquidity ratios, profitability ratios, solvency ratios etc. Another effective indication of corporate performance in predicting financial solvency of a firm is Altman's Z-score. This is nothing but a combination of financial ratios to form an index of profitability. The ratios used to calculate Z-score are working capital to total assets, retained earnings to total assets, EBIT to total assets, market value of equity to total liabilities and sales to total assets [4].

In Bangladesh the Z score does not apply to every situation. It can only be used for forecasting if the company being analysed can be compared to the database. The Z-score formula for predicting bankruptcy was developed in 1968 by Edward I. Altman, a financial economist and professor at the Leonard N. Stern School of Business at New York University. The Z-score is a multivariate formula for a measurement of the financial health of a company and a powerful diagnostic tool that forecasts the probability of a company entering bankruptcy within a 2 year period. A good way to measure the possibility of bankruptcy is to use Z score model [2]. Therefore many companies in Bangladesh are suffering from financial distress risk due to very poor management capability and operating inefficiency although its reflection to the stock price is absent from the market in many instances. The Altman Z score, model though may not be fully applicable for companies in Bangladesh, yet proves its strong validity and correctness in predicting financial status of the Z category companies [9].

The Problem Statement of this research is to "Measure the financial performance of the banking sector in Bangladesh by using various standard of ratio as current ratio, Retained earnings to total assets ratio, return on assets ratio, book value of equity to total liabilities ratio and linking all of them together to find out the impact on profitability through the use of Altman Z Score".

Purpose of the Study

1. To measure the financial performance of Bangladesh Banking Sector using Altman's Z-score test and ratio analysis.
2. To test the correlations of five ratios with Z-score.
3. To measure the short-term financial position between five banks through liquidity ratios.
4. To analyse the short-term profitability position between five banks through profitability ratios.
5. To analyse the efficiency between five banks through efficiency ratios.
6. To analyse the leverage of five banks through financial leverage ratios

Literature Review

Altman's Z-score

The Altman Z-Score (Named on Edward Altman, New York University professor) is a combination of five financial ratios to estimate the financial position of a company and also a toll for predict corporate bankruptcy. Though Altman planned to invent the Z-Score in the 1960s, the concept of trying to predict which companies would bankrupt was new in that time. Altman use a statistical analysis called multivariate analysis to investigate some traditional ratio-analysis. These give him a concept that not only the effects of several ratios on the "performance of company" bankruptcy model, but to consider how those ratios affected each other's in this model. Edward I. Altman [2], after evaluating 66 companies Altman developed Z-Score model, half of them was filed for bankruptcy between 1946 and 1965. He started investigating his model with 22 ratio, then he classified them into five categories. They are:

1. Liquidity Ratio
2. Profitability Ratio
3. Leverage Ratio
4. Solvency Ratio
5. Activity Ratio

Edward I. Altman [2], Altman model is 90% accurate in classifying the bankrupt firms and 80% accurate in speculating the next financial situation. In 2009, Morgan Stanley strategy analyst, Graham Secker, used the Z-score to rank a basket of European companies. He found that the companies with weaker balance sheets underperformed the market more than two thirds of the time. Morgan Stanley also found that a company with an Altman Z-score of less than 1 tended to underperform the wider market by more than 4%. The Altman model has been used in air transport to successfully predict carrier failures as early as the 1980s where it correctly presaged the bankruptcy filings of both Braniff and Continental [10], and in subsequent years to track airline financial performance. Because of the significant increase in the use of leasing to finance assets in this industry, that model has become less reliable over time. Jhon Aiyabei [11], analyze the financial performance of small business firms based on MDA for the measurement and significance of financial distress. Lin Lin and Jenifarpisse [12], used Conditional probability analysis (CPA) model to determine merger acquisitions to prediction of the corporate failure.

The Z-Score model was based on 66 sample of manufacturing company; half of them were same pair groups. The formula for the Z-Score is:

$$Z = 6.56T1 + 3.26T2 + 6.72T3 + 1.05T4$$

T1 = (Current Assets-Current Liabilities) / Total Assets

T2 = Retained Earnings / Total Assets

T3 = Earnings before Interest and Taxes / Total Assets

T4 = Book Value of Equity / Total Liabilities

This equation gives a coefficient from the result of step by step multiple discriminate analysis or MDA regression (Table 1). Richard D [13], there is a reverse situation for ratios value. High ratios increase the Z score and minimize the risk of failure, on the other hand low ratios increase the risk of failure. The values were derived from the

Situation	Z-Score	Indicator	Remarks
1	Less than 1.1	Insolvent	The score indicates a high probability of distress within this time period.
2	Among 1.1 and 2.66	Healthy	There is a good chance of the company going bankrupt within the next 2 years of operations
3	2.6 and above	Secure	The company is considered 'Safe' based on the financial figures only.

Table 1: Z-Score and survivability indicators.

intercept of Z score. Altman [2], found that the values of the Z were 1.1 and 2.66. Firms with scores of <1.1 fit a bankruptcy profile, while firms with scores>2. 6 fit the solvency profile. Scores between the two values lie in what Altman [2] called the "gray zone" where profiling is more difficult. If the analyst wanted one key score in place of the "gray zone," he argued for a 2.6 cut off because that zone contained.

T1 working capital / total asset

Working capital is needed for day-to-day operations. Working capital is a common measure of a company's liquidity, efficiency, and overall health. It includes cash, inventory, accounts receivable, accounts payable and the portion of debt due within one year.

Positive working capital generally indicates that a company is able to pay off its short-term liabilities almost immediately. Negative working capital generally indicates a company is unable to do so.

The formula of Working Capital to Total Asset is:

$$Working\ Capital\ to\ Total\ Asset\ Ratio = \frac{Working\ Capital}{Total\ Asset}$$

There are several ways to evaluate a company's working capital. Such as, by calculating the inventory-turnover ratio, the receivable ratio, the payable ratio, the current ratio and the quick ratio.

Working capital management is a very important factor, which has a direct positive effect on profitability as well as liquidity of the company. Liquidity and profitability are both the two different sides of same coin. Optimum level of liquidity guarantees a firm to meet their short term debts and the proper management of flow can be promised by a profitable business. The most important items inside determination of working capital are inventories of the corporation, its accounts receivables and payables [14]. The management of working capital frequently considered a tool to maintaining competence of the business inside their operations. Working capital is often assessed by lenders to judge the financial short term paying back ability in difficult financial period [15].

There is a strong linear relationship between profitability of the firm and its working capital efficiency. The ability of the company to earn profit can be referred to as the profitability of that company. Profit is determined by deducting expenses from the revenue incurred in generating that revenue. The amount of profit can be a good measure of the performance of a company, so I can use profitability as a measure of the financial performance of a company. Proper Working capital management ensures that the company increased its profitability. Effective working capital management is very important due to its significant effect on profitability of company and thus the existence of company in the market. Efficient working capital management involves planning and controlling current assets and current liabilities in a manner that eliminates the risk of inability to meet due short term obligations on the one hand and avoid excessive investment in these assets on the other hand [14,16].

Mobeen Ur Rehman and Naveed Anjum [15], empirically examine the effects of working capital management on the profitability of Pakistan cement industry. Secondary Data was collected from Annual Reports and the sample size is 10 consisting of Pakistan cement Companies listed in KSE from 2003-2008. The relationship between working capital management and profitability is examined using statistical tools. The result accepts the hypothesis that there is a positive relationship between working capital management and profitability on the cement sector of Pakistan. Deloof [14,17], discussed that most firms had a large amount of cash invested in working capital. It can therefore be expected that the way in which working capital is managed will have a significant impact on profitability of those firms. Using correlation and regression tests he found a significant negative relationship between gross operating income and the number of days accounts receivable, inventories and accounts payable of Belgian firms. On basis of these results he suggested that managers could create value for their shareholders by reducing the number of days' accounts receivable and inventories to a reasonable minimum. The negative relationship between accounts payable and profitability is consistent with the view that less profitable firms wait longer to pay their bills.

T2 retained earnings / total assets

The retained earnings of a company are the percentage of net income this is not paid out as dividends to its shareholders and it is retained to reinvest or to pay down debt that is accumulated over the year. The retained earnings to total asset ratio is calculated as follows:

$$Retained\ Earnings\ to\ Total\ Assetsratio = \frac{Retained\ Earnings}{Total\ Asset}$$

Total assets refer to the total amount of assets that is owned by an organization. And the assets must have the economic value that is expended over time to yield a benefit for the owner. Assets are also classified on the balance sheet as either current assets or long term assets. A current asset, such as an account receivable is expected to be liquidated within one year. A long-term asset, such as a fixed asset, is expected to be liquidated in more than one year.

Through retained earnings to Total Assets I measure the extent to which a company relies on debt or leverage on that particular year. The lower the outcome of ratio, the more a company is funding assets by borrowing instead of through retained earnings which again increases the risk of bankruptcy if the firm cannot meet its debt obligations

Retained Earnings/Total Assets indicates how much assets will be financed from retained earnings. The increase in retained earnings will give capital adequacy to the firm and which indicates favorable impact on debt to equity ratio [18].

Retained Earnings to Total Assets measures the amount of reinvested earnings or losses, which reflects the extent of the company's leverage. Companies that have low RE/TA are financing capital expenditure through borrowings rather than through retained earnings. Companies which have high RE/TA suggest a history of profitability and the ability to stand up to a bad year of losses [19].

Retained earnings is the account which reports the total amount of reinvested earnings or losses of a firm over time. The account is also referred to as earned surplus. It should note that the retained earnings account is subject to manipulations. In addition the RE\TA ratio measures the leverage of a firm. those Firms with high RE. Relative to low RE, financed their assets through retention of profits and have not utilized as much debt [2].

Retained earnings to total assets are an indicator of the "cumulative profitability" of the firm overtime which indicates the efficiency of management in manufacturing, Sales, Administration and other activities [20].

Retained earnings to total assets measures profitability that reflects the company's age and earning power [21].

Retained earnings represent the accumulation of earnings that have remained within the entity. Retained earnings can be affected by reorganizations and stock dividend declarations, if so, consideration should be given to readjusting retained earnings. To increase retained earnings a company must generates profits either through operations or the profitable sell-off of assets or division or the forgiveness of the debt [22].

The ratio indicates the ability of a firm to earn profit and thereby securing retained earnings. Normally a firm has higher retained earnings, a firm will not starve for liquidity crunch and also the firm can reinvest in the appropriate venture at cheaper cost [23].

T3 Operating earnings / total assets

CI Staff [5] this is a variation on return on assets, which is net income divided by total assets. This ratio assesses a firm's ability to generate profits from its assets before deducting interest and taxes. It Measures operating efficiency apart from tax and leveraging factors. It recognizes operating earnings as being important to long-term viability.

Earnings before interest and tax (EBIT) to total assets ratio indicates a proportion between the measure that shows company's profitability and company's assets [8]. It measures the productivity of the firm's assets notwithstanding any tax or leverage factors. "Since a firm's ultimate existence is based on the earning power of its assets, this ratio appears to be particularly appropriate for studies dealing with corporate failure" [2]. In short, it represents general profitability of the company's assets. EBITDA would not be a very accurate measure of a bank's financial position as it takes into account depreciation and amortization which would not be applicable to the nature of a bank's operations.

This ratio is calculated by dividing the total assets of a firm into its earnings before interest and tax reductions. Vineet Chouhan, Bibhas Chandra and Shubham Goswami [24], Predicting financial stability of select BSE companies revisiting Altman Z score In essence, it is a measure of the true productivity of the firm's assets, abstracting from any tax or leverage factors. Since a firm's ultimate existence is based on the earning power of its assets, this ratio appears to be particularly appropriate for studies dealing with corporate failure. Furthermore, insolvency in a bankruptcy sense occurs when the total liabilities exceed a fair valuation of the firm's assets with value determined by the earning power of the assets. (EBIT/TA) is a version of return on assets (ROA), an effective way of assessing a firm's ability to squeeze profits before factors like interest and tax are deducted.

This ratio is used to evaluate the company's ability to generate operating profit with existing asset. When the company has high profit with low asset, it has a relatively low chance of getting default. It is due to the dollar of asset that is able to generate a larger amount of operating profit. On the other way, lower income might not be enough to cover company's daily expenses (Thai, 2014)Earnings before interest and tax (EBIT) to total assets ratio indicates a proportion between the measure that shows company's profitability and company's assets [25]. In short, it represents general profitability of the company's assets. Data to calculate this ratio is collected from the income statement and balance sheet.

There are no general norms for this ratio. It is recommended to compare this ratio to those of the companies, working within the same industry.

$$EBIT\ to\ Total\ Asset\ Ratio = \frac{EBIT}{Total\ Asset}$$

Earnings before interest and taxes (EBIT) equal net income, plus interest expense, plus taxes. Assets (Total assets) - a balance sheet item, representing what a company owns

T4 Market value of equity / book value of total liabilities

This is a measure of a company's financial leverage. It is reciprocal of the familiar debt-equity ratio. Debt-equity ratio relates the amount of a firms' debt financing with the amount of equity financing. Market Value of Equity is the total current market value of all common and preferred shares on the other side Book Value of Total Liabilities is the sum of all current and long-term liabilities of a firms' balance sheet. If a company has no debt that is unlevered firm, there is some sort of benefit with debt. By acquiring debt financing firm get extra money for investment and make a tax shield from the debt [26]. That is the leverage and debt-equity ratio show the picture how a firm using the debt to maximizing profit. What is considered a "high" debt-to-equity ratio differs depending upon the industry, because some industries tend to utilize more debt financing than others. There is no single value above which would be deemed a high debt-to-equity ratio. For calculation of debt-equity ratio I have to divide firm's equity with the total amount of debt.

$$Equity\ to\ Debt\ ratio = \frac{Market\ Value\ of\ Equity}{Book\ Value\ of\ Total\ Liabilities}$$

VikasTyagi, describes that a higher debt-equity ratio generally means that a company has been aggressive in financing its growth with debt [27]. This can result in unpredictable earnings as a result of the additional interest expense. If a lot of debt is used to finance increased operation, the company could potentially generate more earnings than it would have without this outside financing. If this were to increase earnings by a greater amount than the debt cost, then the shareholders benefit as more earnings are being spread among the same amount of shareholders. However, the cost of this debt financing may outweigh the return that the company generates on the debt through investment and business activities and become too much for the company to handle. This can lead to bankruptcy, which would leave shareholders with nothing.

The debt-equity ratio also depends on the industry in which the company operates. If capital intensive industries as auto manufacturing tend to have a debt-equity ratio above 2, while personal computer companies have a debt-equity of under 0.5 [28]. The financial industry, for example, typically has a higher debt-to-equity ratio. This is for the fact that banks and other financial institutions borrow money to lend money, which results in a higher debt-equity ratio. There are more sectors that have high capital structure so they have higher debt-equity ratios, such as services, utilities and the industrial goods sector. As a result, investors must look at a company's historical debt-to-equity ratio figures to determine if there have been significant changes that could indicate a red flag. In addition, investors must also make comparisons between other similar companies and the industry as a whole to determine if a particular firm has what could be considered a high debt-to-equity ratio.

Optimal debt-equity ratio is considered to be about liabilities = equity, but the ratio is very industry has this type ratio because it depends on the proportion of current and non-current assets. The more non-current the assets and equity is required to finance these long term investments [29]. A higher total debt-to-equity ratio indicates that the sector has been increasing the relative share of debt in external financing, whereas a lower debt-to-equity ratio indicates that the sector is financing a decreasing proportion of its activities through debt as compared to financing through their equity. Variations in the market value of equity can also cause changes in the ratio. Therefore, if a financial corporation's ratio is 3.5 it means that the liability outstanding is 3. 5 times larger than their shareholder's equity. Higher debt can result in volatile earnings due to additional interest expense as well as increased vulnerability to business solvency [29]. However, opposing to what many believe, debt is not necessarily a bad thing, it can be positive, provided it is used for productive purposes such as purchasing assets and improving processes to increase net profits. Also, the debt-to-equity ratio is more significant when relate over a period of time. Non-consolidated debt data gives important info about the total liability of the financial corporation's sector. For these reason Edward I. Altman [2] us this ratio as a variable for his Z-Score model for a better concept of a firms' financial performance.

Research Framework

Z = 6.56T1 + 3.26T2 + 6.72T3 + 1.05T4

T1 = (Current Assets - Current Liabilities) / Total Assets

T2 = Retained Earnings / Total Assets

T3 = Earnings before Interest and Taxes / Total Assets

T4 = Book Value of Equity / Total Liabilities

Research Questions

Q_1: What is the relationship between Working Capital to Total Assets and Z-score?

Q_2: What is the relationship between Retained Earnings to Total Assets and Z-score?

Q_3: What is the relationship between EBIT to Total Assets and Z-score?

Q_4: What is the relationship between Market Value of Equity to Total Liabilities Z-score?

Hypothesis

Ho_1: There is a negative relationship between Working Capital to Total Assets and Z-score.

Ha_1: There is a positive relationship between Working Capital to Total Assets and Z-score.

Ho_2: There is a negative relationship between Retained Earnings to Total Assets and Z-score.

Ha_2: There is a positive relationship between Retained Earnings to Total Assets and Z-score.

Ho_3: There is a negative relationship between EBIT to Total Assets and Z-score.

Ha_3: There is a positive relationship between EBIT to Total Assets and Z-score.

Ho_4: There is a negative relationship between Market Value of Equity to Total Liabilities and Z-score.

Ha_4: There is a positive relationship between Market Value of Equity to Total Liabilities and Z-score.

Research Design

Research design is crucial as it acts as a blueprint for the collection, measurement and analysis of data. In this study, I have selected ex post facto design, because this study required structured and précised way to show the relationship among different variables and to test hypotheses.

The method of data collection

Under the method of data collection, I have selected secondary data through annual report. Because I wanted to communicate with different employees of banks by asking them many questions.

Researcher control of variables

In ex post facto research I uses historical data that cannot be manipulated by researchers. In my research my dependent variable is financial performance and that cannot be changed by me. My research could be stated as ex post facto design.

Degree of research question crystallization

My study was Formal study as I tried to explain the relationship among different variables.

Purpose of the study

My study was designed for testing hypotheses quantitatively which required a good number of samples which reflected the investor.

The time dimension

I focused on longitudinal study. I have studied on 29 different banks of Bangladesh as samples for and they did not need to be studied again for the same study. I have analyzed6 years annual repot data.

The topical scope

The topical scope for my research is statistical study. I used statistical analysis to collect quantitative information because it is designed for breadth instead of depth.

The research environment

My research occurred in actual environment conditions. My research environment could be specified as stimulation. This option was chosen because I had to receive information from historical data and relationships in variables of my study were required.

Sampling

In Bangladesh, the total number of banks is 64 where state-owned banks are 4, private commercial banks are 32, Islamic commercial banks are 8, foreign banks are 09 and specialized banks are 11. So, this is not possible to take all the banks as a research data for the research and it is also not possible to evaluate all the banks financial performance. For this reason to obtain a probable result, a sampling procedure has been conducted.

Sample unit: For doing the research, I have taken private commercial banks and state-owned banks as a sample unit to evaluate the financial performance and to find out what effects will occur on profitability.

Sample size: For getting a better result, I have taken different level of private commercial banks as a sample size and those are Bank Asia

Limited, AB Bank Limited, Brac Bank Limited, Dautch Bangla bank Limited, Dhaka Bank Limited, Agrani Bank Limited, Basic Bank Limited, Easter Bank Limited, IFIC Bank, Janata Bank, Mercantile Bank Limited, Mutual Trust Bank Limited, One bank Limited, Premier Bank Limited, Prime Bank Limited, Pubali Bank Limited, Rupali Bank Limited, Shahjala Bank Limited, Social Islami Bank Limited, Standard Bank Limited, South East Bank Limited, Trust Bnak Limited, The City Bank, United Commercial bank Limited, Islami Bank Limited, Exim Bank Limited, ICB Islamic Bank Limited, Fist Security Islami Bank Limited, Uttara Bank Limited and it will help me to complete my research. The total sample size for the research is 29.

Sample procedure: The most important step for sampling is that how I do my research and collect data for getting the proper information. It is not sure that the providing information after the research is accurate because the research is based on secondary data and the total sample size is only 29. For that reason, this sample procedure will be probability sample procedure.

Data Analysis

In 2009, Z-Score of Bank Asia Limitedis1.829080966 so that bank was performing good as this is greater than 1.1 so bank's financial position was healthy up to 2011. From 2011 to 2014, Bank Asia Limited's performance was below 1.1 and that is declining trend of performance. On an average Z-Score value is 0.946211502, this is also stating the fact that the Bank Asia was insolvent. From Table 2, we can see that Bank Asia Limited's overall financial position is insolvent and trend shows that performance is getting worse.

In 2009, Z-Score of AB Bank Limited are 5.555341493 so that bank was performing good as this is greater than 2.6 so bank's financial position was secure. In 2010 AB Bank Limited was healthy. From 2011 to 2014, AB Bank Limited's performance was below 1.1 and that is declining trend of performance. On an average Z-Score value is 1.658249831, this is also stating the fact that the AB Bank Limited was insolvent. From Table 3, we can see that AB Bank Limited's overall financial position is Healthy and trend shows that performance is getting worse.

In 2009, Z-Score of Brac Limited is -0.045822189 so that bank was performing poorly as this is less than 1.1 so bank's financial position was insolvent. From 2010 to 2014, Brac Bank Limited's performance was below 1.1. On an average Z-Score value is 0. 021480171, this is also stating the fact that the Brac Bank Limited was insolvent. From Table 4, we can see that Brac Bank Limited's overall financial position is insolvent and trend shows that performance is getting better.

In 2009, Z-Score of Dautch Bangla Bank Limited is 1.005247418 so that bank was performing poorly as this is less than 1.1 bank's financial position was insolvent. From 2010 to 2014, Dautch Bangla Bank Limited's performance was below 1.1. On an average Z-Score value is 0.812640457, this is also stating the fact that the Dautch Bangla Bank Limited was insolvent. From Table 5, we can see that Dautch Bangla Bank Limited's overall financial position is insolvent and trend shows that Z-score volatility is too high.

In 2009, Z-Score of Dhaka Bank Limited is 1.224478092 so that bank was performing good as this is greater than 1.1 so bank's financial position was healthy. From 2011 to 2014, Dhaka Bank Limited's performance was below 1.1 and that is declining trend of performance. On an average Z-Score value is 1.041098355, this is also stating the fact that the Dhaka Bank Limited was insolvent. From Table 6, we can see that Dhaka Bank Limited's overall financial position is insolvent.

In 2009, Z-Score of Agrani Bank Limited 0.003339096 so that bank was performing poorly as this is less than 1.1 so bank's financial position was Insolvent. From 2010 to 2014, Agrani Bank Limited's performance was below 1.1 and that is declining trend of performance. On an average Z-Score value is 0.084776014, this is also stating the fact that the Agrani Bank Limited was insolvent. From Table 7, we can see

Year	Z-Score	Indicator	Average
2009	1.829080966	Healthy	
2010	1.268538299	Healthy	
2011	1.451911972	Healthy	
2012	0.530534185	Insolvent	0.946211502
2013	0.360403495	Insolvent	
2014	0.236800094	Insolvent	Insolvent

Table 2: Data analysis of Bank Asia..

Year	Z-Score	Indicator	Average
2009	5.555341493	Secure	
2010	1.052672451	Healthy	
2011	0.967978315	Insolvent	
2012	1.018492668	Insolvent	1.658249831
2013	0.759504208	Insolvent	
2014	0.595509853	Insolvent	Healthy

Table 3: Data analysis of AB Bank limited..

Year	Z-Score	Indicator	Average
2009	-0.045822189	Insolvent	
2010	-0.286252537	Insolvent	
2011	-0.106734377	Insolvent	
2012	-0.113000077	Insolvent	0.021480171
2013	0.039942471	Insolvent	
2014	0.640747732	Insolvent	Insolvent

Table 4: Data analysis Brac Bank limited.

Year	Z-Score	Indicator	Average
2009	1.005247418	Insolvent	
2010	0.455119337	Insolvent	
2011	0.679372597	Insolvent	
2012	1.000651292	Insolvent	0.812640457
2013	0.92297793	Insolvent	
2014	0.812474169	Insolvent	Insolvent

Table 5: Data analysis of Dautch Bangla Bank limited.

Year	Z-Score	Indicator	Average
2009	1.224478092	Healthy	
2010	0.986605678	Insolvent	
2011	1.003653894	Insolvent	
2012	1.046265571	Insolvent	1.041098355
2013	0.985375779	Insolvent	
2014	1.000211114	Insolvent	Insolvent

Table 6: Data analysis of Dhaka Bank limited.

Year	Z-Score	Indicator	Average
2009	0.003339096	Insolvent	
2010	-0.162509365	Insolvent	
2011	-0.002784539	Insolvent	
2012	-0.38602878	Insolvent	0.084776014
2013	0.532524765	Insolvent	
2014	0.524114909	Insolvent	Insolvent

Table 7: Data analysis of Agrani Bank limited.

that Agrani Bank Limited's overall financial position is insolvent and trend shows that performance is getting better.

In 2009, Z-Score of Basic Bank Limited is 5.824081263 so that bank was performing good as this is greater than 2.6 so bank's financial position was secure. From 2010 to 2013, Basic Bank Limited's performance was more than 1.1 and that indicate that bank was in healthy financial position. In 2014 Basic Bank Limited was insolvent. On an average Z-Score value is 2.29114436, this is also stating the fact that the Basic Bank Limited was healthy. From Table 8, we can see that AB Basic Bank Limited's overall financial position is Healthy and trend shows that performance is getting worse.

In 2009, Z-Score of Eastern Bank Limited is 1.153197804 so that bank was performing good as this is greater than 1.1 so bank's financial position was healthy. In 2010, Eastern Bank Limited's financial position was insolvent. On an average Z-Score value is 2.329345782, this is also stating the fact that the Eastern Bank Limited was healthy. From Table 9, we can see that Eastern Bank Limited's overall financial position is Healthy.

In 2009, Z-Score of IFIC Bank Limited is 1.153197804 so that bank was performing good as this is greater than 1.1 so bank's financial position was healthy. In 2010 IFIC Bank Limited was insolvent. From 2011 to 2014, IFIC Bank Limited's performance was below 1.1 and that is declining trend of performance. On an average Z-score value is 2. 29345782, this is also stating the fact that the IFIC Bank limited was Healthy. From Table 10, we can see that IFIC Bank Limited's overall financial position is Healthy and trend shows that performance is getting better.

In 2009, Z-Score of Janata Bank Limited is 0.853929515 so that bank was performing poorly as this is less than 1.1 so bank's financial position was insolvent. In 2010, Janata Bank Limited's financial positionwas insolvent. From 2011 to 2014, Janata Bank Limited's performance was below 1.1 and that is declining trend of performance. On an average Z-Score value is 0.364374669, this is also stating the fact that the Janata Bank Limited was insolvent. From Table 11, we can see that Janata Bank Limited's overall financial position is insolvent and trend shows that performance is getting worse.

In 2009, Z-Score of Mercantile Bank Limited is 0.633749043 so that bank was performing poorly as this is less than 1.1 so bank's financial position was secure. From 2010 to 2014, Mercantile Bank Limited's performance was below 1.1 and that is declining trend of performance. On an average Z-Score value is 0.284227138, this is also stating the fact that the Mercantile Bank Limited was insolvent. From Table 12, we can see that Mercantile Bank Limited's overall financial position is insolvent and trend shows that performance is getting worse.

In 2009, Z-Score of Mutual Trust Bank limited is 0. 857734615 so that bank was performing poorly as this is less than 1.1 so bank's financial position was insolvent. From 2010 to 2014, Mutual Trust Bank Limited's performance was below 1.1 and that is declining trend of performance. On an average Z-Score value is 0.434647794, this is also stating the fact that the Mutual Trust Bank Limited was insolvent. From Table 13, we can see that Mutual Trust Bank Limited's overall financial position is insolvent and trend shows that performance is getting worse.

In 2009, Z-Score of One Bank Limited is 0.786361994 so that bank was performing poorly as this is less than 1.1 so bank's financial position was insolvent. From 2010 to 2014, One Bank Limited's performance was below 1.1 and that is declining trend of performance. On an average Z-Score value is 1.658249831, this is also stating the fact that the One Bank Limited was insolvent. From Table 14, we can see that One Bank Limited's overall financial position is insolvent and trend shows that performance is getting worse.

In 2009, Z-Score of Premier Bank Limited is 0.566145952 so that bank was performing poorly as this is less than 1.1 so bank's financial

Year	Z-Score	Indicator	Average
2009	5.824081263	Secure	
2010	1.68190398	Healthy	
2011	2.065936981	Healthy	
2012	1.887564213	Healthy	2.29114436
2013	1.251097364	Healthy	
2014	1.03628236	Insolvent	Healthy

Table 8: Data analysis of Basic Bank limited.

Year	Z-Score	Indicator	Average
2009	1.153197804	Healthy	
2010	0.790681447	Insolvent	
2011	0.974474574	Insolvent	
2012	1.613475164	Healthy	2.329345782
2013	7.303866779	Secure	
2014	2.140378925	Healthy	Healthy

Table 9: Data analysis of Eastern Bank limited.

Year	Z-Score	Indicator	Average
2009	1.300918718	Healthy	
2010	0.294460975	Insolvent	
2011	0.48758785	Insolvent	
2012	0.776261564	Insolvent	0.788318078
2013	0.944799603	Insolvent	
2014	0.925879757	Insolvent	Insolvent

Table 10: Data analysis of IFIC Bank limited.

Year	Z-Score	Indicator	Average
2009	0.853929515	Insolvent	
2010	-0.038248682	Insolvent	
2011	0.332854105	Insolvent	
2012	-0.018923182	Insolvent	0.364374669
2013	0.613824369	Insolvent	
2014	0.442811891	Insolvent	Insolvent

Table 11: Data analysis of Janata Bank limited.

Year	Z-Score	Indicator	Average
2009	0.633749043	Insolvent	
2010	-0.04099097	Insolvent	
2011	0.295482843	Insolvent	
2012	0.228788627	Insolvent	0.284227138
2013	0.366022244	Insolvent	
2014	0.22231104	Insolvent	Insolvent

Table 12: Data analysis of Mercantile Bank limited.

Year	Z-Score	Indicator	Average
2009	0.857734615	Insolvent	
2010	0.405209564	Insolvent	
2011	0.221274934	Insolvent	
2012	0.391701809	Insolvent	0.434647794
2013	0.496142395	Insolvent	
2014	0.235823448	Insolvent	Insolvent

Table 13: Data analysis of Mutual Trust Bank limited.

position was insolvent. From 2010 to 2014, Premier Bank Limited's performance was below 1.1 and that is declining trend of performance. On an average Z-Score value is 0.239339886, this is also stating the fact that the Premier Bank Limited was insolvent. From Table 15, we can see that Premier Bank Limited's overall financial position is insolvent and trend shows that performance is getting worse.

In 2009, Z-Score of Prime Bank Limited is 0.706791386 so that bank was performing poorly as this is less than 1.1 so bank's financial position was insolvent. From 2010 to 2014, Prime Bank Limited's performance was below 1.1 and that is declining trend of performance. On an average Z-Score value is 0.434565403, this is also stating the fact that the Prime Bank Limited was insolvent. From Table 16, we can see that Prime Bank Limited's overall financial position is insolvent and trend shows that performance is getting worse.

In 2009, Z-Score of Pubali Bank Limited is 0.640405829 so that bank was performing poorly as this is less than 1.1 so bank's financial position was insolvent. From 2010 to 2014, Pubali Bank Limited's performance was below 1.1 and that is declining trend of performance. On an average Z-Score value is 0.630899433, this is also stating the fact that the Pubali Bank Limited was insolvent. From Table 17, we can see that Pubali Bank Limited's overall financial position is insolvent and trend shows that performance is getting worse.

Year	Z-Score	Indicator	Average
2009	0.786361994	Insolvent	
2010	0.763556365	Insolvent	
2011	0.804434889	Insolvent	
2012	0.755744723	Insolvent	
2013	0.333915303	Insolvent	**0.636124015**
2014	0.372730818	Insolvent	**Insolvent**

Table 14: Data analysis of One Bank limited.

Year	Z-Score	Indicator	Average
2009	0.566145952	Insolvent	
2010	0.372788267	Insolvent	
2011	0.225097445	Insolvent	
2012	0.226028772	Insolvent	
2013	0.028946429	Insolvent	**0.239339886**
2014	0.017032451	Insolvent	**Insolvent**

Table 15: Data analysis of Premier Bank limited.

Year	Z-Score	Indicator	Average
2009	0.706791386	Insolvent	
2010	0.214538365	Insolvent	
2011	0.419962411	Insolvent	
2012	0.436021111	Insolvent	
2013	0.461624627	Insolvent	**0.434565403**
2014	0.36845452	Insolvent	**Insolvent**

Table 16: Data analysis of Prime Bank limited.

Year	Z-Score	Indicator	Average
2009	0.640405829	Insolvent	
2010	0.760551291	Insolvent	
2011	0.506470636	Insolvent	
2012	0.692683577	Insolvent	
2013	0.62797331	Insolvent	**0.630899433**
2014	0.557311955	Insolvent	**Insolvent**

Table 17: Data analysis of Pubali Bank limited.

In 2009, Z-Score of Rupali Bank Limited is 0.058272868 so that bank was performing poorly as this is less than 1.1 so bank's financial position was insolvent. In 2014, Rupali Bank Limited's financial position was healthy. From 2010 to 2013, Rupali Bank Limited's performance was below 1.1. On an average Z-Score value is 0.599435625, this is also stating the fact that the Rupali Bank Limited was insolvent. From Table 18, we can see that Rupali Bank Limited's overall financial position is insolvent and trend shows that performance is getting better.

In 2009, Z-Score of ShahjalaIslami Bank Limited is 1.749143504 so that bank was performing good as this is greater than 1.1 so bank's financial position was healthy. From 2010 to 2014, ShahjalaIslami Bank Limited's performance was greater than 1.1. On an average Z-Score value is 11.412860203, this is also stating the fact that the ShahjalaIslami Bank Limited was healthy. From Table 19, we can see that ShahjalaIslami Bank Limited's overall financial position is healthy.

In 2009, Z-Score of Social Islami Bank Limited is 1.590300694 so that bank was performing good as this is greater than 1.1 so bank's financial position was healthy. In 2010, Social Islami Bank Limited's financial position was insolvent. On an average Z-Score value is 1.199321565, this is also stating the fact that the financial position of Social Islami Bank Limited was healthy. From Table 20, we can see that Social Islami Bank Limited's overall financial position is healthy.

In 2009, Z-Score of Standard Bank Limited is 1.796279978 so that bank was performing good as this is greater than 1.1 so bank's financial position was healthy. In 2010, Standard Bank Limited's financial position was insolvent. From 2011 to 2014, Standard Bank Limited's performance was below 1.1 and that is declining trend of performance. On an average Z-Score value is 0.88747442, this is also stating the fact that the Standard Bank Limited was insolvent. From Table 21, we can see that Standard Bank Limited's overall financial position is insolvent and trend shows that performance is getting worse.

In 2009, Z-Score of South East Bank Limited is 1.090556628 so that

Year	Z-Score	Indicator	Average
2009	0.058272868	Insolvent	
2010	0.275236565	Insolvent	
2011	0.384638674	Insolvent	
2012	0.848787637	Insolvent	
2013	0.91508542	Insolvent	**0.599435625**
2014	1.11459259	Healthy	**Insolvent**

Table 18: Data analysis of Rupali Bank limited.

Year	Z-Score	Indicator	Average
2009	1.749143504	Healthy	
2010	1.366876664	Healthy	
2011	1.327528111	Healthy	
2012	1.550718232	Healthy	
2013	1.34577502	Healthy	**1.412860203**
2014	1.137119685	Healthy	**Healthy**

Table 19: Data analysis of Shahjala Islami Bank limited.

Year	Z-Score	Indicator	Average
2009	1.590300694	Healthy	
2010	1.073512152	Insolvent	
2011	1.272193784	Healthy	
2012	1.260119769	Healthy	
2013	0.998814661	Insolvent	**1.199321565**
2014	1.000988327	Healthy	**Healthy**

Table 20: Data analysis of Social Islami Bank limited.

bank was performing good as this is greater than 1.1 so bank's financial position was healthy. In 2010, South East Bank Limited's financial position was insolvent. From 2011 to 2014, South East Bank Limited's performance was below 1.1 and that is declining trend of performance. On an average Z-Score value is 10.889008076, this is also stating the fact that the South East Bank Limited was insolvent. From Table 22, we can see that South East Bank Limited's overall financial position is insolvent and trend shows that performance is getting worse.

In 2009, Z-Score of Trust Bank Limited is 1.48206737 so that bank was performing good as this is greater than 1.1 so bank's financial position was healthy. In 2010, Trust Bank Limited's financial position was insolvent. From 2013 to 2014, Trust Bank Limited's performance was below 1.1 and that is declining trend of performance. On an average Z-Score value is 0.916365639, this is also stating the fact that the Trust Bank Limited was insolvent. From Table 23, we can see that Trust Bank Limited's overall financial position is insolvent.

In 2009, Z-Score of The City Bank Limited is 2. 220814453 so that bank was performing good as this is greater than 1.1 so bank's financial position was healthy. In 2010, The City Bank Limited's financial position was insolvent. From 2011 to 2014, The City Bank Limited's performance was below 1.1 and that is declining trend of performance. On an average Z-Score value is 0.87299446, this is also stating the fact that the financial position of The City Bank Limited was insolvent. From Table 24, we can see that The City Bank Limited's overall financial position is insolvent and trend shows that performance is getting worse.

In 2009, Z-Score of United Commercial Bank Limited is 0.781932915 so that bank was performing poorly as this is less than 1.1 so bank's financial position was insolvent. In 2010 United Commercial Bank Limited's financial position was insolvent. From 2011 to 2014, United Commercial Bank Limited's performance was below 1.1 and that is declining trend of performance. On an average Z-Score value is 0. 685883956, this is also stating the fact that the financial position of United Commercial Bank Limited was insolvent. From Table 25, we can see that United Commercial Bank Limited's overall financial position is insolvent and trend shows that performance is getting worse.

In 2009, Z-Score of Islami Bank Limited is 7.129397337 so that bank was performing good as this is greater than 2.6 so bank's financial position was Secure. In 2010, Islami Bank Limited's financial position was insolvent. From 2011 to 2014 Islami Bank Limited's performance was below 1.1 and that is declining trend of performance. On an average Z-Score value is 1.800897889, this is also stating the fact that the financial position of Islami Bank Limited was healthy. From Table 26, we can see that Islami Bank Limited's overall financial position is healthy and trend shows that performance is getting worse.

In 2009, Z-Score of EXIM Bank Limited is 1.164116124 so that bank was performing good as this is greater than 1.1 so bank's financial position was healthy. In 2011, EXIM Bank Limited's financial position was secure. On an average Z-Score value is 1.793443355, this is also stating the fact that the financial position of EXIM Bank Limited was healthy. From Table 27, we can see that EXIM Bank Limited's overall financial position is healthy.

In 2009, Z-Score of ICB Islami Bank Limited is -0. 0075826 so that bank was performing poorly as this is less than 1.1 so bank's financial position was insolvent. In 2010, ICB Islami Bank Limited's financial position was insolvent. From 2011 to 2014 ICB ISLAMI Bank Limited's

Year	Z-Score	Indicator	Average
2009	1.796279978	Healthy	
2010	0.592112559	Insolvent	
2011	0.732562673	Insolvent	
2012	0.884250629	Insolvent	0.88747442
2013	0.782236726	Insolvent	
2014	0.537403958	Insolvent	Insolvent

Table 21: Data analysis of Standard Bank limited.

Year	Z-Score	Indicator	Average
2009	1.090556628	Healthy	
2010	0.849597337	Insolvent	
2011	0.672516914	Insolvent	0.889008076
2012	0.981172769	Insolvent	Insolvent
2013	0.881130829	Insolvent	
2014	0.859073981	Insolvent	

Table 22: Data analysis of South East Bank limited.

Year	Z-Score	Indicator	Average
2009	1.48206737	Healthy	
2010	0.634523868	Insolvent	
2011	1.097505114	Insolvent	
2012	1.324424294	Healthy	0.916365639
2013	0.570335631	Insolvent	
2014	0.389337558	Insolvent	Insolvent

Table 23: Data analysis of Trust Bank limited.

Year	Z-Score	Indicator	Average
2009	2.220814453	Healthy	
2010	0.205350775	Insolvent	
2011	0.708555943	Insolvent	
2012	0.514108175	Insolvent	0.87299446
2013	0.86043952	Insolvent	
2014	0.728697891		Insolvent

Table 24: Data analysis of The City Bank limited.

Year	Z-Score	Indicator	Average
2009	0.781932915	Insolvent	
2010	0.296402526	Insolvent	
2011	0.843486952	Insolvent	0.685883956
2012	0.946095679	Insolvent	Insolvent
2013	0.790134743	Insolvent	
2014	0.457250922	Insolvent	

Table 25: Data analysis of United Commercial Bank limited.

Year	Z-Score	Indicator	Average
2009	7.129397337	Secure	
2010	0.712007674	Insolvent	
2011	0.842267254	Insolvent	
2012	0.820851464	Insolvent	1.800897889
2013	0.632854304	Insolvent	
2014	0.668009303	Insolvent	Healthy

Table 26: Data analysis of Islami Bank limited.

Year	Z-Score	Indicator	Average
2009	1.164116124	Healthy	
2010	0.750045444	Insolvent	
2011	5.181350825	Secure	
2012	1.404541155	Healthy	1.793443355
2013	1.288380016	Healthy	
2014	0.972226567	Insolvent	Healthy

Table 27: Data analysis of Exim Bank limited.

performance was below 1.1 and that is declining trend of performance. On an average Z-Score value is -1.126189731, this is also stating the fact that the financial position of ICB Islami Bank Limited was insolvent. From Table 28, we can see that ICB Islami Bank Limited's overall financial position is insolvent also negative and trend shows that performance is getting worse.

In 2009, Z-Score of First Security Islami Bank Limited is 0.989124679 so that bank was performing poorly as this is less than 1.1 so bank's financial position was insolvent. In 2010, First Security Islami Bank Limited's financial position was insolvent. On an average Z-Score value is 0.997654317, this is also stating the fact that the financial position of First Security Islami Bank Limited was insolvent. From Table 29, we can see that First Security Islami Bank Limited's overall financial position is insolvent and trend shows that performance is getting worse.

In 2009, Z-Score of Uttara Bank Limited is -0.599078531 so that bank was performing poorly as this is less than 1.1 so bank's financial position was insolvent. In 2010, Uttara Bank Limited's financial position was insolvent. On an average Z-Score value is -0.751652157, this is also stating the fact that the financial position of Uttara Bank Limited was insolvent. From Table 29, we can see that Uttara Bank Limited's overall financial position is insolvent and trend shows that performance is getting worse.

The failure in Gray area, bankruptcy cannot easily be predicted so all year data shows that all banks are insolvent. The score indicates a high probability of distress within this time period. From Figure 1, we can see that on average Basic Bank, Eastern Bank, Islami Bank and EXIM Bank Limited's performance comparatively better than other banks. As all banks use their fixed Liability (Fixed Deposit) as working capital most of them have negative working capital. Uttara Bank and ICB Islami Bank have negative financial performance.

Based on the level of mean, the condition of banks is not good because here highest mean is T2 between T1-T4. Median is affective to protect bankruptcy because the level of median is 0.757624466 that is lower number then proper number of standard. Minimum Z score is -3.353078608 and average Z-Score is 0.79913588 and it shows that all sample banks are insolvent during the time period. Standard Deviation of Z-score is comparatively higher than T1, T2, T3 and T4 (Table 30).

Correlation of T1 with Z is 0.688157 and it is positive hence the null hypothesis is rejected and alternate hypothesis is accepted. Also correlation of T2 with Z, T3 with Z and T4 with Z are positive so null hypothesis is rejected and alternate hypothesis is accepted (Figure 2). So all null hypothesis will be rejected and all alternate hypothesis will be accepted (Table 31).

From Table 32, it can be found that coefficient of T1=6.56, T2=3.26, T3=6.72 and T4=1.05 and Constant C=-5.75E-10. As R^2=100%, all independent variable together explain the dependent variable. As a result all alternate hypothesis will be accepted and all null hypothesis will be rejected. Here, Significance level is 0.01 and our Probability (F-Statistics) is 0 (Table 33). So Significance level is 0.01 greater than

Year	Z-Score	Indicator	Average
2009	-0.0075826	Insolvent	
2010	-2.258630792	Insolvent	
2011	-3.008525749	Insolvent	
2012	-3.353078608	Insolvent	-1.126189731
2013	0.944799603	Insolvent	
2014	0.925879757	Insolvent	Insolvent

Table 28: Data analysis of ICB Islami Bank limited.

Year	Z-Score	Indicator	Average
2009	0.989124679	Insolvent	
2010	0.4542641	Insolvent	
2011	1.002467048	Insolvent	
2012	1.296142167	Healthy	0.997654317
2013	1.381026755	Healthy	
2014	0.862901154	Insolvent	Insolvent

Table 29: Data analysis of First Security Islami Bank limited.

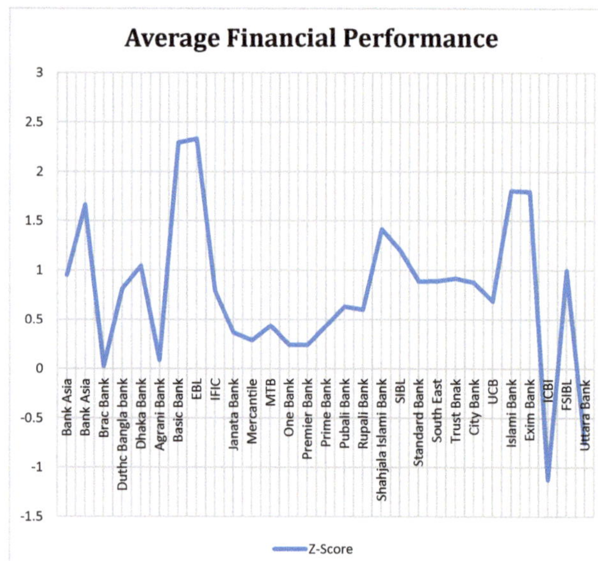

Figure 1: Average financial performance.

Year	Z-Score	Indicator	Average
2009	-0.599078531	Insolvent	
2010	-0.782417352	Insolvent	
2011	-0.327403766	Insolvent	
2012	-0.721857246	Insolvent	-0.751652157
2013	-1.028852892	Insolvent	
2014	-1.050303155	Insolvent	Insolvent

Table 30: Data analysis of Uttara Bank limited.

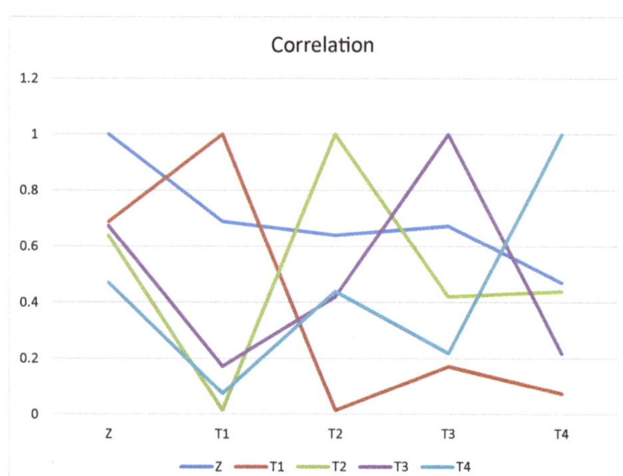

Figure 2: Correlation.

	Z	T1	T2	T3	T4
Mean	0.79913588	0.011474992	0.01186953	0.083804399	0.116190192
Median	0.757624466	0.007265134	0.00964133	0.079863541	0.089687656
Maximum	7.303866779	0.999496369	1	0.667849565	1.13207154
Minimum	-3.353078608	-0.249722417	-1.05443415	-0.080724046	-0.364242531
Std. Dev.	1.187709592	0.109992254	0.147218575	0.064100823	0.191040839

Table 31: Descriptive Statistics.

	Z	T1	T2	T3	T4
Z	1	0.688157	0.638977	0.673559	0.470427
T1	0.688157	1	0.014205	0.171937	0.074284
T2	0.638977	0.014205	1	0.419615	0.438622
T3	0.673559	0.171937	0.419615	1	0.218286
T4	0.470427	0.074284	0.438622	0.218286	1

Table 32: Correlation.

Variable	Coefficient	Std. Error	t-Statistic	Prob.
C	-5.75E-10	3.78E-10	-1.52114	0.130094
T1	6.56	1.92E-09	3.42E+09	0
T2	3.26	1.69E-09	1.93E+09	0
T3	6.72	3.61E-09	1.86E+09	0
T4	1.05	1.21E-09	8.69E+08	0

Table 33: Regression.

the Probability (F-Statistics), as a result all alternate hypothesis will be accepted and all null hypothesis will be rejected. And the model is good fit (Table 34).

Significance of the Study

The aim of this research was to analyse the financial performance of Bangladeshi banks using statistical analysis of summary financial information and selected financial ratios. Here are some significant finding of this research:

- Here, R2=100%, all independent variable together explain the dependent variable. As a result all alternate hypothesis will be accepted and all null hypothesis will be rejected.
- Significance level is 0.01 greater than the Probability (F-Statistics), as a result all alternate hypothesis will be accepted and all null hypothesis will be rejected.
- Correlations of T1, T2, T3 and T4 with Z are positive so null hypothesis is rejected and alternate hypothesis is accepted.
- Based on the level of mean, the condition of banks is not good because here highest mean is T2 between T1- T4.
- Median is affective to protect bankruptcy because the level of median is lower number then proper number of standard.
- Based on minimum Z score and average Z-Score they show that financial position of 22 banks are insolvent and 7 banks are healthy during the time period.
- Standard Deviation of Z-score is comparatively higher than T1, T2, T3 and T4.
- Some banks have negative working capital, so they cannot liquidate day to day business. But banks cover that liquidity by using long-term Liability (Fixed Deposited).
- Most of banks have low equity than liability. Because they are taking more deposit than loans.

R-squared	1	Mean dependent var	0.799136
Adjusted R-squared	1	S.D. dependent var	1.18771
S.E. of regression	2.72E-09	**Log likelihood**	3187.484
Sum squared resid	1.25E-15	**F-statistic**	8.26E+18
Prob(F-statistic)	0		

Table 34: Alternate Hypothesis.

In all testes all the null hypothesis are rejected, so we can say that there is a relationship between the independent variables and the dependent variable.

Conclusion

The financial sector of Bangladesh is mostly small and developing. This sector resides of banking and an emerging capital market. The banking sector in the country comparatively more developed than the equity market, even though both are developing in international benchmark (Table 34). The basic reasons of the Bangladeshi financial sector barriers are lack of market discipline due to lack of rivalry in the banking industry. Excessive government involvement and political influences, economic and political corruptions, operational and managerial disorganization and incompetence result vicious cycle. For this reasons we are far away from economic development, industrialization, and social progress [30]. From this research it is found that most of Islamic Banks are doing well than other banks. Their Z-Score is better comparing to standard. Most of the state-owned bank used to follow the traditional working procedures few years ago. But our state owned banks are now doing better than before for adopting of IT. By managing working capital and credit risk all Banks will do better in Future. Those banks that have negative Z-Score they should take some immediate steps to reduce doubt about their going concern. So after this research with sample size of 29 banks, it can be easily understand that on an average all rivalry banks are doing better and soon they will overcome their existing problems.

References

1. Beaver WH (1966) Financial Ratios as Predictors of Failure, J Account Res: Empirical Research in Accounting: Selected Studies 4: 71-111.
2. Altman EI (1968) Financial Ratios, Discriminant Analysis and Prediction of Corporate. J Fin 23: 589-609.
3. Altman EI (1994) Corporate Distress Diagnosis: Comparisons Using Linear Discriminant Analysis and Neural Networks (the Italian Experience). J Banking Financ 18: 505-529.
4. Mahtab N (2013) Financial Performance of Conventional and Islamic Banks in Bangladesh: An Analysis Based on Rati.
5. Staff C (2012) The Altman Z-Score. American Association of Individual Investors.
6. Altman EI (1995) Emerging Markets Corporate Bonds: A Scoring System. Salomon Brothers Inc, New York, USA.
7. Lawrence EC, Robert M (1986) Corporate Bankruptcy Prediction and the Impact of Leases. J Bus Financ Account 13: 571-585.
8. Chieng JR (2013) Verifying the Validity of Altman's Z" Score as a Predictor of Bank Failures in the Case of the Eurozone. National College of Ireland, Ireland.
9. Chowdhury A (2009) Rationalities of Z-Category shares in Dhaka Stock Exchange: Are they in financial distress risk? BRAC University Journal 1: 45-58.
10. Gritta R (1982) Bankruptcy Risks Facing the Major U.S. Airlines. Journal of Air Law & Commerce 36: 83-108.
11. Aiyabei J (2002) Financial Distress: Theory, Measurement and Consequence. The Eastern Africa Journal of Humanities and Sciences.
12. Piesse LL (2003) Financial risk assessment in takeover: The effect of bidder firm shareholders wealth. International Journal of Risk Assessment and Management 4: 332-347.
13. Richard D, Bahram A. (2008) An Update on Airline Financial Condition and Insolvency Prospects Using the Altman Z Score Model, Transportation Research Forum 47: 133-138.
14. Agha H (2014) Impact of Working Capital management on profitability. European Scientfic Journal.
15. Rehman MU, N Anjum (2013) Determination of the impact of working capital management on profitability.
16. Eljelly A (2004) Liquidity-Profitability Tradeoff: An empirical Investigation in an Emerging Market. Int J Commerce Management 8: 48-61.
17. Deloof M (2003) Does Working Capital Management Affects Profitability of Belgian Firms? Journal of Business Finance & Accounting 10: 573-587.
18. Kasilingam DG (2012) Profitability and solvency analysis of a manufacturing company using dupont and Altman model.
19. Mamo AQ (1968) Applicability of Altman model in predicting financial distress of commercial banks in Kenya.
20. Muthukumar G, Sekar M (2014) Fiscal Fitness of Select Automobile Companies in India: Application of Z-score and Springate Models.
21. Sasivimol M, Polwat L (2014) Applying Emerging Market Z-Score Model to Predict Bankruptcy: A Case Study of Listed Companies in the Stock Exchange of Thailand.
22. Lucarelli A (2013) Using the Z- scores as a turnaround tools.
23. Parvez A (2014) Evaluating the financial Health of Steel authority of India limited using Altman's Z Score Model.
24. Chouhan V, Chandra B (2014) Predicting financial stability of select BSE companies revisiting Altman Z score. International Letters of Social and Humanistic Sciences 26: 92-105.
25. Thai GA (2014) A Revisited of Altman Z-Score Model for Companies Listed in Bursa Malaysia. International Journal of Business and Social Science 5: 197-206.
26. Miller MA (1963) Corporate income taxes and the cost of capital: A correction. American Economic Review 53: 433-443.
27. Tyagi V (2014) A Study to Measures the Financial Health of Selected Firms with Special Reference to Indian Logistic Industry: An Application Of Altman's Z Score. Industrial Engineering Letters 4: 43-51.
28. David PLL (2012) Bankruptcy and Financial Standing Models Application for SMEs. The Seventh International Conference on Software Engineering Advances.
29. OECD (2013) Financial Balance Sheets. National Accounts of OECD Countries.
30. Abdullah M (2015) In Industry Wise Contribution to Bangladeshi Gross Domestic Product: In Which industry we should emphasize more.

14

Continuous Process Improvement (CPI) in Pakistani Banking Sector for Improving Overall Performance

Saeed MS[1]* and Nasar A[2]

[1]*Business Management, Glasgow Caledonian University, Glasgow Business School, Glasgow, UK*
[2]*Government Model Degree College (for Boys), Lahore, Pakistan*

Abstract

The purpose of this paper is to study the implementation of CPI in the bank, and to analyse the merits and its effect on the competitiveness of banking in order to develop PBS (Processing Bank System). The theoretical structure, features and the functions of the CPI theory has progressed after the thorough investigation. Then a hybrid theoretical model of CPI-PBS was developed. The PBS dynamic optimisation system has been developed through the implementation of Lean Six Sigma (LSS) and then we put up an empirical example to indicate the performance of CPI model. Finally the research reached to the conclusions after the thorough analysis. Firstly, the implementation of CPI theory has a healthy impact to service industries, however, the appositeness and conceivability should be taken into account. Secondly, the amelioration of process in commercial banks is an effective, constant progressing process and we can achieve a good synergism effect that the imperative amalgamation of CPI theory and PBS thinking. Finally, it should be realised that the LSS alone was not sufficient and PBS should be considered. The idea and model of the CPI with the methodology of LSS should be combined. Then we identify the issues and steps of the implementation of CPI to management banks.

Keywords: Continuous process improvement; Banking sector; Performance; Department of defense

Introduction

The international economic system moved to integration. Pakistani integration due to its interest and drift has entered into global market. The period of post economic crisis rests on the global economy and high tech as essential elements. The banking sector was the victim as a result of the US subprime mortgage crisis and this crisis alert the banking sector. At that time it was an inexorable choice to set up banking management model globally and persist to build up the core competitiveness. Processing Bank System (PBS) is an extremely used model of management for many banks with an international level. The banking industry of Pakistan made some progress when they started to research the framework of PBS since 2006. The development of PBS was a serious issue in order to promote it in an effective manner from the aspects of strategic implementation and certain techniques.

The commercial banks need CPI (Continuous Process Improvement) to accommodate to the present financial promotion and the global trend for increasing their core competitiveness for the sake of understanding PBS productively. As its core management to develop PBS should remodel moderately to the management strategy specifically strategic core business, the pursuit of efficiency and organizational change. The theory of CPI is an approach that guided the organization to understand and ameliorate the process effectively. It is a theory that is customer oriented and it implemented all types of tools to understand the systematic management. Thus the requirement of CPI is not only the changes in the external environment, but also from their own internal requirements for commercial banks.

CPI has been implemented in managing all kinds of procedures to administer the frequent transformation in our worldwide surroundings. This is also a verified proficient method in the Department of Defense (DOD) [1]. But after investigating the functions of CPI theory, we discovered that it hardly ever talked about business accomplishment or achievement from the perspective of the service industry, particularly in banking services, which is the most serious subject matter in service operations and the centre of attention of a majority of the study is typically on the military issues or medical concerns. Currently, service operations encompass more than 40% of the GDP in Pakistan and are hastily rising globally, and banking services is the utmost grave issue in the service industry. This research filled these spaces.

Based on the above research, this investigation examined Pakistani commercial banks, i.e. how to construct PBS in outlook of CPI and by structured approach.

The objectives of this research are: we look at the CPI theory, Processing Bank System (PBS) theory and Lean Six Sigma (LSS) theory. After that we explain the similarities and dissimilarities between the theories of CPI and LSS and the relationship between them. The development of commercial banks PBS on national and international level has been explored in this paper. The CPI theoretical has been investigated and improved from the theoretical system, core ideas, implementation tools and the techniques. The theory of the CPI and PBS thinking has been integrated in order to present a CPI-PBS hybrid deployment model in this paper. This conceptual model uses the techniques of LSS as the major tool for implementing CPI theory. The Key Performance Indicator (KPI) has been used between the macro and micro level in the CPI-PBS hybrid deployment model as a control node. After the careful analysis, the study applies a process improvement model that is appropriate to the commercial banking system.

The objective of commercial banks can be achieved at the end. The study explained the PBS framework from the two stages of strategic

***Corresponding author:** Muhammad Sajid Saeed, PhD in Business Management, Glasgow Caledonian University, Glasgow Business School, Glasgow, Cowcaddens Rd, Lanarkshire G4 0BA, Scotland, UK
E-mail: msaeed14@caledonian.ac.uk

deployment and financial practices which proved the feasibility and acceptance by the case from bank C. Then it explored various departments' operations so as to strengthen them and to increase the internal operation control of the banking sector. It examined the feasibility and application of the CPI implementation in order to develop PBS. It identifies the issues of the CPI application to management banks. The rest of the part of the paper is divided as follows. Section 2 includes the literature review; section 3 describes the development of the PBS model; section 4 discusses the case study; conclusion, recommendations has been discussed in the last section.

Literature Review

CPI and applications

Quality is a continuous quest and CPI is a continuous effort to eradicate and identify the roots of the issues [2]. CPI system is a technique that needs the integration of all the development activities to achieve the operational objectives. CPI system is a customer oriented learning that guides the organization innovation of thinking and process development with CPI tools to comprehend all types of systematic management for instance revolution thinking, flowcharts, process diagrams, knowledge discovery tools and much more [3,4].

CPI is a strategic process to develop a feasible improvement trend in the productivity, feature, decision making process and revolution process. It is an approach to expand the benefits and revolution performance, cost management, product discrimination and improvement in the resource [5]. We explore to learn the things what makes them happen and then utilize this knowledge to lessen the changes, eliminate those activities that are worthless to the organization and improve the customer satisfaction when we are dealing with the process improvement [6]. The main objective of CPI is the self-examination of processes. That is a method of feedback [2]. The motive of CPI theory is to identify, lessen and eradicate the processes of poor quality to make it more efficient.

The focus of CPI is additional and continual steps in order to stay away from the abrupt changes. It is a form of advancement [3]. The components above are the most strategically components of CPI [7]. The more strategic components involve decisions that how to enhance the delivery process value and how much flexibility is important in the process to meet the varying needs [8]. Some analysers express CPI as a meta- process for some systems of management for instance Project Management, Quality Management and Business Process Management [9]. Wilson and Dobson saw it as a system part through which feedback from both the customer and process were estimated against organizational goals [10].

The management process does not necessarily mean that it needs to be implemented by management solely but it makes decisions about the design and implementation of the delivery process [9]. There are many techniques to comprehend CPI [2]. The main focus is on the small improvements rather than extensive change and makes an effort to remove the worthless activities. CPI is significant for organization because Pareto's Principle (the 80/20 rule) applies. It is said that 80% of all problems report the processes, whereas the remaining 20% report people [11].

The main focus on CPI is on the four key elements that need a comprehension and support to promote the current CPI strategies for the advancement of greater enterprise level. The first key element is broad-based organized CPI implementation method that emphasize mainly on why a safe plan is required and how to implement the best result. The second key element is an emphasis on the implementation of CPI confined to a structure of objectives that are oriented to outcome based metric. The third key element laid stress on the combination and management of CPI project. The fourth and final key element decides how good the organisations and projects are improving with the training, certification and techniques of CPI. Continuous improvement is a successful achievement to improve the processes, product and services. These achievements can pursue step-by-step advancement over time or breakthrough advancement altogether [12]. There are plenty of examples for the implementation of CPI techniques into lower costs, reduced cycle times and productivity gains [4,9]. CPI is an approach that has been acquired successfully in management processes in order to manage abrupt changes in the environment globally. CPI consists of the implementation of a diverse range of tools for instance, Six Sigma, Lean and Theory of Constraints (TOC) in Department Of Defence (DoD).

In Department Of Defence (DoD) CPI is a strategic methodology for the advancement in the field of accuracy, quality, efficiency, cycle times, less consumption of resource and cycle times [1]. The things done within the Department Of Defence (DoD) are directed by the process. They have the process of acquisition for creating and obtaining their defence system, processes for maintaining the tools, processes for presenting travel claims and others. As a result, the productiveness, effectiveness and quality of our work are operated by the processes we utilize to do our work [13]. CPI presents techniques, tool and ideology that can be utilized to advance the system we work with. It is implemented on a continuous basis, which results in the efficacy and effectiveness. DOD is now acquiring these implementations and gripping the knowledge obtained from these unique pockets of CPI success [14]. Consequently, the strategic approach for the advancement in the field of accuracy, quality, efficiency, cycle times, less consumption of resources and cycle times has been achieved [1].

The CPI has been verified as an important tool for the advancement of the achieving efficiency within DOD. For instance, the Air Force implemented CPI to improve the management process concerning medical and lessens the flow time on giving authorizations from 97 hours to 1 hour. The Army utilized a Lean approach to enlarge the mean time between overhaul for helicopter engines by 300%. Within two years the Navy lessen the cycle time for F404 jet engines by 78%. Similarly the Marine Corps implemented tools of TOC to lessen the repair cycle time for CH-46 helicopters by 40%. These favourable outcomes and others similar to them exhibit CPI's ability to implement outstanding, compatible practices to perform a diverse range of operational requirements.

These good practices decide for huge improvement on the business level. CPI aims at building each process more and more efficient. The theory named Kaizen put emphasis on the increasing effect of improvements on small levels. This theory Kaizen operated on the unsolicited and tangled change [3]. Nobody realizes an effective, management or running department like those operating in it each day. Some published reports specified this additional approach can yield in 100% efficiency across the duration of 12-18 months [8,12]. But the improvement will differ from organization to organization stated by how inefficacious an organization was at the time when reestablishment start. Because of the incremental nature of the variations the investments in CPI are generally small.

Continuous process improvement (CPI) and processing bank system (PBS)

The requirement of CPI is not only from the external variation environment, but also from their internal requirements for the commercial banks. The banking sector experienced the pressure of the American sub-prime mortgage crisis. The extreme ferocious competition has been experienced by the Pakistani commercial banks in domestic and foreign markets. The commercial bank experienced the constant ferocious competition in the market and also in the customer market maturing as a service industry. In general the demand for the products and services has been tremendously increasing. In order to develop PBS, the core of management should slowly change into the strategy oriented management that is strategic core business, seeking of effectiveness and quality and the organizational change. CPI theory is an ideology and a technique that manages the organization to comprehend and improve the process effectively. Therefore, we need CPI to observe the existing financial deepening and the global trend to put emphasis on customer, to increase their core competitiveness, to answer seriously to the market competition idea in order to realize PBS [15].

The Processing Bank System (PBS) indicates a commercial bank management model which is extremely used as a management model for many international banks. This management model is customer and market oriented that mainly focuses on the key rules of business within the marketing, accounting and management system. According to the definition of Deloitte's, PBS is the services of banks from work, uncertainty, rules and quality to apply the five principles to front, central and background processes. Furthermore, the bank cannot be too hasty in avoiding risks, according to these five principles. The working of PBS puts emphasis on the vertical management on area of distinct business and it also emphasizes on dealing with the business of monitoring, accounting, billing and customer oriented management and a great number of middle and background business.

The quality of PBS is to adapt its conventional operating methodology and to create an up to date banking model that put emphasis on customer with the support of IT technology, with the qualities to organizational modernization and process advancement, modification and designing, with resource integration in all fields. PBS incorporates the flexible capacity of the latest bank and competitiveness by keeping balance, understandable duties and rights, team harmony to become accustomed to the rapid revolutionizing market.

In order to build a PBS effectively than we have to indicate the Business Process Reengineer (PBR). The simple definition of PBR mentioned in the Davenport introducing book-Reengineering the Corporation: A definite Business Evolution [13]. They explained BPR that it is a continual methodology that demands intense dedication and creativity of the top management. This type of incremental alterations to create PBS comprised of four levels that is the identification of process, improvement, reengineering and homing.

Lean six sigma (LSS) and processing bank system (PBS)

Lean Six Sigma (LSS) is the ideal model that is the integration of six sigma theory and lean production theory. CPI which is implemented on DOD is built on three supportive, but different perspectives that is Lean, Sigma and TOC [1]. Lean Six Sigma has been extensively used and built in all kinds of management processes as an important tool of the CPI theory [16]. As we are familiar with the modification on a large scale, early adopters of Lean Six Sigma for accounting services for instance Merrill Lynch, Bank of America and Vanguard have broken the potential of this technique to build billions of dollars in reducing the cost of business and customer service rates which has been improved up to 25%. This methodology of management has four important elements: 1. Please greatly your customers with the quality and speed, 2. Improve processes consistently, 3. Cooperation for maximum gain, 4. build decisions on facts and data [17]. LSS combines Six Sigma and Lean manufacturing, gripping the benefits of the two models of management to build up for the shortage of single management model to gain "1+1>2" team effort and acquire the top quality management effectiveness. LSS has put emphasis on the satisfaction of the customer and its working focus on systematized processes, lessen volatility to stabilize and enhance the interests of all as a management philosophy [18]. LSS focus on the Critical Success Factors (CSF) so as to put emphasis on the cultural development, process concentration, management support and select the right person, right method and tools. Then it becomes a strong supportive toll to the CPI theory.

LSS is an advance strategic methodology based process. The performance of the organization working depends on the performance of the core process. Banks apply considerable importance to the processes that is the financial sector building. But the concentration of the commercial bank management resides in the effective process management [18]. PBS is an efficient organization process with the management as a beginning point; for the present it means that its management of the system and the operating procedures will also be initiated from the process as a plan or outline for work [19]. Therefore LSS would be a powerful support to create PBS. All of the financial industry is intimately associated with the process. The bank of America implements the six sigma process firstly as the key management tool to bank services industry in order to research the evolution of PBS on national and international bank.

The business operations have a powerful consistency, repetition and comparatively more systematized business processes in the bank. These features are extremely worthy for the LSS thinking and perspective for improving the business processes. Nevertheless the evolution of information technology is a business. The equipment or computer cannot entirely substitute the service resources to give it to the customers. LSS builds decision by data, although the immense financial transaction data and extremely information oriented acquisition system to obtain problem solving data for creating eccentric conditions for "making decision by data" [20].

Unlike the typical sense of sequence, the greatest difference of PBS value sequence is that it is a process based on a closed loop. The value source that arrives from the group of customer value is not only the termination of the whole value chain. In fact, it is also the potential of some powers and associates which operates the entire bank operations from the bank evolution in the channel development. Therefore the model of the entire value chain of PBS can be concluded as: ACFC ("At Customer, for Customer"). At customer belongs to the viewpoint of the customer's status through its own products, marketing, maintenance and running of IT system, channel management et al. so the value of PBS arrives from the Voice of the Customer (VOC). It is a well said that who comprehends the customers will be victorious in the market [21].

Developing PBS deployment framework

Operations are seen in the circumstances of customer belief and needs, requirements of resource and technology and the operational environments. The fundamental ideas of CPI are set into use through a methodology of CPI deployment that should alter how we consider and think about work. It gives satisfaction to the customers that is value oriented, but not task oriented with the importance defined by the customer. The aim of PBS is to fulfil the requirements of customers and increase the core competence. In order to realize the core competitiveness, the Pakistani banks require CPI. The banking business operations have a strong consistency and repetition and comparatively more uniform transaction process. These features are best fitting for LSS thinking and methodology to comprehend improvement in business process [15,18]. The two processes, i.e., planning and implementation and each step in the CPI-PBS hybrid deployment model has been shown in the Figure 1. These two processes of planning and implementation are supportive. The outcomes from the implementation are sending back to the planning cycle like the implementation of CPI-BPS that is guided by the deployment planning (Figure 1).

Step 1: Initial process

The first process of the hybrid development model CPI-PBS is planning. The CPI deployment model is initiated with the evolution of CPI, innovation statement and is accompanied by a strategic approach on how to create the innovation a reality. The concentrated innovation, understandable vision and strategic oriented plan present the structure to acquire the goals of the organization. There are five factors that could help to comprehend them.

1. Innovation and developing orders that promote teamwork, inter departmental teamwork and adjustment between objectives and measures.
2. Emphasize on decreasing the limitations to acquire more suitable usage of resources and potential.
3. Maintain a speed of improving achievements.
4. Improved principle for the decision making and analysis.
5. Enlarging viewpoint on the complete value stream.

The target of CPI is a brief, explicit and quantitative explanation of the role of organization with the goals altogether. The mission of the CPI in a future sight is that it briefly explains how the organization will manage the business. It also shows a break between the existing and future state. The strategic approach gives the actions on a high level that can be taken over the time span of the plan to create the innovation a reality. The objective is to depict all inclusive and integrated road map for the organization that give strength to its objectives or aims for mission completion. The strategic approach must be an active contract

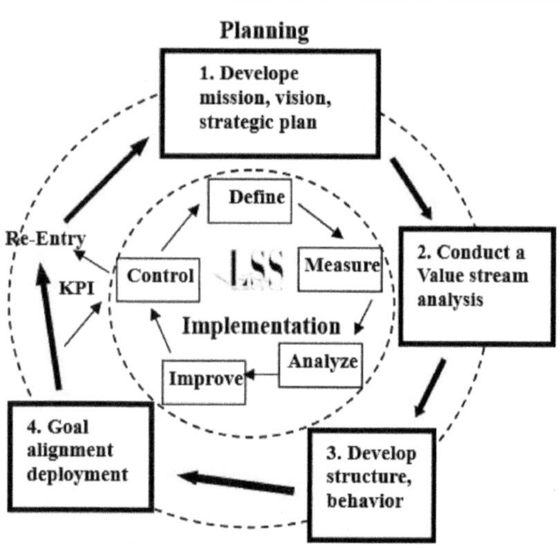

Figure 1: CPI-PBS hybrid framework.

that explicitly focuses on the surroundings in which the operation of the organization takes place.

Adopting Lean philosophy tool the second level of the deployment model arises that account for the establishment of the value stream map and managing the analysis linked to it.

A value stream incorporates the overall planning, implementation, services and products that move on to a process in order to build up the customer value. Through vision, mission and strategic approach, the first goal is to orient the processes to support that direction. And the best method is a value stream mapping process that guides to demonstrate the opportunities for the improvement. Value stream mapping and analysis put emphasis on the customer value and it commonly comprised the existing state map development which explains the current process. It also discovers improvement chances and a future state map that illustrates the future process which are desired and the gap research analysis expose capable leverage points for the improvement in the process. The organizational value stream mapping activities usually comprised of the analysis and association of the two processes that is value added and non-value added. A value stream map holds all the activities that are needed to yield a service or a product to the customer and utilizing a value stream map to the initial document that how we perform our jobs currently and can point out those processes or actions that counts no value to the customers [22]. The analysis of value stream helps to teach the series of efforts we put in the addressing process ineffectiveness with efficient projects of CPI. At multiple levels, the value stream analysis is managed inside an enterprise and is normally achieved as a top down action.

The third stage of the deployment model is called as "develop structure and behaviour". This process makes an organizational structure and training certification program to make CPI successful within an organization [23]. The target completion on the basis of the cost wise and effectiveness successfully relies on the encouraging infrastructure development. The success of any strategy or a plan is totally relying upon the strong teamwork [24].

A CPI support team gives training of CPI and does smoothly the CPI management of initiatives, work team manages each step individually and peer should also be used to enhance the performance as desired conduct by the CPI committee. The champion expresses the main values and builds up the foremost expectations for the mission and innovation of an enterprise within this framework. The champion also requires to build an association with all the components of the enterprise concerning the CPI meaning and its goals. The champions must share through the organizational hurdles and trickle in covering these connections and make it continual for instance in the champion sponsored town hall meetings in General Electric. The leading committee is the main channel for the champions in order to keep up the CPI effort oriented to the expectations. The team of CPI also gives the technical skills and stable approach. This permits CPI to be a repeatable methodology that is established in the attitude and speech of the organization and eventually it becomes a defining part of its culture. The CPI working team acquires the peer groups input when desired and maintains alternatives for the improvements. Peer groups work inside and outside the functional areas to share skills, best applications and standard. The hierarchy is finished with the development of peer groups of CPI that gives moral support and share information outside the organization and explore methods to actively boost the outputs across many methodologies.

The fourth stage in the deployment of the CPI-PBS is the

orientation and deployment of the goals. One of the main parts to move forward in an organization in a cooperative way is through the deployment and orientation of the objectives. The objectives should be developed for the support of an organization and be uniform with the high level commands objectives. There should be an unambiguous association between the objectives of the commands and reporting sub units. It is mandatory that the achievement of goals progress can be precisely considered and observable. The output should be the metrics and it is completely based on the tool for day to day operations and oriented with the objectives of organizations. These objectives need to be computed through the considerate developed metrics. These metrics will teach the working on daily basis, whereas an organization carries on its vision. There must be a straightforward, distinguishable and an easy going connection between every metrics and more than one objective. The efforts of CPI should be opted and executed with the goals of the organization and work hard to achieve the effective value stream.

Re-entry and KPI

The entire process should be reviewed at irregular intervals in order to check if the organization is moving forward toward the end state by the innovation and mission in the strategic plan. This needs to get back to the start and again visiting the steps of mission, innovation and strategic plan. Between the two levels of deployment model that is macro level and micro level the study used key performance indicators (KPI) as the control node. This process has been shown in the Figure 1 with the KPI.

Key performance indicators are essential as they estimate the process improvements in banks or organizations and can improve the efficiency and performance. These indicators are used to tell the execution of the organization strategic approach and KPI system is the notification for the organizational strategic approach and plan variations. All the steps should be visited again in the same way so as to make it sure that the organizations are moving forward in the right direction. This feedback performs to do some activities of planning as the continuous improvement process [1].

Step 2: DMAIC process

Implementation is the second process of the CPI-PBS hybrid deployment cycle. Once the basis of the CPI deployment model has been developed with the four planning activities then the implementation phase comes based on the LSS theory and it is comprised of five phases. The DMAIC project technique has five stages:

Define the problem: it mainly focuses on the goals of the project and customer voice.

Measure key aspects: it includes some features of the existing process and data being gathered.

Analyse the data: it is used to look into the cause and effect relationships. It also tells what the relationships are and an effort to make it sure that all the ingredients have been taken into account. It also explores the main causes of the flaws under proper analysis.

Improve or optimize the current process: it is based on the DOE (Design of Experiments) methodologies, analysis, mistake proofing and quality work to make a new, future state process (He et al.)

Control the future state process: this process ensures the variations before the result gets faulty. Control systems are executed for instance SPC (Statistical Process Control), visual work places and production boards so that the process is operated consistently.

For the implementation of the operational plan, terms need to be identified first and instructed in the techniques of CPI. Targeted processes are formed on utilizing the value stream maps by using the LSS techniques. With the implementation of LSS classic process – DMAIC against the operational plan is controlled utilizing the formerly metrics. CPI is a strategic approach for acquiring the operational levels. It increases the existing execution by representing and uniform positive outcomes delivered by the staffs. Feedback through teams, committees, peers and CPI winners is used for improving the outcomes.

Case Study

The essential condition in this case is as follows: there areas even windows that are serviced by the Bank C staff, and the windows that are being utilizing are only three. However the customers hardly utilize ATM as long as the queue arrives in the windows that are serviced by the staff. The service time of twenty seven customers is shown in the Figure 2 and we can determine that the average service time to be 104 second. We research the data from the bank C and reach to the conclusions as follows. The average arrival evaluates every customer that is 132 people per hour and present Poisson distribution. Similarly the average service rates for each window are about 35 people per hour and presents exponential distribution. On the whole there were three windows in service and fewer customers around 13:30 however the quantity adds up at a fast speed. At 13:30 roughly the window is added in which there are four windows service at that time. Approximately 14:10 another window is added again (Figure 2).

Define

Problem Description: The Bank C has a high rate of queue as it has an average service time of 104 second and also there is a great distance between the satisfaction and hope of the customers. The customer would move to another bank if the bank C didn't improve the effectiveness.

Aim Description: it improves the efficiency of service and increase the service amount to 60 persons per hour. A SIPOC diagram (a tool that is used to find and classify the process kinds to the suppliers, process, input, output or customers) have been drawn considering the service process and we can sketch the flow diagram for the service system of Bank C as shown in Figure 3.

Measure

In this phase of measuring, the timing of each level should be measured as well as we study our idea about the data and sample that has been gathered and measure the appraisal system data when required. We can reach to a conclusion that there is a straightforward correlation

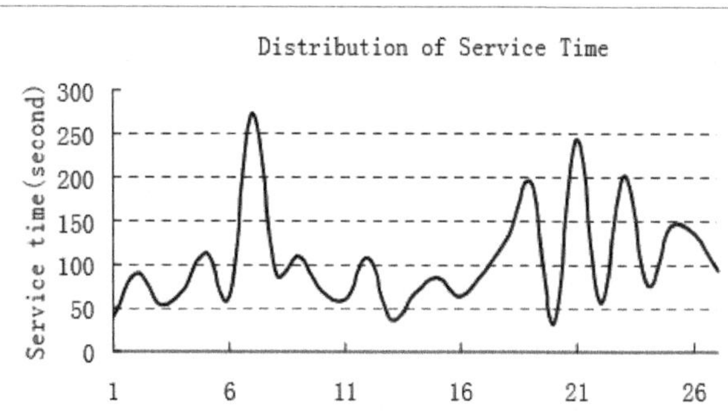

Figure 2: Service distribution time.

between the issues occurring in the queue of the savings bank and the amount of service window as well as the customer's service time.

Analyse

We obtain the service time as well as service window inside the main levels of the service process and find that they are greatly powerful with the queue quantity. We can look at the queue system from the Table 1 that the queue system of Bank C is unreasonable. It is due to the data of the first line that the probability of the customers waiting in the queue when arrived system is 94.3%, the average queue time of each customer is 0.4714 hours (28.3 minutes) that is 16 times greater than the average service time of 104 second. But the probability of seven customers is 66.3% of the system that is unreasonable for the customer. The Bank C should improve the efficiency to enlarge the service window while facing extremely strong competition. And this should be done if we expand the service window and lessen the service time. Now we will study the two methods as follows that is by expanding the service window, same queue standard and it is like creating customer route. The service rate of every system is 35 persons per hour and the result is shown in the second line of Table 1.

If the second method is adopted by not enlarging the service window, but we can enlarge counting money machine set up management information system of the customers in order to lessen the service time of every business and to build the service quantity ranging from 35 to 60 persons per hour.

The result can be seen in the third line of Table 1 in which the average queue time of each customer lessens the hours from 0.4714 hours to 0.0204 hours, whereas in the average stayed time the hours reduce from 0.5 hours to 0.0371 hours for each customer. The probability of 7 customers in a system reduces greatly from 66.3% to 1.49% at the same time. Therefore the outcome in the improvement of system and reducing service time is more suitable enlarging the service window. The time analysis decreasing the time and create the quantity of customer in system reduces greatly and as the customer quantity increases from 35 to 60 persons, therefore the probability that at least 7 customers in a system decreases to 1.49%.

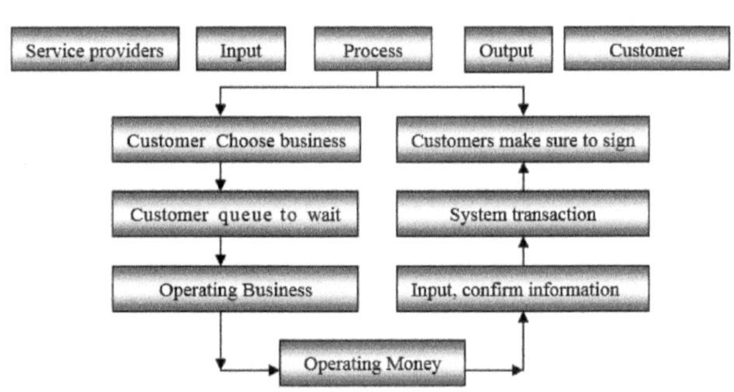

Figure 3: SIPOC of banking system (Source: Wang et al. [11]).

Improve

Considering the design analysis, we can utilize two techniques so as to decrease service time by enlarging current counter machine and build MIS of the customer. Other actions can be taken at the same time to understand the objective for instance enlarging the service window and delay for the service by queue machine take a lot of benefits of the system resources.

Control

We create the improved measures that are incorporated in the daily management and then set up the performance analysis standard so as to keep up the improved performance and to get rid of rebound. We can see important performance improvement after applying LSS project through methodical analysis of bank service. The service efficiency and the bank competitiveness has been increased. Therefore, we finished project of LSS and continuously seeking for a new project.

How to make it constant effectively improved? We should first define a key performance index (KPI) in order to make it a regulating point by keeping in mind the requirements of the banks. The LSS project is operated again if any problem arises each time and do not meet the needs of KPI.

Conclusion

The improvement of process in commercial banks is a strong, continual advancing process. As a fully developed international banking model, PBS is a strong management model for Pakistan to create an advance commercial bank. In order to realize PBS efficaciously, the systematic perspective in strategic level as well as an efficient operation way in the execution level is required. CPI is a verified approach that has been adopted strongly in all kinds of management processes to manage the high speed changes in the global environment. For the sake of realising PBS, the commercial banks of Pakistan require CPI to adapt to the existing financial deepening and the trend on international level in order to enlarge their core competitiveness. LSS has been extensively used and built in all kinds of management processes as an important tool. The banking sector fixes huge importance to the processes. PBS is an organizational oriented process as an initiative in the management. Therefore LSS technique would be a powerful support to create PBS. The existing conditions and issues of the commercial banks in Pakistan based on the research have created a theoretical model of process advancement: the hybrid deployment model named CPI-PBS, and implemented LSS as an important tool to create a dynamic optimization system process. Then it did a conceptual verification of this methodology at the same time. We can achieve great experience and show its effectiveness and approval by the case of bank C, but for the present time to build an implication for this type of study.

Project	Symbolised by	Before improvement		After improvement
		4 windows	5 windows	
Probability of no customer	P_0	0.06	0.23	0.45
Average number of queued customer	L_q	15.56	2.60	0.67
Average number of customers in system	L_s	16.5	2.80	1.22
Average queue time for each customer	W_q	0.47	0.10	0.02
Average waited time for each customer	W_s	0.50	0.13	0.04
Probability of customers prior to queue	P_w	0.94	0.77	0.55
Probability of at least 7 customer in system	P_s	0.66	0.16	0.02

Table 1: Service comparison before and after improvement.

The research reaches to the conclusions through the study as follows: 1. the implementation of CPI theory has a great impact to service industries in fact it should consider the effectiveness and efficiency. 2. PBS is an excellent management model for Pakistan to create a modern commercial bank. 3. The associated technique and ideology of CPI with the BPS can acquire the best teamwork management effect. 4. LSS is a powerful operational method to build dynamic optimization system of PBS. 5. To realize that PB, LSS was not enough. It should combine the idea, model system of CPI with the technique and model of LSS. The research proposed a process improvement model through careful analysis and research that is adjustable to the commercial banks of Pakistan and pick out the problems and preventives of implementation of CPI to management banks.

References

1. Sicilia JD (2008) Department of Defense Lean Six Sigma Deployment. Department of Defense pp: 1-21.
2. Plenert G (2011) Strategic Continuous Process Improvement. McGraw Hill Professional.
3. Vance DE (2009) Reengineering, Process Mapping, Continuous process Improvement and Outstanding. Corporate Restructuring pp: 151-167.
4. Protzman C, Whiton F, Kerpchar J, Lewandowski C, Stenberg S, et al. (2016) The Lean Practitioner's Field Book: Proven, Practical, Profitable and Powerful Techniques for Making Lean Really Work. CRC Press.
5. Anand G, Ward PT, Tatikonda MV, Schiling DA (2009) Dynamic capabilities through continuous improvement infrastructure. Journal of Operations Management 27: 444-461.
6. Bookman L, Troy R, McCaffrey M, Randolph G (2010) Using quality-improvement methods to reduce variation in surfactant administration. Quality Safety Health Care 19: e23.
7. Kreitner R (2008) Principles of Management. (11thedn) Cengage Learning.
8. Han KH, Park JW, Jo YH (2008) Process-Centered Knowledge Model for Continuous Process Improvement. Proceedings of the 2008 IEEE IEEM pp: 42-46.
9. Malheiros V, Paim FR, Mendonca M (2008) Continuous Process Improvement at a Large Software Organization. Software Process Improvement and Practice 14: 65-83.
10. Wilson SB, Dobson MS (2008) Goal Setting: How to Create an Action Plan and Achieve Your Goals. (2ndedn) AMACOM Div American Management Association.
11. Wang L, Herve DBG, Shen Y (2012) Continuous Process Improvement in Banking Sector and a Model Design for Performance Enhancement. International Journal of Business and Management 7: 130-141.
12. Knapp KJ (2009) Cyber Security and Global Information Assurance: Threat Analysis and Response Solutions: Threat Analysis and Response Solutions. IGI Global.
13. Davenport TH (2013) Process Innovation: Reengineering Work through Information Technology. Harvard Business Press.
14. Linnean Ⅲ HW (2007) AFO21: Identifying potential failure points in sustaining continuous process improvement across the air force. Alabama: Air command and staff college, Air University.
15. Küng P, Hagen C (2007) The fruits of Business Process Management: an experience report from a Swiss bank. Business Process Management Journal 13: 477-487.
16. Snee RD (2010) Lean Six Sigma – getting better all the time. International Journal of Lean Six Sigma, 1: 09-29.
17. Narula V, Grover S (2015) Six Sigma: Literature Review and Implications for Future Research. International Journal of Industrial Engineering and Production Research 26: 13-26.
18. Furterer SL (2016) Lean Six Sigma in Service: Applications and Case Studies. CRC Press.
19. Debela T, Hagos A (2011) The Design and Implementation of Business Process Reengineering in the Ethiopian Public Sector: An Assessment of Four Organizations. African Books Collective.
20. Hayler R, Nichols M (2007) Six Sigma for Financial Services: How Leading Companies Are Driving results with Lean, Six Sigma and Process Management. The McGraw-Hill Companies.
21. Agustiady T (2013) Communication for Continuous Improvement Projects. CRC Press.
22. Hines P, Rich N (1997) The seven value stream mapping tools. Int J Oper Prod Man 17: 46-60.
23. Kofman F, Repenning N, Sterman J (1994) Unanticipated side effects of a successful quality programs: exploring a paradox of organizational improvement. Alfred P. Sloan School of Management pp: 1-45.
24. Klein KJ, Sorra JS (1996) The challenge of innovation implementation. Academy of Management Review 21: 1055-1080.

An Empirical Analysis to Assess the Impact of Inconsistency of Exchange Rate on Share Market: A Case Study of London Stock Exchange

Hossain SA*

Teaching Assistant, London college of business management and Information technology, UK

Abstract

This study evaluated the impacts of inconstancy of exchange rate on the London Stock Exchange (LSE). An assessment of writing on inconstancy of exchange rate and stock exchanges was led coming about into detail of an observational model. The Regression model was utilized as a part of making the relationship between conversion standard instability and securities exchange execution. The study utilized month to month United Kingdom information for the period August, 2004 - July, 2014. The information recurrence chose guaranteed a sufficient number of perceptions. An extremely feeble relationship between money instability and the share trading system was affirmed. The exploration finding is upheld by past studies. US premium rates were found to have a positive effect on Market capitalisation. Also GBP volatility makes greater impact on the money supply.

This study prescribed that, since the United Kingdom securities exchange is not by any means presented to the negative impacts of inconstancy of exchange rate, government can utilize conversion scale as an arrangement device to pull in outside portfolio speculation. The feeble relationship between inconstancy of exchange rate and money markets proposes that the LSE could be advertised as a safe business for remote speculators. Nonetheless, financial specialists, investors and portfolio directors still need to be vigilant concerning the overflows from the remote swapping scale into money markets. Despite the fact that there is a powerless relationship between GBP inconstancy and stocks in United Kingdom, this does not so much imply that financial specialists and portfolio administrators require not screen the improvements between these two variables.

Introduction

Rationale

The trend of volatility has been regarded as one of most prominent difficulties or the UK economy in recent years. Despite the fact that exchange markets, various firms and various industries are working together for diminishing the GBP volatility, in the same way as, vitality worth producers mentioned lowering the costs with diverse arrangements, steadiness inside conversion scale also been regarded as a long shot. For UK, Instability additionally has made an economy dilemma and it is introducing the as lower weight currency against EURO. Volatility of currency is mainly functioning as an important reactor for the UK economy growth. Exchange rate unpredictability caused basically by the tsunami of structural movements in the worldwide economy. In most of the cases, it is influencing stocks too. It is exceptionally critical for strategy creators to comprehend the relationship between fluctuations of exchange rate and stock market. Likewise there are such a large number of debates around nature's domain also. Analyzing fluctuations of exchange rate will provide such important knowledge which will determine the factual impacts exchange rate on London Stock Exchange (LSE).

Relevance to the management study

The Exchange rate ideal has changed fundamentally inside most recent 100 years. Since the starting till now guidelines have changed namelessly. Just extravagant nations had fluctuating exchange rates and level cash a while ago. Anyway, by the end of the century the parameter has been changed. It is not any more similar to the recent past. It has now ended up more evident to try for a coasting conversion standard. To extra, these drifting trade rates have affected the stock exchanges not at all like different apparatuses of economy. In purpose of certainty, decision is significantly more confounded than some time recently. In the Bretton Wood framework, one of the significant concerns of approach producers is the vitality of unpredictability of exchange rates. This evident to be, a projecting adaptability of exchange rates framework. Instability of exchange rates has significant derivations inside financial commercial center, especially stock markets. Above analysis settled the point of exchange rate and share market importance for any kind of management. It is very much relevant to the management studies and therefore, the study significance is higher for study of management.

Purpose of the project and achieving aim

Various researches have proved that exchange rate fluctuation has impacted on the stock market. It has been regarded as one of the top priority of business and finance area. This has prejudiced researcher to involve a research on such subject. Researcher aims to define the impact of exchange rate fluctuation on LSE. Below objective and question certainly will provide a greater idea about the impacts.

Research Objective

Research objective is "to measure the impact of inconstancy of exchange rate on the London Stock Exchange (LSE)".

***Corresponding author:** Hossain SA, Teaching Assistant, London college of business management and Information technology, United Kingdom
E-mail: ssahossain@gmail.com

Research question

- Research question is "what the impact of inconstancy of exchange rate on the London Stock Exchange (LSE)?

Structure

The paper report is separated into 6 tiers. Introduction, is the essential portion is the that demonstrated the foundation besides assorted establishments for the work report including research background, research objective, research question and targets and the essentialness of the study. Literature Review is second portion which kept an eye out for the aide perspectives of research. Overview of LSE and exchange rate is the third portion that outlines LSE (London Stock Exchange) and exchange rate summary. Research methodology, is the fourth portion that explains the procedure of the research, research plan where the research method and technique moreover the parts of vital and optional research and information get-together have been tended to. Data presentation and analysis, is the fifth portion where data assortment is done and then analyzed accordingly. Discussion is the sixth portion where all the results are discussed and evaluated whether it matches the objectives or not. Conclusion is the section of the where researcher addresses the proposal and further proposal on the research to conclude the work (Figure 1).

Literature Review

Introduction

A few scholastics, for example, Ross [1,2] furnished speculations with evidences on exchange rate fluctuation and stock market. Not, one or the other has provided such important models that actually can identify the actual relationships of exchange and stock market. This chapter is divided into two parts. First researcher will present the theoretical base and provide the gathered empirical evidences of exchange rate fluctuations.

Flow oriented model

Relying on the grounds of microeconomics Flow oriented model was established. is focused around the grounds of microeconomics. Flow oriented model shows associating connection presence which runs from exchange rate to stock prices. As such, stock costs are influenced through fluctuations of exchange rate. Saleh [3] mentioned that flow oriented model involves that worldwide intensity along with offset of exchange points that are influenced through exchange rate. Thusly it makes influences the future and present expected association's money stream and qualities of the stock. Local currencies positive reception captures a floating framework can regulate organization's increase and aggressive execution of trading stocks [4]. In this manner they maintain their cost of stock. Joseph accepts it that it can affect the data and yield costs, intensity of associations which are influenced through progressions within return rate.

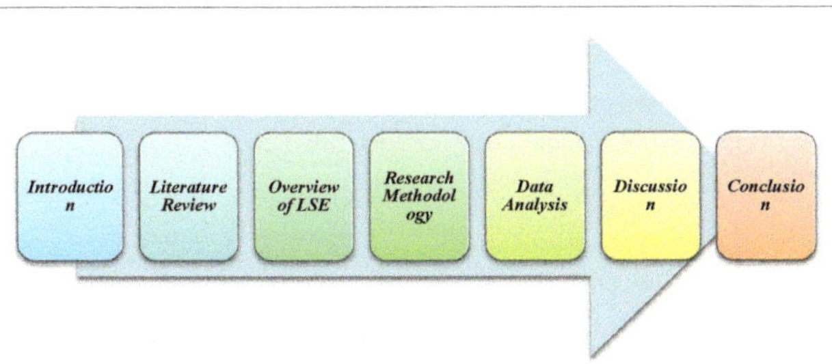

Figure 1: Structure of study.

Adverse consequences of exporters are conspicuous whether rate of trade. Subsequently, worldwide aggressiveness would be decreasing. Thusly, lessening benefit would influence the residential aggressiveness of the association. Resultantly, a discouraging correspondence between household money and stock cost might be perceived. In any case importing firms are profited if the trade rates acknowledge through encouraging the lessening in info costs. Low costs for the last items and administrations would be made by the decrease in expenses. Therefore benefits will be supported by the expanded deals. The appeal of the association in the residential securities exchange will build and the normal level of stock costs will be helped. Subsequently, the pattern of the effect relies on upon whether the organizations work essentially in an import or trading industry [3].

Legitimacy of flow orient model's

Aggarwal [5] mentioned about the flow orient model that it is backed through procurement of proof. Author also inspected the relationship of exchange rate and stock price. This concentrated the relationship of US exchange weighted conversion standard and US securities exchange files of every month within the period of 1974 and 1978. The optimistic correspondence within US securities exchange records and the exchange rate volatility is found in the study that presumes two variables are interrelated with a consistent style along with the flow orient model. In between the period of 1980 to 1986, US dollar and US stock price maintained a link that is downbeat. This figure was achieved through the monthly figures [6]. This also represented the flow model. Casualty and cointegration research was used by Bahmani and Sohrabian [7] for investigating the exchange rate and stock price correlation. To add on it, Fang and Miller investigated same kind of research on Korea of a period 1997 to 2002. Bhattacharya and Mukherje, Chow, et al., Solnik, Young and Frank all established a verification that flow oriented model is not consistent [8-11].

Stock oriented model

In spite of the fact that the remote cash business is overwhelmed by the worldwide capital developments, a clear issue with the stream arranged model was brought up by Pilbeam [12] as being that they don't identify with the global monetary developments. This model's fundamental nature provides the capital record parity of installments. Money related record for determining the exchange rates were pushed by this stock oriented model. While exploring this stock oriented model, Adjasi and Biekpe confirmed the supply and request for possessions are likened through swapping scale. In this way, value developments of fiscally held holdings are affected altogether by the possibilities of relative money developments. In this manner swapping scale developments may affect or be affected by the stock value developments. Harmony of stock within currency business sector decides the supply and interest for coinage; the money related model suggests. Financial model distinguishes the swapping scale as a relative stake cost.

Legitimacy of stock oriented model

To a large extent, present value of asset is influenced by expected rate of return. Three variables that determine the exchange rate are relative national yield, relative cash supply and the relative premium rates. These variables also focuses on the on the stock trade rates. Friedman [13] established such financial model that incorporates the costs of stock. Friedman [13] has also outlined the interest determination for elevating the trading system of share. For accompanying capacity the model is demonstrated below $E(R_i) = R_f + [E(R_m) - R_f]xB_i$

$$m_t = p_t + \alpha y_t - \beta i_t + \chi s_t$$

Portfolio balance model

Portfolio balance model hypnotizes a negative relationship in between the exchange rate and costs of stock. It mainly expresses the effect of exchange rate on costs of stock. For building the interest strength and the stake of national and international, the part of trade rates and all-inclusive spread portfolios are assumed by the model Stavárek [14]. Using immediate and roundabout channel, the energy about residential coin is headed by an expand in local stocks costs. A conversion standard with a negative relationship is relied upon to be headed by stock cost since the local riches is lessened by decline in the stock cost, which thus prompts lower cash request and premium rates as far as the household prospect [15]. Along these lines one currency gratefulness and inflows of capital will be headed to the circumstance.

The accompanying mathematical statement exhibits the business sectors which the model comprises of; where the aggregate of outside securities if, residential securities B and cash M would characterize the aggregate riches W. The model is

$$W = M + B + e^F$$

Welfens [16] mentioned that rather than the residential security markets, securities exchange is incorporated through a modified approach of portfolio offset.

Practical validity of portfolio balance model

Richard, et al. [17] examined the interface of exchange rate and costs of stock in Australia. While determining the exchange rate and costs of stock author involved the granger causality test and which clashed with the portfolio theory approach. Ajayi, et. al depicted the connection in between these two variables. Bahmani and Sohrabian [7] utilized the causality research for realising the connection in between the exchange rate and stock exchange. Many other authors like, frank and Young, Aggarwal [5,11] used this model for realising the same relationship. However, Sonen and Hennigar [6] determined a negative association of this relationship.

Hypothesis of efficient market

The data that is accessible for securities and reflects on the costs of securities is known as efficient market hypothesis. This mainly works on the productivity of the capital market where handling data is initiated by theories. Security cost increases the value of characteristics. Kasper [18] commented that it creates effective business speculation.

Practical validity of efficient market hypothesis

Business like proof supportive EMH gets to be noticeable when return to of alterably overseen common stores is surpassed by the reappearance of business sector midpoints. The current stock costs after the report of a takeover in the UK has been considered by Firth (; cases Mandal [19]. Semi-solid structure effectiveness of (United Kingdom) securities exchange and the completely quick alteration for offering costs to their right levels were noticeable in the conclusion from study of Firth.

Capital Asset Pricing Model (CAPM)

Capital Asset Pricing Model (CAPM) is a model that actually works with a facilitating set for forecasting yield of the asset for the year. It was developed in the 60's. Yield of the asset [σ2] is displayed by the icon. This model explicates doubt about estimation where yield's standard deviation is charecterized [20]. Grosman and Livingstone mentioned that the mathematical statement CAPM is anticipated by the yield of stock. The model is

$$E(R_i) = R_f + [E(R_m) - R_f]xB_i$$

As per the solution, the yield got for initiating interest in danger free securities, Rf must equivalent the anticipated yield of any dubious stock i-E (Ri). The yield adjusted stands on an unsafe possession which is biased through precise factors.

Validity of CAPM

Roll evolved an empirical test with stock indicator and other features of markets and identified it as hard for empirical test. Taylor [21] also supported the critique of roll. Fama and McBeth (1973) found the correlation of risk and return which is positive. Taylor [21] suggested that their firm and market ratio was very much reliable and CAPM actually calculates the evident.

The arbitrage pricing theory and its practical validity

Drake and Fabozzi proposed the model APT (Arbitrage Pricing Theory) for Differentiating CAPM's market danger, one set of risky factors make impact on an advantage's normal yield. Model APT (Arbitrage Pricing Theory) creates a direct relationship of the yield on a basis of benefit with the H component. Vernimmen [22] mentioned that APT counts the Yield stock.

Discussion

From, above theories researcher found that Richard [17] examined the interface of exchange rate and costs of stock in Australia. While determining the exchange rate and costs of stock author involved the granger causality test and which clashed with the portfolio theory approach. Ajayi depicted the connection in between these two variables. Therefore, researcher followed portfolio model for this research paper.

Empirical Analysis

The conduct of unpredictability of stock exchange has been broadly contemplated utilizing the Regression structure spearheaded by Engel and further created by Bollerslev, and others. These studies endeavored to explore the relation of exchange rates and stock costs association within the rising monetary markets and industrialized nations. Notwithstanding, the aftereffects of some of these studies are uncertain. The present study might take a gander at studies that have been carried out in creating nations, developing markets and in created nations.

Developing Countries

Adjasi and Biekpe [12] researched the relationship between stock costs and swapping scale development in Ghana, South Africa, Egypt, Kenya, Mauritius and Nigeria. Vector Auto Regressive cointegration (VAR) was utilized by them and drive reaction investigation for focusing the short run linkage and long run linkage within stock costs and exchange rates. Long run relationship standard between stock costs and the conversion are discovered from their study in Tunisia, where swapping scale devaluation drove down stock costs. A short-run mistake adjustment display likewise demonstrated comparative results.

Adjasi, Harvey and Agyapong [12] utilized the Exponential Generalized Autoregressive Conditional Heteroskedascity (EGARCH) display in making the relationship between conversion standard unpredictability and securities exchange instability in Ghana. In their study, it was discovered that there was negative relationship between swapping scale unpredictability and securities exchange returns, deterioration in the nearby cash prompts a build in stock exchange returns over the long haul. Moreover, there was instability determination in the vast majority of the macroeconomic variables; current period's rate had an impact on conjecture change of future rate. It was likewise uncovered that an expand (diminish) in exchange shortfall and desire in future climb in exchange shortage will diminishing (build) stock exchange unpredictability. Furthermore, the buyer value file demonstrated a solid association with stock exchange instability. This implied that a build in buyer value prompted an ascent in securities exchange unpredictability. At long last, there was the vicinity of influence impact and instability stuns in stock profits for the Ghana Stock Exchange.

Pilinkus and Boguslauskas examined the short-run relationship between stock exchange costs and macroeconomic variables in Lithuania. One of their macroeconomic variables was swapping scale. The Augmented Dickey Fuller test was utilized to check the stationary of the chose time arrangement since a spurious relapse may happen if a period arrangement is not stationary. The study utilized the Impulse reaction capacity to test the presence of the short-run relationship between securities exchange costs and macroeconomic variables. As the consequences of the Impulse reaction capacity are dependable just with a stationary time arrangement the information was transformed into stationary after the second distinction. The consequences of the study unmistakably showed that macroeconomic variables are critical determinants at stock exchange costs in Lithuania. Their study presumed that unemployment rate, swapping scale, and transient premium rates adversely impact securities exchange costs. Through the Error Correction model, Subair and Salihu explored the impacts of exchange rateinstability on the Nigeria securities exchanges. It was observed that the swapping scale instability produced by means of GARCH procedure pushes a stronger negative effect on the Nigeria securities exchanges. Notwithstanding, the rate of swelling and premium rate did not have long run association with securities exchange promotion since the significant member in the business sector was the administration. In light of this, it was proposed that a facilitated money related and monetary strategy ought to be placed set up to check mate the vacillation of swapping scale so as to extend the profundity of the Stock Market.

Olugbenga analyzed the long-run and short-run impacts of exchange rate on stock exchange advancement in Nigeria in excess of 1985:1–2009:4 utilizing the Johansen cointegration tests. A bi-variate model was pointed out and observational results demonstrated a huge positive stock exchange execution to swapping scale in the short-run and a noteworthy negative stock exchange execution to conversion standard over the long haul. The Granger causality test indicated solid proof that the causation runs from swapping scale to securities exchange execution. This suggested that varieties in the Nigerian securities exchange are clarified by exchange rate instability. The study reasoned that the negative impact of exchange rate on Nigerian stock exchange execution could have been an aftereffect of overwhelming degrading of the coin since the presentation of the structural alteration program in 1986.

General evaluation

An investigation of studies from creating nations was directed and it was watched that there is no general accord concerning the connection between swapping scale and the stock exchange. Whilst a few studies found that swapping scale unpredictability pushes a stronger negative effect on the securities exchanges, others found that there is no relationship between these two variables. It was additionally watched that diverse studies connected distinctive methodologies to attain their targets. Confirmation of remarkable connections between trade rates and the stock exchange has been seen in various African nations. Notwithstanding, because of the distinctive approachs that were utilized by diverse studies furthermore the way that studies were directed in distinctive nations, diverse results could be acquired.

Developing markets

Murinde and Abdalla explored associations within stock cost and exchange rate among the rising monetary markets like, Philippine, Pakistan, Korea, India. The inspiration was to make the causal linkages between heading costs in the outside trade business sector and money markets; the linkages had suggestions for the on-going endeavors to create stock exchanges in rising economies all the while with an approach shift towards freely skimming trade rates. A bivariate vector autoregressive model was connected as an estimation strategy and the study utilized month to month perceptions on the IFC stock value list and the genuine viable swapping scale in excess of 1985:01 - 1994:07. Their finding has strategy suggestions; it recommended that separate governments ought to be mindful in their execution of swapping scale strategies, given that such approaches have repercussions on their securities exchanges.

The essential instinct behind Karoui's examination was that the instability of the stock returns could be incompletely clarified by the unpredictability of the money rates. The study concentrated on the accompanying 18 rising nations which are- Turkey, Thailand, Taiwan, South korea, South Africa, Russia, Philippines, Poland, Peru, Mexico, Malaysia, Indonesia, India, Hungary, Colombia, Chile, Brazil, Argentina. The study discovered a huge relationship between cash rate instability and stocks returns unpredictability for an expansive piece of the records mulled over. Additionally, a positive relationship between the outside conversion standard instability and the stock return unpredictability in an expansive piece of the division records concentrated on was found.

Spirits explored the degree of instability overflows between stock returns and exchange rate changes for six Latin American budgetary markets to be specific: Venezuela, Colombia, Chile, Brazil, Argentina and Mexico one European monetary market, and Spain in the 1998-2006 periods. The study partitioned the example into sub periods, before and after the presentation of the Euro and it connected the EGARCH technique to model unpredictability. The results demonstrated that the instability of stock returns influences the unpredictability of trade rates; nonetheless, no proof of instability transmission in the inverse course was found. The after effects of the study are predictable with those of Kanas and Yang and Doong who both discovered proof of instability overflows from stock comes back to trade rates. However the results vary on the proof of overflows in the inverse course from trade rates to securities exchanges. Spirits' study found that in spite of the fact that unpredictability overflows are substantially less pervasive from the different two-sided trade rates to the stock exchanges in the nations inspected, and also less steady crosswise over nations and about whether than the overflows from stock exchanges to trade rates.

Agrawal and Srivastav observationally inspected the motion between the unpredictability of stock returns and development of Rupee-Dollar trade rates, as far as the degree of interdependency and causality. Supreme estimations of information were changed over to log ordinary structures and checked for typicality. Application of Jarque-Bera test yielded facts that confirmed non-typical conveyance of both the variables. These postured inquiries on the stationary of the two arrangements. Stationary of the two arrangements was checked with ADF test and the results demonstrated stationary at level structures for both the arrangement. The coefficient of relationship between the two variables was registered, which showed slight negative connection between them. This cleared a path for deciding the course of impact between the two variables. Granger Causality test was connected to the two variables and it demonstrated unidirectional causality running from stock comes back to trade rates, that is, a build in the reappearances of Nifty brought on a decrease in the trade rates yet the opposite was not discovered to be genuine.

Eissa, Chortareas and Cipollini inspected the vicinity of unpredictability overflows between ostensible trade rates and stock returns in three nations: Egypt, Morocco and Turkey. The study considered day by day division files in Egypt, Morocco and Turkey. The multivariate GARCH show that was utilized did not deliver proof of cross-business sector impacts for the general stock lists returns. Anyway it was seen that a bidirectional stun and unpredictability overflows between trade rates and stock returns existed at the business division level. These discoveries were considerably more declared in Egypt and Turkey. The diverse results were because of the distinctive swapping scale administrations/approaches received by the three nations. While trade rates in Egypt and Turkey were permitted to buoy, Morocco took after an all the more firmly oversaw exchange rate administration.

In an alternate study in Turkey, Yıldiz and Ulusoy inspected the impact of conversion standard unpredictability on Turkish stock returns utilizing month to month information for the period 1987-2010. The squared residuals from the Autoregressive Moving Average (ARMA) models were utilized to create a measure of exchange rate unpredictability and after that tried against Turkish stock returns. The month to month shutting file estimations of the Istanbul Stock Exchange 100 Index (ISE) were utilized as a part of request to acquire Turkish stock returns. The consequences of the study underlined that Turkish exporters did not consider exchange rate instability as a vital issue.

General Evaluation

Above observational investigation writing in developing markets demonstrated that there is no exact congruity among the studies directed to analyze the effect trade rates on securities exchange in developing markets. A few systems have been utilized with distinctive methodologies to test the connection between trade rates and the share trading system. Procedures, for example, the Engel-Granger Causality, Johansen Cointergration, GARCH, and ARMA were utilized by different studies. On the other hand, results from these studies are uncertain; there are blended results as to the connection between the two variables. There are differentiating results and a conclusion can't be attracted as to the relationship between conversion standard and stocks. This legitimizes the need of more research around there to help existing writing.

Developed countries

Aggarwal [5] inspected the relationship between trade rates and stock costs by taking a gander at the association between progressions in the US exchange weighted exchange rate and changes in US securities exchange records every month for the period 1974 to 1978. The study found that the exchange weighted exchange rate and the US securities exchange records were emphatically connected amid this period. The study reasoned that developments in the swapping scale could specifically influence the stock costs of multinational firms by impacting the estimation of its abroad operations, and in roundabout way impact household firms through affecting the costs of its fares and/or its foreign made inputs.

Results demonstrated that nations like France, Germany, and Hong Kong don't display solid proof of positive commitment to swapping scale vacillations. This suggested that deteriorating neighborhood coinage are connected with climbing US stock exchanges, recommending a negative effect of exchange rate vacillations on the US/nearby value market association. Factual confirmation exhibited in Mun's study showed that higher exchange rate variability, generally, helped higher nearby value market instability however to a lower US value market unpredictability.

As far as their causality examination, Morales' results demonstrated an unidirectional causal relationship structure the trade rates to the stock costs on account of Hungary, Poland and Czech Republic. There was likewise proof of causality from the Hungarian exchange rateto the United Kingdom stock costs, from the Polish trade rates to the United Kingdom stock costs, from the Czech Republic exchange rateto the United Kingdom stock costs and from the Slovakian trade rates to the United Kingdom stock costs. At long last, the study likewise discovered proof of causality from the stock costs to the stock costs on account of Hungary to United Kingdom, United Kingdom to Poland, and the United States to Poland.

In an alternate study, Korsgaard analyzed the relationship between firm esteem and exchange return predictability in the accompanying European nations; Denmark, Spain and German. An alternate numerous relapse models was created and resultantly, the typical Ordinary Least Squared (OLS) technique was supplanted by the Newey-West standard slips test. The information on Danish, Spanish and German organizations was synchronized such that the time compass went from May 2001 to October 2008. Conversion standard instability was tried against stock returns. The discoveries proposed that stock returns are to a certain degree delicate to swapping scale instability.

Sekmen inspected the impacts of exchange rate instability, utilizing the squared residuals from the autoregressive moving normal (ARMA) models, on stock returns for the U.S for the period 1980 to 2008. The study tried the impact of exchange rate unpredictability on the benefits of firms in the US utilizing the squared residuals from the ARMA model to create appraisals of unpredictability. In general, the study found that conversion standard instability adversely influenced US stock returns.

Evaluation

Table 1 explicates that a few studies, for example, those by Aggarwal [5] help the view that there is a relationship between exchange rate and stock exchanges. Others by Morales, Nieh and Lee [23] and Alagidede, Panagiotidis and Zhang demonstrate that there is no relationship between trade rates and the share trading system. The table also demonstrates that distinctive methods were utilized by diverse studies to acquire results. Studies utilized the EGARCH, Johansen system, Granger Causality Tests and the Autoregressive moving normal (ARMA), Regression models for estimation purposes. Diverse results were gotten in created nations. This may have been created by distinctive elements and diverse monetary circumstances that every nation was laid open to. Studies led in created nations are uncertain; the results are blended. From the table, it can be seen that Chi, Fang and Yang FU emphasises on the relationship of exchange rate and stock exchange can be followed up by either EGARCH or

Regression analysis. This advocates this study in looking at the effect of swapping scale and securities exchange London.

Overview of Exchange Rate Policy and LSE

Exchange rate history of UK

Exchange rate administration ideal has changed fundamentally inside most recent 100 years. Since the starting till now principles have changed secretly. Just extreme nations had drifting trade rates and level cash awhile ago. However, the parameter changed by end of the century. It is no more like some time recently. It has now gotten to be clearer to try for a gliding exchange rate. To extra, these gliding trade rates have affected the securities exchanges dissimilar to different instruments of economy.

A history of LSE (London Stock Exchange)

One of the most seasoned stock trade businesses of the world is London Stock. It began exchanging more than 300 years back. London Stock Exchange quickly raised to wind up most vital monetary establishment of the City since Starting its life in the cafés of London in the seventeenth century, Years after years, London Stock Exchange has been reliably heading the method for developing a solid, generally directed securities exchange. By today it exists in the heart of the world monetary group. In 1995, it touched one of the breakthroughs including AIM (Alternative Money Investment) into their administrations. In 2007, it developed with Borsa Italiana and shaped London Stock Exchange Group.

Exchange rate policy and maintenance

Exchange rate approach is a basic part of arrangement contentions identifying with worldwide intensity and macroeconomics concerns. Farrell and Todani, contend that developments in return rates can have a huge effect on financial development, vocation, expansion and the equalization of instalments and on the prosperity of people. Exchange rate progressions influence macroeconomic components, for example, expansion, monetary development, vocation creation and salary appropriation. Financial arrangement creators subsequently need to nearly screen exchange rate improvements to settle on the right choice. Exchange rate improvements are a critical part of the economy which the legislature should dependably stand watch on. The consequence of having unseemly conversion standard arrangements would be a misaligned Exchange rate. This misalignment has been rebuked for an arrangement of monetary fiascos endured by economies around the globe. Expand in globalization has likewise made the exchange rate approach to be one of the key determinants of both inner and outer strength. Exchange rate administration strategy of United Kingdom.

In UK, exchange rate administrations have developed from being altered, to oversee skimming lastly to free drifting in the year 2000. The appropriation of the expansion focusing on administration in the year 2000 had suggestions on the way with which the swapping scale strategy is led. The Bank of England decided to direct expansion focusing on and having an adaptable exchange rate. The expansion focusing on skeleton, as in any state where it is connected has permitted the conversion scale to buoy and there are no exchange rate targets. Under an unadulterated expansion focusing on administration that the Bank of England decided to direct, the national bank has constrained control in the outside trade market. When the GBP devalued forcefully against the primary monetary forms, the Bank of England consistently abstained from interceding in the remote trade business sector to backing the GBP. The estimation of the GBP swapping scale was regardless is controlled by the strengths of interest and supply in the remote trade market. Despite the fact that the swapping scale is seen as an essential transmission system for fiscal approach that could influence swelling and financial development, the Bank of England is of the view that a lot of worry about conversion standard security can affect the wrong arrangement reaction.

The globalization process has permitted budgetary transactions and cash to moderately move crosswise over national limits and this has made the conversion scale to be a standout amongst the most critical instruments for dealing with the nation's economy. UK is no special case to this. Hentz (2005:18) prominent that exchange rate now be a standout amongst the most vital costs in the economy. As a consequence of this, general conversion standard arrangements are currently being coordinated to some proximate goals, including outside parity, interior offset, and micro financial productivity (Boker, Boraine, and Krafchik, 1993:138). The inquiry, nonetheless, of attaining proximate goals (for instance inside and outside offsets) are truly chosen by the decision of exchange rate administration.

The decision of Exchange rate administrations has been a focal choice confronting policymakers in very nearly all economies around the globe. The conversion standard has essential ramifications for exchange, inflation, Gross Domestic Products (GDP), budgetary markets and numerous different parts of the economy. Diverse exchange rate administrations could be worked to attain the picked targets these incorporate settled trade rates, free skimming and a mixed bag of halfway administrations, for example, movable peg or creeping peg.

Economic Indicators of LSE

Structural, administrative and mechanical changes over the previous decade have made the LSE to have numerous positive progressions. Numerous positive improvements have been recognized and as an aftereffect of this "the LSE is on the radar screen of numerous universal financial specialists today". Positive improvements have been portrayed by noteworthy changes in the financial pointers predominantly made out of, in addition to everything else, complete volume what's more estimation of shares exchanged on the LSE, All Share Index, Liquidity and business capitalisation. This area might inspect the patterns that have been going on the LSE in manifestation of graphical and numerical dissection. Graphical and numerical dissection serves to break down the patterns in the monetary markers on the LSE. This will give a measuring stick of assessing the general execution of the LSE. The aggregate volume and estimation of shares exchanged on the LSE, market capitalization, liquidity on the LSE, All Share Index are the monetary pointers broke down by this study.

Research Methodology

Introduction

This exploration expects to assess the effect of swapping scale instability on London Stock Market. Section 2 concentrated on writing audit of speculations and clarifications identified with the point. This part explains the philosophy to perform the examination. This predominantly incorporates the models and related variables picked for exploration, foreseen priori, research standard, information gathering and exact examination procedure of information.

Style of Research

Research philosophy

The term that portrays a change of learning and the way of

information is known as exploration theory [24]. It impacts real perspective of the association in the middle of learning and the procedure through it is created. Saunders [24] specified around three examination methods of insight epistemology, philosophy and axiology.

Epistemology

Scientist should work from a position of common researcher when assets give information. At times, specialist might picked reality where information are considered as true. In this viewpoint scientist can contend that gathered information less open and therefore more target. All things considered, specialist would view question through sentiments and demeanour.

Positivism

One positivism system acknowledges the truth may be explored prevented from securing annoying the made case. This technique may be performed really if the reality of the situation is reliable (Levin, 1988). It has a couple of mixtures. Alavi and Carlson, communicated all trial investigates are positivist in nature.

Interpretivism

Saunders [24], said in regards to the examination rationale where expert commonly go about as a social performing craftsman to perceive change of human. It is known as Interpretivism. It generally focuses on human contrasts as opposed to considering matters like, machines. Remenyi, communicated that interpretivism has subjective point of view.

Realism

Saunders [24], raise legitimacy as an epistemological locus. Genuineness is focused on the inclination of truth. It truly infers that dissents subsist autonomously on individual's mind. Free identity of people is the center motivation behind legitimacy theory.

Pragmatism

The rationale that stands amidst a position of interpretivism and positivism is known as calm mindedness. It practices focused solicitation for the examination. Solicitation may be seen as an on-going strategy. Segregating deduction picks waverings and request and over the long haul attested in topple. Saunders [24], said there is no true position to get.

Chosen philosophy

Fundamental objective of the momentum exploration is to discovering effect of swapping scale instability. This money based paper will be examining optional information which are true and accessible. Enough measure of learning is accessible is around also. Consequently scientist likes to work with epistemological reasoning.

This exploration objective affirms that examination conducts both subject and item. Therefore the flow examination affirms that it remains in an in the middle of positivism and interpretivism and practices center request and discriminating thinking. Along these lines the analyst plans to practical methodology of epistemological reasoning.

Research approach

Ghauri and Gronhaug, expressed that while channeling an exploration scientist needs to spare the apparent information without any preference. Result may match supremely with speculations and laws perceived around. Exploration methodology is required so as to discover reality and false and finishing the examination.

Inductive

An inductive technique of investigation is performed with down to business annotations by re-searcher. Contingent upon it, researcher improvises distinctive hypotheses, begins new theories and adds them to routine speculations. Grazino communicated that this procedure remains closer to the recouped data and high-lights on incitation. As needs be new made hypotheses could be all the more compelling.

Deductive

Bryman and Bell said that examiners fortifies theory from the open theories in deductive approach of investigation. Later on master performs the investigation and find precise results. Cooper and Schindler tagged that conclusions give the vital in deductive technique. Grazino et al. refered to that deductive approach principally focuses on the actuations recouped from theories. From speculations it starts and later on it is observationally investigated later on.

Chosen approach

Fundamental objective of the flow examination is to discovering effect of conversion standard instability. This money based paper will be inquiring about optional information which are genuine and accessible. Enough measures of information and speculations are accessible around too. Scientist does not expect to manufacture theory namelessly and build new hypothesis. As opposed to that, scientist likes to fabricate speculations on the premise of made hypothesis, inspect information and give genuine result. In this manner analyst will pick inductive methodology of exploration.

Quantitative technique

Quantitative technique for exploration predominantly depends on the strategy of information accumulation, dissect them and produce numeric information resultant. Results are clarified by diagrams or detail in this system for exploration [24].

Qualitative strategy

Qualitative strategy for examination mostly depends on the hypotheses and clarifications investigate them and create non-numeric information resultant. Results are clarified by hypotheses and clarifications in this strategy for examination [24].

The picked system

Principle objective of the momentum examination is to discovering effect of conversion standard instability. This account based paper will be looking into auxiliary information which are genuine and accessible. Numeric examination will give conclusions. These will be clarified too. Accordingly scientist will pick both qualitative and quantitative technique for the exploration.

Saunders [24] referred to that there are 2 sorts of exploration techniques Specified routines change in the standings numeric and non-numeric information.

Data Analysis

Analyse model

So as to measure the effect of money unpredictability on the stock exchange in United Kingdom, this study emulated Subair's model.

Subair utilized the regression model to explore the effect of swapping scale instability on money markets execution in London. His study utilized the accompanying model:

This present study might change Subair's model. The informative variables that are incorporated in this current study's model are: money supply (M3)fares, GBP volatility, Market capitalization and US premium rates. The model should, in this way, take the structure:

Lsmc=f(GBPVOL,MC,M3,USINT (4.1)

Meaning of Variables

LSMC is the characteristic logarithm of the stock exchange capitalisation (LSE). Market promotion is the piece of the pie value for every offer increased by the quantity of shares exceptional. Market underwriting will change in accordance with progressions in offer cost and the quantity of shares issued. Financial specialists focus an organization's offer esteem by taking a gander at its market promotion. Olalere held that, in United Kingdom, the conversion scale has a more noteworthy effect available promotion than stock costs. This is the motivation behind why market underwriting instead of stock costs is picked in this study.

Gbpvol is the US/GBP Exchange rate - The US dollar has been utilized as a part of perspective of the predominance of the dollar in universal transaction and also close connections between the United Kingdomn and US economies. Since 2001 the LSE execution takes after the GBP swapping scale.

M3 is utilized to catch cash supply. M3 is utilized to be a sign of the aggregate sum of cash supply accessible in the economy. M is the broadest measure of cash thus it is utilized to gauge the whole supply of cash inside an economy. Bhattacharya and Mukherjee [8] likewise utilized this variable when they were leading a study on the way of the causal relationship between stock exchange and macroeconomic totals in India.

US investment rates - The expanded openness of the United Kingdomn economy permits the USA financial advancements to assume a urgent part in value costs in United Kingdom. The US premium rates have been assuming an immense part in deciding interest in developing markets. The LSE pulls in an extensive measure of remote investment from institutional financial specialists in the created world, including the US (Ocran, 2010). Subsequently changes (particularly diminishes in premium rates) in the US premium rates will make speculators to move far from the US and look for appealing venture ends of the line, for example, United Kingdom. Thus the United States investment rates are essential in clarifying the offer cost on the LSE.

Expected priori

Cash Supply - The indication of M3 is relied upon to be sure. Higher M3 additionally bestows additional liquidity to the securities exchanges since the overabundance cash is channelized into the stock exchanges, along these lines pushing up the business capitalisation. Thus, stock valuations climb as a quick response to an expand in M3. The productive business sector theory (EMH), as formalized by Fama [2], proposes that changes in macroeconomic variables, for example, cash supply can impact the conduct of securities exchange exercises. In an effective business, present and additionally past data on the development of these essential macro-variables are completely reflected in possession.

US investment rates: The US premium rates sign is required to be negative. A lessening in the US investment rate is relied upon to cause the stock costs to climb. When US premium rates fall, financial specialists move their speculation from the US to United Kingdom since it is a developing business sector. This build in speculation will result in the stock costs to climb because of the accessibility of numerous purchasers on the stock trade. In this way a negative relationship is relied upon to exist between the US premium rates and the stock exchange costs.

GBP Volatility: The indication of the GBP unpredictability is required to be negative. At the point when there is expanded unpredictability, speculators won't contribute much on stocks. It would be unsafe to contribute and they will take their venture somewhere else. This will result in stock costs to decline. Hence a negative relationship is perceived on the stock costs. Adjasi [12] (additionally discovered a negative relationship between conversion standard vacillations and the London securities exchange returns.

Information for the study should be acquired from optional sources, for example, the Johannesburg Stock Exchange and the United Kingdom Revenue Services, Statistics United Kingdom, United Kingdom Reserve Bank, and Department of Trade and Industry. Ostensible figures should be utilized for the study. The study utilizes month to month United Kingdom information for the period 2000 – 2010. The information recurrence chose should be month to month to guarantee a satisfactory number of perceptions. A perception lower than this (yearly or quarterly) won't give enough perception of which a solid conclusion might be drawn as the information won't be a sufficient representation of unpredictability while a higher recurrence will be influenced by impacts of settlements and clearing deferrals which influence returns over a shorter inspecting interims. The results from month to month data are more exact and are better equipped to catch the elements between trade rates and the LSE. The information should first test for stationary or the request of incorporation of the information arrangement keeping in mind the end goal to dispose of spurious relapse results. This should be carried out utilizing the Augmented Dickey Fuller system and the Phillip Peron test. This is the center of the following are

The ADF Test

Mernard held that the Dickey Fuller tests figure an autoregressive model and test whether the coefficient is measurably unique in relation to one. On the off chance that it is not, it will be important to distinction the arrangement to accomplish stationary. The Dickey Fuller test is of the model:

A significant issue with normal D.f test is that their discriminating qualities are pre dispositioned if there is autocorrelation in the residuals of the D-F relapse. To redress this, Dickey and Fuller (1981) concocted the increased rendition of the Dickey Fuller Test. They included the same number of slacked variables as important to evacuate any autocorrelation in the residuals. The ADF methodology controls for higher-request connection by including slacked contrasts terms of the ward variables to the right hand side of the relapse held that the Augmented Dickey Fuller will, then, take the structure: For the reasons of this study the Augmented Dickey Fuller is utilized.

Phillips peron test

In spite of the fact that the ADF is a standout amongst the most generally utilized tests5, it some of the time carries on inadequately, particularly in the vicinity of serial connection. As a consequence of this, Phillips and Peron created a more far reaching hypothesis of unit root non stationarity. The tests are like the ADF tests, however they fused programmed adjustment to the DF methodology to take into consideration auto correlated residuals. The Phillips Peron test performs better than (or at any rate and additionally) the ADF test regarding near force and yields tighter certainty interims. Notwithstanding this, the Phillips and Peron tests are non-parametic tests of the invalid of the unit root and are viewed as all the more influential, as they utilize reliable estimators of the change. The Phillips Perron unit root test contrasts from the ADF tests for the most part by the way they manage serial association and hetero scedasticity in the slips.

Conclusion

This part set out the model which decides the effect of money instability on stocks. Included in this model are variables that are liable to influence the operation of money markets. These variables are the local investment rates, US premium rates, GBP unpredictability, aggregate mining creation and fares. For stationarity/unit roots purposes, the model utilized the Dickey-Fuller and the Phillips Perron tests. Indicative tests, for example, the Normality test, Ramsey RESET test and the LM test were talked about. The regression system has been picked as the estimation method for the effect of coin unpredictability on money markets in United Kingdom. The succeeding section will run the talked about preparatory examination of the information and the last regression model utilizing the econometric bundle EVIEWS 7. At long last, demonstrative tests should be performed on the residuals.

Data Analysis

Introduction

The past section set the systematic structure and assessed the model and estimation methods to be utilized as a part of this study. This section introduces the primary aftereffects of relapse on month to month information for the period from August 2004 to July 2014. The effect of exchange rate inconstancy on stock exchange is evaluated utilizing three macroeconomic variables. It is through this part that the destination of this study might be accomplished. The fundamental target of this study has been to research the exchange rate inconstancy on the stock exchange in United kingdom.

This part is separated into 4 sub-segments. The primary exhibits the consequences of enlightening detail. This is done by descriptive statistics. This part has mainly followed the market capitalisation exchange rate fluctuation. The second part, Collinearity test, took after by stationarity tests for finding mean and variance change in the third area. Final test, regression is performed on the last part for finding the result of research question.

Descriptive statistics of market capitalisation and exchange rate fluctuation in last 10 years

Xuezheng, Rusell and Tiao held that numerous monetary arrangements, for example, returns on stocks and remote trade rates, show leptokurtosis and time-shifting unpredictability. These two gimmicks have been the subject of broad studies following the time when Mandelbrot (1963) and Fama (1965) initially reported them. In this respect it is important to perform some engaging facts to look at if the GBPvol and MC display time differing instability and leptokurtosis qualities. The two primary variables of the study are inspected in light of the fact that these variables focus the estimation system for the study. The facts of the GBPvol and MC arrangement are shown in Table 2 below.

Descriptive Statistics

Table 2 demonstrates the spellbinding detail of the GBPvol variable. Correspondingly, skewness and kurtosis speak to the way of flight from typicality. Emenike contends that in an ordinarily disseminated arrangement, skewness is 0 and kurtosis is 3. The coefficient of skewness measures asymmetry. The GBPvol esteem for skewness is .462 and it reflects positive skewness. A positive skew demonstrates that the tail on the right side is longer than the left side and the majority of the qualities lie to the left of the mean. Additionally, if skewness is sure, the normal extent of positive deviations is bigger than the normal size of negative deviations. The coefficient of the GBPvol variable is showing that there is asymmetry within GBPvol. Thus, a variable that takes after a typical dissemination ought to be symmetric. The coefficient of kurtosis measures the peakedness of dissemination. The quality for kurtosis is -1.083 and this recommends that there is peakedness in the GBPvol. Kurtosis coefficients have values short of what 0. From this it could be watched that the GBPvol variable displays noteworthy deviations from ordinariness. The coefficient of kurtosis is -1.083 and it is more modest than zero. This shows noteworthy lerptokurtosis. A dissemination with a coefficient bigger than 3 is said to be leptokurtic and unified with a coefficient more modest than 3 is platykurtic. The MC variable reflects positive skewness with an estimation of 4.6 and this demonstrates that there is asymmetry in the MC variable. Defusco, Mcleavey, Pinto, Runkle (2006) held that a few specialists accept that speculators favour positive skewness, all else measure up to that is, they ought to lean toward portfolios with appropriations offering a moderately vast recurrence of uncommonly huge settlements. The

Study	Methodology	Findings
Choi, Fang and Yong Fu (2009) (New Zealand)	EGARCH	The exchange rate affected the stock market
Moracles (2007) (Czech republic, Hungary, Poland and Slovakia)	Regression Analysis, Johansen technique, Cointegration, Vector Error, Correction Modelling and the standard Granger Casuality test	No evidence of stock prices and exchange rates moving together either in the long-run or in the short-run was found.
Alagidede, Panagiotidis and Zhang (2010)	Cointegration tests and Granger casuality test	There is no long-run relationship between two variables.
Sekmen (2011)	ARMA	Exchange negatively stock returns rate volatility affected U.S

Table 1: Evaluation Studies.

	N	Minimum	Minimum	Mean	Std. Deviation	Variance	Skewness		Kurtosis	
	Statistic	Statistic	Statistic	Statistic	Statistic	Statistic	Statistic	Std. Error	Statistic	Std. error
GBP/USD	119	1.42	2.07	1.7117	.17257	.030	.462	.222	-1.083	.440
Market Capitalization	119	414193.00	793432.00	5689427.899	1.12448E5	1.264.E10	.143	.222	27.981	.440
Valid N	119									

Table 2: Descriptive Statistics.

estimation of kurtosis demonstrates that the MC variable has high circulation than a typical conveyance. The kurtosis worth is 27.981 and this demonstrates leptokurtosis.

From the month to month standard deviation, it might be seen that the MC is substantially more unpredictable than the Gbpvol henceforth there is requirement for it to be caught under the relapse model. Overall, both the Gbpvol and MC variables don't adjust to typical dissemination however show negative skewness and leptokurtic appropriations. Deviations from typicality of time arrangement information have been seen by past studies. Emenike watched that the Stock return arrangement don't fit in with typical appropriation yet show negative skewness and leptokurtic dispersion. Agrawal and Srivastava, likewise recognized that these variables are non-ordinarily dispersed.

Finding the linear correlation between variables

Collinearity Test: Collinearity was performed to see in there is no direct correspondence between illustrative variables. Rationale behind suspicion of no multicollinearity is if two variables are collinear it gets to be hard to divided the individual impact of every variable on the ward variable. So as to check multi collinearity among autonomous variables, a correspondence examination was performed. The closer the r coefficient approaches ± 1, paying little mind to the course, the stronger is the current affiliation demonstrating a more straight relationship between the two variables. Notwithstanding, a recommended dependable guideline is that if the pair insightful relationship between two repressors is high, in abundance of 0.8, multicollinearity may posture genuine issue. The association examination results are accounted for in Table 3 underneath.

Table 3 demonstrates that the most elevated relationship coefficient worth is 0.984which is low. It is well beneath 0.8. Since the most noteworthy correspondence numbers are higher than 0.8, the results plainly demonstrate that none of the autonomous variables are exceptionally corresponded and multi collinearity amongst free variables exist.

Finding the mean and changes in variance

Stationarity test : On the off chance that the mean and fluctuation are consistent about whether, then the arrangement is stationary. Stationarity is vital for standard econometric hypothesis. Without it we can't get predictable estimators. One method for telling if a procedure is stationary is to plot the arrangement against time. Graphical representations taking the manifestation of time arrangement plots provide for us especially valuable methods for imagining data and leading similar dissects about whether. In the event that the chart crosses the mean of the specimen commonly, risks are that the variable is stationary; overall that is an evidence of diligent patterns far from the mean of the arrangement. On the off chance that the mean and difference change, then the arrangement is non-stationary. To identify if an arrangement is stationary graphical plots were carried out on watched estimations of the information. It demonstrates the GBPVOL and MC plots.

Model		Colinearity Statistics	
		Tolerance	VIF
1	Market Capitalization	.826	1.210
	US interest rate	.984	1.016
	Money supply	.821	1.218

Table 3: Elevated relationship coefficient.

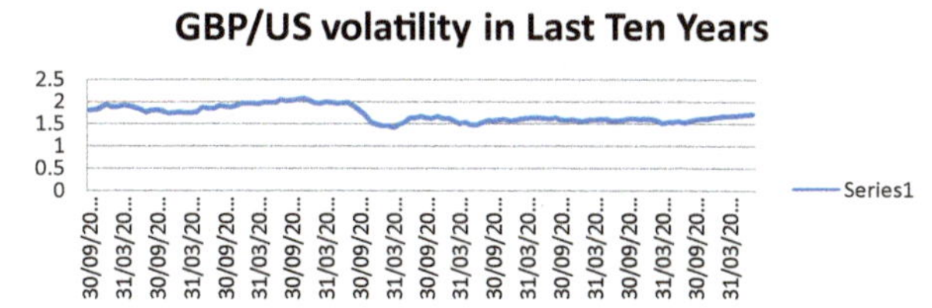

Figure 2: GBP/US Volatility in last ten years.

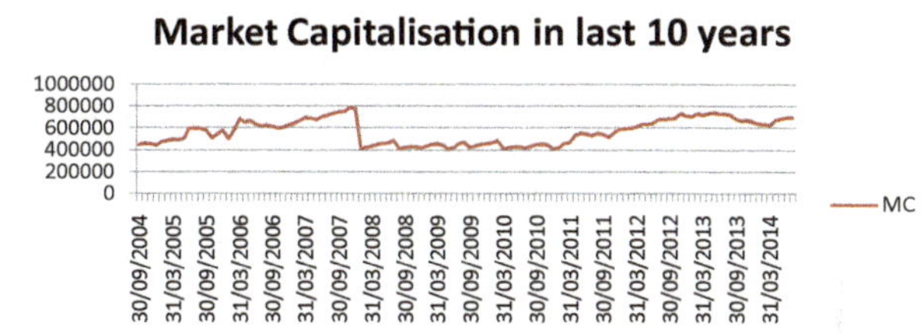

Figure 3: Market Capitalisation in last ten years.

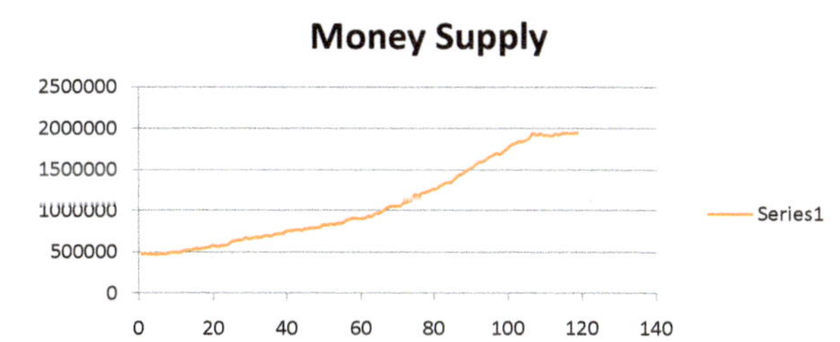

Figure 4: Money supply rate.

It proposes that the GBPVOL variable shows changes about whether. The level information demonstrates no propensity to come back to its mean demonstrating the requirement for differencing. The arrangement plot of the MC information shows that the arrangement is fluctuating about whether. This demonstrates that it is not stationary. The two variables have a period variation mean and change proposing that they are not stationary in their levels. The MC arrangement has a fluctuating conduct and with such a fluctuating example, a period arrangement is non-stationary, it doesn't demonstrate a propensity of mean inversion (Figure 2).

Graphical representations taking the manifestation of time arrangement plots was additionally done on the other informative variables; US premium rate, Money supply (M3). Their diagrams are shown in Figure 3 underneath.

Figure 4 demonstrates that the M3 information arrangement is emphatically straightly drifted and subsequently it is in this way non-stationary. The arrangement likewise demonstrates no inclination of coming back to its mean.

Figure 5 demonstrates that the Interest rate information arrangement is emitted and non- straightly drifted and subsequently it is stationary. The arrangement additionally demonstrates inclination of coming back to its mean.

Notwithstanding visual assessment, formal econometric tests were connected to unambiguously choose the genuine nature of time arrangement. Essential examination of graphical presentation of the information demonstrated conceivable non-stationary of the variables

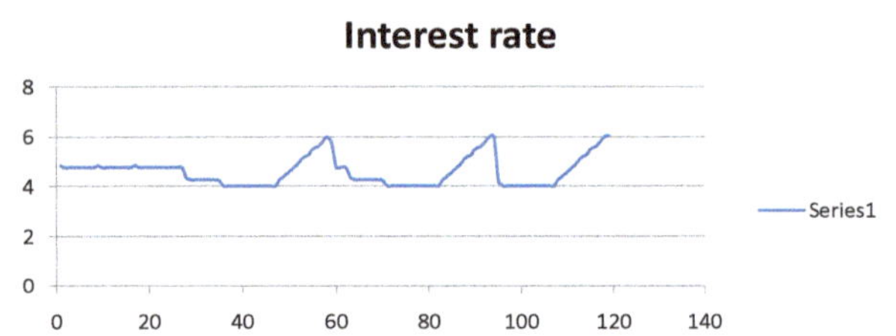

Figure 5: Interest rate.

which encourages for unit root testing. This study emulated the standard methodology of unit root testing by utilizing the Augmented Dickey Fuller (ADF) test. Since the ADF test is regularly reprimanded for low power, the study supplements this test with the Phillips Perron (PP) test. Results from these tests are indicated in the tables underneath.

ADF test: In the event that the mean and change are consistent about whether, then the arrangement is stationary. Stationary is key for standard econometric hypothesis. Without it we can't get steady estimators. One method for telling if a methodology is stationary is to plot the arrangement against time. Graphical representations taking the type of time arrangement plots provide for us especially valuable methods for imagining data and leading similar examines about whether. On the off chance that the chart crosses the mean of the example ordinarily, risks are that the variable is stationary; overall that is an evidence of constant patterns far from the mean of the arrangement. In the event that the mean and fluctuation change, then the arrangement is non-stationary. To discover if an arrangement is stationary graphical plots were carried out on watched estimations of the information. Figure 2 demonstrates the GBPVOL and MC plots.

Figure 2 proposes that the GBPVOL variable shows vacillations about whether. The level information demonstrates no inclination to come back to its mean showing the requirement for differencing. The grouping plot of the MC information shows that the arrangement is fluctuating about whether. This demonstrates that it is not stationary. The two variables have a period variation mean and fluctuation recommending that they are not stationary in their levels. The MC arrangement has a fluctuating conduct and with such a fluctuating example, a period arrangement is non-stationary, it doesn't demonstrate a propensity of mean inversion.

Graphical representations taking the manifestation of time arrangement plots was additionally done on the other illustrative variables; POR, Export Money (M3).

It demonstrates that the M3 information arrangement is emphatically straightly slanted and henceforth it is along these lines non-stationary. The arrangement additionally demonstrates no propensity of coming back to its mean.

Notwithstanding visual review, formal econometric tests were connected to unambiguously choose the real nature of time arrangement. Essential investigation of graphical presentation of the information showed conceivable non-stationary of the variables which encourages for unit root testing. This study took after the standard strategy of unit root testing by utilizing the Augmented Dickey Fuller (ADF) test. Since the ADF test is regularly condemned for low power, the study supplements this test with the Phillips Perron (PP) test. Results from these tests are demonstrated in the tables underneath (Table 4).

The results from the ADF tests are given in tables. The results are organized as per level information arrangement and for first contrasts in the information arrangement.

Table 4 demonstrates that all variables were not stationary in levels. The p- estimations of the variables all being more noteworthy than 0.05 show that we couldn't dismiss the invalid theory of the presence of unit establish in levels for all variables. Be that as it may, the variables are stationary will be stationary after first differencing them. The greatness of the p –values (short of what 0.05) are huge, demonstrating that the variables are stationary from the start contras

PP Test: The results from the Phillip Perron test are given in Table 5 beneath.

In applying the Phillips Peron test to the variables, MC and TMP were discovered to be stationary at levels. On the other hand, the test detail of M3, POR, USINT and GBPVL were short of what the discriminating worth at 1% and 5% individually and subsequently not stationary. In any case, these variables achieved stationary after the first differencing. The discriminating qualities at 1% and 5% were 3.480818 and 2.883579 individually.

After the stationary tests, graphical plots were carried out to watch the way of the mean and difference of the stationary information. The graphical plots of the differenced variables are appeared.

It demonstrates that the initially differenced variables hint at coming back to its mean recommending that the arrangement is pitifully stationary. In the wake of differencing, the run arrangement plot shows that the information has a steady area and fluctuation, in spite of the fact that the example of the residuals demonstrates that the information leave from the model in a methodical way. The same is seen in the other four illustrative variables.

		ADF test (intercept)		ADF (Trend and intercept)	
Variables		Levels	1ST Difference	Levels	1ST Difference
M3 (P value)		1.931176 0.9998	9.723775** 0.0000	-2.274915 0.4442	-10.03535 0.0000
GBPVOL (P value)		2.224457 0.1987	8.076612** 0.0000	-2.340393 0.4090	-8.085405 0.0000
USINT (P value)		-1.769695 0.3941	-4.679856** 0.0002	-1.764772 0.7162	-4.670071 0.0002
MC (P value)		-0.786105 0.8191	-6.921686** 0.0000	-2.561822 0.2985	-7.155631 0.0000
Critical values	1%	3.480818	3.480818	4.036310	4.036310
	5%	-2.885654	-2.885654	3.447699	3.447699
** and * denotes rejection of the null hypothesis at 1% and 5% respectively					

Table 4: Unit root/stationary test: ADF test.

		Phillips perron (intercept)		Phillips perron (Trend and intercept)	
Variables		Levels	1ST Difference	Levels	1ST Difference
M3 (P value)		1.194002 0.9980	-10.49386 0.0000	-2.122939 0.5279	-10.59217 0.0000
MC (P value)		10.51483 0.0000		-11.11609 0.0000	
GBPVOL (P value)		-2.143811 0.2281	-8.037357 0.0000	-2.245581 0.4602	-8.046197 0.0000
USINT (P value)		1.357667 0.6011	-4.581038 0.0002	-1.467586 0.8358	4.527591 0.0020
Critical values	1%	3.480818	3.480818	4.036310	4.036310
	5%	-2.883579	-2.883553	-3.444487	2.883753
** and * denotes rejection of the null hypothesis at 1% and 5% respectively					

Table 5: Unit root/Stationary tests: Phillips person tests.

Exchange rate vs Market capitalization

Researcher performed regression analysis here. Researcher aimed to find the inconstancy of exchange rate impact on market capitalization. Picked invalid theory here is that there is no such association in the middle of enhancement of monetary position and availability to Market Capitalization. Reverse theory is that there is association in the middle of them. Utilizing SPSS programming figuring is carried out. Bivariate relapse examination results are demonstrated in above tables. Model rundown table gives R2 = to the relapse model. R2 delineates level of variety between two variables. If there should arise an occurrence of loaner's originations of change of their monetary circumstance for 88.6% of the aggregate variety in Market Capitalization. The ANNOVA table outlines the F degree planned for the relapse model. This detail assesses centrality of the facts for the general relapse. More prominent F proportion gives more noteworthy change inside the ward variable which is illuminated by the free variable. F degree here assigns the relapse show that is profoundly noteworthy at the 0.000 level. The relapse coefficient table demonstrates the dock named "Unstandardized Coefficients" uncovers the unstandardized relapse coefficient for better budgetary positions, 0.168. T-test demonstrates the centrality level of relapse coefficient which is (0.000) here. Investigation above rejects the invalid speculations that demonstrate existing associations in the middle of 2 variables which could be seen specifically above sober minded bend of total likelihood. Hence, it demonstrates that conversion standard instability has more noteworthy effect on Market Capitalization.

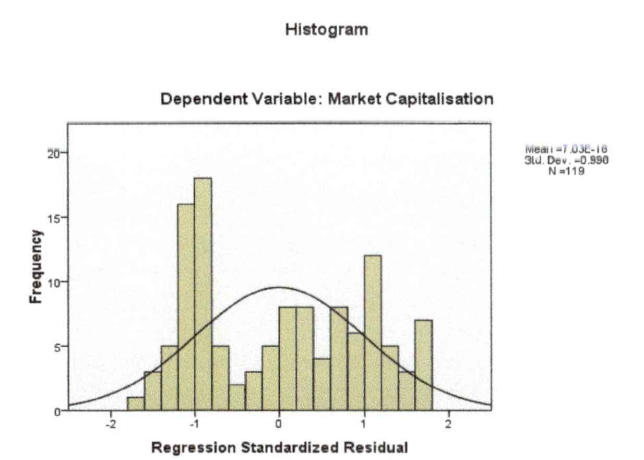

Figure 6: Exchange rate vs Market Capitalisation.

Exchange rate vs Interest rate

Researcher performed regression analysis here. Researcher aimed to find the inconstancy of exchange rate impact on Interest Rate. Picked invalid theory here is that there is no such association in the middle of enhancement of monetary position and availability to Interest Rate. Reverse theory is that there is association in the middle of them. Utilizing SPSS programming figuring is carried out. Bivariate relapse examination results are demonstrated in above tables. Model rundown table gives R2 = to the relapse model. R2 delineates level of variety between two variables. If there should arise an occurrence of loaner's originations of change of their monetary circumstance for 88.6% of the aggregate variety in Interest Rate. The ANNOVA table outlines the F degree planned for the relapse model. This detail assesses centrality of the facts for the general relapse. More prominent F proportion gives more noteworthy change inside the ward variable which is illuminated by the free variable. F degree here assigns the relapse show that is profoundly noteworthy at the 0.000 level. The relapse coefficient table demonstrates the dock named "Unstandardized Coefficients" uncovers the unstandardized relapse coefficient for better budgetary positions, 0.168. T-test demonstrates the centrality level of relapse coefficient which is (0.000) here. Investigation above rejects the invalid speculations that demonstrate existing associations in the middle of 2 variables which could be seen specifically above sober minded bend of total likelihood. Hence, it demonstrates that conversion standard instability has more noteworthy effect on Market Capitalization (Figure 6, Tables 6 and 7).

Exchange rate vs Money Supply

Researcher performed regression analysis here. Researcher aimed to find the inconstancy of exchange rate impact on market capitalization. Picked invalid theory here is that there is no such association in the middle of enhancement of monetary position and availability to Money Supply. Reverse theory is that there is association in the middle of them. Utilizing SPSS programming figuring is carried out. Bivariate relapse examination results are demonstrated in above tables. Model rundown table gives R2 = to the relapse model. R2 delineates level of variety between two variables. If there should arise an occurrence of loaner's originations of change of their monetary circumstance for the aggregate variety in Money Supply The ANNOVA table outlines the F degree planned for the relapse model (Figures 6 and 7). This detail assesses centrality of the facts for the general relapse. More prominent F proportion gives more noteworthy change inside the ward variable which is illuminated by the free variable. F degree here 3.740 assigns the relapse show that is profoundly noteworthy at the 0.000 level. The

Model	R	R Square	Adjusted R Square	Std. Error of the Estimate	Change Statistics				
					R Square Change	F Change	df1	df2	Sig. F Change
1	.208[a]	.043	.035	.56438	.043	5.309	1	117	.023

a. Predictors: (Constant), GBP/USD

b. Dependent Variable: US Interest Rate

Table 6: Model Summary[b] of Exchange rate vs interest rate.

Model		Sum of Squares	Df	Mean Square	F	Sig.
1	Regression	1.691	1	1.691	5.309	.023[a]
	Residual	37.268	117	.319		
	Total	38.959	118			

a. Predictors: (Constant), GBP/USD

b. Dependent Variable: US Interest Rate

Table 7: Anova.[b]

relapse coefficient table demonstrates the dock named "Unstandardized Coefficients" uncovers the unstandardized relapse coefficient for better budgetary positions, 0.168. T-test demonstrates the centrality level of relapse coefficient which is (0.000) here. Investigation above rejects the invalid speculations that demonstrate existing associations in the middle of 2 variables which could be seen specifically above sober minded bend of total likelihood. Hence, it demonstrates that conversion standard instability has more noteworthy effect on Money Supply (Tables 8 and 9).

Discussion and Conclusion

The principle goal driving this study has been to analyze the effect of currency fluctuations on stocks market in United Kingdom. To accomplish this destination, a few appraisals were performed. Firstly, an outline of the advancements of the GBP and the stock exchange was carried out. An outline of the advancements of the GBP swapping scale and the share trading system was important as this gives a premise to our understanding of the reason for its fluctuation. The exchange rate in United Kingdom has been described by respectable fluctuation and these were seen to spill into money markets. Changes in the GBP have extensive impacts on the route with which the stock exchange works.

An evaluation of writing on exchange rate fluctuation and securities exchanges was led and from it an exact model was tagged. It was seen that there is a blended supposition as to the relationship that exist between conversion scale and the share trading system. The study utilized month to month United Kingdom's information for the period August, 2004- July, 2014. The information recurrence chose guaranteed a satisfactory number of perceptions. The variables utilized within the study were GBP conversion standard, market capitalisation; supply of money (M3), and United States premium rate. Spellbinding facts were utilized to explore the factual properties of the two principle variables; exchange rate standard and business capitalisation. Results demonstrated that these two variables were absolutely skewed and notwithstanding this they had fat tails. The study utilized the regression model to measure the effect of exchange rate fluctuation on the share trading system of LSE.

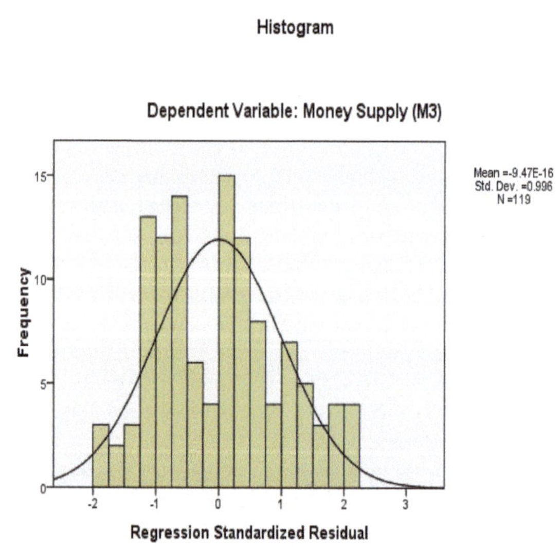

Figure 7: Exchange rate vs Money Supply.

The imperative experiences of the results could be abridged as takes after

To begin with, the examination reported powerless relationship between exchange rate fluctuation and the stock exchange. This result is not steady of the assumption that the instability encompassing conversion scale business sector misshapes proficient speculation distribution. Showcases that are presented to cash instability generally confront extensive vulnerability about the reappearances of venture ventures. This can prompt interruption of these organizations on stocks. Unpredictability influences the stream of data about the nature of undertakings to speculators and subsequently twists asset distribution.

Results from this study did not discover any confirmation that backing the above declaration. Actually, unpredictability was seen to bring positive effects on the stock exchange in United Kingdom. This may be a consequence of the accompanying;

1. The organizations on the LSE now understand the negative effects of coin unpredictability and thus have created measures that pad against the impacts of cash instability.

2. Cavallo held that "working together in an economy that is occasionally presented to turmoil in relative costs implies that business visionaries must face generous vulnerability about the benefit of option tasks. Under this situation, a key peculiarity is the capacity to adjust to a nature's domain". Organizations and firms working on the LSE have taken different instruments to fence against swapping scale hazard. Results from this study propose that the LSE has approached towards educational productivity in any event as for swapping scale and cash supply unpredictability. The frail relationship between money unpredictability and stocks appear to give prove that the LSE

Model	R	R Square	Adjusted R Square	Std. Error of the Estimate	Change Statistics				
					R Square Change	F Change	df1	df2	Sig. F Change
1	.608[a]	.369	.364	3.95317E5	.369	68.474	1	117	.000

a. Predictors: (Constant), GBP/USD

b. Dependent Variable: Money Supply (M3)

Table 8: Model Summary[b] of Exchange rate vs Money Supply.

Model		Sum of Squares	Df	Mean Square	F	Sig.
1	Regression	1.070E13	1	1.070E13	68.474	.000[a]
	Residual	1.828E13	117	1.563E11		
	Total	2.898E13	118			

a. Predictors: (Constant), GBP/USD

b. Dependent Variable: Money Supply (M3)

Table 9: Anova.[b]

is not a proficient business sector. Results propose that organizations on the LSE can utilize swapping scale data to anticipate the future conduct of stocks. This results in the organizations' capability to gauge the developments that the GBP would take later on consequently empowering them to pad against the future variances of the GBP. As a consequence of this, money unpredictability won't influence the stock operations on the LSE.

3. The frail relationship between conversion scale unpredictability and the stock exchange may have been brought on by the diverse variables that influence each of these businesses. The variables/news that causes changes in return rates may be unique in relation to the components that cause changes in stock costs. Under such situation, there ought to be no connection between the said variables (Muhammad and Rasheed, 2011). On the off chance that there were normal elements that impact both swapping scale unpredictability and securities exchange, then a solid relationship between these two money related variables would have been found.

Second, stocks was seen to be influenced by other macroeconomic variables to be specific: premium rates, aggregate mining generation, cash supply and the United States premium rates. Premium rates were seen to have a negative effect on stocks. This is upheld both by monetary hypothesis and various studies including that of Alam and Uddin. Expands in premium rates builds the opportunity expense of holding cash and consequently substitution in the middle of stocks and enthusiasm bearing securities and thus falling stock costs. In different words, climbs in premium rates propel speculators to put less in stocks and this, subsequently, prompt a fall in business sector capitalisation.

Aggregate mining creation was likewise seen to have a negative effect on securities exchange capitalisation; a build altogether mining generation prompted a decrease in securities exchange capitalisation. A build in the supply of cash was seen to have a positive effect on the stock exchange. Expand in cash supply prompts build in liquidity that eventually brings about upward development of ostensible value costs. Li discovered a comparative bring about a study which evolved an examination of cash supply and stock exchange relation in Europe.

In conclusion, the results demonstrated a optimistic relationship within US premium rate and market capitalisation. The estimation of the US premium rates was sure; implying that an expand in US premium rates will prompt an ascent in business sector capitalisation. The US investment rates sign was required to be negative yet comes about have demonstrated the positive. This may be the way that developing markets like United Kingdom are still seen as alluring by speculators paying little mind to other macroeconomic elements, for example, world premium rates.

Indicative tests on the model demonstrated a steady and strong model. The Q-detail test demonstrated that there was no serial association in the residuals. Issues of ARCH were additionally killed by the GARCH model. In any case, the typicality test demonstrated that the residuals were not typically disseminated and this situation is confronted by a few studies.

Policy implications and recommendations

The discoveries from this study have various strategy suggestions. Firstly, the frail unpredictability transmission from the GBP to stock exchange may be characteristic of expanded utilization of supporting instruments by firms on the LSE. Additional supporting instruments needs to be placed set up to guarantee the disposal of negative impacts of GBP unpredictability. These supporting instruments ought to be proficient and they ought not contort the ordinary working of the LSE. There has been sizeable proof in backing of hypotheses recommending that relative value instability gives motivations to ambitious people to embrace more "flexible" however less beneficial generation advances, empowering them to oblige money volatility8. Supporting operations are, on occasion, expensive and can diminish the execution of the organizations.

Besides, Since the United Kingdom n stock exchange is not by any stretch of the imagination presented to the negative impacts of money unpredictability. Important arrangement creators in government can utilize swapping scale as an approach instrument to pull in remote portfolio speculation. In addition, the capacity of the LSE to support against the negative impacts of cash instability could be utilized as a device to pull in outside financial specialists to stocks. The capacity of securities exchanges to pad against macroeconomic vulnerabilities has been connected with created nations' stock exchanges, for example, the United States and United Kingdom. Be that as it may, this has additionally been seen, in this study, and this demonstrates that the LSE could be showcased as a safe business for remote financial specialists. The feeble unpredictability transmission from the conversion scale business to money markets shows that there is prospect for remote speculators to differentiate their interests in these two businesses.

Thirdly, The LSE needs to keep up its co-operation with world class stock exchanges, for example, the LSE. This may be one of the reasons the LSE can pad negative impacts of coin unpredictability. Macroeconomic overflows from created nations are normally difficult to manage however in the event that there is some joining between the LSE and created nations, news about any conceivable improvements in these business sectors will achieve the LSE quick and measures to manage any conceivable impacts of these macroeconomic advancements will be placed set up route before the businesses are influenced.

In conclusion, Investors, brokers and portfolio chiefs still need to be vigilant on the overflows from the remote conversion standard into stocks. In spite of the fact that there is a feeble relationship between GBP instability and the share trading system in United Kingdom , this does not so much imply that speculators and portfolio chiefs require not screen the improvements between these two variables. Different methodologies to ensure money markets from the hurtful impacts of cash instability need to be brought into stocks. These instruments would then be utilized to further fence against trade hazard. Conversion standard incited instability is a pressing issue in United Kingdom and numerous different nations that have adaptable swapping scale administrations.

Possible regions for further research

Swapping scale unpredictability is at the center of the boiling over verbal confrontation on the execution of conversion standard administrations. This worry was fortified by the huge developments in ostensible trade rates that portrayed world budgetary markets since the move to an oversaw skimming conversion scale framework in 1973. A significant concern of approach producers at the downfall of the Bretton Wood framework is the outcome of swapping scale instability saw to be a noticeable peculiarity of an adaptable conversion standard framework. Money unpredictability has respectable ramifications in the monetary markets, particularly the stock exchange.

The GBP has been the most unstable among rising monetary standards over the recent years. United Kingdom 's late measures to diminish the GBP's unpredictability haven't had a craved effect as the cash's vacillation is powered by worldwide financial shakiness and capital inflows from created nations (Davies, 2010). United Kingdom has encountered significant and proceeded with money unpredictability amid the recent years notwithstanding of solid monetary basics. Pretorius and de Beer (2002) note that the stressing instability of the GBP brought about the erGBP of the Myburgh Commission of investigation into the devaluation of the GBP. Policymakers and scholastics have progressively pondered about the way of the money instability emergencies, the variables in charge of their spread and especially whether a nation with apparently suitable residential and outer essentials can experience the ill effects of cash emergency.

"The joining of the LSE into the world business has been supported by the proceeded with development and improvements it has been making. Mboweni contends that amid 2001, the LSE entered into two concurrences with the London Stock Exchange (LSE) to accommodate co-operation in admiration of information dispersal and the likelihood of remote participation and double essential postings on both trades. The relations with the London Stock Exchange (LSE) have been solid and have to a great extent enhanced the operations on the LSE. The LSE Tradelect, which is the LSE's completely robotized exchanging framework, is worked under the permit from the LSE. These and different improvements have helped the LSE's worldwide standing and this has enhanced LSE's effectiveness and its risks of pulling in financial specialists both generally and abroad. This has made it to be one of the best performing stock trades on the planet.

It is recognized that United Kingdom 's ostensible conversion scale unpredictability is among the most astounding of all merchandise exporters and developing markets and that, in time of "unnecessary instability", money developments don't go about as a stun absorber reflecting changes in relative costs, however as a "wellspring of powerlessness". Notwithstanding real upgrades in the organization of financial and fiscal approach, money instability discourages speculators in tradable products and administrations outside of the merchandise segment. "The GBP remains to some degree unstable; however the level of instability has been decreased. At present, the relative instability is joined by a coin that is over-esteemed as in monetary assets are redirected into limited territories of venture, establishing a shaky framework for what's to come"

Knedlik kept up that expanded unpredictability of trade rates in developing markets is additionally ascribed to the more modest size of their economies and therefore the littler size of the business for their money. Higher swapping scale instability in developing business sector nations is in this way a reasonable desire and reflects principal contrasts in the structure of economies. Regardless, it is evident that a real snag for effective arranging in the business area, and the powers would have wanted to have more prominent conversion scale soundness. Yet, under the current circumstances, conversion scale variances are most likely unavoidable. Unstable money related streams now and then created by advancements in different monetary forms make the accomplishment of swapping scale steadiness almost unimaginable (Van de Merwe and Mollentze, 2009).

Benita and Lauterbach (2004) demonstrated that conversion standard unpredictability have genuine financial expenses that influence value steadiness, firm benefit and a nation's solidness. Swapping scale unpredictability has suggestions for the monetary arrangement of a nation particularly money markets. Conversion standard instability produces quality of vulnerability as the fluctuation of expected benefits climbs and its net present worth falls. Stock exchange assumes an extremely essential part in evaluating financial states of any nation through enhanced stock returns normally meant by higher benefit to firms. This thusly causes financial development and the other way around. Essentially stock trade business serves as a channel through which surplus trusts are moved from Lender-Savers to Borrower-Spenders who have deficiencies of stores. In view of this reason, instability in stock costs can essentially influence the execution of the budgetary area and the whole economy.

Also, cash instability prompts the issues of conversion scale hazard. Swapping scale danger, or money danger, is the hazard that a business' operations or a venture's worth will be influenced by progressions in return rates. Case in point, if cash must be changed over into alternate money to make certain venture, changes in the estimation of the coin with respect to the US dollar will influence the aggregate misfortune or increase on the speculation when the cash is changed over back. This danger typically influences organizations yet it can likewise influence singular financial specialists who make global speculations. Subsequently trade danger is higher under states of conversion scale unpredictability.

The majority of the studies that looked to analyze the relationship between conversion scale unpredictability and the share trading system, including this one, focused on utilizing month to month information to inspect the relationship that exists between the two variables. Then again, it must be noted that day by day information or week by week information give more helpful comes about that month to month information. It is along these lines, recommended that the centrality of this present study's results could be enhanced by applying day by day or week by week information.

Utilizing more incessant perceptions better catches flow of conversion scale and stock exchange interrelationships.

References

1. Branson W, Halttunen H, Masson P (1977) Exchange rate in the short run: The dollar Deutsche mark rate, European Economic Review 10: 303-324.
2. Fama EF, French RK (2004) The Capital Asset Pricing Model: Theory and Evidence.
3. Saleh G (2009) The Dynamic Relation Between Stock Prices and Exchange Rates in Egypt, Saudi Arabia and UAE. United States, UMI.
4. Choi JJ, Papaioannou MG (2009) Credit, Currency, or Derivatives: Instruments of Global Financial Stability. U.K, Emerald Group Publishing.
5. Aggarwal R (1981) Exchange Rates and Stock Prices: A Study of the US Capital Markets under Floating Exchange Rates, Akron Business and Economic Review.
6. Soenen LA, Hennigar ES (1988) An Analysis of Exchange Rates and Stock Prices: The U.S Experience between 1980 and 1986.
7. Bahmani OM, Sohrabian A (1992) Stock Prices and the effective exchange rate of the dollar, Applied Economics 24: 459-464.
8. Bhattacharya B, Mukherjee J (2003) Causal Relationship Between Stock Market and Exchange Rate. Foreign Exchange Reserves and Value of Trade Balance: A Case Study for India.
9. Chow EH, Lee WY, Solt MS (1997) The exchange rate risk exposure of asset returns.
10. Solnik B (1987) Using financial prices to test exchange rate models: A note. J Financ, 42: 141-149.
11. Franck P, Young A (1972) Stock Price Reaction of Multinational Firms to Exchange Realignments.
12. Pilbeam K (1998) International Finance. 2nd ed. UK, Basingstoke: Mac Adjasi C, Harvey SK, Agyapong D (2008) Effect of Exchange rate volatalitity on the Ghana stock exchange. African Journal of Accounting, Economics and Banking research.

13. Friedman M (1988) Money and the Stock Market, Journal of Political Economy 96: 221-245.

14. Stavárek D (2004) Linkages between Stock Prices and Exchange Rates in the EU and the United States, Cech Republic, Silesian University in Opava School of Business Administration in Karviná Department of Finance.

15. Aydemir O, Demirhan E (2009) The Relationship between Stock Prices and Exchange Rates Evidence from Turkey, Int Res J Financ Eco, 23: 207-215.

16. Welfens PJ, Ryan C (2007) Financial Market Integration and Growth: Structural Change and Economic Dynamics in the European Union. London, Springer.

17. Richards ND, Simpson J, Evans J (2009) The Interaction Between Exchange Rates and Stock Prices: An Australian Context, Int J Eco Financ 1: 3-23.

18. Kasper LJ (1997) Business Valuations: Advanced Topics. USA, Green wood Publishing.

19. Mandal BN (2009) Global Encyclopaedia of Welfare Economics: The Principle of Population. India, Singh Global Vision for Publishing

20. Herekar H (2006) Capital Asset Pricing Model (CAPM) for Dummies.

21. Taylor (2005) An Empirical Evaluation of the Capital Asset Pricing Model.

22. Vernimmen P, Quiry P, Fur Y, Dallochio M, Salvi A (2005) Corporate Finance: Theory & Practice. England, John Wiley and Sons.

23. Nieh CC, Lee CF (2001) Dynamic relationship between stock prices and exchange rates for G-7 countries, The Quarterly Review of Economics and Finance 41: 477-490.

24. Saunders M, Lewis P, Thornhill A (2007) Research Methods for Business Students, Harlow: Pearson Education Ltd.

Impact of Macro Variables on Karachi Stock Exchange

Rabia N* and Khakan N
University of Lahore, Lahore, Pakistan

Abstract

In this paper we have studied that impact of macro variables on Karachi stock exchange. Karachi stock exchange is very interesting topic for the discussion. Karachi stock exchange is known as one of the oldest stock exchange of Asia. Karachi stock exchange is the largest stock exchange of Pakistan. Karachi stock exchange is the dependent variables and inflation, interest rate and exchange rate and GDP are the independent variables. We have taken the data from period 1992 to 2012. We have found that there is 80 %variation. Therefore we can say there is a strong relationship among the variables. While other variables have shown that GDP, interest rate and inflation has strong relationship with kse stock index while interest rate have negative relationship with Karachi stock exchange. The increase and decrease the stock prices will affect the performance of the economy. In this paper researcher want to found out the fundamental marc variables which have impact on stock exchange and also want to found out that what are the impact of these variables on the government policies like monetary and facial policy. Fundamental macro variables are export, money, supply, interest rate.

Keywords: Facial policy; Monetary policy; Asia; GDP; interest rate; Inflation

Introduction

Karachi stock exchange is very interesting topic for the discussion. In this paper we have find out impact of macro variables on Karachi stock exchange. Karachi stock exchange is known as oldest stock exchange of Asia Karachi stock exchange is the largest stock exchange of Pakistan. Stock market means the prices of securities which are traded in stock exchange. Stock exchange has a vital role for the fostering capital formation. Stock exchange has a main role for the healthy economy of any country. Stock exchange is work as a channel between stock investors and stock borrowers. In the words simple stock market is place where we can trade securities. According to different approaches statues that stock market contain two types of investors. One approaches says that investors use their different techniques to overcome the stock market prices and market is insufficient there. The second approaches says that all the investors have the same information ad cannot beat the stock prices. Koh says that share price depends upon the effect of macro variables. Khenet et al. analysis that stock market performances are affected because macroeconomic variables are flotation in nature [1-4]. Lee and Wang in Thailand stock exchange and stock return have positive relationship. Mohamed et al. analyzed that impact of different variables on stock return. Bollersley investors are very attractive towards the profits. With the help of determination of value of demand and supply we can know prices of securities which are traded in stock market as daily basis. The fluctuation in stock market due to different factors like economic and political behavior of country. Karachi stock exchange also reacts due to these factors. In simple words during business hours buyers and sellers exchange their holdings. Stock exchange is the place where investors seek reward in the shape of capital gain. Exchange investment projects are useful to mobilize the nation's saving. Stock market is the channel between savings and borrower's. According to leading stocks of world reported that negative growth ranging from Pakistan 50.8% and china 2.7% during the facial year. Since the last decade the Pakistani stock market was highly disturbed due to financial crises. In March 2005 stock market was crashed in year 2005. The second collage was observed in year 2006. The biggest crash in the may 2008 to January 2009 it was the worst crash in the history of Pakistan. Karachi stock exchange was dropped more than 12 thousand points. There are many reasons due to which prices of demand and supply increases and decrease and have impact on market behavior. According to different researches increase in inflation will increase in the income of demand and supply. The main reason for inflation of any country is there is inverse relationship between demand and supply. According to different economist view that increase in prices of things will indicate the inflation. In other words inflation means expansion of money supply. Many researchers have proved that the rate on inflation has impact on the stock market volatility. Commonly we can say inflation has two main parts 1) expected inflation 2) unexpected inflation. Expected inflation rate is plan one year to year between economists and consumer. Unexpected inflation means that what we can expect between economic and consumers. In this study has shown that main effect of unexpected inflation is due to redistribution of wealth. After the world war 2 in USA the inflation rate is between 3% to 6% for many years which has impact On the performance of the stock market inflation created natural bias. Due to inflation in the world every country has worst stock market. In this paper also explores that if government could not control the inflation then worst stock market ratio will increase. In the high inflation many assets failed to keep up. Government should control it soon otherwise stock will be collapse over 95%. Morever, many studies has shown that in the period of high inflation dividend will increase in consumer prices. For the policy point of review stock prices and inflation has relationship. According to famar stock market are reflect from the macroeconomic variable therefore it is efficient. Chakravarity shows that stock market and inflation relationship. Mukherjee has shown there is two way causation between stock market performance and inflation. Inflation is due to increase rate and volatility. Inflation has very huge impact on the economic competitiveness. This study has shown that how there is relationship between interest rate and inflation rate. According to

***Corresponding author:** Rabia N, University of Lahore, Lahore, Pakistan
E-mail: rabianajaf@hotmail.com

different hypothesis high inflation shows high uncertainty. According to Li henggua inflation and stock prices has multiple relationships [5]. According to Zhaorang shows that we cannot consider impact of inflation on stock prices a single factor. Modern economy has common feature is called stock market. Stock market is famous for the development of the economy. After the stock market failure government has enable of raise financing for new projects. The status of investment in stock market is long term. Any variable which has impact on economy also impact of stock exchange [6]. According to different economist's inflation is one of the factors which have negative impact of stock exchange. We can measure stock market performance with the help of market capitalization. In this paper we discuss the following issue like 1) what is correlation between stock market and inflation 2) how much correlation between stock market liquidity and inflation. In all the countries inflation caused by monetary authorizes. Therefore, we can say impact of inflation on the stock market has implications on policy market. All the studies shown that stock market performance has effect on the economy [7-9]. The basic characteristics of this Indian economy that it has strong economic growth. A unique feature of this economy is that it has become second faster economy of the world. In the financial year 2008, 2010 the GDP growth has average near about 6.8% [10]. The target growth rate is 8% and the growth of Indian s service sector was 9.5% in 2008-2009. The best feature of Indian economy that it has high growth. In recent years Asian economy was facing crisis and Indian economy has proven its strength. According to different research foreign exchange reserves has record level in June [11-15]. In June 2009, the foreign exchange reserves were reaching a record level of $300. In May 2002, the Indian rupees were in strength as compared to dollar $1=rs 43.51. In 2004, the inflation rate contained at 5.5% in 2006 the inflation rate was at 6% and slow down at the beginning of the year 2009 was 9% (Figures 1-4 and Table 1).

Scope of Study

The scope of this study is find nature and strength of relation between stock return and inflation, and interest rate.

Objectives

1) What are the relationship between stock market and inflation?

2) What are the relationship between stock market and interest rate?

3) What are the relationship between stock market and exchange rate?

Methodology

The purpose of this study is to measure that affect of marc variables on the stock prices of Karachi. We explained the research model by

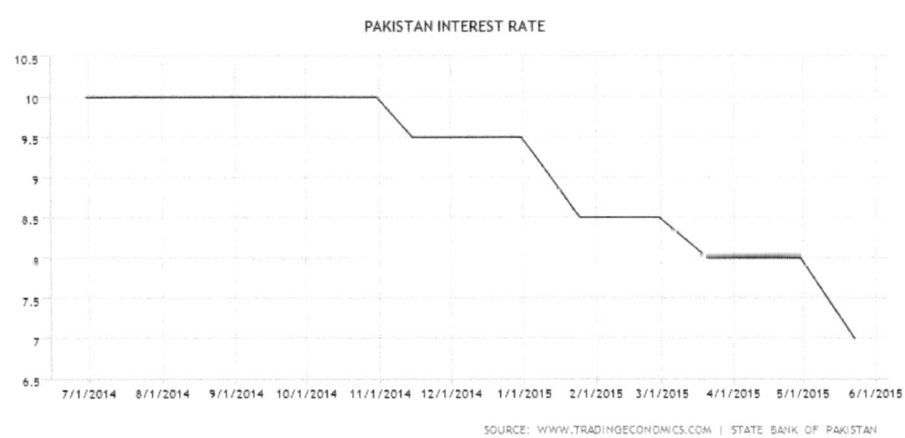

Figure 1: Pakistani interest rate.

Figure 2: Pakistani Growth rate.

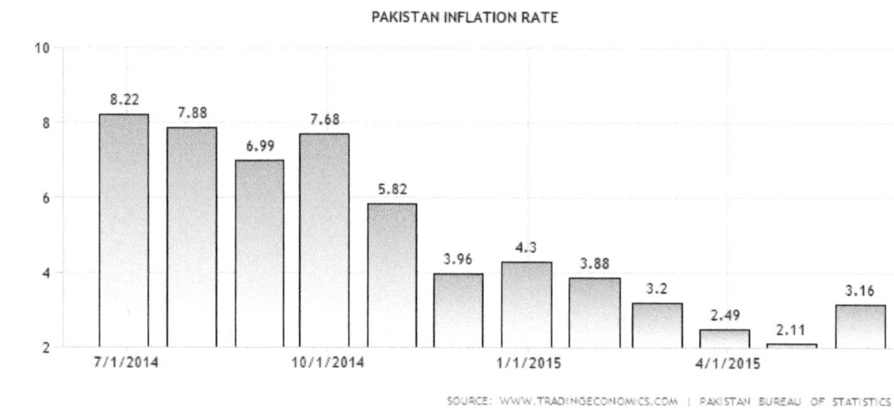

Figure 3: Pakistani inflation rate.

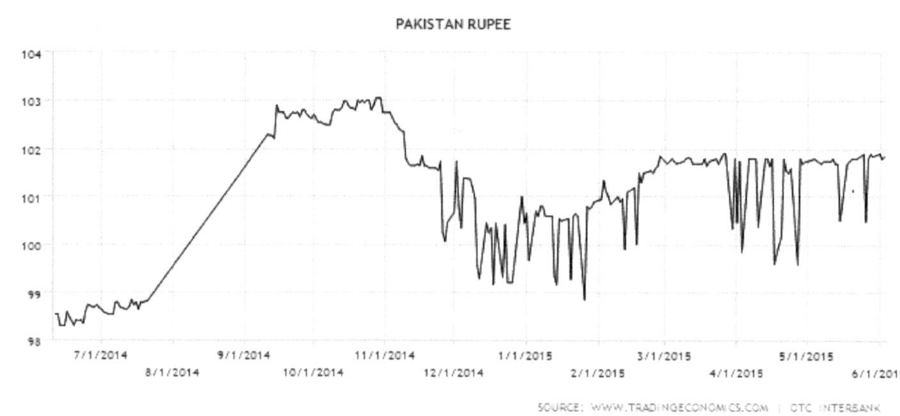

Figure 4: Pakistani rupee.

No.	Market	%
1	United States	47.7
2	Japan	10.3
3	United Kingdom	10.4
4	France	4.3
5	Canada	3.4
6	Germany	2.8
7	Switzerland	2.7
8	Italy	2.2
9	Australia	2.1
10	Netherlands	2.1

Table 1: Top Ten Biggest Stock Markets in the World (% of Total).

using the different variables. In this model Karachi stock exchange is the dependent variables and other are independent variables. We use yearly data from 1992 to 2012 (Figures 5 and 6).

The model:

$Y=a+b1(x1)+b2(x2)+b3(x3)+b4(x4)+e$

$Y=a+b1(\Delta exc)+b2(\Delta gdp)+b3(\Delta inflation)+b4(\Delta int\ rate)$

Where y =dependent variable

X1=exchange rate

X2=GDP

X3=inflation

X4=interest rate

Statistical tools

For the interpretation of the model we have used Pearson product movement correlation coefficient and multiple regression models. Table 2 shows that there is positive relationship between Karachi stock prices and exchange rate and there is negative relationship between interest rate and Karachi stock prices. At the end 100% change in independent variable will lead to 5.3033% change in stock prices [16]. For the purpose of checking that data is significant or not we use t ratio.

Method

Table 2 shows the relationship between dependent variables and independents variables.

$\Delta kse\ 100\ index=a+b1(\Delta ex)+b2(\Delta IR)+b3(\Delta inf)+b4(\Delta GDP)$

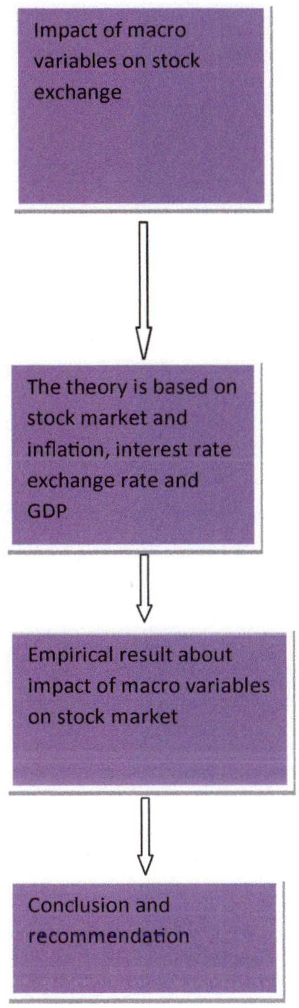

Figure 5: Research Framework.

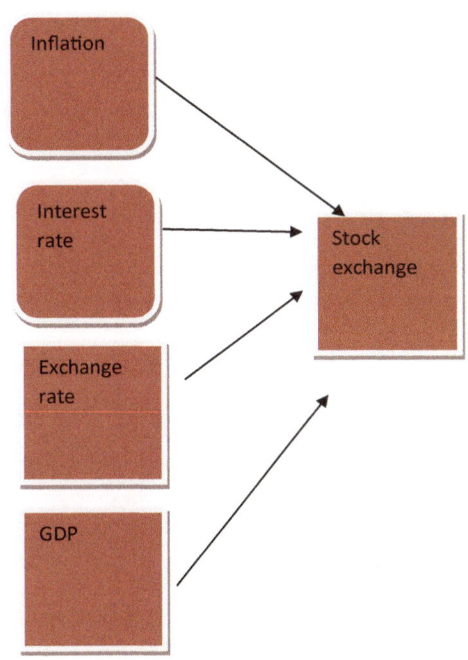

Figure 6: Theoretical framework.

All the data have shown that change in the independent variable will cause change in dependent variable. Table 2 shows that exchange rate, interest rate and gdp has positive and inflation show the negative relationship.

R2

R2 is used to checking that data is fit or not. It ranges normally form 0 to. The value of r2 is 0.8098 which is nearest to 1. It means there is 80% variation and this model is good fit.

Pearson's product movement correlation co efficient:

The purpose of person's product movement correlation is the show the relationship is positive and negative. It is represented by p and denoted by greek letter. It ranges from +1 to -1.

GDP and KSE 100 index

After the evaluation of data in Tables 6 and 10 shows that have not strong relationship. The model suggests that there is 15.5% correlation is present (Table 3-4).

F ratio

The purpose of f ratio is that overall model is significant or not. For this purpose we use a confidence interval. The value of f ratio in Table 4 is 15.9593 which shows that exchange rate and stock prices are the positive relationship.

Sample size	20
Coefficient of determination R^2	0.8098
Readjusted	0.7591
Multiple correlation coefficient	0.8998
Residual standard deviation	21.3378

Table 2: Relationship between dependent variables and independents variables.

Independent variables	Coefficient	Std. Error	Partial	T	P
(Constant)	-65.7771				
Exchange	1.5386	0.3921	0.7119	3.926	0.0015
Interest	-2.3135	2.3151	-0.2499	-0.998	0.3336
Inflation	4.1828	1.3476	0.6255	3.105	0.0074
GDP	5.3033	3.0641	0.4081	1.732	0.1041

Table 3: Relationship between dependent variables and independents variables.

Source	DF	Sum of Squares	Mean Square
Regression	4	29065.1541	7266.2886
Residual	16	6829.5823	455.3056

Table 4: Relationship between dependent variables and independents variables.

F-ratio	15.9593
Significance level	P<0.002

Table 5: Relationship between dependent variables and independents variables.

Variable	R
Exchange	0.7558
Interest	-0.4301
Inflation	0.4649
GDP	0.1538

Table 6: Relationship between dependent variables and independents variables.

Interest rate and kse stock prices:

Tables 5-9 shows that there is negative relationship between stock exchange and interest rate and correlation is insignificant because value of 0.585 is greater than 0.05. The study of nishat and shaheen in 2007 shows that there is negative correlation between interest rate and stock prices. When inflation rates moved to high then government should try to control hyper inflation. Increase the rate of has a bad impact on stock prices [17,18].

Inflation rate and kse 100 index

Tables 10 and 11 shows that there is moderate positive relationship between inflation and stock prices index and the p value is less than 0.05 therefore correlation is significant. For all the tables it has shown that independent variables shows positive and negative and weak correlation [19-21].

Conclusion

We have discussed the brief summary of the paper that changes in the macroeconomic variable have impact on the stock exchange prices in any nation. There are no variables which have impact on the stock prices. There are three types of stock exchange in Pakistani economy. 1) Islamabad stock exchange, 2) Karachi stock exchange, 3) Lahore stock exchange. Karachi stock exchange is one of biggest stock exchange of Pakistan economy and it has capacity to capture 76% of the capital market of Pakistan. Karachi stock exchange is the backbone four economies. In the Table 1 r2 is used to check that model is good or not. Value of r2 shows that model is good. And we used the t test to check that individual significant and f test is used to check that model is significant or not. According to Pearson's correlation model shows that exchange rate and stock prices have positive correlation. There is a moderate positive correlation between inflation and stock exchange. The relationship between interest rate and stock prices is negative. All these relationship has shown that there is not strong correlation among the variables.

		KSE	Exchange
KSE	Correlation Coefficient Significance Level Pn		0.757 0.0002 20
Exchange	Correlation Coefficient Significance Level Pn	0.757 0.0002 20	

Table 7: Relationship between dependent variables and independents variables.

		KSE	Interest
KSE	Correlation Coefficient Significance Level Pn		-0.431 0.0585 20
Interest	Correlation Coefficient Significance Level Pn	-0.431 0.0585 20	

Table 8: Relationship between dependent variables and independents variables.

		KSE	Inflation
KSE	Correlation Coefficient Significance Level Pn		0.466 0.0388 20
Inflation	Correlation Coefficient Significance Level Pn	0.466 0.0388 20	

Table 9: Relationship between dependent variables and independents variables.

		KSE	GDP
KSE	Correlation Coefficient Significance Level Pn		0.155 0.5172 20
GDP	Correlation Coefficient Significance Level Pn	0.155 0.5172 20	

Table 10: Relationship between dependent variables and independents variables.

		Exchange	Interest	Inflation	GDP
Exchange	Correlation Coefficient Significance Level Pn		-0.437 0.0547 20	0.194 0.4158 20	-0.219 0.3567 20
Interest	Correlation Coefficient Significance Level Pn	-0.437 0.0547 20		0.345 0.1382 20	-0.418 0.0657 20
Inflation	Correlation Coefficient Significance Level Pn	0.194 0.4158 20	0.345 0.1382 20		-0.098 0.6788 20
GDP	Correlation Coefficient Significance Level Pn	-0.219 0.3567 20	-0.418 0.0657 20	-0.098 0.6788 20	

Table 11: Relationship between dependent variables and independents variables.

Recommended

1) Practitioners and analysts should try to prediction about the future stock prices.

2) They should find out the stock market movement.

3) Investors should forecast how financial market changes.

References

1. Adrangi (1998) Impact of the Inflation Evidence 20: 63-76.
2. Bakshi (1996) About Inflation, Asset Prices and Interest Rates. Review of Financial Studies 10: 342-277.
3. Caporale (1998) Correlation between Inflation and Stock Prices, 9: 268-269.
4. Charles, Adjasi (2008) What is the Effect of Exchange Rate on the Indian Stock Exchange, Banking and finance Research 3.
5. Chatrath (1999) Relationship between Inflation and growth rate 9: 439-449.
6. Choudhry (1998) Relationship between Inflation and Rates of Return: University of Sadina, Department of Banking.
7. Dicky (1979, 1981) Likelihood Ratio with a Unit Root. Econometric 40: 1059-1074.
8. Engle (1988) Co-integration and estimation and testing. Econometric 57: 253-278.
9. Fama (1982) Relationship between Stock Returns and Money. African Economic Review 73: 547-567.
10. Fama (1978) Relationship Asset Returns and Inflation. J financ 57: 2012323.
11. Fisher (1931) The Theory of Interest.
12. Fraser (2000) Has shown The UK Stock Market's Relationship with and American Stock Markets.
13. Gallagher L (2005) The Stock Return- and Inflation. Economics Letters 77: 149-158.
14. Geetha, et al. (2011) What are The Relationship between Inflation and Stock Market: Evidence from Mal China. Int J Eco financ 1: 1-18.
15. Geske (1981) What is impact of Fiscal and Monetary Linkage between Stock Returns and Inflation? 9-83.

16. Graham (1996) Inflation, Real Stock Returns, and Monetary Policy. Applied Financial Economics 8: 27-37.

17. Granger (1989) Discuses about the different recent developments in a concept of causality. J Eco 37: 199-214.

18. Granger (1997) A bivariate Causality between Stock Prices and Exchange Rates.

19. Greenspan, Allen (1996) What Do Budget Deficits Do? Issues and Options: 139-148.

20. Hamrita (2007) The Multi-Scale Interaction between Interest Rate and inflation.

21. Hardouvelis GA (1988) The predictive power of recent monetary regimes. Journal of banking 44: 339-358.

Optimal Premium Subsidy and Its Impact on Individual Choice for Insurance Coverage

Mahito Okura[1]* and YingYing Jiang[2]

[1]Associate Professor, Faculty of Contemporary Social Studies, Department of Social System Studies, Doshisha Women's College of Liberal Arts, Kyoto, Japan
[2]Part-time Instructor, Faculty of Economics, Meiji Gakuin University, Tokyo, Japan

Abstract

The purpose of this article is to analyze whether a government premium subsidy is desirable by using a game theoretic approach. From our analysis, the following main results are derived. When policyholder's effort for lowering accident probability is not considered, government conducts premium subsidy when the fraction of policyholders is small. In contrast, when policyholder's effort is considered, whether government conducts premium subsidy is ambiguous even if the fraction of policyholders is small.

Keywords: Government; Premium subsidy; Insurance demand

Introduction

The importance of sharing risks via the insurance market has been addressed by many previous studies [1-3]. However, it is always difficult for an individual to get full insurance coverage at a reasonable cost due to the failure of private insurance market. In general, factors such as market imperfections and existence of informational asymmetries between an individual and insurer which generate problems such as moral hazard and/or adverse selection are responsible for market failure.

Insurer would prefer to provide an incomplete coverage or conduct some monitoring activities in order to avoid incurring possible losses caused by individual's opportunistic behavior [4-6]. In the latter case, a full insurance coverage would probably become more expensive due to increase in transaction cost resulted from monitoring activities in relation to policyholder's behavior. In some cases, an insurance coverage itself would become unaffordable or unavailable if asymmetric information problems are significant enough that complicated and specialized insurance contracts associated with high costs become indispensable [7].

Previous studies have also shown that an individual may favor a partial coverage or no coverage at all if she does not have sufficient knowledge and/or information regarding certain risks and/or insurance coverage [8-11]. Moreover, Anderson [12] and Kaplow [13] suggest that an ex post government relief program (e.g., grants, low-interest loans) against financial losses undermines an individual's willingness to pay to be fully insured, which is known as a problem of charity hazard [14-16]. Although government relief can be efficient if insurance markets suffer more inefficiency from market imperfections other than moral hazard [17].

Given the presence of market failures and, in some cases, the resulting absence of markets for insurance, the overall distribution of risks would presumably be sub-optimal and if the total cost of individual's risk-bearing is consequently significant, then government intervention may be desirable [18]. More specifically, government intervention in certain markets as a supplier of insurance (e.g., public health care) can be cost-effective because all uncertainty will be borne publicly and the total of the costs of risk-bearing goes to zero as the population of taxpayers becomes large [7,19].

Government can also intervene in insurance markets by providing a government-sponsored reinsurance program, which has been relatively effective in dealing with natural disaster hazards [20]. Government can intervene in insurance markets by means of a financial subsidy as well, which is more likely to be used in the agricultural and health service sectors by taking the form of premium subsidies or tax subsidies. Regarding catastrophe risks, government involves not only in the form of reinsurer, but also in the form of tax subsidies [21].

The cost efficiency of such government interventions, however, has been controversial because the intervention itself may generate inefficiencies due to new problems such moral hazard and/or adverse selection associated with the intervention [22]. For example, Nelson and Loehman [23], and Hazell [24] have pointed out that a public subsidy might be a costly solution to the market imperfections of agricultural insurance, although it is still preferred by many governments, especially in developing countries. Barnett and Skees [25] also suggested that participation rate of Federal Crop Insurance in the United States is not proportional to the increase in premium subsidies. Meanwhile, regarding the health service sector, Feldstein and Friedman [26] and Pauly [27] asserted that tax subsidies have caused large welfare losses, despite the fact that they contributed to the growth and development of health insurance in the United States.

On the other hand, Stiglitz [28] and Greenwald and Stiglitz [29] argued that government interventions (e.g., taxes and subsidies) in imperfect markets particularly those caused by the existence of imperfect and costly information, can be Pareto-improving and make everyone better off. Moreover, Akerlof [30] addressed that in the case of "trust" being considered an important element in market transactions, for example, as conducted in developing countries, the value of government intervention increases more than would otherwise be the case.

Given the aforesaid background of government intervention, this article focuses on the case in which government intervenes in a market with a low penetration rate by taking the form of premium subsidy.

***Corresponding author:** Mahito Okura, Faculty of Contemporary Social Studies, Department of Social System Studies, Doshisha Women's College of Liberal Arts, Kyoto, Japan, E-mail: mokura@dwc.doshisha.ac.jp

From our analysis, the following main results are derived. When policyholder's effort of lowering the probability of an accident is not considered in case the fraction of policyholders is small, premium subsidy conducted by government is desirable under which an individual chooses to purchase full coverage while the social welfare is maximized which consists of the welfare of policyholders, non-policyholders and insurance firm. In contrast, when policyholder's effort is considered, whether government should conduct premium subsidy is ambiguous even if the fraction of policyholders is small.

The remainder of this article is organized as follows. Section 2 builds a model and explains game structure of this model. Section 3 develops the model to derive the condition in which government conducts premium subsidy when policyholder does not conduct the effort. Section 4 provides a further analysis by introducing effort for lowering accident probability and investigates the effect of effort. The major findings of this article are summarized in Section 5.

The Model

Suppose that there are weakly risk-averse identical (potential) individuals, a risk-neutral insurance firm, and the government. One type of individuals has two types of initial assets. The first type is liquid assets such as salary and bonuses, which is denoted by $w_L > 0$. The second type is fixed assets such as a house and vehicle, which is denoted by $w_F > 0$. In contrast, another type of individuals has only liquid assets. Assume that a fixed asset has the potential to incur damage, and the individual considers purchasing insurance for covering the damage. In contrast, it is assumed that there is no possibility of losing the amount of the liquid asset. After purchasing insurance, the policyholder chooses whether the effort of lowering the probability of an accident is conducted in "effort case" section. Because that effort is not observable by others, the policyholder chooses the effort only if it is profitable. π_i represents the accident probability and $i \in \{0,1\}$ where "0" and "1" indicate the cases of no effort and effort, respectively. Thus, it is natural that $0 \le \pi_1 < \pi_0 \le 1/2$.

Effort can lower the accident probability, but the policyholder has to incur the cost involved. Effort cost is assumed to be constant and represented by $k > 0$. The following four-stage game is considered.

In the first stage, the government decides both the subsidy rate, which is denoted by $s_i \in [0,1]$, and the tax rate, which is denoted by $t_i \in [0,1]$. The government subsidizes a portion of the insurance premium from tax revenue. Thus, the policyholder actually pays the insurance premium. To apply the premium subsidy, the government imposes a tax on each liquid asset w_L such as income tax. $\beta \in (0,1]$ denotes the fraction of policyholders involved. Then, the government chooses both the subsidy rate and the tax rate to satisfy the following equation which specifies that the government revenue and expenditure are equal:

$$t_i w_L = \beta s_i p_i \tag{1}$$

where $p_i > 0$ represents the insurance premium. Then, the government chooses the subsidy rate in accordance with the following equation:

$$s_i = \frac{t_i w_L}{\beta p_i} \tag{2}$$

In the second stage, the insurance firm chooses the insurance premium. For simplicity of the model, the amount of damage is assumed to be equal to w_F. Thus, when the policyholder purchases full insurance, the insurance money is equal to w_F. In the third stage, the policyholder chooses the insurance coverage rate, which is represented by $\alpha_i \in [0,1]$. In the fourth stage, the policyholder chooses whether to conduct the effort.

In this situation, the expected utility for the policyholder, which is denoted by EU_i, can be written as follows:

$$EU_1 = \pi_1 u(w_L + w_F - \alpha_1 p_1 - (1-\alpha_1) w_F) + (1-\pi_1) u(w_L + w_F - \alpha_1 p_1) - k \tag{3}$$

$$EU_0 = \pi_0 u(w_L + w_F - \alpha_0 p_0 - (1-\alpha_0) w_F) + (1-\pi_0) u(w_L + w_F - \alpha_0 p_0) \tag{4}$$

By using the computation in Asai and Okura [31], the certainty equivalent, which is denoted by CE_i, can be derived as follows:

$$CE_1 = (1-t_1) w_L - \alpha_1 (1-s_1) p_1 - \pi (1-\alpha_1) w_F - \frac{r}{2}\pi(1-\pi)\{(1-\alpha_1) w_F\}^2 - k \tag{5}$$

$$CE_0 = (1-t_0) w_L - \alpha_0 (1-s_0) p_0 - \pi (1-\alpha_0) w_F - \frac{r}{2}\pi(1-\pi)\{(1-\alpha_0) w_F\}^2 \tag{6}$$

where $r \ge 0$ represents the policyholder's degree of absolute risk aversion.

No effort case

In this section, we consider the case in which policyholder's effort is excluded. To analyze this game, we temporarily remove the fourth stage from the original game and a three-stage game is considered by backward induction. Because policyholder does not conduct the effort, subscript of all variables in this section is surely zero.

We first investigate the third stage. The optimal insurance coverage rate has to satisfy the following first-order condition:

$$\frac{\partial CE_0}{\partial \alpha_0} = -(1-s_0) p_0 + \pi_0 w_F \{1 + (1-\pi_0)(1-\alpha_0^*) r w_F\} = 0 \tag{7}$$

where the asterisk represents the equilibrium value. From equation (7), we show

$$\alpha_0^* = \frac{\pi_0 w_F \{1 + (1-\pi_0) r w_F\} - (1-s_0) p_0}{\pi_0 (1-\pi_0) r w_F^2} \tag{8}$$

Further, consider the second stage. The expected profit of the insurance firm, denoted by $E\Pi_0$, is:

$$E\Pi_0 = \alpha_0^* (p_0 - \pi w_F) \tag{9}$$

Then, substituting equations (2) and (8) into equation (9), we have

$$E\Pi_0 = \frac{(p_0 - \pi_0 w_F)\left[t_0 w_L + \beta\{\pi_0 w_F \{1 + (1-\pi_0) r w_F\} - p_0\}\right]}{\pi_0 (1-\pi_0) r \beta w_F^2} \tag{10}$$

The optimal insurance premium has to satisfy the following first-order condition:

$$\frac{\partial E\Pi_0}{\partial p_0} = \frac{t_0 w_L + \pi_0 \beta w_F \{2 + (1-\pi_0) r w_F\} - 2\beta p_0^*}{\pi_0 (1-\pi_0) r \beta w_F^2} = 0 \tag{11}$$

From equation (11), the optimal insurance premium can be derived as follows:

$$p_0^* = \frac{1}{2\beta}\left[t_0 w_L + \pi_0 \beta w_F \{2 + (1-\pi_0) r w_F\}\right] \tag{12}$$

Also, substituting equation (12) into equation (8), the optimal insurance coverage rate can be rewritten as:

$$\alpha_0^* = \frac{1}{2} + \frac{t_0 w_L}{2\pi_0 (1-\pi_0) r \beta w_F^2} \tag{13}$$

From equation (13), we find the larger the tax rate (and the subsidy rate), the larger the optimal insurance coverage rate. However, there is an upper limit for the tax rate because $\alpha_0 \leq 1$ has to be satisfied. Let $\overline{t}_0$ be the upper limit of the tax rate. The government can choose a tax rate beyond $\overline{t}_0$. However, even if such a tax rate is chosen, the policyholder will not change the insurance coverage rate. Thus, it is not desirable for the government to choose a tax rate beyond $\overline{t}_0$. Then, we have

$$\alpha_0^* = \frac{1}{2} + \frac{t_0 w_L}{2\pi_0(1-\pi_0) r w_F^2} = 1 \Rightarrow \overline{t}_0 = \frac{\pi_0(1-\pi_0) r \beta w_F^2}{w_L} \tag{14}$$

In contrast, $\alpha_0^* = 1/2$ is realized when the tax rate (and the subsidy rate) is zero. Thus, the premium subsidy offered by the government always raises the optimal insurance coverage rate. Substituting equation (12) into equation (2), the subsidy rate is:

$$s_0 = \frac{2t_0 w_L}{t_0 w_L + \pi_0 \beta w_F \{2 + (1-\pi_0) r w_F\}} \tag{15}$$

$s_0 < 1$ is always satisfied if and only if $t_0 \leq \overline{t}_0$ is satisfied.

Further, substituting equations (12), (13), and (15) into equations (6), and (10), the certainty equivalent of the policyholder and the expected profit of the insurance firm are derived as:

$$CE_0 = \frac{1}{8}\left[-\pi_0 w_F \{8 + 3(1-\pi_0) r w_F\} + \frac{2w_L\{t_0 + 4\beta(1-t_0)\}}{\beta} + \frac{t_0^2 w_L^2}{\pi_0(1-\pi_0) r \beta^2 w_F^2}\right] \tag{16}$$

$$E\Pi_0 = \frac{\{t_0 w_L + \pi_0(1-\pi_0) r \beta w_F^2\}^2}{4\pi_0(1-\pi_0) r \beta^2 w_F^2} \tag{17}$$

Lastly, we investigate the first stage. In this stage, the government actually chooses both the premium subsidy and the tax rates. However, both rates are related in equation (15), and the problem at this stage can be reduced to derive the optimal tax rate. It means that if government chooses strictly positive tax rate $t_0^* > 0$, government chooses strictly positive premium subsidy $s_0^* > 0$ and vice versa. It is assumed that the government chooses the tax rate for maximizing social welfare, which consists of the welfare of policyholders, non-policyholders, and the insurance firm. Then, the social welfare, denoted by SW_i, is shown as:

$$SW_i = \gamma\{\beta CE_i - (1-\beta) t_i w_L\} + (1-\gamma) E\Pi_i \tag{18}$$

where $\gamma \in [0,1]$ represents the weight of consumers' welfare used to calculate the social welfare.

Substituting equations (16) and (17) into equation (18), we obtain

$$SW_0 = \frac{1}{8\pi_0(1-\pi_0) r \beta^2 w_F^2}\left[-\pi_0^2(1-\pi_0) r \beta^2 w_F^3 \{8\beta\gamma + (1-\pi_0) r \{(2+3\beta)\gamma - 2\} w_F\}\right.$$
$$\left. + 2\pi_0(1-\pi_0) r \beta w_F^2 w_L \{-t_0\{(2+3\beta)\gamma - 2\} + 4\beta^2\gamma\} + t_0^{\,2} w_L^2 \{2 - (2-\beta)\gamma\}\right] \tag{19}$$

Equation (19) is the quadratic and convex functions of t_0, and so the value to minimize social welfare is uniquely determined. This value is denoted by $\hat{t}_0$, and the first-order condition can be shown as:

$$\frac{\partial SW_0}{\partial t_0} = -\frac{w_L}{4\beta^2}\left\{\beta\{(2+3\beta)\gamma - 2\} - \frac{\{2-(2-\beta)\gamma\}\hat{t}_0 w_L}{\pi_0(1-\pi_0) r w_F^2}\right\} = 0 \tag{20}$$

From equation (20), we have:

$$\hat{t}_0 = \frac{\pi_0(1-\pi_0) r \beta \{(2+3\beta)\gamma - 2\} w_F^2}{\{2-(2-\beta)\gamma\} w_L} \tag{21}$$

From equations (14) and (21), the following relationships are indicated:

$$\hat{t}_0 \geq 0 \Leftrightarrow \gamma \geq \frac{2}{2+3\beta} \tag{22}$$

$$\hat{t}_0 \geq \overline{t}_0 \Leftrightarrow \gamma \geq \frac{2}{2+\beta} \tag{23}$$

From equations (22) and (23), the following three cases are possible.

Case 1: $\gamma \leq 2/(2+3\beta)$

From equation (22), we find $\hat{t}_0 \leq 0$. Then, the social welfare function in equation (19) is a monotone increasing function of t_0 in the range of $[0, \overline{t}_0]$. Thus, the government chooses $t_0^* = \overline{t}_0$ and full insurance is realized.

Case 2: $2/(2+3\beta) \leq \gamma \leq 2/(2+\beta)$

From equations (22) and (23), we find $0 \leq \hat{t}_0 \leq \overline{t}_0$. Then, social welfare is maximized in either t_0=0 or $t_0 = \overline{t}_0$ in the range of $[0, \overline{t}_0]$. To find the optimal tax rate that maximizes social welfare, two situations, $t_0 = 0$ and $t_0 = \overline{t}_0$ are compared. Let SW_0^t and SW_0^0 be the social welfare in the case of $t_0 = \overline{t}_0$ and $t_0 = 0$, respectively. Then, social welfare in each tax rate can be computed as:

$$SW_0^t = \pi_0 w_F \{-\beta\gamma + (1-\pi_0) r w_F \{1 - \gamma(1+\beta)\}\} + \beta\gamma w_L \tag{24}$$

$$SW_0^0 = \frac{1}{8}\left[8\gamma\beta w_L - \pi_0 w_F \{8\beta\gamma + (1-\pi_0) r w_F \{(2+3\beta)\gamma - 2\}\}\right] \tag{25}$$

Also define $f_0 \equiv SW_0^t - SW_0^0$. Then, f_0 is calculated as:

$$f_0 = -\frac{1}{8}\pi_0(1-\pi_0)\{(6+5\beta)\gamma - 6\} r w_F^2 \tag{26}$$

From equation (26), the following relationship can be confirmed:

$$SW_0^t \geq SW_0^0 \Leftrightarrow \gamma \leq \frac{6}{6+5\beta} \tag{27}$$

Because $2/(2+3\beta) < 6/(6+5\beta) < 2/(2+\beta)$, the value of γ that satisfies equation (27) surely exists. Then, we find:

If $\frac{2}{2+3\beta} \leq \gamma \leq \frac{6}{6+5\beta}$, then $t_0^* = \overline{t}_0$ and full insurance is realized.

If $\frac{6}{6+5\beta} \leq \gamma \leq \frac{2}{2+\beta}$, then $t_0^* = 0$ and partial insurance ($\alpha_0^* = 1/2$) is realized.

Case 3: $\gamma \geq 2/(2+\beta)$

From equation (23), we find $\overline{t}_0 \leq \hat{t}_0$. Then, the social welfare function in equation (19) is a monotone decreasing function of t_0 in the range of $[0, \overline{t}_0]$. Thus, the government chooses $t_0^* = 0$ and partial insurance ($\alpha_0^* = 1/2$) is realized.

By combining the above three cases, the following two possible results are derived.

If $0 \leq \gamma \leq \frac{6}{6+5\beta}$, then $t_0^* = \overline{t}_0$ and full insurance is realized.

If $\frac{6}{6+5\beta} \leq \gamma \leq 1$, then $t_0^* = 0$ and partial insurance ($\alpha_0^* = 1/2$) is realized.

The above results show that whether the premium subsidy is desirable depends on the weight of consumers' welfare γ and the fraction of policyholders β. If γ and/or β are relatively small, then the government introduces a premium subsidy and full insurance is realized. In contrast, if γ and/or β are relatively large, then the government does not offer a premium subsidy and partial insurance is realized.

Effort case

It is easy to verify that $CE_1 \geq CE_0$ is the condition in which policyholder chooses the effort in the fourth stage of the game. However, introducing policyholder's effort may change the condition whether government conducts premium subsidy. For example, the government may want to lower the optimal tax rate in the case of $0 \leq \gamma \leq 6/(6+5\beta)$ for lowering the optimal insurance coverage rate and conducting the effort. To investigate the effect of the effort, we re-examine two situations, $0 \leq \gamma \leq 6/(6+5\beta)$ and $6/(6+5\beta) \leq \gamma \leq 1$.

First, consider the case where $0 \leq \gamma \leq 6/(6+5\beta)$. In this situation, the policyholder never chooses to conduct the effort because full insurance is chosen. Thus, the optimal tax rate is surely $\bar{t}_0$. Then, the government may be able to increase the social welfare by lowering the tax rate, because this leads to lowering the optimal insurance coverage rate, and then the policyholder voluntarily conducts the effort. Let $\tilde{t}_1$ be the maximum tax rate at which the policyholder conducts the effort. Then, $\tilde{t}_1$ can be derived by solving $CE_1 = CE_0$. Of course, $\tilde{t}_1$ does not necessarily exist, because $\tilde{t}_1$ is never greater than $\bar{t}_1 = \pi_1(1-\pi_1)r\beta w_F^2/w_L$ that is the upper limit of the tax rate when policyholder conducts the effort. In the latter analysis, it is assumed that $\tilde{t}_1$ always exists. Let $\tilde{\alpha}_1$ be the insurance coverage rate in the case of $\tilde{t}_1$. From same manner deriving equation (13), we find that $1/2 \leq \tilde{\alpha}_1 \leq 1$. In addition, SW_1^t represents the social welfare when the tax rate is $\tilde{t}_1$. Then, the difference between the two social welfares, which is defined by $g \equiv SW_1^t - SW_0^t$, can be computed as:

$$g = \{-\gamma(1-\beta)\tilde{t}_1 w_L + (1-\gamma)E\Pi_1\} - \{-\gamma(1-\beta)\bar{t}_0 w_L + (1-\gamma)E\Pi_0\} \quad (28)$$

From the same manner deriving equation (19), we have

$$E\Pi_1 = \frac{\{t_1 w_L + \pi_1(1-\pi_1)r\beta w_F^2\}^2}{4\pi_1(1-\pi_1)r\beta^2 w_F^2} \quad (29)$$

Then, if $g \geq 0$ is realized, the government chooses $\tilde{t}_1$ instead of $\bar{t}_0$. There are two kinds of conditions to realize $g \geq 0$, as shown below.

In the case that $E\Pi_1 - E\Pi_0 - (1-\beta)(\bar{t}_0 - \tilde{t}_1)w_L \geq 0$:

$$\gamma \leq \frac{E\Pi_1 - E\Pi_0}{E\Pi_1 - E\Pi_0 - (\bar{t}_0 - \tilde{t}_1)(1-\beta)w_L} \quad (30)$$

In the case that $E\Pi_1 - E\Pi_0 - (1-\beta)(\bar{t}_0 - \tilde{t}_1)w_L \leq 0$:

$$\gamma \geq \frac{E\Pi_1 - E\Pi_0}{E\Pi_1 - E\Pi_0 - (\bar{t}_0 - \tilde{t}_1)(1-\beta)w_L} \quad (31)$$

where $\bar{t}_0 \geq \tilde{t}_1$ is always satisfied, because $\bar{t}_0 \geq \bar{t}_1$. The denominator on the right-hand side of equations (30) and (31) represents the change in the expected profit for the insurance firm, represented by $E\Pi_1 - E\Pi_0$, and the welfare of non-policyholders, represented by $(\bar{t}_0 - \tilde{t}_1)(1-\beta)w_L$, when the tax rate changes from $\bar{t}_0$ to $\tilde{t}_1$. From equations (30) and (31), we easily find that $SW_1^t \geq SW_0^t$ is always realized for all $\gamma \in [0, 6/(6+5\beta)]$ when $E\Pi_1 \geq E\Pi_0$. Thus, the government chooses $\tilde{t}_1$, while the policyholder chooses $\tilde{\alpha}_1 \in [1/2, 1]$ and conducts the effort. In this situation, the change from $\bar{t}_0$ to $\tilde{t}_1$ improves the social welfare of non-policyholders, because the tax rate becomes lower and the expected profit for the insurance firm is increased because $E\Pi_1 \geq E\Pi_0$, while the social welfare of policyholders is the same because $CE_1 = CE_0$. Consequently, it is desirable for all parties to choose the tax rate $\tilde{t}_1$.

In contrast, when $E\Pi_1 \leq E\Pi_0$, equation (31) is the unique condition because there exists no γ that satisfies equation (30), since $E\Pi_1 - E\Pi_0 - (1-\beta)(\bar{t}_0 - \tilde{t}_1)w_L \leq 0$. However, we cannot know whether γ satisfies equation (31) and so whether the government chooses $\bar{t}_0$ or $\tilde{t}_1$ is ambiguous.

Next, we consider the case where $6/(6+5\beta) \leq \gamma \leq 1$. In this situation, the policyholder chooses partial insurance $\alpha_i^* = 1/2$. Assume that the policyholder decides to conduct the effort in the case of $\alpha_i^* = 1/2$. Then, we compare two kinds of situations, $t_1 = 0$ and $t_1 = \tilde{t}_1$. Let $E\Pi_1^0$ be the expected profit of the insurance firm in the case of $t_1 = 0$ and SW_1^0 be the social welfare when the tax rate is zero and policyholder conducts the effort. If we define $h \equiv SW_1^t - SW_1^0$, we can show that

$$h = \{-\gamma(1-\beta)\tilde{t}_1 w_L + (1-\gamma)E\Pi_1\} - (1-\gamma)E\Pi_1^0 \quad (32)$$

Then, if $h \geq 0$ is realized, the government chooses $\tilde{t}_1$ instead of zero. From equation (32), the following condition for satisfying $h \geq 0$ is derived:

$$\gamma \leq \frac{E\Pi_1 - E\Pi_1^0}{E\Pi_1 - E\Pi_1^0 + \tilde{t}_1(1-\beta)w_L} \quad (33)$$

Because expected profit of the insurance firm is an increasing function of t_i by equations (17) and (29), $E\Pi_1 \geq E\Pi_1$ is always satisfied. Thus, it is possible to realize $\tilde{t}_1$, but whether the government chooses zero or $\tilde{t}_1$ is ambiguous.

The above analysis shows that there are three kinds of optimal tax rates 0, $\tilde{t}_1$, and $\bar{t}_0$ and three insurance coverage rates, 1/2, $\tilde{\alpha}_1$, and 1. To know which optimal tax rate and insurance coverage rate are realized, we define the following two variables, which are the right-hand side of equations (31) and (33):

$$\gamma_1 \equiv \frac{E\Pi_1 - E\Pi_0}{E\Pi_1 - E\Pi_0 - (\bar{t}_0 - \tilde{t}_1)(1-\beta)w_L} \quad (34)$$

$$\gamma_2 \equiv \frac{E\Pi_1 - E\Pi_1^0}{E\Pi_1 - E\Pi_1^0 + \tilde{t}_1(1-\beta)w_L} \quad (35)$$

To guarantee the above two variables, $0 \leq \gamma_1 \leq 6/(6+5\beta)$ and $6/(6+5\beta) \leq \gamma_2 \leq 1$ are assumed to be satisfied. First, consider the case of $E\Pi_1 \geq E\Pi_0$. From equation (33), the following results are derived.

If $\gamma \in [0, \gamma_2]$, then $t_i^* = \tilde{t}_1$ and $\alpha_i^* = \tilde{\alpha}_1$ are realized.

If $\gamma \in [\gamma_2, 1]$, then $t_i^* = 0$ and $\alpha_i^* = 1/2$ are realized.

Next, consider the case of $E\Pi_1 \leq E\Pi_0$. From equations (31) and (33), the following results are derived.

If $\gamma \in [0, \gamma_1]$, then $t_i^* = \bar{t}_0$ and $\alpha_i^* = 1$ are realized.

If $\gamma \in [\gamma_1, \gamma_2]$, then $t_i^* = \tilde{t}_1$ and $\alpha_i^* = \tilde{\alpha}_1$ are realized.

If $\gamma \in [\gamma_2, 1]$, then $t_i^* = 0$ and $\alpha_i^* = 1/2$ are realized.

From the results in this analysis, we derive the following implications. First, the smaller γ, the larger t_i^* and α_i^*. Second, unlike no effort case, whether government conducts premium subsidy is ambiguous even if β is small. It is easy to verify that γ_2 becomes the critical value whether government conducts premium subsidy. However, the relationship between γ_2 and β is unclear because $\tilde{t}_1$ is a function of β and $\tilde{t}_1$ is neither monotone increasing nor decreasing function of β. This result shows whether premium subsidy conducted by government is surely desirable depends on whether policyholder's effort is considered when the fraction of policyholders is small.

Concluding Remarks

The main findings of this article are summarized as follows. When policyholder's effort for lowering accident probability is not considered, and the fraction of policyholders is small, government conducts premium subsidy which stimulates an individual to choose full insurance coverage while maximizes social welfare which consists of policyholders, non-policyholders and insurance firm. In contrast, when policyholder's effort is considered, it becomes ambiguous whether premium subsidy is desirable even in the case of small fraction of policyholders.

This result suggests that, as a means of fostering the growth and development of insurance industry, a premium subsidy policy by government will probably be more effective when the targets are underdeveloped or in the rudimentary stage at least when policyholder's effort is not necessarily considered. Concretely, a government grant will facilitate the dissemination of knowledge and/or information regarding insurance and increase its penetration rate. Meanwhile, achieving sustainable growth in the insurance sector will ultimately lead to an improvement in social and economic welfare.

This finding is consistent with prior studies that assert government intervention can be Pareto-improving in a market associated with imperfect and/or costly information [28,29]. It also helps to explain why agricultural insurance programs in most developing countries would be assisted by a subsidy from the government. As a matter of fact, it has also been empirically supported by some recent studies on China's Cooperative Medical Scheme, a government-subsidized voluntary health insurance program in rural regions [32,33].

However, our study is only focused on a short-term contract. A further analysis based on a long-term contract and/or a repeated contract should be considered. Moreover, the problem of moral hazard between the insurance firm and the government also deserves special attention, because insurance firms may be reluctant to pursue sound practices such as risk classification and/or loss assessment when they know the government will eventually pay the bill.

Acknowledgements

This article was originally presented at the 18th Asia-Pacific Risk and Insurance Association Annual Conference in Moscow, Russia, in 2014. We would like to thank the participants of this conference for helpful comments on earlier versions of this article. This work was supported by JSPS KAKENHI Grant Numbers JP24730362 and JP15K03727.

References

1. Arrow KJ (1964) The Role of Securities in the Optimal Allocation of Risk-bearing. Review of Economic Studies 31: 91-96.
2. Debreu G (1959) Theory of Value: An Axiomatic Analysis of Economic Equilibrium. Wiley, New York.
3. Rothschild M, Stiglitz JE (1976) Equilibrium in Competitive Insurance Markets: An Essay on the Economics of Imperfect Information. Quarterly Journal of Economics 90: 629-649.
4. Pauly MV (1974) Overinsurance and Public Provision of Insurance: The Roles of Moral Hazard and Adverse Selection. Quarterly Journal of Economics 88: 44-62.
5. Kunreuther H, Ginsberg R, Miller L, Sagi P, Slovic P, Borkan B, Katz N (1978) Disaster Insurance Protection: Public Policy Lessons. Wiley, New York.
6. Spence M, Zeckhauser R (1971) Insurance, Information, and Individual Action. American Economic Review 61: 380-387.
7. Arrow KJ, Lind RC (1970) Uncertainty and the Evaluation of Public Investment Decisions. American Economic Review 60: 364-378.
8. Kunreuther H (1976) Limited knowledge and insurance protection. Public Policy 24: 227-261.
9. Kunreuther H (1984) Causes of Underinsurance against Natural Disasters. The Geneva Papers on Risk and Insurance 31: 206-220.
10. Tversky A, Kahneman D (1974) Judgment under Uncertainty: Heuristics and Biases. Science (New Series) 185: 1124-1131.
11. Zhou-Richter T, Browne MJ, Gründl H (2010) Don't They Care? Or, Are They Just Unaware? Risk Perception and the Demand for Long-Term Care Insurance. Journal of Risk and Insurance 77: 715-747.
12. Anderson DR (1974) The National Flood Insurance Program- Problems and Potential. Journal of Risk and Insurance 41: 579-600.
13. Kaplow L (1992) Government Relief for Risk Associated with Government Action. Scandinavian Journal of Economics 94: 525-541.
14. Browne MJ, Hoyt RE (2000) The Demand for Flood Insurance: Empirical Evidence. Journal of Risk and Uncertainty 20: 291-306.
15. Lewis T, Nickerson D (1980) Self-Insurance against Natural Disasters. Journal of Environmental Economics and Management 16: 209-223.
16. Raschky PA, Weck-Hannemann H (2007) Charity Hazard: A Real Hazard to Natural Disaster Insurance? Environmental Hazards 7: 321-329.
17. Kaplow L (1991) Incentives and Government Relief for Risk. Journal of Risk and Uncertainty 4: 167-175.
18. Akerlof GA (1970) The Market for 'Lemons': Quality Uncertainty and the Market Mechanism. Quarterly Journal of Economics 84: 488-500.
19. Arrow KJ (1963) Uncertainty and the Welfare Economics of Medical Care. American Economic Review 53: 941-973.
20. Lewis CM, Murdock KC (1996) The Role of Government Contracts in Discretionary Reinsurance Markets for Natural Disasters. Journal of Risk and Insurance 63: 567-597.
21. Denlea Jr. LE (1996) How Catastrophe Risk Is Shaping Insurance Politics. Journal of Insurance Issues 19: 85-93.
22. Lee K (1992) Moral Hazard, Insurance and Public Loss Prevention. Journal of Risk and Insurance 59: 275-283.
23. Nelson CH, Loehman ET (1987) Further Toward a Theory of Agricultural Insurance. American Journal of Agricultural Economics 69: 523-531.
24. Hazell PBR (1992) The Appropriate Role of Agricultural Insurance in Developing Countries. Journal of International Development 4: 567-581.
25. Barnett BJ, Skees JR (1995) Region and Crop Specific Models of the Demand for Federal Crop Insurance. Journal of Insurance Issues 18: 47-65.
26. Feldstein M, Friedman B (1977) Tax Subsidies, the Rational Demand for Insurance and the Health Care Crisis. Journal of Public Economics 7: 155-178.
27. Pauly MV (1986) Taxation, Health Insurance and Market Failure in the Medical Economy. Journal of Economic Literature 24: 629-675.
28. Stiglitz JE (1989) Markets, Market Failures, and Development. American Economic Review 79: 197-203.
29. Greenwald B, Stiglitz JE (1986) Externalities in Economies with Imperfect Information and Incomplete Markets. Quarterly Journal of Economics 101: 229-264.

30. Arrow KJ (1970) Political and Economic Evaluation of Social Effects and Externalities. In J Margolis (ed.) The Analysis of Public Output, Columbia University Press, New York: 1-30.
31. Asai Y, Okura M (2011) How Do Cost and Regulation Change Loss Control Activities and Insurers' Monitoring? Journal of Insurance Issues 34: 172-188.
32. Wang H, Yip W, Zhang L, Wang L, Hsiao W (2005) Community-based Health Insurance in Poor Rural China: The Distribution of Net Benefits. Health Policy and Planning 20: 366-374.
33. Wagstaff A, Lindelow M, Jun G, Ling X, Jungcheng Q (2009) Extending Health Insurance to the Rural Population: An Impact Evaluation of China's New Cooperative Medical Scheme. Journal of Health Economics 28: 1-19.

18

Interest Rate Risk - A Comparative Study of Public and Private Sector Banks in India

Reeta*

Lovely School of Business, Lovely Professional University, India

Abstract

The Indian banks are exposed to so many risks like interest rate risk, liquidity risk, credit risk and exchange rate risk which affect the net interest income and profitability of the banks. This paper is aimed at measuring interest rate risk in public and private sector banks in India with the help of gap analysis. It is also found whether there is any difference in the level of interest rate risk in the selected public and private sector banks of India. The findings revealed that both the private sector banks and public sector banks are exposed to interest rate risk.

Keywords: Private sector banks; Public sector banks; Gap analysis; Assets-Liability mismatch

Introduction

These days, The Indian Economy is going to be a world class economy. The Indian banking industry is one of the most important parameter of the Indian economy which is also adopting new advancements in terms of technology, diversification and expansion. But it is also true that this sector is exposed to so many risks and interest rate risk is one of them. Financial transactions are fraught with ample risk not only because of changes in exchange rates but because of changes in interest rates also. With growing preference for floating interest rates since 1980s, the interest rate risk or exposure has become more significant. Interest rate risk is the risk to earnings or capital arising from movements in interest rates. Sometimes it moves in the favour of the lender, but then the debt burden of the borrower gets bigger. When it moves in the favour of the borrower, the lender has to suffer loss on account of interest. So in banking sector interest rate risk is considered the most important area which affects earnings and liquidity in banks. So it is necessary for the management of the bank to focus on the methods to measure this risk accurately and then do sound efforts to mitigate this risk.

Literature Review

Carter David A examines that interest rate derivatives can be used to mitigate the exposure of interest rate risk in banks [1]. He measured the level of interest rate risk by considering the absolute value of the 12-months maturity gap analysis. Dhanani A determined various factors like interest rate fluctuations, use of borrowed funds etc. due to which interest rate risk arise [2]. He found that UK companies should hedge their interest rate risk to manage volatility in their profit and cash flows. Shashi Srivastava measured interest rate risk in SBI and ICICI bank and found that SBI is more exposed to interest rate risk as compared to ICICI bank [3]. He analyzed interest rate exposure by using various methods like assets-liability mismatch, gap analysis and sensitivity anlaysis and suggested to use interest rate derivatives to hedge this risk. Reeta analysed the measurement and management tools of interest rate risk used in Indian firms [4]. She found that interest rate risk is considered the most important risk in Indian firms and maximum firms use gap analysis and Maclay's Duration analysis to measure the level of interest rate risk. She also discussed various factors like monetary policy, inflation rate and fluctuations in money market which are responsible for interest rate changes.

VN Prakash Sharma examined the effect of interest rate changes on net interest income and on profitability of the Bank of Baroda and ICICI bank [5]. She used earning sensitivity analysis, duration gap analysis and rate adjusted gap to measure the level of interest rate risk.

Objectives of the Study

- To discuss the importance of interest rate risk in Indian Banks
- To compare the level of interest rate risk using Gap Analysis in selected public and private sector banks.

Research hypothesis

H_0 There is no significant difference in the level of interest rate risk in public and private sector banks in India.

H_1 There is significant difference in the level of interest rate risk in public and private sector banks in India.

Research Methodology

The study is analytical in nature. In this paper efforts are done to find out the prevailing level of interest rate risk in the Indian banks. For analysis top 5 banks are selected from public sector as well as from private sector on the basis of sales maximization and value of assets. The study is based on secondary data which has been collected from Indian Banking Association(IBA), Reserve Bank of India, moneycontrol.com, annual reports of the banks and Capita-line Plus database. Data is compiled for the financial year 2011-2015. Assets-Liability Mismatch and Gap analysis have been done to measure interest rate risk. Independent t-test has been used to evaluate the significance of results. SPSS and MS-Excel are used for analysis [6].

Analysis and interpretation

Asset- liability management: For banks and financial institutions assets and liabilities are most important factors which get affected

***Corresponding author:** Reeta, Assistant Professor, Lovely School of Business, Lovely Professional University, Phagwara, Punjab 144411, India
E-mail: reeta.clonia@gmail.com

because of interest rate changes. So doing proper match of assets and liabilities are advisable to mitigate the effect of interest rate changes. In the balance sheet of banks balances with banks and money at call, investment and advances are given at the assets side and in liabilities side deposits and borrowing are shown. When interest rate rises, it will affect both the assets as well as the liabilities. Now what will be the overall impact of this interest rate rise it depends on the total amount of assets and liabilities which a bank has? If interest rate sensitive assets of a bank are more as compared to interest rate liabilities then this interest rate changes will be beneficial for the concerned bank and vice versa. Here in the Table 1 interest rate sensitive assets and interest rate sensitive liabilities are shown of the selected private and public sector banks. The researcher compared the Rate Sensitive Assets (RSA) and Rate Sensitive Liabilities (RSL) of private sector banks with the public sector banks and found gap analysis which is shown with the help of Figure 1. Mean value of RSA and RSL are calculated for the financial year 2011-15 to evaluate the overall gap of public and private sector banks. Table 1 and Figure 1 show that except Bank of India (Rs. -1813 cr.) all selected banks have RSA>RSL, it means they all have positive Gap and any changes in interest rate will positively affect the banks' net interest income and profitability [7]. But in case of Bank of India profitability will be affected negatively due to any changes in interest rates so it has to use some hedging techniques to mitigate interest rate exposure. In public sector banks SBI has the highest gap i.e. Rs. 607680 cr. and in case of private sector banks ICICI bank has the highest gap of Rs. 428111 cr (Table 1 and Figure 1).

Table 2 shows year wise gap analysis of each selected bank for the period of 2011 to 2015 and it shows the fluctuations of assets and liabilities throughout the research period. This table depicted that on an average all the banks either private or public (except Bank of India) have positive gap in maximum years. In 2011 three public sector banks (Punjab National Bank, Canara Bank and Bank of India) have negative value of gap. In case of private sector banks not even a single bank has negative gap in any year which is a symbol of appropriate assets-liability management.

Descriptive statistics and hypothesis testing: This paper is aimed to compare the level of interest rate risk using gap analysis in private and public sector banks so mean and standard deviation are calculated of public and private sector banks using SPSS which is shown in the Table 3. Here it shows that there is a difference in the mean value and the standard deviation of private and public sector banks. To check the homogeneity of variances of public and private sector banks Levene's test has been used and to check the significance of the mean difference independent t-test has been applied with the help of SPSS. Table 4 depicts that significance value under Levene's test is 0.591>0.05 so t-test assuming equal variance is applicable here. Result of t-test using equal variance shows that t statistics of 0.209 (Sig. 0.840>0.05) indicate that there is no significant difference in the level of interest rate risk in private and public sector banks which means that the interest rate risk is the most important risk for public and private sector banks and both the sector are doing proper assets-liability management to make their

Interest Rate Sensitive Assets and Liabilities (Mean Value computed in Crores for Financial Years from 2011-2015)										
Assets\Banks	**ICICI**	**HDFC**	**AXIS**	**KM***	**INDUSIND**	**SBI**	**PNB**	**CB***	**BOI***	**BOB***
Balances with Banks and money at Call+	175351	92453	87748	15657	33806	454254	160361	175461	319327	765286
Investments +	1658483	1134874	1049625	246935	188399	3705005	1285659	1158001	1002368	1028864
Advances +	2973135	2527237	2040566	472132	458881	10359540	3148962	2634075	3048112	3338621
Total RSA	4806060	3754504	3177939	734723	681085	14518799	4594982	3967538	4369807	5132771
Liabilities										
Deposits+	2934384	3139346	2530684	505518	530961	12303043	4073645	3741819	4015644	4701296
Borrowings +	1444474	311799	468680	147551	118094	1608077	404360	205945	355976	289075
Total RSL	4378858	3451145	2999364	653069	649055	13911120	4478005	3947764	4371620	4990371
GAP (RSA-RSL)	428111	303419	178575	81654	32030	607680	116977	19774	-1813	142401
Source: Capita-Line Data Base, Calculation done by Author										
*KM: Kotak Mahindra Bank, CB: Canara Bank, BOI: Bank of India, BOB: Bank of Baroda										

Table 1: Assets-Liability Mismatch between private and public banks.

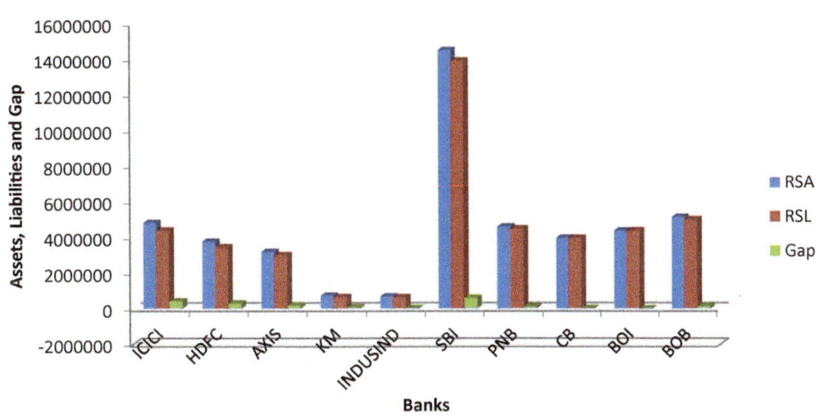

Figure 1: RSA, RSL and gap analysis of private and public banks.

Bank Wise Annual GAP Analysis in crores						
Banks\Year	2015	2014	2013	2012	2011	Average
ICICI	567737.3	487595.3	460527.1	333908.5	290785.8	428111
HDFC	447667.8	314128.8	347334.3	282966.2	124995.8	303419
AXIS	275058.4	235770.7	197816.8	120066.5	64162.6	178575
KOTAK MAHINDRA	119058.4	95759.3	73842.8	61320.6	58290.9	81654.4
INDUSIND BANK	56391.5	37560.7	39973.9	12283.8	13942.3	32030.4
STATE BANK OF INDIA	720877.1	786828.8	735615.3	522107.9	272968.9	607680
PUNJAB NATIONAL BANK	164768	165963.3	167602.5	99601.7	-13050.9	116977
CANARA BANK	25391.6	26172.1	64788.6	23523.9	-41006.5	19773.9
BANK OF INDIA	-9125.1	17932.7	-3574.2	49812.2	-64110.2	-1812.9
BANK OF BARODA	234256.1	196599.3	210636.9	46596.2	23915	142401
Source: Capita-Line Data Base, Calculation done by Author.						

Table 2: Bank Wise Gap Analysis for the period 2011-2015.

	Banks	N	Mean	Std. Deviation	Std. Error Mean
GAP	Private	5	204758	162246	72558.7
	Public	5	177004	248485	111126

Table 3: Group statistics.

		Levene's Test		t-test for Equality of Means				
		F	Sig.	t	df	Sig. (2-tailed)	Mean Difference	Std. Error Difference
GAP	Equal Variances Assumed	0.312	0.591	0.209	8.000	0.840	27754.196	132716.6
	Equal variances not assumed			0.209	6.886	0.840	27754.196	132716.6

Table 4: Hypothesis testing using t-test.

gap value positive so the benefit of interest rate changes can be achieved and negative exposure can be hedged (Tables 3 and 4).

Conclusion

Hence on the basis of the analysis done above it can be said that both the banks either it is private sector or public sector have been facing interest rate risk during the research period of the study but on an average except Bank of India all the banks have done their assets-liability management very well and they have positive value of gap throughout the research period and this thing has been proved by t-test also which shows that there is no significant difference in the level of interest rate risk in both sector banks. By doing this assets-liability management banks will be able to mitigate interest rate exposure up to a large extent and when their RSA>RSL they can always get benefit of interest rate changes in terms of increased net interest income which leads to increase liquidity and profitability of the banks.

Research Implications and Future Work

This study is helpful for the selected banks for research to evaluate their performance and to develop some other innovative techniques to measure and manage interest rate risk. This study will also provide help to govt. to evaluate public sector banks and to instruct the officials of the public sector banks (in this research Bank of India has negative gap) to focus on proper assets- liability management to convert negative gap into positive. This study is done at small level by selecting 5 sample banks from private sector and 5 sample banks from public sector, in future this research can be done at large level by selecting all the banks of private sectors and public sectors to get more specific results. The research period of the study also can be expended to do further research.

References

1. David CA, Sinkey JF (1998) The use of interest rate derivatives by end users: The case of large community banks. Journal of Financial Services Research 14: 17-34.
2. Dhanani A (2005) Interest Rate Risk Management - An Investigation into the Management of Interest Rate Risk in UK Companies. Research Executive summary Series published by CIMA 2: 1-7.
3. Srivastava S, Srivastava D (2015) Interest Rate Risk Management: A Comparative Study of State Bank of India and ICICI Bank. International Journal of Management and Social Sciences Research (IJMSSR) 4.
4. Reeta (2013) Measurement and Management strategies of Interest Rate Risk-A Study in Indian Perspective. GGGI Management Review 1: 7-11.
5. Sharma VNP, Santhosh NG (2016) Interest Rate Risk Management: A Comparative Study of Bank of Baroda and ICICI Bank. IOSR Journal of Economics and Finance (IOSR-JEF) 7: 01-04.
6. Froot KA, Scharfstein DS, Stein JC (1994) A framework for risk management. Harvard Business Review pp: 91-102.
7. Charumathi B (2008) Asset Liability Management in Indian Banking Industry - with special reference to Interest Rate Risk Management in ICICI Bank. Proceedings of the World Congress on Engineering, London, UK.

Job Satisfaction Levels among Employees of Private Commercial Banks at Chuadanga District in Bangladesh

Rahman M[1*], Ashraf A[2], Hasan N[1], Hoshen S[1], Chowdhury RHK[1] and Moni MA[3]

[1]*Department of Business Administration, First Capital University of Bangladesh, Shahnaz Mansion, Alamdanga Road (Pouro College Para), Chuadanga-7200, Bangladesh*
[2]*Department of Marketing and Finance, Frostburg State University, Frostburg, Maryland, USA*
[3]*Faculty of Medicine, University of Sydney, New South Wales, Australia*

Abstract

Job satisfaction among employees in banking sector is an important issue. The purpose of the study is to measure the level of job satisfaction among bank employees from socio-demographic context at Chuadanga District, in Bangladesh. The cross-sectional study sample consisted of 56 (male 89.3% and female 10.7%) respondents and used semi-structured questionnaire containing pre-coded and open-ended questions. The job satisfaction was estimated using dimension index. Thereafter, ANOVA-test and t-test were used to estimate the level of job satisfaction. In this study, several indicators, such as, salary, sympathetic view to officers, increment allocation method, welfare facilities, bonus facilities, reward, working with present colleagues, leadership style, leave rules, job security, performance appraisal and evaluation process, working schedule and teamwork were recorded higher level of job satisfaction among bank employees. Significance means variation of low level of job satisfaction were found among age (76.04%), designation (72.31%), salary (70.77%), marital status (83.36%), service period (68.27%) and working environment (79.38%) which can be recovered by ensuring equitable and competitive compensation system, periodical increments, allowances, promotion, redesigning of working hour and environment, opportunities to participation in decision making and effective training and development program. More studies are essential to spotlight the issue that helps stakeholders to formulate strategies.

Keywords: Job satisfaction level; Socio-demographic factors; Dimension Index; ANOVA-test and t-test

Introduction

Banking sector plays a vital role for the overall economic development of a country. Since Bangladesh is a developing country, financial institutions, especially banking sector, have significant contribution in the development process [1]. With the opening up of the banking sector, a dramatic change has been observed in agriculture, business and other sectors which have brought higher employment opportunities, increases in income level, and changes in consumption pattern. Consequently it emerges a competitive environment in the country. Specifically, with the expansion of private banking business, along with customized services, has created a severe implied competition in this sector [2]. This competition has made the service gap wider as private banks offer better services to their internal and external customers [3]. As better services of banks depend on employees, Job satisfaction is one of the most widely researched areas in organization behavior and human resource management [4].

According to Locke, job satisfaction is a pleasurable or positive emotional state which is the result from the appraisal of one's job experiences [5]. Allport stated job satisfaction is a person's attitude towards the specific job [6]. Herzberg stated that, job satisfaction can be perceived as a motive for people who work in a company. Experimental studies have found that it is important to satisfy the needs of employee, as job satisfaction is a predictive factor for job performance, counterproductive work behavior, and turnover intentions [7,8]. Satisfied employees are an asset of a company that works like a team to fulfill the goals [9]. Studies revealed that potential employees make their decisions based on their perception of their values that the organization will place on them [10,11]. Employees' desires are perceived as being satisfied when the organization meets or exceeds their expectations [5,12-14]. Efficient human resource with higher job satisfaction level in banks determines not only the performance of the bank but also affect the growth and performance of the entire economy [15]. Job dissatisfaction affects the quality of service, raises worker's voice and creates unrest which affects the degree of customer satisfaction [16-18]. Since job satisfaction has a significant relationship with the performance of the work force, overall productivity and profitability of the organization [19,20]. This scenario has created an urge to the bank policy makers to identify the underlying reasons of job satisfaction and brought them into consideration [2,16]. Job satisfaction is important because most of the people spend a major portion of their life at working place [21]. Only economic factor has never satisfied human. It is always of greater interest to know why people work and at which level and how he/she satisfied with the job [22].

Several studies have been steered in Bangladesh over job satisfaction and most of them are revealed the factors or indicators responsible for job satisfaction like as, Anjom et al. have found that because of smart remuneration, attractive compensation package, dignity, smooth career growth, job security, pension funds, provident fund, gratuity, incentives, and lots of other benefits fresh graduates had fascination for banking sector jobs in Bangladesh [23]. Ahmed revealed that recruitment and selection, training & development, salary & benefits, and reward have positive effect on employees' job satisfaction whereas supervisory role and job security has adverse effect [24]. Uddin et al.

***Corresponding author:** Mostafijur Rahman, Department of Business Administration, First Capital University of Bangladesh, Shahnaz Mansion, Alamdanga Road (Pouro College Para), Chuadanga-7200, Bangladesh
E-mail: mostafizrumgt@gmail.com

conducted a study on the employees of the general insurance companies in Bangladesh and found that pay and promotional potential, well-organized chain of command and general working condition have positive relation with job satisfaction where poor team spirit and poor job security have negative relation [25]. Rana found a positive and significant relationship between job satisfaction and human recourse management practices like team work environment, job autonomy and behavior of leadership. It is also inferred that male and female workers have significantly different level of job satisfaction [26]. Masum et al. conducted a study on private university academics which revealed that compensation package, supervisory support, job security, training and development opportunities, team cohesion, career growth, working conditions, and organizational culture and policies are positively associated with the academics' job satisfaction. Amongst them, compensation package, job security, and working conditions were most significant contributors [27]. Hossain showed that working conditions, pay, fairness, and promotion significantly influenced employee job satisfaction in Bank but individual factors such as age and gender did not [16]. According to Rahman employee training and job satisfactions have a significant positive relationship with organizational effectiveness [1]. Mahmud et al. showed job satisfaction of bank officers is significantly dependent upon compensation, promotion opportunities, rewards, relation with boss and coworkers [28]. Rubel et al. revealed that three works related variable have statistically significant predictive relationship with job satisfaction which were role conflict, job autonomy, job stress [29]. Islam and Islam showed that salary, efficiency in work, fringe supervision, and co-worker relation are the most vital factors connecting to job satisfaction [3]. Majumder the employees are dissatisfied with compensation package followed by reward and motivation, career growth, training and development, management style, and job design and responsibilities [30].

However, there is no significant study in Bangladesh that measures the level of job satisfaction of bank employees. Therefore our aim of the study is to measure the level of job satisfaction in context of socio-demographic characteristics.

Data and Methodology

Source of data

For our study we have considered seven branches of seven private commercial banks at Chuadanga district in Bangladesh. The cross-sectional study sample consisted of 56 (male 89.3% and female 10.7%) bank employees who were interviewed from March to April 2016 using semi-structured questionnaire containing pre-coded and open-ended questions. Sample has been selected randomly without considering any biasness. Banks that are considered for our study are Dutch Bangla Bank Limited, BRAC Bank Limited, Shahjalal Islami Bank Limited, United Commercial Bank Limited, Mercantile Bank Limited, Islami Bank Bangladesh Limited and First Security Islami Bank Limited. A semi-structured questionnaire was developed using job satisfaction forces to which the respondents were asked to react using a five Bi-polar scale ranging from strongly satisfied =1 to strongly dissatisfied =5. All the questions were derived from the previous studies and from general perception of job satisfaction.

In this study, several independent variables were considered (Table 1).

Measuring level of job satisfaction and outcome

We asked 13 questions (indicators) to bank employees to measure the levels of job satisfaction, such as, "Are you satisfied with your current salary?", "Are your Bank is sympathetic to officers?", "Are you satisfied with your increment allocation method?", "Are you satisfied with the welfare facilities?", "How much are you satisfied with the bonus facilities?", "Are you satisfied with the reward organization providing for the quality of your efforts?", "How much are you Prefer working with present colleagues?", "Are you satisfied with Leadership style?", "Are the leave rules cover average requirements adequately?", "Are you satisfied with Job Security policy of the bank?", "Are you satisfied with the Performance Appraisal & Evaluation Process?", "Are you satisfied with Working Schedule?" and "Does your organization promote an atmosphere of teamwork?" Each question was categorized into five responses: 1=strongly satisfied, 2=satisfied, 3=Neutral, 4=Dissatisfied, 5=strongly dissatisfied. Then the five categories were coded dichotomously: 1=Satisfaction, 2=Dissatisfaction. Thereafter, the "dimension index" formula was used to estimate the levels of job satisfaction (defined as to "what extent bank employees are satisfied") followed by selected indicators. The internal reliability of the indicators was evaluated using Cronbach's alpha, which was 0.91, suggesting high internal consistency. The index was then constructed using the sums of weighted binary input variables, whereby maximum and minimum values were chosen for underlying dimensions. Performance in this dimension index was expressed as a unit-free index ranging from 0 to 1 [31]. The dimension index is shown below:

Dimension Index=(Actual Value-Minimum Value)/(Maximum Value-Minimum Value).

Actual values were obtained by summing the binary responses (1=satisfaction, 0=dissatisfaction) for 13 indicators for each respondent, with maximum and minimum value of 13 and 0, respectively. Individual scores were converted into percentages by multiplying each score by 100.

Statistical analysis

Descriptive statistics was used as percentages where it was appropriate. The continuous scores of job satisfaction based on the dimension index were tested using ANOVA-test and t-test. These statistics tested the differences of job satisfaction among various categories of each independent variable. Statistical significance was accepted at $P<0.05$. Statistical analyses were carried out using SPSS software (version 20.0).

Results

Table 2 showed the socio-demographic characteristics of the employee. Among the employees, 46.4% belonged to 30-35 age group, 91.1% was master degree holder and Muslim, 42.9% working as training assistant officer/assistant officer/junior officer/assistant officer cash, 30.4% withdraw monthly salary between 26,000 and 35,000, and more than 45,000, 76.8% were married, 64.3% employees live in semi-urban area, 42.9% service period <36 month.

According to Table 3, we observed that around 73.2% employees were satisfied with their salary. Other indicators, such as, sympathetic view to officers, increment allocation method, welfare facilities, bonus facilities, reward, working with present colleagues, leadership style, leave rules, job security, performance appraisal and evaluation process, working schedule and teamwork were found satisfactory among 71.4%, 58.9%, 50%, 60.7%, 58.9%, 53.6%, 58.9%, 33.9%, 50%, 58.9%, 67.9% and 73.2% employees respectively. In contrast (3.6%) employees were found dissatisfied with their salary and (5.4%) with sympathetic view to officers, (5.4%) with increment, (10.7%) welfare facilities, (3.6%) bonus, (8.9%) reward, (7.1%) working with colleagues, (7.1%) leadership style, (10.7%) leave rules, (5.4%) job security, (8.9%) performance appraisal

Variables name	Categories
Gender	1=Male
	2=Female
Age of the respondents (in years)	1 ≤ 30
	2=30-35
	3 ≥ 35
Religion of the respondents	1=Islam
	2=Hindu
Education of the respondents	1=Honors degree
	2=Master's degree
Designation of the respondents	1=Training Assistant Officer/Assistant Officer/Junior Officer/Assistant Officer Cash
	2=Officer
	3=Senior Officer/Principal Officer/Executive Officer/Grade- ii
	4=Senior Principal Officer/ Senior Executive Officer /Grade-i
Salary of the respondents	1 ≤ 2500
	2=25,001-35,000
	3=35,001-45,000
	4 ≥ 45,000
Family member of the respondents	1 ≤ 3
	2=4
	3 ≥ 4
Marital status of the respondents	1=Married
	2=Unmarried
Geographic Location of the respondents	1=Rural
	2=Semi-Urban
	3=Urban
Family income of the respondents	1 ≤ 45000
	2=45000-65000
	3 ≥ 65000
Service period of the respondents (in month)	1 ≤ 36
	2=36-60
	3 ≥ 60
Working Environment	1=Participative
	2=Autonomy

Table 1: Covariates.

& evaluation, (5.4%) working schedule, (1.8%) teamwork. Besides few employees were found highly satisfied and few were highly dissatisfied and some were neither satisfied nor dissatisfied.

Table 4 represented the level of job satisfaction among bank employees in context of socio-demographic factors. Significance mean differences were found among the categories of some selected socio-demographic factors, such as, age of the respondents, designation, salary, marital status, service period and working environment (Table 4). Low levels of job satisfaction were found among employees of 30-35 age group (76.04%), where officer (72.31%), had salary 35,001-45,000 (70.77%), were married (83.36%), with long service period (68.27%) and were working in autonomous environment (79.38%). On the other hand, high levels of job satisfaction were found among employees age >35 (100%) and <30 (91.03%), working as a SPO/SEO/Grade-I (98.10%) and O/PO/EO/Grade-ii (96.58%), withdraw salary ≤2500 (96.79%) and >45,000 (96.40%), Unmarried (94.67%), with service period 36-60 (95.19%) and <36 (91.67%) and with participative working environment (91.32%). On the other hand no significance mean differences were found among these factors namely, family income, geographic location, family member, education, religion and gender.

Figure 1 represented male is more satisfied than their female counterpart considering the indicators, such as salary, bank's sympathetic view, bonus, reward, working with colleagues, leave rules, job security, appraisal and evaluation and working schedule other than increment, welfare facilities, leadership style and teamwork.

Figure 2 showed that female were highly dissatisfied than male except these indicators like as increment, welfare facilities, leadership and teamwork.

Figure 3 illustrated that senior employees were more satisfied than other two junior category employees for the indicators of salary, bank's sympathetic view, bonus, reward, working with colleagues, leave rules, job security, appraisal and evaluation, working schedule, welfare facilities and leadership style and most junior employees also same satisfied for increment and teamwork like the senior.

Figure 4 represented that employees age 30-35 were dissatisfied for all indicators.

Discussions

In this study, we observed that more than 80% bank employees were satisfied with their job. We considered several job satisfaction indicators, such as salary, sympathetic view to officers, increment allocation method, welfare facilities, bonus facilities, reward, working with present colleagues, leadership style, leave rules, job security, performance appraisal and evaluation process, working schedule and teamwork. A higher portion of the respondents was satisfied based on selected job satisfaction indicators during the study period.

Title/variables	Number	Percentage (%)
Gender		
Male	50	89.3
Female	6	10.7
Age of the respondents (in years)		
<30	18	32.1
30-35	26	46.4
>35	12	21.4
Religion of the respondents		
Islam	51	91.1
Hindu	5	8.9
Education of the respondents		
Honors degree	5	8.9
Masters degree	51	91.1
Designation of the respondents		
TAO/AO/JO/ACO	24	42.9
Officer	15	26.8
SO/PO/EO/Grade- ii	9	16.1
SPO/SEO/Grade-i	8	14.3
Salary of the respondents		
≤2500	12	21.4
25,001-35,000	17	30.4
35,001-45,000	10	17.9
>45,000	17	30.4
Family member of the respondents		
<=3	17	30.4
4	16	28.6
>4	23	41.1
Marital status of the respondents		
Married	43	76.8
Unmarried	13	23.2
Geographic Location of the respondents		
Rural	5	8.9
Semi- Urban	36	64.3
Urban	15	26.8
Family income of the respondents		
<45,000	17	30.4
45,000-65,000	19	33.9
>65,000	20	35.7
Service period of the respondents(in month)		
<36	24	42.9
36-60	16	28.6
>60	16	28.6
Working Environment		
Participative	31	55.4
Autonomy	25	44.7

Table 2: Socio-demographic characteristics of bank employees.

Variables	Highly satisfied	Satisfied	Neutral	Dissatisfied	Highly dissatisfied
Are you Satisfied with your salary	3 (5.4%)	41 (73.2%)	5 (8.9%)	2 (3.6%)	5 (8.9%)
Are your Bank is sympathetic to officers view	1 (1.8%)	40 (71.4%)	8 (14.3%)	3 (5.4%)	4(7.1%)
Are you Satisfy with your increment allocation method	2(3.6%)	33 (58.9%)	16 (28.6%)	3(5.4%)	2 (3.6%)
Are you satisfied with the welfare facilities	2 (3.6%)	28 (50%)	15 (26.8%)	6 (10.7%)	5 (8.9%)
How much are you satisfied with the bonus facilities	2 (3.6%)	34 (60.7%)	15 (26.8%)	2 (3.6%)	3(5.4%)
Are you satisfied with the reward organization provide for your qualitative efforts	4 (7.1%)	33 (58.9%)	11 (19.6%)	5 (8.9%)	3(5.4%)
How much are you Prefer working with present colleagues	7 (12.5%)	30 (53.6%)	12 (21.4%)	4 (7.1%)	3(5.4%)
Are you satisfied with Leadership style	6 (10.7%)	33 (58.9%)	9 (16.1%)	4 (7.1%)	4 (7.1%)
Are the leave rules cover average requirements adequately	2 (3.6%)	19 (33.9%)	21 (37.5%)	6 (10.7%)	8 (14.3%)
Are you satisfy with Job Security policy of the bank	2 (3.6%)	28 (50%)	17 (30.4%)	3(5.4%)	6 (10.7%)
Are you satisfied with the Performance Appraisal & Evaluation Process	1 (1.8%)	33 (58.9%)	14 (25.0%)	5 (8.9%)	3 (5.4%)
Are you satisfied with Working Schedule	3 (5.4%)	38 (67.9%)	6 (10.7%)	3 (5.4%)	6 (10.7%)
Does your organization promote an atmosphere of teamwork	---	41 (73.2%)	12 (21.4%)	1 (1.8%)	2 (3.6%)

Table 3: Responses on the different factors of job satisfaction.

Title/variables	Number	Mean level	P values
Gender			
Male	50	86.0%	0.705
Female	6	85.9%	
Age of the respondents (in years)			
<30	18	91.03%	0.019
30-35	26	76.04%	
>35	12	100%	
Religion of the respondents			
Islam	51	86.0%	0.952
Hindu	5	86.2%	
Education of the respondents			
Honors degree	5	86.2%	0.808
Masters degree	51	86.0%	
Designation of the respondents			
TAO/AO/JO/ACO	24	86.54%	0.049
Officer	15	72.31%	
SO/PO/EO/Grade- ii	9	96.58%	
SPO/SEO/Grade-i	8	98.10%	
Salary of the respondents			
≤2500	12	96.79%	0.016
25,001-35,000	17	76.92%	
35,001-45,000	10	70.77%	
>45,000	17	96.40%	
Family member of the respondents			
< = 3	17	94.12%	0.235
4	16	86.54%	
>4	23	79.60%	
Marital status of the respondents			
Married	43	83.36%	0.013
Unmarried	13	94.67%	
Geographic Location of the respondents			
Rural	5	90.77%	0.488
Semi Urban	36	88.25%	
Urban	15	79.0%	
Family income of the respondents			
<45,000	17	76.47%	0.092
45,000-65,000	19	84.62%	
>65,000	20	95.38%	
Service period of the respondents(in month)			
<36	24	91.67%	0.005
36-60	16	95.19%	
>60	16	68.27%	
Working Environment			
Participative	31	91.32%	0.002
Autonomy	25	79.38%	
Total	56	85.99%	

Table 4: Mean level of job satisfaction based on dimension index.

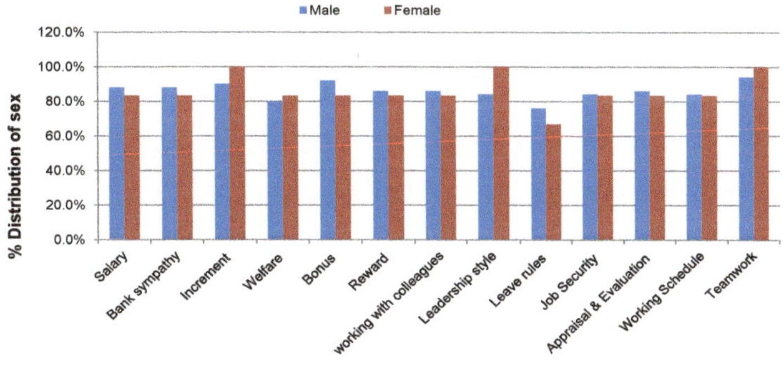

Figure 1: Differences of job satisfaction between sexes.

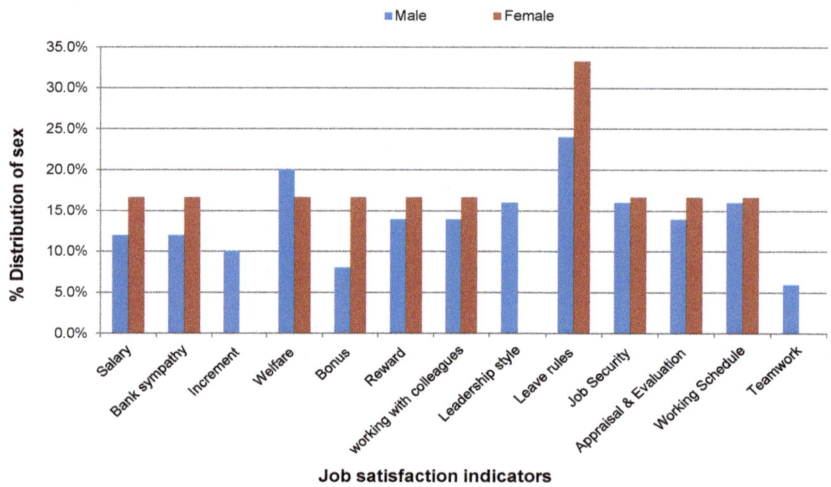

Figure 2: Differences of job dissatisfaction between sexes.

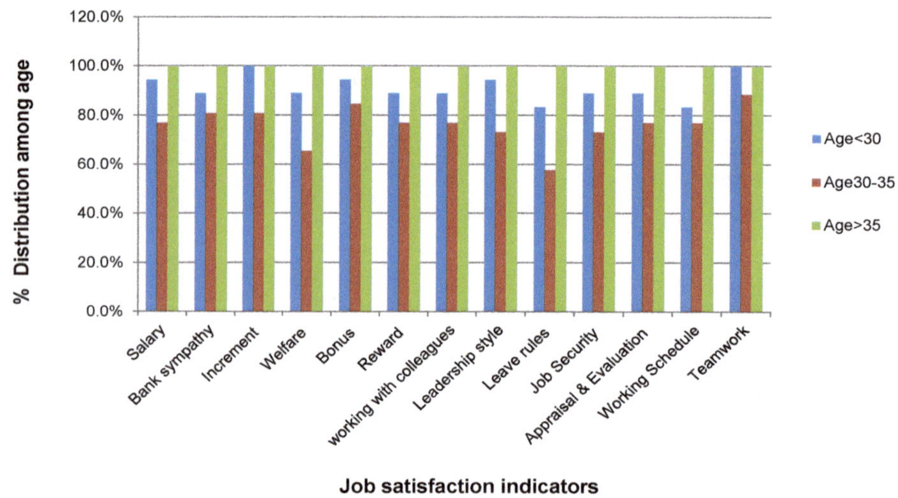

Figure 3: Differences of job satisfaction among age group.

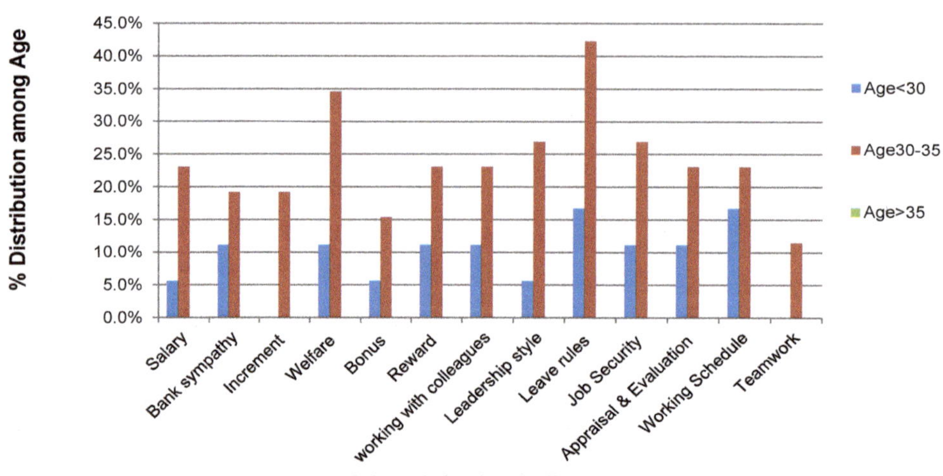

Figure 4: Differences of job dissatisfaction among age groups.

Several studies have been conducted in different countries, like, Malaysia, Pakistan, India, UAE, Europe and Western Europe along with Bangladesh regarding this issue. Some similar job satisfaction indicators, such as, policy, administration, salary, reward, recognition, training, fairness, compensation and benefits, promotion, career development, interpersonal relations and working conditions were used to identify the proportions of satisfaction [16,22,24,32-34].

According to numerous studies, various demographic characteristics such as education, age, sex, income, occupation and race have an influence on job satisfaction [2,28,35]. However, we estimated the levels of job satisfaction in the context of socio-demographic factors using dimension index in this study. No significant studies were available to compare the appropriate match. In our study, significance variations in satisfaction levels have been found among the categories of age, designation, salary, marital status, service period, and working environment.

Job satisfaction level of newly joined and young age employees are high because of designation, participative working environment and higher opening salary on bank than other job. But with the passes of year satisfaction level decrease because promotion, increment and rewards facilities aren't increasing at a desired level. Empirical study showed that less salary, noisy working environment, delay of promotion, demographic and biographical characteristics, working hours, training and development and job insecurity reduce job satisfaction level and become cause of employee turnover [21]. Study showed that female workers have lower level of job satisfaction than their male counterparts because male officials dominate most of the organizations [36,37]. Workers with higher educational level would tend to be more satisfied with their job than workers with lower educational level [38,39].

Limitations of the Study

One of the major limitations was the small sample size. Some employees denied to give information may limit our study. Another limitation is only private banks were included in this study. However, it represented a clear picture of the level of job satisfaction among employee in Bangladesh.

Conclusion and Recommendation

Based on the aim of this study, various socio-demographic factors, such as, age, designation, salary, marital status, service period and working environment showed significance interclass variations in satisfaction levels among employees. However, the overall level of job satisfaction was high. In spite of this factors, management should focus on different issues, such as, transparence, equitable and competitive compensation system, periodical increments, allowances, promotion and other compensations, redesigning of working hour and environment, opportunities to participation in decision making and effective training and development program regarding job satisfaction among bank employees. More research on job satisfaction is essential to formulate the strategies to keep the employees satisfied with their job.

Acknowledgments

We are very grateful to Mohammad Rocky Khan Chowdhury, Lecturer at the Department of Public Health, First Capital University of Bangladesh, Chuadanga for his cordial help in statistical analysis and guide to prepare the article. Thankful to the authority of all banks for their warm assists by giving information. Also thanks to the whole authority of First Capital University for their pleasant support.

References

1. Rahman H (2014) Training and job satisfaction for organizational effectiveness: A case study from the banking sector. Central European Business Review 3: 27-34.
2. Uddin MK, Kabir MJ (2015) Satisfaction towards Banking Profession: A Comparative Study on Male and Female Executives. IIUC STUDIES 12: 127-138.
3. Islam MS, Islam MM (2014) A comparative study of job satisfaction in banking. A case study of public and private bank sectors. European Journal of Business and Management 6: 105-111.
4. Opkara JO (2002) The impact of salary differential on managerial job satisfaction: A study of the gender gap and its implications for management education and practice in a developing economy. The Journal of Business in Developing Nations 8: 65-92.
5. Locke EA (1976) The Nature and Causes of Job Satisfaction. In: Dunnette MD (ed.), Hand book of Industrial and Organizational Psychology, Rand McNally, Chicago, IL, pp: 1297-1343.
6. Belias D, Koustelios A, Aspridis G, Varsanis K, Koffas S (2016) Personal traits and job satisfaction of people who work into the Greek banking sector. International Journal of Strategic Innovative Marketing, pp: 41-55.
7. Hwang W, Ramadoss K (2017) The job demands–control–support model and job satisfaction across gender: The mediating role of work–family conflict. Journal of Family Issues 38: 52-72.
8. Qazi S, Jeet V (2017) Impact of prevailing HRM practices on job satisfaction: A comparative study of public and private higher educational institutions in India. International Journal of Business and Management 12: 178-187.
9. Soodan V, Pandey A (2017) Impact assessment of leadership style on job satisfaction of NGO employees in Uttarakhand-India. International Journal of Management & Social Sciences 6: 6-12.
10. Rousseau DM (1995) Psychological contracts in organizations: Understanding written and unwritten agreements. Thosand Oaks, Sage, CA.
11. Rynes SL (1993) Who's selecting whom? Effects of selection practices on applicant's attitudes and behavior. In: Schmitt N and Borman W C (eds.), Personnel Selection in Organizations. Jossey Bass, San Francisco, pp: 171-202.
12. Hackman JR, Oldham GR (1976) Motivation through the design of work: Test of a theory. Organizational Behavior and Human Performance 16: 250-279.
13. Hanny M, Northam M (2000) Low cost strategies for employee retention. Compensation and Benefit Review 23: 65-72.
14. Rust RT, Stewart GL, Miller H, Pielack D (1996) The satisfaction and retention of frontline employees: A customer satisfaction measurement approach. International Journal of Service Industry Management 7: 62-80.
15. Devi S, Suneja A (2013) Job satisfaction among bank employees: A comparative study of public sector and private sector banks. International Journal of Research in Management, Science & Technology 1: 93-101.
16. Hossain MS (2014) Job satisfaction of bank employees in Bangladesh. Research Journal of Finance and Accounting 5: 1-8.
17. Hossan CG, Sarker AR, Afroze R (2012) Recent unrest in RMG sector of Bangladesh: Is this an outcome of poor labor practices? International Journal of Business and Management 7: 206-218.
18. Noe RA, Hollenbeck JR, Gerhart B, Wright PM (2007) Human Resource Management: Gaining a competitive advantage. McGraw-Hill, USA.
19. Saba I (2011) Measuring the job satisfaction level of the academic staff in Bahawalpur colleges. International Journal of Academic Research in Business and Social Sciences 1: 12-19.
20. Santhepparaj AS, Alam SS (2005) Job satisfaction among academic staff in Private Universities in Malaysia. Journal of Social Sciences 1: 72-76.
21. Chahal A, Chahal S, Chowdhary B, Chahal J (2013) Job satisfaction among bank employees: An analysis of the contributing variables towards job satisfaction. International Journal of Scientific & Technology Research 2: 11-20.
22. Rahman MM, Gupta AD, Huq SM (2012) Job satisfaction of female employees in financial institutions of Bangladesh: A study on selected private commercial banks in Chittagong. Global Journal of Management and Business Research 12: 49-55.
23. Anjom W, Akther S, Karim AM (2016) Factors affecting the fascination for banking sector jobs in Bangladesh: An empirical study conducted among the fresh graduates in Chittagong. Australasian Journal of Business, Social Science and Information Technology 2: 216-224.

24. Ahmed RU (2015) A comparative research on job satisfaction and human resource management practices: Empirical investigation of few commercial bank employees in Bangladesh. International Journal of Human Resource Studies 5: 290-300.

25. Uddin MJ, Chowdhury MM, Yasmin M, Akter A (2016) Job satisfaction of the employees of the general insurance companies in Bangladesh. Global Disclosure of Economics and Business 5: 7-18.

26. Rana MS (2015) Job satisfaction effecting factors of employees in Bangladesh banking sector. International Journal of Economics, Finance and Management Sciences 3: 352-357.

27. Masum AKM, Azad MAK, Beh LS (2015) Determinants of academics' job satisfaction: Empirical evidence from Private Universities in Bangladesh. PLoS ONE 10: e0117834.

28. Mahmud MT, Hasan MT, Ashifa SM (2014) Determinants of job satisfaction: A comparative study in the banking sector of Bangladesh. International Journal of Economics and Empirical Research 2: 22-28.

29. Rubel MMC, Rokon MAA, Kabir ME (2014) The influence of job related variables on apparel merchandisers' job satisfaction in Bangladesh. International Journal of Modern Communication Technologies & Research 2: 31-36.

30. Majumder MTH (2012) Human resource management practices and employees' satisfaction towards private banking sector in Bangladesh. International Review of Management and Marketing 2: 52-58.

31. Chawdhury MRK, Rahman MS, Mondal MNI, Saye A, Billah B (2015) Social impact of stigma regarding tuberculosis hindering adherence to treatment: A cross sectional study involving tuberculosis patients in Rajshahi City, Bangladesh. Japanese Journal of Infectious Diseases 68: 461-466.

32. Kitana A, Karam AA (2017) The relationship between work environment into women's career development and job satisfaction in the United Arab Emirates: A large scale sampling. International Journal of Business and Management Invention 6: 22-28.

33. Parveen S, Khan AA (2014) Dynamics influencing job satisfaction of employees: a study of Indian banking sector. International Journal of Management and Commerce Innovations 2: 212-224.

34. Javed M, Rafiq M, Ahmed, M Khan M (2012) Impact of HR Practices on Employee Job Satisfaction in Public Sector Organizations of Pakistan. Interdisciplinary Journal of Contemporary Research in Business 4: 348-363.

35. Reiner MD, Zhao J (1999) The determinants of job satisfaction among United States Air Force's security police. Rev Public Personnel Adm 19: 5-18.

36. Vrinda NN, Jacob NA (2015) The impact of job satisfaction on job performance. International Journal in Commerce, It & Social Sciences 2: 27-37.

37. Sattar (2014) A Job satisfaction of district officers: A global perspective. Global Journal of Management and Business Research: A Administration and Management 14: 68-80.

38. Griffin RG, Dunbar RLM, McGill ME (1978) Factors associated with job satisfaction among police personnel. Journal of Police Science and Administration 6: 77-85.

39. Ahmed S, Uddin MN (2012) Job satisfaction of bankers and its impact in banking: A case study of Janata Bank. ASA University Review 6: 95-102.

Measuring the Performance of the Kuwaiti Banking Sector Before and After the Recent Financial Crisis

Atyeh MH[1]*, Yasin J[2] and Khatib AM[1]

[1]School of Business, Australian College of Kuwait
[2]School of Business, Australian College of Kuwait

Abstract

The objective of this research is to investigate the determinants of the performance of the Kuwaiti banking sector before and after the recent financial crisis over the period of 2006-2012. The data utilized is based on the yearly financial statements of the Kuwaiti banks that are listed on Kuwait Stock Exchange over the same period. There are several methods have been used to identify the determinants which impact the performance of the banking sector. In this research, a ratio analysis technique is considered efficient and more reliable method than other approaches. Other factors such as trend, government regulations and other economic factors are also included. The study found that the overall banking sector performance increased considerably in the first two years of the analysis. A significant change in trend is noticed at the onset of the global financial crisis in September 2008, reaching its peak before the global financial crisis. This resulted in decreasing the profitability, return on equity, assets and capital.

Keywords: Banking sector; Financial performance; Financial ratios; Interest spread rate; Kuwait stock exchange (KSE); Growth ratios; Financial crisis

Introduction

The banking industry in general is an old industry and it is one the major factors behind the development of the countries' economies due to the contribution that it provides to the countries and societies.

In Kuwait the banking sector is different than the banking sectors in other countries. The banking sector in Kuwait is considered one of the major sectors that are contributing to the Kuwaiti economy. The banks in Kuwait are divided into two categories which are the traditional banks and the Islamic banks.

The study will be based on the yearly financial statements of all the Kuwaiti listed banks form (2006-2012) except Warba Bank which will be excluded due to the unavailability of its data since it's a newly established bank.

The performance measurement of the banking sector will include an analysis for some internal factors that have a direct affect on the banking sector performance in Kuwait such as the interest rates and the financial ratios. Other factors will be considered such as external factors will be considered such as the growth rates and the Kuwait stock Exchange (KSE) movements during that period since the banks that are included in this research are all listed on the KSE.

Our main source of data and financial information are the Kuwait Stock Exchange website, banks websites and Zawya research in addition to the available market news and information.

Literature Review

In light of the change in the economic, market conditions and new management needs, banks started to work on improving their capabilities to measure their performance after the recent financial crisis that took place in 2008.

Measuring the performance of the banking sector in general is related to many factors that directly affect this kind of institutions. One of these factors is the cost management which requires a better management. Other factor is about managing the relationship with the clients which requires a deeper relationship, in addition to the pricing decisions and its appropriation to the market.

Many scholars have discussed measuring the performance of the banking sector tools and devices such as Tarawneh et al. [1-5]. Measuring the performance of the banking sector topic has received high attention by the researchers over the previous years [6]. However, little research has been done on measuring the banks performance in the gulf region in general and Kuwait in particular.

Some researchers have discussed the banking institutions performance and focused mainly on the cost efficiency and the key performance indicators. However, Isik et al. and Berger et al. in their study believe that looking on both profit efficiency and cost would lead to a more accurate results than focusing on the cost efficiency only[7,8].

The literature on measuring the banks performance shows that the accounting indicators are the main tools such as the profitability and cost financial ratios [5]. However, other researchers have criticized using these accounting tools to measure the performance and recommended using other approaches such as Berger and Humphrey [9].

Many scholars from many countries have implemented the performance indicators method to measure the banks performance, whilst other researchers suggest that the use of these indicators could lead to incorrect results. Some of the researchers that criticized the previous method are Marginson from Australia, Barnett from the United Kingdom [10,11].

Modell and Vakkuri et al. in their research recommend using the financial performance indicators due to the importance of the results that it would lead to. De Kool and Weick confirm the conclusion of the

***Corresponding author:** Dr. Atyeh MH, Assistant Professor, School of Business, Australian College of Kuwait, E-mail: m.atyeh@ack.edu.kw

previous two studies and add that this measurement tool makes sense and a good management method [12-15].

Samad examined the performance of the banking sector in Bahrain and used the financial ratios of seven commercial banks over the period from 1994 to 2001[16]. The performance of these banks was compared to Bahrain banking sector which was considered as a benchmark. The study results indicate that these commercial banks are less liquid, less profitable with a high credit risk.

Methodology

This paper uses the ratio analysis approach to examine the performance of the banking sector in Kuwait. The study relies on the financial statements of the past seven years from 2006 till 2012 for the banks that are listed on Kuwait stock exchange.

This research paper is different than other studies in in two things they are the methodology and the sample coverage. The methodology used in this research is the ratio analysis method considering the banking industry financials for the period after 2009 financial crisis until 2012 and compared to the period before the financial crisis, 2006 to 2008.

Using the ratio analysis method to measure the performance of the banking industry shows clearly the effect of the recent 2008 subprime breakdown on the banking industry and identifies the banking sector weaknesses and strengths [16].

Data and descriptive statistics

The number of observations for each bank is 7 observations while the total number observations are estimated to be 63 observations are shown in Table 1.

Results and Discussion

Below are the average major financial ratios of the banking sector in Kuwait for the period between 2006 and 2008 (before the financial crisis) and the period between 2009 and 2012 (after the financial crisis) (Table 2).

Financial ratios

Return on Assets (ROA) is an indicator of how profitable the company is relative to its total assets. Moreover, it gives an idea of how the management is using its assets efficiently to generate profits. In our case, the banking sector seems to be having a stable ROA rate of 1% between year 2006- 2008 (before the financial crisis) and 2009- 2012 (after the financial crisis).

Return on Equity (ROE) is the amount of net income returned as a percentage of shareholders equity. In addition, it measures the banking sector profitability by revealing how much profit the bank generates with the money shareholders have invested. The Table above shows that the ROE during the period from 2006 till 2008 (before the financial crisis) was 14% while the period after the financial crisis between 2009 and 2012.

Concerning the Return on Capital (ROC), it measures the returns of the Banking sector as a percentage of its capital. Therefore, ROC in years 2009 till 2012 has witnessed a decrease by 18% if we compare to the period before the financial crisis.

Net Profit Margin (NPM) indicates how the company effectively is controlling the cost and expenses whether it was operating or non-operating expenses. In our case the banking sector profitability seems to be decreased by nearly the half after the recent financial crisis, 23% if we compare to 46% before the financial crisis period.

Spread in Interest Rare (SIR) is the difference between the average of the interest received and interest paid by the banks. The net interest rate spread is a key determinant of the banking sector profitability. I our case, the average SIR decreased after the financial crisis by 1% to become 4% (2009-2012) after it was 5% (2006-2008).

Growth ratios

The table below shows the growth percentages of the major indicators for both periods 2006-2008 (before the financial crisis) and 2009-2012 (after the financial crisis) (Table 3).

It is clear from the figures above that the recent financial crisis has affected the performance of the banking sector in Kuwait negatively. Through looking at the major financial ratios for the two periods mentioned, we conclude that the average growth in total assets was decreased to 7% after it was 20% in the period before the crisis. Regarding the total liabilities, it seems to be decreased as well to 6% after it was 22%. While growth ratio of total equity was increased to 12% after it was 5%. In terms of the net income, and due to the decrease in the banking sector profits that we have seen above, the growth rate I income seems to be decreased by 6% if we compare the income growth rates of the two periods.

The Figure 1 shows that the movement of the Kuwait Stock Exchange (KSE) index over the period tested in the study from year 2006 till 2012. It is clear that the KSE index sharply declined in September 2008 which is the beginning of the financial crisis. Hence,

#	Bank Name	Ticker	Observations
1	National Bank of Kuwait	NBK	7
2	Gulf Bank of Kuwait	GBK	7
3	Commercial Bank of Kuwait	CBK	7
4	Ahli Bank of Kuwait	ABK	7
5	Kuwait International Bank	KIB	7
6	Burgan Bank	BURG	7
7	Kuwait Finance Bank	KFH	7
8	Boubyan Bank	BOUBYAN	7
9	Ahli United Bank	AUB	7
No. of Obs.			**63**

Table 1: Number of Observations for Each Bank.

Ratios	Average 2009-2012	Ratios	Average 2006-2008
Interest Received	5%	Interest Received	8%
Interest Paid	2%	Interest Paid	2%
Spread in Interest Rate	4%	Spread in Interest Rate	5%
Return on Assets	1%	Return on Assets	1%
Return on Equity	5%	Return on Equity	14%
Return on Capital	24%	Return on Capital	42%
Net Profit Margin	23%	Net Profit Margin	46%

Table 2: Average Major Financial Ratios Of The Banking Sector.

Growth Rates	Average 2009-2012	Growth Rates	Average 2006-2007
Total Assets	7%	Total Assets	20%
Total Liabilities	6%	Total Liabilities	22%
Total Equity	12%	Total Equity	5%
Net Income	-16%	Net Income	-22%

Table: 3 Growth percentages of the major Indicators.

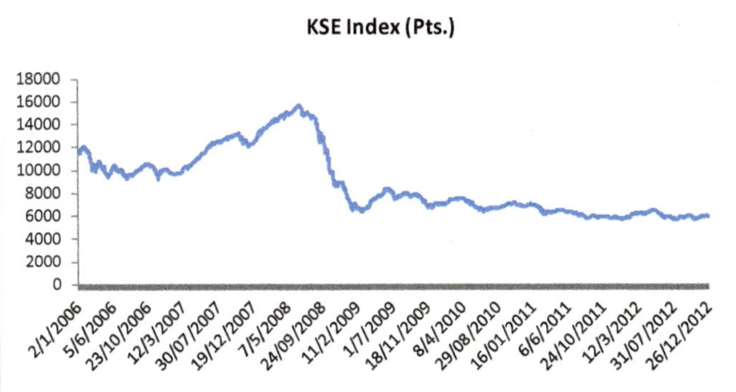

Figure 1: The Movement of The Kuwait Stock Exchange.

we conclude that the Kuwaiti banking sector performance is moving in parallel with the movement of the KSE index which is directly effect by the global market.

Summary and Conclusion

This research paper measured the performance of Kuwait banking sector over the period between year 2006 to 2012 to include the effects of September 2008 financial crisis.

The results indicate that the overall banking sector performance in terms of profitability, capital, equity and assets has been declined since September 2008 up to 2012 as the banks' operating environment deteriorated due to the global financial crisis and a slowing economy.

Despite these alarming features, Kuwaiti banks have managed to continue with their normal day to day business during the global financial crisis. Kuwaiti banks' low leverage and profitability allowed them to remain liquid and well-capitalized; avoiding any need for extraordinary liquidity or government support.

References

1. Tarawneh M (2006) A Comparison of Financial Performance in the Banking Sector: Some Evidence from Omani Commercial Banks. International Research Journal of Finance and Economics 3: 103-112.
2. Halkos G, Salamouris D (2004) Efficiency measurement of the Greek commercial banks with the use of financial ratios: a data envelope analysis approach. Management Accounting Research 15: 201-224.
3. Webb RM (2003) Levels of efficiency in UK retail banks: a DEA window analysis. International Journal of the Economics of Business 10: 305-322.
4. Lacewell SK (2003) Do Efficient Institutions Score Well Using Ratio Analysis? An Examination of Commercial Banks in The 1990s. Journal of Commercial Banking and Finance 2: 17-33.
5. Yeh QJ (1996) The Application of Data Envelopment Analysis in Conjunction with Financial Ratios for Bank Performance Evaluation. Journal of the Operational Research Society 47: 980-988.
6. Seiford LM, Zhu J (1999) Profitability and Marketability of the Top 55 U.S. Commercial Banks Management Science 45: 1270-1288.
7. Isik I, Hassan MK (2002) Cost and Profit Efficiency of the Turkish Banking Industry: An Empirical Investigation. The Financial Review 37: 257-280.
8. Berger AN, Mester LB (1997) Inside the black box: What explains differences in the efficiencies of financial institutions? Journal of Banking and Finance 21: 895-947.
9. Berger AN, Humphrey DB (1997) Efficiency of financial institutions: International survey and directions for future research. European Journal of Operational Research 98: 175-212.
10. Marginson S (1995) Universities and the new perpetual motion. Campus Review 5: 8–9.
11. Barnett R (1992) Improving Higher Education: Total Quality Care. Buckingham: The
12. Society for Research into Higher Education and Open University Press 26: 472-475.
13. Modell S (2004) Performance measurement myths in the public sector: A research note. Financial Accountability and Management 20: 39-55.
14. Vakkuri J, Meklin P (2006) Ambiguity in performance measurement: a theoretical approach to organisational uses of performance measurement. Financial Accountability and Management 22: 235-250.
15. De Kool D (2004) Monitoring and utilization: surveillance, struggle, symbol or source of inspiration, Conference of the European Group of Public Administration. 1-4 September, Ljubljana, Slovenia.
16. Weick KE (1995) Sense making in Organizations. Sage: Thousand Oaks, CA.
17. Samad A (2004) Bahrain Commercial Bank's Performance during 1994-2001. Credit and Financial Management Review 10: 33-40.

Implementation of Basel Capital Ratios by Indian Banks

Rai A, Viswanathan KG* and White N

Frank G. Zarb School of Business, Hofstra University, Hempstead, NY 11549, USA

Abstract

In 2010, central banks, in conjunction with the Basel Committee on Banking Supervision, proposed new capital standards: Basel III, to supplement Basel I and II. Guidelines issued by the Reserve Bank of India required Indian banks to begin following Basel III standards in 2013. Full implementation is expected by 2019. This study examines Basel I, II and III's impact on Indian banks. We find transitioning from Basel I to Basel II had the greatest impact on foreign banks because the new standards required additional capital reserves for market and operational risk.

Keywords: Basel capital standards; Reserve Bank of India; Basel implementation in India

Introduction

In 1988, the Bank for International Settlements (BIS) located in Basel, Switzerland, proposed a set of minimum capital requirements that required banks holding risky assets to increase their capital reserves. Based on borrowers' creditworthiness, assets were divided into four groups with specified risk weights as shown in Table 1.

Holding government bonds or loans was considered risk-free and therefore carried a risk weight of zero. Loans to government agencies were considered slightly risky, resulting in a risk weight of 20%; loans to individuals and corporations were deemed riskiest, and assigned a risk weight of 100%. After applying the above weights to convert all assets into risk-weighted assets, banks were required to set aside a minimum Tier 1 capital equivalent to four percent of the risk-weighted assets (RWA). They also were required to hold a minimum combined Tier 1 and Tier II capital equivalent to eight percent of RWA [1].

In 1992, Basel I was successfully adopted by banks throughout the world [2]. Basel I's adoption accomplished one of the committee's main objectives: creation of a common global standard that permitted cross border comparison of banks' risk profiles. Basel II improved loan classifications and required additional capital to be held against market and operational risk as banks expanded beyond traditional lending into trading and investment banking [3]. The new standards were adopted in Europe and by several Asian countries in 2007. The United States postponed the adoption deadline to 2008, but the financial crisis in 2008 scuttled Basel II before it was fully implemented.

At the height of the crisis in 2009, Basel 2.5 was adopted, significantly increasing the amount of capital held by banks. In 2010, Basel III was introduced with additional requirements that included a new classification for large banks considered too big to fail, SIFIs (systemically important financial institutions). The new standards added a non-risk based leverage ratio, liquidity coverage ratio (LCR) and Net Stable Funding Ratio (NSFR), and introduced additional capital requirements for countercyclical and conservation buffers. Basel III reduced reliance on external ratings agencies because of their poor performance in predicting banks' creditworthiness during the financial crisis. Basel III continues to be modified; in 2016 BIS announced additional rules that include strengthened risk weights, (these had been weakened over the years), and the creation of a lower bound for capital requirements; prior to the crisis, many internal models underestimated capital requirements [4]. The new standards, yet to be formally proposed, are referred to as Basel IV.

In 2004, the Reserve Bank of India (RBI) adopted most of the recommendations outlined in Basel II. In 2008, foreign banks operating in India and Indian banks with large presences overseas began reporting in compliance with Basel II. Other banks scheduled for adoption (except for Local Area and Regional Rural banks) had to implement the adopted recommendations by 2009. In March 2013, the same set of banks began implementing of Basel III, with full adoption expected by 2019.

Study objectives

a. To determine whether capital ratios differ across the four classification of Indian banks: State Bank of India (SBI) banks, nationalized banks, private sector banks and foreign banks.

b. To compare changes in capital ratios across banks between Basel I, II and III.

Research Methodology

The study period extends from 2008 to 2015, when continuous data on capital ratios are available from the RBI. We use a test of means to measure the statistical differences in capital ratios under Basel I, II and III for the four sets of banks.

Description of variables

Risk-based capital ratios require the estimation of risk-weighted assets and Tier I and Tier II capital.

Tier I capital includes the following:

a. Paid-up capital (ordinary shares), statutory reserves, and other disclosed free reserves, if any;

b. Perpetual Non-cumulative preference shares (PNCPS) eligible for inclusion as Tier I capital, subject to laws in force from time to time;

c. Innovative perpetual debt instruments (IPDI) eligible for inclusion as Tier I capital; and

***Corresponding author:** Viswanathan KG, 221A Weller Hall, 134 Hofstra University, Hempstead, NY 11549, USA, E-mail: finkgv@hofstra.edu

d. Capital reserves representing surplus from sale proceeds of assets.

Tier II capital includes undisclosed reserves, revaluation reserves, general provisions and loss reserves, hybrid capital instruments, subordinated debt and investment reserve account. Both Tier 1 and II have some deductions, such as intangible assets, that reduce the amount of capital requirement.

The formula for determining sufficiency for Basel I standards requires banks to keep a minimum Tier I ratio of 4% and Tier I and Tier II ratio of 8%, as shown below:

$$\text{Tier I ratio} = \frac{\text{Eligible Tier 1 Capital}}{\text{Risk - Weighted Assets}} > 4\%$$

$$\text{Total ratio} = \frac{\text{Eligible Tier I and II Capital}}{\text{Risk - Weighted Assets}} > 8\%$$

The RBI requested Indian banks to hold a minimum of 8% for total capital ratio but in 1999 they increased it to 9%. They also recommended a minimum of 6% for Tier I capital ratio.

One weakness of Basel I is the lack of differentiation between consumer and commercial loans. A risky loan to a real estate company carried the same risk weight as a loan to a stable and mature company. Consequently, the United States proposed that borrower classifications be based on ratings provided by external ratings agencies such as S&P and Moody's. Other countries, notably Germany objected. German firms rarely borrowed from public markets; therefore, their debt was not rated. Negotiating countries compromised by agreeing that banks could use either external rating agencies or internally generated rating models if the models were approved by their respective regulators. The new standards, termed Basel II, were approved in 2004 and included requirements for holding additional capital for market and operational risk. The RBI implemented Basel II in 2008 and allowed banks to use external ratings to classify loans with risk weights that were slightly different from those proposed by Basel.

Table 2 provides an example of the risk weights that could be applied to public sector enterprises (PSEs) in India.

Tier I and Total capital were to be estimated as follows:

$$\text{Tier 1 Capital ratio} = \frac{\text{Eligible Tier 1 Capital}}{\text{Credit Risk RWA} + \text{Market Risk RWA} + \text{Operational Risk RWA}}$$

$$\text{Total Capital (CPAR) ratio} \frac{\text{Eligible Total Capital}}{\text{Credit Risk RWA} + \text{Market Risk RWA} + \text{Operational Risk RWA}}$$

Basel III has added an additional layer to capital requirements [5]. The new standards include a Tier I common equity capital ratio in addition to the Tier 1 capital and Total capital (CRAR) ratios, as shown below. The Tier I common equity capital ratio is comprised primarily of common shares, stock surplus and statutory reserves and Basel's specified minimum of 4.5%.

$$\text{Common Equity Tier 1 capital ratio} = \frac{\text{Common Equity Tier 1 Capital}}{\text{Credit Risk RWA} + \text{Market Risk RWA} + \text{Operational Risk RWA}}$$

In addition, Basel III required banks to set aside capital for conservation and countercyclical buffers. The conservation buffer limits the size of bonuses that banks can pay their executives, restricts dividend declarations and banks' ability to repurchase shares. Lehman Brothers' repurchase of nearly $1 billion in shares immediately before its collapse in 2008, is cited as a reason for the last restriction. Similarly, the countercyclical buffer is intended to force banks to hold additional capital during high growth periods because expected falls might be higher than during a moderate increase in the business cycle.

The minimum ratio guidelines issued by RBI are higher than those proposed by Basel, as shown in Table 3.

Table 3 shows the RBI requires a minimum ratio of 5.5% for the common equity Tier 1 ratio, one percent higher than that mandated by Basel. In addition, the conservation buffer increases the total capital ratio by another 2.5%. If the countercyclical buffer is included, the minimum total capital ratio can reach 14%.

Data

Our study will compare the differences in the total capital ratios (CRARs) estimated by banks under the three different standards. We compare two sets of capital ratios. Our first test compares ratios under Basel I and II for the years 2008 to 2012. By 2008 most banks in India were reporting Basel II ratios [6]. We separate the sample into four categories provided by the RBI:

SBI and Associates State Bank of India associates include all majority owned subsidiaries such as State Bank of Hyderabad, State Bank of Bikaner, State Bank of Jaipur, State Bank of Patiala, State Bank of Mysore and State Bank of Travancore.

Nationalized Banks There are 20 nationalized banks in 2008 in the sample provided by RBI. These are major banks in India and include Canara Bank, Syndicate Banks and Vijaya Bank. In 2015, the addition of Bharatiya Mahila Bank Limited increased the number to 21.

Private Sector Banks In 2008, there were approximately 22 private sector banks including HDFC and ICICI bank. In 2015, the number was reduced to 20 banks.

Foreign Banks There were 29 foreign banks in 2008; in 2015, the number increased to 44 banks. These include banks of varying sizes

Borrower category	Risk weight
Government bonds and loans	0%
Government agency bonds and loans	20%
Mortgages	50%
Loans to individuals and corporations	100%

Table 1: Borrowers' creditworthiness.

S&P/Fitch ratings	Moody's ratings	Risk weight %
AAA to AA	Aaa to Aa	20
A	A	50
BBB to BB	Baa to Ba	100
Below BB	Below Ba	150
Unrated	Unrated	100

Table 2: Basel II and risk weights for PSEs by external ratings.

S.No	Regulatory Capital for Indian Banks under Basel III	As % of RWA
(i)	Minimum Common Equity Tier 1 Ratio	5.5
(ii)	Capital Conservation Buffer (comprised of Common Equity)	2.5
(iii)	Minimum Common Equity Tier 1 Ratio plus Capital Conservation Buffer [(i)+(ii)]	8
(iv)	Additional Tier 1 Capital	1.5
(v)	Minimum Tier 1 Capital Ratio [(i) +(iv)]	7
(vi)	Tier 2 Capital	2
(vii)	Minimum Total Capital Ratio (MTC) [(v)+(vi)]	9
(viii)	Minimum Total Capital Ratio plus Capital Conservation (vii) + (ii)	11.5

Source: Section 4.2 RBI Master Circular DBR.No.BP.BC.1/21.06.201/2015-16

Table 3: Regulatory Capital for Indian Banks under Basel III.

such as the Royal Bank of Scotland, Hong Kong and Shanghai Banks and Sonali Bank Limited from Bangladesh.

Since most banks had implemented Basel III by 2013, the second test compares bank ratios under Basel II and Basel III for the years 2013 and 2016.

We tabulate the capital ratios in two ways. First, for each bank in the sample, the mean CRAR (capital to risk-adjusted assets ratio) is computed regardless of whether banks reported under both Basel I and Basel II. Therefore, we have an unmatched sample. Second, mean CRARs are estimated only for banks that reported Basel I and Basel II ratios, creating a matched sample. Similarly, mean CRARs for matched and unmatched banks reporting ratios under Basel II and Basel III are estimated [7,8]. The results between the two groups are not qualitatively different, so we only report the unmatched sample results. The t-tests determine whether the differences in the two regimes are statistically significant.

Results

Table 4 shows a comparison of the Basel I and Basle II mean CRARs as reported by the banks.

There appears to be a substantial difference in the capital ratios reported by banks; foreign banks report the largest ratios in every year, and under Basel I and II. With the exception of 2008, capital ratios for the State Bank of India (SBI) and the Nationalized Banks are higher under Basel II than Basel I. In 2009-2012, the increase in both groups' capital ratios exceeds 1%; with the exception of changes in the SBI in 2011, all differences are statistically significant. Under Basel II, capital ratios in private sector banks increased slightly, but not significantly. In contrast, the ratios for foreign banks dropped under Basel II. Although the changes are not statistically significant, the average change exceeded negative 3%. One explanation for the differences between foreign and domestic banks is Basel II's requirement that additional capital by held for banks subjected to market and/or operational risks. SBI and nationalized banks do not engage in trading and or hold as many off-balance sheet instruments as do private and foreign banks in India. Also, banks with direct government ownership have lower operational risk than banks with other ownership structures. Private and foreign banks must set aside additional capital for operational risk. Private banks tend to be more profitable, as shown by Agarwal and Yadav (2015), but they also take on extra risk [1].

Table 5 shows the transition by Indian banks from Basel II to Basel III. The transition began in 2013 and it is expected to be fully implemented by 2019. The table shows the comparison for four years from 2013-2016 with N reported as the larger of the unmatched banks.

The data for some banks are limited between 2013 and 2016. However, the overall results indicate that all banks experienced a decline in capital-to-asset ratios when they transitioned from Basel II to Basel III. In 2013, the 2.23% decline for SBI banks was statistically significant. In 2014, the ratio decline was not significant but equaled 8.18%. Thereafter, ratio changes for SBI banks dropped to less than 1%. Ratios reported by nationalized banks also declined but the reductions were less than one percent. Ratio changes for the ratios reported by private sector banks were small, with two years of increases and two of small declines. Finally, the capital to asset ratios reported by foreign banks dropped substantially, but not significantly, with a large decline of -22.18% in 2015.

Overall, it appears that the transition from Basel I to Basel II had the most significant impact on foreign banks. For foreign banks, ratios dropped because Basel II required additional capital for market and operational risk. The transition to Basel negatively affected most banks

Unmatched Sample	2008				
	Basel I	Basel II	Diff	N	P-Value
SBI and Associates	12.6	12.52	-0.08	7	0.889
Nationalized Banks	11.78	11.91	0.13	20	0.793
Private sector banks	15.81	16.22	0.41	22	0.928
Foreign Banks	29.58	27.13	-2.45	26	0.632
Unmatched Sample	2009				
	Basel I	Basel II	Diff	N	P-Value
SBI and Associates	12.07	13.34	1.27	7	0.033**
Nationalized Banks	12.03	13.14	1.11	20	0.000***
Private sector banks	15.8	15.99	0.19	22	0.928
Foreign Banks	27.96	28.52	0.57	25	0.904
Unmatched Sample	2010				
	Basel I	Basel II	Diff	N	P-Value
SBI and Associates	12.31	13.51	1.19	7	0.008***
Nationalized Banks	12.04	13.19	1.15	20	0.002***
Private sector banks	16.03	16.61	0.58	22	0.747
Foreign Banks	33.17	29.97	-3.2	29	0.511
Unmatched Sample	2011				
	Basel I	Basel II	Diff	N	P-Value
SBI and Associates	11.87	12.94	1.07	6	0.112
Nationalized Banks	12.15	13.45	1.3	16	0.000***
Private sector banks	18.76	19.28	0.52	14	0.726
Foreign Banks	42.72	36.9	-5.82	16	0.292
Unmatched Sample	2012				
	Basel I	Basel II	Diff	N	P-Value
SBI and Associates	11.74	13.26	1.52	6	0.005***
Nationalized Banks	11.74	12.89	1.15	20	0.000***
Private sector banks	14.05	14.89	0.84	20	0.476
Foreign Banks	41.5	36.65	-4.85	33	0.509

Table 4: Comparison of Mean Capital-to-Asset Ratios under Basel I and II.

Unmatched Sample	2013				
	Basel II	Basel III	Diff	N	P-Value
SBI and Associates	10.29	8.07	-2.23	6	0.009***
Nationalized Banks	12.19	NA	NA	20	-
Private sector banks	14.72	14.43	-0.29	20	-
Foreign Banks	38.13	31.21	-6.92	38	0.277
Unmatched Sample	2014				
	Basel II	Basel III	Diff	N	P-Value
SBI and Associates	8.85	0.67	-8.18	6	0.129
Nationalized Banks	11.85	11.05	-0.8	20	0.007***
Private sector banks	14.25	14.22	-0.03	20	0.972
Foreign Banks	41.31	37.22	-4.09	39	0.632
Unmatched Sample	2015				
	Basel II	Basel III	Diff	N	P-Value
SBI and Associates	12.13	11.53	-0.59	6	0.035**
Nationalized Banks	11.68	11.22	-0.46	20	0.136
Private sector banks	13.38	14.07	0.69	20	0.439
Foreign Banks	54.81	32.63	-22.18	39	-
Unmatched Sample	2016				
	Basel II	Basel III	Diff	N	P-Value
SBI and Associates	12.59	11.68	-0.91	6	0.362
Nationalized Banks	11.84	11.23	-0.61	20	0.149
Private sector banks	13.54	14.69	1.15	21	0.381
Foreign Banks	NA	33.84	NA	39	-

Table 5: Comparison of Mean Capital-to-Asset Ratios under Basel II and III.

but the greatest impact was felt by foreign banks. Our results suggest that Basel III requirements are more stringent than those under Basel I and II.

Conclusion

The Basel Committee on Banking Supervision has released three sets of rules for bank capital over the last three decades beginning with Basel 1 I 1992, Basel II in 2004 and Basel III in 2010. Most central banks have adopted the rules including the Reserve Bank of India. This study compares the Basel ratios reported by banks in India for the period 2008-2012 when Basel II replaced Basel I and 2013-2016 when Basel II replaced Basel II. The results show that the transition from Basel I to Basel II increased the ratios for domestic banks, but decreased them for foreign banks. The most likely explanation is that foreign banks were engaged in additional activities than traditional banking such as trading and investment banking and incurred more risk-weighted assets. The transition from Basel II to Basel III was negative for most banks but foreign banks again showed the largest decline. However, since the full implementation of Basel III will not take place until 2019, we will have to wait to learn if its impact will increase in the future.

References

1. Agarwal P, Yadav AK (2015) A Comparative Study of the Public and Private Sector Bank with Special Reference to Punjab National Bank and HDFC Bank. Journal of Business & Financial Affairs 4: 155.
2. Basel I (2015) Reserve Bank of India - Master Circular - Master Circular - Prudential Norms on Capital Adequacy.
3. Basel II (2015) Reserve Bank of India - Master Circular - Prudential Guidelines on Capital Adequacy and Market Discipline - Implementation of the New Capital Adequacy Framework.
4. Basel III (2015) Reserve Bank of India - Master Circular - Basel III Capital Regulations.
5. Basel III (2011) A global regulatory framework for more resilient banks and banking systems. Bank of International Settlements.
6. Cannatta F, Quaqliariello M (2009) The role of Basel II in the subprime financial crisis: Guilty or not guilty? Carefin Working Paper.
7. Gavalas D, Syriopoulos T (2014) Basel III and its Effects on Banking Performance Investigating Lending Rates and Loan Quantity. Journal of Finance and Bank Management 2: 17-52.
8. Saunders A, Million-Cornett M (2014) Financial Institutions Management - A Risk Management Approach. (8th edn.), McGraw Hill Companies, New York.

The Impact of Electronic Banking on Customers' Satisfaction in Ethiopian Banking Industry (The Case of Customers of Dashen and Wogagen Banks in Gondar City)

Worku G[1], Tilahun A[1] and Tafa MA[2*]

[1]*Faculty of business and economics (FBE), University of Gondar, Gondar, Ethiopia*
[2]*Dashen Bank S.C., Sierra Leone St, Addis Ababa, Ethiopia*

Abstract

This study presents what impact electronic banking has on customer satisfaction in comparing with traditional brick and mortar banking service, its relationship with that of age, occupation and education, its impact on branch visits, the level of customer understanding about e-banking and the opportunities and challenges of e-banking. The paper tried to see all the above among 402 properly filled and returned questionnaires of e-banking customers and interview with four branches of the two commercial banks which have started e-banking service in Gondar city when this study was conducted. The study used tables, percentages, chi-square independency test to see the relationship between demographic characteristics and e-banking, independency t-test to see the visits of branches before and after e-banking by customers is significant or not and regression analysis test has been conducted to explain the variables which determine customers' satisfaction in e-banking. The results of the study implied t that majority of users of e-banking are the young, the educated, salaried and students, business men and women are not actively using the service of e-banking and there is also a relationship between e-banking and demographic characteristics, e-banking currently provided for saving and current accounts holders only, e-banking has improved customer satisfaction, reduced frequency of bank hall for banking service, reduced waiting time for customers, there are customers who don't know the fee charged for being e-banking users, the bank customers' satisfaction increased after being e-banking users, enabled customers to control their account movements and there is high opportunity to expand e-banking service in the city.

Keywords: Electronic banking; Customers' satisfaction; Ethiopian banking industry; Dashen and Wogagen banks; Gondar city

Introduction

Background of the study and the study area

Customer satisfaction is a measure of how products and services supplied by a company meet or surpass customer expectation. Customer satisfaction is also defined as the number of customers, or percentage of total customers, whose reported experience with a firm, its products or its services (ratings) exceeds specified satisfaction goals [1]. And yet another definition of customer satisfaction is it refers to the extent to which customers are happy with the products and/or services provided by a business. Further definition of customer satisfaction is it is a term generally used to measure a customer's perception of a company's products and/or services. It's not a straight forward science however, as customer satisfaction will vary from person to person, depending on a whole host of variables which may be both psychological and physical. The usual measures of customer satisfaction involve a survey with a set of statements using a Likert Technique or scale [2].

Technology is making a tremendous impact upon service companies in general and the financial services sector is no exception. The application of information and communication technology concepts, techniques, policies and implementation strategies to banking services has become a subject of fundamentals importance and concerns to all banks and indeed a prerequisite for local and global competitiveness in banking industry. As a result of this technological improvement business environment in financial sector is extremely dynamic and experience rapid changes and demands banks to serve their customer electronically. The evolution of e-banking started from the use of Automatic Teller Machine (ATM) and Finland is the first country in the world to have taken a lead in e-banking [3]. E-banking has been widely used in developed countries and in developing economies; however, the spread of e-banking is much limited. As suggested by Claessens, Glaessner and Klingebiel, developing countries in general have an advantage as they can learn from the experience of advanced economies [4]. Today, almost all banks are adopting electronic banking as a means of enhancing service quality of banking services. They are providing electronic banking to their customers to increase customers' satisfaction in banking service.

A study by Kumbhar on customer satisfaction towards e-banking services of ICICI bank in Chennai, India, which considered factors affecting on customer' satisfaction: an empirical investigation of ATMs service and examined that the cost effectiveness of ATM service were core service quality dimension and it was significantly affecting on overall customer satisfaction in ATM service provided by commercial banks [5].

Though there are few researches done about electronic banking in Ethiopia electronic banking is a useful topic to study how to make it applicable using the available Information Communication Technology infrastructures together with the existing financial and legal frameworks so that the quality of services in Ethiopian banking

***Corresponding author:** Milion Assefa Tafa, Master in MBA, Dashen Bank S.C., Sierra Leone St, Addis Ababa, Ethiopia, E-mail: milionassefa@yahoo.com

sector can be enhanced for the future. Moreover Internet banking has been widely studied in developed countries and also to some extent in developing countries but not in Ethiopia. Very few studies have been done in developing countries, and it has not been well investigated in Ethiopia. Customers in Ethiopia are late adopters of the Internet and its applications with regards to electronic baking. It looks that electronic banking is facing difficulties in Ethiopia. Ethiopian banking system is still underdeveloped compared to the rest of the world and electronic payment systems are at an embryonic stage. Among 15 commercial banks in Ethiopia very few of them are engaged with the diffusion of e-commerce. Moreover among several services of e-banking, they are limited to ATM service. Creating an electronic banking in Ethiopia is the same as to building a web business for all who are participating in the economy of the country. This leads the country to the electronic business (e-business). The e-business, e-commerce is about using electronic techniques to create opportunities, create new markets, new processes and growth the creation of wealth using electronic mediums [6]. The development of Ethiopian banking system has largely been affected by the dominance of cash. In Ethiopia, cash is a king since the bulk of personal consumption is done through the medium of cash. For being companies in particular this has resulted in problems of cost and delay, arising from the counting bundling, transporting and depositing of large volumes of cash, as well as the risk and inconvenience of dealing with counterfeiting and the treatment of damaged notes.

Though there is no official statistic on the banking services of the country it is estimated that out of a total population of 80 million, less than 10% are getting banking services. Cash remains as the main method of payment especially among individuals. Although the number of bank account holders is increasing since the liberalization of banking industry in the country, the account holders are mainly high-income earners and urban areas. This may due to the concentration of bank branches at the major cities and towns. The payment system is manually handled using papers that moves from banks to National Banks of Ethiopia (NBE). To improve the payment system of the country, the NBE is working on the modernization of the national payment system project that encompassed the following components

- ➢ RTGS (Real Time Gross Settlement)
- ➢ ACH (Automatic Clearance House)
- ➢ Central/National Switch and
- ➢ Central Security deposit (CSD).

Up on the accomplishment of this assignment, there will be a switching company with unique brand that will be connecting all ATM machines and POS terminals from the currently fragmented card alliances. The unification of card alliances will ensure the effective usage of card payment infrastructure, bringing more convenience for card users and providing access to small banks.

From the experience of other countries banking services, electronic payment systems are found to benefit commercial banks by extending bank customer base, reducing operating costs, enhancing customer services and improving banks competitive advantages. For example, some proactive banks have considered cards as the strategic products to broaden their customer base, cut down paper work, invoices and cashier services and build competitive advantage over other banks without card products.

Electronic banking is in an embryonic stage in the country. The current e-banking services being delivered in the country are

- ➢ Automatic Teller Machine (ATMs)
- ➢ POS (Point of Sale)
- ➢ Online book transfer which is not considered as transaction by the NBE.

But there are no mobile transaction banking service and online banking. National Bank of Ethiopia made CORE banking system mandatory since June 2011 in order to facilitate the payment of the banking system and also a mandatory to use electronic banking that is enable banks to provide mobile, internet and card banking services. After the directive has been issued all commercial banks operating in the country are on the way to get the system from different companies.

The other development of e-banking in the country is the establishment of a company called Eth Switch S.C. It is established by all commercial banks currently operating in the country and NBE for national Electronic Fund Transfer (EFT). The Company will enable clients to transact money from a nearby ATM with payment cards of any bank included in the system. It is a company of industry wide established with a registered capital of 80 million birr equally contributed banks operating in the country and the NBE as shareholders.

In Ethiopia there are more than 18 million mobile holders which provide more opportunities for financial institutions to reach the un-banked areas. The numbers of mobile holders are near to fold of the number of bank account holders in the country. The number of ATMs available in the country has reached 194 by the end of 2011, much lower than the number of ATMs operated by commercial banks in Kenya, which stood at 1,979 during the same time. Zemen bank has launched prepaid bank cards which can be used without opening a deposit account at the bank. The cards will have preloaded funds, which can be withdrawn from ATMs or used to make purchases from POS terminal. The prepaid cards will be given to the cardholders with a personal identification number (PIN) to withdraw the cash. The prepaid cards can be used as gift cards or employee salary or expense cards, which can avoid the need to carry around a large amount of cash. The cards can be preloaded with a minimum of 100 Br. And a maximum of 50,000.00 Br. and reloaded after the previous funds have been fully utilized. The bank will take a commission each time a card is loaded.

The Ethiopian banking industry also entering in to this ICT based service to customer in order to bring efficiency in operation by minimizing operating cost thereby increasing customer satisfaction and profitability. The state owned Commercial bank of Ethiopia is pioneer in introducing electronic banking service in the country with eight ATMs machine in 2001 in Addis Ababa and then followed by Dashen Bank. Currently Zemen bank and Wogagen bank are also providing the service. In the specific area in which the study conducted, Gondar city, while this thesis was being done there were 12 commercial banks with 20 branches. But only two commercial banks, Dashen and Wogagen banks, provide electronic banking service using ATM and POS. Dashen bank has started the service since March 2010 and currently having 3 ATMs located one at the branch and two in Gondar University in different campuses and 25 POSs located in different retail shop, supermarket, hotels, etc. Wogagen bank started the service since June 2012 and currently having one ATM located in Taye Belay Hotel and 17 POSs located in different retail shop, supermarket, hotels, etc.

Statement of the problem

The introduction of electronic banking in to the banking sector is to bring customer satisfaction there by to enhance the banks' profitability. Unless this technology bring increase customer satisfaction than the traditional brick and mortar branches customer may perceive as the same as different branches rather than a new means of delivery channels. Daniel and Mols described that compared to ordinary banking system electronic banking is providing the competitive advantage by lowering the cost and providing best satisfaction of customer needs [7,8]. The old age people are generally shy of use of ATM because of perceived risk of failure, complexity, security, and lack of personalized service [9]. Applegate also described the benefit of e-banking from customer point of view [10]; convenient and valuable source to deal with funding because it provides convenience to access account 24/7 that is access is not limited to banking operation hours and available around the clock, wherever the customer's located. Abraham described several benefits of electronic banking like transferring money, collecting receivable, paying bill, productivity gains, transaction cost reduction, customer service improvement and at the same time establishing a means to control the overall activities on bank accounts [6]. Study conducted in Nigeria revealed that 47% of customer that used electronic banking products and services are satisfied with the quality of the products and efficiency of the delivery [11]. A study conducted by Philipos L about customer satisfaction and electronic banking service on some selected banks of Ethiopia listed that currently there are some factors which affect customer satisfaction in electronic banking service in selected banks (commercial banks of Ethiopia, Wegagen bank, and Zemen bank) of Ethiopia [12]. Those are machine out of order, machine out of cash, no printing statements, cards get blocked, frequent breakdown of ATM service, unreliability of ATM service, lack of sufficient technicians in all bank who solve breakdown of ATM machine, lack of sufficient alternative system which substitute ATM service for the customer when temporary problem happen in the machine, lack of convenience of E-bank service, lack of mobile banking service, lack of reliable Tele-banking, lack of credit card service, under-development of technological infrastructure, low level of relevant knowledge creation and innovation, interruption of network, lack of suitable and regulatory frame work for e-commerce, resistance to changes in technology among customers and service providers as result of fear of risk, lack of fair distribution of E-banking service in all over Ethiopia during his pretest of this study. In his study result he found that customer satisfaction in e-banking has significant relationship with convenience, reasonable and fair fees (charges) during transaction, efficient service of e-banking, privacy, security, reliability and responsiveness of employees to solve e-banking service failure and these variable determined 84% customer satisfaction in e-banking and he also recommended for future researcher to investigate the impact of e-banking on customer satisfaction, customer loyalty and customer retention. Belay Deribe and Ebisa Deribie in their study of evaluation of customer satisfaction on bank services in Jimma Commercial bank of Ethiopia found that 25% of their sample responded that there was no any change the benefits they got from e-banking in comparison to ordinary banking and 17% of their sample respondents replied that they got best benefits at best level through e-banking banking service than ordinary banking [13]. Abenet Yohannes, in his study of key factors that determine adoption of internet banking in Ethiopia 85% the sample respondents of them do agree that internet banking enables them to manage their account better than the ordinary banking, occupation has an impact on the adoption of internet banking, demographic factors have a relationship with the adoption of internet banking and education levels are regarded as an influential factor in consumers, use of internet banking services with high education levels being particularly significant [14]. Empirical evidence implies that customer, patronage for and reaction to a particular product depend on their level of understanding of what the product can do and what they stand to benefit there from Balachandher [15]. The researcher here want to answer the above problems and findings against his findings that is to investigate the impact of e-banking on customer satisfaction e-banking that have been recommended by other researchers for future study, to explain the problem listed by other researchers in the particularly study area, to know customer view about what they feel about over all activities of bank account movement control, to see the relationship of e-banking variables listed by other researchers which determined customer satisfaction in e-banking would look like in the study area and the researcher believes that previously no research has been done in this specific topic in the city to provide empirical evidence of the impact on customer satisfaction of e-banking.

Research questions

- What are the impacts of e-banking on customers' satisfaction in comparison to traditional mortar and brick, banking service?
- Does increment of customers' satisfaction in banking service is related to e-banking?
- Does usage of e-banking has reduced the visits of mortar and brick branches and waiting time for customers and the services are available 24/7?
- Does satisfaction in e-banking services related to age, occupational and educational status in the city?
- What is the level of understanding of customers about e-banking?
- How customers see the challenges and opportunities of e-banking in the city?
- Do customers know that there is a fee charged for getting e-banking services?
- Does e-banking service help customers' more than ordinary banking in controlling their accounts movements?
- How customers see their relationship with employees after they have started e-banking service?

Research hypothesis

In addition to answering the research questions the study tested the following hypothesis.

H0: There is no relationship between customers' satisfaction in e-banking than ordinary banking and demographic characteristics

Ha: There is relationship between customers' satisfaction in e-banking than ordinary banking and demographic characteristics

H0: There is no significant difference between branch visits after e-banking and before e-banking

Ha: There is significant difference between branch visits after e-banking and before e-banking

H0: There is no relation between customers' satisfaction in e-banking than ordinary banking with customer knowledge about e-banking, availability and improvement of account control movements

Ha: There is relation between customers' satisfaction in e-banking than ordinary banking with customer knowledge about e-banking, availability and improvement of account control movements

Objective of the study

General objectives: To assess and examine the impact of e-banking on customers' satisfaction in Ethiopian banking industry with particular emphasis in Gondar city in comparison with the ordinary mortar and brick banking system.

Specific objectives:

➢ To describe the age, gender, marital status, occupation and educational status of e-banking users in the city specifically.

➢ To see the relationship of customers satisfaction in e-banking than ordinary banking service with age, occupation and education.

➢ To assess the level of customer understanding of e-banking customers and does it has reduced cycle time for customers.

➢ To know customers responses related employees relationship after using e-banking and e-banking impacts on controlling their movement on their accounts.

➢ To know customers understanding about the fee charged and do they get the service 24/7.

➢ To see if e-banking service has reduced the visits of branches for customers.

➢ To list the major challenges and opportunities of e-banking from customers point of view.

➢ To suggest necessary actions that should be considered by the commercial banks in order to increase the impact of e-banking on customer satisfaction.

Significance of the study

First the study will be useful for Ethiopian commercial banks in order to see the impacts of e-banking on customers' satisfaction in comparison with the ordinary mortar and brick banking system. Second it helps in understanding what attitude customers' have towards e-banking and what actions should the banks take in order to benefits from the opportunities and how to overcome the challenges. Third study can be used by other researcher as a reference who wants to study further in this or related areas or to serve as a reading material for anyone who is interested. Last but not least this research will alert bankers tomorrow's problems today in order to get the intended customers satisfaction as this service can be said it is at infant stage in the country.

Scope and Limitations of the Study

Scope of the study

In assessing the impact of e-banking on customers' satisfaction customers of two commercial banks that is Dashen and Wogagen bank which were chosen because these banks were the only banks that have started to provide at least one electronic banking payment systems to customers in the city are considered the population study of the. The study will also see whether or not the usage is related to age, educational status and occupation. Last but not least the study will see do customer know about what e-banking means and how they see the challenges and opportunities of e-banking in the city.

Limitations of the study

The basic limitation of this study is that it only considers customers perspective of e-banking and it does not take in to consideration what perspective do all bankers employees have on the technology. Second it does not include bank customers who do not use the current e-banking which would help to compare the attitude of e-banking users and non-users towards e-banking. Third it is also limited to banks customers only that started e-baking service it doesn't fully cover those which do not start it. Fourth most available data of previous research conducted may not explain specific to our country context of the area. Last but not least the study only covers one city that is Gondar city.

Organization of the study

The study is organized in to five chapters. The first chapter deals with background of the study, statements of the problem, objective of the study, the research questions, and scope and significant of study, limitations of the study, and definitions of terms and organization of the research. The second chapter presents previous related research done on e-banking, and customer satisfaction both which done in the country and outside country (empirical study) and theoretical background of issues related to e-banking. The third chapter explains types and source of data that will be used for the study, sampling techniques used to determine the sample size, method of statistical data analysis tools and collection. The fourth chapter presents the analysis and result of the study that will be arrived using descriptive and inferential statistical tools. The last chapter will present conclusion and recommendation of the study.

Meaning of E-Banking

The concept of electronic banking has been defined in many ways; Daniel defines electronic banking as the delivery of banks' information and services by banks to customers via different delivery plat forms that can be used with different terminal devices such as personal computers and mobile phone with browser or desktop software, telephone or digital television [7].

According to Abid and Noreen electronic banking defined as any use of information and communication technology and electronic means by a bank to conduct transactions and have interaction with stakeholders [16].

Stan also defined electronic payment as a system of payment whereby transaction takes place electronically without the use of cash. Magembe BAS and Shemi AP defined electronic banking (e-banking) is nothing but e-business in banking industry [17]. E-banking is a generic term for delivery of banking services and products through electronic channels, such as the telephone, the internet, the cell phone, etc. The concept and scope of e-banking is still evolving. It facilitates an effective payment and accounting system thereby enhancing the speed of delivery of banking services considerably [18]. Ovia argues that electronic banking is a product of e-commerce in the field of banking and financial services [19]. In what can be describe as business to consumer domain for balance enquiry request for cheque books recording stop payment instruction balance transfer instruction account opening and other forms of traditional banking service. Banks are also offering payment services on behalf of their customer who shop indifferent e-shops.

Saleh M Nsouli and Andrea Schaechter also defined electronic banking as per the following chart concluding that e-banking is providing banking products and services through electronic delivery channels (Figure 1) [20].

In simple words, e-banking implies provision of banking products and services through electronic delivery channels. Electronic banking has been around for quite some time in the form of automatic teller machines (ATMs) and telephone transactions. In more recent times, it has been transformed by the internet –a new delivery channel that has facilitated banking transactions for both customers and banks [21].

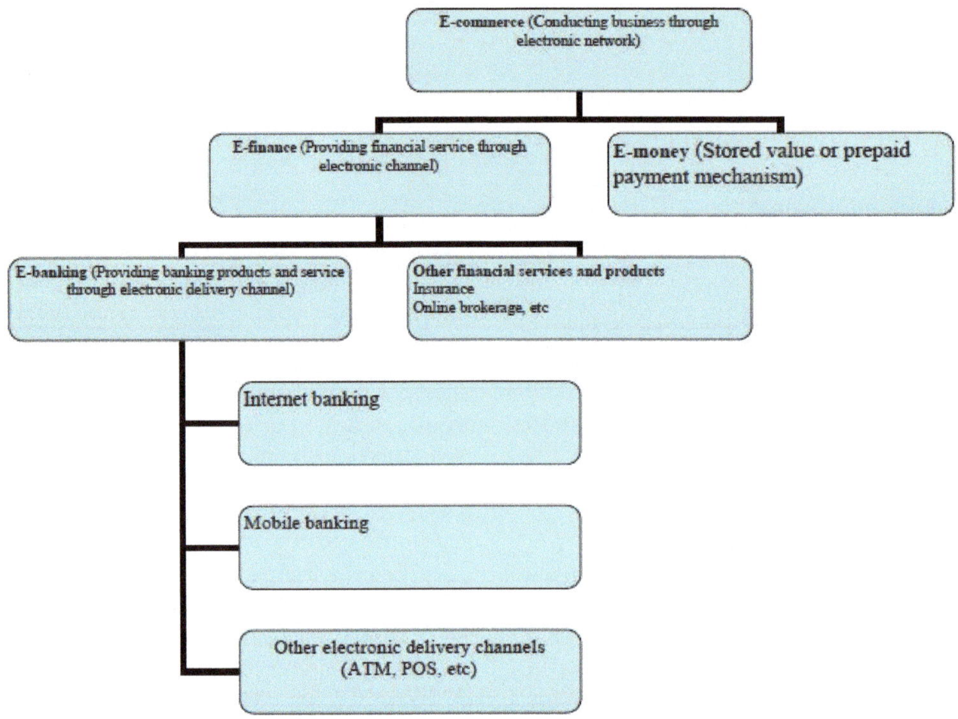

Figure 1: Flow chart of electronic banking.

Types of e-banking

There are many electronic banking delivery channels to provide banking service to customers. Among them ATM, POS, mobile banking and internet banking are the most widely used and discussed below.

ATM: Automated Teller Machine (ATM) is a machine where cash withdrawal can be made over the machine without going in to the banking hall. It also sells recharge cards and transfer funds; it can be accessed 24 hours/7 days with account balance enquiry [22].

Internet banking: Internet banking allows customers of a financial institution to conduct financial transactions on a secure website operated by the institution, which can be a retail or virtual bank, credit union or society. It may include of any transactions related to online usage. Banks increasingly operate websites through which customers are able not only to inquire about account balances, interest and exchange rates but also to conduct a range of transactions. Unfortunately, data on Internet banking are scarce, and differences in definitions make cross-country comparisons difficult [23].

POS: Point of sale (POS) also sometimes referred to as point of purchase (POP) or checkout is the location where a transaction occurs. A 'checkout' refers to a POS terminal or more generally to the hardware and software used for checkouts, the equivalent of an electronic cash register. A POS terminal manages the selling process by a salesperson accessible interface. The same system allows the creation and printing of the receipt. Because of the expense involved with a POS system, the eBay guide recommends that if annual revenue exceeds the threshold of $700,000, investment in a POS system will be advantageous. POS systems record sales for business and tax purposes. Illegal software dubbed 'zappers' is increasingly used on them to falsify these records with a view to evading the payment of taxes [24].

Mobile banking: Mobile banking (also known as M-banking, mbanking) is a term used for performing balance checks, account transactions, payments, credit applications and other banking transactions through a mobile device such as a mobile phone or Personal Digital Assistant (PDA). The earliest mobile banking services were offered over SMS, a service known as SMS banking. Mobile banking is used in many parts of the world with little or no infrastructure, especially remote and rural areas. This aspect of mobile commerce is also popular in countries where most of their population is un-banked. In most of these places, banks can only be found in big cities, and customers have to travel hundreds of miles to the nearest bank. The scope of offered services may include facilities to conduct bank and stock market transactions, to administer accounts and to access customized information [25].

Customer satisfaction

According to Hansemark and Albinsson [26], satisfaction is an overall customer attitude towards a service provider, or an emotional reaction to the difference between what customers anticipate and what they receive, regarding the fulfillment of some need, goal or desire. Oliver defined satisfaction as a judgment following a consumption experience-it is the consumer's judgment that a product provided (or is providing) a pleasurable level of consumption-related fulfilment [27]. Kotler defined satisfaction as a person's feelings of pleasure or disappointment resulting from comparing a product's perceived performance (or outcome) in relation to his or her expectations [28]. Satisfaction can be associated with feelings of acceptance, happiness, relief, excitement, and delight. Most research confirms that the confirmation or disconfirmation of pre-consumption expectations is the essential determinant of satisfaction. This means that customers have a certain predicted product performance in mind prior to consumption. During consumption, customers experience the product performance and compare it to their expected product performance level. Satisfaction judgments are then formed based on this comparison. The resulting judgment is labelled positive disconfirmation if the performance is better than expected, negative disconfirmation if it is worse than expected and simple confirmation if it is as expected. In short, customers evaluate product performance by comparing what they expected with what they believe they received.

Customer satisfaction in e-banking

During the recent years, the development of e-channels has dramatically changed the rules and operation in the banking industry [29]. Aladwani mentioned that while the industry has moved instantly to deploy and offer new banking services via e-channels for customers and in consequence the e-banking services have boomed promptly [30]. Today, several financial institutions are endeavouring to emphasize customer–oriented services. For this sake, it is crucial to implement new banking services in order to develop and keep better relationships with customers. Hence building up competitive predominance almost depends on customers' satisfaction with banking service. It is recognized that banks gaining higher customer satisfaction will have a conspicuous marketing ascendancy because the higher customer satisfaction is associated with greater revenues, increased cross-sell rations, higher customer retention and bigger market share [31].

A study conducted by Athanassopoulous examined the impact of customer satisfaction on customers' behavioural responses [32]. The findings of the study indicated that when customers assessed customer satisfaction to be high, they either decided to stay with the existing service provider or subdue their negative behavioural intensions. Customer satisfaction is also found to have strong positive association with word-of mouth communication. The research results confirm prior research and indicate that the customer satisfaction dimensions are not industry specific, but also country specific. The authors suggest developing strategies to enhance behavioural responses to customer satisfaction and prohibit negative ones. Such strategies can include meeting customers desired service levels, preventing service problems from occurring, dealing effectively with dissatisfied customers, solving service problems effectively when they occur and dealing with customer complaints positively.

A study by Kumbhar on customer Satisfaction towards E-banking services of ICICI bank in Chennai [5], India which considered factors affecting on customers' satisfaction: an empirical investigation of ATMs service and examined that the cost effectiveness of ATM service were core service quality dimension and it was significantly affecting on overall customer satisfaction in ATM service provided by commercial banks. However, result of factor analysis indicates that cost effectiveness, easy to use and security and responsiveness were also influence customer satisfaction. Therefore, banks should concentrate their efforts on these dimensions for cater better ATM service to satisfy their customers.

Hazra attempted to examine a contribution of various dimensions of service quality in customers' satisfaction. A result of the study indicates that, all 13 variables were found significant and were good predictors of overall satisfaction in e-banking. However, A result of principle component analysis indicates that, perceived value, brand perception, cost effectiveness, easy to use, convenience, problem handling, security/assurance and responsiveness are important factors in customers satisfaction in e-banking it explains 48.30% of variance. Contact facilities, system availability, fulfilment, efficiency and compensation are comparatively less important because these dimensions explain 21.70% of variance in customers' satisfaction. Responsiveness, easy to use, cost effectiveness and compensation are predictors of brand perception in e-banking and fulfilment, efficiency, security/assurance, responsiveness, convenience, cost effectiveness, problem handling and compensation are predictors of perceived value in e-banking. Therefore, banker and e-banking service designers should think over these dimensions and make possible changes in the e-banking services according to the customers' expectations and need of the time. It will help to enhance service quality of e-banking and increase the level of customers' satisfaction in e-banking.

Zeinthaml expressed their view customer satisfaction is an ambiguous and abstract concept. Actual manifestation of the state of satisfaction will vary from person to person, product to product and service to service. The state of satisfaction depends on a number of factors which consolidate as psychological, economic and physical factors. The quality of the service is one of the major determinants of customer satisfaction and many researchers and experts mentioned that, service quality can be enhanced by using advanced information and communication technology (ICT) [33].

Kumbhar expressed that today almost all banks are adopting ICT as means to enhance service quality of banking services. They are providing ICT based e-service to their customers which is called as e-banking, internet banking or online banking etc. It brings convenience, customer centricity, enhance service quality and cost effectiveness in the banking and increasing customer satisfaction in banking services. Even know, customers are also evaluating their banks in the light of e-service era [5].

Ahmed described that electronic commerce is now thought to hold the promise of a new commercial revolution by offering an inexpensive and direct way to exchange information and to sell or buy products and services. This revolution in the market place has set in motion a revolution in the banking sector for the provision of a payment system that is compatible with the demands of the electronic marketplace [11].

Bank customers' taste and desire have begun to raise the stakes of expectation of exceptional services. Customers want to transact their banking transactions at any time and location convenient for their life style. They want to pay their regular household bills, buy and sell stocks and shares [34].

Research conducted in some countries on customers' perception and reaction to electronic banking products and services and others on customer satisfaction concluded that the few e-banks that face liquidity problems in so called advanced countries as a results of negative perception their customers have of the services. In fact, in some countries, e-banking products and services are not very popular because customers do not consider them as better alternative to traditional banking service [15]. Worst still; findings of few researches reveal that some customers view these e-developments as nothing to talk about. The success of e-banking depends squarely on customer' satisfaction of the e-products and e-services. Therefore banks need to make a lot of effort in creating awareness among existing and prospective customers about the benefits of the products and services. Study conducted in Nigeria revealed that 47% of the respondents that use electronic banking products and services are satisfied with the quality of the products and efficiency of the delivery. This calls for concern.

The study also revealed that customers' enjoying electronic banking services are still not satisfied with the quality and efficiency of the services [11]. Another study conducted in one of Nigerian bank,

Unit bank, has shown that an effective electronic banking system has improved its customer's relationship and satisfaction [24].

Wise and Ali argued that many banks want to go invest in ATMs to reduced branch cost since customers prefer to use them instead of a branch to transact business [35]. The financial impacts of ATMs are a marginal increase in fee income substantially offset by the cost of significant increases in the number of customer transactions. The value proposition however, is a significant increase in the intangible item; customer satisfaction. The increases translate into improved customer loyalty those results in higher customer retention and growing organization value. Ala et al. study results analysis revealed that there is a variation in the effect of e-banking functionality factors on satisfaction and empirical evidence in this research suggest that e-banking factors have a significant degree of influences on satisfaction and outcomes of satisfaction [36]. In their study they conclude that e-banking positively influences customer satisfaction in Jordan commercial banks. The study also find that influence of e-banking on customer satisfaction would differ according to the personal variable that is gender, age, marital status, educational level, computer literacy, and internet accessibility. Although waiting for service is a fact of life, excessive waiting can impair significant satisfaction and economic impacts. Bank professionals also experience adverse effects of long queues and waiting time including a growing frustration associated with the inability to provide timely and appropriate service delivery. A third study made in Nigerian banks revealed that there is a significant relationship between electronic payment and banking services, direct relation between high level of automation of banking firm services and improvement of services delivery and it is a must to invest in electronic payment system before it can compete effectively in the new age as well as increase customer satisfaction [22].

E-banking can offer speedier, quicker and a dependable service to the customers for which they may be relatively satisfied than that of manual system of banking. E-banking system not only generates latest viable return, it can get its better dealings with customers [37].

Thornton and White have compared seven distribution channels (ATM, EFTPOS, credit card, cheques, human teller, telephone and Internet) with a view to a set of variables affecting their usage. They concluded that customer orientations such as convenience, service technology, change, knowledge, computer, and internet affected the usage of different channels. The usage of ATM, EFTPOS, and telephone increased as customers were more oriented towards change, knowledge, computer and confidence. Polatoglu and Ekin argued that early adapters and heavy users of internet banking services were more satisfied with the service compared to the other customer groups [38]. According to Joseph and Stone, the ability in order to deliver services via technology appears to be correlated with high satisfaction with services deemed most important to customers [39]. Furthermore Moutinho and Smith emphasized that human and technology based delivery channels were greatly linked with the customer perceptions of how these bank services were delivered to them and pointed out that these perceptual outcomes would affect the level of bank customer satisfaction, retention and switching [9]. Before the shift of technology customers were facing a lot of problems like handling a lot of money and transferring of these money, submission of utility bills and waiting in a long queue by banks and mostly deposit holders were unaware of how to get benefits from bank product s and services like bank loans, credit cards, ATM cards etc. So if we go back five to ten years we can see the quite difference between two banking systems.

Zohra and Kashif study of electronic banking in Pakistan revealed that reliability, learning and feedback are very important for the satisfaction of the customers [40]. This study also revealed those customers are not satisfied by the downloading time of website banks in Pakistan. If clients are not happy with the banking products, prices or services offered by a particular bank, they are able to change their banking partner much more easily than in the physical or real bank-client relationship. Abraham described that currently available research findings about adoption of electronic banking are not enough in Ethiopia to the development of electronic services as required [6]. Doll results showed that there is a relation between customer satisfaction in e-banking and reliability, responsiveness, assurance and empathy [41].

Yohannes in his study of key factors that determine adoption of internet banking in Ethiopia findings revealed that demographic factors including age, income, education level and occupation have a relationship with the adoption of internet banking [14]. In his study, the age group 30-39 accounts for 52% of internet banking users, which is relatively high proportion of younger users and based on his data, concluded that age has an impact on the use of internet banking in Ethiopia. In his study findings education levels were regarded as an influential factor in consumers' use of internet banking services with high education levels being particularly significant. In the study, 81% of internet banking users have a higher education level (diploma or degree), whereas only 34% of non-users have tertiary education level qualification and confirmed that education levels have an impact on the use of internet banking in this study. In the study 80% of the users were employed and concluded that occupation has an impact on the adoption of internet banking. 85% of the study sample agreed that internet banking enables them to manage their account better. 95% of users agree that internet banking allows them to conduct transactions at any time, from any location, with time savings being the end result. Thus internet banking eliminates time and place constraints. The results indicated that internet banking charges are a key factor in motivating the use of internet banking.

Kumbhar in his study has shown that there is a positive relationship between age, education and profession [42]. In the study 82.10% of the respondents were male and the rest were female and age wise 54.70% of the respondents were 35 and below and 9.50% were above 50. The study result also showed that in order to increase customer satisfaction and its further adoption bankers should enhance service quality of alternative banking services. It also mentioned that many researchers from USA, UK, Finland, Malaysia, Taiwan etc. have proved that technology have positive impacts on customers' satisfaction in banking industry. Ala' Eddin and Hassan in their study in which 70.40% were male, age wise 71.60% of the users of e-banking were 35 or below and below 45 accounts 7.8% and educational level e-banking customers participated in the study that only 8.40% were high school complete or less and the rest 91.6% were above high school [36]. The study also investigated that fees determined by Jordan banks were an important element to facilitate the using of e-banking which was reflected on the customer satisfaction. Jayaraman in their study of demographic factors in adaption of retail internet banking in Klang valley, Malaysia, found that gender, age, education, occupation and annual income were negatively related to adoption of internet banking [43]. Only race has positive relationship with internet banking usage and gender and annual income exhibit a significant negative relationship with adoption. Paul in his study entitled ATM: The new horizon of e-banking on commercial banks customers in Odisha, Hyderabad, India out of the 300 sample, 61.33% were male and 38.66% were female and most of the respondents (30.66%) belong to 25-35 age groups [44]. Regarding education most of the customers were qualified that is 68.34 of them have degree and above. Out of total respondents 28% were students, 24.33% were self-employed, 8.33% were professionals where as 19.33% were belong to the house hold group. In the study he also found reasons why people prefer ATM were time saving, faster transaction, easy to use, easy banking anytime/anywhere and also reasons why customers do not prefer ATM were lack of knowledge, lack of security and ATM Machine problem. Timothy in his study 61.40% of the respondents were male and the rest female, age wise 66% of the respondents were 35 and below and educational level 97.70% were diploma and above it and the study has also shown electronic banking service had significant influence on customers' satisfaction in Nigeria [23]. Ahmed in his study of the impacts of e-banking on customer satisfaction in Nigeria showed that in contrary to the expectations the visits of customer bank hall per month has increased by 11% after using e-banking, much need to be done in the area of creating awareness about the availability of electronic banking products and service, how they operate and their benefits a head of providing the service, only 47% of customers of e-banking have satisfied with e-banking service and 82% of the respondents of the sample respondent consider human teller very important and important [11]. Sampson E found that e-banking services have been able to cut costs, save time and offer services at the expenses of man-hour to the satisfaction of customers [45]. Sultan in his study has found that there exists an indirect relationship between fee charged in e-banking and customer satisfaction and there is direct relationship between the problems faced in e-banking and customer satisfaction. Zohra and Kashif in their study have shown that the users do not understand about what meant mobile banking is and suggested that it is crucial to create awareness about the usage of mobile device and familiarize people with its benefit in order to increase customer satisfaction [40]. Salman and Kashif study result showed that the awareness of customers in e-banking was poor that is more number of customers do not know what e-banking meant, e-banking has totally reduced interaction with bank employees and it enabled customers to control their accounts movements more than ordinary banking. Empirical evidence implies that customer' patronage for and reaction to a particular product depend on their level of understanding of what the product can do and what they stand to benefit there from Balachandher [15].

Philipos in his study of customer satisfaction and e-banking service in some selected banks of Ethiopia found out that customer satisfaction in e-banking has significant relationship with convenience, reasonable and fair fees (charges) during transaction, efficient service of e-banking, privacy, security, reliability and responsiveness of employees to solve e-banking service failure and these variable determined 84% customer satisfaction in e-banking [12]. Hasan et al. in their survey of on relationship between customers, satisfaction and electronic banking features found that easy access, design, transaction speed, security, information content and customer support of electronic banking have meaningful and positive relationship with electronic banking [46]. Fenuga in his study the effect of electronic payment on customer satisfaction in Nigerian banks have also deduced that electronic payments have affected an average increased in the customer service delivery and customer satisfaction [22]. Deribe and Deribie in their study of evaluation of customer satisfaction on bank services in Jimma commercial bank of Ethiopia found that 25% of their sample responded that there was no any change the benefits they got from e-banking in comparison to ordinary banking and 17% of their sample respondents replied that they got best benefits at best level through e-banking banking service than ordinary banking [13].

Gardachew in his study electronic banking in Ethiopia-Practices, opportunities and challenges listed that the main opportunities were opportunities offered by ICT through e-learning programs, late adaptor opportunities, the help given by UNECA, World Bank and UNCTAD and commitments of the government in considering ICT as an indispensable tool to alleviate poverty and the state GTP [47]. Low level of internet penetration and poorly developed telecommunication, lack of suitable legal and regulatory framework, frequent power interruption, absence of financial networks that links different banks, high cost of internet, high rate of illiteracy and political instabilities in neighbouring countries were the challenges he had listed. Tewodros described that Ethiopian banking system is one of the most underdeveloped compared to the rest of the world [48]. In Ethiopia cash is still the most dominant medium of exchange and Electronic-banking is not well known, let alone used for transacting banking issues. Key challenges in technology and e-banking applications are: new technologies, internet and telecommunication, lack of suitable legal and regulatory framework for banking, political instabilities in neighbouring countries, high rates of illiteracy, integration of different financial networks, frequent power interruptions, resistance to changes in technology among customers and staff. Ayana Gemechu in his study the adaption of electronic banking system in Ethiopian banking industry (Barriers and driver) indicated that, the major barriers Ethiopian banking industry faces in the adoption of electronic banking are, security risk, lack of trust, lack of legal and regulatory frame work, lack of ICT infrastructure and absence of competition between local and foreign banks [49]. The study also identified perceived ease of use and perceived usefulness as a driver of adopting E-banking system. E-banking system, such as ATM, mobile banking, internet banking and others were not well adopted by Ethiopian banking industry. This is due to low level of ICT infrastructure and lack of legal frame works at NBE, which can initiate banking industry to implement the system. In addition to the above two basic factors affecting adoption of e-banking in Ethiopia, result of the study also shows that security risk and lack of trust on the use of technological adoption are other major barriers for the system. The level of security risk associated with e-banking product or service, such as ATM, internet banking, mobile banking and others, pose different challenges to different banks. Improvements are required to ensure client confidence. Lack of competition among local and foreign banks is also another challenge for the adoption of e-banking in the country.

Challenges and opportunities of e-banking

The changing financial landscape has brought with it new challenges for bank management and regulatory and supervisory authorities. The major ones stem from increased cross-border transactions resulting from drastically lower transaction costs and the greater ease of banking activities, and from the reliance on technology to provide banking services with the necessary security [20]. While electronic banking can provide a number of benefits for customers and new business opportunities for banks, it exacerbates traditional banking risks. Even though considerable work has been done in some countries in adapting banking and supervision regulations, continuous vigilance and revisions will be essential as the scope of e-banking increases. In particular, there is still a need to establish greater harmonization and coordination at the international level. Moreover, the ease with which capital can potentially be moved between banks and across borders in an electronic environment creates a greater sensitivity to economic policy management. To understand the impact of e-banking on the conduct of economic policy, policymakers need a solid analytical foundation. Without one, the markets will provide the answer, possibly at a high economic cost. Further research on policy-related issues in the period ahead is therefore critical [20].

The primary challenge for banks is to provide consistent service to customers irrespective of the kind of channel they use. The more a bank relies on electronic delivery channels, the greater the potential for reputation risks. There are some serious implications of international e-banking. It is a common argument that low transaction costs potentially make it much easier to conduct cross-border banking electronically. For many banks, cross-border operations offer an opportunity to reap economies of scale. But cross-border finance also needs a higher degree of cross-border supervision. Such cooperation may need to extend to similar supervisory rules and disclosure requirements (for efficiency and to avoid regulatory arbitrage) and some harmonizing of legal, accounting and taxation arrangements [21].

Major concerns of electronic transactions are the issues of security and privacy. In the developed countries like France, 3 out of 40 purchases on line and the remaining 37 are reluctant to use on line services and the reason is security and privacy which is the major threats to perform online business. It is not only the duty of industry but also the duty of government assuring people to perform secure electronic transactions [50].

When we see the challenges and opportunities of e-banking in Ethiopia only 20% of the Ethiopian households are connected to IT network and a large number of people are served by one bank branch even compared to other African countries. Un-served market, stable and secure political environment, rapidly growing mobile infrastructure, availability of delivery channels (outlets), safe and sound financial sector are the most important opportunities in Ethiopia.

Low level of financial literacy of the public, level of readiness and capacity of financial institutions to provide service, infrastructure, insufficient cash flow in rural areas limited potential agents, and presence of a few branches in rural areas are some of the challenges facing the country. Legal and related issues, the importance of looking in to the role of newly emerging third party technical providers, reconsidering pre-paid balance requirements and widening the scope of mobile banking service are also critical [51].

Abraham described in Ethiopian, among the known common problems which are related to electronic banking few of them are listed below [6].

- Lack of banking services through the web or other electronic means such as using mobile phone.
- Data and network security and privacy.
- Lack and limitation of government policies, regulations and e-commerce laws, as well as legislation to protect workers and to make the Internet secure.
- Weak telecommunications.
- Broken and slow Internet connections.
- Lack of Internet awareness.

But in recent years the Ethiopian government has a grand plan for the improvement of ICT infrastructures hoping for Ethiopia to leapfrog into the information age.

Banking in Ethiopia faces numerous challenges to fully adopt and adopt e-banking application and seize the opportunities presented by ICT applications in general. Key challenges of for e-banking applications are: Low level of internet penetration and poorly developed telecommunication infrastructure, lack of infrastructure for telecommunications, internet and online payments impede smooth development and improvements of e-commerce in Ethiopia. Lack of suitable legal and regulatory framework for e-commerce and e-payment: Ethiopian current laws don't accommodate electronic contracts and signature.

Ethiopia has not yet enacted legislation that deals with e-commerce concerns including enforceability of the validity of electronic contracts, digital signatures and restricts the use of encryption technologies. High rate of illiteracy: low literacy rate is a serious impediment for the adoption of e-banking in Ethiopia as it hinders the accessibility of banking services. For citizens to fully enjoy the benefits of E-banking, they should not know only how to read and write but also possess basic ICT literacy. High cost of internet: The cost of internet access relatively to per capita income is a critical factor. Compared to the developed countries, there is higher cost of entry in to e-commerce market in Ethiopia. These include high start-up investment costs of computers and telecommunication and licensing requirements. Absences of financial networks that link different banks, frequent power interruption: lack of reliable power supply is a key challenge for smoothly running e-banking in Ethiopia. Resistance to changes in technology among customers and staff due to lack of awareness on the benefits of new technologies, fear of risk, lack of trained personnel in key areas, tendency to be content with the existing structures and people may be resistance to new payment systems [48].

Research Methodology

Types and sources of data

Primary data and their sources: The sources of the primary data for this study were e-banking customers of Dashen and Wogagen bank and the branch managers of the four branches of these two commercial banks in the city.

Secondary data and their sources: The secondary data were used for supporting the study and to get the findings of other researchers in the area (empirical study). The sources of secondary data were library books, newspapers on business, magazines on business, a bilingual quarterly magazine published by public relation of NBE (Birtu), annual reports of different commercial banks, reports of national bank of Ethiopia, internet sources, reports made by Ethiopian Bankers' Association on establishing national electronic payment system, Fortune News Paper which focus on business reports, and other related materials were used.

Sampling techniques and sample size

The population of this study was e-banking customers of Dashen and Wegagen bank in Gondar city and questionnaires were distributed using simple random sampling techniques and these banks were chosen because in the specific area in which the study conducted, Gondar city, while this thesis was being done there were 12 commercial banks with 20 branches. But only two commercial banks, Dashen and Wogagen banks, provide electronic banking service using ATM and POS. Dashen bank has started the service since March 2010 and currently having 3 ATMs located one at the branch and two in Gondar University in different campuses and 25 POSs located in different retail shop, supermarket, hotels, etc. Wogagen bank started the service since June 2012 and currently having one ATM located in Taye Belay Hotel and 17 POSs located in different retail shop, supermarket, hotels, etc. The total number of e-banking customers of Dashen Bank was 14,000.00 while the total customers of Wegagen bank were 400.00. Taro Yamane (1967) provided simplified formula and table to calculate simple size. As per the formula that is

$n=\frac{N}{1+N(e)^2}$ the sample size will be $\frac{14,400}{1+14,400(0.05)^2}=390$ and the researcher assumed 90% response rate and totally distributed 420 questionnaires but 402 were filled completely and used for the study.

Methods of primary data collection

To collect the relevant data or information the following methods of data collection were used in the study.

Questionnaire: It was one of the methods of primary data collection that was employed in this study.

Interview: Direct structure interview has been made with Ato Yemane Teka branch manager of Dashen Gondar area branch on 11-03-2013, with Ato Daniel Hailu branch manager of Dashen bank Jantekel area branch on 11-03-2013, Wro. Meseret Mekonnen branch manager of Fasiledes of Wogagen bank on 09-03-2013 and Ato Tadesse Alebel branch manager Gondar branch of Wogagen bank on 01-03-2013 in order to triangulate the sample of the study respondents' responses.

Methods of data analysis

In order to facilitate the interpretation the finding of the study both descriptive and inferential statistic were employed in analyzing this study and were done using SPSS version 20. Tables, percentage, linear regression, chi-square independence test statistic and paired sample t-test were specifically used in the study.

Data Analysis and Result of the Study

Analysis and result

Demographics of respondents: The descriptive analyses for demographics profile of respondents which indicated out of 402 respondents 30.85% were female and the rest 69.15% were male. In terms of age as Table 1 depicts 94.53% of 402 were respondents whose age was between 18 and 35. From the sample respondents there were no respondents whose age were 51 and above. Marital status of the respondents 73.88% single and 24.88% married and 1.24% separated and there were no divorced and widowed from the sample respondents participated. Educational status results shows that 86.56% of the respondents current educational status is university degree and above. There were no respondents who were illiterate or less than primary education level. Occupational results of the respondents showed that salaried and students were the majority users which account 94.28%, business men/women accounts 1.24% and there were no respondents from pensioner category in the sample respondents under consideration.

The interview responses support the above result obtained from customers that is the educational level the educated, occupationally salaried and employees, age wise the young generation, gender males are the dominant and marital status single are the majority of the users (Table 1).

Hypothesis testing: Here the researcher also tests whether there is a relationship between customers' satisfaction in e-banking than ordinary banking (Ordinal level measurement) and demographic characteristics (Nominal level measurement). Since the two are categorical variables for testing the hypothesis, a statistical test chi square test for independence was employed to test if there is a significant relationship in between the two through the use of SPSS statistical package.

Ho: There is no relationship between customers' satisfaction in e-banking than ordinary banking and demographic characteristics.

Ha: There is relationship between customers' satisfaction in e-banking than ordinary banking and demographic characteristics (Table 2).

Since the P-value is <0.05 the null hypothesis is rejected that is there is a relationship between demographic characteristics and satisfaction in e-banking service than ordinary banking service. The result of the chi square independence result shows that there is a relationship between demographic characteristics and customer satisfaction in e-banking than ordinary banking and in addition the

Demographic	Frequency	Percent	Cumulative percent
Gender			
Female	124	30.85	30.85
Male	278	69.15	100.00
Total	402	100.00	
Age			
18-24	218	54.23	54.23
25-35	162	40.3	94.53
36-50	22	5.47	100.00
51-60	0	0.00	0.00
Total	402	100.00	100.00
Marital status			
Single	297	73.88	73.88
Married	100	24.88	98.76
Separated	5	1.24	100
Divorced	0	0	0
Widowed	0	0	0
Total	402	100.00	100.00
Current educational status			
Less than primary	0	0.00	0.00
Primary	3	0.75	0.75
High school	20	4.98	5.73
TVET	5	1.24	6.97
Diploma	26	6.47	13.44
University degree	239	59.45	72.79
Master's degree	101	25.12	98.01
Doctorate	8	1.99	100.00
Other	0	0.00	0.00
Total	402	100.00	
Occupation			
Unemployed	18	4.48	4.48
Student	213	52.99	52.99
Salaried	166	41.29	41.29
Business man/woman	5	1.24	1.24
Pensioner	0	0.00	0.00
Other	0	0.00	0.00
Total	402	100.00	100.00

Source: Compiled from questionnaires

Table 1: Demographics profile of respondents.

Demographic character	Value	df	Asymp. sig. sig. (2 sided)
Gender	154.405	4	0.000
Age	1108.86	12	0.000
Marital status	533.432	8	0.000
Educational status	53.716	16	0.000
Occupation	679.169	12	0.000

Source: SPSS analysis result

Table 2: Chi-square test for independence result.

results of descriptive statistics results highly support this therefore the statistical hypothesis is rejected and the research hypothesis accepted. This study result supports the study result of Vijay in which 82.10% of respondents were male, 54.70% of the sample respondents age were 35 and below, 90.60% of the participants education level were degree and above occupationally where 36.30% and 4.20% were businessmen and retired respectively and the rest where salaried and students which found that there is relationship between demographics characteristics and customer satisfaction in e-banking [43]. This study result also supports the result of study of Abenet Yohannes the study of key factors that determine the adoption of internet banking in Ethiopia in which his findings revealed that demographic factors have relationship with the adoption of internet banking in Ethiopia and also found that the majority of the users are younger and most of the current users of internet banking in the country are the educated which he described diploma and above diploma holders [14]. In contrary this study result is against the study result of Jayaraman in Klang Valley, Malysia, about the study of demographic factors in adoption of retail internet banking factors that found that there is no relationship between gender, age, education, occupation and annual income with that of adoption of retail internet banking and only race has relationship [44].

Types of bank accounts: From the result of the sample respondents 96.52% of 402 respondents were users of saving accounts and the rest 3.48% were users of current account and from the 96.52% who use saving account all them were ordinary saving holders. There are no sample respondents for checking saving and other types of accounts from respondents. The interview responses support this result of customers that is the interview result found that the bank provide the service for ordinary saving account holders and current account holders and all most majority of the users are ordinary saving account holders and there is no time limit set as pre condition for customers to be e-banking users (Table 3).

Frequency of branch visits: The Table 4 depicts those who visits the branch in a month (from once per month up to ten per month) accounts 42.79% before the introduction of e-banking service but those respondents who visits the branch in month after using e-banking service (from once per week up to seven per week) accounts only 36.57%. From this table it can also be seen that only 46.01% of the sample respondents started to use e-banking on account opening and the rest 53.99% was either were customers who were users of the bank before e-banking service or started to use e-banking service after using the ordinary banking. The result of this study is against the findings of Ahmed B who found in contrary to the expectation the visits of customer bank hall per month has increased by 11% after using e-banking service in his study of the impacts of e-banking on customer satisfaction in Nigeria [11].

The interview responses of the branches which is justified by the transaction that had been transacted on ATM or POS would haven transacted on branches said that there is no question that it has reduced the visit of branches for customers (Table 4).

Here the researcher also tests whether the difference of branch visit before and after introduction of e-banking is significant. For testing the hypothesis, a statistical test called independent samples t-test was employed to test the significance difference of branch visit and to compare the means of branch visits before e-banking and branch visits after e-banking through the use of SPSS statistical package.

Banking service	Frequency	Percent	Cumulative
Types of account			
Saving	388	96.52	96.52
Current	14	3.48	100
Loan	0	0.00	0.00
Other	0	0.00	0.00
Total	402	100	0.00
Types of saving account			
Checking saving	0.00	0.00	0.00
Ordinary saving	388	96.52	96.52
Other	0	0.00	96.52
Total	388	96.52	96.52

Source: Compiled from questionnaires

Table 3: Types of banking account respondent use.

Frequency of visits	Frequency	Percent	Cumulative
After the introduction of e-banking			
Once per week	109	27.11	27.11
Twice per week	41	10.20	37.31
Three times per week	11	2.74	40.05
Four times per week	8	1.99	42.04
Ten times per week	3	0.75	42.79
Twice per month	23	5.72	48.51
As necessary	12	2.99	51.50
I don't know	10	2.49	53.99
Started e-banking on opening account	185	46.01	100.00
Total	402	100	
Before the introduction of e-banking			
Once per week	97	24.13	24.13
Twice per week	29	7.21	31.34
Three times per week	11	2.74	34.08
Four times per week	5	1.24	35.32
Six times per week	3	0.75	36.07
Seven times per week	2	0.50	36.57
Once per month	15	3.73	40.30
Twice per month	15	3.73	44.03
Once in three month	12	2.99	47.02
Only if ATM does not work	145	36.07	83.09
As needed	24	5.97	89.06
I don't know	44	10.94	100.00
Total	402	100.00	

Source: Compiled from questionnaires

Table 4: Frequency of branch visit of the customers.

a) Statement of hypothesis

H0: There is no significant difference between the branch visits after e-banking and before e-banking.

Ha: There is significant difference between the branch visits after e-banking and before e-banking.

b) Decision rule

Reject H0 if P value is <0.05 and accept H0 if P value is >0.05 (Table 5).

Since the P value is <0.05 the H0 is rejected that is the difference of branch visit before and after introduction of e-banking is significant at 95% confidence level. This means the result indicates the mean of branch visits before e-banking is statistically significantly different from the mean of branch visits after e-banking.

Using the Cohen's rule that is small effect for $0.1 < r < 0.3$

- Medium effect for $0.3 < r < 0.5$

- Large effect for $r > 0.5$

$$r = \sqrt{\frac{t^2}{t^2 + df}}$$

$$r = \sqrt{\frac{(-15.284)^2}{(-15.284) + 40}}$$

r = 0.92 which implies the introduction of e-banking in the banks have large effect on frequency of branch visits of customers which supports the output of independence sample test.

Satisfaction in e-banking service and e-banking delivery channel: The response of customers question which compare the satisfaction of customer between ordinary banking and e-banking 95.02% of the 402 respondents said that e-banking has given them more satisfaction than ordinary banking and only 4.98% said they are dissatisfied. The responses for e-banking service delivery channel 96.02% use ATM and 3.98% use both ATM and POS no user of internet banking and mobile banking and other types of delivery channels. The interview responses support the results obtained from customers that is the four branches said that the types of e-banking service delivery channels currently provided by them are ATM and POS and majority of the users use ATM to transact and from the oral feedback they got from customers the technology has given more satisfaction to customers (Table 6).

Waiting time: The result of the sample respondents in the table below the percentage of the respondents who said average waiting time per routine transaction before using the e-banking service 5 minutes or below accounts 48% while the respondents who said average waiting time per routine transaction after using e-banking 5 minutes or below accounts 76.64%. The result support the finding of Sampson that said e-banking services have been able to save time at the expense of man-hour to the satisfaction of customers (Table 7) [46].

Fee charged: Out of 402 respondents 250 or 62.19% respondents said yes that means they know the fee charged for being e-banking service and the rest 29.60% said that the did not pay any fee for being e-banking users and 8.21% they don't know whether they pay fee or not. Ala'Eddin and Hassan in their study of e-banking functionality and outcomes of customer satisfaction investigated that fees determined by Jordan banks were an important element to facilitate the using of e-banking which was reflected on the customer satisfaction and the study of Sultan findings revealed that the existence of relationship between fee charge for e-banking service and customers' satisfaction [36]. Though there are 29.60% of customers who said they did not pay any fee for being e-banking users and 8.21% who do not know whether they pay fee or not for being e-banking users the interview responses obtained from the banks there is a fee charged for being e-banking user which is for ATM 0.25 cents/100.00 birr and 0.50 cents/100 birr for POS users (Table 8).

Customers' responses about their perspective on e-banking: This part presents the result of 10 questions asked for customers to express their degree of agreement and disagreement for the questions summarized in the table below. Customers' responses about their

Mean	Std. deviation	Std. error mean	F	t	df	Sig. (2-tailed)
2.2927	1.55312	0.24256	18.956	-15.284	40	.000
6.0000	0.00000	0.00000				

Source: Compiled from SPSS result

Table 5: Independent samples test and group statistics.

	Frequency	Percent	Cumulative percent
More satisfaction after using e-baking			
Yes	382	95.02	95.02
No	20	4.98	100.00
Total	402	100.00	
E-banking channel			
ATM	386	96.02	96.02
POS	0	0	96.02
Both ATM and POS	16	3.98	100.00
Mobile banking	0	0	100.00
Internet banking	0	0	100.00
Other	0	0	100.00
Total	402	100.00	

Source: Compiled from questionnaires

Table 6: Satisfaction and e-banking delivery channel.

Waiting time	Frequency	Percent	Cumulative
Average time per routine transaction before e-banking			
I don't know	51	12.69	12.69
above one hour	110	27.36	40.05
31 min-1 hour	158	39.3	79.35
16-30 minutes	41	10.20	89.55
15 minutes	8	1.99	91.54
6-10 minutes	16	3.98	95.52
1-5 minutes	17	4.23	99.75
within seconds	1	0.25	100.00
Total	402	100.00	
Average time per routine transaction after e-banking			
I don't know	9	2.24	2.24
31 min-1 hour	11	2.74	4.98
16-30	28	6.97	11.95
11-15 minutes	14	3.48	15.43
6-10 minutes	56	13.93	29.36
1-5 minutes	272	67.65	97.01
within seconds	12	2.99	100
Total	402	100.00	

Source: Compiled from questionnaires

Table 7: Waiting time.

Fee charged	Frequency	Percent	Valid percent	Cumulative percent
Do you pay for using e-banking				
Yes	250	62.19	62.19	62.19
No	119	29.6	29.6	91.79
I don't know	33	8.21	8.21	100
Total	402	100	100	

Source: Compiled from questionnaires

Table 8: Fee charged.

knowledge of e-banking 62.19% of 402 respondents strongly agree that means they know what meant e-banking means. There were no sample respondents who strongly disagree that they do not know what e-banking means and 0.75% said they disagree and the study results improve the result of the study of Salman and Kashif about knowledge of users of e-banking in Pakistan bank customers and found that customers knowledge what meant e-banking is poor but the result of this study shows that it is against the study findings of Zohar and Kashif in which they found the users of mobile banking, one elements of e-banking, do not understand what mobile banking is though they are users of the service. From the interview responses obtained the banks have not provided any official practical training for customers to increase the awareness of customers about e-banking and said since the bank provide brief description during the card taking process the believe that at least customers know the basics of e-banking.

From the result of the response as it can be seen from the table below those who said they do strongly agree that there is a direct relationship between their banking service satisfaction and electronic banking and electronic banking service providing service up to their expectation accounts 66.42% and 70.15% respectively. The result can be supported by the findings of the study of Kumbhar which revealed the enhancing service quality of e-banking will increase customers' satisfaction and he also supported this by mentioning the findings of many researchers from USA, UK, Finland, Malaysia, Taiwan proved that technology have a direct positive relationship with customers' satisfaction in banking industry and also the study of Hasan in their survey of relationship between customers' satisfaction and electronic banking features found that easy access, design, transaction speed of electronic banking have direct relationship with customers' satisfaction in e-banking [43,47].

The table below shows that availability of the service 24/7 in which 53.23% said they strongly agree or agree that they do get the service 24 hours a day and seven days a week and those who responded that they disagree and strongly disagree that is they do not get the service 24/7 account 22.89% and 11.44 respectively. The interview responses about the availability that is 24/7 the two branches of Dashen branches said except power failure, network problems and some technical problems the provide the service 24/7 and the two Wegagen branches said that since they have stand by generator for the ATM said that they are providing the service as much as possible.

The level customers' satisfaction improvement after using e-banking service accounts 90.55% for strongly agree or agree and those who said disagree and strongly disagree account 2.98% which reveals from the sample respondents most of them said there is an increase in their satisfaction in e-banking than ordinary banking. The result of the study is against the findings of Ahmed who found only 47% of Nigerian banks e-banking customers responded the improvement of their satisfaction in e-banking than ordinary banking [11]. This study also disprove the findings of Deribe and Deribie in their study of the evaluation of customer satisfaction on bank services in Jimma Commercial bank of Ethiopia found that 25% of the sample respondents that there is no change the satisfaction and the benefits they got from e-banking and ordinary banking and only 17% of them said they got best benefits and satisfaction through e-banking service than ordinary banking [13]. But the findings of this study is supported by the findings of Fenuga from his study the effects of electronic payment on customers satisfaction in Nigerian banks customers that electronic payment system have affected customer satisfaction increment by large than ordinary banking [22].

Concerning the relationship of customers with employees before and after the introduction of e-banking 51% said that they strongly disagree or disagree that e-banking has reduced their relationship with the bank employees. These findings disprove the findings of Salman and Kashif which they found that e-banking totally reduced the interaction with bank employees.

Comparison of e-banking and employees about their service to customers those who said strongly agree or agree accounts 67.42% that is e-banking is doing for them everything what employees do for them but this disprove the findings of Ahmed which found 82% of the respondents of the sample study still consider human teller very important and important than e-banking [11]. The interview responses about this the four branches said that since the types of the service provided by e-banking is limited said that the technology is not providing same as what employees do.

Concerning improvement of controlling their account movements 75.87% of the sample respondents said that they strongly agree or agree that e-banking has improved in controlling their account movements after being e-banking customers which is supported by the result of the study of Salman and Kashif.

The interview responses support this that is the four branches said that since customers could see their balance now and then without any fear said that e-banking is better in controlling their account movements.

Concerning the opportunity exists in expanding e-banking service in the city 48.61% of the respondent responded that they either strongly agree or agree that there is high opportunities in expanding e-banking service in the city and 38.80% the sample respondent said that they strongly agree or agree that challenge for electronic banking is high in expanding e-banking service in the city.

The interview responses about the opportunity of e-banking by the four branches said that there is high opportunity in expanding the technology the main once are the existence of large number of users, the growth of the city from time to time and the eagerness of customers to use the technology and the challenge is not high and the main once would be power failure, getting secured place in keeping ATM and network failure (Table 9).

The researcher here also test whether e-banking has impact on customers' satisfaction where e-banking variables are considered independent and customer satisfaction as dependent variables. The independent variables are knowledge of customers about e-banking (I1), 24/7 availability (I2) and improvement of controlling account movement (I4). For testing the hypothesis, a statistical test called liner regression analysis test was employed through the use of SPSS statistical package.

a) Statement of hypothesis

H0: There is no relation between customers' satisfaction in

		Strongly agree	agree	Undecided	Disagree	Strongly disagree	Total
1	I do understand what meant by electronic banking	62.19	33.58	3.48	0.75	0	100.00
2	There is a direct relationship between my banking service satisfaction and electronic banking service satisfaction and electronic banking service	66.42	30.09	1.99	0.75	0.75	100.00
3	Electronic banking is providing banking service satisfaction up to my expectation	70.15	17.41	4.48	5.97	1.99	100.00
4	I do get the service of electronic banking 24 hours per day and 7 days a week	33.58	19.65	12.44	22.89	11.44	100.00
5	The level of satisfaction, I am getting from electronic banking service is higher than ordinary banking service	53.73	36.82	6.47	1.49	1.49	100.00
6	Using electronic banking avoid to relationship with bank employees	9.44	10.95	28.61	30.35	20.65	100.00
7	Electronic banking can do everything for me as employees do	34.83	32.59	13.93	11.94	6.71	100.00
8	Controlling of my bank account has improved after using electronic banking	40.05	35.82	12.44	8.71	2.98	100.00
9	The opportunities for electronic banking service expansion in the city is high	19.65	19.15	19.15	27.87	14.18	100.00
10	The challenges for electronic banking expansion in the city is high	26.62	21.39	24.88	13.18	13.93	100.00

Source: Compiled from questionnaires

Table 9: Customers' responses about their perspective on e-banking.

e-banking than ordinary banking with customer knowledge about e-banking, availability and improvement of account movements.

Ha: There is relation between customers' satisfaction in e-banking than ordinary banking with customer knowledge about e-banking, availability and improvement of account movements.

b) Dependent variable (D1): Customers' satisfaction.

c) Independent variables (I4, I1 and I2): Customers' knowledge about e-banking, availability of e-banking service 24/7 and customers' account movement control (Tables 10-12).

From the above model summery R = 0.915 which shows there is a positive relationship (direct effect) between customer satisfaction in e-banking than ordinary banking with knowledge of e-banking, availability (24/7) and improvement customer in controlling their account. R^2 implies that the above three variables contributed for customer satisfaction 83.70% where the rest 16.30% explained by other variables. F is 682.105 at a significance level of 0.000 which implies the rejection of H0 which means there is a relationship between customer satisfaction and availability (24/7), knowledge of customers about e-banking and improvement of customers in controlling their account movements.

Interview responses

The interview responses of the four branches concerning age, gender, occupational, marital status and others are presented here to triangulate with customers responses. Dashen Gondar area branch answered that concerning gender and marital status the branch have no any recorded data or observation to express which category dominate. But concerning the age status of the users of e-banking from actual observation youth is the majority of the users and to describe in number age that ranges from 18 up to 30 are dominant. About educational status the branch replied that since most of their customers are Gondar University employees, Israel embassy employees and Gondar university students the branch guessed that 90% of them are diploma and above diploma holders. In occupational category since majority of their users are Gondar university employees, Israel embassy employees and Gondar university students most of them can be said students and salaried and confirmed that business men are rare to use this technology. Dashen Jantekel area branch replied that in age status of the users majority of them are youth and the status of the gender though there is no much gap as the branch believes it could be said

Model	R	R square	Adjusted R sqaure	Std. error of the estimates
1	0.915	0.837	0.836	0.32154

Predictors: (Constant), I4, I1, I2

Table 10: Model summary.

Model 1	Sum of square (a)	df	Mean square (b)	F	Sig.
Regression	211.567	3	70.522	682.105	0.000
Residual	41.149	398	0.103		
Total	252.716	401			

a. Dependent variable D1
b. Predictors: I4, I1, I2

Table 11: ANOVA.

Model 1	Unstandardized coefficients		Standardized coefficients	t	Sig.(a)	Collinearity	
	B	Std. error	Beta			Tolerance	VIF
(Constant)	-0.045	0.025		-1.794	0.074		
I1	0.603	0.053	0.456	11.377	0.000	0.255	3.927
I2	0.054	0.028	0.097	1.892	0.059	0.154	6.487
I4	0.302	0.036	0.407	8.452	0.000	0.177	5.663

[a]Dependent variable D1

Table 12: Coefficients.

majority of them are males. Concerning marital status since students are majority of their customers' of e-banking replied that most of them are single and in educational status it could be said that educated that is degree students or degree holders are the majority once and occupationally salaried and students are the majority users. Failedes Wegagen branch replied that since the bank started this service in the city it is too short that it could not be said anything concerning the gender status, marital status, education and occupation and about the age status the branch expects that the young generation would be the majority of the users. Gondar Wegagen branch replied that since the bank have few numbers of customers it could not be said much about this but the branch expect young generation, educated and business men could be the majority of users since they need money now and then but the branch replied that it could not say anything about gender and marital status.

The interview responses of the four branches concerning account holders type that is for which types of bank account holders the banks provide the service of e-banking and the researcher used this to triangulate with customers responses. Gondar Dashen area branch replied that concerning account type ordinary saving account holders are the main users and as a general currently they are not providing e-banking service for time deposit, checking saving account holders, over draft account holders and loan account holders. Gondar Jantekel area branch replied that all most all users are ordinary saving account holders and though the bank provides e-banking service to current account holders the branch said that the majority of them due to the limits on one time withdrawal they are not willing to use but they do have few customers but the bank could not provide the service for over draft account holders. Fasilades branch replied that the bank provides the service for ordinary saving account and current account holders but said that majority of the users is saving account holders. Wegagen Gondar branch responded that currently majority of the users are saving account holders but in the future the branch expects that current account holders would be business men if the bank increase limit on one time withdrawal.

The interview responses of the four branches concerning if there is any time limit set as a pre-condition to be e-banking user are presented here to triangulates with customers responses. Dashen Gondar area branch replied that there is no any time limit set by the bank to get the service and whenever a customer opens either ordinary saving account or current account the branch's employees give brief description about all the benefits of the technology and related issues like security issue, charges maximum amount of withdrawal per a transaction and then if the customer become willing the bank provides standardized form and contractual agreement to be filled and signed by the customer and after checking the form is filled and signed properly by the customer the branch transmit it to head office. Therefore in general in the branch if a customer wants the service it could be given immediately and the only time a customer wait to use the service is one up to two weeks until the personalized electronic card is received from Addis Abeba. Gondar Jantekel area replied that except the time it takes for preparing the card any one can be the users of the service immediately. The two Wegagen branches said that there is no any time limit set as pre condition to be the user of the service except 3-4 days in personalizing the electronic card.

The interview responses of the four branches concerning types of e-banking delivery channels they provide are presented here to triangulate with customers responses. Gondar area Dashen bank replied that most of their customers use ATM and there were rare cases of POS in comparison with ATM and Jantekl area Dashen bank branch replied that from the branch's experience around 98% of them use ATM and 2% use POS and from this 2% of POS users 50% are foreigners. The two branches of Wegagen said that all most all customers use ATM but their bank has been working in creating awareness among customers that customers develop the habit of paying payments through POS.

The interview responses of the four branches about comparison of customers' satisfaction in e-baking and ordinary banking and frequency of branch visits before and after e-banking are presented here to triangulate with customers' responses. Gondar area Dashen bank branch replied that there is no question that the technology has given more satisfaction as customer get it 24/7, standardized service, quicker and near to their residence. The branch also said that e-banking totally reduced the visit of branch and said that if ATM fails for one hour due to various reasons the branch would be full of people. Jantekel area Dashen branch responded that it has reduced the visits of the branch which could be seen from the transaction on ATM and even some customers have been even totally do not visit the branch after they take the personalized electronic card and about satisfaction it could not be compared as e-banking gives more satisfaction than ordinary banking from oral feedback of customers it got. Fasiledes Wegagen branch said that concerning satisfaction from the oral feedback of customers it depends on customer that is those people who are specifically older do not like the technology and for the young it gives them more satisfaction. About the frequency of the branch visits it has reduced and that the very purpose of the technology is to avoid branch visits of customers now and then. Gondar Wegagen branch replied that from oral customers' responses it has increased customer satisfaction and for the visits of the branch since this technology is as a substitute of building branch there is no question for the reduction of branch visit otherwise those transaction transacted on ATM would have been taken in the branch.

The interview responses of the four branches issue related to fee charged for being e-banking user are presented here to triangulate with customers responses. Dashen Gondar area branch responded that there is a payment charged from customers for being e-banking users that is POS users 0.50 per birr 100.00 and for ATM users 0.25 birr per 100.00 birr. Gondar Dashen Jantekel area branch responded that there is a payment the same as described above but there is a great problem that most of the customers do not like to read the contractual agreement whenever they sign to be e-banking users that describe the rate of e-banking charge and because of this there were cases that customer complain when they see the debit amount on their passbook. The two Wegagen branches responded that the rate payment is the same as Dashen bank that is for ATM 0.25 for every 100.00 birr and for POS 0.50 birr for every 100.00.

The interview responses of the four branches concerning official training given for customers about the service of e-banking and the level of awareness of customers about e-banking are presented here to triangulate with customers responses. Gondar area Dashen bank responded that the branch has not given any official training and it is difficult for the branch to say the level of awareness of customer about e-banking. Dashen Jantekel area branch replied that the bank has not given any official training for customers but since the bank give brief orientation whenever a customer take the card said that it is possible to say that customers know at least the basic of e-banking. Wegagen Fasiledas branch responded that unless they are aware of it they could not have taken the card but concerning the training said that until now the bank has not provided official training. Wegagen Gondar branch responded that customers know what electronic banking means since the branch provides to customers about e-banking whenever they fill the form and sign the contractual agreement to take the card and whenever they take the card but has not given any official training for customers.

The interview responses of the four branches concerning whether the service is available 24/7 and does e-banking gives service like employee provide to customers are presented here to triangulate with customers responses. Gondar area Dashen bank responded that it could be said that customers are getting more than what employees provide when we compare the service availability with that of ATM and POS but said that the total types of the service provided by ATM and POS with that of employees provide more types of the service as example mentioned currently ATM and POS are not accepting deposit but employees do, about the availability of the service except for power failure and some technical problem customers are getting 24/7. Jantekel Dashen branch responded that the technology is not providing the whole service as employees do and 24/7 except when ever power failure, network failure or technical problem happened and in comparison to the ordinary banking service replied that the technology is providing better service for customers. Fasiledes Wegagen branch replied that there is no question that the types of the service provided by e-banking and employees differ and since the bank has stand by generator for ATM and most of POSs said that the bank is providing 24/7. Gondar Wegagen branch responded that from the oral feedback got from customers that most of them are telling more than happy in using the technology and comparing the service what employees is providing with that of e-banking said that the branch could not say that it is providing as employees provide. For instance employees might give the criteria for taking loan to customers but the technology does not and the bank is providing the service 24/7 as much as possible.

The interview responses of the four branches whether e-banking has enabled to control customers account movement better than ordinary banking are presented here to triangulate with customers responses. Dashen Gondar area branch responded in this aspect that the situation is the same whenever customers withdraw from e-banking they can see their balance and whenever they withdraw using passbook they can see on it. Jantekel area Dashen bank said that the technology enabled customers to control their account movement in a better way but said that most customers strongly believe the bank that they take only the money without checking the movements of their accounts that is from the experience customers most of the times do not concentrate on their remaining balance amount. Gondar Fasildes branch replied that there is no much difference in between the two if customers want it. Wegagen Gondar branch said that the technology is better for customers in controlling their account movement.

The interview responses of the four branches about the issues related to the opportunities and the challenges of e-banking in the city are presented here to triangulate with customers responses. Dashen Gondar area branch replied that the opportunities of e-banking in the city can be said it is good and the main challenge is blackout. The availability of large number of users and the growth of the city from time to time can be seen as opportunity and also described that Gondar Dashen bank branches are one of the top branches which have highest number of transactions in number though not in amount. Jantekel area Dashen bank responded that the development of e-banking comparing the city found in the same rank is in a better condition and said this witness there is high opportunity to expand the technology. For the challenge in expanding the technology in the future mentioned that getting secured place, blackout and network failure. The two branches of Wegagen branches responded that the challenge would be getting secured place in putting ATM and the main opportunities are the eagerness of customers in using the technology and the development of the city from time to time.

Conclusions and Recommendations

Conclusions

Based on the result of the descriptive analysis study it can be concluded that the majority of current e-banking users are youth between the age of 18 up to 35, gender wise the males are the dominant users, occupationally salaried and students are the majority users and business men/women are not active participant in using the service, educational level diploma and above diploma holders are the majority users and the banks do not keep full record of their customer profile in standardized way for easy reference. There is a relationship between demographic characteristics and customer satisfaction in e-banking than ordinary banking. The banks are currently providing e-banking service for ordinary saving account holders and current account holders and in the city there are only two e-banking delivery channels of which ATM the most widely used and POS service is not well known among customers like that of ATM even this channels provide limited in comparison to bank hall service given by the banks' employees. E-banking service highly reduced the visits of bank hall, waiting time for service, there customers who do not know the existence of fee charged for being e-banking users though they have been being charged and there also customers who do not know what e-banking means and the banks except providing the card have not given any organized training for customers in order to create awareness about e-banking. E-banking has improved customer satisfaction than ordinary banking, enabled customers to control their account better than the ordinary banking, there is high opportunity in expanding the service and the banks have not taken any empirical study or customer survey to measure customer satisfaction in the technology. Customers' knowledge about e-banking, availability of the service 24/7 and improvement of customers in controlling their account are more sensitive variable which determine customer satisfaction in e-banking. To put it in a net shell e-banking has impact in improving customer satisfaction, impact in reducing waiting time for customers to get bank service and impact in improving customers to control their account movements.

Recommendations

The banks should work much in increasing the number of users from all aspects that is from gender, age, educational status, occupationally and should do great job in making- business men/ women to be the users of e-banking and also should keep all rounded personal profile of customers to retrieve easily whenever needed and bankers should determine which customers with which demographic characteristics are more sensitive to e-banking service satisfaction. The banks should add other e-banking service delivery channels like mobile banking and internet banking in addition to existing delivery channels, also try to provide e-banking service for other types of account holders and encourage customers to use POS like ATM. E-banking service should expand as much as possible in order to reduce the visits of bank hall for customers and to get investment cost advantage than opening bank hall as the current rent price per year for opening bank hall is much greater than buying an ATM machine. All Customers should be awaked to know the existence of e-banking service charge; official trainings should be organized by the banks for customers in order to increase customers' awareness about e-banking rather than providing the card only. Current account holders should be encouraged to use e-banking service as the users of this type of account are business men and women who need money now and then which increase the revenue generated from the service when they use now and then. The banks should exceed the promise of providing 24/7 rather than under delivering 24/7 availability that is the banks should ensure that at no time should service cease as a result of network problem, power failure and other technical problems. Should increase the effort to keep customers satisfaction above the current level and should conduct survey to measure customers' satisfaction empirically. The types of service provided by e-banking should be increased for instance to accept the deposits and the banks should exploit the opportunities in expanding e-banking by mitigating the challenges. Finally more emphasis should be given by the banks on those aspects which have more impacts in determine customers' satisfaction in e-banking. Future researchers try to determine customers' satisfaction of in e-banking if it depends on banks including other geographic areas, other variables, include customers who do not use e-banking and banks which do not provide e-banking service currently (Appendixes A and B).

References

1. Farris PW, Bendle NT, Pfeifer PE, Reibstein DJ (2010) Marketing Metrics: The Definitive Guide to Measuring Marketing Performance (2nd edn.), Pearson Education, Upper Saddle River, New Jersey.
2. Westbrook RA (1980) A Rating Scale for Measuring Product/Service Satisfaction. Journal of Marketing pp: 68-72.
3. Mishra RK, Kiranamai J (2009) E-banking: A case of India. ICFAI Journal of publication Administration 5: 55-65.
4. Claessens S, Glaessner T, Klingebiel D (2000) E-finance in emerging markets: Is leapfrogging possible? Financial Markets, Institutions & Instruments 11: 1-125.
5. Kumbhar VM (2011) Factors affecting customer satisfaction: Some evidence from Indian banks. Romania Knowledge Management Research & Practice 3: 1-14.
6. Abraham H (2012) Challenges and Opportunities of Adapting electronic banking in Ethiopia.
7. Daniel E (1999) Provision of electronic banking in the UK and the Republic of Ireland. International Journal of Bank marketing 17: 72-83.
8. Mols NP (1998) The behavioral consequence of PC banking. International Journal of bank marketing 16: 195-201.
9. Moutinho L, Smith A (2000) Modeling bank customer satisfaction through mediation of attitudes towards human and automated banking. International Journal of bank marketing 18: 124-134.
10. Applegate LM, Holsapple CW, Kalakota R (1996) Electronic commerce: Building blocks of new business opportunity. Journal of organizational computing and electronic commerce 6: 1-10.
11. Dogarawa AB (2005) The impacts of e-banking on customer satisfaction in Nigeria. University of Zaria-Abuja Nigeria. MPRA Paper, University Library of Munich, Germany pp: 1-13.
12. Bambore PL (2013) Customer satisfaction and electronic banking service on some selected banks of Ethiopia. International Journal of Research in Computer Application & Mana 3: 133.
13. Deribe B, Deribie E (2012) Evaluation of customer satisfaction on bank services: An empirical analysis (Jimma commercial bank of Ethiopia). Basic Research Journal of Business Management and Accounts 1: 64-71.
14. Yohannes A (2010) Key factors that determine adoption of internet banking in Ethiopia.
15. Balachandher KG, Vaithilingam S, Ismail N, Prasad R (2001) Electronic banking in Malaysia: Note on evolution of service and consumer reactions. Electronic banking pp: 135-147.
16. Abid H, Noreen U (2006) Ready to e-bank: An exploratory research on adoption of e-banking and e-readiness among customers and commercial banks in Pakistan. Spider 31: 1-31.
17. Magemhe S, Shemi AP (2002) Challenges and opportunities for adapting electronic commerce in developing country: The Botswana perspective. IAABD Conference proceedings, Port Elizabeth.
18. Uppal RK, Jantana R (2007) E-banking in India: challenges and opportunities SBN: 8177081373 pp: 266.
19. Ovia J (2001) Internet banking: Practices and Potentials in Nigeria, A paper presented at a seminar organized by the institute of Chartered Accountants of Nigerian (ICAN) Lagos Sheraton Hotel and Towers, Lkeja.
20. Nsouli SM, Schaechter A (2002) Challenges of the e-banking revolution. A quarterly magazine of the IMF.
21. Nitsure RR (2003) E-banking challenges and opportunities. Economic and Political weekly 38: 5377-5381.
22. Fenuga OJ (2010) The effect of electronic payment on customer service delivery. International Journal of Economic Development Research and Investment.
23. Timothy AT (2012) Electronic banking service and customer satisfaction in the Nigerian banking industry. International Journal of business and management tomorrow.
24. Olorunsegun S (2010) The impacts of electronic banking in Nigeria banking system.
25. Tiwari R, Buse S (2007) The Mobile Commerce Prospects: A Strategic analysis of opportunities in the banking sector. Hamburg University Press pp: 1-236.
26. Hansemark OC, Albinson M (2004) Customer Satisfaction and Retention: The experiences of Individual Employees. Managing Service Quality 14: 40-57.
27. Oliver RL (1997) Satisfaction: A Behavioral Perspective on the Consumer. McGraw Hill, New York.
28. Kotler P (2000) Marketing management (6th edn.), Longitudinal Assessment of customer, Prentice-Hall LaBarbera, New Jersey.
29. Gunasekaran A, Love PED (1999) Current and future directions of multimedia technology in business. International Journal of information management 19: 105-120.
30. Aladawani AM (2001) Online banking: A field study of drivers, development, challenges and expectations. International Journal of Information management 21: 213-225.
31. Gonzalez ME, Quesada G, Picado F, Eckelman CA (2004) Customer satisfaction using QFD: An e-banking case. Managing service quality 14: 317-330.
32. Athanasssopoulous A, Gounraris S, Sthaakopuoulos V (2001) Behavioral responses of customer satisfaction: An empirical study. European Journal of marketing 35: 687-707.
33. Zenithal VA, Parasuraman A, Malhotra A (2000) Marketing science institute and Dell star.
34. Carse HT (1999) The effect of information technology on banking services: Economic review. Federal Reserve bank of Richmond 77: 16-28.
35. Victoria W, Muhammad A (2009) Customer relationship management in banks with special reference to Bangladesh. Southwest review of international business research pp: 45-57.
36. Eddin A, Al-Zubi H (2011) E-banking functionality and outcomes of customer satisfaction: An empirical investigation in Jordan commercial banks. International Journal of marketing studies 3: 50-65.
37. Nupur JM (2010) E-banking and customer' satisfaction in Bangladesh: an analysis. International Review of Business Research Papers 6: 145-156.
38. Polatoglu VN, Ekin S (2010) An empirical investigation of the Turkish consumers' acceptance of internet banking services. International Journal of Bank Marketing 19: 156-165.
39. Joseph M, Stone G (2003) An empirical evaluation of bank customer perceptions of the impacts of technology on service delivery in the banking sector. International Journal of retail and distribution management 31: 190-202.
40. Zohra S, Kashif R (2011) Relationship between customer satisfaction and mobile banking adoption in Pakistan. International Journal of Trade, Economics and Finance 2: 537-544.
41. Doll WJ, Torkzadeh G (1988) The measurement of end-user computing satisfaction. MIS quarterly 12: 259-274.

42. Kumbhar VM (2012) Alternative banking channels and customer satisfaction in Satara City: An empirical study of public and private sector banks. International Journal of business and management tomorrow 1: 1-24.

43. Munusamy J, Run ECD, Chelliah S, Annamalah S (2012) Adoption of Retail Internet Banking: A Study of Demographic Factors 17: 1-14.

44. Paul S (2013) ATM: The New Horizon of E-Banking. Science, Technology and Arts Research Journal 2: 148-152.

45. Sampson E (2005) Technological developments and global banking innovation: Zenith Economic Quarterly.

46. Darvish H, Moayeri MR, Faradonbe MM, Naderifar AR (2013) A survey on relationship between customer satisfaction and electronic banking features: A case Study of Tejarat bank in Iran. Management Science Letters 3: 425-430.

47. Fekadu GW (2010) Electronic banking in Ethiopia-Practice, opportunities and challenges.

48. Sisay TA, Muvva VBR (2011) E-Business: Application of software and technology in selected Ethiopian Banks: Issues and challenges. International Journal of Computer Science Issues 8: 190.

49. Bultum AG (2012) Adoption of Electronic banking system in Ethiopian Banking industry: Barriers and driver.

50. Abbasi Z (2001) E-security issues in Pakistan.

51. Birutu (2012) A quarterly magazine of the National Bank of Ethiopia. 113: 10-20.

The Role of Accounting Reform in Deterring Corruption Practices in the Public Sector: A Case Study in Kurdistan Region

Ghaffoori A*

Department of Accounting, Essex Business School, UK

Abstract

There is an increasing focus on the subject of corruption around the world. The aim of this research is to investigate the impact of accounting reform on Kurdistan region with respect to corruption. The methodology used in this study is the qualitative interpretive method and the main tool for collecting data was the semi-structured interviews, through a case study on the Kurdistan region (Iraq). According to the literature and findings of this research, there is a relationship between the accounting system and corruption. Further, an efficient accounting system is regarded as one of the effective anti-corruption strategies. The Kurdistan region can increase the level of accountability and transparency in the public sector by reforming its current accounting processes, which will thus lead to the reduction in cases of corruption. Some essential changes have been suggested by the respondents to increase government accountability and transparency such as shifting from cash-basis to accrual-basis accounting, adopting international accounting standards, changing budget system from input-line to performance programme budget system, strengthening audit especially external auditors, updating the accounting curriculum and computerising the accounting system. These will improve the accounting system and thus aid in fighting corruption.

Keywords: Accounting; Corruption; Kurdistan region; Public sector

Introduction

Corruption is a very complicated and debatable phenomenon. Many definitions have been used to determine its meaning, while there is no one universally accepted definition [1]. However, corruption, in simple terms, means a person or an organisation who takes advantage of money or position, whether in the public sector or the private sector in order to achieve purely individual gains [2].

Corruption is a barrier that postpones the economic development of a country [3]. The World Bank indicated in its annual report, in 1997, that corruption is a serious threat that hinders the social and economic development, increases social inequality, and perpetuates poverty [4]. In addition, it impedes the enhancement of the quality of general services which are delivered by governments for the poor citizens and rural areas, especially in the developing countries. Its impacts are not only on the government institutions or private sector, but also on the society as a whole [5].

Spector states that in the developing countries, corruption is regarded as the most dangerous problem and has more negative impacts there than in the developed countries [6]. Sandholtz and Koetzle argue that corruption is a big challenge for developing countries [7]. Further, Koetzle argues that corruption has affected many aspects of life and created many economic, financial, educational, administrative, and social problems. Thus, fighting corruption in developing countries is regarded as the essential step towards economic development.

Corruption occurs in public and private sectors and has negative impacts on both these sectors. In the private sector, it reduces competition, weakens efficiency, and effectiveness, and increases the cost of businesses. In the public sector, it increases the general expenses, decreases the amount of taxation and thus, increases financial deficits and creates macroeconomic uncertainty [8]. Therefore, fighting corruption is not limited to only the government, but all parties that take part in this fight.

In this regard, one of the anti-corruption strategies suggested by the previous literature is the reformation of accounting systems. Malagueño et al. explain that corruption has a relationship with the accounting system. Any country can strive to reduce the level of corruption by strengthening its accounting and auditing systems [9].

According to Ouda, the accounting system in many developing countries is still traditional and unable to fight corruption. Therefore, this paper aims to study the impact of accounting reforms on corruption practices in the Kurdistan region of Iraq (which is the case study of this research) [10].

The research aim

As the accounting system in majority of developing countries is traditional and weak, including the Kurdistan region (case study), the study aims to investigate the role of accounting reforms in deterring corruption practices in the public sector in the Kurdistan region (more information about Kurdistan region is provided in chapter three).

The research question

With regard to the corruption practices, Kurdistan region, like many other developing countries, is suffering from a high level of corruption in its government structure. As for its financial and accounting system, there is a lack of proper accounting system. Thus, the main research question is "What is the role of accounting reform in deterring corruption practices in government sector in Kurdistan region?"

The important of the research

Through reviewing the literature on this subject, it can be concluded

***Corresponding author:** Arsalan Ghaffoori, Department of Accounting, Essex Business School, Wivenhoe Park, Colchester CO4 3SQ, UK
E-mail: aqmgha@essex.ac.uk

that there are a considerable number of studies about corruption and its negative impacts in developing countries. However, there is no particular case study on the Kurdistan region about corruption and the relationship with its accounting system. This research will be important, because it is regarded as the first study of the Kurdistan region about accounting system and corruption.

The research methodology

The method chosen for this research is the qualitative interpretive approach. It uses a case study (Kurdistan region). The tool for collecting data is semi-structured interview (research methodology chapter three).

Organization of the research

In order to achieve the research aim, this research has been divided into five chapters.

Chapter one deals with the introduction. It illustrates the background of the research, research aim, the research question, the methodology, and the research importance.

Chapter two is the literature review, which explains corruption and its main definitions, other topics such as corruption in developed and developing countries, corruption and its relationship with accounting system, accounting system in developing countries and finally formulated the research question.

Chapter three talks about the methodology. It illustrates the chosen qualitative method, interpretive paradigm, case study, and background information about the Kurdistan region, steps in case study, and the semi-structured interview process.

Fourth chapter is about data analysis and discussion. It includes the themes of interview process and discusses the findings.

Chapter five refers to the conclusion, limitations and ethical considerations.

Literature Review

Introduction

This chapter constructs the research question through reviewing relevant previous literature. It explains why accounting system is regarded one of the anti-corruption strategies. Relevant literatures have been reviewed in order to make establish a connection between different studies. The review focuses on the relationship between corruption and accounting system and the extent to which accounting reform is a necessary in preparing countries to fight corruption.

Background

Corruption is considered to be a big human concern. It is found in all civilisations and societies throughout history, regardless of the civilisation‘s size and level of prosperity [11]. Throughout history, each civilisation had contributed in developing corruption concepts. Further, factors such as cultural, ethical, and political, and management systems may have contributed to the occurrence and the increase of corruption [12].

Corruption is a global problem and has negative impacts on all countries around the world. There is no doubt that corruption is the most dangerous problem in the 21st century, particularly in the poor and developing countries [13]. Since the last decade of the 20th century, corruption has been considered a main player in the global agenda [14]. It has drawn the attention of many academic researchers around the world [15].

Definition of corruption

There is a necessity of having a clear understanding of corruption phenomenon. This section will discuss many definitions of corruption that have been developed by scholars in order to provide a clear understanding.

Lambsdorff argues that corruption is a very complex phenomenon that is not easy to define, due to its several types and forms [16]. Along the same lines, Rabl claims that there is no comprehensive definition of corruption [17]. However, there are some definitions that express the main features of corruption.

The common definition of corruption is the use of public office for private gain [13]. A similar definition was given by the Transparency Organisation in 2006, the abuse of entrusted power for private gain' [18]. According to these definitions, corruption is linked only to the public sector, even though, the fact is that corruption occurs in both public and private sectors. For example, a person may try to use his/her position in a private organisation for personal gain [7].

It is clear from the above definitions that corruption in any form is an illegal act; some of these forms are fraud, bribery, nepotism, extortion, speed money, graft, embezzlement, pilferage, falsification and manipulation of records, theft, kickbacks, and influence peddling. Corruption primarily happens in the public sector. It also happens in other areas of governance, such as the enterprise sector, political parties, and NGOs [19].

Categories of corruption

USAID classifies corruption into two categories: systemic and spontaneous [20]. Firstly, the systemic corruption is usually found in communities where corrupt practices are widespread and perennially. In these communities, corruption is common and a way of life; people use it in order to gain private interests. It seems that systemic corruption is widespread in developing countries, where the political governance system is weak. Secondly, spontaneous corruption often occurs in developed communities that control ethics in the public sector.

Forms of corruption

According to the argument of Deflem [21], there are two types of corruption: monetary and bureaucratic. With regard to the framework of this research, monetary corruption of the public sector will be studied. The monetary corruption includes many forms such as bribery, fraud, embezzlement, favouritism, and money laundering. The terms have been explained as follows:

Bribery is regarded as a common form of corruption [22]. It is an amount of money that is received by an official person, who has a post either in the public sector or in the private sector, when he/she fulfils a particular task for a particular person [23].

Fraud is described as something that is similar to financial injuries [24]. Fraud is usually regarded as an economic scandal that involves such terms as swindle and deceit. Fraud occurs when an official person, who is responsible to perform a particular task, performs these tasks illegally by manipulating the documents for his private gain [25].

Embezzlement may be regarded as a kind of theft [25]. It happens when a dishonest agent steals from his employer by abusing or misappropriating the assets of an organisation for private gain [25].

Further, Okafor adds another view point entrusted power for private gain" [18,26]. According to these definitions, corruption is linked only to the public sector, even though, the fact is that corruption occurs in both public and private sectors. For example, a person may try to use his/her position in a private organisation for personal gain [7].

Corruption in developed countries

Campos et al, explains that corruption is a global problem and does not directly relate to a particular country or region [13]. Corruption is without borders, that exists everywhere and creates various problems for governments, firms, businesses, people, and society in many countries, whether they are developed or developing. However, certainly, the level of corruption in developing countries is higher than in developed countries. In the light of this, Sandholtz and Koetzle state that corruption has a priority for discussion in agendas of international platforms such as the International Monetary Fund, World Trade Organization, and World Bank [7]. As a result, many suggestions are being proposed internationally for developing anti-corruption strategies and helping poor nations to fight corruption.

In relation to developed and industrialised countries, there are studies which indicate that the level of corruption recently has increased in developed countries. For instance, MacDonald and Majeed conducted a study about corruption in European countries [27]. According to the result, corruption has increased in many European countries. They state those three decades ago, the average level of corruption in European countries was 0.74 units. This level has increased to 2.12 units in 2007. They state that "this is an alarming figure and surely needs to be rapidly addressed. Further, they argued that corruption cases can be found even in countries known as corruption-free such as Finland, Sweden, and Denmark.

Another study that supports this argument indicates that about European countries [28]. The author states that, for many years corruption was seen as a problem only for poor countries, while economic crises in European countries strongly indicates that controlling corruption is difficult. For instance, in countries like Greece, Italy, Portugal, and Spain, economic situation has regressed rather than progressed. According to Special European Survey, 79% of the participants fully or partially agreed that corruption exists in their countries.

These studies reveal that there is no country without any instances of corruption. It rejects the idea of economists and development practitioners that corruption is a problem only for developing countries. However, it is important to acknowledge that in developing countries, the level of corruption is relatively high, where a systemic corruption exists, hence, calling for more efforts to fight corruption.

Corruption in developing countries

The economic and political situations in developing countries indicate that there are very small numbers of developing countries that have low levels of corruption cases [3]. Thus, corruption poses a significant challenge for the developing countries and is regarded as a serious threat. It has created many economic, financial, cultural, educational, management and social problems [7]. Shabbir and Anwar argue that in developing countries [29], if the level of corruption increases by 1%, it will lead to a decline in the gross domestic products by about 3%. In addition, Lambsdorff conducted a study and reached a similar result [16]. The result of the study shows that corruption affects investment, especially foreign investment, reduces the general domestic product (GDP), generates poor institutional quality, increases public expenditure, and reduces the income and tax collection, international capital flow, and international goods and aids.

Another important sector had been influenced by corruption is the education sector. A recent study conducted by Campos et al. illustrates that corruption affects the education process. The study collected data from 50 countries [13]. According to the study's findings, corruptors have taken advantage of the education budget because countries usually allocate high percentages of budget, about 30% yearly, for this sector. The education budget is not spending according to the requirement of the sector. Further, in regard to the teaching process in education centres, the scientific and logical rooting at the graduation of students has been disregarded, thus, yielding poor education outcomes. As stated by Chapman, corruption permeates the day-to-day transactions at the classroom, school, and district levels. The real damage to a society occurs when entire generations of youth are mis-educated by example to believe that personal success comes not through merit and hard work, but through favouritism, bribery, and fraud. Such lessons have the potential to undermine civil society well into the future [30].

According to the studies which have studied the impacts of corruption in developing countries, it is clear that corruption has brought many problems for these countries. Nonetheless, few arguments have been made regarding the positive impacts of corruption. For example, Bardhan argues that corruption affects positively the economy of a country and increases the effectiveness of the private sector and encourages trade [31].

Another argument about the positive impact of corruption has been made by Rock and Bonnet [32]. They claim that corruption in new industrialised countries such as East Asian countries has positive impacts on investments and has increased growth. For instance, Leff argues that in such an environment, bribery could help investors by providing an opportunity to attain government licenses [33]. It may allow businesses to avoid unnecessary and heavy delays. Further, corruption could increase the investments by lowering the risk of a volatile government. The government may intervene harmfully in an investor's project.

However, it seems that the positive impacts may be the case only for a short time, and at some stages, the growth trends will decrease due to corruption causing distractions in the socio economic system of a country. In other words, corruption will naively impact the citizens, especially the poor people and those who have no relationship with the political authority [1].

Thus, through the above discussion, it is clear that in the developing countries systemic corruption exists and therefore its impacts are higher than in the developed countries. Therefore, in developing countries fighting corruption becomes more difficult than in developed countries. They need to take into account many the political aspects, management and control system, and the ethical, social, and cultural aspects.

According to many studies, which have been conducted on the subject of corruption, this chapter aims to display the link between corruption and the country's accounting system. If, in a country, an efficient accounting system exists, the level of corruption could possibly be low.

Corruption and accounting system

Everett et al. conducted a study, examining the role of accounting in the global fight against corruption [34]. They state that accounting and auditing systems have an important role in any organisation. According to them, accounting is an information system that provides information about economic entities through financial statements and reports. These statements and reports are important for decision makers. Audit is a monitoring system, which provides neutral and professional opinions about the financial statements. Further, they state that, Accounting serves a dual role: Financial statements provide information about economic transactions, and the auditing profession serves as a monitoring mechanism to check on the accuracy of this information Accounting as an information system, and auditing as a monitoring or check on the accuracy of the accounting information system, provide an enormous potential for establishing accountability and detection of corrupt activities [34].

A similar argument is made by Malagueño et al. [9]. They conducted a study to discover the existence of a relationship between accounting and auditing and the level of corruption. The authors have collected data by a cross-country survey. They found out practical evidence that the level of corruption in a country enormously depends on its accounting and audit systems. According to the findings, financial reports with high transparency and disclosure show a lower level of corruption. Malagueño et al. argue that any country will be able to reduce the level of corruption by strengthening its accounting and audit systems [9].

They point out that stakeholders can assess the organisation's performance through accounting and audit reports; these reports allow them to make decisions in a relevant time. However, since a poor accounting and control system does not provide accurate financial reports they become less reliable for stakeholders while making decisions. In addition, poor accounting and auditing systems generate a situation that makes it easier for employees to work against accounting and auditing rules for fulfilling private gains. In this context, state this is an important discovery because if, as our research suggests, better accounting and audit systems are associated with less perceived corruption, then governments may be able to decrease corruption by improving accounting and audit standards thus improving their business climate, encouraging investment by both nationals and foreigners and increasing overall their productivity and GDP.

Another study has been conducted by Wu about corruption in corporate sector of Asian countries [35]. The author indicates that the accounting system is one important element of a management system and has a great role to detect cases of corruption, especially the bribery and fraud cases. In addition, he found out that many Asian countries still have a poor accounting and control system. He claims that the main factors that have led to the financial crisis in the Asian countries in 1997 were the low quality of accounting and auditing standards. He states that, as a result, some Asian countries have changed their accounting systems and adopted International Accounting Standards (IAS) and some other modern accounting techniques to avoid financial crisis in the future. Currently, one can see a considerable progress in relation to accounting and auditing aspects.

These studies reveal that accounting and audit systems are an important element in the organisational structure for all organisations whether in the public or private sector. They also show that there is a relationship between the accounting system and corruption practices. When good accounting and auditing systems exist, there is low level of corruption and vice versa. However, the question here, in relation to developing countries, is about the ability of accounting system to answer the requirements of new age and its potential to fight corruption.

Accounting system

Before illustrating the accounting system in developing countries, there is a need to understand to the role of accounting system in general. Accounting is an information system which is regarded as an essential part in an organisational structure. It provides financial information to the related parties, whether internal or external. Audit is a part of the accounting system which verifies the information provided by the accounting system. Accounting and auditing system together work to produce accurate, relevant, comparable, and transparent information. Thus, in this case, accounting system is considered to actively contribute in a country's economic development [36]. The accounting contribution was confirmed by the World Bank. The World Bank in 1997 emphasised the role of an accounting system in strengthening a country's economic development by stating that, —there is no doubt that weak accounting and auditing capabilities, as well as the high incidence of financial mismanagement in the public and private sectors are major constraints to sustainable economic development.

Traditionally, the role of an accounting system is merely to provide financial information about an organisations' performance for interested parties, in order to facilitate decision making. However, the role of an accounting system has evolved significantly, especially in the developed countries. It now ensures concepts of transparency and accountability, not only in public organisations, but also in the private organisations and in the wider scope of national economic development as well. In other words, it provides to citizens the financial and non-financial information about an organisations' performance, whether they are public or private. In addition, it has an active role in the socio-economic development by providing information about the general national income, general resources, social values, fairness, and environmental considerations [29].

Accounting change

Barth et al. argue that some factors have affect the accounting system [37]; these include increasing international trades, international flow capital and foreign investment, financial crisis and accounting scandals, information technology and globalization process. These factors have encouraged accounting federations and associations in some developed and industrial countries to invent and change the existing accounting system to improve it to deal with the new and competitive era. As a result, the international accounting and auditing standards have been issued.

The majority of countries, especially developed countries, made the essential changes in their accounting system and adopted these international standards. In the light of this, Mangualde state that [38], over the last 30 years, the public sector has passed through a wave of reforms worldwide, usually towards the adoption of business-like practices as a way to better manage the public resources. With respect to financial reporting, these reforms have as cornerstones the adoption of accrual-accounting (AA) in place of the traditional cash-basis accounting and the discussions towards the use of a set of international accounting standards (IAS) such as the International Public Sector Accounting Standards (IPSAS) or the International Financial Reporting Standards (IFRS).

For example, Ouda states that some developed countries such as New Zealand, UK, and Australia and a few countries in Asia such as Malaysia, Singapore, Thailand, and Philippines have made essential changes in the government sector [10]. This reform had positive impacts, which have increased productivity and efficiency in the public sector. Ouda gives an example of a situation in New Zealand. He argues that New Zealand was suffering from economic crises, when the government implemented a chain of economic reforms. One element of these reforms was the government sector reform aimed to overcome the economic and financial crises. The public sector schemes for reform were:

- Separating private sector operations from government operations.
- Strengthening the accountability and transparency in the government sector.
- Designing management performance system to appraise the public sector performance.
- Shifting from an input-based budget to line performance-based budgeting system.
- Shifting from cash based to accrual accounting.
- Strengthening both internal and external auditing systems.

Another example of the public sector reform in a Latin American country is of Brazil. Mangualde indicates that the main purpose of accounting reforms, in Brazil, was to obtain more accounting disclosure and transparency in the government sector [38]. The outcomes of accounting reform in Brazil were: provision of more reliable accounting information to stakeholders in the country, strengthened accountability and transparency in the corporate sector, encouraged management practices, and thus increased productivity and efficiency and better allocated resources in the general budget.

However, in many developing countries, accounting system is still traditional and unable to perform the role expected of it, as in developed countries. Therefore, it needs some essential changes.

Accounting system in developing countries

Briston indicates that in the past, accounting system in developing countries was essentially designed and imposed by the colonial countries in order to meet their needs, rather than being helping in meeting the requirements of the host country [39]. These systems are most unlikely to be completely suitable for the different economic situation. Currently, these systems are inappropriate even for the colonial countries themselves. Similarly, Piers et al. claim that in many developing countries accounting records are routinely designed and poorly managed. The citizens cannot access the general and financial information. The researchers point out some problems, for instance, delayed closing accounts, incomplete transactions, weak internal audit, poor management accounting, deficient and incorrect records, and non-auditable systems and non-computerised system.

Hopper et al. indicate that transparency and accountability are regarded as the essential requirements of good governance [40]. Transparency comes with accountability; this is necessary as citizens require access to general information in order to judge government performance [40]. However, Mimba et al. claim that in the developing countries, the public sector is usually characterised by low institutional ability, weak procedures and practices, lower levels of accountability, inadequate transparency, and limited access to information and high level of corruption [41]. Similarly, Svensson claims that most anti-corruption strategies depend on the strengthening accountability and transparency in the public sector. The main assumption is that better government system, regulations, and rules will increase transparency and thus will deter corruption practices. However, in many developing countries, regulation, management system, and financial institutions are weak and are often corrupt themselves. Therefore, it can be concluded that conventional systems and regulations are ineffective. Keeping this in mind, the testing and adoption of new systems and tools to enhance and increase accountability in the public sector should be at the frontline of research on corruption.

Another accounting problem in relation to developing countries is accounting staff. Pratap and Quintin argue that accounting staff and human resources are insufficient in many developing countries [42]. In addition, their accounting qualifications are not adequately sophisticated to deal with different financial situations. Therefore, developing countries should modify their accounting systems to meet their needs and to be suitable for contemporary institutions. In addition, they should design training programs to produce well-qualified accountants in order to be able to run and manage a new accounting system.

In this regard, The World Bank provides advice and suggestions for developing poor countries, fighting corruption, and modifying financial and management systems. In 1994 in its annual reports provided some suggestions about fighting corruption. It suggests that any country that desires to establish anti-corruption strategies should enhance its accounting system in the following ways:

- Adopting strong financial and management accounting system.
- Creating and developing their original professional accounting and audit standards.
- Implementing and supporting modern accounting standards such international accounting standards.

Another international organisation also plays a role in this regard, which is the United Nations Development Program (UNDP). In 2011, (UNDP) has proposed the development of countries through some reforms which are: management and accounting reforms that increase the independence of internal and external auditors and design computerised systems.

Chapter conclusion

To sum up, the literature review has illustrated three points: firstly, the corruption phenomenon in developing countries is regarded a serious problem which impedes their economic development. Secondly, a financial system has weaknesses especially in relation to accounting and auditing system, where there is no accountability and transparency in the public sector. Thirdly, there is the need for comprehensive change in the accounting and auditing system.

In light of this result, one can formulate the research question which is, "What is the role of accounting reform in deterring corruption practices in government sector in Kurdistan region?"

Methodology

Introduction

The methodology opted for this research is the qualitative interpretive approach. The philosophical aspects of qualitative research depend on the interpretive approach to the social world and on the description of the human beings experiences [43]. Qualitative approach is a method for investigating and understanding a social phenomenon. As it is defined by [44], it is a form of social inquiry that focuses on the way people interpret and make sense of their experiences and the world in which they live. Further, researchers use qualitative approaches to explore the behaviours, perspectives, feelings, and experiences of people and what lies at the core of their lives [44]. The steps of qualitative research include determining the research question, collecting and analysing data, structuring general themes, interpreting the data and writing the results [45].

The scientific research process depends upon the philosophical lenses through which a researcher sees the world. These lenses make sense of the world, and about what is going on. Philosophical lenses help a researcher to work out the research questions he/she needs to ask, and what he/she might need to do to be able to get the answers to the research questions [46].

Social research and philosophical viewpoints

Social research is a process of seeking the truth. It includes gathering, analysing, interpreting, and reporting information. Therefore, the research process aims to predict and describe a phenomenon that has taken place in the surrounding environment of an organisation. Eventually, it is a methodical inquiry that provides information and knowledge to guide decision-makers [47].

Therefore, a researcher looking for truth must follow a particular philosophical approach which contains significant and meaningful assumptions about epistemology (theory of knowledge) and ontology (theory or the nature of being) [48]. These epistemological and ontological assumptions will clearly underpin the procedures and strategies of the research process. Before discussing the philosophical issues, it is useful to understand epistemology and ontology. Epistemology relates to the question of what is or should be considered knowledge. The essential point here is that social sciences can be investigated using the same method of the natural sciences. Ontology relates to the nature of reality. Through these assumptions researchers view the world.

Interpretive paradigm

Ryan et al. claims that the essential difference point for interpretive research paradigm is the assumption that social phenomena, including management and accounting, is not natural phenomena, but is socially constructed. These kinds of research follow an interpretive epistemological assumption which is predicated upon the belief that there are differences between people and the things of the natural sciences and, therefore, require the social researcher to recognise the subjective and social meaning of social phenomena. The interpretive paradigm promoters claim that it is necessary to understand the differences between human thoughts in our world as social researchers [49]. The ontology of the positivism paradigm assumes that reality is objective and exterior of human beings. However, the ontology of interpretive paradigm assumes that reality is socially constructed and its meanings are given by people [50].

Collis et al. explains that the interpretive paradigm accentuates the subjective aspects of social motion by focusing on the meaning of social phenomena, rather than the measurement. The interpretive paradigm is unlike the positivist paradigm that does not focus on the generalisation of findings. But, the findings can be approachable and have a broad reflection, particularly in cases where there are enough similarities to the primary research. Likewise, the ontology of this research is subjectivism (interpretivism) which emphasises that social phenomena and their meanings are being investigated by social actors [51]. Bryman and Bell indicate that this means that social phenomena are not only constructed through social interplay, but that they are in a continual case of revision.

The epistemological position of this research is interpretive and the ontological position is subjective, because the researcher believes that the topic of the research cannot be investigated by positivism (objectivism) paradigm. The topic cannot be recognised just by senses and stay at a distance, but by it needs to interplay with people who live and work in the real context of the phenomenon. Furthermore, the interpretive paradigm seems more appropriate in that the research is more qualitative, rather than quantitative research that deals with statistical data to get the answers of the research questions.

However, the main drawback of interpretive research is that firstly, the findings cannot be generalised because it gives way to subjectivity during collecting, analysing and interpreting.

Secondly, the outcomes from interview process can be interpreted from different perspectives by another researcher. Thirdly, because the number of respondents is small, a general theory cannot be built for a particular case. Fourthly, the questions are designed by the researcher that may lead to bias because he/she has his/her own perceptions and views about the subject. Finally, the results rely on the extent to which the respondents are honest with their answers [52].

The reason for selecting qualitative approach for this research study is: this research focuses on one case study, which is about the Kurdistan region and involves an in-depth investigation about the relationship between corruption and the region's accounting system. Therefore, interpretive approach will aid in the research, where the aim is to understand the enablers of corruption within the public sector.

Case study

There are different methods for gathering data for a research, and this considerably relies on the subject of the research study [45]. A case study, in this context, has been selected as the method for collecting data. The case study research is an intensive study about a single organisation, group, society or a country. Case study research is a methodical way to investigate a particular event or a particular phenomenon in its real and social context [53]. As it is defined by Yin in 1994, an empirical inquiry that investigates a contemporary phenomenon within its real-life context, especially when the boundaries between phenomenon and context are not clearly evident [54].

Robson looks at the case study as a strategy for scientific research to collect empirical data regarding a particular phenomenon [55]. In this context, he defines case study as —a strategy for doing research which involves an empirical investigation of a particular contemporary phenomenon within its real life context using multiple source of evidence.

A case study is a good tool for a researcher who would like to obtain information about the context of the research and its procedures [56]. The reason for adopting a case study is the flexibility and exploratory of the case study [55]. Yin claims that to answer questions such as how, why, and what of the result, a case study is a relevant tool to get these answers [54]. In addition, Easterby-Smith et al., have a similar argument they argue that the case study method is more interested in providing a clear picture of a particular phenomenon and behaviour [50].

Strengths and weaknesses of case studies

The key features of performing a case study are flexibility in design, holistic in view (it allows one to gather different perspectives about the same phenomenon or case at the same period of time), dynamic process, and more reflexivity of the researcher regarding the impact of the research process [56]. Furthermore, an individual case study in qualitative research provides the researcher an opportunity to examine, investigate, and deeply analyse a phenomenon under study when there is a lack of proper literature review [49].

However, case studies pose some of the following disadvantages:

1- The difficulty for the researcher to decide the scope of the case study.

2- The difficulty for the researcher to consider him/herself to be a neutral observer and the difficulty of reliability and validity of evidence.

3- The difficult for the researchers in accessing information that may be confidential to the organisations, which are under study [57].

Of the above, the last point is the most common disadvantage, especially in the developing countries because, where the majority of organisations either public or private, neither desire to share information nor let employees reveal information. The researcher of this study has experienced this difficulty during the semi-structured interview process.

Steps in a case study

Any researcher in order to conduct a case study research should follow the following steps [58].

Preparation: The researcher must survey the available theories which could be possibly applicable to the case study in question. This survey of previous theories will determine the path for the researcher to approach the case study.

Collecting evidence: The preliminary survey of theories will give indication of some sort of evidence which should be reviewed for the case study. Such evidence contains documentation, interviews, researcher observations and participant observations.

Assessing evidence: During the collection of evidence the researcher should confirm the reliability and validity of evidence. Reliability means the extent to which the evidence is independent. Validity means the extent to which the data is true.

Identifying and explaining themes: In a case study, different patterns and themes often appear. It is important for the researcher to link and connect the different themes and issues with the existing literature. In this regard, some themes and patterns will need further investigation, expansion of the model, collection of new evidence, and re-interpretation of the findings in order to harmonise the different themes. More importantly, in any single case study, the researcher should select the study's scope and limitations at the beginning of the research process.

Theory elaboration: If conflicts emerge among the themes and existing theories, it is important for the researcher to gather new evidence in order to solve these conflicts. In this regard, theories can be expanded to meet the requirements of the new situations.

The last step of a case study is writing a report about the main findings of the research study. This step will make the case study and its explanations clear and understandable to the readers. This not only includes writing down the findings of the research, but also the provision of sufficient evidence to persuade the readers that the researcher has a proper understanding about different aspects of the case study [59].

The researcher, adhering to the above steps, has gathered reliable and valid findings.

Methods and types of a case study

The researcher can use either the quantitative or qualitative methods or both in a single case study [46]. In addition, Scapens states that there are many types of case studies such as descriptive, illustrative, experimental, and exploratory. This research follows the explanatory qualitative case study. Explanatory case studies focus on particular cases in order to explain reasons for a particular practice in such cases [58].

This research is an explanatory case study of Kurdistan region and uses qualitative method to investigate the research question. Scapens argues that case study is very common in management, business, and accounting research since the focus is usually on an organisation or a sector [58].

There are many methods in a case study research to collect data such as textual analysis, observation, focus groups, semi-structured interviews and triangulation [59]. Since the research question focuses on the explanatory characteristic, how can reforms in the accounting system in Kurdistan region affect the corruption cases? the method of semi-structured interview was found to be a suitable tool to gather the required data.

The interview, in general, is regarded as one of the most effective methods for collecting qualitative data and has been broadly adopted in qualitative research. Usually, there are three different types of interview processes: structured, unstructured, and semi-structured. The last type is mostly preferred as it provides a free atmosphere for the interviewees.

The semi-structured interview has enabled the researcher to talk openly and freely with the respondents, unlike the structured interview, wherein the respondents cannot answer broadly in a structured interview. However, in the case of the respondents, semi-structured interviews may make them feel more convenient as they are given the opportunity to demonstrate and clarify their answers in long answers rather than in short answers [60].

The semi-structured interview is widely popular with researchers, because itis more flexible than other types of interview methods and in addition it gives scope for the respondents to reveal important facets of human behaviour. It is regarded as a powerful means of collecting data [61].

Furthermore, Schensul et al. indicate that the effectiveness of an interview could be maintained by considering the following points [62]:

(1) The story of the interviewee should be followed.

(2) The relationship should be maintained; and

(3) The interviewer‘s bias should be avoided.

Background information about Kurdistan region

Kurdistan region is a federal part of Iraq. It is located in the north of the country, borders Iran to the east, Syria to the west, and Turkey to the north. The area of this region is more than 80,000 square kilometres and its population is estimated to be more than 5.5 million. The Kurd people in Kurdistan region consist of about 95% and the remaining 5% comprise the Turkmen, Assyrians, and Armenians. The formal language of the region is Kurdish (the formal webpage of Kurdistan Regional Government (www.krg.org).

The regional capital city of Kurdistan region is Erbil. The Kurdistan region geographically includes four main big cities, which are Erbil (the capital city), Sulaymaniyah, Duhok, and Kirkuk city (the richest oil city in the world). However, the last city (Kirkuk) is characterised by disputes between the central government of Iraq and the Kurdistan regional government; therefore, it is still politically governed by central government of Baghdad [63].

The Kurdish people have rebelled against the Saddam Hussein regime in 1991 after the first Gulf War. The first government, which is the Kurdistan Regional Government (KRG), was founded in July 1992 by the approval of Kurdistan Parliament after the first democratic election in May 1992 [64].

Kurdistan region has been constitutionally recognised by the Iraqi central government since 2003, after the Second Gulf War, when the Saddam Hussein regime was overthrown by the U.S army. Nowadays, the Kurdistan region has constitutional and official institutions, such as the presidency institution, parliament, government, judicial authority, and the private military forces that are known as Peshmerga [65]. More importantly, Kurdistan region is trying to become an independent state.

Currently, the Kurdistan Region has made significant improvement towards achieving a political and economic stability by practicing principles of democracy and hard work. Thus, it has become a prosperous and peaceful place among the other violent and unstable parts of Iraq [66]. However, Kurdistan region like many other parts of Iraq and other developing countries suffer from rampant corruption.

Despite the Kurdistan region having made significant progress with regard to the political and economic aspects (www.krg.org), there are many other areas that are still following traditional and out of date methods such as its financial and accounting system, banking and insurance system, and information technology. These areas suffer from real weaknesses that need reforms or essential changes in order to be able to deal with the current situations of their society.

Interview process

Initially, a preliminary field conversation was conducted through the formal interview. This early conversation was considered very useful to facilitate answers to the research question. The process of research includes elaborating the research question, collecting data, analysing the data, building general themes and making interpretations.

Selecting respondents

This research focuses on aspects of reform in government accounting and general budget, and their anticipated impacts on corruption practices. Therefore, it needs a detailed analysis and examination of the themes by the respondents who have a better understanding of the research topic.

The respondents were recruited from the Kurdistan government to allow the generation of valid and reliable data. The respondents have been recruited and interviewed from different government entities and organisations; these respondents include auditors, accountants, lectures from universities and other education institutions.

The researcher has contacted the interviewees through emails and social media platforms such Facebook. During this, many managers, accountants, auditors, academics, employees and other specialists have been contacted. A total of 10 semi-structured interviews through Skype were performed.

Interview guide

As a foundation for conducting these interviews, a short background about the research topic was given to respondents by emails. These explanations served as a guide to the interviews. The interview guide involved background of the research topic and questions related to the topic.

For coherence, the set of respondents in different institutions were asked identical questions. This helped the researcher to reduce the bias that may occur, especially if the researcher had interviewed only one category of respondents. In addition, this helped the researcher to collect information that could not have been acquired from only one category of respondents.

The amount of time spent for each interview was about 60 minutes. The semi-structured interviews were recorded and transcribed. All interview conversations have been performed in the Kurdish language. The researcher has tried to guide the interviewees towards the related subjects and to probe new issues emerging during the discussion. A short summary after each interview was written and reviewed. The issues of the subject which required additional investigation and discussion were prepared and added to the next interview guide.

Before the interview process began, respondents were asked to sign a consent form, but the researcher realised that this was very difficult for them. At the beginning of the interview process, the researcher introduced himself and explained a short background of the research topic and its main aim. The respondents were asked to acknowledge their approval orally.

Finally, the interview process was performed in the Kurdish language and translated to the English language. After transcribing interviews, to get general idea, a broad reading was done. New and important issues that required further explanation were highlighted.

The data were coded and revised systematically. Finally, the data were analysed and assessed manually.

Interview questions

The type of questions used in the interview was open-ended. The semi-structured interview was adopted for two reasons: firstly, there was a set of themes about accounting and corruption that required intensive investigation. Secondly, the questions linked to these themes could not be answered in closed-end questions or yes‘ and no‘ questions. The open-ended questions allow the interviewees to reveal their opinions smoothly and freely.

The interview consisted of three main open-ended questions, in addition to some other probing questions to support and promote the main questions.

Question 1: What are the common forms of corruption practices in the public sector in the Kurdistan region? Or in other words the opportunities for practicing corruption in the public sector.

Question 2: What are the main gaps and problems in the government accounting system in the Kurdistan region?

Question 3: In your opinion, what are the main aspects of accounting system that need essential changes in order to become more transparent and accountable and thus can be used as an anti-corruption strategy?

Chapter conclusion

In this chapter, the methodology of the research was discussed in general. Also, different methodology aspects were included such as the definitions of qualitative method, philosophical approaches in social research, information about the case study, and a background about Kurdistan region; in addition, semi-structured interviews and some other information about the interview process and the interview questions have been highlighted in this section.

Findings and Discussion

Introduction

Saunders et al. argue that in qualitative research, there is a difficulty in finding a logical path to approach the collected data and analysis as it provides broad guidelines [49]. In order to overcome this difficulty, Saunders et al. suggest summarising, classifying, and structuring are the main steps of analysing data of the qualitative research. For this reason, the data have been summarised by reducing long statements into short statements. The results of the interviews have been categorised and themes have been developed. These themes have been examined keeping in mind the literature review and filling the gaps between the existing literature and the present study.

First theme: Forms of corruption in the Kurdistan region

In Kurdistan region, according to the answers of all interviewees, corruption is quite common and obvious. It is a widespread phenomenon in the entire government structure. The interviewees stated that bribery, fraud, abuse of public position and accounts manipulation, tax and customs evasion are the common forms of corruption in this region.

There are some areas in the public sector which are considered to be the most corrupt.

Below is the brief discussion of each of them:

1. Procurement, contracts, and government tenders: Essentially, these three areas have a strong relationship with money and thus are subject to corruption. Government employees and concerned parties exploit the weak systems and legal gaps and the lack of appropriate procedures and legal controls [67]. In this case, corrupt practitioners, in some procurement commissions, usually find suitable opportunities to gain private advantages by the conclusion of fictitious government contracts and tenders. In Kurdistan region, there is no appropriate system, especially an accounting system to deal with the prevention of each and every one of these important cases. The interviewees have illustrated that in the majority of corruption cases accountants and other employees function as intermediaries and brokers of corruption. The most common type of corruption in Kurdistan region is the procurement process. The employee who is responsible to purchase goods receives a bribe. The interviewee (R3) stated that: "This form of corruption is a frequent case in the general sector. For instance, the purchase commissions manipulate items in terms of quality, quantity, and price. According to my practical knowledge, most cases which I have reviewed have no adequate control in public organisations to review the purchase process. Further, import of construction materials is one of the situations where corruption cases occur frequently, since the price of construction items is difficult to investigate."

2. General resources collection: Resources, here, refer to different government taxes, customs, and other government resources. In these cases, money is also involved. Through the exploitation of these positions, the discounts and benefits are granted illegally in exchange for bribes and special favours. These areas have significantly reduced the national resources. For instance, in Kurdistan region, there are more than 10 international border crossing customs [68]; for e.g., the annual revenue of International Ibrahim Khalil crossing which is located between Kurdistan region and Turkey is about 350 million US dollars. However, only little amount returns to the general government treasury.

3. Granting of approvals, licenses and permits: This is another area that attracts corruption in the public sector. In Kurdistan, regional private companies, investors, and business owners usually pay bribes for approvals for starting a business. Government officials do grant approvals only after receiving the kickbacks of the applicant.

4. Bureaucratic corruption is widespread in Kurdistan region. There is a survey that shows 3.7% of citizens have reported paying bribes in Kurdistan [69].

5. Misuse of government resources: This includes the use of resources and government positions for fulfilling private gains. In these cases, an employee tries to obtain financial benefits from the use of government cars for private purposes of the employee or relatives such as brother, cousin, and family. Usage of mechanisms, equipment, buildings, and public facilities by employees for purposes different than those are allowed is also a form of corruption.

6 Exploitation of public office: People who are in a high position in Kurdistan government exploit their positions for financial gains. They spend most of their time searching for ways and means to enable them to increase the size of their wealth at the expense of the general interest. They also try to legitimise their illegal behaviours by exploiting the weakness of general system. For instance, the interviewee (R2) stated that: "While setting a proposal for a certain project, they exaggerate the cost of the project, for e.g. if the real cost of the project (A) 1 million US dollars, they inform government that the project needs 1.5 million dollars. On the other hand, while implementing the project they try to purchase materials of low quality with low price."

7. Smuggling funds: Some government officials in the Kurdistan region smuggle money which are obtained illegally. They deposit this in banks and capital markets in foreign countries. Others participating in money laundering buy properties outside of Kurdistan region. An interviewee (R9) stated that: "Many managers and employees who have high positions such as those working in tax authorities and customs own houses in Turkey and Dubai."

8. Tax and customs evasion: Many firms, businessmen, and investors from the private sector pay bribes to government officials in order to avail tax reductions or exemptions for a long time, or ease customs duties or be exempted or excluded by manipulating laws and procedures. Further, some traders pay bribes in order to import goods of low quality and thus, ease customs duties.

Determining the various forms of corruption is a difficult task. The points mentioned above do not necessarily limit the manifestations of corruption. The forms of corruption in Kurdistan region are manifold making it difficult for the researcher to discuss out all of them.

Second theme: Current accounting system in the Kurdistan region

The second theme is about the current government accounting system in Kurdistan region, which is based on the cash-basis system, where the majority of accounting procedures are processed manually.

Cash-basis system: The cash-basis system is the foundation for Kurdistan region's accounting. According to the cash-basis principles, transactions are recognised and recorded only when cash is paid or received. This means the revenues, expenditures, assets, and liabilities are only recognised when cash is received or paid [70]. As a result, the books of accounts are unable to show the real financial situation. The following are some shortages of the cash-basis system.

Firstly, the cash-basis system is unable to show real assets and liabilities accounts. It is unable to provide the government with adequate information about the total assets and liabilities in a given year, due to which some money is not paid or received on time (IFAC 97). Under cash-basis, a liability or asset is recorded only when a monetary transaction related to these occurs. As a result, a large amount of assets and liabilities are not revealed in the financial statements when appraising government's financial position and performance [71]. Furthermore, the accrued expenditures are also not recognised at the end of the year. Therefore, it can be seen how the cash-basis system misleads the financial situation of the government [72].

Secondly, earned revenues are not revealed under the cash-basis system. According to this system, the revenue is recognised in the financial reports when cash is received. In addition, the cash basis does not differentiate between current receipts and capital receipts [10].

Thirdly, under cash-basis accounting, information about total costs of goods and services is not reported until the cash is paid during the financial year. This indicates that the cash payments do not indicate general costs of the organisation during the period [10].

Lastly, the general value of inventory consumed during the period is not disclosed by the cash-basis system. As a result, the cash system is unable to adjust and measure real inventory accurately [70]. As the interviewee (R4) said: "From my point of view, cash-basis opens the doors for corruptors to achieve their private gains. So, as a consequence of applying the cash system, a large amount of the state's liabilities, revenues, costs, and expenses are not recorded in financial reports and are not paid attention to, during the appraisal of the government's financial situation and outcomes, or selecting expected revenue demands. In addition, the accrued expenditures of the government are similarly not recognised at the end of the fiscal year."

To sum up, cash-basis is ineffective in showing the real fiscal and economic position of governmental organisations. As a result, the government is unable to show appropriate transparency and accountability about its operations and activities. As discussed above, some of the shortages of the government accounting system are likely to be related to this very ineffective system. However, there are some other problems that have connection with accounting structure in general. The interviewee (R2) said that: "There is a chaos in the accounting aspects in Kurdistan region, where there is no uniform national accounting to be followed by all entities whether in public or in private sector."

The interviewees stated that different government institutions have different accounting systems. The harmonisation and coordination do not exist. This definitely leads to a case of uncertainty and discrepancy as far as the procedures and practice of accounting system are concerned. Some of the discrepancies arise due to the following factors:

- Government accounting is applied by the government sector.
- The Uniform Accounting System is applied by industrial and commercial sectors.
- Accounting system for investment activity is according to the investment plans of the Ministry of Plan.
- Accounting systems applied in banks and insurance companies.
- Different accounting systems in the private sector.

Also, in the Kurdistan region, there is a lack of accounting legislation. The accounting legislation is an important element to organise the accounting aspects. The interviewee (R7) said: "In the Kurdistan region thousands of national and foreign companies are working in different sectors and industries. Each company follows a particular accounting system and procedures, especially the foreign companies. These companies have contact with the government of Kurdistan in relation to taxes, exemptions, and fines. In this case, there is an opportunity for government officials to manipulate financial statements for those companies in regard to paying taxes, fines or granting licenses. Because there is no uniform accounting legislation about those aspects."

It is natural that these systems differ in terms of registering, recording, bookkeeping, accounting principles and rules, preparing financial statements and financial disclosure which will overall lead to different results. To sum up, in Kurdistan region, the government accounting system is based on the cash system. In addition, the government accounting system does not provide the necessary information about government activities and performance. There is no adequate transparency and accountability; citizens do not have opportunity to get information about government's activities. As a result, it can be concluded that the present accounting system in Kurdistan region suffers from the following flaws:

- It is unable to provide comprehensive financial statements and reports in a relevant time.
- It does not adhere to the international accounting principles.
- It is unable to provide appropriate information for general budget purposes.
- It is unable to provide information for financial analysis purposes.

Finally, in the Kurdistan region, some accounting problems are related to accounting staffs.

The next theme will illustrate this problem.

Third theme: Staff qualifications and accounting education

An accounting system has six main components: principles and procedures, data, software, information technology, internal control, and human resource. The human resource part (accountants and who runs the system) is the main input for an accounting system [73].

In regard to the situation of Kurdistan region, the government accounting is managed by less capable and ineligible accountants and auditors. Referring to the Kurdistan situation, it was observed that the majority of government accountants and auditors do not have competent accounting knowledge and information. In this context the interviewee (R3) stated: "In Kurdistan region managers generally are less trained. Thus, they choose low accounting systems because they do not have proper knowledge about new accounting tools and procedures. For instance, in the public manufacturing sector, traditional cost system (job system) is still in use. Overhead costs are usually allocated according to job system. This opens the door for employees to manipulate the transaction because it is not accurate system."

Further, some accountants and auditors in the public sector basically do not have accounting certificates. As is stated by the interviewee (R10): "If you look to some government organisations in different ministries, you can see many employees in the accounting departments do not have accounting certification. For example, the general manager of the Regional Central Bank does not have accounting certification."

This lack of qualified staff is regarding the critical problem in the public sector in Kurdistan region. This includes the lack of qualified clerks, accountants, and auditors. This shortage may relate to the fact that there is no proper accounting education in universities and institutions. In the universities, old accounting curriculum is still in use and not updated. About this problem the interviewee (R5) said: "In 2007, in my final year of bachelor's degree, I had one module, which was Auditing, the book for this module was published in 1970."

In addition, in this region, many lecturers and faculty staffs are also not knowledgeable about contemporary accounting issues. Finally, the universities and higher education institutions in the Kurdistan region are not in a position to offer proper accounting education that meets the requirements of the new contemporary and market economy. Teachers and faculty staff who are teaching accounting do not have the ability to teach new accounting methods and standards. The interview (R7) stated: "From my practical experience, in Kurdistan region new graduation of accountants, they do not have sufficient knowledge about accounting issues. This tells us that universities and other educational institutions in our region do not provide suitable accounting education that meets the requirements of contemporary challenges."

Fourth theme: The role of auditors

Accountants should participate in efforts to reduce corruption as they hold sensitive positions in the management structure [74]. Besides accountants, auditors are also essential in deterring fraud and corruption practices. Internal auditors, in particular, have a wide attention and understanding of events which are happening during the financial year [75]. Auditors are regarded as the eyes and ears of management and they can deliver a vital role in the anti-corruption strategies. Correspondingly, external auditors encourage managers, employees, and accountants to stay away from manipulative transactions and falsifying financial statements. Both internal and external auditors can contribute to improving regulations of an organisation. As is stated by Virginia et al. [76], Traditionally, the role of external auditors has been perceived as the most important factor in detecting and preventing financial statement fraud. In recent years, however, the entire corporate governance system (board of directors, audit committee, top management team, internal auditors, external auditors, and governing bodies) is responsible for ensuring the integrity, transparency, and quality of financial statements.

However, the situation in Kurdistan region is different. Many accountants and auditors are involved in corruption cases instead to preventing it. On the one hand, as stated in the previous theme, accountants and auditors are generally not qualified to practice accountancy. On the other hand, in any profession there are some ethical standards and considerations that should be taken into account by the practitioners of these professions. However, as stated by the interviewee (R4): "Through reviewing many big corruption cases, it is clear that there is an agreement between who work in accounting departments particularly auditors and private sector to legitimise the illegal acts e.g. paying bribe to an external auditor to hide real profit to be used to tax evasion."

Fifth theme: General budget system

The general budget is the process to determine general resources and expenditures for the subsequent period normally for a year, based on previous data and facts according to scientific principles. Initially a budget process is included four stages; formulation, setting, implementation and control [77].

In the Kurdistan region, the general budget process is regarded a suitable sphere for practicing corruption. All respondents have agreed that setting and implementing of budget process have essential gaps. For instance, setting the budget is not based upon any scientific strategies, as for the majority of government projects, the essential costs are randomly determined and exaggerated. For instance, the interviewee (3) stated that: "There was a project, which was (the establishment of a big general hospital), in Sulaymaniyah city, its cost was 100 million dollars. Through the audit process we realised that the money has allocated for this project more than five times."

Further, people do not have enough information about the sources of government income. There is no transparency about the allocation of general resources in the budget and the government expenditures. The process of implementing the budget also does not follow the instructions. There is no adequate control to observe the stages. Moreover, the general budget system does not adapt to the international standards. There are some serious delays in setting and executing the budget. The budget delay became a normal matter in this region. For example the interviewee (R8) said: Maybe every year the process of preparing and approving the general budget has been postponed, e.g. the general budget for 2013 was approved in the middle of July 2014. This, in my opinion, opens a door for practicing corruption because spending general expenditures is not based on new budget instructions as well as collecting government resources such as taxes and customs."

Sixth theme: Forms of accounting reform in Kurdistan region

The last question of the interview process was in your opinion what are the essential forms of accounting reform process in Kurdistan region? The interviewees were referred to various forms of reform. The main forms were summarised as follows.

Shifting from cash-basis to accrual-basis: There is another kind of accounting, which is the accrual-basis. Producing financial statements under accrual-basis is more transparent and includes all the financial events which have happened during a specific period [78]. Further, Hepworth indicates that the accrual-basis system provides more transparent information and is more reliable than cash-basis. Accrual-basis also recognises revenues and expenses, apart from the cash receipts and payments [79].

In this regard, Torres states that accrual-basis accounting is a powerful weapon to combat fraud and corruption in government sector [80]. Further, Torres adds: accrual-based fiscal indicators provide better information about the sustainability of fiscal policies, provide a stronger basis for government accountability and a better measure of the effects of government policies [they also] provide better measures of organizational efficiency and effectiveness, and reduce opportunities for fraud and corruption [80].

Therefore, in fighting corruption, accrual-basis is more relevant than the cash-basis method. This is so because financial statements and reports based on accrual-basis provide accurate information about:

- How a government funds its activities and to what extent meets its cash requirements.
- How it allows users to evaluate a government performance and its abilities to meet its commitments and liabilities.

- Government financial situation and its commitments and liabilities.
- Government revenues and their sources and how these resources are allocated in general budget.
- The financial position of the government and the changes in it during a given year.
- Information for national economic planning and GDP [81].

Thus, according to the answers of the interviewees, switching to the accrual-basis accounting systems is necessary as the traditional cash-basis is now regarded to be outdated and no longer adequate, especially because it is unable to show the correct financial position, planning, and control in public sector organisations. Therefore, the first priority of the government of Kurdistan region is shifting from cash-basis to accrual-basis in order to be able to fight against corruption.

Adopting the International Accounting Standards (IAS): The IASs are a set of international standards that were invented by international organisations and federations of accounting. The main aim of IASs is providing international harmonisation and coordination in relation to accounting issues. Further, financial statements under IAS have comparability, accuracy, reliability, and validity [82].

Adopting IASs has possibly many benefits; for example, it leads to the national and international coordination of a country. It encourages values such as accountability, responsibility, transparency, and fairness [37]. These values are essential for the enhancement of the operations within the public sector. In regard to corruption issues, it will enable a country to fight corruption better due to these accounting international efforts [83]. Therefore, the interviewees suggested, the Kurdistan government create national accounting standards, while taking into account the cultural and social considerations, all the while keeping in line with IASs.

Budget reform: An accounting system has a direct relationship with the general budget of a country [84]. Therefore, another aspect of reform is the general budget reform. Audio (2013) argues that the lack of a proper accounting system could possibly undermine the role of the budget. The budget system is linked to the accounting system. Therefore, the budget should depend on the basis of accounting used; thus, budget reform makes accounting reform unavoidable. In this regard, Kudo in 2010 states that [85], public reform policies that include restructuring of government institutions and public organizations, modernization of budgeting processes, rationalization of financial policy and its implementation, change of human resource management, renewal of public management and public service delivery, review of public/private partnership, and use of Information and Communication Technology (ICT') to improve the managerial process as well as to communicate better with the citizens.

The government of Kurdistan can overcome the shortcomings of the traditional budget, which is the line-item budget, by shifting to the program-performance budget. This new budget can improve the allocation process and provide a basis for choosing between the attainable alternatives. The program-performance budget, organises the link between the inputs and the outputs and it tries to use the resources efficiently and effectively in order to achieve the target objectives. In short, it focuses on government expenditures and their outcomes and provides information that can be used to appraise general budget outcomes. Similarly, Ouda argues that applying the program-performance budget can [10]:

- Limit the general expenditures to the items allocated in the general budget.
- Make the implementation of budget easier and more transparent, accountable, and manageable; and
- Make general budget flexible and adaptable to all-economic situations and conditions.

Accounting education: The outcomes of this situation are the shortage of professional accountants in the government sector. There is the need to add contemporary accounting curriculum to universities and institutions in order to provide student competencies and skills that will help them to deal with illegal behaviours and corruption cases. The main challenge is the lack of qualified accounting staffs who are able to understand these new requirements and thus be able to run the new accounting system. For example, one part of accounting reform will include adopting the international accounting standards. It is difficult for accountants and auditors to follow these standards without previous information and understanding.

Therefore, this situation calls for a proper accounting education in the Kurdistan region. Thus, in order to overcome this problem, Kurdistan government is required to renew and develop the accounting curriculum in universities and introduce contemporary and necessary subjects related to accounting issues.

Strengthening the auditing system through the Supreme Audit Board (SAB): SAB has the authority to audit and control all organisations, whether public or private. It is regarded as safety valve, which makes sure that organisations follow the necessary legislations and rules in their accounting and auditing processes. In many countries, SAB has the absolute authority [86]. However, in Kurdistan region SAB fails to perform its real role and is not independent. Therefore, SAB is required to be powerful and authorised entirely. SAB can also take action to prevent and minimise corruption. As the interview (R2) stated that: "The Kurdistan government should reinforce laws that should guarantee SAB's independence by reinforcing laws, allow publishing a wide range of its reports, give them authority entirely to check the different level of public sector organisations at any time, and implement its recommendations. Further, SAB should be responsible for the recruit, hire, firing its staff."

The government of Kurdistan should grant SAB an adequate power to access the records of all public organisations in a timely manner, have authority to question and interview managers and their employees at any time, and they show complete cooperation with the SAB staff. In addition, the new regulations should provide punishments for those who do not comply with the requirements and regulations or do not provide necessary information for the SAB staffs.

Information technology: The information technology has an impact in many fields, accounting system being one of the fields which was significantly affected by the information technology [87]. In addition, currently, accounting processes mainly depend on computer programmes particularly in the developed countries.

As stated in the second theme, the traditional accounting system is based on manual work, therefore, the Kurdistan government should consider using the design information technology in the public sector. The interviewee (R5) stated: "From my practical experience, I realised that the information system in Kurdistan region is inefficient and has some limitations, for example, it's unable to provide reliable, accurate, and up-to-date information in a cost-effective way. Thus, designing a network to connect all government organisations with each other is regarded a good step forward towards fighting corruption."

To sum up, the interviews made clear that the corruption phenomenon is disseminated from the high level government officials to the low level. According to the findings of the study, many cases of corruption are found to be the result of the ineffective accounting and budget system of the Kurdistan region. Some aspects of reform, as suggested by the respondents, may help the government to address the weaknesses of its accounting and budget system and thus fight corruption easily. However, on the one hand, besides the aim of fighting corruption there are also some challenges that make the reform process necessary.

Seventh theme: Challenges towards accounting reform

Globalisation: Globalisation is imposing significant pressure on countries across the world to make radical changes to the systems, accelerate responsiveness, and open the doors for increasing local and foreign competition. Globalisation demands governments and organisations to harmonise their goals with each other. The harmonisation process may increase economic development and decrease discrepancies in goals between the private and public sector on the one hand and between the national and international goals on the other hand. Therefore, there is a need for proper government system in order to be able to deal with globalisation and its requirements [88].

International pressure: Some concerned international organisations such as The World Bank (WB), International Transparency Organisation (IT), and International Monetary Fund (IMF) are pressurising countries, particularly the developing and transitional economy countries, to make changes in their political, economic, and financial fields. These organisations require countries to be transparent and accountable. In addition, they encourage countries to reform their accounting systems by granting international loans and aids [89].

National coordination and integration: Another reason to make changes in one's accounting budget system is to achieve coordination and integration among different public organisations. Ouda argues that in many Arab countries [10], the national financial strategic planning has tended to be scrappy and there is no synergy and coordination at the national level. There is no relation between budget objectives and the macroeconomic objectives; there is a cause of financial chaos. As a result, many government projects are prone to implementation failure or long delays. A way for governments to overcome this problem is by reforming their accounting and budget system. Such a reform will force all government organisations to adopt the same system and procedures and thus, will unite the efforts towards achieving national objectives.

Conclusion, Limitations, Ethical Considerations

Conclusion

The findings of this research explain that Kurdistan region is suffering from various forms of corruption in its public sector. Corruptors often use accounting and budget procedures to legitimise their corrupt practices for deriving private gains on account of public resources. With regard to the accounting and budget system, there are some serious shortages and gaps in the operations and procedures of the government sector. These gaps have seeped into the heart of many accounting and budget procedures.

According to the statements of all respondents of the study, the government accounting system follows the cash-basis approach and is thus, outmoded and cumbersome. The system does not record assets, liabilities, revenues, and expenditures unless they result in cash transactions of a particular financial year; thus, making many of them invisible.

The budget system is based on the line-item system. This system does not accurately show the amount of general resources and expenditures. Thus it does not afford an appropriate accountability and transparency, in the process preventing people from accessing government information. In addition, the allocation process is not based on any scientific method, and for a majority of government projects the costs are allocated randomly.

In Kurdistan region, internal and external audits are weak. The Supreme Audit Board (SAB) does not play its role effectively, as it is still not independent. For many government projects, SAB cannot investigate their costs and only observes their execution stages. Also, with respect to the accounting staff, in Kurdistan region, many accountants and auditors are not qualified. Therefore, these shortages and gaps within the public sector have led to an increase in the corruption practices.

The following essential reform steps have been suggested by respondents: shifting from cash-basis to accrual-basis and line-item budget to performance programme budget, strengthening the role of audit and SAB, changing the accounting curriculum, training accountants and auditors and designing information technology. It is believed that these steps may aid to some extent in deterring the corruption practices.

However, this research does not assert that an effective accounting system is the only solution to deter the corruption practices in the public sector of Kurdistan region. There may be other variables such as the political, social, cultural, and legal systems that also affect the corruption phenomenon in a country, and these should not be ignored. This is considered to be a limitation and to address this, future research can be conducted to investigate corruption practices in depth by taking into account these variables.

Limitations

Despite the sensible power of qualitative research, some limitations have been noted during the study. The limitations are with respect to the chosen approach, methodology, and methods followed. Johnson has identified three main disadvantages to qualitative research: firstly, its failure to manage independent variables, secondly, it may lead to incorrect interpretation, and thirdly, it presents a weakness of power to randomise. These problems cannot be overcome entirely; they are also relative from a case study to another [14].

Taking this into consideration, it can be said that this research was conducted amidst these limitations. The researcher has encountered some constraints. The process of recruiting respondents was considered the most difficult task and was time consuming, because the distance between the researcher, the environment of the case study (with refer to Kurdistan region), and the topic was very sensitive, and the respondents paid attention to some considerations such as political, social, and cultural.

The second was the limitation of generalizability as the number of respondents was small, which makes it difficult to generalise the findings. The researcher tried to involve a large number of respondents; however, due to the scope and limitations of time, the number of interviewees was limited to only 10. In regard to subjectivity, the researcher tried to mitigate its impacts as much as possible in order to increase the reliability and validity of data.

The third limitation is with respect to the semi-structured interview, which is characterised by linguistic variability, wherein the phrases and words used may have different meanings. It is difficult for a researcher to interpret them and put them in correct places [90]. Since the interviews were conducted in Kurdish, in this case, the answers were more likely to lose some essential meanings when translated to English language.

In the final face-to-face interview, wherein the topic of discussion was the corruption and accounting in Kurdistan region, the researcher did not have the opportunity to travel to the area of the study in order to collect primary data. The information was collected via an online Skype session. Thus, the information gathered through this kind of interview is considered to be less reliable than a face-to-face interview.

Ethical considerations

The ethical considerations have been fulfilled by the researcher at the outset of the field work. The researcher has obtained the ethical approval form which was made mandatory by the university. As part of the ethical consideration, the respondents were required to review the consent form and sign it, before taking part in the interview. All interviewees have signed the consent form. The respondents were assured of anonymity and confidentiality their names would not be revealed. The questions were designed to collect confidential data from the respondents without revealing their names. Further, the results of the interviews were personally transcribed by the researcher to protect the respondent's anonymity.

Acknowledgements

- First of all, it would not have been possible without the help of ALLAH then the prayers of my parents.
- I would like to express my deepest gratitude to my supervisor, Dr. Pinar Guven-Uslu, for her wonderful guidance, without her I would never have been able to finish my dissertation.
- Also, I would like to thank my wife (Nihaya) for her help and patience with me.
- Finally, I would also like to thank my brother Mr. Ameer who was always supported me and arranged for me the interview process with respondents in Kurdistan region.
- This dissertation would not have been possible without their help and support.

References

1. Mauro P (1998) Corruption: causes, consequences, and agenda for further research. Finance and Development 35: 11-14.
2. Tanzi V, Davoodi H (1998) Corruption, public investment, and growth. Springer Japan pp. 41-60.
3. Khan M (2006) Determinants of corruption in developing countries: the limits of conventional economic analysis. International Handbook on the Economics of Corruption pp. 216-244.
4. World Bank Report (1997) Helping Developing Countries Combat Corruption.
5. Hwang J (2002) A note on the relationship between corruption and government revenue. Journal of Economic Development 27: 161-176.
6. Spector BI (2005) Fighting corruption in developing countries: strategies and analysis. Bloomfield, CT: Kumarian Press p. 312.
7. Sandholtz W, Koetzle W (2000) Accounting for corruption: Economic structure, democracy and trade. International studies quarterly 44: 31-50.
8. Bhargava VK, Bolongaita EP (2004) Challenging corruption in Asia: Case studies and a framework for action. World Bank Publications.
9. Malagueño R, Albrecht C, Ainge C, Stephens N (2010) Accounting and corruption: a cross country analysis. Journal of Money Laundering Control 13: 372-393.
10. Ouda HA (2003) Public Sector Accounting and Budgeting Reform: The Main Issues Involved with Special focus on the Arab World. Economic and Social Commission for Western Asia (ESCWA), Beirut, Lebanon.
11. Haller D, Shore C (2005) Corruption: anthropological perspectives. Pluto Press.
12. Génaux M (2004) Social sciences and the evolving concept of corruption. Crime, law and social change 42: 13-24.
13. Campos NF, Dimova RD, Saleh A (2010) Whither corruption? A quantitative survey of the literature on corruption and growth.
14. Johnston M (2005) Keeping the answers, changing the questions: Corruption definitions revisited 35: 61-76.
15. Mo PH (2001) Corruption and economic growth. Journal of comparative economics 29: 66-79.
16. Lambsdorff JG (2006) Causes and consequences of corruption: what do we know from a cross section of countries. International handbook on the economics of corruption 1: 3-51.
17. Rabl T (2008) Private Corruption and Its Actors: Insights into the Subjective Decision Making Processes. Pabst Science Publishers.
18. Transparency International 2004 Annual Report (2004), University Press, USA.
19. Kaufmann D (1997) Corruption: the facts. Foreign Policy 107: 114-131.
20. USAID (2005) USAID Anticorruption Strategy. Washington DC, USAID.
21. Deflem M (1995) Corruption, law, and justice: A conceptual clarification. Journal of Criminal Justice 23: 243-258.
22. Vargas-Hernández JG (2009) The multiple faces of corruption: typology, forms and levels. Forms and Levels pp. 1-19.
23. Amundsen I (2000) Corruption: definition and concepts. Bergen: Utstein Anti-Corruption Resource Centre.
24. Singleton TW, Singleton AJ (2006) Fraud auditing and forensic accounting. (4thedn) John Wiley and Sons.
25. Andvig JC, Fjeldstad OH, Amundsen I, Sissener T, Søreide T (2001) Corruption: A review of contemporary research. Chr. Michelsen Institute. Approaches, SAGE, London.
26. Okafor B (2004) Strategic approach to reduction of employee, theft fraud and embezzlement. Niger Account 37: 3-5.
27. MacDonald R, Majeed MT (2011) Causes of corruption in European Countries: History, law, and political Stability. University of Glasgow University of Glasgow.
28. Mungiu-Pippidi A (2013) Controlling corruption through collective action. Journal of Democracy 24: 101-115.
29. Shabbir G, Anwar M (2007) Determinants of Corruption in Developing Countries. The Pakistan Development Review 46: 761-764.
30. Chapman D (2002) Corruption and the education sector. Sectoral Perspectives on Corruption, prepared by MSI Sponsored by USAID, DCHA/DG.
31. Bardhan P (1997) Corruption and development: A review of issues. Journal of economic literature 35: 1320-1346.
32. Rock MT, Bonnett H (2004) The comparative politics of corruption: Accounting for the East Asian paradox in empirical studies of corruption, growth and investment. World Development 32: 999-1017.
33. Leff NH (1964) Economic Development through Bureaucratic Corruption. American Behavioural Scientist 8: 8-14.
34. Everett J, Neu D, Rahaman AS (2007) Accounting and the global fight against corruption. Accounting, Organizations and Society 32: 513-542.
35. Wu X (2005) Corporate governance and corruption: A cross-country analysis. Governance: An International Journal of Policy, Administration and Institutions 18: 151-170.
36. Kimbro MB (2002) A cross-country empirical investigation of corruption and its relationship to economic, cultural, and monitoring institutions: An examination of the role of accounting and financial statements quality. Journal of Accounting, Auditing and Finance 17: 325-350.

37. Barth ME, Landsman WR, Lang MH (2008) International accounting standards and accounting quality. Journal of accounting research 46: 467-498.

38. Mangualde BR (2013) Perceptions of benefits and challenges of public sector accounting reforms: a cross-sectional comparison between Brazilian and English local governments. University of Birmingham, England.

39. Briston RJ (1978) The evolution of accounting in developing countries. International Journal of Accounting Education and Research 14: 105-120.

40. Hopper T, Tsamenyi M, Uddin S, Wickramasinghe D (2009) Management accounting in less developed countries: What is known and needs knowing. Accounting, Auditing and Accountability Journal 22: 469-514.

41. Mimba NPSH, Helden GJV, Tillema S (2007) Public sector performance measurement in developing countries: A literature review and research agenda. Journal of Accounting and Organizational Change 3: 192-208.

42. Pratap S, Quintin E (2006) The informal sector in developing countries: Output, assets and employment. Research Paper, UNU-WIDER, United Nations University (UNU), Japan.

43. Patton MQ (2005) Qualitative research. John Wiley & Sons, Ltd.

44. Holloway I, Wheeler S (2013) Qualitative research in nursing and healthcare. John Wiley & Sons.

45. Creswell JW (2013) Research design: Qualitative, quantitative, and mixed methods approaches. Sage publications.

46. Bryman A (2003) Quantity and quality in social research. Routledge.

47. Cooper DR, Schindler PS, Sun J (2006) Business research methods. McGraw-hill, New York.

48. Guba EG, Lincoln YS (1994) Competing paradigms in qualitative research. Handbook of qualitative research 2: 163-194.

49. Saunders M, Lewis P, Thornhill A (2009) Research methods for business students. Financial Times/Prentice Hall, Harlow, England.

50. Easterby-Smith Mark, Thorpe R, Jackson PR (2008) Management Research. Business and economics, SAGE pp. 1-351.

51. Zimmer L (2006) Qualitative meta-synthesis: a question of dialoguing with texts. Journal of advanced nursing 53: 311-318.

52. Ghauri PN, Grønhaug K (2005) Research methods in business studies: A practical guide. Pearson Education.

53. Gerring J (2006) Case study research: principles and practices. Cambridge University Press.

54. Yin RK (1994) Case Study Research: Design and Methods, SAGE, London p. 240.

55. Robson C (1993) Real world research: A resource for social scientists and practitioners- researchers. Massachusetts: Blackwell Pushers.

56. Eisenhardt KM (1989) Building theories from case study research. Academy of management review 14: 532-550.

57. Baxter P, Jack S (2008) Qualitative case study methodology: Study design and implementation for novice researchers. The qualitative report 13: 544-559.

58. Scapens RW (1990) Researching management accounting practice: the role of case study methods. The British Accounting Review 22: 259-281.

59. Strauss A, Corbin J (1994) Grounded theory methodology. Handbook of qualitative research pp. 273-285.

60. Bryman A, Bell E (2007) Business Research Methods. Oxford.

61. Louise Barriball K, While A (1994) Collecting Data using a semi-structured interview: A discussion paper. Journal of advanced nursing 19: 328-335.

62. Schensul SL, Schensul JJ, LeCompte MD (1999) Essential ethnographic methods: Observations, interviews, and questionnaires. Rowman Altamira p. 318.

63. O'Leary B, McGarry J, Salih K (2006) The future of Kurdistan in Iraq. University of Pennsylvania Press.

64. Karim KH, Koyi H, Baziany MM, Hessami K (2011) Significance of angular unconformities between Cretaceous and Tertiary strata in the north western segment of the Zagros fold-thrust belt. Geological Magazine 148: 925-939.

65. McGarry J, O'Leary B (2009) Must pluri-national federations fail? Ethnopolitics 8: 5-25.

66. Aslan S (2011) Everyday forms of state power and the Kurds in the early Turkish republic. International Journal of Middle East Studies 43: 75-93.

67. Basheka BC (2009) Procurement planning and local governance in Uganda: a factor analysis approach. International Journal of Procurement Management 2: 191-209.

68. Chorev M (2007) Iraqi Kurdistan: The internal dynamics and statecraft of a semistate. Al Nakhlah: The Fletcher School Online Journal for Issues Related to Southwest Asia and Islamic Civilization pp. 1-11.

69. Doski SA (2015) The necessity of issuing a corporate governance code for the Kurdistan Region. Journal of Finance and Accountancy 18: 1-19.

70. Jones R, Pendlebury M (2000) Public sector accounting. Business and Economics, Financial Times Princeton Hall p. 278.

71. Peter VM (2005) From cash to accrual budgeting and accounting in the public sector: The Dutch experience. Public Budgeting & Finance 25: 32-44.

72. Frederick TC (1983) Cash or Accrual Basis Accounting-Which System is better for the Law Firm. Legal Econ 9: 51.

73. Romney M, Steinbart P, Mula J, McNamara R, Tonkin T (2012) Accounting Information Systems. Australasian Edition, Pearson Higher Education, AU.

74. Harding N, Ren M (2007) The importance in accounting of ambiguity tolerance at the national level: Evidence from Australia and China. Asian Review of Accounting 15: 6-24.

75. Balkaran L (2013) Auditing the Corporate Governance Effort in an Organization. EDPACS 48: 12-18.

76. Virginia A, Eleni K, Dimitrios P, Chrysoula X (2009) The role of financial accounting information in strengthening corporate control mechanisms to alleviate corporate corruption. University Macedonia.

77. Lienert MI (2005) Who controls the budget: the legislature or the executive? International Monetary Fund. London: SAGE Publications Inc., London: Thomson Learning. pp. 38-47.

78. Dechow PM (1994) Accounting earnings and cash flows as measures of firm performance: The role of accounting accruals. Journal of accounting and economics 18: 3-42.

79. Hepworth N (2003) Preconditions for successful implementation of accrual accounting in central government. Public Money & Management 23: 37-44.

80. Torres L (2004) Accounting and accountability: recent developments in government financial information systems. Public Administration and Development 24: 447-456.

81. Vinnari EM, Näsi S (2008) Creative accrual accounting in the public sector: milking 'water utilities to balance municipal budgets and accounts. Financial Accountability and Management 24: 97-116.

82. Wallace RO (1990) Survival strategies of a global organization: The case of the International Accounting Standards Committee. Accounting Horizons 4: 1.

83. Scofield B, Wilhelm P (2004) International accounting standards and corruption. Mimeo, University of Texas, Permian Basin.

84. Ateetanan P (2001) Country Report Thailand. In 12th International Workshop for Information Policy and Management in the Public Sector, November, Tokyo, Japan.

85. Kudo H IIAS (2012) What Capacity-Building needed for the trustful CIO? : How to educate and train new generation of CIOs in Japan. International Congress Mérida, Yucatán, Mexico.

86. Dye KM, Stapenhurst R (1998) Pillars of integrity: the importance of supreme audit institutions in curbing corruption. Economic Development Institute of the World Bank.

87. Hollander A, Denna E, Cherrington JO (1999) Accounting, information technology, and business solutions. McGraw-Hill Higher Education.

88. Fulin C (2002) Overcoming institutional barriers and sociocultural conflicts in China. Newsletter.

89. Godfrey AD, Devlin PJ, Merrouche MC (2001) A diffusion-contingency model for government accounting innovations. In International Comparative Issues in Government Accounting. Springer US pp. 279-296.

90. Willig C (2008) Introducing qualitative research in Psychology: Adventures in theory and method. (1stedn), Open University Press, UK.

To analyze the Comparative Financial Performance Analysis of Islamic and Conventional Banks in Pakistan

Naeem B*

Comptroller of Accounts at Packages Limited, Accounting, Lahore, Pakistan

Abstract

This exploration study was directed to make correlation of money related execution of 5 Islamic banks and 5 routine banks in Pakistan from 2008-2015. To survey the money related execution of Islamic and routine banks enlightening insights was utilized for the inner determinants of CAMEL model. To check whether there is critical distinction or not in execution of Islamic and traditional banks one way ANOVA was used. To assess those components which impact the execution of banks Regression was implemented. On the premise of discoveries it is reasoned that there is noteworthy contrast in execution of Islamic and conventional banks in significant terms.

Keywords: Camel model; Financial performance; Islamic and Conventional banks; ANOVA

Introduction

Background

Financial and economic activities are mainly supported by banking sector in any country [1]. The system of banking which is based on the rules of Islamic laws and economics are known as Islamic banking system. Islamic banking is mainly based on 2 rules which are prevention of interest and also sharing of profit or loss [2]. The concept of Islamic banking is not only confined to prohibition of interest but also to avoid from immoral activities [3]. Most of the studies related to Camel model are conducted which influence the financial performance of conventional banks. Those components which influence the money related execution of Islamic banks is an under looked into range. The exact studies which are identified with the determinants of the benefit of the Islamic banks are not very many [4]. Exact studies identified with the correlation of money related execution of Islamic and conventional banks are not very many. Along these lines with a specific end goal to fill the hole in the writing near money related execution investigation of Islamic and conventional banks is required [5].

Problem statement

In Pakistan Islamic banks initiated their operations in year 2002. Internal factors which are broadly categorized as Camel model are named as capital adequacy, asset quality, management quality, earning quality and liquidity."

This study will look at those components which influence the money related execution of Islamic and conventional banks in Pakistan. In Pakistan administration, diverse administrative powers, investors and partners will have far reaching examination of the Islamic and traditional banks.

Research gap

In Pakistan very few studies are conducted which have analyzed comparative financial performance analysis of Islamic and conventional banks [6]. According to Hunjra and Bashir, there is need of comparative financial performance analysis of Islamic banks and conventional banks to fill the gap in literature [5].

Research objectives

- To determine internal factors of banks that influence profitability of Islamic and Conventional banks and consider which segment of banking is more profitable in Pakistan?
- To examine the impact of internal factors of banks on the basis of profitability in Islamic and conventional banks in Pakistan?

Research questions

- How internal factors of bank influence the profitability of Islamic and Conventional banks to check which banking sector is more profitable?
- What is the impact of internal factors of banks on profitability of Islamic and conventional banks?"

Research hypothesis

- H1: The internal factors of Islamic banks have significant relationship with ROA as compare to conventional banks
- H2: The internal factors of Islamic banks have significant relationship with ROE as compare to conventional banks

Literature Review

Saving money framework based upon the standards of Islamic laws and financial matters is known as Islamic managing an account framework. Benefit and misfortune sharing and premium disallowance are two noteworthy overseeing principles of Islamic managing an account [2]. Islamic managing an account can be characterized as keeping money in view of traditions and grounds of shariah and Islam. Islamic managing an account not just disallows enthusiasm as it's a constrained idea additionally limit shameless exercises [3]. A particular normal for Islamic saving money is sharing of benefit and misfortune [7]. Operations of First Islamic bank began in 1963 by the

***Corresponding author:** Bilal Naeem, Comptroller of Accounts at Packages Limited, Accounting, Lahore, Pakistan, E-mail: bilalnaeem123@hotmail.com

name of Mitghamr sparing bank. In any case, this bank was shut in 1967 because of political impact [8].

There are 396 Islamic banks working in 53 nations with aggregate assets of 442 billion US dollars. Around the globe number of no standard banks offering Islamic windows are 320 having complete assets of 200 billion US dollars. Yearly development rate of Islamic managing an account is 15% [2]. In the blink of an eye at least 500 Islamic money related establishments are working far and wide. Inside components are the elements that are all in all influenced by the choices and strategies of bank administration. [9]. As indicated by Olweny and Shipho [10], CAMEL structure is recommended by Basel Council on Bank Supervision and IMF as model to assess the execution of banks. This model is utilized for the inner components of the bank's execution. In creating economies routine of utilizing CAMEL show as a part of saving money studies is constrained. Wirnkar and Tanko in their study utilized CAMEL show as a part of request to study execution of managing an account division of Nigeria [11]. Ferrouhi in his study utilized CAMEL model to assess the execution of FIs of Morocco amid the time of 2001 to 2011.Profit mirrors the execution of the bank and considered as the most vital and basic variable which decide the survival of the banks [12]. Return on resource (ROA) and Profit for Value (ROE) are utilized to gauge the execution of the banks due to specific points of interest of these gainfulness proportions. ROA and ROE are broadly utilized proportions [13] (Figure 1).

Hypothetically, 2 key proportions utilized most ordinarily and most broadly as benefit measures are profit for resources (ROA) and profit for value (ROE). The purpose for is that both ROA and ROE relate nearly to the key things in bank's budgetary articulation. Return on value can be ascertained by separating the net wage after assessments with aggregate value capital. Return on resource can be characterized as the proportion of wage to aggregate resource. Financial execution of banks measured by profit for resources (ROA) and profit for value (ROE). The capacity of administration of bank regarding benefit era out of advantages of bank is reflected by ROA, and it is ascertained as the proportion of net benefit after assessment (NPAT) to aggregate resources. On the other edge ROE, is the impression of the value come back to shareholders [14].

It is critical to understand that ROA and ROE both are utilized to gauge the bank execution in Islamic and additionally traditional banks. Numerous studies utilized ROA and ROE to quantify the benefit of

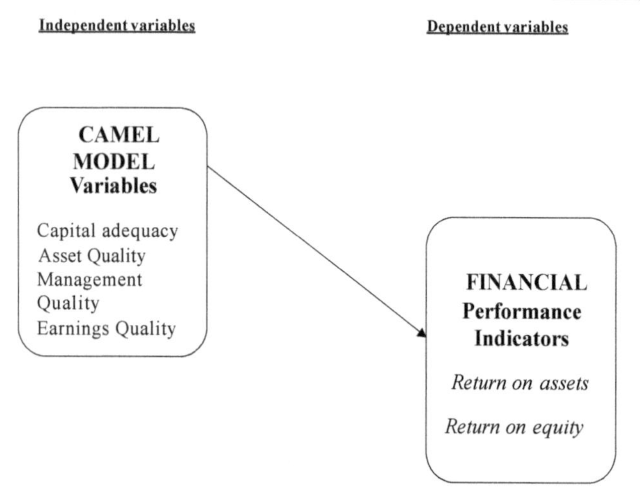

Figure 1: Theoretical framework.

the banks paying little respect to look into on Islamic or conventional banks. These studies are Sufian et al. [13,15].

Moin looked at the monetary execution of first Islamic bank in Pakistan with a gathering of 5 conventional banks for a time of 2003-2007 [6]. He found that Islamic bank is less gainful, less unsafe furthermore less effective contrasted with Routine banks. Be that as it may, there is no huge contrast in liquidity between the two arrangements of banks.

Beck et al. looked at the two sorts of keeping money and their budgetary execution crosswise over numerous nations, amid late emergency and reason that however both sorts of managing an account were influenced by the emergency, Islamic banks had higher capitalization combined with higher liquidity holds bringing about better monetary execution of Islamic banks.

Comprehensively, different exact studies have been directed to look at the budgetary execution of Islamic saves money with that of conventional banks in various districts amid various periods. In any case, the volume of such inquires about is constrained because of the way that the information of Islamic banks have been inaccessible because of their late development.

Ansari and Rehman directed a study on the money related execution examination of Islamic and conventional banks situated in Pakistan for the time of 2006 – 2009. Three Islamic and Three conventional banks were chosen for the study. Eighteen diverse budgetary proportions, which spoke to benefit, liquidity, hazard and dissolvability, capital adequacy, sending and operational proficiency, were used. Autonomous example t-test and ANOVA was utilized to decide the importance of mean contrasts of these proportions between and among banks. They discovered that in contrast with conventional banks, Islamic banks were exceedingly fluid, less unsafe and operationally proficient.

Return on resource is utilized to quantify the execution of the banks. ROA is ascertained by isolating the Net-Working Salary with Aggregate Resources. Swarnapali and Shah utilized ROA to quantify the execution of the banks [14].

Return on value is utilized as the intermediary to quantify the execution of the banks. ROE is measured by Net-Working Pay/Add up to Value. Ali, Akhthar and Ahmed; Sufian and Habibullah utilized ROE to decide the execution of banks [13,15].

Capital adequacy is considered as the inward element which impacts the execution of the banks. It is dictated by the isolating the aggregate value with aggregate resources, a similar intermediary for estimation of Capital adequacy is bolstered by Rao and Lakew; Dealer; Qudah and Jaradat utilized capital sufficiency proportion as inside variable which impact the execution of the bank [16].

Propelling advances is one of the real elements of the banks and consider as fundamental wellspring of gaining for the banks. It can be figured as the proportion of NPLS (Non-Performing Credits) and aggregate advances.

Administration quality is third critical segment of the CAMEL Demonstrate. Intermediary used to ascertain administration quality is Add up to Advances to Aggregate Stores (TA/TD): This proportion endeavors to measures the capacity and productivity of bank's administration to change over accessible stores while barring different assets e.g. value capital, and so forth into higher gaining progresses.

Winning capacity of the monetary foundations can be resolved as the proportion of aggregate salary to aggregate cost [8]. Liquidity can be measure by venture resource proportion (Add up to Speculations/ Add up to Resources) [5].

Methodology

The essential motivation behind this examination study was to play out the relative investigation of the Islamic and conventional banks working in Pakistan. This study expects to decide how bank's interior variables impact on gainfulness of Islamic and Routine banks and which saving money section is more beneficial. Quantitative approach and enlightening outline is utilized for research.

In Pakistan a few banks are working in both surges of managing an account that is Islamic and conventional saving money. With a specific end goal to play out the similar money related execution investigation just those banks are considered which can either delegated Islamic or conventional. There are five full fledge Islamic banks performing operations in Pakistan i.e. Meezan bank, Bank Islami Pakistan, Burj bank, Dubai Islamic bank Pakistan and Al Barka bank Pakistan Five conventional banks considered of proportionate size as far as branch system as Islamic banks was chosen i.e. Comfort inspecting was utilized in this study (Table 1).

Information is gathered from the reviewed money related proclamations of the banks. Shah and Jan utilized money related explanations to gather information for assessment of monetary execution of the banks in their exploration contemplates [15].

Data analysis

In this study regression examination is utilized. Numerous specialists utilized these investigation systems. Dawood utilized clear and regression examination to decide the variables influencing the money related execution of the Islamic and routine banks [1]. CAMEL model is utilized to check the effect of inward bank particular factors on the execution of Islamic and conventional banks in Pakistan. Numerous regression models is utilized and explained by utilizing STATA. T-test is utilized to check the mean contrasts of the Islamic and conventional banks. Hunjra and Bashir utilized T-test as a part of their study to test the mean contrasts of various proportions of Islamic and routine banks [5]. One way ANOVA is utilized to decide distinction in execution of Islamic and routine banks in light of the segments of CAMEL model."

One-Way ANOVA

One path examination of difference is utilized to figure out if traditional and Islamic banks are performing distinctively or not. CAMEL model is utilized with the end goal of assessment of contrast in the execution of the both surges of saving money. Fundamental standard for acknowledgment and dismissal is that if significant value is under 0.05 reject the invalid speculation and the other way around.

Capital adequacy: As far as capital sufficiency Islamic and conventional banks are performing diversely and this distinction in execution is measurably huge as p-esteem for capital adequacy is 0.0296 which is under 0.05 subsequently, we have rejected invalid speculation.

Islamic Banks	Conventional Banks
Meezan Bank Limited	Bank Al-Habib
Bank Islami Pakistan Limited	JS Bank
Al-Baraka Bank	Summit Bank
Dubai Islamic Bank	Habib Metropolitan Bank
Burj Bank	Silk bank"

Table 1: List of Islamic banks and conventional Banks.

Management quality: There exists no distinction in execution of Islamic and conventional banks when measured as far as administration quality. Scientist don't dismiss the invalid speculation in light of the fact that the p-esteem is 0.0678 which is more noteworthy than 0.05 which demonstrates that measurably inconsequential distinction wins in execution of Islamic and traditional banks as far as administration quality.

Earning quality: There exists no distinction in execution of Islamic and conventional banks when measured as far as acquiring quality. Specialist don't dismiss the invalid theory in light of the fact that the p-esteem is 0.9138 which is more noteworthy than 0.05 which demonstrates that measurably unimportant distinction wins in execution of Islamic and conventional banks regarding procuring quality.

Liquidity: There exists no distinction in execution of Islamic and conventional banks when measured as far as liquidity. Scientist don't dismiss the invalid theory on the grounds that the p-value is 0.0688 which is more prominent than 0.05 which demonstrates that measurably irrelevant distinction wins in execution of Islamic and routine banks as far as liquidity.

Asset quality: As far as resource quality Islamic and conventional banks are performing contrary and this distinction in execution is measurably critical as p-value for capital sufficiency seems to be 0.0002 which is under 0.05 consequently, we have rejected invalid speculation (Table 2).

Regression analysis: In this segment scientist will demonstrate the aftereffects of regression investigation. This will expand how subordinate factors will reaction when autonomous factors change. Effect of interior factors in view of CAMEL model and ROA and ROE will be checked by utilizing the six regression models as done by Faizulayev, in his study [17].

Regression results: The regression outcomes about show that various bank-particular inner components essentially impact the benefit of banks as measured by ROA and ROE at 95% certainty level (since their p-values are> 0.05) (Table 3). Variables having critical effect on the gainfulness of the banks are CPA (Capital adequacy), ASQ (Resource quality), LIQ (Liquidity) and MNQ (Administration quality), as finished up by the past looks into [15,18,19]. Benefit of the banks are required to increment when capital adequacy increments and resource quality proportion diminishes which demonstrates that nonperforming advances to aggregate advances proportion is diminished. Furthermore, despite the fact that we expected administration quality to be emphatically related to benefit as built up by Faizulayev in his study [17].

Then again, it is expected that acquiring quality has positive impact on gainfulness of the banks yet in this study procuring quality has no effect on the execution determinants of the banks. Relationship of procuring quality is demonstrated measurably irrelevant these outcomes are in accordance with the examination concentrate on directed by Faizulayev [17].

Capital adequacy of Islamic banks has negative huge connection with ROA and ROE while, in routine banks capital sufficiency has negative critical connection with ROA and negative inconsequential connection with ROE. Administration quality has positive huge connection with ROA and ROE of both Islamic and conventional banks. Liquidity and Resource quality both has negative critical effect on Islamic and also traditional banks.

Measures of financial performance	Squares of Sum	Degree of freedom	Square of mean	F	Significance level
Capital Adequacy					
Between Groups	0.04623540	1	0.06424463	5.13	0.0296
Within Groups	0.748044391	78	0.018641221		
Total	0.796197902	79	0.011167353		
Management Quality					
Between Groups	0.03624463	1	0.03624463	3.27	0.0678
Within Groups	2.56246527	78	0.029754629		
Total	2.75585537	79	0.029763437		
Earning Quality					
Between Groups	4.83216846	1	4.83216846	0.01	0.9138
Within Groups	26763.3210	78	346.281414		
Total	26773.5354	79	341.877481		
Liquidity					
Between Groups	0.125413793	1	0.125413793	3.38	0.0688
Within Groups	2.49257617	78	0.042755327		
Total	2.67476349	79	0.035799230		
Asset Quality					
Between Groups	0.363843423	1	0.363843423	23.84	0.0002
Within Groups	1.18374719	78	0.014372539		
Total	1.61646914	79	0.017854730		
ROA					
Between Groups	10.6655847	1	10.6655847	1.61	0.2142
Within Groups	613.175364	78	7.65693279		
Total	611.874859	79	6.14124103		
ROE					
Between Groups	5454.14674	1	5454.14674	11.34	0.0013
Within Groups	43543.514	78	531.875437		
Total	43446.5743	79	231.257658		

Table 2: One-way ANOVA.

Variables	Islamic Banks"		Conventional Banks"	
	Return on" assets	Return on" equity	Return on assets	Return on equity
Capital adequacy	-16.97568 (-4.63)***	-123.1534 (-3.130)***	-33.01143 (-2.89)***	67.50153 (1.12)
Management quality	12.64047 (3.14)***	97.87637 (3.01)***	15.12472 (1.77)**	132.2899 (2.31)**
Earning quality	.011021 (1.64)*	.0733364 (1.04)	-0.0165028 (-0.30)	-0.0928568 (-0.22)
Liquidity	-21.65150 (-5.23)***	-168.8149 (-3.83)***	-21.65085 (-1.86)**	-192.5492 (-2.15)**
Asset quality	-16.68670 (-4.23)***	-73.28685 (-2.51)**	-23.66546 (-4.93)***	-117.1521 (-2.87)***
Constant	4.77631 (4.26)	37.82154 (4.13)	5.150147 (1.72)	-38.68768 (-1.53)
R Squire	0.6812	0.5187	0.7513	0.2554
F –statistics	7.09	4.45	4.67	3.93
Prob>F	0.0010	0.0013	0.0015	0.0039

*,**,***denote significant levels at 10%, 5% and 1% respectively.

Table 3: Regression results.

T Test of all ratios: (2008-2015): The outcomes uncovered that a normal of routine banks ROA is superior to ROE of Islamic bank from 2008 to 2015. Moreover, measurably there is no contrast between the two means at 5% level of hugeness. ROE of Islamic banks is persistently better as contrast with ROE of routine banks amid 2008-2015 (Table 4).

The Capital adequacy proportion of Islamic Banks and conventional Banks are 14.11063% and 11.97143% individually with mean distinction of 3.90681%. Along these lines, Islamic banks performed prevalent than Routine Banks, as far as Capital adequacy, amid the study time frame. The specimen supreme t-value is 2.4106.

Administration quality is another vital component of the CAMEL Show. The proportion in this fragment includes subjective investigation to gauge the proficiency and viability of administration. The administration of bank takes essential choices relying upon its hazard observation. The Administration nature of Islamic Banks and conventional Banks are 51.61586% and 74.42177% separately with mean distinction - 23.56641%. Accordingly, conventional banks performed superior to anything Islamic Banks, as far as Administration productivity, amid the study time frame. The specimen supreme t-value is -1.3867.

The earning quality of Islamic Banks and conventional Banks are 2.136455% and 1.57357% separately with mean contrast 0.4904717%. Hence, Islamic banks performed superior to anything Routine Banks, as far as Profit quality, amid the study time frame. The example outright t-esteem is 0.1610.

Liquidity of Islamic Banks and conventional Banks are 0.5401476% and 0.6045102% individually with mean contrast - 06.56641%. In this manner, routine banks performed superior to anything Islamic Banks, as far as Liquidity, amid the study time frame. The example outright t-value is - 1.3873.

Variables	Type of bank	Number	Mean difference	Standard Deviation	t-value
Return on assets	Islamic	40	-0.0106431	1.388605	-1.2834
	Conventional	40	.6563567	3.6927421	
	Combined	80	.3758576	2.690134	
	Diff		-0.6750413		
Return on equity	Islamic	40	3.013268	11.20631	3.2314
	Conventional	40	-13.21812	30.73638	
	Combined	80	-5.193873	21.86145	
	Diff		12.62134		
Capital adequacy	Islamic	40	0.1411063	0.1061404	2.4106
	Conventional	40	0.1197143	0.06345173	
	Combined	80	0.1418468	0.1139307	
	Diff		0.0351578		
Management quality	Islamic	40	0.5161586	0.2372672	-1.3867
	Conventional	40	0.7442177	0.1312570	
	Combined	80	0.6798986	0.1765624	
	Diff		-0.2335371		
Earning quality	Islamic	40	2.136455	21.53463	0.1610
	Conventional	40	1.57357	13.25718	
	Combined	80	1.631224	17.67463	
	Diff		0.4301624		
Liquidity	Islamic	40	0.5401476	0.2403571	-1.3873
	Conventional	40	0.6045102	0.1412623	
	Combined	80	0.5735693	0.1458944	
	Diff		-0.0645713		
Assets quality	Islamic	40	0.0631526	0.05374328	-4.1714
	Conventional	40	0.1883024	0.2042931	
	Combined	80	0.1934354	0.1210315	
	Diff		-0.1213124		

Table 4: T Test of All Ratios: (2008-2015).

The asset quality of Islamic Banks and conventional Banks are 6.31526% and 18.83024% separately with mean contrast -12.13124%. Subsequently, conventional banks performed superior to anything Islamic Banks, as far as Resource quality, amid the study time frame. The example outright t-value is - 4.1714.

Discussion and Results

The motivation behind this exploration was to survey the execution of banks in the Pakistan over the period 2008-2015 by method for the Camel display approach. Elucidating insights of the information demonstrated that Islamic banks beat conventional banks in capital sufficiency, administration quality, and liquidity and resource quality where as traditional banks overwhelm Islamic banks regarding procuring capacity. These outcomes are reliable with the past studies [17,19-21].

To test whether the distinctions in execution were noteworthy, one-way ANOVA tests were done, and discovered measurably huge contrasts in the execution of Islamic and traditional banks. On the premise of discoveries it is reasoned that there is huge distinction in execution of Islamic and conventional banks as far as capital adequacy and resource quality though, as far as administration quality, winning quality and liquidity there is no huge contrast in the execution of Islamic and conventional banks. These outcomes are reliable with the consequences of past studies [6,22-25].

The regression outcomes demonstrated that few bank-particular inner components altogether affect the gainfulness of banks. Capital adequacy, resource quality, Liquidity and administration quality are all inside elements with critical factual effect on gainfulness as likewise finished up by past studies [15,18,19]. Then again, other inner element income quality which is probably emphatically related with bank execution applied no impact on the benefit pointers ROE and ROA in light of the fact that they are factually immaterial. These discoveries are like those reported by Faizulayev in his study led in 2011 [17].

Capital adequacy of Islamic banks has negative noteworthy connection with ROA and ROE though, in traditional banks capital sufficiency has negative critical connection with ROA and negative inconsequential connection with ROE. Administration quality has positive huge connection with ROA and ROE of both Islamic and traditional banks [26,27]. Liquidity and Resource quality both has negative critical effect on Islamic and additionally traditional banks.

Research limitations

- Information of Islamic windows of traditional banks is not considered in this study.
- Inside determinants of money related execution of banks other than CAMEL are not considered in this examination concentrate on.
- NIM (Net Premium Edge) is intermediary used to quantify the execution of banks is excluded on the grounds that Islamic banks don't produce premium salary.
- Outer components like Gross domestic product and expansion are additionally overlooked.

Future recommendations

It is suggested that information of Islamic windows of routine banks ought to be considered in future studies. Also inward determinants of budgetary execution and additionally outside determinants of banks other than CAMEL ought to be considered in future studies.

References

1. Dawood U (2014) Factors Impacting Profitability of Commercial Banks in Pakistan for the Period of (2009-2012). International Journal of Scientific and Research Publications 4: 1-7.
2. Nasser SA, Muhammed DD (2013) Introduction to history of Islamic banking in Malaysia. Humanomics 29: 80-87.
3. Khalid S, Amjad S (2012) Risk management practices in Islamic banks of Pakistan. The Journal of Risk Finance 13: 148-159.
4. Elseify E (2013) Comparative Analysis of Qatari Islamic Banks Performance versus Conventional Banks Before, During and After the Financial Crisis. International Journal of Business and Commerce 3: 11-41.
5. Hunjra AI, Bashir A (2014) Comparative Financial Performance Analysis of Conventional and Islamic Banks in Pakistan. Bulletin of Business and Economics 3: 196-206.
6. Moin MS (2008) Performance of Islamic Banking and Conventional Banking in Pakistan: A Comparative Study. School of Technology and Society, University of Skovde, Sweden.
7. Chong and Liu (2007) Islamic banking: Interest-free or interest-based. Pacific-Basin Finance Journal 17: 15-30.
8. Erol C, Baklaci HF, Aydogan B, Tunç G (2014) Performance comparison of Islamic (participation) banks and commercial banks in Turkish banking sector. EuroMed Journal of Business 9: 114-128.
9. Frederick NK (2015) Factors Affecting Performance of Commercial Banks in Uganda: A Case for Domestic Commercial Banks. International Review of Business Research Papers 11: 95-113.
10. Olweny T, Shipho TM (2011) Effects of Banking Sectoral Factors on the Profitability of Commercial Banks in Kenya. Economics and Finance Review 1: 1-30.
11. Wirnkar AD, Tanko M (2008) Camels and banks performance evaluation: The way forward. Working Paper, SSRN.
12. Muda M, Shaharuddin A, Embaya A (2013) Comparative analysis of profitability determinants of domestic and foreign Islamic banks in Malaysia. International Journal of Economics and Financial 3: 559-569.
13. Sufian F, Habibullah SM (2009) Bank specific and macroeconomic determinants of bank profitability: Empirical evidence from the China banking sector. Frontiers of economics in china 14: 274-229.
14. Swarnapali RMNC (2014) Firm Specific Determinants and Financial Performance of Licensed Commercial Banks in Sri Lanka. Proceedings of the 3rd International Conference on Management and Economics Ruhuna, University of Ruhuna, Sri Lanka pp: 247-252.
15. Ghenimi A, Omri MAB (2015) Liquidity Risk Management: A comparative study between Conventional and Islamic Banks. Journal of Business Management and Economics 3: 25-30.
16. Rao KRM, Lakew TB (2012) Determinants of Profitability of Commercial Banks in a Developing Country: Evidence from Ethiopia. International Journal of Accounting and Financial Management Research (IJAFMR) 2: 1-20.
17. Faizulayev A (2011) Comparative Analysis between Islamic Banking and Conventional Banking Firms in terms of Profitability, 2006-2009. Jeddah: Eastern Mediterranean.
18. Javaid S, Anwar J, Zaman K, Gafoor A (2011) Determinants of Bank Profitability in Pakistan: Internal Factor Analysis. Mediterranean journal of social sciences 2: 59-78.
19. Rahman S, Farzand A, Kurshed I, Zafar A (2012) Parameters of conventional and Islamic Bank's profitability in Pakistan: Evaluation of Internal Factor. Research Journal of Finance and Accounting 3: 11-18.
20. Rozzani N, Rahman R (2013) Camels and Performance Evaluation of Banks in Malaysia: Conventional Versus Islamic. Journal of Islamic Finance and Business Research 2: 36-45.
21. Momeneen W, Tahir A, Tariq M, Hanif M (2012) Comparative Performance Study of Conventional and Islamic Banking in Pakistan. International Research Journal of Finance and Economics 83: 1-17.
22. Samad A (2004) Performance of Interest-free Islamic banks vis-à-vis Interest-based Conventional Banks of Bahrain. IIUM Journal of Economics and Management 5: 1-15.
23. Metwally M (1997) Economic Consequences of Applying Islamic Principles in Muslim Societies. International Journal of Social Economics 24: 941-957.
24. Gul S, Irshad F, Zaman K (2011) Factors Affecting Bank Profitability in Pakistan. Romanian Econ J 14: 61-87.
25. Dixon R (1992) Islamic Banking. International Journal of Bank Marketing 10: 32-37.
26. Mehta A (2012) Financial Performance of UAE Banking Sector- A Comparison of before and during Crisis Ratios. International Journal of Trade, Economics and Finance 3: 381-387.
27. Jaffar M, Manarvi I (2011) Performance comparison of Islamic and Conventional banks in Pakistan. Global Journal of Management and Business Research 11: 60-66.

Permissions

All chapters in this book were first published in JBFA, by OMICS International; hereby published with permission under the Creative Commons Attribution License or equivalent. Every chapter published in this book has been scrutinized by our experts. Their significance has been extensively debated. The topics covered herein carry significant findings which will fuel the growth of the discipline. They may even be implemented as practical applications or may be referred to as a beginning point for another development.

The contributors of this book come from diverse backgrounds, making this book a truly international effort. This book will bring forth new frontiers with its revolutionizing research information and detailed analysis of the nascent developments around the world.

We would like to thank all the contributing authors for lending their expertise to make the book truly unique. They have played a crucial role in the development of this book. Without their invaluable contributions this book wouldn't have been possible. They have made vital efforts to compile up to date information on the varied aspects of this subject to make this book a valuable addition to the collection of many professionals and students.

This book was conceptualized with the vision of imparting up-to-date information and advanced data in this field. To ensure the same, a matchless editorial board was set up. Every individual on the board went through rigorous rounds of assessment to prove their worth. After which they invested a large part of their time researching and compiling the most relevant data for our readers.

The editorial board has been involved in producing this book since its inception. They have spent rigorous hours researching and exploring the diverse topics which have resulted in the successful publishing of this book. They have passed on their knowledge of decades through this book. To expedite this challenging task, the publisher supported the team at every step. A small team of assistant editors was also appointed to further simplify the editing procedure and attain best results for the readers.

Apart from the editorial board, the designing team has also invested a significant amount of their time in understanding the subject and creating the most relevant covers. They scrutinized every image to scout for the most suitable representation of the subject and create an appropriate cover for the book.

The publishing team has been an ardent support to the editorial, designing and production team. Their endless efforts to recruit the best for this project, has resulted in the accomplishment of this book. They are a veteran in the field of academics and their pool of knowledge is as vast as their experience in printing. Their expertise and guidance has proved useful at every step. Their uncompromising quality standards have made this book an exceptional effort. Their encouragement from time to time has been an inspiration for everyone.

The publisher and the editorial board hope that this book will prove to be a valuable piece of knowledge for researchers, students, practitioners and scholars across the globe.

List of Contributors

Agrawal P
Research Scholar, Department of Business Administration, DDU Gorakhpur University, Gorakhpur

Yadav AK
Associate Professor, Department of Commerce, DDU Gorakhpur University, Gorakhpur

Al Ghammari KA and Ahmed EM
Binary University, Faculty of Business, Multimedia University, Malaysia

Khaliq IH
Pacific Western University (USA), Warid Telecom, Pakistan

Naeem B
Department of Management Sciences, COMSATS Institute of Information Technology, Lahore, Pakistan

Khalid S
Department of Education, University of Sargodha, Sargodha, Pakistan

Affes H and Hakim NH
Lecturer at the Faculty of Sciences, Faculty of Economics and Management of Sfax, University of Sfax, Tunisia

Prasad S
Associate Professor in Marketing, Regional College of Management, Bhubaneswar, India

Malyadri P
Principal, Government Degree College, Osmania University, Hyderabad, India

Sirisha S
Assistant Professor, ITM-Business School, Warangal, India

Ishaq AB, Karim A, Ahmed S and Zaheer A
Department of Finance, Army Public College of Management and Sciences (APCOMS), University of engineering and technology, Taxila, Pakistan

Chung TF
Taylor's University, 47500 Subang Jaya, Selangor, Malaysia

Ariff M
University Putra Malaysia, 43400, Serdang, Selangor, Malaysia

Sarkodie EE and Addai I
Department of Accounting Studies Education, College of Technology Education, Kumasi, Ghana

Asiedu DK
University of Education, Winneba, College of Technology Education, Kumasi, Ghana

Asiedu E
Servicio Nacional De Aprendizaje (SENA) Neiva, Huila, Colombia

Agrawal P
Research Scholar, Department of Business Administration, DDU Gorakhpur University, Gorakhpur

Yadav AK
Associate Professor, Department of Commerce, DDU Gorakhpur University, Gorakhpur

Veron JF, Wang I, Duong H, Dang VNT, Pham HNA, Wallace D and Ramiah V
UniSA Business School, University of South Australia, Australia

Babatolu Ayorinde
Department of Accounting, Federal University of Agriculture, Abeokuta, Ogun State, Nigeria

Oyewo Babajide
Department of Accounting, University of Lagos, Nigeria

Abdullah M
Assistant Professor, Independent University, Dhaka, Bangladesh

Saeed MS
Business Management, Glasgow Caledonian University, Glasgow Business School, Glasgow, UK

Nasar A
Government Model Degree College (for Boys), Lahore, Pakistan

Hossain SA
Teaching Assistant, London college of business management and Information technology, UK

Rabia N and Khakan N
University of Lahore, Lahore, Pakistan

Mahito Okura
Associate Professor, Faculty of Contemporary Social Studies, Department of Social System Studies, Doshisha Women's College of Liberal Arts, Kyoto, Japan

YingYing Jiang
Part-time Instructor, Faculty of Economics, Meiji Gakuin University, Tokyo, Japan

Reeta
Lovely School of Business, Lovely Professional University, India

Rahman M, Hasan N, Hoshen S and Chowdhury RHK
Department of Business Administration, First Capital University of Bangladesh, Shahnaz Mansion, Alamdanga Road (Pouro College Para), Chuadanga-7200, Bangladesh

Ashraf A
Department of Marketing and Finance, Frostburg State University, Frostburg, Maryland, USA

Moni MA
Faculty of Medicine, University of Sydney, New South Wales, Australia

Atyeh MH and Khatib AM
School of Business, Australian College of Kuwait

Yasin J
School of Business, Australian College of Kuwait

Rai A, Viswanathan KG and White N
Frank G. Zarb School of Business, Hofstra University, Hempstead, NY 11549, USA

Worku G and Tilahun A
Faculty of business and economics (FBE), University of Gondar, Gondar, Ethiopia

Tafa MA
Dashen Bank S.C., Sierra Leone St, Addis Ababa, Ethiopia

Ghaffoori A
Department of Accounting, Essex Business School, UK

Naeem B
Comptroller of Accounts at Packages Limited, Accounting, Lahore, Pakistan

Index